GEORGIA

A Guide to Its Towns and Countryside

American Guide Series

Published by TUPPER & LOVE Atlanta

GEORGIA

A Guide to Its Towns and Countryside

9696

REVISED AND EXTENDED BY GEORGE G. LECKIE

Foreword by RALPH McGILL

Illustrated

A TUPPER & LOVE BOOK

Printed and bound in the United States of America

Library of Congress Catalog Card Number 54–10344

Foreword

ONE EVENING in the early summer of 1943 I attended a small dinner in still embattled London. The host was Mr. Brenden Bracken, then a member of Mr. Winston Churchill's war-time cabinet. He introduced a guest who had produced several excellent books requiring both a scholarly background and patiently detailed research, and said of him:

"To do this work it is not really necessary that one be a gentleman, but it is a positive requirement that he be a scholar of ability. Happily, in our guest tonight, the two are met and I am rejoiced to present a scholar and a gentleman."

This story intruded itself into my mind as I read, *Georgia, a Guide to Its Towns and Countryside* as revised and extended by George G. Leckie. Happily in him the two are met, and I am rejoiced to have the privilege of writing this brief foreword to what is, without any doubt at all, a long needed and valuable contribution both to those who wish to know a great deal about the history of Georgia, and those who desire merely to travel up and down it and enjoy the great variety of interests it has to offer: scenic, historical and economic.

The first edition of this volume in the American Guide Series, was published in 1940 as compiled and written by workers of the Writer's Program of the Works Projects Administration during the depression years. It was the product of many minds and hands and was, in general, very well done. It quickly became, as indeed did all other state guide books, a much-sought-after and necessary sort of volume. Somehow our states had never done much of a job of recording either their history or their social and economic development in guide form. So, it was a quite natural development that within a few years the various Guide books became almost collectors' items to be hoarded and lent with care.

It was, however, the unhappy fate of almost all the Guide books to become, in very considerable measure, out of date by the time they were published. They were a relief work product of the depression. The material, gathered patiently across several very lean years, appeared in 1940 when the acute recession had spent itself and Georgia, along with the rest of the nation, was already started on the amazing acceleration of change and growth which were to be a part of the Second Great War's flexing of our national muscles, and of the extraordinary industrial, technological and scientific developments which followed.

Since 1940 Georgia has undergone dramatic and exciting change, as is evident to both the eye and the mind. She has escaped from the tyranny of the row crop into the green pastures. Great dams have been built (and are a-building) on her rivers. Her burgeoning cities testify both to the revolution in agriculture and the coming of industry to absorb those no longer required on the land.

All this drama of change is faithfully, and entertainingly, recorded and evaluated in this revision.

But, for me at least, the best part of it is the writing done on the cities of the state. Here the author contributes something which the first edition lacked—a true and lively story and history of the cities. Since the first edition was the work of many hands, it was inevitable the story of the cities should have been pedestrian and pedantic. In this new edition they are a joy. George Leckie has clothed the carefully detailed data of the cities in the attractively styled words of a fine writer and scholar. I think it not at all far-fetched to say that the citizen of our state, and that of any other state or country who may travel within our borders, may have from his stories of our cities a really comprehensive basic history of Georgia. The writing style holds one. It is a pleasure and a delight to read what he has written. When one has finished with "the cities" one has a very real "feel" of Georgia and of the historical forces which helped to shape the present.

Mr. Leckie and his publishers have done us all a great service in this revision and extension of the valuable but out-dated Guide.

RALPH McGILL

Acknowledgment

THE FIRST edition of *Georgia: A Guide to Its Towns and Countryside,* "compiled and written by workers of the Writers' Program of the Work Projects Administration in the State of Georgia," was published in 1940 by the University of Georgia Press, at Athens. Written under such auspices, the book was accordingly sensitive to the conditions of the time. It is this edition that serves as the substantial model for the present revision.

The present edition has been revised and extended that it might bring within its scope the period from 1940 to about 1952. A considerable part of the task consisted in recording the extraordinary multiplication of modern industrial and agricultural techniques in the state, with the installations and environmental changes, both physical and social, that always accompany an alteration in the agents of production.

During the period, among Federal projects, the U. S. Army Corps of Engineers, for example, has constructed four major dams to serve both as means to soil and water conservation and for the production of hydroelectric power. As a part of an imposing list of increased and improved services, the state of Georgia has added what by comparison with other states must be an exceptional number of state parks —some originally Federal conservation projects—for purposes of natural conservation and to serve as recreation areas. Modified by both Federal and state agencies, the clog of custom in Georgia of raising cotton and corn excessively has been eased, and diversified farming has taken a firm hold on the habits of the farmers in a manner significant for the prosperity and social advancement of its rural population. Much land has been converted to grass and the uses of grazing; soil conservation measures have been applied to checking erosion; reforestation and forest-care measures to insure the future of Georgia's forest products have gained recognition widely; the north Georgia broiler industry, with its operational center at Gainesville, has grown to be

#1 in the nation; the state's Department of Agriculture has developed an important system of Farmers' Markets to serve as regional outlets for farm products; and the changes in the industrial scene are a complex story in themselves. This list is neither systematic nor complete. But it is suggestive of the basic complex of changes shaping what one may well call the New Georgia, in keeping with the wider expression "New South."

It would have been impossible for the present editor to cover such an extensive and detailed scene had it not been for the unfailing assistance rendered him by both organized sources and interested individuals. Important among the sources were the chambers of commerce throughout the state, agencies of both the Federal and state governments, and a long list of individuals possessed of special information. Because of the basic nature of the project the help of the State Highway Department was essential, and Mr. Roy A. Flynt, State Highway Planning Engineer, deserves special mention for the patience and generosity with which he met this need. Typical of help rendered by specifically qualified individuals is that of Mrs. Annette McDonald Suarez, Randolph County Historian; of Mrs. Marianna K. Blaum who developed the story on the state's Battey Memorial Hospital; and, of James A. Cragon, a past president of the Appalachian Trail Club, whose firsthand information was important for Tour 13 A covering the Appalachian Trail in Georgia. Like Odysseus, Ralph McGill, of the *Atlanta Constitution,* should be called "the man who was never at a loss," since at need he unfailingly suggested some device by which an over-modest or stubbornly obscure fact might be made public or enlightened. In the absence of a systematic index of photographs covering the state, for there is none such existing, illustrations had to be taken where found. When possible, credit for these has been given in the List of Illustrations.

A note of warning. Though the numbers appearing in the present edition for road mileage are given with apparently decimal exactitude, they are based on reckonings that are sometimes now inexact because of Georgia's current road construction program. The mileage figures should be taken as likely rather than as literal, and checked by a recent road map, or by the Rand McNally *Georgia Pocket Map.*

Published ostensibly as a handbook for tours, the GUIDE soon after its initial appearance found a use implicit in the organized and well-indexed material it contained—that of serving as a handbook of ready information about the state as a whole. This perennial use has dictated the integration of Part One: The General Background, of the old edition, with Section Two: Cities, and Section Three: Tours. Its generalizing and bridging function has been absorbed into the regional material of the separate cities and tours. This change provides a special focus for the multiplicity of facts that grow dense about any time and place. Perhaps this feature can be perfected in later revisions.

In addition to these generalities, the editor would like to add a comment on the period covered in the revision by way of a quotation from *Plutarch's Lives*. Reflecting on Pericles' works administration policy for ancient Athens during a time of troubles, Plutarch has Pericles say in justifying his program to the people, ". . . . that it was good reason, that, now the city was sufficiently provided and stored with all things necessary for war, they should convert the overplus of its wealth to such undertakings as would hereafter, when completed, give them eternal honour, and for the present, while in process, freely supply all the inhabitants with plenty. With their varieties of workmanship and occasions for service, which summon all arts and trades and require all hands to be employed about them, they do actually put the whole city, in a manner into state pay; while at the same time she is both beautiful and maintained by herself." * Similarly in Georgia, undertakings that might have required several generations of men were brought somehow within the brief confines of a single political era.

GEORGE G. LECKIE

May 9, 1954
Little Creek Farm
Roswell, Georgia

* Quoted from The Modern Library Edition of *Plutarch's Lives* by the permission of Random House.

Contents

Part Three: Appendices

List of Illustrations

xv

...Blue Ridge, Brunswick, Canton, Chamblee, Columbus, Cordele, Dallas, Dockstation, Dublin, Gainesville, Griffin, Hinesville, La-Grange, Madison, Manchester, McDonough, McRae, Newnan, Perry, Reidsville, Rutland, Sylvania, Thomaston, Thomasville, Thomson, Tifton, Perry, Valdosta, Ville Rica, Washington, and Waycross. Current account information may be obtained from the State Highway Department, Atlanta, or the Division Offices of the State Highway Department at Gainesville, Augusta, Macon, Savannah, and Tifton.

General Information

Railroads: Twelve Class 1 railroads, with some 6,015 miles of main line track, and a number of smaller railroads which, however, have decreased in recent years either because they were discontinued or absorbed into main line companies. The foregoing figures exclude side tracks and switching yards. The Class 1 lines are: Alabama Great Southern R.R.; Atlanta & West Point R.R.; Atlantic Coast Line R.R.; Central of Georgia Ry.; Charleston & Western Carolina Ry.; Georgia R.R.; Georgia & Florida R.R.; Georgia Southern & Florida Ry.; Louisville & Nashville R.R. (L. & N.); Nashville, Chattanooga & St. Louis Ry. (N. C. & St. L.); Seaboard Air Line Ry.; and Southern Ry.

Highways: Twenty-six US numbered highways, of which thirteen traverse several of the southeastern states in the United States. Highways patrolled by State Police; a few counties provide their own. Filling stations are well distributed, but many close at dark. State gasoline tax 6¢. Since there are no stock laws in several counties of south Georgia, motorists are warned to watch for cattle and pigs. A copy of the *Uniform Traffic Code and Department of Public Safety* (Official Rules and Regulations of the State of Georgia) may be obtained by addressing the Georgia Department of Public Safety, P. O. Box 1456, Atlanta 1, Georgia. A copy of the official map of the Georgia State Highway System may be obtained from the State Highway Department, Atlanta, Georgia. State Patrol Headquarters are located in the following places: Albany Radio Station, Atlanta, Americus, Athens, Blue Ridge, Brunswick, Canton, Cartersville, Cedartown, Cordele, Dalton, Donalsonville, Dublin, Gainesville, Griffin, Hinesville, LaGrange, Madison, Manchester, Milledgeville, McRae, Newnan, Perry, Reidsville, Swainsboro, Sylvania, Thomaston, Thomasville, Thomson, Tifton, Toccoa, Valdosta, Villa Rica, Washington, and Waycross. Current detour information may be obtained from the State Highway Department, Atlanta, or the Division Offices of the State Highway Department, at Gainesville, Augusta, Macon, Savannah, and Tifton.

Bus Lines: The major bus carriers operating in Georgia are: Atlantic Greyhound Corporation; Atlantic Stages, Inc.; Continental Crescent Lines, Inc.; Georgia-Florida Coaches; Modern Coach Corporation; Service Coach Lines, Inc.; Smoky Mountain Stages, Inc.; Southeastern Greyhound Lines; Southeastern Motor Lines, Inc.; Southeastern Stages, Inc.; Southern Stages, Inc.; Teche Greyhound Lines; Tennessee Coach Co.; and the Queen City Coach Co.

Waterways: Two principal seaports, Savannah and Brunswick, of which Savannah is by far the more important.

Airlines: Five scheduled airlines link thirteen Georgia cities (Albany, Athens, Atlanta, Augusta, Brunswick, Columbus, LaGrange, Macon, Moultrie, Rome, Savannah, Valdosta, and Waycross) so completely that the communities are only minutes apart and less than three hours from the major markets of New York and Chicago. The major lines are: Delta-C&S Air Lines, of Atlanta; Capital Airlines, of Washington, D. C.; Eastern Air Lines, of New York City; National Airlines, of Miami; and Southern Airways, of Birmingham, Alabama.

Motor Vehicle Laws (*digest*): Maximum speed 60 m.p.h. daytime, 50 m.p.h. night; 10 m.p.h. at slow signs; non-resident drivers of vehicles properly registered under the laws of another state are exempt from registration for 30 days. Either hand signals or lights, or mechanical signals must be used for stops and turns. Turns on traffic lights vary in cities. Full stop must be made at unsafe grade crossings. Driver's license required. Minimum age for drivers, sixteen. Two front lights and one rear must be in good order; horn, windshield wiper, rear view mirror inside or outside, and noise-preventing muffler are all required to be in good order.

Prohibited: Passing streetcar on left; passing vehicle on left without sounding horn; passing schoolbus or streetcar while passengers are getting on or off; driving into a boulevard without stopping; passing to left of a vehicle where no passing zone is marked on pavement. Bright lights are prohibited in some cities.

Liquor Laws: State laws permit the sale of light wines and beer; county option on sale of whisky.

Accommodations: First-class commercial hotels in large cities of uniformly good quality; although accommodations in small towns vary widely in quality, a good number have new, comfortable hotels. Motels and motor courts have increased in recent years. The Georgia Motor Club, an affiliate of AAA, has offices in Atlanta, Albany, Columbus, Macon, Rome, and Waycross; two other affiliates of AAA exist: the East Georgia Motor Club in Augusta, and the Savannah Motor Club in Savannah. The winter resorts of south Georgia generally have more luxurious accommodations than the summer resorts of the north Georgia mountains. Most hotels have no seasonal fluctuations in rates.

Climate: The climate is generally mild. Topcoats needed for spring and autumn evenings in the mountains. Sudden rain may be expected, but this varies considerably from season to season. Throughout the state sudden changes make weather predictions difficult, and travelers should be well provided with wraps from November through April.

Recreation Areas: Admission is free to all state parks (see Index under State Parks for names, accommodations, and locations). Information is obtainable from the Department of State Parks, 418 State Capitol Building, Atlanta. For information about the vast Chattahoochee National Forest, address the Forest Supervisor, Gainesville, Georgia. Refer to Okefenokee National Wildlife Refuge in the Index for information about its several entrance accommodations. For information concerning accommodations in the various Federal Reservoir Areas, see Index under that title. In the mountain sections of north Georgia are many small summer resorts including Cloudland, Lakemont, Clayton, and Tate. Recreation is afforded by several large lakes formed in the course of hydroelectric power development.

Fishing and Hunting: The Georgia Game and Fish Commission issues from time to time a booklet of seasonal rules and regulations. Address the Game and Fish Commission, 412 State Capitol, Atlanta. With the purchase of fishing and hunting licenses is included a subscription to the quarterly magazine *Georgia Game and Fish.* •

Poisonous Snakes and Plants: Rattlesnake, water moccasin (cottonmouth), and highland moccasin (copperhead, sometimes miscalled a pilot snake) found in rural and wooded areas of entire state; coral snake (not a pit viper but extremely lethal), in extreme south Georgia. Poison ivy grows in some locations.

Information Service: Address the Georgia State Department of Commerce, 100 State Capitol, Atlanta; and for Atlanta specifically, the Atlanta Convention & Visitors Bureau, Rhodes Haverty Building, Atlanta 3, Georgia.

Annual Celebrations: Tomato Festival—late May—Glenville; Blessing of the Fleet—June—Thunderbolt; Poultry Festival—June—Gainesville; Watermelon Festival—June, July—Cordele; Boat Regatta—June, July—St. Simons; Tobacco Festival—August—Moultrie; Masters Golf Tournament—2nd week in April—Augusta; Women Title Holders Golf Match—last week in March—Augusta; Dogwood Festival—mid-April—Atlanta; Rose Festival—last Friday in April—Thomasville; Pine Tree Festival—April—Swainsboro; Georgia Mountain Fair—end of August—Hiawassee, sixteen counties participating; Ham & Egg

Show (many minor ones), the major one—March—Fort Valley; Camellia Shows, throughout the central and lower part of the state during January and February; Georgia Tours of Gardens and Homes—March and April—in about eight cities; Plum Nelly Art Show—October—Plum Nelly; Kennesaw Mountain Seminar—first Friday and Saturday in October—Kennesaw National Battlefield Park; no one Cotton Festival, various towns have their own and pick their contestant for the Georgia Maid of Cotton Contest who competes with contestants from other cotton states for the final honor.

*

PART ONE

CITIES

*

Athens

Railroad Stations: Thomas and Mitchell sts. for Central of Georgia Ry.; foot of Broad St. for Georgia R.R.; College Ave. and Ware St. for Seaboard Air Line Ry. and Gainesville Midland R.R.; Hoyt and Hull sts. for Southern Ry.

Airport: The Athens Municipal Airport is located three miles east of Athens, just off the county highway to Winterville. It is served by Southern Airways with four flights daily; facilities for private planes, service, etc. Transportation from the city by means of taxi-cabs, $1.00 per passenger.

Taxis: 20¢ a passenger within city limits; 10¢ additional for each suitcase or large parcel.

Traffic Regulations: Right, left and U turns at all intersections except where traffic lights indicate otherwise. Right turns on red light, provided full stop is made. Speed limit in business district 15 m.p.h.; in residential, 30.

Accommodations: 5 hotels, tourist homes, 3 motels.

Information Service: Athens Chamber of Commerce, Civic Hall, Washington St.

Football: Sanford Field Stadium, University of Georgia North Campus.

Baseball: Old Sanford Field, Lumpkin St., for University of Georgia games.

Swimming: American Legion Pool, Lumpkin St., small fees for adults and children.

Golf: Athens Country Club, 2 m. NW. on US 129 (Jefferson Rd.), 18 holes; nominal fee for non-residents.

Radio Stations: WGAU (1340 kc.), WRXC (960 kc.); Television, 3 Atlanta channels.

Motion Picture Houses: 5 including one for Negroes; 2 drive-ins.

Annual Events: Little International Livestock Show, Hardman Hall, State Agricultural College, May; American Legion Fair and Carnival, on Legion grounds, 500 block Lumpkin St., October; Athens Agricultural Fair, October; four football games during fall months; Livestock auctions every week at N. E. Georgia Livestock Auction, Inc., Barn on Winterville Road.

ATHENS (771 alt.; 28,180 pop.), on a hill partly embraced by the Oconee River, is known both as the home of the University of Georgia and as a city of distinguished ante-bellum houses. Greek porticoes with pediments and impressive Doric columns make up the dominant architectural theme. Early boxwood gardens, oaks and elms grown stately with years, and white-blossomed magnolias emitting the rich oil of their perfume in the summer air, seem to recreate continually the romantic tradition of the Deep South.

In the early years of Athens' existence it was like many another col-

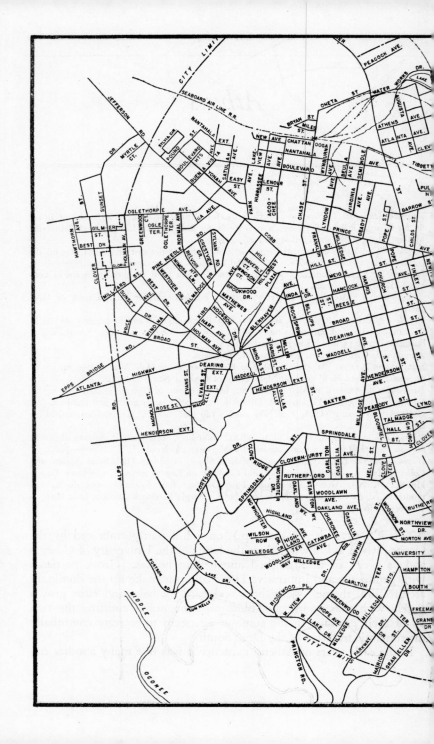

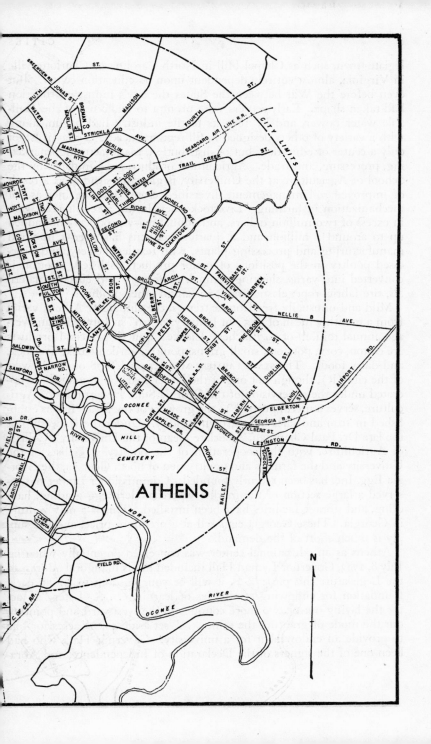

ATHENS

N

legiate town, such as Chapel Hill in North Carolina or Charlottesville in Virginia, almost entirely dependent upon its education center. But even before the War between the States the city's industrial function had taken shape. Early settlers were prompt to make use of the available water power, and by 1830 its textile industry had begun, along with a variety of others designed to fill regional needs. Today it is not only a center of education, but of distribution, manufacturing, marketing, processing, and trade. Agricultural production, stimulated by the School of Agriculture at the University, is growing steadily as a result of improved soil management, diversified crops, and the increase of mechanization in farming. Livestock sales during a recent year were in excess of two million dollars, and annual dairy products sales added up to around a million and a quarter. Athens has over a hundred manufacturing and processing plants, with textiles, hosiery, and processed poultry in the positions of major products as listed. Cotton is converted into yarns, sheeting, flannel, upholstery and curtain materials, tire fabric, rope, elastic braid, rugs, and other products.

Mild and unusually free from extremes, the climate of Athens varies from a monthly mean of 43.5° in January to 79.6° in July, with an average annual rainfall of 49.7 inches. Clarke County's principal products are cotton, corn, potatoes, small grains, poultry, garden truck, livestock, and dairy foods. The STATE FARMERS MARKET on US 78 one mile west of the city (R), though not one of the larger markets among those operated under the supervision of the Georgia State Department of Agriculture, serves a useful purpose to the growers of the area. It was established in 1949 and sales have grown steadily. Under the leadership of the late Dr. Paul Chapman, Associate Dean of the University's College of Agriculture, with the cooperation of the poultry specialists of the University and the farmers and poultrymen of north Georgia, the Georgia Egg, Inc. has been recently founded. Commissioner Linder has reserved a large section of the market where modern egg grading, handling, and storage facilities have been installed. This is a new venture in Georgia. These Georgia eggs sell at a premium price, and the supply is much short of the demand.

Athens as an educational center was conceived potentially when on July 8, 1783, Governor Lyman Hall included in his inaugural address to the Legislature this plea: ". . . it will be your wisdom to lay an early foundation for endowing seminaries of learning . . ." Later "an act for the laying out of two more counties to the westward and pointing out the mode of granting the same . . ." set aside 40,000 acres for sale to provide an endowment for a university. Governor Hall, who had been one of the signers of the Declaration of Independence, and Abraham Baldwin, an alumnus of Yale and an educational philosopher, were appointed, among others, on a board of trustees. But it was Baldwin who supplied the idea for a state university somewhat as Plato supplied the idea for a state in his *Republic*. Baldwin's charter, which was legally passed in 1785, read as follows in Sec. XIV. "All public schools instituted or to be supported by funds or public monies in this State, shall be considered as parts or members of the University, and shall be under the foregoing directions and regulations." The depth and latitude given to the word "university" in the Charter were exceptional in their scope, especially for the times. Some important history was to be conditioned by it as the years accumulated. Despite Baldwin's resolution in promoting his idea of a state university, funds grew slowly: the state was young and preoccupied in getting physical possession of itself, ready cash was restricted, and the generality of men indifferent.

Some degree of enthusiasm came to a head for the enterprise in 1800, and in 1801 Josiah Meigs, a former student of Baldwin at Yale, was elected president; a committee was appointed to settle upon a site for the college or first group of buildings. Eventually a tract of land recessed into a bend of the Oconee River was chosen; it was covered with massive oaks, and possessed of a freely flowing spring of sparkling water. Earth, air, water, and place prescribed a happy situation for a town. John Milledge, later governor, donated 633 acres here as the site for the institution, and the committee chose the auspicious name, Athens, with the ease of Adam after the creation.

In the fall of 1801 Meigs hastily pushed the construction of a few log and frame buildings, and sold lots in the new town site to raise money for the college, since the legislature's bounty of 40,000 acres, consisting of wild lands plentiful in the state, was not exactly a fluid asset. With the advent of a handful of young men seeking the higher learning, the college came into existence properly with its first convocation. The peaceful Cherokee did not interfere, and in 1805 the first permanent building was completed.

The college was not exactly born with a silver spoon in its mouth, and the apathy of the legislature to its needs was the only constant feature of its affairs. This attitude persisted until, after the War between the States, the provisions of the Morrill or "Land-Grant" Act seduced the legislature into virtue. By this time, with Georgia's industrial revolution coming to a head in 1890 in the widespread popular move to establish cotton mills, even the most "practical mind" could hardly fail to entertain some notion of the rôle of professional and technical training in the complex of factors engendering the neotechnic world. The reasons for the early apathy are doubtless socially intricate, but may be chiefly attributed to the fact that the more affluent planters and merchants, acting as the leaders of the period, tended to send their sons "East" to college, while those in more modest positions saw no need for the higher learning. Too, the situation was aggravated by a strong anti-formal, and hence anti-rational bias in the religious sects that tardily but thoroughly took hold upon the people from around 1840 onward. The denominational struggles to gain possession of the college, while not atypical of the times, were inconvenient to sound learning and truth.

Taken against a backdrop of wilderness and Indians, the curriculum does appear on the odd side, with its emphasis on the classics and the study of Greek, and some mathematics and physics, at least at moments when these were not being burnt as vanities by the religious powers. Posed against the present it may seem even odder, if possible—at a time when hard-boiled minds regard technical means as instruments of social salvation in themselves. But no better books on political wisdom have ever been written than those of the Greeks and Romans. What the young state needed was to find some degree of political stability and hence order for itself in an almost newly-born nation. Men might expect to use the physical environment in simple mechanical ways, but the notion of coercing it by a complete technical mastery to be learned at institutions was then hardly more exact than Aladdin's relation to his wonderful lamp.

What the young liberal artists were learning was not how to manage physical affairs but human. This they did by rehearsing among themselves the motives of power by means of the mind's native tongue, its written and spoken symbols with which it comes to terms with itself and other men, in a community of meaning and purpose. The sense of the day was necessarily dramatic and personal: the measure of affairs entirely in the human scale. So the young men orated and debated as sharply as Greek sophists or as judiciously as Roman senators, especially in those colleges within the college, the literary societies, one located in Demosthenian Hall and the other in Phi Kappa Hall. If this did not lead expeditiously to a mastery of the industrial arts (and their theoretical superstructures in advanced study), and of the sorts of social technics by which a few men contrive to manage many in order to sustain such arts efficiently, it did promise much in the way of a civil society that was primarily open and expanding and where the measure of success was strictly human, such as courage or justice.

The mid-nineteenth century was marked in Georgia by a rising interest in girls' schools, especially as the North-South storm became more lowering, and it was felt that the image of woman in the Southern idyl might be fractured by the impact of northern school influences. Of these, Lucy Cobb, opened in 1859 and one of the most beloved, lasted the longest.

Meanwhile the college commencement acquired a state-wide meaning as a sort of seasonal drama of the social and political year. Not only did graduates return to keep the old conversations going; men of affairs gathered to have their laurels further gilded by academic favors. The literary societies, Demosthenian and Phi Kappa, were an organic part of the ceremony. In fact their exhibits of address and oratory served as the focus of dramatic interest, and certainly more aptly than today's elephantine football spectacles. But this course of events came to an end with the terrible year 1862 when, aroused by the secessionist eloquence of Thomas R. R. Cobb, so large a part of the student body enlisted in the Confederate Army that the college closed in 1863.

Educationally it was the close of an era. The long argument with the intellectual and imaginative models of Greece and Rome had come to an end. When the institution was able to resume its function of state leadership, in any serious sense, that is, the scene was not only agricultural but industrial, and even agriculture was becoming technical and systematic. A philosophy of education that could find no way to advance except by disfiguring the humanistic images of the past, would eventually become ascendent under the name of progress. This was to cause some curious agonies in the southern soul as it sought to adjust its basic pieties to the new learning.

The increase in population, caused by the many refugees who remained after the war, led to the incorporation of Athens as a city in 1872, and about that time it became the seat of Clarke County. Urbanization had begun in Georgia with its associated mercantile developments, as the plantation owners functionally displaced by emancipation were forced to contrive a new life. The bitter herbs of Reconstruction were not invigorating to the body, nor did they teach the lesson that the North designed, since the Southern mind elaborated in fancy what it was denied in fact; the "Old South" became one of its chief articles of export. And yet the South was learning with amazing speed how to row in fortune's boat. A radical change was at work behind the stereotyped image of plantation gentility. Between 1882 and 1886 there was an estimated forty per cent increase in the regional wealth of the South.

Although the Lumpkin Law School, originally a private institution established in 1859, became part of the school at Athens in 1867, it was the acceptance in 1866 of the conditions of the Morrill Act of 1862 that marked the sharpest change. If funds for the higher learning had been meager before the war, they were more so, and understandably, during

Reconstruction. Making a virtue out of a necessity, the state became the recipient of Federal funds in accordance with the Morrill Act which required the establishment of an agricultural and mechanical college.

This movement favored a split between the older education and the new. The new means tended to become technical operations increasingly directed to economic ends. In contrast, the older tradition had taken from the Greek and Roman heritage a way of life that sought wisdom in accumulated moral experience, especially in the sense in which the ideas of personal dignity and salvation were strengthened by Christian doctrine. But on the material side the old education had failed to relieve poverty, infection, misery, and in short a painfully meager level of subsistence for the masses. Henceforth, emphasis must fall on technical skill, to effect balance. The Jeffersonian principle of discovering and fostering the gifted individual, with its associated emphasis on a political democracy of individual rights, had to make way for the Jacksonian principle of raising the human average, with its emphasis on economic democracy and mass improvement. This is the key to the New South.

Although according to report it was discovered in 1871 that $90,000, all the interest accumulated for five years on the Land-Grant fund, had been peculated by the Reconstruction government, nevertheless on May 1, 1872, the State School of Agriculture and Mechanic Arts began operation, at Athens but in separation from the college. Meanwhile North Georgia Agriculture College at Dahlonega was established as an extension of the use of the Morrill Fund and as a part of the "university," in the sense of Abraham Baldwin's Sec. XIV of the original charter, referred to above. Thus an institution not located at Athens became an adjunct of the "university." In further extension of this principle the State Medical College, established in 1829 and located at Augusta, was redesignated as the Georgia Medical College and a part of the "university." Finally, the Constitution of 1877 specified that appropriations for education, except those for the "elementary branches of an English education," be made to the "university." Appropriations were so made, but in the name of each institution which became equally with the parts at Athens an adjunct of the "university."

In 1892 the teacher training movement got under way at Athens in old Rock College which was renamed Gilmer Hall in honor of George R. Gilmer who established a fund to train teachers for elementary teaching. The State Normal school began as a further stage of this movement in 1892. In 1904 the Normal School was made a part of the "university" by an act of the legislature appropriating $25,000, if the sum be matched. Ten thousand from George Foster Peabody, another from James M. Smith, and five from a state-wide drive satisfied the condition. This was of course not the day of astronomical finance and monumental public works. With the creation of the Board of Regents in 1931, the State Normal School's teacher training was soon assimilated by the Department of Education of the University of Georgia. The State Normal School became known as the Co-ordinate College, and freshman and sophomore girls were domiciled there.

In 1931 the general assembly placed all publicly supported schools and colleges—and this included the University of Georgia in the local sense—under one managerial board, the regents of the University System of Georgia, with quite elastic powers of organization and direction. The virtues of this in brief were: one governing body—the regents; a single executive officer—the chancellor; one appropriation, made to the regents and to be distributed by them for the common good; a council composed of members from the various adjunct institutions, with deliberative and exploratory functions, though not executive. Reports from this council are reviewed by the chancellor and then transmitted to the regents for action. On January 1, 1932, the Board of Regents unified in itself functions formerly carried out by nearly four hundred people, and assimilated to itself the separate powers of twenty-six institutions. The schools or colleges at Athens still separate, were absorbed into the University of Georgia which in turn became an adjunct of the University System. And hence the ambiguity in the word "university" became articulated at last.

Since the Reorganization Act in 1931 and between that time and 1942, for example, more support has been forthcoming from the general assembly for the expansion of the University System's physical plants and equipment than in all the years from 1785 to 1931. According to John C. Meadows' analysis of this situation in his *Modern Georgia*, "It will be noted that all funds available for buildings from the state, from trust funds, or gifts have been matched by funds either from the Public Works Administration or the Works Progress Administration." Apparently, like the Morrill Act, this is another instance of virtue by seduction, as well as of a vastly expanding awareness of the function of education in an increasingly complex world in need of simplification.

The University of Georgia is now divided into eleven schools and colleges, each of which is concerned with instruction in some special field of knowledge. It now includes Franklin College; the School of Law; the School of Pharmacy; the College of Agriculture; the Peabody School of Forestry—founded in 1906 and the oldest in the South; the

Peabody College of Education; the College of Business Administration founded in 1913; the Henry W. Grady School of Journalism which began in 1915 and was named for the distinguished journalist in 1921; the School of Home Economics; the School of Veterinary Medicine begun in 1946; and the Graduate School. *The Atlanta Journal and Constitution,* for Sunday, April 12, 1953, reports that the Board of Regents have under consideration a Campus Development Plan designed ultimately to take care of ten thousand students as distinguished from the present 4,700. "Aside from having ultra-modern buildings which will group all allied courses of study into centers of learning, the campus—now split in two by [a] valley-like depression which provides a beautiful bowl for Sanford Stadium—will be welded together by [a] road system and the grading of the two hills now known as Ag Hill and Main Campus." The development of the University System and the expansion of the University of Georgia have gone far toward giving existence to Abraham Baldwin's idea of a public university.

THE UNIVERSITY OF GEORGIA CAMPUS

The area of the University of Georgia is known as North Campus and South Campus. North Campus, entered on foot by way of the Georgia Arch from Broad Street near its intersection with Lumpkin, is the older area, while South Campus, roughly the section south of Sanford Stadium and Stegeman Hall, is newer and includes the College of Agriculture.

1. The GEORGIA ARCH, at the main entrance to the campus on Broad Street, is a simplified version of the one depicted on the state seal. The cast-iron arch, placed in 1856, is decorated with a design of leaf and branch, and supported by three slender fluted columns. The older structures, set about the long grassy quadrangle, are uniform neither in style nor material, but suggest age and repose in their setting of trees and shrubbery.

2. DEMOSTHENIAN HALL, on the right immediately beyond the Academic Building, is a small, square, two-story building of cement-covered brick with a simple elliptical-arch doorway and central Palladian window. It was completed in 1824. The ceiling of the upper floor is designed in the Sir Christopher Wren manner, with a pleasant central medallion and molded plaster frieze. It houses the university's first literary society, founded in 1803. The Demosthenian Society developed the custom of making famous men honorary members, and its membership, for example, included Andrew Johnson, Henry Clay, and William Cullen Bryant. Among its regular members were Crawford Long, the first physician to use ether in an operation; Robert Toombs, oratorical

and military hero of the Confederacy; and Henry Timrod, the poet; not to mention many others whose names are a part of Georgia's history.

3. THE CHAPEL, next to Demosthenian Hall, is a cement-covered brick building with massive Doric columns supporting a Greek pediment above a portico the length of the front. Completed in 1832, it was the first permanent assembly hall of the college. Commencement exercises were held in this old building for nearly a century, until a larger enrollment made the custom impracticable. During the War between the States Federal troops quartered on the campus used the front columns as rifle targets. Dominating its auditorium is a large painting of the interior of St. Peter's in Rome "so located that the scene in the picture appears to be a continuation of the auditorium itself." The painting is by George Cooke, a Virginia artist (1783-1857); it was presented to the school by Daniel Pratt, of Prattville, Alabama.

4. PHI KAPPA HALL, across from Demosthenian Hall and the Chapel, is a two-story red brick building with four simple Doric columns supporting the unornamented pediment above its portico. It was built in 1836 for the Phi Kappa Literary Society, which was organized in 1820 largely through the efforts of Joseph Henry Lumpkin. To signify the political trend of the literary as it then moved their understanding, the Phi Kappa members adorned their walls with portraits of presidents of the United States. In selecting their honorary members, they were even more inclusive than their Demosthenian rivals, for they extended invitations to Andrew Jackson, James K. Polk, James Buchanan, Jefferson Davis, John Tyler, and Napoleon III. When the hall was used as a storehouse during the War between the States, its valuable library was damaged irreparably.

5. OLD COLLEGE, a three-story, red brick structure of post-Colonial design completed in 1805, was modeled after Connecticut Hall at Yale, Josiah Meigs having brought the plans with him when he came from Yale in 1801. The building was named Franklin College to honor Benjamin Franklin who had served the Georgia colony as its London agent; and this name is still applied to the College of Arts and Sciences. A plaque on the exterior wall of the second story marks the room once occupied by Crawford W. Long and Alexander H. Stephens. Roommates in college, these two men are Georgia's representatives in Statuary Hall of the National Capitol. In the vicinity of Old College are several buildings, originally residences, dating back to the first half of the 19th century.

6. HAROLD HIRSCH HALL, occupied by the Lumpkin Law School, is behind and to the right of Old College. It was built in 1932 largely

through alumni contributions and named for Harold Hirsch, a prominent lawyer and alumnus. The building is designed in the Greek Revival style. The Alexander C. King Law Library contains more than fourteen thousand volumes. On the library walls hang seven engravings which William Starr Basinger, an 1846 alumnus, bought from the Arundel Society of England. These engravings are from Raphael's original designs for the Sistine Chapel tapestries.

The Lumpkin Law School was founded in 1859, when the question of secession and states' rights had kindled Georgia to excitement over legislative affairs. The founders, William Hope Hull, Thomas R. R. Cobb, and Joseph Henry Lumpkin, were well-known attorneys, and Lumpkin, for whom the school was named, was the first Chief Justice of Georgia's Supreme Court.

7. At left from the Law School is PEABODY HALL, completely renovated in 1953, in which is centered the College of Education, and at right is the Commerce-Journalism Building of red brick with Ionic columns.

8. Directly behind and opposite Old College, at the end of a quadrangle, is the new ILAH DUNLAP LITTLE MEMORIAL LIBRARY, completed at a cost of $2,300,000, in the summer of 1953. This library, along with the South Campus Library (located beyond Sanford Stadium in front of Conner Hall), contains more than 283,000 catalogued volumes in addition to many uncatalogued manuscripts, maps, and pamphlets. The number of subscriptions for newspapers and periodicals adds up to some 2,300. Among items of special interest is the DeRenne Library from Wormsloe (*see* SAVANNAH), acquired in 1938. Among the prized documents of this collection are letters of Harman Verelst, Oglethorpe's private agent, of James Wright, last Colonial governor, and of General Nathanael Greene, Colonial patriot. William Stephens' *Journal of the Proceedings in Georgia* (1742), a copy of the *Cherokee Phoenix,* and photostat files of the *Royal Georgia Gazette* are other rare items of Georgiana. The university libraries serve as a depository for publications of the U. S. government.

9. Behind the Commerce and Journalism Building, facing on Lumpkin Street, is the LANDSCAPE ARCHITECTURE BUILDING, which, dating from about 1840, formerly served as a professor's home. The architectural details of the building have recently been renovated and the precision of its style restored. In the rear is the old kitchen and smoke house, to which have been added several formal gardens, in keeping with the style of the buildings. From this point a pair of steps leads down to the Founders' Memorial Garden which is on a somewhat lower level. The serpentine wall enclosing the garden is reminiscent of those Mr. Jefferson had built among the Ranges at the University of Virginia. Work

was begun on the Garden in 1939, and is sponsored by both the Garden Club of Georgia and the Department of Landscape Architecture.

10. Behind the Ilah Dunlap Little Library is LECONTE HALL, to the left of which is Baldwin Hall and to the right Park Hall, the former with Corinthian columns, the latter with Doric, and both pedimented in the Greek manner. These buildings illustrate the way in which the style of the old Chapel has been continued in modern buildings.

11. Further along West Campus Road, and beyond Woodruff Hall to the left, is MEMORIAL HALL (L), situated on a high hill overlooking the campus. This building with its Ionic portico was erected in 1923 by friends and alumni to honor university students who died in World War I. Reed Hall which stands between Memorial and Milledge Hall is one of the newest dormitories for freshmen men. It houses about five hundred students.

12. SANFORD STADIUM (L) which was dedicated in 1929 is a large oval concrete structure in a natural ravine, with a seating capacity of 33,000. It is named for S. V. Sanford, a former chancellor. For the dedication, Yale broke a precedent by coming south to play against the Georgia Bulldogs, who won 15-0.

13. Farther north and just off Lumpkin Street is a group of three buildings, the central one of which is JENNIE BELLE MYERS HALL which provides housing for 467 women.

14. THE STATE COLLEGE OF AGRICULTURE, Cedar Street and College Drive, a department of the university, has a campus of several hundred acres and a farm of several thousand. There are nine main buildings, barns for dairy and livestock, greenhouses, poultry buildings, and many other special buildings. In its major fields of specialization, the college prepares students for the various types of agricultural activities, for careers in associated business and industry, and for service in the sundry farm agencies of the state and Federal government. The college offers degrees in Agriculture, Agricultural Engineering, and Landscape Architecture.

15. LUCY COBB DORMITORY, Milledge Ave. between Reese St. and Hancock Ave., a three-story stone building with long piazzas decorated in lacy iron work, housed Lucy Cobb Institute from the 1860's well into the twentieth century. This school for girls was known throughout the South for its tuition in gentle manners and old-fashioned accomplishments. Its founding followed an article in the *Southern Watchman* in which Mrs. Williams Rutherford, writing under an assumed name from modesty, deplored the lack of attention given to the education of young southern ladies. Her brother, General T. R. R. Cobb, reading the article and reportedly unaware of its authorship, was moved

to appeal to the people of Athens, canvass for subscriptions, and to contribute largely himself. Lucy Cobb Institute was opened in 1859 and named for the general's young daughter recently dead.

From 1880 until 1928 the institution was directed by Miss Mildred Lewis Rutherford, the general's niece. "Miss Millie," always a champion of southern tradition, was a woman of effective personality, commanding presence, and fearlessly outspoken opinions. Two years after her death, with declining interest in the old institution, the university annexed the building as a dormitory for women students.

OTHER POINTS OF INTEREST

16. The HOWELL COBB HOUSE (*private*), 425 Hill Street, is a two-story, white frame house of Greek Revival design. The classic portico is adorned with Doric columns, a small overhanging balcony, and a wide piazza enclosed by an iron balustrade. General Howell Cobb, having built a similar house at the head of Pope Street, one block from Prince Avenue in 1835, built this house in 1850. Howell Cobb was Secretary of State under President Buchanan and a staunch Union man throughout the time of troubles that was defined by the 1850 compromise. But he later changed in favor of secession as the political situation grew more tumid. A brother of General T. R. R. Cobb, of Confederate fame, he was governor from 1851 to 1853. When Joe Brown, Georgia's individualist wartime governor, defied President Jefferson Davis over the right of states to raise their own armies, Cobb was among Brown's bitterest opponents, foreseeing that Brown's action could only multiply confusion and disorder in Confederate counsels.

17. The DOUBLE-BARRELED CANNON, SW. corner Hancock and College avenues, faces an old residence, built in 1830 by James Tinsley, and restored in 1949 to serve as the Athens Regional Library. The inventor of the cannon, John Gilleland, devised a plan for chaining the balls together in order to mow the enemy down in great numbers. Unhappily, he failed to synchronize the firing of the two barrels. Report has it that when tested, the chain broke, one ball demolishing a Negro cabin, the other plowing up an acre of ground and killing an innocently browsing calf in a distant field. The muse of invention has often been pictured as somewhat melancholy.

18. The T. R. R. COBB HOUSE (*private*), 194 Prince Ave., is a white frame dwelling with a Doric portico, a small balcony, and octagonal wings. The clapboarded exterior walls are formalized by Doric pilasters at the corners. This house, built between 1830 and 1840, was bought by Cobb about 1843, at which time the octagonal wings were added. General Cobb, an ardent secessionist and a man of oratorical gifts, was influen-

tial in causing Georgia's break with the Union and in drafting the new Confederate constitution.

19. The JOSEPH HENRY LUMPKIN HOUSE (*private*), 248 Prince Avenue, was built about 1845 by Lumpkin, a co-founder of the Lumpkin Law School and Georgia's first chief justice. The house is an excellent example of Greek Revival architecture, with a large Doric portico around the front and two sides, and a hanging balcony above the entrance. For a period following 1869 the house was occupied by the Home School, established by Mme. Sophie Sosnowski, a political refugee from Poland, who came to Athens in 1862 to teach at Lucy Cobb.

20. The CAMAK HOUSE, 279 Meigs Street, was built around 1830 by James Camak, first president of a branch of the Georgia State Bank established in Athens in 1834. The house, constructed of brick later painted white, is predominantly Georgian Colonial in style, having a raised basement and a small piazza of wrought iron. From the time it was built until the Cherokee were removed in 1838, the house actually stood within the confines of the Cherokee Nation. After remaining in the family for five generations, it became the Masonic Temple in 1949.

21. The BENJAMIN H. HILL HOME (*now the residence of the president of the university*), 570 Prince Ave., is a white clapboard house of Greek Revival design, with an imposing Corinthian peristyle of fourteen columns around the front and two ends, and with a typical balcony above the entrance. Fiske Kimball, the architect and author, has designated it as the "most superb" in Athens, of the Greek Revival mode. The front garden, with its oaks, cedars, magnolias, cherry laurels, gardenia, tea olive, and formal plantings of box, follows the old-fashioned southern plan, with its avoidance of open lawn. A Doric colonnade in the rear overlooks another garden and a pleasing early cottage.

Built in 1855 by Thomas Grant of Virginia the house did not come into Hill's possession until 1869, when he moved from LaGrange. Benjamin Hill (*see* TOUR 3) was a prominent Georgia statesman despite an interval of unpopularity when he advocated coming to terms with Reconstruction. Later he was elected to the U. S. House of Representatives, and afterwards to the Senate. It is claimed that he influenced President Hayes' decision to withdraw Federal troops and end the military occupation, thus terminating Reconstruction in Georgia and leading to the Constitution of 1877. The house was bought by the University of Georgia in 1949.

22. The HENRY GRADY HOUSE (*private*), 634 Prince Ave., was built about 1845 by General Robert Taylor. Henry Grady's mother rented the house as a residence for a short time after the death of her husband in the War between the States. Later, as managing editor of the *Atlanta*

Constitution, Grady did much towards building up the character and distinction of that newspaper, and his inspired imagination but equable, progressive attitude did much to promote understanding between the South and North.

Thirteen monumental Doric columns, said to represent the original colonies, enclose the Greek Revival portico on three sides of the house. Heavily linteled windows extending to the floor level are flanked by paneled pilasters. Grady often referred nostalgically to this house in later years as "the house with tall columns and spacious verandas." The school of journalism at the university is named for him.

23. The E. K. LUMPKIN HOME (*private*), 973 Prince Avenue, a two-story brownstone house with corner quoins and a wrought-iron piazza, was built between 1845 and 1850. Here in 1891 the Ladies' Garden Club was founded, the first organization of its kind in the United States. In 1939 this fact was confirmed by a tribute from the National Council of State Garden Clubs. The house is now owned by the Young Harris Methodist Church, which stands nearby.

24. The CO-ORDINATE COLLEGE, Prince and Oglethorpe aves., was originally the State Normal School, opened in 1895. When the control of the state colleges was vested in the Board of Regents in 1932, this institution was reorganized as an integral part of the university. The ten buildings are set on a sixty-acre campus. With the recent removal of residence for freshmen and sophomore women to Jennie Belle Myers Hall on Ag Hill, the university's use of the Co-Ordinate College area has come to a close. It is now used as a Naval Training Center.

25. GILMER HALL (*private*), Prince and Oglethorpe Aves., a brownstone dormitory with iron-railed piazzas and a large bracketed gable, was erected 1856-60 and was called Rock College because built of native stone. It was first occupied as a preparatory school for Franklin College. It was used as a hospital during the War between the States and afterwards as a sort of rehabilitation center or training school for Confederate soldiers. In 1895 the building was given to the new State Normal School, and its name was changed to Gilmer Hall in honor of Governor George R. Gilmer (1829-1831), who bequeathed an endowment fund for the training of Georgia teachers. Thus a precedent was enlarged into a new institution.

26. Many of the old houses, in various localities, are occupied by sororities or fraternities. One of these is the SIGMA ALPHA EPSILON HOUSE, 247 Pulaski Street, built by Ross Crane about 1842. White, with tall square columns and a hanging balcony above a well-proportioned door, the house is distinctly framed by its box hedge immediately in front of it and by handsome magnolias on its extensive lawn. The oldest Greek-

letter social fraternity, Σ. A. E. came to Franklin College in 1866 after being founded at the University of Alabama, the chapter of which is now known as Mother Mu.

27. The FERDINAND PHINIZY HOUSE (*private*), 250 South Milledge Avenue, from around 1857, is one of the interesting exceptions to the Greek Revival style. Its double-porch and the precise elegance of its ironwork suggest Mobile or New Orleans. This avenue has other houses of interest.

Atlanta

(Upon approaching the city on principal US highways, and especially with regard to north-south routes, transients not familiar with Atlanta should inquire about the Central Expressway and its arterial adjuncts—parts of which are now complete, others under construction.)

Railroad Stations: Terminal Station, Mitchell and Spring streets, for Central of Georgia Ry., Atlanta & West Point R.R., Seaboard Air Line Ry., and Southern Ry.; Union Station, 2 Forsyth Street, for Atlantic Coast Line R.R., Louisville & Nashville R.R., Nashville, Chattanooga & St. Louis Ry., and Georgia R.R.; also, Peachtree Station, 1688 Peachtree Street, for Southern Ry.

Bus Station: Greyhound Bus Depot, 169 Carnegie Way, for Southeastern Greyhound, Southeastern Management Co., Atlantic Greyhound, Teche Greyhound, Southeastern Stages, Southeastern Motor, Dahlonega (Roswell, Cumming) Bus; Trailways Bus Depot, 212 Spring Street, N. W., Modern Trailways, Smoky Mountain Trailways, Crescent Trailways, Tennessee Coach Co.

Airport: Atlanta Municipal Airport at Hapeville, 9.2 m. S. of City on US 41, for American Air Lines, Capital Air Lines, Eastern Air Lines, Delta-C & S Air Lines, North American Air Lines, and Southern Airways; special bus, fare $1.15, stops at principal hotels, Terminal Station, and downtown ticket offices of air lines.

Taxis: 50¢ in business district for one to five passengers; 50¢ for first 1½ miles; 10¢ each additional ⅖ mile; hand baggage free.

Local Busses: Trolley fare 15¢ straight; shoppers' busses limited to principal business section, 5¢.

Traffic Regulations: Speed limit in downtown area 25 m.p.h.; elsewhere 35 m.p.h. One-way streets indicated by signs. Right turn permitted on red light *where indicated* after full stop; left turn on green light only. All vehicles must stop six feet behind trolleys or busses except at safety islands. Ample off-street but limited curb parking in downtown area; no parking at yellow curbs; parking on R. of street strictly enforced in all areas. Differential speed limits on the Central Expressway strictly enforced by motor police, at all hours.

Accommodations: Some 70 hotels including 7 for Negroes (*see* Yellow Pages, Classified Section of Atlanta Telephone Directory); motor courts and motels on principal highways.

Tourist Information Service: Atlanta Chamber of Commerce, Volunteer Building, Broad, Luckie and Forsyth streets; AAA. Georgian Terrace Hotel, 659 Peachtree Street, N. E.; Dixie Motor Club, 627 Peachtree Street, N. E.; Atlanta Convention and Visitors' Bureau, Rhodes-Haverty Bldg., 134 Peachtree.

Theaters and Motion Picture Houses: Tower Theater, Peachtree Street between Linden Street and North Avenue; Atlanta Municipal Auditorium, corner Courtland Street and Gilmer Street, for occasional concerts and operas; some 65 motion picture houses including a number for Negroes.

18

Radio Stations: WSB (750 kc.); WGST (920 kc.); WATL (1380 kc.); WAGA (590 kc.); WBGE (1340 kc.); WEAS (1010 kc.); WQXI (790 kc.); WERD (860 kc.); WGLS (970 kc.); WTJH (1260 kc.).
Television: WSB-TV Chan. 2; WAGA-TV Chan. 5; WLWA-TV Chan. 11.
Parks in the Atlanta System offering golf and often other facilities not listed, such as playgrounds, picnic areas, etc.: Adams Park, located in Cascade Heights in SW. Atlanta, at 2300 Wilson Drive, 18-hole golf course (swimming pool, lake, football, softball, tennis); Atlanta Memorial Park, Bobby Jones Golf Course, 18 holes, 384 Woodward Way, N. W. (tennis courts—lighted 13); Chastain Memorial Park, North Fulton Golf Course, Powers Ferry Road, 18 holes (swimming pool, lake, football, baseball, tennis courts—9, and lighted—6); James L. Key Golf Course—9 holes, end of Kalb Avenue, S. E.; Piedmont Park, 9-hole golf course (swimming, football, softball, baseball); John A. White Golf Course, Huff Road and Cascade Avenue, S. W., 9-hole golf course (football, baseball, tennis courts—4). Atlanta has more than fifty other recreational parks offering a variety of facilities.
Baseball: Ponce de Leon Park, 650 Ponce de Leon Avenue, N. E., Southern League (Atlanta Crackers); seats 14,500.
Football: Grant Field (Georgia Tech Stadium), corner of North Avenue and Techwood Drive, N. W.; seats 35,000; home of the "Yellow Jackets."
Annual Events: Flowering of dogwood trees in residential sections, usually first and second weeks of April—special sightseeing tours by transit company; the Atlanta Flower Show Association's exhibit, latter part of March, at the Atlanta Biltmore Hotel; the Camellia Show at the Atlanta Biltmore Hotel, February 13 and 14; Egleston Home and Garden Tours, April and May; "Holiday Houses" usually open ten days before Christmas, homes decorated for Christmas by local garden clubs; the Horse Show, Chastain Memorial Park, in May; May Festival for children at Wren's Nest, home of Joel Chandler Harris, 1050 Gordon Street (exact date may vary due to weather); Auto Races, at Lakewood Park, July 4 and also Labor Day; Southeastern World's Fair, first week in October; the Atlanta Art Association's Southeastern Annual Exhibition, at the High Museum, latter part of September and early October; Georgia–Georgia Tech Freshman Football Game, Grant Field, Thanksgiving; Joel Chandler Harris Memorial Service (inquire from Wren's Nest), annual banquet, December 9; numerous conventions throughout the year.

ATLANTA (1,050 alt., 331,314 urban pop.; metropolitan pop., 668,-022), the capital of Georgia, is generally recognized as the functional center of the Southeast in regard to commerce, industry, transportation, communication, and finance. Hence it is also a center of the service, clerical, and managerial arts typical of the American productive and commercial genius. It is the offspring of an exceptional topographical situation, and the railroads that this situation made possible.

Let a straight line be drawn on a map from Boston, through New York, to New Orleans; and another, from Chicago to Miami. These will form an immense X that intersects itself at a point slightly northeast of Atlanta. Roughly, the northeast leg of the X's New Orleans–Boston axis will lie just east of the great Appalachian chain, extending southwest from the St. Lawrence Valley in Canada's Quebec Province to the Coastal Plain of Alabama. Early expansion to the west funneled

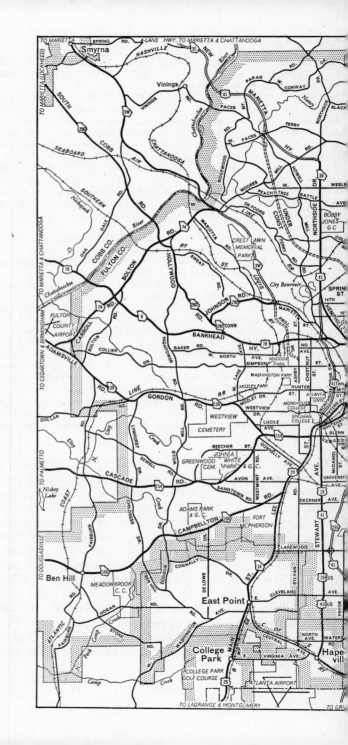

out of the singularly few breaks in the Appalachian chain into the rich
Ohio River Valley and into the Mississippi area. One of these outlets
will be seen to lie on the Chicago-Miami axis of the X, just at Chattanooga, with an easy downgrade to Atlanta. It is the "swag" at the
great spur of the Appalachian where the ridge exhibits a major fault
before rising again to its last crest in Alabama. Likewise a line from
Minneapolis–St. Paul to Miami and one from Kansas City to Savannah
will intersect nearly at Atlanta. A glance at air and railroad maps and
at those for communication lines will show that the great X is a sort of
general equation for a complex of regional functions making up a
crucial part of the industrial physiology of the American body economic.

Nurtured by the rich pecuniary imagination of the early nineteenth
century, the Georgia railroads began to spread out over the state like
acquisitive fingers. From the upcountry a natural line of trade pointed
like a magnetic needle towards the opening in northwest Georgia to
the Ohio Valley. Climbing by the vast terraces that make up Georgia's
Coastal Plain and by the Piedmont ridges, the railroads to the northwest were persuaded by the logic of the terrain to converge towards a
point on the Piedmont Plateau, later to be named Atlanta.

Think of Chicago as the civic enlargement of its stockyards and of
the surrounding rich grain areas, and thus as an organic function of its
region; of New York as a many-chambered shell secreted by its stock-
exchange (and of all that the word "exchange" can mean), but as not
organic to its region: the one primarily producing, the other primarily
exchanging. Then—to the extent that primary functions can be descriptive—Atlanta may be seen in the order of American cities as a partial
mixture of the elements determining Chicago and New York. It is
productive, and also organic to the extent that its decidedly diversified
industries draw upon the Southeast for materials, though it is not the
civic enlargement of any one of these, such as cotton. It is engaged,
and critically, with the complex forms of exchange (finance, transportation, communication, distribution, etc.) characteristic of a neotechnic
economy—including an imposing pyramid of clerical and managerial
skills needed to record and direct such operations. But it is not a pecuniary empire within its own confines.

Founded little more than a century ago and burned in its youth by
Sherman—who recognized it for the artery of economic life that it is,
Atlanta quickly recovered. Not being in any irreparable sense tied to
the plantation type of economy as such, and hence to the fate of the
cotton oligarchy, it seemed to thrive on Reconstruction, and on the acceptance of that industry and its complementary mercantilism implied
by the defeat of the Confederacy.

Unlike most sizable cities of the South, such as Savannah, Mobile, or New Orleans, Atlanta's youth precludes the existence of any genuinely old houses, and the old families are importations from other sections. Not that it is estranged from the familial images of the Old South. These still move the daily imagination. On the benign side they work toward conserving good taste and to provide a sense of social style. As for the reverse side, the Southeast has never been reconstructed to the extent of explicitly accepting all the provisions of the Constitution. Thus it remains in the position of a church which, though absorbed into a larger whole, still exercises a local rite otherwise proscribed. Atlanta is too much *of* its scene, to be unaffected by what from the standpoint of democracy is a tragic predicament, as witness its 1907 race riot. But at times and especially in recent years, exemplary policies have promised much towards good civic health in this respect. Atlanta's discharge of the social duties arising from the common blood flowing through the hearts of men may eventually establish the model for a new regional morality.

Gay, modern, colorful, energetic, and alert, Atlanta in its prime can well afford to substitute the cheerful realism of its present, and what this means for the future, for the traditional Southern uses of the past. Such white columns as it has—and Atlanta has a very high position with regard to good architectural taste among American cities—should be taken as symbolic of its energy and managerial skill, and not as monuments over the grave of a dream. Restless, assertive, sprawling in all directions and taking in smaller towns in its incessant push towards growth, the city in 1952 annexed eighty-two square miles, with approximately 100,000 residents, as part of an extensive civic plan of improvement for its area. Atlanta is one of a group of cities that have undertaken to think their way into a New South.

Atlanta's history, characteristic of its vigorous growth, is a narrative of energetic personalities and rapid changes. First mention of the region is found in Revolutionary War records dated August 1, 1782, which state that a secret emissary had been delegated to report on rumors of friction between the Cherokee and Creek Indians at The Standing Peachtree. Named, according to legend, for an Indian peach on a nearby mound, The Standing Peachtree was a Creek settlement on the southern bank of the Chattahoochee River, approximately seven miles from the present site of Atlanta. The story is that the Creeks won the region south of the river from the Cherokee as a trophy in a series of Indian ball games.

Because of the disturbance between the Creek and Cherokee, Lieutenant George R. Gilmer, later governor of Georgia, was commissioned in 1813 to erect a fort at The Standing Peachtree; he and twenty-two recruits constituted the first white settlement in the Atlanta area. After his departure, The Standing Peachtree grew into an important trading post and gateway to northern Cherokee lands.

The founding of Atlanta was due to the creative imagination of certain pioneer railroad entrepreneurs. In 1836 representatives of Georgia's existing railroads devised a plan whereby the state should build a railroad through the mountains of north Georgia to connect the proposed termini of their lines at the Chattahoochee River, with the Tennessee River. In December a law was steered through the legislature permitting the construction of the proposed line from the Chattahoochee north to Ross's Landing, later Chattanooga. To avoid having the southern end of the state line, afterwards named the Western & Atlantic, terminate in the immense silence of the pine woods, without transportation affiliates for the rest of Georgia, the Georgia Railroad from Augusta to Union Point and the Central of Georgia from Savannah to Macon were pushed northward. The meeting point on the Chattahoochee required by the terrain became the southern terminus of the Western & Atlantic. A little post office known as White Hall was nearby, but the area involved took its name Terminus from the engineer's final stake.

Terminus soon became a trading center for the surrounding country, with two stores, a sawmill, and a railroad office. In 1843 the settlement was incorporated as the town of Marthasville in honor of Martha Lumpkin, daughter of the Governor. When the Georgia railroad was completed in September of 1845, it was decided that the town should be given a name descriptive of its function, and it was named Atlanta: "from Atlanta to the Atlantic." Although the cars of the Macon & Western (formerly the Monroe Railroad) reached Jonesboro for the first time in the fall of 1845 with a load of salt, the tracks were not operating to Atlanta itself until the following year.

So rapidly had the town's commercial importance grown that on December 29, 1847, Atlanta was reincorporated as a city. Its new corporate limits were within a circle, the center of which was the Western & Atlantic zero milepost near the southwestern corner of Wall Street and Central Avenue. With the completion of the Atlanta and West Point Railroad in 1853 connections were established with Montgomery, Alabama, and points westward.

The new county of Fulton was created from DeKalb County on December 20, 1853, and Atlanta was made its seat. It is commonly said that it was named for Robert Fulton of steamboat fame, but it may have been for Hamilton Fulton, an English civil engineer, appointed by the Board of Public Works created by the legislature in 1825 to organize a system of canals. Like most men who supply the formal plans without which men of action are absurdly blind in regard to pioneer enterprises, he was discredited and the board abolished a year later. In the same year that the county was created, the Holland Free School, the city's first publicly sponsored educational institution, was opened in the old Angier Academy on the southwest corner of Forsyth and Garnett streets. In 1854, when the population numbered around 6,000, the Athenaeum Theater was opened, and the first city hall built. Though severely sober in its style, the *Georgia Gazetteer* broke its routine to call the city hall "a splendid building." The Atlanta Medical College was founded in 1855 by physicians of the city, and that same year a charter was granted to the Atlanta Gas Company, and the city was illuminated by Christmas Day. A city directory of 1859 gives 11,500 as Atlanta's population.

By the late 1850's discourse had so deteriorated between the North and South that a Georgia periodical commented, ". . . it is the settled determination of many planters and merchants to have direct trade with Europe—to send our produce there, in our own bottoms, and bring back the goods we do not see fit to manufacture. *Non-intercourse* in regard to the North, in the minds of thousands is now the settled policy." The Gate City Guards and the Atlanta Grays were organized and began to hold drill exercises. Since it was in the nature of things that Atlanta must become an important military and hospitalization center as well as supply depot for the Confederacy, the secession of Georgia from the Union on January 19, 1861, simply confirmed its destiny. Confederate forces put the city under martial law in April, 1862. Large factories and warehouses were established for the manufacture and storage of supplies during the war's course, and it is estimated that as many as 80,000 wounded soldiers were quartered in the city.

On March 22, 1863, instructions were given Colonel Lemuel P. Grant to plan fortifications for the defense of Atlanta; by April of next year breastworks and batteries were ready to withstand the expected attack. When General John B. Hood superseded General Joseph E. Johnston in command of the Confederate army on July 17, 1864, General Sherman was already moving his men into position around the line of defense. On July 22, two days after General Hood's desperate attempt to break the advancing Union line at the Battle of Peachtree Creek, the fierce encounter known as the Battle of Atlanta occurred in the southeastern part of the city, principally along what are now Moreland and DeKalb avenues. Despite heavy losses on both sides, the battle was ambiguous. A few days later, however, a brief conflict at Ezra Church in southwest Atlanta convinced Sherman that it would be too costly to take the city by assault. Some of the largest siege guns used in the war were hauled down from Chattanooga, and Atlanta was bombarded for the rest of July and through the hot days of August. Meanwhile Sherman separated Atlanta from its external sources of supply as one breaks away the claws of a crab.

By the end of August all Confederate means of communication with Atlanta were lost except the Central Railroad (formerly the Macon & Western). Finding the city irreducible by bombardment, General Sherman swung a decisive section of his army toward Jonesboro, twenty miles south, in an effort to cut the final life line. General W. J. Hardee was sent to meet it, but his force was too small, and the result was a telling Confederate defeat at the Battle of Jonesboro, September 1, and the seizure of the railroad. Hood evacuated Atlanta that night by way of the McDonough wagon road, and on September 2 the mayor formally surrendered the city to Colonel John Coburn.

Within the next few days General Sherman ordered the removal of all citizens from the city. This was a shock since the terms of surrender specified that the lives and property of all citizens were to be protected. Sherman supplied teams of horses for transporting the refugees to Rough and Ready, a settlement one mile south of the present Hapeville, and Hood furnished additional teams from there to Lovejoy Station, ten miles farther south. With the evacuation completed, Sherman reorganized his army and gave orders for the destruction of Atlanta. On November 15, the day after a night of fire, looting, and drunkenness on the part of his troops, Sherman and his army resumed their march toward the sea, having dispersed the population and razed all but some 400 of Atlanta's 4,500 houses and commercial buildings.

Rehabilitation in Atlanta was soon under way. By January, 1865, many citizens had returned to the city, and after the Confederate surrender there was an influx of people from the North and others from parts of the South. In keeping with the pattern of good sense in its history, on June 24, 1865, at the first public forum held after Atlanta's surrender, its citizens formulated reconstruction plans and prudently resolved to co-operate with the Union commercially. This also carried a suggestion of political assent. At first the confusion of local finances, reduced at the collapse of the Confederacy to barter until Union money should circulate, made it necessary to appeal for food supplies. Immediate steps were taken to reorganize business and repair the wrecked railroads. An occupying army may be politically and socially a bitter draught, but commercially it has its advantages. One may recall that in Margaret Mitchell's *Gone with the Wind* winsome Scarlett O'Hara made use of a certain wallet of Union gold and greenbacks obtained by quick resolution. In 1866, after Atlanta became headquarters for Federal reconstruction in this section, the population was estimated at 20,228, almost twice what it was when Sherman attacked.

The Young Men's Library Association was established in 1867, and in the next year the *Atlanta Constitution,* oldest existing newspaper in the city, was founded. Later its editor, Henry W. Grady, was to make articulate the city's dream of a New South, and in this he was helped by Joel Chandler Harris, who, for example, spoke in the *Sunday Gazette,* of the folly of adhering to a "period that was soul-destroying in its narrowness." However, lest the historical images of the period seem too precise, one should consider Grady's arrangements for the unveiling of the Benjamin H. Hill statue in 1886. Jefferson Davis had been invited, and that General John B. Gordon's reputation might be purged of its railroad associations, Grady arranged for the two celebrities to appear together. At the height of the dedication ceremony "a solitary horseman rode out of Peachtree Street toward the monument. He was mounted on a fine horse and wore the uniform of a lieutenant general of the Confederate army." The horseman was General James Longstreet, and the Confederate leaders sat together for the rest of the ceremony. General Longstreet had turned Republican in 1882 and for good. Whether Grady arranged the Longstreet part of the above Confederate epiphany is not clear.

In 1870 the first board of education was elected, and within three years several public schools were opened to 4,000 children. The year 1870 also saw the opening of the DeGive Opera House, one of the finest theatres of the South. Its cars drawn typically enough by mules rather than horses, the first street railway began operating the year afterward. Atlanta's importance as a railroad center was further increased in 1873 by the construction of the Atlanta & Charlotte Air Line Railroad—the survey for which had been made before the war—and of the Georgia Western. Atlanta had now become the second largest city in the state, surpassed only by Savannah.

A constitutional convention had met in Atlanta on December 9, 1867, at the order of Major General Pope, who was in charge of the reconstruction government. Atlanta offered the state free office space for ten years, and a capitol site, if that body would adopt a resolution to make the city the state seat of government. The proposal was accepted on February 27, 1868, and upon ratification of the constitution the same year, Atlanta became the state capital. Since the convention of 1867 was under Republican auspices, and in fact is commonly called the Carpetbag Convention, angry objections broke out against the removal of the capital from Milledgeville. But when the constitutional convention of 1877 submitted the issue to the people, the selection of Atlanta was confirmed, it having by then become a leading center of industry and commerce.

After the war the Freedman's Bureau, helped by charitable interests from the North, underwrote the education of the liberated Negroes. Atlanta University was established in 1867. It has continued to grow, and today a complex of associated colleges, it is the most important center in the world for Negro education.

The International Cotton Exposition, held in 1881, focused the attention of the nation on the potentialities of this region as a manufacturing center and attracted investments from solid Republicans, now called Eastern capitalists and not Yankees. The fair buildings afterward were taken over by the Exposition Cotton Mills. A second and more ambitious undertaking was the Cotton States and International Exposition, held in 1895 in the area that is now Piedmont Park. Its purpose was to revive and exercise the impression made by the 1881 Exposition upon the national eye. Its images of progress included the advances made by the Negro since Emancipation. Booker T. Washington made one of the principal addresses. Signs of the times were a contribution of $200,000 by the Federal government towards the expenses of the Exposition, and its opening by President Cleveland's young daughter who pressed a telegraph button in Boston. If the exposition did not achieve anything as synoptic of the age as the intricate wonder of glass and iron girders at the Paris Exposition of 1899, known as the Machine Hall, it did indicate that the Industrial Revolution, however belatedly and however shyly, was drawing the South into common bond with the nation's destiny.

The expansion of industry and manufacturing in the late nineteenth century was accompanied by a decided upswing in Atlanta's population. The perfect circle, ". . . one mile from the State Depot in every direction," set in 1847 by the General Assembly as the area of the city, turned into a figure less geometric but more organic as Atlanta spread out along its ridges. Atlanta's youth as a manufacturing center was an advantage to the city. No vested property interests operating with obsolete equipment slowed up the introduction of new industrial techniques. Moreover, coal and iron as the essential factors in the production and transmission of mechanical power were soon to give way to natural gas and electrical energy. This meant that the city would escape much of the factory filth and blight which along with their smokestacks are features of older manufacturing centers. It is also true that Atlanta's distributive function began to take the upper hand over its manufacturing development.

The greatest physical catastrophe to the city since the Siege of Atlanta was the fire that started on May 21, 1917, near Decatur Street, and rapidly burned the section about Boulevard from Decatur Street to Ponce de Leon Avenue. About 2,000 dwellings and business houses were destroyed and property damages were estimated at over five million dollars.

During World War I Atlanta's topographical situation made it one of the large centers for troop training. From September, 1917, through November, 1918, more than 230,000 soldiers and officers were mobilized at Camp Gordon, in the Chamblee area to the north of the city. For several years after the war houses were built by new citizens, as well as by old inhabitants who moved into newly developed residential sections. Industrial corporations opening distribution units in Atlanta required office space, and Atlanta's midtown skyline came into existence with its multi-storied buildings. Candler Field, established in 1925, was later selected by principal airlines as an airport, and by 1934 the new three-million dollar post office was completed.

After World War I with the great improvement of rapid transit vehicles, and especially of the automobile now made cheap by assembly-line methods, the concentration of population in American cities began to find relief by an inverse movement to the suburbs. In the area around Atlanta this movement tended to appear as a double image. Increasing land prices tempted the holders of small farms to sell, and frequently to move to Atlanta, while those able to do so moved outward. For the most part the city's slums received the inflow. But the outward movement has a further aspect. Factories, especially of the assembly type, such as that of John Deere at Chamblee, of General Motors at Doraville, and of the Ford Motor Company at Hapeville, are instances on another functional level. With World War II and the vast increase in consumer buying power, resulting from the policies of the Roosevelt administration, new industries flowed into Atlanta. The metropolitan enlargement of Atlanta had become the dominant feature of its evolution. In 1947 the General Assembly created the Metropolitan Planning Commission, a deliberative and advisory group, for the purpose of developing an "overall master plan for Fulton and DeKalb Counties." Actual adoption is a matter for local government.

Faced with the certainty in recent years that if something were not done, its midtown business section was doomed by premature high traffic pressure, Atlanta looked about for the doctor. H. W. Lochner and Company was retained to make a study of its highways problem at the request of the State Highway Department. From a 1946 bond issue voted jointly by the people of Atlanta and Fulton County, the sum of $16,600,000 was allocated for carrying out the revised Lochner Plan. The Central Expressway, under construction and partially completed by the Atlanta–Fulton County Joint Bond Commission, the Georgia State Highway Department, and the Federal Bureau of Public Roads, is a six lane north-south route. It is designed to conduct interregional traffic through a painfully obstructed area, and to bring suburban traffic from the north and south into the downtown business district, though not through it. Since work began, more than twelve miles of the project have been completed or let to contract, though not the connector or midsection needed to tie the present north and south trunks together.

To date almost all of the $16,600,000 allotment has been exhausted, and in addition $16,000,000 from state and Federal sources. Meanwhile a 1952 city-county bond issue is available for an additional $12,700,000. It specifies completion of the midtown connector, as well as enabling other construction, and it is matched by state and Federal funds. A breakdown of the sums spent shows that Federal and state funds have mostly gone for construction costs; the acquisition of rights of way, time consuming and costly, accounts for the greater part of the bond fund. The present Central Expressway is the main artery of a complete circulation system planned to take care of Atlanta's present congestion and to keep it fluid for years to come. Atlanta is beginning to learn that the collective conditions imposed on life by the industrial factory and the office disfigure life unless relieved by the formal and also moral uses of reason.

Atlanta ranks first among the cities of the Southeast as a railroad and distribution center. The Atlanta shop of the Pullman Company, established in 1926 and the company's sixth, has become one of the most important parts of the system. Atlanta is the third largest telegraph and the third largest telephone switching center in the world. Most of the Federal Departments and Agencies are represented in Atlanta, there being 76 such establishments, 36 of which, employing over 20,000 persons, are regional in scope. The rest serve the state and the Atlanta Metropolitan Area. Atlanta has no dominating industry, but its 1,625 factories turn out more than 3,000 different commodities. In addition to the many locally owned and operated industries, over 3,300 of the nation's leading business organizations have branches in Atlanta for manufacturing or for warehousing and distributing purposes.

Twelve major airline routes serve Atlanta. The in and out daily schedule of planes is 214. The Atlantic Coast Line, the Atlanta & West Point Railway, the Central of Georgia, the Georgia Railroad, the Louisville & Nashville Railway, the Nashville, Chattanooga & St. Louis, the Seaboard Air Line Railway, and the Southern Railway, all serve Atlanta.

Atlanta's altitude of 1,050 feet above sea level, which is not exceeded by any other city of 200,000 or over except Denver, accounts for its relatively cool weather in summer. As Atlantans know to their joy, while northern areas are in the grip of a heat wave Atlanta will often be pleasantly temperate. Based on a period of forty-five years, Atlanta's January mean temperature is 43.2°, and in July 78.1°; its annual rainfall, 49.30 inches. Visitors from more rigorous parts, especially in winter, are always impressed with the fresh greenness of the grass, not to dwell upon the formal beauty of the numerous evergreens, especially broadleafed, that are used in great abundance. When there is no late frost and spring is favorable, the dogwood displays itself everywhere with fabulous generosity.

Atlanta has twenty-three golf courses, 14 with eighteen holes and 9 with nine holes, of which seventeen are municipally owned. In all, the city maintains 146 parks, squares, and spaces for public use, making up a total area of around 2,350 acres. Atlanta has its own symphony orchestra which began in 1944 as the Youth Symphony. The name was changed to Atlanta Symphony Orchestra in January of 1947. During the 1952-53 season the orchestra joined the American Symphony Orchestra League, and the Atlanta Symphony Library of Music was founded by the Atlanta Junior League. Several small affiliated instrumental groups have developed: The Atlanta Symphony Little Symphony (30 pieces), the Atlanta Symphony String Quartet, the Atlanta Symphony Woodwind Quintet, and the Atlanta String Ensemble (12 pieces). Also seasons of grand opera, light opera, and popular concerts are given annually in Atlanta. The high quality of the Atlanta Music Club's annual series is shown by the following selections from its 1953-54 group: the Sadler's Wells Ballet, the Detroit Symphony Orchestra, and a dramatization of Stephen Vincent Benét's *John Brown's Body,* starring Tyrone Power, Raymond Massey, and Anne Baxter, with a chorus of twenty voices directed by Walter Shumann. Among the institutions of higher learning in the metropolitan area are Emory University, Oglethorpe University, Atlanta University and its associated colleges, the Atlanta Division of the University of Georgia, Agnes Scott College, and the Georgia Institute of Technology.

By 1980 it is highly probable in terms of present trends that metropolitan Atlanta will house and supply the means of livelihood for a million and a quarter people. New residential areas—nearly all of which will tend to be peripheral in location—will absorb additional acreages to accommodate the homes, schools, churches, and shopping centers demanded by the increase in population. Since at present the greater part of the new industrial acreage is in extensive districts located around the periphery of the urban area, residential sections have tended to follow these work areas, and convenient shopping centers have developed. At the same time the Central Business District in the hub of the city's extensive expressway and transit system continues to supply specialized shopping and services not available elsewhere within the metropolitan area or for that matter elsewhere in the Southeast. The pattern that is emerging as likely for the future metropolis, as the age of mobility itself moves on, is that of sub-centers of industry, residences, and business tied to the heart of the central city by rapid transportation routes.

POINTS OF INTEREST
(DOWNTOWN)

FIVE POINTS, at the intersection of Peachtree, Decatur, and Marietta streets and Edgewood Avenue, is a wedge-shaped area, constituting Atlanta's hub, from which principal thoroughfares radiate to all parts of the metropolitan area. In recent decades steel and concrete office buildings have grown above the low brick buildings of the 1880's and '90's. Many of the city's important financial establishments are grouped about this section. Traffic pours through the area, lights change, police whistles blow insistently, and crowds of hurrying people surge and flow. Important civic occasions are usually publicized from Five Points.

Soon after the incorporation of the city in 1847, this section became its natural center. The city drilled an artesian well here in 1884 that was 2,044 feet deep, and a tank and pump were installed to supply water to downtown establishments.

1. The OLD LAMPPOST, NE. corner Whitehall and Alabama streets, preserved as a relic of the War between the States, was first lit on Christmas Day, 1855. At its base is a hole torn by a shell during the siege of Atlanta in 1864. The gas was again connected for the *première* of the screen version of *Gone with the Wind* in December of 1939, and the lamp now burns as a memorial to the South of the period.

2. The ATLANTA DIVISION, University of Georgia, 24 Ivy Street, S. E., urban unit of the University System of Georgia, is situated two blocks east of Five Points in the midtown heart of the city. The seven-story classroom building at 24 Ivy Street, once a concrete and brick garage

and office building, was converted into an educational building able to accommodate 5,000 students each quarter. Over one hundred classrooms, eight laboratories, several assembly rooms, clinic, three restaurants, academic and administrative offices, music and art studios, provide for the educational activities of the students, many of whom are employed in businesses and industries in metropolitan Atlanta.

The Atlanta Division's new $2,000,000 Georgia marble and granite library and administration building overlooks Hurt Park at the corner of Gilmer and Courtland streets. With the drill field and two R. O. T. C. buildings on Courtland Street, the gymnasium-auditorium, the seven-story classroom building and parking lots at 20-32 Ivy Street, the institution's downtown properties have an appraised valuation of $7,000,000.

Unique services for students include a work-scholarship plan through which qualified Georgia high school graduates earn their educational and living expenses. The only state-chartered Student Credit Union in the country and a book-rental system supply other financial help.

Established as a branch of Georgia Tech in 1914, and called Tech Evening School of Commerce, the institution in 1933 was made an independent one by the Regents of the University System, and renamed Georgia Evening College. In 1934 the Atlanta Junior College was established. The two were known as the University of Georgia Center.

Outgrowing seven locations, including a remodeled building on the old Sheltering Arms property at 223 Walton Street now occupied by the Southern College of Pharmacy, and the old Georgia Baptist Hospital building at 162 Luckie Street, the college finally came to rest at 24 Ivy Street in August, 1945. Classes began in the converted garage building the following spring.

By action of the Regents of the University System of Georgia the college was designated as a branch of the University of Georgia in the fall of 1947, to be known as the Atlanta Division, University of Georgia. This was in line with a policy developed by large universities located in small towns, of having urban branches in nearby metropolitan centers.

The academic courses of the Atlanta Division are accredited by the Southern Association of Schools and Colleges, and lead to the Bachelor of Business Administration degree, and the degree of B. S. in Nursing Education. Other programs include art, music, drama, education, certain general studies, and those in twenty concentration fields of business administration and economics.

3. HENRY GRADY MONUMENT, Marietta and Forsyth streets, was unveiled on October 21, 1891, as a memorial to Henry Woodfin Grady, direct-

ing genius of the *Atlanta Constitution,* whose vision of the New South did so much to ease sectionalism and to re-imagine its destiny. Draped female figures, representing *Memory* and one of her daughters, *History,* are set on two sides of a large granite pedestal, which is surmounted by a bronze figure of Grady delivering an address. Alexander Doyle was the sculptor.

Grady, born in Athens on May 24, 1850, devoted his life to furthering the peace and prosperity of his native state. Two orations especially: *The New South,* delivered before the New England Club of New York City in 1886, and *The South and Her Problems,* delivered at the State Fair at Dallas, Texas, in 1887, gave him a national reputation. His most eloquent address, *The Race Problem,* was delivered in Boston ten days before his death on December 23, 1889. He had begun work for the *Constitution* in October of 1876.

4. The ATLANTA PUBLIC LIBRARY, formerly known as the Carnegie Library (*open 9 A.M.-9 P.M. Monday through Friday; 9 A.M.-6 P.M. Saturdays*), 126 Carnegie Way, occupies a two-story building constructed of native white marble, the old wing being conventionalized Ionic and the new wing modern in style. On the façade above the arched windows of the old wing's second story are carved the names of distinguished authors. Many innovations in color, lighting, equipment, and furnishings have been introduced in the new wing. Ackerman and Ross of New York were the architects of the old wing, Toombs and Creighton of Atlanta of the new.

The library is an outgrowth of the Young Men's Library Association organized on June 30, 1867. The old wing was opened to the public in 1902, the new on December 1, 1950. Including Georgiana, genealogy, and Southern history, on January 1, 1953, the book collection of the library numbered 212,983 volumes. In addition, its Fine Arts Department has an excellent collection of recordings, films, and prints. The library system as a whole consists of 15 white and three Negro branches, and a bookmobile is maintained for service to rural areas.

5. The FEDERAL RESERVE BANK, 104 Marietta Street, N. W., of the Sixth Federal Reserve District, has its main office in Atlanta, with branches at Birmingham, Jacksonville, Nashville, and New Orleans. The bank and its branches serve a territory that includes all of the states of Alabama, Florida, and Georgia, the eastern three-quarters of Tennessee, and the southeastern halves of Louisiana and Mississippi. As of September 1, 1953, the bank had 1,290 employees, of whom 537 were at the Atlanta office, 168 at Birmingham, 235 at Jacksonville, 130 at Nashville, and 220 at New Orleans.

Within the area of the Sixth District, there were on September 1,

1953, 1,229 commercial banks, of which 363 were member banks of the Federal Reserve System, *i.e.* 291 national banks, and 72 state chartered banks. The member banks of the Sixth District in mid-1953 had $7.4 billion in total resource. In September 1953, the resources of the Federal Reserve Bank of Atlanta amounted to $2.5 billion. As the depository of the member bank reserves and as a banking institution with the right of issue and discount, the Federal Reserve Bank of Atlanta occupies a key position in the banking affairs of the Southeast.

The Federal Reserve Bank of Atlanta is one of twelve regional Federal Reserve Banks. Each Reserve Bank is a separately incorporated institution, having its own board of directors. The Reserve Banks themselves operate under the general supervision of the Board of Governors of the Federal Reserve System with headquarters at Washington, D. C. The member banks, the reserve banks, and the Board of Governors compose a banking system that is peculiarly a product of the American democratic process. Quite literally, the Board of Governors represents the essential link between government and the private interests of our banking system. In adjusting the country's money supply towards a stable economic growth, the Board of Governors plays the primary rôle through its authority over changes in member bank reserve requirements, its participation in open market operations, and its approval of changes in discount rates at the Federal Reserve Bank.

The Federal Reserve Bank of Atlanta opened for business on November 16, 1914. It was first housed in rented quarters in the Hurt Building, but on October 1, 1918, moved to its present location. The original building of Georgia white marble is Greek in style, the composite order being used throughout. The front is colonnaded, with an ornamental balustrade. In 1952 the bank acquired the property occupied by the Atlanta Georgian Building, and now has the John Silvey Building under purchase agreement. The bank is shortly scheduled to begin a six-story building which will occupy the space between the present bank building and the Silvey Building.

On the northwest corner of the bank is a plaque with the following information:

Site of the First Mercantile Business, 1839. The general store of Johnson and Thrasher. Home, 1842-45, of Mrs. and Mrs. Willis Carlisle and their daughter Julia Carlisle (Withers), 'Atlanta's First Baby,' born August 17, 1842. First Presbyterian Church was built here in 1850. Rebuilt, 1877, and occupied until 1915.

6. CANDLER BUILDING, SE. corner Peachtree and Houston streets, built 1904-06, rises to a height of seventeen stories and was for so many years

Atlanta's only skyscraper that "as tall as the Candler Building" became
an established local simile. The exterior to the fifth floor line and the
interior are of white native marble, with the other exterior stories granite. French, Italian, English, and Scottish sculptors were employed to
do the elaborate carving. A series of panels carved on the façades represents the liberal arts and the sciences. At the Houston Street entrance are two 26-foot engaged columns cut from single blocks of marble. In two niches above the grand staircase are busts of Asa G.
Candler's parents, and carved in high relief in an ornate frieze are the
heads of Alexander H. Stephens, Charles J. Jenkins, General John B.
Gordon, General Joseph E. Wheeler, Sidney Lanier, Joel Chandler
Harris, and Eli Whitney.

7. The ATLANTA MUNICIPAL AUDITORIUM, Courtland Street between
Edgewood Avenue and Gilmer Street, N. E., consists of a Main Building and Annex. The Main Building, formerly the Auditorium-
Armory, was built during 1908-09 at a cost of more than $200,000; in
1938, through Works Progress Administration assistance, the entire
building was renovated. The Auditorium proper seats 5,000 people
and has a total of 10,290 square feet of floor space suitable for exhibits.
Taft Hall, off the lobby, has 4,000 square feet of exhibit space and is
suitable for group and other similar meetings. The second floor contains Committee Rooms 1 and 2, seating 150 and 250 respectively. On
the third floor is an exceptionally fine ballroom, with 7,500 square feet
of clear maple hardwood floor, and equipped with a piano and over
100 tables and more than 400 chairs, for dances and parties.

In 1953 the new floor was put on the stage of the main auditorium,
the orchestra pit was filled in, and the city purchased a portable raised
floor for the arena, that concert goers might see the stage from any
seat. The entire building having been air-conditioned in 1953 at a cost
of $256,000, its many civic uses were increased.

In 1948 the Auditorium Annex on the left was built at a cost of
$550,000, adding three rooms to the existing building. Exhibit Hall 1
on the lobby floor contains 5,500 square feet of unobstructed exhibit
space, and Exhibit Hall 2 and 3 contain 5,400 and 7,000 square feet of
exhibit space, respectively. Obstructing columns make these two unsuitable for seated shows.

JOEL HURT PARK, across Courtland Street directly in front of the Auditorium, has an electric fountain with changing lights, on the edge of
its pleasant oval green.

8. GRADY HOSPITAL, 36 Butler Street, occupying some twenty buildings
contained in a two-block area, began as a municipal charity hospital,
built in 1891-92 as a memorial to Henry W. Grady who had promoted

such an institution before his death. Under the City of Atlanta from 1892 to 1945, it was transferred to the Fulton–DeKalb Hospital Authority, January 1, 1946.

Among its historical antecedents are the Atlanta Medical College founded by Dr. D. G. Westmoreland in 1854 and the Southern Medical College, chartered in 1878. In 1898 these colleges were joined to form the Atlanta College of Physicians and Surgeons. Founded in 1905, the Atlanta School of Medicine was merged in 1913 with the Atlanta School of Physicians and Surgeons to form a new school but with the old name of Atlanta Medical College. In need of endowment, teaching connections, and hospital facilities, Atlanta Medical College legally became the School of Medicine of Emory University in 1915. The old buildings by agreement came to serve as a part of Grady Hospital. The University has provided professional services to the hospital's ward and clinic patients, and the hospital has furnished teaching opportunities and facilities required by the Medical School. The hospital's total expenditures for the year ending December 31, 1952, were $3,384,474.50, of which $1,337,459.17 went for the professional care of patients.

The HUGHES SPALDING PAVILION was dedicated June 22, 1952, primarily to serve Negroes who are not eligible for medical care in charity hospitals. Divided into 4-bed wards, semi-private and private rooms, the five-story building of cream brick with green marble trim has a capacity of 116 beds and 33 bassinets. Its cost of around one and three-quarter millions was divided between state, hospital, and Federal sources, in conformity with the Hill-Burton Act, with the government providing over $1,000,000, other sources about equal amounts the one with the other.

The THOMAS K. GLENN MEMORIAL BUILDING, corner of Butler and Armstrong streets, recently completed, houses the medical education and research staff of the Emory University School of Medicine. The entire vacant block contained by Armstrong, Butler, Gilmer, and Pratt streets, has been bought for Emory University for the construction of the new Grady Hospital, of 1,000 beds. Construction is expected to begin in 1954 and to cost around twenty millions.

9. BIG BETHEL A. M. E. CHURCH, NW. corner of Butler Street and Auburn Avenue, is the largest Negro church in Atlanta. Constructed of granite blocks, and with a circular tower and spire, the building is marked by large electric signs. The present one was built in 1922 after a fire destroyed the older building.

Big Bethel Choir, composed of male and female voices, made a national reputation because of its singing of Negro spirituals and especially for its presentation of *Heaven Bound,* a medieval miracle play with a regional accent.

10. The ATLANTA DAILY WORLD BUILDING, 210 Auburn Avenue, N. E., houses the only daily newspaper in the world published by Negroes (*i.e.* every morning except Mondays). The *World,* founded in 1928 by the late W. A. Scott, was published first as a weekly. Circulation increased so rapidly that in 1931 the publishers organized a syndicate which now owns a semi-weekly in Birmingham, and one in Memphis. It prints weekly papers for six other Southern cities.

11. DECATUR STREET, for about five blocks southeast of Five Points, was once the center of a fashionable residential section, but has now taken on a more cosmopolitan air as the principal trading and amusement center of the Negro population.

12. The STATE CAPITOL, Washington Street between Hunter and Mitchell streets, was completed in 1889 at an approximate cost of a million dollars. Built not of Georgia marble but Indiana limestone and modeled after the national capitol, it is one of the few buildings of such scope to be raised within the sum appropriated. Edbrooke and Burnham were the architects. The capitol grounds, provided with native trees and shrubs, form the setting for heroic monuments, and tablets commemorating Georgia personalities and events.

Within the hallways and rotunda, which are finished in Georgia marble, are numerous life-sized oil paintings of prominent state leaders, as well as collections of historical and literary interest. A marble bust of Benjamin Harvey Hill is the work of Alexander Doyle. Through the efforts of the U. D. C., many historic flags, some battle torn, have been preserved and are on display.

The capitol dome, rising 237 feet above ground, is reached by a staircase from the top floor of the building. Surmounting the dome is an allegorical figure with torch in one hand, a sword in the other.

The GEORGIA STATE MUSEUM has its exhibition cases arranged around the corridors of the upper floor area. Well classified and effectively presented and arranged, the exhibits are of natural resources, minerals, fossils, early pottery and Indian relics, birds, serpents, small animals. There are dioramas (miniature scenes reproduced three-dimensionally with the help of figures, colors, and perspective) of native industries and historical locales. A detailed *Directory* of 72 printed pages has been prepared by Curator Annette McLean.

The STATE LIBRARY (*open 8:15-4:30 Mon.-Fri.; 8:15-12 Sat.*), on the third floor, has an extensive collection of Georgia materials. These are isolated from other items, closely catalogued, and expertly serviced. Thus a source of general and special information at all levels about the state is available, second to none, and making the library a public relations medium with a world-wide list of correspondents. State legislative, judicial, and administrative officers, members of the legal professions, and citizens interested in questions of law, legislation, and government, make constant use of the library's major collection of materials. Valuable help is rendered by the librarian and aids who are experienced in these specialized fields.

A periodical, *The Georgia Commentary,* edited by the State Librarian, has for the last four years been published at intervals. The last issue was Number 8 for June 1953.

The STATE OFFICE BUILDING (*open 8-4 Mon.-Fri.; 8-12 Sat.*), Capitol Square SW. of Capitol, houses the State Department of Education, Department of Public Works, and Department of Education. The six-story building, built of marble and granite in 1939, has six bronze relief figures by Julian Harris embossed on the black marble spandrels. Augustus Constantine was the architect. The entrance to the State Highway Department is at left on the corner. New buildings, to cost some $9,800,000, will be the JUDICIAL BUILDING on Capitol Square at the corner of Washington and Mitchell streets, the LABOR-OFFICE BUILDING behind the Judicial Building, both of six stories, and the four-story AGRICULTURAL BUILDING on Capitol Square at the corner of Hunter and Washington streets.

13. The CITY HALL (*open 8:30-5 Mon.-Fri.; 8:30-12:30 Sat.; observation tower same hours*), 56 Mitchell Street, S. E. (between Central Avenue and Washington Street), was erected in 1929 at a cost of more than a million dollars. The dignified 14-story building, Gothic in detail and modern in mass, is of the set-back type of architecture. Its outside walls are terra cotta, its main entrance and lobby walls finished in Georgia travertine. The bronze doors of the four elevators are inscribed with the seal of Atlanta, bearing a phoenix and the legend "Resurgens 1847-1864, Atlanta, Georgia." The building, designed by G. Lloyd Preacher, is on the site of headquarters occupied by General Sherman in 1864. There is an excellent panoramic view of the city from the observation tower.

14. The FULTON COUNTY COURTHOUSE, corner of Pryor and Hunter streets, is a nine-story and basement building, completed in 1914, and originally intended primarily to accommodate the county superior, civil, and criminal courts, and their associated offices. In the classical style, the exterior is of granite up to the second story and of glazed terra cotta beyond. As the county grew, its enlarged and also increasing services, such as Taxes, Welfare, Education, Civil Service, Purchasing, Farm Promotion, etc., functions not pertinent to the courts, re-

quired office space which had to be found in the Courthouse. The recent $20,000,000 Fulton County bond issue provided $2½ million to build the New County Administration Building adjacent to the Courthouse.

The NEW ADMINISTRATION BUILDING, 165 Central Avenue, S. W., is of seven stories, faced with Georgia marble. Associates Barili and Humphreys—Toombs and Creighton were the architects. Next to it is the new Juvenile Court Building and a parking garage for personnel. The old Courthouse is now being rehabilitated for the use of the courts and their auxiliary services and needs.

An added feature of civic dignity is the park approved by the Georgia general assembly. It will occupy the block opposite City Hall and between the New Administration Building and Capitol Square. With the completion of the state's Judicial Building and Labor Office Building on the right side, and the Agricultural Building on the left side, of Capitol Square, an imposing vista will unfold with the Capitol as its focal center. An orderly and monumental use of open spaces of this sort suggests those imagined by the early civic planners of the Republic, as, for example, between the Capitol and White House, in Washington, D. C.

15. CHURCH OF THE IMMACULATE CONCEPTION (Roman Catholic), SE. corner Central Avenue and Hunter Street, erected in 1869 to replace an earlier frame building damaged by bombardment during the Battle of Atlanta, is the oldest church building in the city. Gothic in design, the church is of red brick with granite embellishments and is partly encircled by an iron picket fence. The interior is softly lighted by tall stained-glass windows. The central altar is carved from white marble. The land on which this building stands was deeded to the Roman Catholics in 1848, and soon afterward a church was erected on the site.

(NORTH ATLANTA)

16. PIEDMONT PARK AND GOLF COURSE, Piedmont Avenue and Tenth Street, N. E. (*picnic areas, grills, day camp, equipped playground, 9-hole golf course, swim pool, lake, football fields—one lighted, baseball diamonds, two lighted softball areas, tennis courts, and fishing*), covers approximately 185 acres of rolling tree-dotted land. Curving asphalt drives lead through landscaped grounds past a lake, a golf course, and recreation areas. In 1887 this tract, then the property of the Gentleman's Driving Club, was used for the Piedmont Exposition which was planned in honor of President Cleveland's visit to Atlanta. Two years later the land was purchased by the Exposition Company, and the Grounds were further improved in 1895 for the Cotton States

A Section of the Atlanta Cyclorama of the Battle of Atlanta

View from Black Mountain Lookout Tower, Chattahoochee National Forest

Forest Road along Rock Creek in the Chattahoochee National Forest

Air Force B-47 Stratojet from the Lockheed Plant, over Stone Mountain

New General Electric Plant in Rome

Tugalo Hydroelectric Dam in Northeast Georgia

Aerial View of Columbus showing the serpentine Chattahoochee

Aerial View of Bibb Manufacturing Plant at Columbus

Eagle and Phenix Mills, Columbus

Atlantic Steel Company, Atlanta

Five Points at night, Atlanta

Rich's Bridge over Forsyth Street, Atlanta

and International Exposition. Atlanta purchased the land for a municipal park in 1904.

The PEACE MONUMENT, near the 14th Street entrance, is a bronze figure of the Goddess of Peace holding an olive branch and commanding a kneeling Confederate soldier to lower his gun. The sculptor was Allen Newman, of New York. The monument, unveiled on October 10, 1911, was presented to the city by the old Gate City Guard, founded in 1857 for the protection of Atlanta.

At the Orme Circle entrance to the park are three lampposts used by the city in its first street lighting system in 1855.

17. ATLANTA ART ASSOCIATION (*open free 9-5 weekdays, and 3-6 P.M. Sundays*), 1262 Peachtree Street, N. E., operates the High Museum of Art, the adjacent Scott Memorial Gallery, and the Atlanta Art Institute. The Atlanta Art Institute has an enrollment at present of fifty full-time and 150 occasional students, and of over 300 children in its Saturday morning classes. The teaching staff consists of four full-time and six part-time instructors.

The Association publishes the *News Bulletin,* assembles loan collections, and arranges lectures. The permanent collection includes a number of Old Masters of the Italian and Northern Schools. Donors include the Samuel H. Kress Foundation of New York, the Atlanta Friends of Art, and many others. A fine collection of paintings by painters living in the Southeast has been assembled through the Purchase Prizes donated each year by Davison-Paxon Company to the Southeastern Annual Exhibition, the largest regional in eight Southeastern states. Other collections include graphic arts, ceramics, and a nucleus of sculpture.

The Association is engaged in active plans for a new Museum and Art School, the first section of which should be open on the Association's Fiftieth Birthday, 1955. This will contain a group of twenty-five Italian Renaissance masterpieces set aside for Atlanta by the Kress Foundation. The present brick and stucco building, of Tudor domestic architecture, containing the High Museum, was the home of Mrs. James Madison High, who presented it to the citizens of Atlanta in 1926.

18. RHODES MEMORIAL HALL or THE GEORGIA STATE DEPARTMENT OF ARCHIVES (*open 8:30-4:30 Mon.-Fri.; 8:30-12 Sat.*), 1516 Peachtree Street, N. W., constructed of Stone Mountain granite and modeled after a Bavarian castle, houses Georgia's official archives consisting of more than 70,000 manuscript book records, and four million paper records. Besides the official state archives, there are some original county records, and a few private collections of manuscripts pertaining to Geor-

gia and Georgians. The department also maintains a small museum on the first floor of Georgia relics, a pictorial collection of Georgia scenes and incidents, and state-owned oil portraits of famous Georgians.

The Georgia Society of the D. A. R. has a library of genealogical and historical books, abstracts of Georgia county records, and Bible and cemetery records. Other patriotic groups have on deposit small collections relevant to their characters, all of which are housed in various parts of the building. These collections may be used during office hours for research purposes. A hand-carved mahogany staircase curves from the foyer to the second floor. A background made by a series of Tiffany painted stained-glass windows depicts *The Rise and Fall of the Confederacy*. Panel 1. shows Jefferson Davis taking the Oath of Office, Panel 2. Stonewall Jackson at First Manassas, and Panel 3. Lee on Traveller bidding farewell to his men at Appomattox.

Rhodes Memorial Hall was originally the residence of A. G. Rhodes, whose heir presented it to the state in 1929. The Georgia Department of Archives and History was established under an Act approved August 20, 1918. The period from 1919-1930 saw the Department established, the official archives assembled, and many of them catalogued. The Reorganization Act of 1931 placed the Department of Archives and History under the Department of State. Lucian Lamar Knight, Georgia author and historian, was appointed in 1919 the first state historian and director of Archives and History.

19. PEACHTREE CREEK is the site of the first of the series of engagements around Atlanta during the summer of 1864. On July 19 the battle lines of the Confederate forces under General Hood had taken a position south of Peachtree Creek to attack Federal troops before they could gain the advantage of crossing the creek. A charge was scheduled for noon on the next day, but the Confederate movement was ill co-ordinated and the attack did not open until mid-afternoon. Desperate fighting in the brief hours before dark resulted in failure for the Confederates and heavy losses on both sides.

20. OGLETHORPE UNIVERSITY, 7200 Peachtree Road, has a campus embracing a 400-acre woodland and a 30-acre lake. The buildings include Lupton Hall, containing administration and classrooms; Phoebe Hearst Hall, girls' dormitory and art studios; Lowry Hall, boys' dormitory and science laboratories. These are all Gothic in style and of Georgia blue granite. In addition, there are a boys' dormitory, a chemistry building, Neil Meyer Memorial Laboratory, and Hermance Stadium with a capacity of 3,000. A coeducational college, Oglethorpe offers courses leading to the B.A. and B.S. degrees. The present faculty numbers 22 and the student enrollment is around 225.

Oglethorpe University is a continuation of the name of Oglethorpe

College, which was founded under Presbyterian auspices at Milledge-ville in 1835. The original college collapsed as an educational institu-tion when its buildings were burned during the War between the States and because of the failure of its endowment invested in Con-federate bonds. The institution was reopened in Atlanta in 1870, but financial difficulties forced it to close within three years. In 1912 a movement began for its revival, and four years later the present insti-tution was opened. Since then a number of substantial donations have been received, some of which are commemorated in the names of Lowry Hall, Phoebe Hearst Hall, and Hermance Stadium. The leg-end on the seal of the university is: *Manu Dei resurrexit*.

In 1944 a new curriculum was organized addressed to the proposi-tion that subject matters may be given a basic moral integration. This curriculum is designed to teach the student to make a life and earn a living, thus establishing a commodious bond between liberal and voca-tional education.

A vault, called the Crypt of Civilization, was built in 1935 under Phoebe Hearst Hall to preserve material illustrative of contemporary American civilization. It contains canned food, cameras, phonographs and records, and encyclopedias on microfilm. The disinterment is scheduled for A.D. 8113.

(DRUID HILLS SECTION)

21. EMORY UNIVERSITY occupies an extensive campus, roughly bounded by North Decatur, Clifton, and Briarcliff roads. Its formal entrance gate is on North Decatur Road. The natural wooded beauty of the grounds has been preserved and enhanced by suitable plantings of flowering trees and shrubs, especially broadleafed evergreens. Most of the buildings, of simplified Italian architecture, are finished in Georgia marble and have red tile roofs.

Desiring to establish a university east of the Mississippi River, the General Conference of the Methodist Episcopal Church, South, de-cided to make Emory College at Oxford (*see* TOUR *17*) the nucleus of a new institution. The university was established in Atlanta in 1914 with a pledge of $500,000 from the city of Atlanta and a gift of $1,000,-000 from Asa G. Candler, Sr., whose family later made further gen-erous contributions. By 1919 the university included schools of medi-cine, law, theology, and business administration in addition to its college and graduate school. Since that date schools of dentistry and nursing have been added, a junior college maintained at Oxford, and one established at Valdosta (*see* TOUR *2*). Emory now has upwards of 4,000 students, and a faculty of more than 500.

Although formerly Emory University was primarily for men, according to a recent decision all departments are now open to women as well. Emory is one of the few universities in the nation that have stressed the development of intramural sports, participating in few intercollegiate contests.

GLENN MEMORIAL CHURCH, on a commanding elevation to the right of the formal entrance gate, is a white stucco building of Georgian design with a tall tower rising from an Ionic portico. The building was presented to the college by Thomas K. Glenn and Mrs. Howard Candler in memory of their father, Wilbur Fisk Glenn. The firm of Hentz, Adler, and Schutze, of Atlanta, designed the church, which was dedicated in 1931.

Set within the campus on the winding entrance road (R) and left of the Glenn Memorial Church is the new RICH MEMORIAL BUILDING which houses the School of Business Administration. This building was given by the Rich Foundation in memory of Morris, Emanuel and Daniel Rich—the three founders of Rich's, Inc. Along the road and across a bridge is the Emory Quadrangle. Around this grassed area are the ASA G. CANDLER LIBRARY, the LAMAR SCHOOL OF LAW, and the CANDLER SCHOOL OF THEOLOGY, and the recently completed HISTORY BUILDING—all in white or pink marble, and of similar design.

Chartered in 1915, the law school was named for L. Q. C. Lamar, a former statesman and U. S. senator, and an alumnus of Emory at Oxford. The theology building was named for Bishop Warren A. Candler, when the school was organized in 1914. On display are a pulpit made for John Wesley and a chair used by Bishop Francis Asbury who was influential in the spread of Methodism in America.

The ASA G. CANDLER LIBRARY (*open 7:50 A.M.-10 P.M. Mon.-Fri.; 7:50 A.M.-6 P.M. Sat.*), N. end of Quadrangle, has more than 220,000 volumes on its shelves. The lower floors contain the offices of administration. On the main floor is a collection of Wesleyana, containing more than 2,600 books and pamphlets of John and Charles Wesley. Of these, 281 are first editions, 481 are manuscripts including portions of John Wesley's account of his stay in Georgia, 89 are autographed letters of John Wesley, and more than 200 are Wesley family letters. This collection of Wesleyana is said to be the most extensive of its kind in this country and perhaps at all.

On the third floor of the library is the Division of Librarianship of the Graduate School, founded as the Southern Library School in 1905, and affiliated with Emory in 1925.

Other buildings near the center of the campus include the new ones for biology, geology, and the basic sciences, built of brick and stucco with limestone trim. Emory University Hospital, a teaching center for

the School of Medicine (*see Grady Hospital under* ATLANTA), dominates the eastern side of the campus. Alongside it is the WOODRUFF
MEMORIAL RESEARCH BUILDING, for investigative and other uses by the
School of Medicine. Established in 1903 as the Wesley Memorial Hospital, Emory Hospital was expanded and moved to its present site in
1922. The name was changed in 1925, when the hospital became affiliated with Emory's School of Medicine. In the new Woodruff Building is the Abner W. Calhoun Medical Library (*open* 9 A.M.-5 P.M.
weekdays) of over 15,000 volumes, and an historical museum display-
ing old pictures, manuscripts, and surgical instruments.

The center for student services at Emory is the $700,000 ALUMNI
MEMORIAL BUILDING, housing alumni headquarters, a music room, meditation chapel, recreation area, and several student activity offices. An
important feature of the building is the Alumni Reception Room furnished as a visitors' lounge and suitable as a meeting place for small
alumni groups.

The gymnasium and field house, with nearly a quarter-million
square feet of floor space, includes several basketball courts, a championship swimming pool, physical training rooms, handball courts,
locker and shower rooms, offices and classrooms, and specially designed
areas for remedial physical education. An extensive system of playing
fields is associated with the building.

Emory has national fraternities whose houses are located along Fraternity Row. Scattered about the campus are ten modern student
dormitories.

Emory's steady development into one of the major universities of
the Southeast has prompted the addition of more than a score of buildings since World War II, and led to the launching in 1952 of a
$40,000,000-program to double the institution's resources in the follow-
ing ten years. When completed this ambitious project will mean the
third doubling of Emory's resources since 1936. The first marked increase was from ten to twenty million dollars between 1936 and 1944.
Now ranking twentieth among the nation's universities in endowment,
in the period 1944-1951 Emory again doubled its resources, bringing its
plant and endowment value to some $42,000,000. The present program
of increase is designed not for physical expansion, but according to
President Goodrich C. White, as "a tool to strengthen all departments
of the university to the point where they will uphold adequately the
ideals of excellence and quality."

22. FERNBANK FOREST AND RECREATION CENTER, 849 Clifton Road, N. E.
contains seventy acres of unspoiled natural woods, a children's nature
museum, wildlife trails, barn theater, day camp sites, motion picture

hall, craft shops, and photographic laboratories. The Druid Hills Golf Club (*private*) is on the other side of Clifton Road.

(*SOUTHEAST SECTION*)

23. OAKLAND CEMETERY, Fair Street between S. Boulevard and Oakland Avenue, is enclosed by an old brick wall. The cemetery, originally a six-acre tract deeded to the city in 1850, was later extended to cover eighty-five acres. The LION OF ATLANTA, on the cemetery grounds, is a copy of the celebrated Lion of Lucerne. Carved from a single block of Georgia marble, it was dedicated to the unknown Confederate dead in Oakland Cemetery on April 26, 1894. The grave of Martha Lumpkin Compton, for whom Marthasville was named before it became Atlanta, is marked by a block of native granite. Among the distinguished Confederate dead is the grave of General John B. Gordon.

Horticulturalists know the cemetery as the regional origin of the famous Burford variety of *Ilex cornuta* or Chinese evergreen holly, specimens of which lend distinction to many Atlanta homes and public buildings. The original two specimens were sent as small plants to T. W. Burford, probably around 1895, at which time he was superintendent of Westview. Now grown to an imposing size, especially for their sort, the original hollies are still in the cemetery. It was first propagated by S. R. Howell of Knoxville, Tennessee, but has since been spread throughout the Southeast.

24. GRANT PARK, Cherokee Avenue and Boulevard, S. E. (*equipped playground, zoo, grills, picnic areas, swimming pool, lake, lighted football field, baseball diamond, lighted softball area, ten tennis courts, six lighted tennis courts, basketball—outcourt, fishing, picnic and dance pavilion, food, and skating rink*), was named for Colonel Lemuel P. Grant, who in 1882 donated a hundred acres of wooded land as the site of a municipal park. Forty-four acres were added later. The zoo with its animals and especially the three elephants, is a great attraction for both young and also not so young.

The SITE OF FORT WALKER, at the crown of the hill near the Atlanta Avenue and Boulevard entrance to the park, is a commanding position held by a Confederate battery during the Siege and Battle of Atlanta in 1864. The park is honeycombed with breastworks. The hill was named in memory of William H. T. Walker, the Confederate general who was killed in the Battle of Atlanta.

The CYCLORAMA BUILDING (*open 9 A.M.-6 P.M. daily, children 25¢, adults 50¢; guided lecture tours at regular intervals, 1st at 9:30, last at 5:30*), facing the Augusta Avenue entrance to the park, houses the colossal *Cyclorama of the Battle of Atlanta*. This battle was fought

July 22, 1864, in the territory around Moreland Avenue for control of the Georgia Railroad.

The building, situated on a high terrace, is approached by a double stairway leading up to a broad esplanade. The front half of the building is made of white terra cotta, while the circular section, especially designed to contain the great canvas, is of stucco. The façade is dominated by a loggia, two stories high, featuring Ionic columns and pilasters.

The scenic moment depicted is the crucial interval at 4:30 P.M., when General Cheatham's troops made a counterattack in an effort to restore their line. Beyond the charging soldiers, the exploding shells, and the rising smoke of the fields lies the small city of Atlanta. Stone Mountain and Kennesaw Mountain can be seen in the distance. Above the confusion of battle, "Abe," the eagle mascot of Union Company C, flies high to avoid the shells. This eagle has since been memorialized on the silver dollar.

The painting is approximately 400 feet in circumference and 50 feet in height, and weighs 18,000 pounds. Suspended from a circular rail, the canvas creates the illusion of a continuous landscape. A striking three dimensional effect is achieved by continuing the action of the picture into the space (about forty feet) between the canvas and the central platform. The irregular terrain of the battlefield is reproduced with 1,500 tons of Georgia clay, ranging in color from white to red. Tree trunks, dynamited and treated to appear shell-torn, green-tinted excelsior simulating grass, and bushes made of wire and plaster add to the immediate effect of reality. Scores of plaster soldiers—fighting, wounded, and dead—are spread over the battlefield. The figures vary in size from twenty-two inches to slightly under four feet, but they are placed in such measure that in perspective they look lifesize. Canvas and foreground merge so skillfully that only a sharp eye can see where one leaves off and the other begins. The ambulance is partly painted and partly done in plaster; the railroad tracks start as pigment on the hanging canvas and extend with actual rails across the field to the opposite side of the picture.

The Cyclorama was painted about 1886, in Milwaukee, Wisconsin, by a staff of German artists. They did similar cycloramas for the battles of Gettysburg and Missionary Ridge, but both were accidentally lost. In the early 1890's the *Battle of Atlanta* was brought to this city and lodged in an Edgewood Avenue building, where it remained until 1898, when it was purchased for $1,000 by G. V. Gress, an Atlanta lumber merchant, and presented to the city.

On the upper floor is a room in which are displayed enlargements of eight pictures of Atlanta and the trenches and breastworks surrounding the city at the time of the Federal siege. The original photographs were taken by General Sherman's official photographer.

The TEXAS, the engine which took part in one of the war's decidedly
dramatic episodes, is in the basement of the Cyclorama Building. At
Marietta, Georgia, on April 11, 1862, James J. Andrews and twenty-
one Union men, disguised as Confederates, boarded the train drawn
by the locomotive *General*. When the crew and passengers detrained
at Big Shanty (now Kennesaw) for breakfast, Andrews and men
seized the *General* and started for Chattanooga. The conductor and
crew took up the chase on foot until they found a handcar at Moon's
Station. At the bridge across the Etowah River they took the *Yonah,*
a spur-engine for the Cooper Iron Works, and continued the chase.
Blocked at Kingston by freight cars that had delayed the *General,* they
changed to the *William R. Smith.* A few miles north of Kingston a
broken track forced them to abandon engine and take out on foot
again. Near Adairsville they found the *Texas,* considered the finest
and fastest on the road. Andrews and his men tried to block the rails
by throwing chunks of wood from the tender across the railroad
tracks, but the pursuing *Texas,* though running backwards, crept up
on them steadily. Five miles out of Chattanooga the *General,* out of
fuel and water, was overtaken, and Andrews and most of his men
were captured. A trial was held at Chattanooga, after which Andrews
and seven of his raiders were brought to Atlanta and executed by
hanging, June, 1862.

The *Texas,* a Danforth and Cook engine, was put on the road in
1856, running in freight service before and after Andrews' Raid. Prior
to 1895 it was equipped for burning coal. In 1907 it was sent to the
Atlanta railroad yards for scrapping, but public sympathy caused it to
be saved as a relic, and in 1911 the City of Atlanta formally accepted
it. In 1927 the locomotive was removed to the Cyclorama Building
and later was completely renovated by employees of the Emergency
Relief Administration. The *General* is on display in the Union Station
in Chattanooga (*see* TENNESSEE GUIDE).

25. The UNITED STATES PENITENTIARY (*open only to immediate relatives
of prisoners and to those having business to transact*), McDonough
Boulevard and Boulevard, S. E., is one of twenty-five varied types
of correctional institutions operated by the Federal Bureau of Prisons,
of the U. S. Department of Justice. Opened in 1902 on a tract of land
given by Atlanta for the purpose in 1899, the institution has served
since for the control and discipline of the more serious types of adult
offenders. Since Atlanta's gift, the city has grown around the institu-

tion, and today it is the only Federal penal institution located directly in a metropolitan area. It is designed to take care of 2,000 inmates, though during the naïve social experiment known as Prohibition the prison was forced to house twice that number.

The penitentiary operates two farms. One adjoins the main institution for the production of fruits and vegetables. More extensive operations are carried on at Honor Farm, a tract of around 1,500 acres located eleven miles from the institution. Some one hundred men live at Honor Farm Dormitory where they learn modern methods of farming while engaged in livestock raising, dairying, swine husbandry, and caring for crops, e.g., the production of tomatoes on a large scale. These practices include soil conservation, terrace building, the planting of cover crops, and other features of land reclamation.

All culinary operations are carried on by trained personnel. Meals are served cafeteria style from stainless steel tables in the dining hall that seats 1,500. Inmates are trained in the preparation and service of food generally as well as in special skills such as butchering and baking. The modern industrial plant uses some 800 men, who with expert civilian supervisors, operate the large textile factories, tailor shop, printing plant, and mattress factory, etc. Thousands of yards of duck and other cotton cloth are woven and made into clothing, mail pouches, tents, mattresses, and other products. The value of the things produced during the fiscal year ending June 30, 1950, was estimated at over six million dollars. The industrial program at Atlanta as at other Federal prisons is managed by Federal Prison Industries, Inc. None of the prison products is sold on the open market. What is not used by the prison community is designed for use by other agencies of the Federal government. Any profits exceeding the various requirements of the institution are turned over to the U. S. Treasury.

26. The CHEVROLET MOTOR ASSEMBLY PLANT (*tours can be arranged by calling the personnel director at the Chevrolet Motor Assembly Plant or the director for the Fisher Body Plant*), McDonough Boulevard and Sawtell Road, is one of ten Chevrolet assembly plants geographically located for the most effective distribution purposes. While frames, chassis parts, and engines are being assembled, and the motors placed on their own wheels for the first time, in the Fisher Body Division next door the body parts are being assembled, and then painted, after which they go to the "body bank," and eventually to the chassis line.

27. LAKEWOOD PARK, Pryor Street and Lakewood Avenue, S. E., the locale of the Southeastern Fair, is located in an area of 366 wooded acres. The original tract of fifty acres was purchased by the city of Atlanta in 1874, and the headwaters of the South River were im-

pounded to form a reservoir for the city water works department. The Lakewood Park Company, organized in 1895, leased the property from the city and converted it into an amusement park. Since 1915 the Southeastern Fair, sponsored in part by the Atlanta Chamber of Commerce, has been held annually, beginning either at the end of September or during the first part of October and lasting eleven days, at Lakewood. The rest of the year is know as the "park season," the amusement features of which center about the one-mile race track, the scenic lake, and a midway.

28. GAMMON THEOLOGICAL SEMINARY (Negro), 9 McDonough Boulevard, S. E., was founded in 1883. Formerly a part of Clark University (*see Atlanta University System below, and also Clark College*), Gammon Theological Seminary is now fully accredited by the American Association of Theological Schools and offers the B.D., S.T.M., and M.R.E. degrees. It is a co-educational institution and has an enrollment of approximately fifty students. On its campus of about thirty acres are: the GILBERT HAVEN MEMORIAL LIBRARY, GAMMON HALL and THAYER HALL (dormitories for men and women), cottages for married students, and BOWEN HALL.

29. WREN'S NEST (*open 9:30 A.M.-5 P.M. weekdays, 2-5 Sundays; small admission*), 1050 Gordon Street, S. W., the former home of Joel Chandler Harris, is a memorial to the creator of the Uncle Remus stories. In 1913 the property was acquired by the Uncle Remus Memorial Association, which sponsors a memorial service in the house on December 9, the author's birthday.

The Wren's Nest is an irregularly shaped frame house with drooping eaves, numerous gables, and elaborate scrollwork. It received its name when a wren built her nest in the mail box and Harris built another mail box so as not to disturb her. A walk leading to the side of the house is made of Georgia pink marble, and each section is inscribed with the name of an author. On display at the Wren's Nest is a collection of autographed letters, pictures, personal possessions, and original editions of Harris' works, more than twenty-five of which were written here.

Joel Chandler Harris (1848-1908), born in Eatonton, was connected with several newspapers, including the *Macon Telegraph* and the *Savannah Daily News,* before he joined the staff of the *Atlanta Constitution* in 1878. That year at the suggestion of the *Constitution's* editor, Evan P. Howell, Harris undertook to write a daily column of humorous sketches and observations. The Uncle Remus saga resulted. Success came almost at once, and in 1880 his first book, *Uncle Remus: His Songs and Sayings,* was published. Next came *Nights with Uncle*

Remus (1883), and other volumes of Uncle Remus stories. His sensitive use of Negro dialect and his unique folk characters made a significant contribution to American letters.

30. On the SITE OF THE BATTLE OF EZRA CHURCH, Mozley Drive at E. end of Mozley Park, is a public playground. At this place General Hood made a third desperate attempt, July 28, 1864, to drive back Sherman's forces. Hardee's and Lee's corps of the Confederate army were involved with the extreme right of Sherman's command by General Logan.

31. BOOKER T. WASHINGTON MONUMENT, before the main entrance to the Booker T. Washington High School, SW. corner of Hunter and C streets, is a memorial to the famous Negro educator. The group of bronze figures, done by Charles Keck, of New York, represents Washington lifting the veil of ignorance from his race. A sentence typical of his philosophy is on the base: "We shall prosper in proportion as we learn to dignify and glorify labor and put brains and skill into the common occupations of life." The monument was erected from funds donated by the teachers and students of Booker T. Washington High School and by white and Negro citizens of Atlanta.

32. ATLANTA UNIVERSITY SYSTEM (administration offices, 223 Chestnut Street, S. W.) (Negro) comprises Atlanta University, a co-educational graduate school conferring the M.A., M.S., M.S.L.S., M.B.A., and M.S.W. degrees; Morehouse College, an undergraduate school for men; and Spelman College, an undergraduate school for women. In 1929, the three institutions, on neighboring campuses, adopted a plan of affiliation whereby they would be so co-ordinated that their combined resources would be available to every student. The three institutions have a total enrollment of approximately 1,644 and an endowment of $12,000,000. Clark College, Morris Brown College, and Gammon Theological Seminary are cooperating institutions, and with Morehouse, Spelman, and Atlanta University, make up what is known as the Atlanta University Center.

ATLANTA UNIVERSITY was established in 1865, when representatives of the American Missionary Association opened a school in a boxcar. With grants from the Federal Freedman's Bureau, the American Missionary Association, and philanthropic individuals, the school grew rapidly. In 1876, the first college class was graduated; in 1930-31, the undergraduate courses were discontinued and all resources of the institution were devoted to graduate work. Atlanta University is the center for graduate and professional courses in the university scheme, and is made up of five professional schools. The School of Education's main objective is to develop men and women for professional leadership in education. It has under its direction a Laboratory School, through seven elementary grades, to give students practical experience in teaching methods. The School of Social Work, the only professional one in the city for training Negro social workers, was organized in 1925 and was admitted to the American Association of Schools of Social Work in 1928. This school, independent before, became a part of the University September 1, 1947. The School of Library Service was established in 1941 through a grant from the Carnegie Corporation. It is accredited by the Board of Education for Librarianship of the American Library Association and by the Southern Association of Secondary Schools and Colleges. The School of Business Administration was organized in September, 1946. The fifth school is the Graduate School of Arts and Sciences.

HARKNESS HALL, the Atlanta University administration building, which houses administrative and faculty offices, a conference room, reception rooms, post office, bookshop and suites for the presidents of the affiliated institutions, was opened in December, 1932. It was dedicated on Sunday, April 16, 1950, in honor of Edward S. Harkness who contributed substantially to the building program of the university after it became affiliated with Spelman and Morehouse Colleges.

DEAN SAGE HALL, the University classroom building, was opened September, 1952, and is the first classroom building since the re-organization of Atlanta University into a graduate institution. A modern three-story edifice, it contains 16 class and seminar rooms, an assembly hall, faculty and student lounges, and suites for faculty and staff members. Made possible through gifts and grants from the General Education Board, the estate of the late Edward S. Harkness and other friends and alumni, Dean Sage Hall is a memorial to Dean Sage of New York City who served Atlanta University for many years as a trustee and chairman of the board.

BUMSTEAD HALL and WARE HALL, the two dormitories for men and for women, provide for 400 students. Connected by the DINING HALL, the three buildings were opened in 1933. The University's heating plant built in 1937 provides light for the University, Morehouse, Spelman, and Clark colleges.

TREVOR ARNETT LIBRARY, named in gratitude for the invaluable services of Trevor Arnett on behalf of education and the development of the Atlanta University System, was financed by a gift from the General Education Board. At present, the library has more than 127,000 bound volumes, and will soon have space for 150,000 more. In addition the Carnegie Art Reference Set of approximately 2,000 prints, color fac-

similes, and photographs, is available. The basement contains a large
room for exhibition purposes, library staff room, storage and delivery
room, and book stacks. On the first floor are four seminar rooms, the
reserve book room, book stacks, and the LINCOLN ROOM, opened February 11, 1953. The Lincoln Room contains the entire collection of
Anna Chittenden Thayer who donated it to the library. Consisting
of letters, pamphlets, books, contemporary newspaper accounts, numerous photographs, handbills, and some three hundred other memo-
rabilia and affiliated items, this is doubtless the most complete collection relating to the Great Emancipator in the South. On the second
floor of the library are additional book stacks, a large reading room,
office of the librarian, the public catalogue, circulation desk, catalogue
department, and work room. The Atlanta University School of Library Service occupies the third floor. The library serves not only
Atlanta University and its collegiate group, but also Morris Brown
College, Clark College, and Gammon Theological Seminary. Extensive enlargements are now in progress.

MOREHOUSE COLLEGE was organized in the year 1867, in Augusta,
Georgia, as the Augusta Institute, but was moved to Atlanta in 1879
and renamed Atlanta Baptist Seminary, at which time full collegiate
powers were granted. In 1912 the name was changed to Morehouse
College in honor of the Reverend Henry L. Morehouse, corresponding
secretary of the American Baptist Home Mission Society. Consisting
of numerous buildings, the college occupies a 13-acre rectangular campus. In 1948, the Samuel Howard Archer Infirmary was erected by
the Federal government, and students are treated by the college nurse
and physician.

THE CHEMISTRY BUILDING, built in 1952-53 at a cost of $600,000, pro-
vides classrooms and laboratories for Morehouse students and students
at Atlanta University. It consists of eleven offices, two classrooms, one
seminar room, an amphitheatre, a departmental reading room, and a
faculty student lounge. It has nine small laboratories for student research, eight large laboratories for graduate and undergraduate work,
five balance rooms, three stock rooms, and several storage closets.

GRAVES HALL and ROBERT HALL are the two main dormitories; SALE
HALL contains classrooms, a reception room, recreation room, and
chapel. The SCIENCE BUILDING contains the Department of Biology.

SPELMAN COLLEGE was founded in 1881 by Sophia B. Packard and
Harriet E. Giles, of Boston. They opened the school with eleven
pupils in the basement of Friendship Baptist Church. In February,
1883, the school acquired the grounds and buildings of old Fort Mc-

Pherson and moved there. Its campus covers twenty-five acres. Legally organized with a charter and board of trustees in 1888, Spelman College granted its first degrees in 1901.

ROCKEFELLER HALL, the administration building, was built in 1886 as the first permanent building of the college. This building represents the first major gift of Rockefeller to education.

SISTERS CHAPEL, dedicated in 1935, is a Greek Revival red brick building with six white columns. Designed by Hentz, Adler and Shutze, of Atlanta, it has a seating capacity of 1,500 and is used for concerts, commencement exercises, and daily chapel services. It was named in honor of John D. Rockefeller's mother and aunt.

The FLORENCE MATILDA READ HEALTH AND RECREATIONAL BUILDING, a gymnasium costing approximately $460,000, was dedicated on December 6, 1951. In 1953, the trustees voted to name the gymnasium in honor of President Emeritus Read.

ABBY ALDRICH ROCKEFELLER HALL, made possible by a gift from John D. Rockefeller as a memorial to his wife, was dedicated on April 12, 1953. This dormitory provides for 96 students, also faculty and guest suites.

SPELMAN COLLEGE NURSERY SCHOOL was opened in the Laura Spelman Rockefeller Memorial Building in the fall of 1930. In 1936, it was moved to Chadwick Hall, where provisions have been made to care for eighty-five children between the ages of eighteen months and five years.

The other college buildings are: MORGAN HALL, which houses the faculty and student dining halls; PACKARD HALL, MOREHOUSE, and BESSIE STRONG, dormitories; LAURA SPELMAN ROCKEFELLER HALL, the home economics building; TAPLEY HALL and GILES HALL, classroom buildings.

MORRIS BROWN COLLEGE (Negro) was founded in 1881 under the patronage of the African Methodist Episcopal Church. Originally located on Boulevard, it was moved in 1932 to the old Atlanta University campus on Hunter and Tatnall streets. With an enrollment of over 600, Morris Brown College offers a four-year college course, and is co-educational. TURNER THEOLOGICAL SEMINARY is maintained by Morris Brown for students desiring theological training.

CLARK COLLEGE (Negro) was founded in 1869 by the Freedman's Aid Society of the Methodist Episcopal Church, and was named Clark University in honor of Augusta Clark Cole who had contributed a large portion of the funds for its founding. In 1940, the name was changed to Clark College. Formerly located on the southeast side of Atlanta, it was removed in 1941 to Chestnut Street, just opposite Atlanta University's administration building. A co-educational institution with about 700 students, the college has three dormitories, PFEIFFER

HALL, ANNIE MERNER HALL, and MERRILL J. HOLMES HALL, a student-union and social building with a cafeteria-dining room and general social rooms, and a large administration and classroom building. A new Home Economics building is now under construction.

33. UNIVERSITY HOMES (Negro), 668 Fair Street, S. W., is a 17½-acre tract developed by the Federal government under the Public Works Administration and completed by April, 1937. It is now administered by the Atlanta Housing Authority. The severely simple fireproof brick buildings contain 675 units ranging in size from two to five rooms. Space is provided in the administration building for a management office, eight stores, offices for doctors and dentists, and a clinic. One central plant manufactures steam for heating all the buildings. Convenient laundries, a kindergarten, and a day nursery are maintained. Approximately 25 per cent of the area is covered by buildings, and the remainder serves for parks, playgrounds, and community activities. It provides homes for a total of some 1,950 people, and cost about $2,500,000.

(NORTHWEST SECTION)

34. TECHWOOD HOMES, Techwood Drive at North Avenue, built at a cost of about $2,875,000 and opened in 1936, was the first all-Federal slum clearance and low-rent housing project completed by PWA in the nation. Covering eleven blocks, a total of twenty-two acres, it consists of 604 units capable of providing quarters for around 1,800 individuals. It is now managed by the Atlanta Housing Authority.

The apartment buildings, severely plain in their rectangular simplicity and economy of detail, are surrounded by landscaped lawns and young trees. All buildings are constructed of steel, hollow tile, and brick, and are insulated with cork; the floors and roofs are made of five-inch reinforced concrete slabs. The apartments range in size from three rooms to duplex units of six rooms, and all are equipped with modern bathrooms, electric refrigerators, electric stoves, and incinerators.

At the southern end of the development is a community playground with wading pools for children. The project provides a number of free laundries completely equipped, a large library room with book repair shop and a librarian's office, a little theater, and a kindergarten. A large brick building houses the administrative offices and the health center.

A dormitory, of the same construction as the apartment buildings, was built in 1935 to accommodate 309 Georgia Tech students.

35. GEORGIA INSTITUTE OF TECHNOLOGY, 225 North Avenue, N. W.

*(visitors welcome to the main campus, academic and research build-
ings open only during routine hours on weekdays; arrangements for
visits by large groups must be made in advance with the Public Relations Office of the Institute; the "T" Room of Brittain Dining Hall,
just off Williams Street next to the Expressway, serves reasonably
priced food to visitors)*, the largest engineering institution in the South
and the third largest in the nation, is the engineering, scientific, and
architectural unit of the University System of Georgia.   Today the
institute consists of the General College, Engineering College, Graduate Division, Engineering Experiment Station, and the Engineering
Extension Division, which includes the Engineering Evening School,
Institute of Public Safety, the Department of Short Courses and Conferences, Department of Industrial Education, and the Southern Technical Institute.   Since 1912, in addition to the regular four-year courses,
Georgia Tech has offered a co-operative plan of engineering education
on a five-year basis in which students alternate between classes and
work in industry in successive quarters.

Both undergraduate and graduate degrees are granted in Aeronauti-
cal, Ceramic, Chemical, Civil, Electrical, Industrial, Mechanical, and
Textile Engineering; Applied Mathematics; Architecture; Chemistry;
Industrial Management; Physics; and Textiles.   In addition, Master of
Science degrees are given in Engineering Mechanics, Public Health
Engineering, Safety Engineering, and Sanitary Engineering, and also
the degrees of Master of Architecture, and Master of City Planning.
The degree of Doctor of Philosophy is offered in Chemical Engineering, Chemistry, and Electrical Engineering.   At the Southern Technical Institute, established at Chamblee in 1948, two-year technical
courses leading to an Associate in Science degree are offered in building construction, civil, electrical, electronics and communications, gas,
fuel, heating and air conditioning, industrial and mechanical technology.

Approximately 17,500 students are now enrolled annually in the
various divisions of Georgia Tech, including some 4,800 regular under-
graduates and 200 graduate students in the day division, 600 students
at the Southern Technical Institute, 3,000 students in the Engineering
Evening School, and the balance in the other units of the Engineering
Extension Division.   The total faculty, administrative and research
staff of Georgia Tech numbers more than 700.

In 1882, the General Assembly of Georgia passed a resolution to
consider the establishment of a technical school in the state, and in 1885
the sum of $65,000 was appropriated for the institution.   Athens, At-
lanta, Macon, Milledgeville, and Penfield offered bids for the new
school, and in 1886 Atlanta was chosen as the site.   Installation services

were held at De Give's Opera House early in October 1886. Since
that time, the school has increased from five acres in land, two buildings, and a plant worth of $65,000 to 121 acres, 57 major buildings, and
$23,500,000.

Based on present development plans, the main campus, extending
from Hemphill Avenue on the west to the Expressway on the east,
and from south of North Avenue to the north of Tenth Street, has
been divided into three major sections. The west section contains the
academic and research functions and the east section the student housing facilities, with the center section between them being devoted to
recreational and sports activities. Architecturally, the buildings range
in style and design from red-brick romanesque of the '90's to the
present-day contemporary functional. The conflict between the various designs is softened by an effective use of landscaping with broad
green lawns, flowering shrubbery, and trees native to the area.

The first group of buildings constructed are typical of the '90's with
their red-brick walls and a conglomerate confusion of various shapes
and forms. This style continued until the advent in 1922 of President
Brittain, who introduced the English Collegiate Gothic design in the
construction of two and one-quarter millions of dollars of additional
buildings. Since 1944, the design of the new buildings has ranged
from the Collegiate Gothic for the new dormitories to the contemporary functional for the new academic buildings.

Dominating the skyline of the campus is the square tower and
pointed steeple of the ADMINISTRATION BUILDING (1888) with the word
TECH in gold and white neon lights emblazoned on each of the four
sides. Surrounding the building on three sides are the other old buildings of the Institute, namely, SWANN (1900), ELECTRICAL (1901), OLD
SHOP (1892), A. FRENCH (1898), LYMAN HALL (1906), KNOWLES (1898),
and CARNEGIE (1906).

Outside of this group, extending west and north are the more recently constructed buildings. On the corner of North Avenue and
Hemphill Avenue is located the DANIEL GUGGENHEIM SCHOOL OF AERO-
NAUTICS (1930), which includes two slow-speed wind tunnels, a small
supersonic wind tunnel, and several laboratories devoted to aeronautical research.

Just north of it is the ENGINEERING DRAWING AND MECHANICAL BUILD-
ING (1938), which contains mechanical laboratories, classrooms and
drafting rooms. Proceeding north along Cherry Street, one comes to
the MECHANICAL ENGINEERING BUILDING (1920) wherein are located machine, welding, gauge, steam and other laboratories as well as classrooms.

Across Cherry Street is the WHITEHEAD MEMORIAL HOSPITAL (1910) for the use of the regular student body. It has a capacity of thirty beds and contains examining and treatment rooms, laboratories, and a diet kitchen.

Next to the hospital on the corner of Cherry and Third Streets is the three-story PHYSICS BUILDING (1923) with up-to-date laboratories, lecture halls, and classrooms. Proceeding east on Third Street, one comes to the CIVIL ENGINEERING BUILDING (1938) (L) which contains classrooms, drafting rooms, and laboratories devoted to hydraulics, fluid-mechanics, highway and masonry building materials, sanitary engineering, and soil mechanics. Besides being utilized for undergraduate and graduate instruction, the laboratories are also extensively used for research.

THE CERAMIC ENGINEERING BUILDING (1924) has classrooms and laboratories with the most complete and up-to-date equipment for research in the processing and usage of non-metallic minerals. Exhibits of the ceramic industry are of great interest to visitors. Directly on the other side of Third Street is the CHEMISTRY ANNEX BUILDING (1942) with a group of well-equipped laboratories devoted to all phases of chemical research. Some outstanding contributions to the field of chemistry have come out of this building.

Continuing east along Third Street, one comes to the ATHLETIC OF-FICE BUILDING (1941) and the combination AUDITORIUM-GYMNASIUM (1937) with a large indoor swimming pool to the rear. Next to the gymnasium is the NAVAL ARMORY (1934), headquarters for the Georgia Tech Naval R. O. T. C., which was one of the first six in the country established in 1926. World War II records indicate that Georgia Tech had more naval officers on active duty than any other institution with the exception of the U. S. Naval Academy. There is a permanent display of modern naval equipment in the Armory open for the inspection of visitors.

South of the gymnasium is an area of two city blocks occupied by the "U" shaped GRANT FIELD STADIUM (1917 and 1948), with a seating capacity of 40,000. This is the home of the nationally famous Georgia Tech football teams, nicknamed the "Yellow Jackets." The most recent addition to the stadium, the West Stands of reinforced concrete, cantilever construction, has been given many architectural awards for its design and layout, which includes the most modern facilities for press, radio, and television.

If one continues north on Cherry Street beyond Third Street, he will enter the center of the new construction at Georgia Tech. First, there is the modern, functional styled RESEARCH BUILDING (1939) with its additions of the CALCULATOR BUILDING (1947) and HINMAN MEMORIAL BUILDING (1950), the home of the State Engineering Experiment Station and the Georgia Tech Research Institute. Located in this group of buildings are some of the most advanced research laboratories in the nation, including the country's largest A.C. Network calculator, micromeritics (research at temperatures as low as —455°), food research, mechanical, etc. Due to the classified nature of some of the research projects, requests for visiting the station must be submitted in writing several weeks in advance.

Next to the station is the new $2,200,000, five-story, PRICE GILBERT LIBRARY (1953), which houses the Institute's million dollar collection of general, engineering, and scientific books. Large view windows are set in the north and south sides of the building, the exterior walls of which are of Roman brick. In addition to the large science-technology and general studies rooms, the contemporary functional building contains many special rooms, such as maps, faculty, graduate studies, etc.

Directly west of the library is the $1,000,000 W. HARRISON HIGHTOWER TEXTILE BUILDING (1948), the most complete facility in the country devoted to instruction and research in textile engineering and textiles. This contemporary functional building is fully equipped with the most up-to-date classrooms, laboratories, and auditorium. There are many exhibits on textiles which should prove very interesting to visitors.

Leaving the textile building, one can continue northeast along Campus Drive to the new $1,000,000 ARCHITECTURE BUILDING (1952), which was designed by Bush-Brown, Gailey & Heffernan, Architects, a firm staffed and operated by professors of the Georgia Tech School of Architecture. This contemporary functional building contains the most modern equipment, classrooms, drafting rooms, laboratories, display hall, and auditorium found anywhere in the United States. The School puts on a series of architectural and other exhibits during the year which are open to visitors. In addition to architecture, there are courses in industrial design and city planning.

Among the many universities and colleges of the nation, Georgia Tech did one of the most outstanding jobs after World War II, in providing permanent housing for both faculty and students. The existing residence halls, located along Williams Street and Techwood Drive, namely, TECHWOOD (1935), BROWN (1925), CLOUDMAN (1931), HARRISON (1939), and HOWELL (1939), were supplemented with the construction of three more at a cost of $1,600,000. These are named after William H. Glenn, John M. Smith and Donigen Dean Towers (1947). In order to aid the married students and faculty, the Institute constructed the $685,000 eight-story BURGE APARTMENT HOUSE (1947), with 66 units on North Avenue, just opposite the old Administration Building. At the same time, it constructed at a cost of $1,330,000 a group of three-story garden-type apartments with 166 units on Tenth Street at Holly Street. Known as the CALLAWAY APARTMENTS (1947), this group consists of buildings named in honor of seven prominent Georgians: GEORGE W. ADAIR, GEORGE GUNBY JORDON, VICTOR ALLEN, GEORGE GORDON CRAWFORD, PAUL HOWES NORCROSS, MAXWELL R. BERRY, and MERCER MCCALL THARPE.

The official residence of the President of Georgia Tech is located on a high hill just south of Tenth and Holly streets, overlooking the main campus. The traditional Georgian styled home is constructed of white-painted brick with imposing square columns in front and back, and is surrounded by beautiful lawns, gardens and trees.

36. THE COCA-COLA COMPANY (*open to visitors Mon. through Fri., 9:00 A.M. to 5:00 P.M.*), 310 North Avenue, N. W., maintains at this address a general office and a syrup manufacturing plant, the latter being one of ten similar plants within the United States. Coca-Cola syrup, made in the Atlanta plant, is shipped to independently owned bottling plants and to authorized wholesalers for distribution to soda fountains throughout the Southeast.

Coca-Cola was first made in Atlanta in 1886 by John S. Pemberton, pharmacist, wholesale druggist and manufacturing chemist, and sale of the new drink was begun that year exclusively through soda fountains. Before his death in 1888, Pemberton sold an interest in the business to Asa G. Candler, also a wholesale druggist. By 1891 Candler (1851-1929) had acquired complete ownership of the product, and early in 1892 organized The Coca-Cola Company.

Until 1899 Coca-Cola was sold to the public only through soda fountains. In that year, however, Mr. Candler granted bottling rights for most of the United States to a couple of Chattanooga citizens, who, during the next few years, granted similar rights to individuals in all parts of the country. As a result, there are now more than 1,100 individually owned and operated Coca-Cola Bottling Plants in the United States, alone.

The Candler family retained a controlling interest in and operated The Coca-Cola Company until 1919, at which time it was sold for $25,-000,000 to a group headed by Ernest Woodruff (1863-1944). Since 1923 the enterprise has been guided by Robert W. Woodruff, under whom it has expanded until Coca-Cola is now available in 86 countries, territories and possessions throughout the world.

37. The FARMERS' MARKET, 1050 Murphy Avenue, S. W., which is operated under the supervision of the Georgia State Department of Agriculture, was officially opened in May, 1941. The market now has around eighty permanent dealers and well over half a thousand people

are engaged in handling and selling the steady flow of farm products moving in and out of the 20-acre area daily.

Soon after the Georgia State Department of Agriculture was established in 1874 it was recognized that a profitable agriculture depends on adequate markets. So long as only a few staple crops were produced, the problem was not acute since every community had its "cotton merchant." But with the introduction of diversified farming the problem became serious. In 1935, a new approach was made. The general assembly authorized the commissioner of agriculture to procure by purchase, lease, gift, or otherwise, necessary market sites on which to conduct Farmers' Markets. The commissioner was also directed to prescribe and collect reasonable charges to pay the cost of operating and maintaining such markets and to promulgate such rules and regulations as might be needed to carry out the provision of the act. Without state finances, but with the cooperation of the city of Atlanta and Fulton County, the first State Farmers' Market was built on a six-acre plot on Gilmer Street between Cortland Street and Piedmont Avenue. Similar markets were established in 1936, with the aid of public-spirited citizens, in Macon, Thomasville, and Valdosta. Eventually, the general assembly, recognizing the complete practicability of such markets, made construction and operating funds available to build a chain with modern facilities throughout the state.

The sales of produce on the market during the remaining months after it opened in May at the Murphy Avenue location amounted to $6,186,000, increasing to $10,000,000 in 1942, $31,000,000 in 1945, $38,000,000 in 1951, and $42,417,251 in 1952, in spite of the 1952 drought. The U. S. Department of Agriculture report shows that carlot deliveries on the market for 1951 amounted to 25,105. This is more than 2,000 carloads for every month of the year. The produce came from forty-six states of the Union, Canada, Cuba, Mexico, Chile, and other foreign sources. Supplies are of course hauled in daily from all over Georgia.

POINTS OF INTEREST IN ENVIRONS

Atlanta Municipal Airport at Hapeville, *9.2 m.* S. of the city; the Ford Motor Company Assembly Plant at Hapeville; the Buick-Oldsmobile-Pontiac Assembly Division Plant of the General Motors Corporation on Peachtree Industrial Boulevard, in Doraville, *14.5 m.* NE. of Atlanta's Five Points downtown; Fort McPherson, *4.2 m.,* Agnes Scott College, *6.8 m.,* Georgia Military Academy, *7.8 m.* (*see* TOUR *3*); Kennesaw Mountain National Battlefield, near Marietta, *21.8 m.* (*see* TOUR *2*); Stone Mountain, *16.3 m.* (*see* TOUR *8*); Barrington Hall, Bulloch Hall, and Mimosa Hall, *21 m.,* in Roswell (*see* TOUR *6*).

Augusta

Railroad Stations: Union Station, 800 block of Walker Street, for Southern Railway; Atlantic Coast Line Railroad; Charleston and Western Carolina Railway; Georgia Railroad; Georgia and Florida Railroad; and Central of Georgia Railway.

Bus Stations: Carolina Scenic States Station, 1128 Greene Street; Trailways Bus Station, 638 Greene Street; and Union Bus Terminal, 1128 Greene Street.

Airports: Bush Field, eight miles south of Augusta on Old Savannah Road, municipal airport, for Delta-C & S, Southern, and Eastern Air Lines. Daniel Field, Wrightsboro and Wheeless Roads, auxiliary municipal airport.

Taxis: Fifty cents minimum, graduated upward by city zones.

Traffic Regulations: Right and left turns at all intersections except where marked otherwise. City uses parking meters. Street signs indicate parking limitations on non-metered streets; no all-night parking on paved streets.

Local Busses: Eight, 10, 12, 15, 20, 30 and one hour schedules. Fare $.10 in city.

Accommodations: Sixteen hotels; 22 motels and motor courts.

Information Service: Augusta Chamber of Commerce, second floor Bell Municipal Auditorium, 700 block of Telfair Street; East Georgia Motor Club, 127 Seventh Street; and AAA Motor Club, 128 Seventh Street.

Golf: Augusta Golf Club, Damascus Road, 18 holes, green fee $1 except Wednesday and Sunday, $1.50; Armed Forces Golf Club, Comfort Road and Magnolia Drive, 18 holes, green fee $2, except week ends, $3 and $4; Augusta Country Club, 18 holes, members and guests only; Augusta National Golf Club, 18 holes, members and guests only.

Baseball: Jennings Park, Fifteenth Street. Team: Augusta Rams, Class A, South Atlantic (Sally) League.

Football: Richmond Academy Stadium, Walton Way and Russell Street.

Motion Picture Houses: 7, including two for Negroes; 4 drive-ins.

Radio Stations: WRDW (1480 kc.); WAUG (1050 kc.); WJBF (1230 kc.); WGAC (580 kc.); and WBBQ (1340 kc.).

Television: Federal Communications Commission has allotted Channels 6 and 12 to city.

Swimming: Lake Olmstead, municipal beach, at Julian Smith Park, west end of Broad Street; Jennings Pool, municipal swimming pool, Fifteenth Street and Walton Way.

Tennis: May Park—6; Jennings Park—12; Allen Park—5; Hickman Park—1.

Annual Events: Women's Titleholders Golf Championship; Masters Tournament, Augusta National Golf Course; Soap Box Derby, held at nearby Camp Gordon; City Tennis Tournament; Augusta City Golf Championship; Sand Hill Garden Club Camellia Show, one of largest and most famous in the nation; Spinsters Club Christmas Ball; Bachelors Club Costume Ball; Augusta Assembly Ball; Exchange Club Fall Fair; Teen Town Follies; Augusta Council of Garden Clubs, Spring and Fall Flower Shows; Beaux Arts Ball; Art Exhibition of Georgia Artists Association; Elizabeth Wright Clothes-Line Art Exhibit; Junior Art Show; Governor's Ball; Elks Club Ball; and Elks Club Annual Christmas Ball.

AUGUSTA [109-483 alt.; 71,508 urban pop.; Metropolitan (Richmond County, Georgia, and Aiken County, South Carolina) pop. 162,013] is Georgia's second oldest city. It was founded, in effect, as a center where the people might "enfort" themselves against the Indian in times of trouble and as a trading post, in 1735, as a part of General Oglethorpe's political policy. It is typical of frontier expansion that the trader is followed by the military, and both are followed by the merchant and lawyer. The arts of the latter two depend upon computation and the written word. And these arts imply the school and especially the church by which God's lively word is heard in the wilderness. Augusta's prime regional function was to serve as a middle term between Savannah and the upcountry, not only with regard to defense and trade, but as introducing in addition to the fort and the market, the school, the church, and the court. And the town's location on the Fall Line—where the Piedmont Plateau meets the Coastal Plain—designed it to be both a center of industry due to its easily available water power, and of agriculture because of the river's rich alluvial deposits and the area's gently rolling terrain. The very Savannah that served as a principal artery of trade and territorial expansion came in time to function as a source of energy by means of which the city itself produced an important part of its trade inventory.

It is no mistake to call Augusta the Industrial Giant on the Savannah. The textile industry alone would justify the epithet, not to mention the nearby Savannah River Project of the Atomic Energy Commission, at Aiken, and the multi-purpose Clark Hill Dam, constructed by the U. S. Corps of Engineers, some twenty miles upriver from Augusta. But giants are monsters, and though gigantism is present, factors indicating a more normal figure of life existed long before the giants came, and may be expected to persist, without carrying matters as far as David did with Goliath. The life-parts of the Augusta region are related one to the other in an exceptional metropolitan-rural balance composed of a well diversified industry and agriculture. Augusta is the center of an agricultural area in eastern Georgia and western South Carolina with soil conservation, crop rotation, and crop diversification established for some time on a practical basis, and with the overt co-operation of bankers, businessmen, and farmers. Among its manufactured products are cotton textiles, brick and tile, kaolin, cottonseed oil and meal, lumber and hardwoods, machinery and mill supplies, mine pumps, candy, bedding, processed foods, flour and meal, bread, soft drinks, dairy products, shirts and pants, brooms, caskets, cigars, furniture, fertilizers, cotton bagging, burlap, chemicals, lubricants, pottery, ice, coffee roasting, and press cloth made from human (Asiatic) hair. That

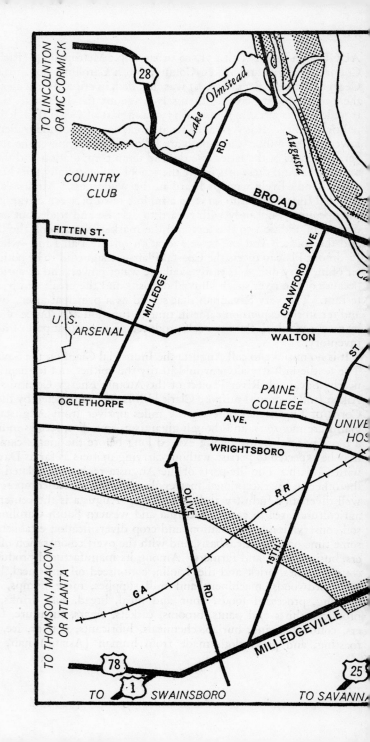

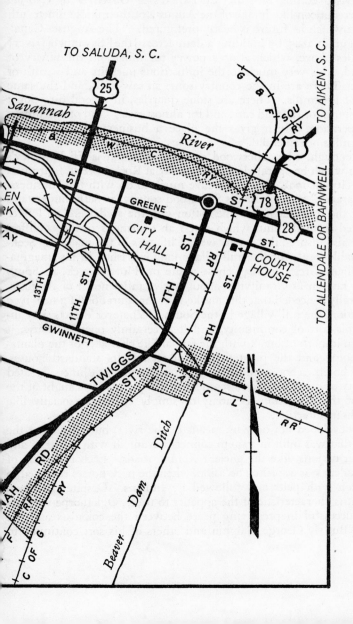

AUGUSTA

TO SALUDA, S. C.

TO AIKEN, S. C.

25

Savannah

River

SOU RY

1

W & C RY ST.

GREENE

78

28

CITY HALL

ST.

ST.

COURT HOUSE

7TH ST.

RR

ST.

5TH

13TH

11TH ST.

ST.

GWINNETT

TWIGGS

ST.

ST.

A

C

L

N

RR

RD.

RY

RR

G

C OF G

F

Beaver Dam Ditch

TO ALLENDALE OR BARNWELL

region is doubtless economically in good health which supplies its needs locally and uses outside markets only for the disposal of surpluses and to purchase alien luxuries. Published articles about Augusta commonly speak of the farmer's money as the backbone of its economy.

The revised edition of Adiel Sherwood's *A Gazetteer of Georgia* gives a stereopticon-like image of the Augusta of the middle nineteenth century in which its future is neatly prefigured. "The Augusta Canal, which begun in 1845, by building a dam across [the] Savannah [river] a few miles above, which affords power for mills and machinery of every kind, adds very much to the industrious pursuits and wealth of the place. There are in the country some 20 saw-mills, and the same number of gristmills. There are stone quarries, in several directions; machine shops for railroad cars, and for almost every kind of machinery are in operation, which gives the place a business-like appearance. Flouring mills are splendid."

Oddly enough, what Sherwood does not mention is Eli Whitney's cotton gin which he operated experimentally at Rocky Creek, four miles from the city, in 1793. It was to have much to do with the "business-like appearance" of Augusta, as Sherwood somewhat flatly understates it. With the introduction of the cotton gin, the seed were no longer handpicked from the lint, which saved an enormous time-cost differential. It also insured that a new way of life was in the making. Seeking a suitable locale for the mill-village long cherished in his imagination, William Gregg in 1845 chose a site on Horse Creek, in South Carolina, known as Granitville, about twelve miles north of Augusta. It is generally conceded that this marked the inauguration of a new type of association, the mill-village in the South. Whatever defects may inhere in this sort of community, and it is certainly open to abuse, it marked an important break with the feudal-like character of the plantation economy and the plantation social scene. Its standard houses, churches, hotels, schools, and other such community adjuncts, created an equality of conditions for a segment of the population caught at the bottom of the plantation hierarchy or simply cut adrift socially like mass without direction.

Trade developed not only by means of the river, but also along the highway that was built in 1740 to connect Savannah with Augusta and the Indian nations, like the ancient Roman roads. Each round-up of the fur traders was a spirited occasion, when the pack horses returned to town laden with pelts and followed by Indians. Despite the usual greed that is characteristic of the appetite to trade, Oglethorpe was singularly successful in preserving peace between the colonists and the Indians. But sly George Galphin and others of his sort continued to exchange trinkets and gay clothing for valuable lands, and the trading post grew vigorously. In 1745 there were five warehouses but no churches, schools, or doctors—those specifics for three great human ills: unlimited desire, ignorance, and pain. The market-fort was yet to feel the need of the civic virtues. But St. Paul's Church was established in 1750, and the following year the Reverend Jonathan Cope came to care for a congregation of more than a hundred souls. When a town is young in a young country its days are very long and change comes slowly at first. Augusta continued for another two decades to serve principally as a fortified market, where the merchant with his scales and balances measured out a sort of justice within an area defined by the fife and drum.

It appears that acuteness in trading is not a savage gift, for in the course of time the Indians fell heavily into debt. In order to bring the claims of white creditors into a state of resolution and to restore commercial ease, Governor Wright called a conference at Augusta in 1773. At this meeting the Indians ceded an area of 2,100,000 acres as far north as the Broad River.

The mixed passions that begot the Revolution created curious fissures among the members of Augusta families as the new balance of republican loyalties began to form. For Augusta like other Georgia cities had its liberty pole and hot-headed patriots. Eventually, in 1776 George Walton, an Augusta citizen, was one of the signers of the Declaration of Independence. The change is shown in the fact that St. Paul's Parish became Richmond County. The Revolutionary period in Georgia stands in an unsteady light, with much shifting back and forth of the symbols of authority between the patriots and the British. But near the close of 1778, when Savannah was lost, Governor John Houstoun and his council took refuge in Augusta, which however fell in its turn. Again in 1780 the seat of revolutionary government was brought to Augusta, this time officially, but soon afterwards the town was overborne by Grierson and Browne, Tory colonels. Browne, who had been tarred and feathered by a patriot mob five years before, had a sharp memory, and persons of the town felt the heavy hand of revenge.

Among later events Fort Augusta, renamed Fort Cornwallis by its British possessors, stubbornly resisted a siege that was lodged against it. Colonel Elijah Clarke attempted a direct assault, but was driven off. It was not until nine months later that Light-Horse Harry Lee contrived to erect a log tower after the ancient tactics, from which his men were able to sweep the interior of the fort with musket fire. On June 5, 1781, the British gave in. Thus Augusta was again in patriot hands, but destitution had become so general in the town that the planters had to pole cargoes of food upriver to the people. The fortunes of war had again reduced Augusta to the status of the frontier economically, and it was forced to re-grow virtually from the roots.

But after the Revolution a fresh source of economic strength began to invigorate the town when tobacco culture migrated from Virginia to Georgia with the settlers. Lands about the city were cleared for the new crop, for tobacco is both voracious and exacting, and thrives best only on new land. In season huge casks of tobacco with axle and shafts were drawn by horses into town. For the rest of the century Augusta was the principal tobacco market of the state. With the shift from Indian trading to a precise agricultural technique as its chief preoccupation, the town began to soften its harsh frontier manners and to assume a style more in keeping with a stable prosperity. In 1783 the Academy of Richmond County was chartered, and began to function two years later in a Bay Street residence. Now the South's oldest newspaper in continuous publication, the *Augusta Chronicle and Gazette* appeared the same year. Augusta was becoming properly civic and assuming the functions of a maturing city.

In 1785 the legislature in Savannah adjourned to meet in Augusta the following year, when it appointed commissioners to choose a favorable location nearer the then center of population and name it Louisville. The new site, though, was not ready until 1796; and hence Augusta remained the state capital for ten years. It was during this time, on January 2, 1788, that Georgia ratified the Federal Constitution. In 1798 Augusta, having undergone the formality of incorporation as a town nine years earlier, was granted a city charter with provision for a council composed of members elected from each district and an intendant chosen by the council.

While Augusta was clearing away its rustic weeds and becoming urbane, William Longstreet was for some fifteen years absorbed in perfecting a steam engine that he had brought forward with the monetary support of Isaac Briggs. Finally he launched an odd craft, with heavy oak boilers banded with iron. A concourse of skiffs rowed by jeering onlookers followed the boat downstream. But Longstreet's dignity was thoroughly salvaged when the boat reversed against the river's current and returned precisely to its dock. Longstreet was about to apply for a patent, but he was stopped by the news of Fulton's nationally more public success reaching Augusta.

The town made another advance in civic maturity when the Thespian Society and the Library Company of Augusta began to function in 1808. In 1810 the Bank of Augusta was chartered, and in 1819 the first arsenal was completed. The War of 1812 brought a brief panic because of mercantile indiscretions among certain trading houses, but it did not seriously delay the town's growth. An important article of the democratic dogma was met when the Augusta Free School Society was established in 1821 to educate children unable to pay the academy tuition. And the Medical Society of Augusta, growing out of an association that began in 1808, was incorporated in 1822. Dr. Milton Antony, assisted by his pupil Dr. Joseph A. Eve, began a school of medicine in connection with the city hospital, a modest frame building equipped to accommodate ten patients normally or twenty-one in an emergency. The Augusta Library Society was organized in 1827. Chartered the following year and opened a few years later, the Medical Academy of Georgia in Augusta was the first in the state. The higher learning in both its liberal and useful phases was now definitely institutionalized and ready to initiate the young into the cultural pattern of the great western tradition.

As the century advanced and cotton supplanted tobacco, Augusta moved ahead as a market for the newer product, partly because of its strategic position but also because sales were conducted in cash. Drivers of cotton caravans announced their arrival by sharply cracking their long whips. Broad Street was jammed with wagons loaded with cotton in 250-pound bags, the packing unit used before the discovery of the cotton press made the bale typical. Some fifteen steamboats and a considerable flock of poled rafts carried burdens of from eight hundred to a thousand bags towards the sea.

In 1837 transportation made a great stride forward when the Georgia Railroad, begun in Augusta, made an initial run on its first twenty miles of track to Berzelia; its engines bore such unlikely names as *Fairy* and *Swallow*. In 1845 work began on the canal that later served the textile industry so well. When a plank road was built up Walton Way in 1850, the Sand Hills area became a year-round place of residence. In 1851 John W. Houghton, a leather merchant, at his death left funds to erect a brick school, free to Augusta children, which was provided with teachers by the city council. The Augusta and Savannah Railroad, now the Central of Georgia, reached Augusta in 1854. Lectures were sponsored by the Young Men's Library Association which had been organized in 1848. The more famous of these lectures presented William Makepeace Thackeray who came to Augusta, during his American tour, to read *The Four Georges,* a series on Kings George I-IV and their eras which appeared sometime later in "Cornhill Magazine," that is, in 1860.

The city went through a somber period in which yellow fever besieged it from 1840 to 1854 with such rigor, especially in the later epidemic, that vehicles were lacking to take away the dead, and wheel-barrows were used to carry them to the cemeteries.

On January 24, 1861, after a singularly polite negotiation, the United States flag was lowered on the arsenal and a white flag with a red star, signifying the Confederacy, replaced it. Because of its geographic situation, water power, and transportation media, Augusta was assigned the responsibility of the Confederate Powder Works. When Sherman left Atlanta for the sea in November of 1864, Augusta of course assumed that it was on the general's list of devoirs and marked for destruction. The Confederate military command ordered the accumulated cotton piled some five or six bales high on Broad Street, with a view to burning it in preference to having it fall into Federal hands. Had not the mayor's good sense prevailed so that the order was remanded, Augusta's defenders might themselves have fired the city. A wing of the Federal army did swing by neighboring plantations, like an erratic thunderstorm in the night, but Sherman was so entertained with Savannah that Augusta was neglected. It was actually not until General Lee's surrender in April of 1865 that the army of occupation took over the city, for the most part without incident.

With the end of Reconstruction and the birth of fresh hope in the 1870's, new industries developed during the next twenty years, bringing about as a complement of their success an advance in population. The cultural life of the city quickened again with its industrial increase, despite a freshet, an earthquake, and a fire. In 1908 an especially memorable flood disabled the city for several days and destroyed several million dollars' worth of property. This flood, and a lesser one in 1912, resulted in the construction of a fourteen-mile levee, financed by a municipal bond issue and completed in 1916. The culminating disaster was the fire of 1916, which destroyed an estimated $2,500,000 in property and wiped out many historic houses. When the city was rebuilt, there was a decided exodus to the higher and more open Sand Hills section. In October, 1929, the river rose to an unusual height and put the levee to the test. Sandbags were piled on top, and there was one ominous rift, but the levee held heroically.

Today the flood antics of the normally sluggish Savannah have been reduced to a steady rhythm of day-by-day industriousness. This has been accomplished under the supervision of the U. S. Corps of Engineers, by the virtual completion of Clark Hill Dam, 21 miles above Augusta, which is a part of the Federal government's multiple-purposed project, with eleven dams in prospect. The dam, which is larger than the Norris in the TVA chain, is an earth-fill and concrete structure. The length of the concrete section is 2,282 feet, though the overall length is slightly more than a mile. A twenty-four foot highway across the top connects Georgia with South Carolina. If the Clark Hill Reservoir is filled to the top of the spillway gates, a lake results that is thirty-nine miles long on the Savannah, twenty-five on Georgia's Little River, and seventeen miles up the Little River in South Carolina. The maximum depth of the reservoir at the dam site is 160 feet, and when the water reaches the top of the spillway 2,900,000 acre-feet of water are impounded.

Year-round navigation to the sea is a basic feature of the inclusive project. The completion of the Clark Hill project carries with it the assurance of a seven-foot channel, and future plans include the increase of this depth first to nine and then to twelve feet. As the plan is carried through, the Central Savannah River area, in eastern Georgia and western South Carolina, of which Augusta is the functional center, will be immensely benefited. Synoptically the benefits are: (1) the addition of a large increase of low-cost hydroelectric power to the potential already available in the area, (2) the confirmation of Augusta as a 12-month barge port with a minimum year-round channel of nine feet, (3) the protection of the city of Augusta and its rich river front soils from the recurrent tolls levied by floods, (4) the establishment of an immense recreation area for the use of the people, like that at Allatoona Lake in northwest Georgia (*see* TOUR 2).

As one result of the Savannah River Project, the E. I. du Pont de Nemours & Company, in the rôle of prime contractor, has advanced the construction of the Atomic Energy Commission's Savannah River Plant, located mostly in Aiken County, South Carolina, adjacent to Augusta, to a point where its operational area is four times greater than that of Washington, D. C. With such a vast development in its front yard, Augusta has been severely taxed to supply facilities and housing. Mercantile figures have increased to such an extent that *The Wall Street Journal,* issue of July 14, 1952, was moved to comment with a high, warm glow, at several column lengths, on the "$4 million weekly payroll" that is bringing a flood—of a different sort—out of the Savannah's energy, for the Augusta area. Meanwhile the atomic bomb is at once the highest advance of American science and an ambiguous symbol of hope and anxiety in the modern world. If true social progress is blocked today, it is not for lack of means but because of an ill-made image of what constitutes success in life.

Industrial Augusta is geographically and economically integrated with some nineteen adjacent Georgia counties and twelve counties in South Carolina, with a population of around seven hundred thousand, known as the Greater Augusta Area. Augusta's industrial products, made for the most part from locally available materials, include principally textiles, then stone and clay, glass, pottery, food and associated items, and lumber and wood products. Iron and coal are readily available from Birmingham and western Tennessee. The city is served by six railroads: the Georgia Railroad, the Charleston & Western Carolina Railway Company, the Southern Railway System, the Atlantic Coast Line, the Central of Georgia Railway Company, the Georgia and Florida Railroad, and also a Belt Line in the city. Four national highways: US 1 from Canada to Key West, US 78 from Charleston to Memphis, US 25 from Port Huron, Michigan, to Brunswick, and US 319, pass through the city, and a large number of interstate long-distance motor lines are routed through it. Airlines operate twenty-two flights daily to and from Augusta. Bush Field which handles both passenger and freight service was used during World War II by the U. S. Air Force as a flight training school and as a base for heavy bombers.

Richmond County is the center of one of the most fertile regions in the Southeast. Rich in natural resources, it has inexhaustible deposits of kaolin and clay, and thirty-two distinct types of soil suitable to an unusual number of crops. Other favorable factors are a 236-day growing season, an annual rainfall of around 47.4 inches, and a year-round mild climate with—during a 52-year period—a January mean temperature of 47.4° and a July mean of 81.2°. These factors favor early planting and the early maturity of crops as well as an unusual interval of available pasture for cattle. Typical field products are cotton, wheat, oats, barley, rye, corn, beans, peanuts, peaches, pecans, pears, apples, plums, and walnuts. Truck gardening is encouraged by a lively demand from the local markets, and exceptionally so with the atomic plant's added population.

Decline of cotton as the principal economic constant of the area's production equation, especially in the 20's, has been attributed to a number of factors: the boll weevil; the costly method of production, that is, by means of small acreage and wasteful tenant farming; the introduction of machinery in place of mules and hands, which suits better the Mississippi Delta and other like areas; and, too, to the advance of synthetic fibers. Nevertheless Augusta has sixteen cotton mills, one large cotton-waste mill, and four cottonseed oil mills. And in spite of the crop diversification that forms along with the application of soil conservation techniques and crop rotations, a basic part of the new agricultural technology, cotton is still the No. 1 crop, and Augusta, once one of the world's largest inland cotton markets, still ranks among its largest ten. The introduction of new pest controls, of improved soil techniques, and of "one variety communities" whose consenting members agree to plant a single sort, thus simplifying the ginning and making possible an automatically graded staple, have served measurably to offset the destructiveness of the boll weevil and to revive hope for cotton.

A decade or so ago livestock production in the area was only a minor economic factor, but at present around $12,000,000 worth of livestock is sold annually in the counties that make up the Twin States Livestock Association, of which sixteen are in Georgia and eleven in South Carolina. The Association's Cow-and-Calf Beef Cattle Program emphasizes the raising of good beef calves at home and their disposal elsewhere to be finished. As a supplement to its program, the Association staged the first Annual Augusta Feeder Calf Show and Sale on October 13, 1948. Local farmers agree quite generally that there is more money and less work in producing one head of cattle than there is in raising one acre of cotton. Meat processing plants in Augusta offer encouragement to this growing industry, and markets are held regularly in the city. The census of pure-bred beef cattle in the area has been in no little part increased through the efforts of the 4-H Clubs, the Future Farmers of America, and the Negro Farmers of America.

Agriculture in the area was slow to accept the wealth of means for progress offered by the neotechnical world. But the heroic efforts of the state extension service and of the various agencies of the U. S. Department of Agriculture have finally brought forward what amounts to a revolution in farming. Agriculture, even today's neotechnical sort, fits the human imagination. In contrast, the industrial worker, a least point in a vastly complicated functional system, is quite commonly involved day by day with some isolated item of routine that makes no sense, and despite the denials of certain economic oracles, no amount of take-home pay can cure the unrest that results. Corporations not infrequently spend a deal of money on public relations and personnel management, but few have equalled the 4-H Clubs, the Future Farmers of America, the Future Homemakers, and the New Farmers of America—in offering a program in which work and recreation are integral to one another and thus are equivalent to *life*.

The new agriculture has added enormously to the well-being of the Augusta farming area, which covers a radius of some fifty miles. The Farmers Market in Augusta, sponsored by the State Department of Agriculture, was organized in 1951 (*see* Points of Interest below), and is already functioning smoothly as a reliable means by which the farmer meets the buyer.

Augusta, often called "The Winter Golf Capital of America," is the location of the (Bobby Jones) Augusta National Golf Course. It is here that the famous Masters Invitation Tournament is played annually in the spring. In addition the city has three other 18-hole championship courses with grass greens. Augusta's attractive trails appeal to horseback riders. The city offers a variety of sports in addition, including polo, tennis, swimming, football, basketball, boxing and wrestling, and professional baseball.

POINTS OF INTEREST
(DOWNTOWN)

1. SIGNERS' MONUMENT, at the conjunction of Greene and Monument streets, is an imposing fifty-foot granite shaft rising from the center of a green. Begun with the laying of the cornerstone on July 4, 1848, it was erected by the state of Georgia in honor of its three signers of the Declaration of Independence. The bodies of Lyman Hall and George Walton are buried beneath the monument. It was intended that the body of Button Gwinnett be included, but he was killed in a duel with Lachlan McIntosh, and his grave has not been located.

2. The CHARLES PHINIZY PLACE, 519 Greene Street, which has served as the Elks Club recently, is a handsome Georgian house built in 1841. It was originally planned as a two-story building over a high basement, but a third story has been added. The usual hand-made red brick of the period was used in its construction. A graceful, iron-railed horseshoe stairway leads to a small entrance balcony at the second floor level. Pink marble is used in the floors and the waist-high dadoes of the basement.

3. The RICHMOND COUNTY BOARD OF HEALTH BUILDING (*open 9-5 week-days*), 503 Greene Street, formerly the Clanton Home, was built in 1848-51 and became county health headquarters in 1934. Greek Revival details are the high basement, the four fluted Doric columns supporting a classic pediment, and the small balcony over the entrance. The delicate iron grillwork used lavishly on the façade is hand wrought, and all the brick used in the construction came from Philadelphia by ship. Silverplated doorknobs and hand-carved woodwork are notable features of the interior.

4. The DE L'AIGLE HOUSE (*private*), 426 Greene Street, a three-story, red brick building, was built in 1818 by Nicholas de l'Aigle, a French *émigré*. The main portion of the house is of Tudor design, but the wide wings, added at a later date, have small Corinthian columns in the Greek Revival manner. The front door is elaborately hand-carved, as are the wood trim and brass work throughout the interior. The sidelights and transom of one of the backdoors are of red Bohemian glass etched with the grape designs typical of the widely distributed decanters and other glass implements in that genre. A graceful mahogany-railed staircase winds up to the ballroom on the third floor. On this floor is a

small, dark room where, it is said, the gentlemen of the old school placed their arms before entering the ballroom. Two large wine cellars with iron-barred windows have ledges for kegs and demijohns. In the back yard is the old kitchen, with a ten-foot fireplace and a large Dutch oven.

5. MAGNOLIA CEMETERY, 702 Third Street (*open 9-5 daily*), was named for the rows of magnolia trees shading its walks and grounds. An older cemetery occupied part of this plot, but the earliest interment recorded since it was taken over by the city bears the date August 5, 1818. Three Augusta poets, Paul Hamilton Hayne, Richard Henry Wilde, and James Ryder Randall, are buried here.

An UPRIGHT CANNON, its mouth buried in the ground, marks the grave of John Martin, a Revolutionary soldier. Supposedly, the cannon figured in a riot, when a mob packed it with such oddments as nails and glass, but when it failed to fire, rather than risk the danger of unloading it, they buried it near the grave.

6. The HOUSE OF DR. E. E. MURPHY (*private*), 432 Telfair Street, is reputed to have been designed by a French architect, probably Gabriel Manigault, of South Carolina, and built as the "Government House" in 1790, when Augusta was the state capital. In 1791, while visiting the city, George Washington was honored by a state banquet in this house. The stucco-covered brick house is of simple, square design in keeping with the architectural simplicity and good taste prior to the Greek Revival idiom. Wings at each end were added at a later date. There are pleasing white Carrara marble mantels and wide floor boards throughout the house. Signs of a social order now gone indeed, old-fashioned service bells hang across the top of the back porch.

7. The NICHOLAS WARE MANSION, 506 Telfair Street, has been remodeled for use as an art school and exhibition hall, and is now owned and used by the Herbert Art Institute. This two-story frame building, ornamented in the Adam style, is considered one of the few almost perfect examples of Georgian architecture in Augusta. The horseshoe entrance steps have balusters with delicate mahogany railings, and inside a handsome elliptical stairway winds to the attic. The house was built in 1818 by Nicholas Ware, and because it cost $40,000, then a large sum though not as considerable today, it was called Ware's Folly. The Marquis de La Fayette, visiting Augusta in 1825, was feted here by a ball.

8. The PUBLIC LIBRARY (*open weekdays*), 540 Telfair Street, began as the Young Men's Library, founded by the association of that name in 1848, but was not opened to the public until 1937. In the same building is the AUGUSTA MUSEUM. Although it was not established until 1933, the museum contains good collections of Indian artifacts, Confederate

relics, rifles, and ceramic art. Of special interest are the pieces of Wedgewood ware made from Georgia clay and a Greek or Roman flagon exhibiting a festival in honor of pagan gods of the harvest.

The building is made of typical hand-made, stucco-covered brick in simple Tudor design. Gothic influence is suggested in the battlemented parapets of the roof, and Renaissance details in the columns of the entrance portico. It was built in 1802 for the Academy of Richmond County and during the War between the States was used as a Confederate hospital. After the removal of the academy to its new quarters on Baker Avenue in 1926, the building stood vacant for two years until it was assigned for the library.

9. The OLD MEDICAL COLLEGE BUILDING, southeast corner of Telfair and Washington streets, is a simple Greek Revival structure of stuccoed brick. Six massive Doric columns of the portico support a plain entablature, above which rises a severe pediment. The building, designed by C. C. Clusky, was erected in 1835 for the Medical Academy of Georgia, the first school of medicine in the state. When the college was moved to University Place in 1911, the building became the manual training shop and science laboratory of the Academy of Richmond County. Abandoned in 1926, when the academy was moved to Baker Avenue, it was made into a garden center by the Sand Hills Garden Club, and is now used as the Augusta Garden Center. Marked by a slab to the left of the entrance is the grave of Dr. Milton Antony, founder of the college, who was the victim of a yellow fever epidemic in 1859.

10. The FIRST PRESBYTERIAN CHURCH, 642 Telfair Street, is a gray, stuccoed brick building of simplified Tudor architecture, showing Gothic influence in its crenelated parapets, rounded Norman arches with mullioned windows, the rose window above the recessed central doorway, and the Chester arch ceiling. Renaissance influence is evident in the three-tiered Georgian tower surmounted by a spire. The church is set on a large tree-shaded lot surrounded by a hand-turned picket fence. It was built in 1812 from the plans of Robert Mills, designer of the Washington Monument. The Austin organ, installed in 1927, is one of the finest instruments in the South.

The MANSE (*private*), NW. corner Telfair and 7th streets, is now a private home, but once served the Presbyterian Church, and was the boyhood home of Woodrow Wilson when his father, the Reverend Joseph R. Wilson, was pastor of the church.

11. SAINT PATRICK'S ROMAN CATHOLIC CHURCH, SE. corner Telfair and Jackson streets, serves a parish that dates from 1810. The church designed by J. R. Nierrusse, of Columbia, South Carolina, and completed

in 1863, is in the Norman style, a stuccoed building with bell tower. Unable to raise sufficient funds for construction, the members of the parish joined the hired workmen each day after their own work was done.

12. The CITY HALL (*open 9-5 weekdays*), Greene and Campbell streets, is a Victorian Gothic building showing a Romanesque influence; an Italian accent is suggested in the red brick and terra cotta ornamentation. It was built between 1888 and 1890 as the Augusta post office at a cost of about $85,000, and it was not acquired by the city until 1916, when the new Federal building was erected.

In the foyer is the *Georgia,* the first steam fire engine purchased by a volunteer fire company, the Georgia Independent, in 1869. Among several old portraits in the building are two of George Washington by unknown artists, one showing the general in uniform, the other, in civilian clothes with stock, lace ruffles, and sword.

13. POETS' MONUMENT, center of green, between McIntosh and Jackson streets, is a granite shaft standing in the green that runs down the center of the street. The city accepted the gift from Anna Russell Cole to honor four Georgia poets: Sidney Lanier, James R. Randall, Paul Hamilton Hayne, and Father Abram Ryan. The last three at one time lived in Augusta.

14. The EVE HOUSE (*private*), 619 Greene Street, erected in 1814, is a two-story frame building distinguished by a high brick basement. This was the home of Dr. Paul Fitzsimmons Eve, who served as a surgeon in the Polish army during the Polish War of 1830. On the green in front of the house a MONUMENT commemorating his services has been erected jointly by the Polish Government and the Medical Department of the University of Georgia. The second-floor iron balcony overhangs the sidewalk.

15. The ALLEN HOUSE (*private*), 613 Greene Street, built in 1859, is a two-story brick structure with a high basement and delicate, vine-covered ironwork of Federal style on the steps, porch, and balcony. The interior plan is unusual because the hallway runs the length of the house on the west side. Three successive generations of Allen men have served as mayors of Augusta.

16. ST. PAUL'S EPISCOPAL CHURCH, NW. corner of Reynolds and Washington streets, with its Doric-columned portico and bell tower surmounted by a small dome, is set behind a brick wall and graceful iron gate. This building, erected in 1918, is a reproduction of the church built almost a century before and destroyed by fire in 1916. It is the fourth on the same site, the first having been established for the men of Fort Augusta in 1750, less than twenty years after Oglethorpe

founded the city. This church was then the farthest outpost of the Church of England on the new continent. A baptismal font, brought from England by the first rector, the Reverend Jonathan Cope, is the only possession saved from the building that burned in 1781. In the crypt beneath the altar is the tomb of Bishop Leonidas Polk, "fighting bishop of the Confederacy," killed at the Battle of Pine Mountain.

The tombs of noted persons in the churchyard include that of General George Brandes Mathews from Virginia, twice governor of Georgia, first from 1787 to 1788 when he slipped into office before he had completed the residence requirement, and again from 1793 to 1796; of Commodore Oliver Bowen, who captured a British powder ship off Tybee Island in 1775; and of William Longstreet, inventor of an early steamboat. It is believed that an Indian chief is entombed upright in the tall brick monument in the southwest corner.

The Celtic cross in the churchyard was placed there by the Colonial Dames to mark the SITE OF FORT AUGUSTA, about which the city developed. At its base is a cannon brought from England by Oglethorpe.

17. The CONFEDERATE MONUMENT, Herald Square, Broad Street, is Augusta's most impressive memorial. The central shaft, carved in Italy from Carrara marble, is seventy-six feet high. The life-size figures, one at each corner of the column, are of General Robert E. Lee and Stonewall Jackson as primary persons of the military Confederacy; General Thomas R. R. Cobb, of Georgia; and General W. H. T. Walker, of Richmond County. At the top of the shaft is a statue of a Confederate private. Designed by Von Gunden and Young, of Philadelphia, the monument was erected by the Ladies Memorial Association at a cost of approximately $17,000 and was dedicated on October 31, 1878.

18. The SPRINGFIELD BAPTIST CHURCH (Negro), SE. corner Reynolds and 12th (Marbury) streets, a red brick building with a gambrel roof, was built in 1910 to house a congregation organized in 1773 as the Silver Bluff or Dead River Church in South Carolina. The congregation of this, the first Negro Baptist church in the New World, was dispersed during the Revolution when many of the Negroes came to Augusta with their masters. Here they were reorganized as the Springfield Baptist Church. Among the six pastors buried in the churchyard is the Reverend Kelly Lowe, who organized the first Negro Sunday School in the nation on January 11, 1869. The wooden school and community house to the rear of the church was originally the St. John Methodist Church (white), moved to this site in 1844.

19. MEADOW GARDEN, Nelson Street, between McKinnie (13th) Street and Jefferson Davis Avenue (15th), (*open 3-6 Wed. during winter, and*

some holidays), was named long before commerce encroached upon the surrounding fields, in the form of business houses, factories, and a canal. The story-and-a-half white frame house with three dormer windows in the steep roof has undergone little change in its more than three half centuries. Severely simple, the building has a porch across the front with slender posts. The property was a gift in 1794 to George Walton, Jr., son of the George Walton who signed the Declaration of Independence, by his godfather, Thomas Watkins. Though available information shows some confusion, apparently Judge Walton, the Signer, used the Walton Home, at 2216 Wrightsboro Road in the Sand Hills section as his summer home, but he is recorded as having died at Meadow Garden in 1804.

Meadow Garden is now owned by the Georgia Division of the D. A. R., which has restored the house and furnished it with period pieces, some of them originally owned by the Waltons. Besides furniture the relics include portraits, prints, clothes, and a cannon used during the Revolution in the defense of Augusta and in the Battle of Ninety-Six, South Carolina.

20. The MEDICAL COLLEGE OF GEORGIA, between Gwinnett and Harper streets, and Railroad Avenue and 15th Street, was chartered in 1828 as the Medical Academy of Georgia. The following year the name was changed to the Medical Institute of the State of Georgia, and in 1833 to the Medical College of Georgia. In 1873 the college became affiliated with the University of Georgia as its Medical Department.

Since 1932 the college has been a unit of the University System of Georgia, controlled by the System's Board of Regents. From 1933 it was designated as the University of Georgia School of Medicine until its older name, the Medical College of Georgia, was restored in 1950. The college has an enrollment of more than three hundred and a faculty of one hundred (above the rank of instructor, including both full-time and part-time teachers). The large red brick building, generally known as the Newton Building, with a mansard roof and ironwork porches was begun in 1870 for the Tuttle-Newton Orphanage, and was converted into the college building in 1911. Near the center of the college campus, the Dugas Building, erected in 1937, and the Murphy Building, erected in 1939, house several of the instructional departments.

Close affiliation is maintained with the UNIVERSITY HOSPITAL, situated on the same tract of land. The main building of the hospital, with three connected wings of semi-classical architecture, was built by the City of Augusta in 1914. The Milton Antony Wing was added in 1934 and the Jennings Wing in 1945. The University Hospital, which accommodates around five hundred patients, is maintained by the City of Augusta.

The Lamar Wing of the hospital, for Negro patients, replaced the Lamar Negro Hospital, established upon the bequest of Gazaway B. Lamar, Augusta financier, who willed $50,000 each to Augusta and Savannah for the building of Negro hospitals. These funds were in the form of claims against the U. S. Government for cotton destroyed during the War between the States. The first Federal payment of $7,000 was increased by a city appropriation of $8,000, and the cornerstone was laid on March 11, 1895.

A new health center building, to be ready by July of 1953, to house the activities of the Richmond County Board of Health is an important adjunct. Among later events, construction has been started on a state general hospital of 800 beds, which will cost some ten million dollars, exclusive of equipment. Contracts have also been let for an administration building for the college, to cost approximately six hundred thousand dollars.

21. The AUGUSTA CANAL, spanned by the Butt Memorial Bridge on Jefferson Davis Avenue, extends nine miles through the city, running from west to east. In 1844, four energetic citizens, realizing the need of Augusta for additional water power, financed a survey for a canal to be filled with water from the Savannah River. Work was begun the following year on a seven-mile project that was completed on November 23, 1846. Six hundred horsepower was developed, but before many years had passed new factories necessitated additional power. Between 1871 and 1875 the widening, deepening, and lengthening of the canal to nine miles increased the horsepower to 14,000. Four cotton mills still derive part of their power from the canal system. Today, however, the Clark Hill Dam serves better as both fact and symbol of Augusta's situation with regard to potential industrial power.

22. The OBELISK-SHAPED CHIMNEY, Goodrich Street, immediately in front of the Sibley Manufacturing Company, one block N. of Broad Street, 176 feet high, stands as a monument to the Confederate Powder Works, of which it is the only remaining part. From 1862 until 1865 this plant, occupying several acres of land, manufactured 2,270,000 pounds of gunpowder under the direction of Colonel George Washington Rains. Since it was the only powder plant in the South, the area about it for several miles was kept under strict guard. It was dismantled in 1871.

23. The OLD WHITE HOUSE, 1822 Broad Street, is now preserved by the Richmond County Historical Association. Built as an inn in 1750, it is generally held to be the oldest extant house in Augusta. Situated on

an eminence above a brick retaining wall, this two-story frame house has a gambrel roof, substantial end chimneys, and a recessed front porch. No house is properly old unless it has its ghost. Standing on the beautiful circular stairway, one may by counting to thirteen, evoke ghostly agents in the form of a groan. The story goes back to the American Revolution when the house was known as McKay's Trading Post. On September 14, 1780, Colonel Elijah Clarke with 500 men attempted to take Augusta from its British possessors, who were under the command of Colonel Grierson and Colonel Thomas Browne, a local Tory. The British, pushed almost to extremity, made a retreat to the trading post which was protected by earthworks and barred windows. Weak from hunger after a four days' siege, they were relieved by the arrival of reinforcements, and the Revolutionists were forced to retreat, leaving Captain Ashby and twenty-eight soldiers behind. The wounded Browne caused thirteen of the soldiers, one for each of the states so the legend runs, to be hanged from an immense hook in the attic, and moved his bed near the door of his sickroom to watch the bodies dangle in the stair well. Indian allies formed a circle about the other prisoners in the front yard and tortured them slowly to death.

(THE HILL)

On THE HILL, Augusta's most beautiful residential section, handsome houses are designed to blend with oak and pine groves and the natural contours of the Sand Hills. Here are green parkways and landscaped gardens, open each spring during the garden club tour, when they are vivid with red flowering quince, wistaria and iris, pink crabapple, and pink and white dogwood. Scattered among the newer and more demanding houses, are to be found examples of the Sand Hills "cottages," variations of the American Farmhouse type, built around 1800. At that time citizens of low-lying Augusta sought to escape the fatigue of the humid summer days and the miasma of the surrounding swamplands by building summer residences on the Sand Hills. Carriages first plowed through the sand of an old tobacco road, called Battle Row because tobacco rollers of the period made a sort of history along its way by lively brawls at the taverns. Later the carriages were able to move more conveniently on a plank road along what is now Walton Way upon payment of a toll collected at the 15th Street gate. By 1861 people were living on the Hill throughout the year, and the village was incorporated as Summerville. When a carline was laid to the arsenal in 1866, an extra team of mules was necessary to pull the car up the grade. Summerville did not become a part of urban Augusta until 1912.

24. The ACADEMY OF RICHMOND COUNTY AND JUNIOR COLLEGE OF AUGUSTA, Walton Way and Baker Avenue, occupy a $375,000 building erected in 1926 of brick and stucco in the modern Collegiate Gothic style. Consisting of the 11th grade, the 12th grade, and two years of college, the academy and the college are a part of the city school system that operates under a Board of Education which has twelve members, one from each of the seven city wards and five from the county. In 1952 the academy and the college had an enrollment of several thousand students and some sixty teachers.

The high school is a modern equivalent of the old Richmond Academy, which was one of the first three public schools in the state. Chartered in 1783, the academy moved two years later into its first building, on Bay Street. When President Washington was in Augusta in May of 1791, Governor and Mrs. Edward Telfair gave a ball in his honor in the building. He also attended an examination of the academy pupils and was sufficiently impressed to send the honor students inscribed copies of the Roman classics, in which the leaders of the day were accustomed to find both their military and their political models. In 1802 the academy moved into the building now occupied by the library, and in 1926 when the junior college was added, transferred into the present structure.

A Spanish convent bell of uncertain age, which, hanging on the porch of the original building, announced the school hours, is a cherished possession of the present school.

25. The OLD WALTON HOUSE (*private*), 2216 Wrightsboro Road, is a two-and-a-half-story, white clapboard house, now owned by Mr. and Mrs. A. W. Harper, collateral descendants of George Walton. Walton, the Georgia signer of the Declaration of Independence, built the house before 1795 as a summer home. The hand-carved exterior and interior trim and the delicate spider web design of the banisters on the first- and second-story porches show clear Colonial detail. Massive end chimneys and numerous windows are important features of its definition.

26. The OLD KILPATRICK HOUSE (*private*), Comfort Road between Buena Vista Road and Magnolia Drive, is a large, square Colonial building that was moved in 1929 from the southwest corner of Greene and 7th streets in downtown Augusta. Its most notable feature is the entrance, with graceful, iron-balustraded and railed horseshoe stairs leading up to a centrally placed Doric-columned portico. The house, built soon after the middle of the eighteenth century, was once a fashionable inn on what was then the Old Post Road to Savannah. In 1825 when

General La Fayette visited Augusta he addressed the populace from the portico in proper republican style.

27. MONTROSE (*private*), 2249 Walton Way, a story-and-a-half clapboarded house, was built in 1849 by Robert Reid. Corinthian columns, reaching from the level of the high brick basement, support the impressive entablature and pediment of the portico at the second-story level. The white columns offer an effective contrast to the yellow clapboards. The mass of the four-columned portico, which dominates the front of the house, is balanced by wings at each end of the building. On the lawn, directly in front of the high steps to the portico, is one of the eight cannon from the dead town of Sunbury (*see* TOUR *1*). During the American Revolution when the British demanded that the Scottish Highlanders at Sunbury surrender Fort Morris, they were cordially invited, "Come and take it." Years later this cannon was presented to Colonel Charles Colcock Jones, the Georgia historian, who lived and wrote at Montrose. Granddaughters of the historian now live there.

28. The MONTGOMERY PLACE (*private*), 2260 Walton Way, now owned by the Applebys, is a two-story white frame building erected about 1830. The large, square house, recently renovated, is built in Greek Revival style and has massive Doric columns rising to the porch roof. An ornamental balcony is suspended over the entrance doorway.

29. The U. S. ARSENAL, Walton Way, between Katherine Street and Monte Sano Avenue, is one of the oldest in the country. The six original buildings, in use since 1829, are built on the sides of a brick quadrangle that encircles a rose garden centered by a stone sundial. The garden was formerly the old parade ground.

The first United States Arsenal at Augusta, built in 1819, was on the Savannah River near the site of the King and Sibley Mills. When an epidemic of "black fever" swept the garrison, higher ground was sought and seventy acres on the Sand Hills bought for $6,000. Suitable buildings were established and the arsenal garrisoned in 1829.

In 1861, five days after Georgia's secession from the Union, the arsenal was surrendered with no more effort than the formality of an exchange of notes between Captain Arnold Elzey, U. S. Army, and Colonel W. H. T. Walker, an officer acting under the authority of Governor Brown. Elzey later chose to side with the Confederacy and became one of its military personnel. The long building near the entrance was built soon afterward for a machine shop where harness, gun-carriages, and other such gear were made.

30. Typically, the Sand Hills "cottage" has the following defining fea-

tures: an A-roof broken by dormer windows, wooden cornices and wainscoting, a height of a story-and-a-half—often above a raised brick basement, a full-length porch supported by slender but well-proportioned posts, a central entrance door with sidelights and fanlight above, and a wide throughway or hall with rooms of full width on each side. The interior woodwork is handcarved and like the exterior details of the house, treated with restrained simplicity and unobtrusive good taste. The CHAFEE COTTAGE (*private*), 914 Milledge Road, is one of these, and the DICKEY COTTAGE (*private*), 728 Milledge Road, is another. The front part of the Dickey house was built in 1857, but the kitchen and pantries were part of the house of Colonel John Forsyth (1780-1841), Governor of Georgia in 1827, and Secretary of State under Andrew Jackson in 1834. Colonel Forsyth, as Minister to Spain during President Monroe's "era of good feeling," helped to negotiate the treaty of 1819 whereby Florida was ceded to the United States and actually transferred two years later, thus ending a long period of territorial unrest for Georgia.

Others are the VERDERY COTTAGE (*private*), 2229 Pickens Road, built about 1802, and the home of Richard Henry Wilde who wrote "My Life Is Like the Summer Rose"; and AZALEA COTTAGE (*private*), 2236 Walton Way, built in 1813.

31. HIGH GATE (*private*), 820 Milledge Road, was built sometime prior to 1800 by slave labor with hand-hewn timber cut from the premises. In 1838 a house that was virtually a duplicate of the original was built in front of the old house, and the two parts are now connected by one-story rooms. The place derives its name from the tall wrought-iron gates of the fence that surrounded the area.

32. OVERTON (*private*), 635 Gary Street, now the J. A. Setze place, is a white frame house showing classical influence in the fluted columns of its two-story portico. John Milledge, Governor of Georgia in 1802, built the house soon after the Revolution. For a site he chose a hill on his 5,000-acre tract so that he could look out over his ample acres from the front porch. Obstructing trees were topped to clear the view, and the effect of this can be seen in the trees today.

OTHER POINTS OF INTEREST

33. PAINE COLLEGE (Negro), 1235 Fifteenth Street (Jefferson Davis Avenue), is a co-educational liberal arts college for Negro youth sponsored by the Methodist and Colored Methodist Episcopal Churches. It is fully accredited by the Southern Association of Colleges and Secondary Schools. There is a beautiful campus of forty acres in which are situated six brick and five frame buildings with a property value of more

than one million dollars. The Warren A. Candler Memorial Library contains a collection of more than 27,000 volumes for use by students of the college and friends from the Augusta community. The college has a bi-racial board of control, and for more than sixty years the faculty has been composed of white and Negro members.

The MUSEUM (*open on application at office*), in Haygood Hall, contains an assemblage of African relics, including carved ivory pieces, grass cloths, woven baskets, two-faced fetishes, native drums, musical instruments, and farming implements. These were brought from Africa by the late Reverend W. E. Tabb, a missionary of the former M. E. Church, South, to the Belgian Congo, Central Africa.

34. The WILLIAM B. BELL MUNICIPAL AUDITORIUM, 712 Telfair Street, erected in 1940, has a seating capacity of 5,054, consisting of the Main Auditorium and the Music hall with 1,000 seats which can be used separately or as a part of the Main Auditorium. In addition there are five committee rooms of various sizes ranging in seating capacity from forty to four hundred, and a large Exhibition Hall, 133 feet by 153 feet, with a seating capacity of 2,000.

35. The FOREST HILLS DIVISION VETERANS ADMINISTRATION HOSPITAL, situated in Forest Hills just west of the city limits, with the Oliver Annex, is surrounded by a 600-acre park that includes an 18-hole golf course designed by Donald Ross. The U. S. VETERANS HOSPITAL NO. 62, Wrightsboro Road between Whitney Street and Maryland Avenue, is in the same general vicinity.

36. The FARMERS MARKET, operated under the supervision of the Georgia State Department of Agriculture, at Hale and 4th streets (or 110 Fifth Street), was established in 1951 when the city's marketing facilities were acquired by the state's Department of Agriculture and the market suitably enlarged. Because of its strategic location which serves a great section of southeast Georgia and a good part of the producing area of western South Carolina, it is growing steadily as an important link in the marketing and distribution system of Georgia.

The records indicate that total sales for the six months' period ending June 3, 1952, amounted to one and a quarter million dollars. This almost equals the total sales for 1951.

37. The AUGUSTA NATIONAL GOLF COURSE (*open to members and guests only*), where the famous Masters Invitation Tournament is played each spring, is northwest of the city. If one follows Broad Street to Lake Olmstead (R), a city recreation area affording water sports and good fishing, and then turns into Washington Road, which leads to Clark Hill Dam, the course will appear on the left at Berckmans Road.

Designed by Alistair McKenzie, the noted Scotch architect, in collaboration with Georgia's beloved Bobby Jones, the course was begun in 1931 and opened in 1934. The fairways are turfed with Bermuda grass which browns off and goes dormant in winter, at which time it is planted with Italian Rye which remains lush through the usual local winter. Three separate fields, including target greens and sanded bunkers, are maintained for practice purposes. Sponsored by a private organization, the Masters is strictly an invitation tournament.

But the area was a special part of Georgia history long before the Augusta National selected it for the course. An avenue of stately magnolias leads to the clubhouse, a broad-porched, stucco house, lived in by Prosper Julius Berckmans on his nursery acres, Fruitlands, from 1858 on. Berckmans was not only famous in Georgia because of the gardens he designed and planted at now historical homes; he achieved an international reputation as a horticulturist of the first rank.

Berckmans in 1850 sought asylum in this country from political and religious disturbances in Belgium, and when his family joined him a year later, a farm was bought at Plainfield, New Jersey. It was during his six years there that he first met Charles Downing and other important men in American horticulture. Apparently, however, the climate in New Jersey did not favor the special techniques that Berckmans brought from the Continent. In any case, in the fall of 1858 Berckmans moved to Augusta, and established the Fruitlands Nurseries by buying a one-half interest in the nurseries of D. Redmond. He soon acquired the entire business, with some twenty-five acres of nursery stock.

Until his retirement in 1907 he worked tirelessly to advance southern horticulture to a position of importance in the nation. F. H. Bailey's *The Standard Cyclopedia of Horticulture* has given him explicit recognition. "Mr. Berckmans spent the major part of his life in an untiring effort to originate, introduce and disseminate fruits and ornamentals of value in the South. Plants, cuttings and seed were imported from all parts of the world to be tested at Fruitlands, and the nurseries became not only an experiment station but a botanical garden as well, from which disseminated many of the most valuable plants of the southern horticulturist, among which are the Honey and Peen-to peaches, Kelsey plum, Japanese persimmon, hardy lemon or *Citrus trifoliata* (Poncirus), Amoor River privet, *Biota aurea nana* (Thuja), besides other fruits and ornamentals." In recognition of his work the University of Georgia conferred the degree of Master of Science upon him in 1880.

The natural beauty of the golf course is greatly augmented by the plantings of unusual trees and shrubs, carefully preserved by the designer. Among the rare specimens is a Spanish cork tree received from the United States Patent Office about 1880; camellias imported around

1861 from Japan and several European countries; forty varieties of foreign azaleas well over half a century old; a Chinese pine past the three-quarters of a century mark; a holly-like tea olive (*Osmanthus aquifolium*) brought from Japan in 1880; and a hardy lemon hedge (*Citrus trifoliata*) propagated from a Japanese plant obtained in 1870. The holes of the golf course have been named for typical trees and shrubs associated with each in the landscaping, as Hole 5—Magnolia, Hole 10—Camellia, and so for others. A cottage has recently been built in the club area for President Eisenhower.

CAMP GORDON, contained in a 56,000-acre area located, roughly, in a triangle between US 78 on the north, US 1 on the south, and State 47 on the west as the base, is about ten miles from Augusta's business district. Construction began officially on August 5, 1941, and the U. S. Corps of Engineers took possession from the contractors in December of 1941. It was named in honor of General John Brown Gordon, soldier of the Confederacy and a business and political figure of Reconstruction days.

Among the famous divisions activated from Camp Gordon during its service training period in World War II were the Tenth Armored, the Fourth Infantry, and the Twenty-Sixth Infantry. The first contingent of WAACS arrived in May, 1943. From June, 1945, until April 14, 1946, the post served as a separation center for troops returning from overseas for discharge. In June, 1948, the post was reactivated to serve as a Signal Corps Training Center. It is now serving as a training school for the Army Military Police Corps, the Signal Corps, and other army units. An expansion program of $5,000,000 was authorized around 1950.

Columbus

Railroad Stations: Union Station, 12th St. and 6th Ave., served by Southern Railway, Seaboard Air Line, and Central of Georgia Railway.

Bus Stations: Trailways Bus Terminal, 1329 Broadway, served by Southern Stages, Capital Trailways, Crescent Stages, Modern Coach Lines, and Southern Motor Lines; Greyhound Bus Station, 319 12th St., served by East Alabama Motor Coach Line, Riley Bus Lines, Atlantic Stages, Teche Greyhound Lines, and Southeastern Greyhound Lines.

Airports: Muscogee County Airport, 5.2 m. from the city, for Eastern Airlines, Delta Airlines, and Southern Airways. Municipal Airport, 1 m. from downtown Columbus, on Victory Drive; no scheduled service. Hangar accommodations at both airports.

Taxis: 25¢ within city limits.

Local Busses: Fare 10¢.

Interurban Busses: Howard Bus Terminal, 319 12th St., service to Fort Benning every half hour. Fares from 21¢ to 26¢, depending on destination at Benning.

Accommodations: 6 hotels, 12 motor courts, several trailer camps.

Informaton Service: Chamber of Commerce, 1338 Broadway; US Highway 27 Association, Ralston Hotel Building; AAA, Kyle Motor Co., 512 12th St.

Athletic Field: Memorial Stadium, Victory Drive and 6th Ave.

Baseball Park: Golden Park, 4th St. and 1st Ave.

Golf: Lion's Municipal Golf Course, 4th St. and 6th Ave.; country club.

Motion Picture Houses: 15, including 4 for Negroes.

Radio Stations: WRBL (1420 kc.); WDAK (1340 kc.); WGBA (1270 kc.). WDAK has a permit to construct a TV-station.

Annual Events: Miss Georgia Pageant, May, sponsored by the Columbus Junior Chamber; Southeastern Invitational Golf Tournament, May or June; Tampa-Troy State Teachers College Football Game, mid-September; Chattahoochee Valley Exposition; Georgia-Auburn Football Game, last week in November; Christmas Parade, last week in November; Peanut Bowl Game, January 1st; Camellia Show, February 14-15.

COLUMBUS (250 alt., 79,611 pop.), the seat of Muscogee County, is the gateway to the resourceful Chattahoochee Valley, in west central Georgia. Just across the Chattahoochee River and reached by a series of bridges, is Phenix City, Alabama, for the most part a residential extension of Columbus. The topography of the area varies from rolling to hilly. Muscogee County's location on the state's Fall Line, partly in the Piedmont and partly in the coastal Plain, though the latter covers the larger part of the county, is the key to the sturdy industrial prosperity of this area. For Columbus stands on a plateau surrounded by slightly rising hills, at the foot of a series of powerful falls on the Chattahoochee, and hence in effect at the head of navigation from the Gulf of Mexico.

Despite the War between the States and several economic sinking spells—more symptomatic of remote ills than local, even in 1929—this brisk upland city has grown astonishingly fast from the water-wheel stage to that of the hydroelectric dynamo, and to its present stature of industrial giant on the Chattahoochee. The unique feature of Western civilization, in distinction from other sorts, has been its theoretical grasp of power joined to its practical exploitation, in connection with the instrumental techniques as the means to life. Its history, so far, can be divided into three consecutive phases of power: that of water-and-wood, coal-and-iron, and of electricity-and-alloys. Each stage has its own way of appropriating and transforming nature's energy, and its families of typically associated skills and consequent social patterns. But the common factor in each is the transfer and multiplication of energy, beyond the product of any likely number of men or animals, and the transformation of this energy by human skills into the thing made from available materials. Columbus reached in little more than a century a stage of development the original cycle of which required nearly ten.

Just as the whole of a person's character can sometimes be inferred from a phrase or gesture, so the whole of a complex industrial history can often be seen in some simple part of it. In the case of Columbus the key image is that of the waterfall, since even hydroelectric power is the flow of water transformed into that of electric current. Though one is visible, the other not directly evident, both are fluid in their behavior, with common mathematical forms. Captain Basil Hall of the British navy had an eye for key images. Visiting Columbus in 1828, when it was being surveyed into lots at the insistence of Governor Forsyth who wanted an outpost against the Indians, Captain Hall afterwards observed in his *Travels in North America,* "The new city was to commence at the lower end of a long series of falls, or more properly speaking rapids, over which this great river dashes in a very picturesque manner. The perpendicular fall being about 200 feet, an immense power for turning mills is placed at the disposal of the inhabitants of the future city. . . ."

In addition to what are now the Georgia Power Company's hydroelectric dams, North Highlands, Goat Rock, and Bartlett's Ferry, and so on towards West Point on the Chattahoochee above Columbus, supplementary power is available, if needed, from the company's statewide network. Also two new dams, the Jim Woodruff (*see* TOUR 6) and the Buford (*see* TOUR 7), of the tri-river Apalachicola-Flint-Chattahoochee

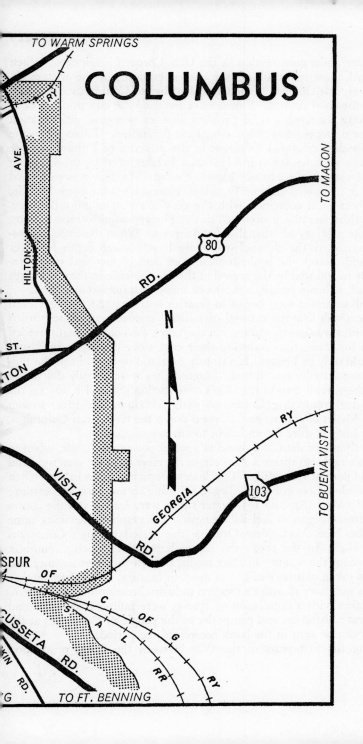

system, are under construction by the U. S. Corps of Engineers. When completed, these will multiply the electric potential of the area, establish a navigable channel in the Chattahoochee to Columbus again, and provide for flood control. Floods have harassed the city since its early days, along its riverfront; a problem that erosion and deforestation along the upper reaches of the river have magnified. Times when the Chattahoochee exhibited its might in the presence of Columbus have been given such names as the Harrison Freshet of 1841, the Pershing Flood of 1919, or the Hoover Flood of 1929. The first was so named because it happened during President Harrison's administration, the second because it coincided with the general's visit to Fort Benning, and the third because it occurred in the Hoover administration, along with quite a galaxy of other ill-starred omens. When the Federal project is completed, the channel will again have enough depth for river traffic, and though the brilliant steamboat days of fact and song, dramatically introduced by the arrival of the *Steubenville* in the city's birth year, 1828, will not return, a means of low-cost transportation will.

Steamboat traffic soon began to flourish and retained its vigor even after the 1850's saw the coming of railroad connections. The burden downstream was mostly cotton, but on return the boats brought needed supplies for trade, thus reducing their cost, since otherwise such supplies could only be brought laboriously overland by dray, until the railroads were actually established. Stagecoaches were already delivering the northern mail, and in the 1830's construction got under way on the first bridge connecting Columbus with Alabama. In 1832, sixteen thousand bales of cotton were shipped down the river from Columbus, a rather lusty gesture for an infant town.

An early use of the Chattahoochee's water power was made, when in 1828 Seaborn Jones threw a dam across the river to make water-ground meal and flour at City Mills. Textile developments began in 1838 when the Columbus Cotton Factory began spinning cotton yarn and carding wool. Between 1840 and 1850 water rights were leased, and the cotton mill industry began to feel its strength. Telegraph connections came when the New York–New Orleans line passed through Columbus around 1848. In the 1850's the railroads began to reach Columbus, which meant the waning of river traffic, though the river steamer had at least a token existence as late as the 20th century. One after another the parts necessary to make a modern industrial community and metropolitan area with a population of 170,645 were falling into order, and with great satisfaction and prosperity to the people of Columbus at the time, as can be seen in the bank records of the period.

During the first years of the War between the States production leapt forward, since economically war is an interval when consumption of industrial products becomes many times in excess of normal; and probably, next to Richmond, Columbus supplied the Confederacy with more manufactured items than any other city. Among these were wool cloth for uniforms, shoes, caps, sabers, bayonets, pistols, cannon, corn meal, oil cloth for belts and cartridge boxes and other things of this sort, white goods and yarn, and some wheat flour. The Columbus Foundry and Machine Shop became the Naval Iron Works, leased by the Confederacy, and besides supplying cannon, made two gunboats, the sorely needed *Muscogee* and *Jackson*. And so affairs stood, for Sherman had felt the lure of Savannah, and it was not until April 16, 1865, a week after General Lee's surrender, that Union forces attacked Columbus. The destruction of mills and public buildings was worthy of Sherman himself, and there was the usual pilfering of shops and homes, but Sherman's lieutenant, General James H. Wilson, found the burning of the 125,000-bale accumulation of cotton in the city a labor of Hercules more or less beyond his strength.

If the general had been able to divert the Chattahoochee, he would have blasted the real vigor of the city at its source. As it was, though Reconstruction was a time of agony, with the social order topsy-turvy, rebuilding moved at such a brisk pace that the city's industries were more numerous and varied by the mid-1870's than they had been before the war. The great step came when, for example, City Mills as well as the Eagle and Phenix Mills began using electric power generated from their own dams. In 1902 North Higlands Dam was constructed for the production of hydroelectric power, to be followed in 1908 by Goat Rock Dam seventeen miles up the Chattahoochee, and this in 1926, four miles farther up, by the Bartlett's Ferry Dam. The reserve of water created by the latter dam was named Lake Harding for R. M. Harding, general manager of the Columbus Electric and Power Company when the dam was built. Covering some ten square miles, the lake which incidentally supplies pleasant fishing and boating as well as a summer residence area, extends to the power dam at Riverview, some distance above which is the West Point Manufacturing Company (*see* TOUR 3).

The Gothic gloom of the early factory with its labyrinth of belts all dependent upon a central power shaft along the middle axis of the building, gave way slowly but surely to the functional economy of the electric motor which, because of the way it receives its power and its tidy compactness, can be located where needed with a trim sort of operational elegance, without congestion. Apparently Columbus entered upon its neotechnic stage smoothly and without social or economic disruption in a sort of natural sequence, which does much to account for its growth in recent years. While the ten years from 1920 to 1930 show a population increase of nearly 28 per cent, from 1930 to 1950 the physical area doubled and the population almost did.

Textiles are still the major industry. Others are food processing, iron and steel works, lumber, chemicals and fertilizer, paper and allied products, printing and publishing, stone, glass, clay, electric units, dyeing equipment for textile mills, wearing apparel, textile equipment and machinery, soft drinks, peanut and pecan products, engines and boilers, refrigerating and ice-making machinery, cotton ginning machinery and packing equipment, and meat packing. The products of many of these plants have a nation-wide reputation. Columbus is located in the heart of the seven states making up the southeastern market: Georgia, Alabama, Florida, Mississippi, Tennessee, North Carolina, and South Carolina. Seven railroad lines, operated by three of the major systems, the Central of Georgia, the Seaboard Air Line, and the Southern Railway, are available for transportation. Three US-designated highways and four state highways, of which US 27 is the most direct route from Chicago to Florida, permit rapid motor transportation by truck lines in all directions, by means of some twelve or more national and local freight lines, ten of which operate terminals in Columbus.

In addition to Lawson Air Force Base and the Phenix City Municipal Airport near by, Columbus has two airports. Muscogee County Airport, 5.2 m. from the business center of the city, serves Delta, Eastern Airlines, and Southern Airways. All runways and taxi-strips are paved and "butterflied" together. It has a competent airport manager; hangar facilities are available, and a modern administration building was completed recently. The Civil Aeronautics Authority has a full-time communications office, and the U. S. Department of Commerce maintains a modern weather station that supplies detailed and regular information and keeps daily records on all weather data. In the city limits, one mile from downtown Columbus, the municipal airport has two landing strips and two runways, with hangar facilities available. Charter service, sales and service, and flight instruction are provided at both airports.

A Department of Recreation is operated as an integral part of the city government, and industrial recreation programs are co-ordinated with the city's program. In 1946 a Master Plan for Recreation was formulated which co-ordinates all of the city's established resources for a year-around sequence. The department operates public park and playground areas, community centers, swimming pools, tennis courts, baseball and softball diamonds, a miniature golf course, a teen tavern, and play fields. Muscogee County has a 202-acre park with swimming pools, lakes for boating and fishing, tennis courts, picnic grills, and camp areas. Memorial Stadium can seat 25,000 persons.

The city has had the commission-manager form of government since 1922. Local public schools have a special reputation for their vocational education and industrial training programs in addition to the usual accredited opportunities offered by urban centers. An off-campus center is operated by the University of Georgia, and another by the Albany State Teachers College, for Negroes, where regular college courses are available. Its four hospitals, well equipped and capably staffed, have a total of 504 beds; one of these is St. Francis Hospital, half the cost of which was contributed by the Catholic Order of St. Francis and the other half by citizens of Columbus. A joint Muscogee County–City of Columbus health department maintains an excellent preventive and sanitation record in the area, in connection with the usual health center services.

Columbus is in an area favorable to agriculture from both the angle of topography and of climate. July's mean maximum temperature is 92.3°, its normal 81.8°; January's mean minimum is 37.6°, its normal 48.3°. The mean annual rainfall is 46.67 inches. Besides helping to keep construction costs low, a mild climate of this sort favors year-around farming, especially cattle or dairy and permanent pasture. Its location on the Fall Line between the Piedmont Plateau and the Coastal Plains provides a variety of soil types that are available for a wide range of crop adaptions. One-crop farming has retreated before the steady advance of agricultural literacy, and diversified farming has brought increased mechanization with it. Dairying leads other agricultural developments, followed by the raising of beef cattle, forestry, truck crops, poultry, peanuts, and swine. Cotton and corn are long established staples. Forestry resources are extensive. Under the forestry training programs, encouraged by the State Forestry Commission and the Federal government, the care and production of timber is assuming a place of increasing importance as a phase of modern agriculture. Of the 42,389 acres of farmland in Muscogee County, 10,814 are in crops for harvest, 15,923 acres in pasture for livestock, and 12,771 acres in forest land. This presents, especially in relation to the diversified industry of Columbus, an exceptionally well-balanced economic equation.

The Columbus area offers an expanding market, raw materials are plentiful, the labor supply is intelligent and co-operative, the city has an industrial tradition, and good transportation and distribution facilities are already established. In addition to its hydroelectric potential, both present and future, solid fuels are available from nearby Alabama, Tennessee, or Kentucky, and gas has been piped from Louisiana.

Nine miles south of Columbus is Fort Benning and the Infantry School, with Lawson Air Force Base adjacent, which supports paratroop training at the Infantry School (*see* TOUR *10A*).

POINTS OF INTEREST

1. The FIRST NATIONAL BANK (formerly Georgia Home Building), SE. corner Broadway and 11th St., is a three-story building erected by William H. Young between 1860 and 1867. Of Italian Renaissance design, it is notable for its narrow, arched windows and for its cast-iron exterior walls that were molded in sections in Pittsburgh, Pennsylvania.

2. The PEASE HOUSE (*private*), 908 Broadway, was built in 1854, the first story being of stuccoed brick and the second of native heart pine. Of the New Orleans or Creole type, it is painted a vivid canary yellow that gives an explicit contrast to the iron grillwork on the upper and lower porches and on the horseshoe stairs curving upward from a lower front court.

3. The OGLETHORPE MARKER, Broadway and 4th St., is a boulder erected by the D. A. R. to commemorate General Oglethorpe's visit to Coweta Town (in what is now Russell County, Alabama) in 1739 to treat with the upper Creek Indians. As a result of this visit Oglethorpe concluded, on August 21, 1739, one of the key treaties among all his quiet negotiations with the American Indians. Not only did this treaty confirm the colony's first title to the eastern territory lying between the Savannah and Altamaha rivers; it provided also for the considerable enlargement of the colony's territory and forestalled a possible alliance of the western Creeks with the Spanish of Florida and the French of Mobile Bay.

4. The CENTENNIAL COTTON GIN PLANT (*open during work hours*), 10th Ave. and 5th St., was organized at Fort Valley in 1876 for the manufacture of cotton gins and ginning machinery. In 1921 the business was moved to Columbus, where continued growth required the building of the present large, modern plant four years later.

5. The LUMMUS COTTON GIN COMPANY (*open Mon.-Thurs. during working hours*), east end of 9th St., one of the largest cotton gin manufacturing plants in the South, was established here in 1869, then in 1872 moved to Juniper, Georgia, and in 1898 back to Columbus. Lummus gins were the first to be equipped with the air-blast system, universally recognized as the most critical improvement in the cotton gin since its invention by Eli Whitney.

6. The TOM HUSTON PEANUT COMPANY (*weekdays, guide service*), SW. corner 10th Ave. and 8th St., is the present development of a notion invented by a Columbus businessman. The first bag of Tom's Toasted

Peanuts, marketed in April, 1925, was packed in a small, one-story building at 4th Avenue and 30th Street. Numbering only three men at that time, the company's working force now runs over a thousand men and women; the products are distributed in thirty-six states.

7. The MUSCOGEE COUNTY COURTHOUSE occupies a well-landscaped city block contained by 9th and 10th streets between 1st and 2nd avenues. Of red brick, the building has its main entrance on the north and south sides, each of which has a recessed portico with five Corinthian columns rising to the frieze, with white marble steps. The second courthouse which had been built in 1840 was razed in 1895 to make way for the present one. At the northern entrance of the area is a CANNON captured by the Federal troops at the Battle of Shiloh. Cast at the Naval Iron Works in Columbus during the War between the States, this cannon was made from household brasses contributed by the ladies of the town —hence the name *Ladies Defender,* crudely incised near the breech.

A small BRASS SALUTE GUN, sometimes called more particularly "Red Jacket," also on the north side, is the property of the Columbus Guards. The gun fired salutes in 1861 upon the secession of each state from the Union and also upon the occasion of Jefferson Davis' inauguration in Montgomery, Alabama, to the presidency of the Confederate States. Later Captain but then Private Thomas E. Blanchard, of the Columbus Guards, says in his diary, "Having carried our cannon with us we took it out and gave the President the first official salute he ever received. I fired the second gun." Thrown into the Chattahoochee River to save it from the Federals, it was later snagged by an anchor and salvaged. Shipped to New York to be sold as junk, it was recovered and returned to Columbus in 1884 by L. H. Chappell, then captain of the Columbus Guards.

8. CHURCH SQUARE, 2nd Ave. between 11th and 12th streets, is an entire block occupied by the FIRST BAPTIST CHURCH and ST. LUKE METHODIST CHURCH. The plot was laid out and reserved as a church square when the town was founded in 1828. With smooth lawn and interlacing trees, it affords a pleasing contrast to the compact squares of the downtown section. The Baptist Church is a brick structure of Greek Revival design with massive Doric columns; the Methodist Church, recently rebuilt, is of Early American (Williamsburg) Colonial design. Both churches date back to the first year of the city.

9. The LION HOUSE (*private*), 1316 3rd Ave., also known as the Ralston Cargill House, is of Greek Revival design, its porch columns influenced by those of the Tower of the Winds near Athens, Greece. An odd feature is the two Nubian lions on abutments at each side of the steps leading up to the porch: one asleep, the other awake. The house, designed

by Stephen Button, an architect of Philadelphia, was built by Dr.
Thomas Hoxey sometime in the 1840's but was not completed. Before
1865 and probably in 1864 the house came into the possession of Augustus Marcelin Allen and his mother, who completed the interior according to the original drawings.

10. At the corner of 4th Ave. and 14th Street is a MARKER commemorating the founding of the Ladies' Memorial Association, in March, 1866,
for the purpose of decorating the graves of Confederate soldiers, on
April 26, Southern Memorial Day. The rite was suggested by Lizzie
Rutherford, later Ellis, while secretary of the Soldiers' Aid Society, a
wartime organization.

11. The PEABODY HOUSE (*private*), 1445 2nd Ave., one-time home of the
philanthropist George Foster Peabody, was built in the 1850's from
brick taken from an earlier building on the corner of 11th Street and
2nd Ave., which was then rebuilt on the new location exactly as it had
been. This made way for the new Presbyterian Church of that period.
Its deep green-shuttered windows, well-proportioned doorway with fanlight, and trim portico with fluted Doric columns, and semi-entabla-
ture, make it one of the most pleasing small houses in the city. The
bricks, once painted gray, now show with time something of their
original warmth. On the eastern and northern sides of the house are
posted signs reading Jackson Street and Bridge Street respectively, their
original names before they were changed in 1885.

12. The MOTT HOUSE (*open during business hours*), SE. corner Mott St.
and Front Ave., a handsome building of Georgian style, is used for general offices by the Muscogee Manufacturing Company. The two-story
brick façade rises to a third story, which is indicated by the high dormer
windows in the mansard roof, the edges of which are decorated by a
finely wrought iron grillwork, over which can be seen a prominent
cupola with four windows in the style of the dormers, in the center of
the roof. Two enclosed chimneys on each end, between which are
spaced two dormer windows, appear at the lower edge of the roof, and
rise well above it. Four fluted Ionic columns support the entablature,
above which is an ironwork grill in the style of the roof railing, and
one also at the entrance level behind the columns of the portico. Originally the Calhoun House, it was next bought by Daniel Griffin, an Irish
civil engineer engaged with the Central of Georgia Railroad. Griffin
landscaped the yard to the river, an area which occupied the whole
block. The house was built sometime prior to 1850. The third owner
was Colonel Randolph Lawler Mott, born in Fauquier County, Virginia, who though a staunch Unionist, retained the good will of the
locality, contributing generously, for example, toward the welfare of

the people as times became difficult. When Columbus was captured by General James H. Wilson, Colonel Mott invited him to make the house his headquarters, which he did for several days. This somewhat odd situation is further accented by the fact that Colonel Mott's son, John R. Mott, was adjutant on General Benning's staff; Benning is the Confederate officer for whom Fort Benning is named.

The Muscogee Manufacturing Company was incorporated in 1867, and organized by Colonel George Parker Swift, originally of Fair Haven, Massachusetts, who had caught an early image of the South's future in cotton manufacturing. The first mill was established on the site of the old Coweta Factory, which had been destroyed by the Federals.

13. The EAGLE AND PHENIX MILLS (*not open to the public*), Front Ave. between 13th and 14th sts., is a large textile plant that is a landmark in Columbus history. The company was organized in 1851 as the Eagle Manufacturing Company. Its building, burnt by Union forces in 1865, was rebuilt, and the company was renamed the Eagle and Phenix Manufacturing Company, changed in 1898 to Eagle and Phenix Mills. Around the turn of the century or in its first decade, the mill began to use hydroelectric power for lighting, and it is claimed that it was the first mill in history to take this critical step, thus making the night shift possible in manufacturing, and by implication leading up to the reorganization of factory power on the basis of electrical transmission.

14. The FONTAINE HOUSE (*private*), 1044 Front Ave., was built by John Fontaine, first mayor of Columbus. Of brick and frame construction and painted white, the old mansion is noted for its fine wrought iron, large Doric columns, and fanlighted doorway set between small pilasters. The interior is elaborate, with frescoed ceilings, solid mahogany doors, and fireplaces of black Italian marble. The spiral staircase winding upward from the central hall is unusual in its combination of massiveness and grace.

15. The COLUMBUS IRON WORKS (*open by arrangement*), SW. corner Front Ave. and Dillingham St., manufactures agricultural implements, cook stoves, ranges, and coal and wood-burning heaters. At the rear of the main plant is the old steamboat landing where Chattahoochee River packets began to dock in 1828. What is believed to have been the first mechanical ice machine in the world was made here in 1872. Invented by Dr. John Gorrie of Apalachicola, Florida, in 1851, it has been placed in the Smithsonian Institution. In 1863 the Columbus Iron Works, then the Naval Iron Works in the service of the Confederacy, produced an unusual breech loading cannon, made from the wheel shaft of the sunken river steamer *John C. Calhoun*. It stands mounted

in the iron works building. The well known Southern Plow Works is now a part of the company.

16. ST. ELMO (*private*), 2810 St. Elmo Drive, was built on the old Stage Coach Road in 1831-32 by Seaborn Jones, prominent lawyer and congressman. It is a stately two-storied Greek Revival house, constructed of brick molded on the premises by slaves. Around the front and two ends, its twelve Doric columns rise to a height of forty feet, lending relief to the massiveness of the building. The dark shutters and black iron grillwork of the swinging balcony offer a sharp relief to the whiteness of the exterior façade. An adjacent smokehouse and circular fountain suggest plantation days.

Originally called El Dorado, its name was changed to St. Elmo by James Jeremiah Slade, who acquired the property about 1875. Augusta Evans Wilson, born in Columbus and a niece of Mrs. Seaborn Jones, often visited this home, and her popular romance *St. Elmo,* published in 1866, contains descriptive references to it. The lasting affection her novel won in many hearts is attested by the appearance of a new edition in the last year or so. Distinguished visitors at St. Elmo have included President James K. Polk, President Millard Fillmore, Henry Clay, and William Makepeace Thackeray.

17. WYNNTON SCHOOL, Wynnton Rd. between Wildwood and Forest Avenue, is a white building of stuccoed brick constructed on the plan of the one-story-and-court, known as the "Columbus Plan" of school architecture. The original Wynnton school, built about 1843, is a small brick structure at the rear of the main building which has been remodeled and is now used as a library.

18. NEHI CORPORATION AND PLANT, 1000 9th Ave., a Columbus institution, produces a soft drink which has gained national acceptance. Nehi, dating from 1925, evolved from the Chero-Cola Company, which was established by Claude A. Hatcher in 1905. With a floor area of six acres, the plant covers almost an entire city block.

19. The BIBB MANUFACTURING COMPANY PLANT (*not open to the public*), W. end of 35th St. in Bibb City, manufactures print goods, tire cord fabric, sheeting, hose yarn, drill, and spun rayon fabric. It contains some 125,000 spindles, over 100,000 of which are in an open floor area that is without partitions, which includes 790,000 square feet of floor space nearly a fourth of a mile long. It presents in one perspective an exceptional technical complex even in a land where the exceptional is the rule. The first mill of this system was established in 1900 on North Highlands, reportedly at Lovers' Leap, an Indian legend spot of the Cowetas and Cussetas. The company began with a modest 20,000

spindles. Bibb City is now an incorporated mill village, with its own civic administration and social organizations for its employees.

20. CITY MILLS COMPANY, 18th Street and 2nd Ave., is the city's oldest existing enterprise. Established when Columbus was founded, the plant has a rock and concrete dam across the river. The old water-powered mill has a capacity of about 2,500 bushels of corn meal daily.

21. W. C. BRADLEY MEMORIAL, located on Wynnton Road, the estate of the late W. C. Bradley, including some nine acres, was given to the city for educational use. The main building is now used for the administrative offices of the Muscogee County School District. Also located here is the new air-conditioned city library, with 50,000 volumes.

22. MEMORIAL STADIUM, Victory Drive and 6th Ave., has a seating capacity of 25,000. It is known regionally as the site of the annual Georgia-Auburn game, and of the Peanut Bowl where high schools play a post-season game on New Year's Day.

POINTS OF INTEREST IN ENVIRONS

Fort Benning and the Lawson Air Force Base: the Infantry School Building, the Jump Towers for parachute training, the Commanding General's Quarters, etc. (*see* TOUR *10A*).

STATE FARMERS MARKET, 318 10th Avenue, just off the main highway between downtown Columbus and Fort Benning, is one of the larger markets that are operated under the supervision of the Georgia Department of Agriculture. The marketing facilities were acquired from the City of Columbus in 1949, and immediate steps were taken towards the construction of a new and enlarged market with modern facilities. In 1949 sales added up to some $3,000,000, and in 1951 had increased to 4½ millions. Serving the southwest section of Georgia and southeast Alabama on a direct route from Florida, the market serves as a meeting point for buyers and sellers of fruits and vegetables in an extensive agricultural area.

Macon

Railroad Station: Terminal Station, Fifth and Cherry Streets, for Georgia R.R., Central of Georgia Ry., Georgia Southern & Florida Railway, Macon, Dublin & Savannah R.R., and Southern Railway.

Bus Station: Greyhound Terminal, 338 Broadway, for Southeastern Greyhound, Southeastern Motor Lines, and Service Trailways. Southern Trailways Terminal, 466 Broadway, for Southern Stages, Southern Trailways, and Southern Transit.

Airport: Cochran Field, 9 m. on State 247, for Eastern Air Lines and Delta Air Lines. Airport Limousine Service $1.25.

Taxis: Zone rates—25¢ first mile, additional rate according to city limits.

Local Busses: Fare 10¢; transfer 1¢ additional.

Traffic Regulations: Right turns may be made on red light; no U turns on Cherry Street, or Broadway in downtown area.

Accommodations: 18 hotels, including 2 for Negroes; numerous boarding houses, tourist homes, 6 modern tourist courts.

Information Service: Chamber of Commerce, Municipal Auditorium, 1st and Cherry Streets. AAA Hotel Dempsey, Mezzanine Floor.

Golf: Idle Hour Country Club, 5.5 m. N. on US 41, 18 holes; Bowden Municipal Golf Course, 18 holes, 4½ m. N. E. on Millerfield Road.

Tennis: Baconsfield Park, North Avenue and Nottingham Drive; Tatnall Square Park, College and Oglethorpe Streets.

Swimming: Lakeside Park, 4 m. S. on US 80; Ragans Park, 2 m. S. E. on US 80; Municipal Swimming Pool, Baconsfield Park, North Avenue and Emery Highway.

Athletics: Municipal Stadium, Morgan Avenue; Municipal Auditorium, Cherry and First Streets; Baseball, Central City Park; 8 city maintained and operated athletic fields, and four private fields.

Theatres and Motion Picture Houses: Municipal Auditorium, Cherry and First Streets; Macon Little Theater, Riverside Drive; 5 motion picture theaters in downtown area, including 2 for Negroes; 5 drive-ins.

Radio Stations: WBML (1240 kc.); WIBB (1280 kc.); WMAZ (940 kc.); WNEX (1400 kc.).

Annual Events: Bibb Flower Show and Middle Georgia Camellia Show, Iris Show, spring; Georgia State Exposition, October. Horse Show and Dog Show, Central City Park.

MACON (334 alt.; 70,252 urban pop.; 135,043 metropolitan pop.), located virtually in the geographical center of the state on the Ocmulgee River and situated on the Fall Line, became from its founding by the legislature in 1823 a strategic center for middle Georgia trade, and as industry developed, for manufactured products, especially textiles. In the early days, boats of fifty tons capacity ascended as far as Macon, though those of thirty could go some fifty miles farther. Pragmatically, this defines its position more or less, as the head of navigation on the Ocmulgee. The location is significant.

The Ocmulgee River, with its source almost on the edge of the Chattahoochee basin, flows from north to south through the middle of the state on a slightly west by east diagonal, and almost exactly parallel to its companion river the Oconee, until it makes an abrupt left turn. Then it soon becomes confluent with the Oconee to form the Altamaha. The Altamaha, the largest river in Georgia the entire drainage basin of which is entirely within the state, joins the Atlantic by way of the old port of Darien, some seventeen miles above Brunswick. Macon was destined by its geography to play the part of an inland port.

As Macon sprang from the wilderness by a creative act of the legislature, it became within the year of its founding a retailing and distributing center for middle Georgia, depending mostly on this agriculturally rich section for its trade and commerce. Lands west of the Oconee were originally distributed by the Land Lottery Act of 1803 for the most part, while those east were allotted by headright warrants, that is, out and out grants made to heads of families. The lottery as a symbol of chance and hence of opportunity expresses very well the dominant note of this westward expansion.

For practical purposes the Fall Line is defined physically as an irregular boundary, running diagonally across the state southwest by northeast, where the red foothills of the Piedmont Plateau merge into the porous and sandy soils of the Coastal Plain. Roughly, the sixty per cent of the state's area south of this demarcation is agricultural while that north is industrial, although of course the actual situation is a mixture, for industrial production is on the march in south Georgia, and all of Georgia is agricultural. Columbus and Augusta are also located along this strategic division of terrain, where water power and river traffic formed an early area of economic opportunity. Being directly on the Fall Line, Macon has the topographical and botanical features of both areas, with flora and disposition of soil in the hilly northern suburbs distinguished typically from those in the southern or coastal section. And this within the 11.2 square miles of the city proper, and not merely in its surrounding Bibb County.

In addition to being situated between the deep-based clays of the Piedmont and the readily tillable soils of the Coastal Plain, Macon is also well located to escape rigorous extremes of temperature. Alternating inflows of moist tropical air from the coast and relatively dry-cold

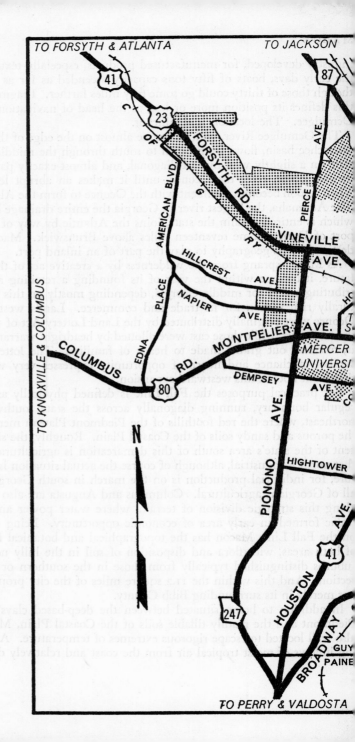

TO FORSYTH & ATLANTA

TO JACKSON

41

23

87

FORSYTH RD.

AMERICAN BLVD.

PIERCE AVE.

VINEVILLE AVE.

HILLCREST AVE.

NAPIER AVE.

PLACE

EDNA

MONTPELIER AVE.

COLUMBUS RD.

MERCER UNIVERSI

DEMPSEY AVE.

TO KNOXVILLE & COLUMBUS

80

HIGHTOWER

PIONONO AVE.

41

247

HOUSTON AVE.

BROADWAY

GUY

PAINE

N

TO PERRY & VALDOSTA

The Price Gilbert Library at Georgia Tech

Ernest Woodruff Memorial Building for Medical Research, Emory University

The Administration Building of Atlanta University for Negroes, Atlanta

Mimosa Hall, Roswell

Valley near Hiawassee

Plantation for pine seedlings

Typical Broiler Houses

Georgia was known as the "Smokehouse of the Confederacy"

The Robert Tombs House, Washington

President's Home, University of Georgia, Athens

Memorial Garden, University of Georgia, Athens

Jim Woodruff Lock, Dam, and Powerhouse in Southwest Georgia

Clark Hill Dam and Reservoir on the Savannah near Augusta

Allatoona Dam and Powerhouse in Northeast Georgia

Site of Buford Dam and Powerhouse

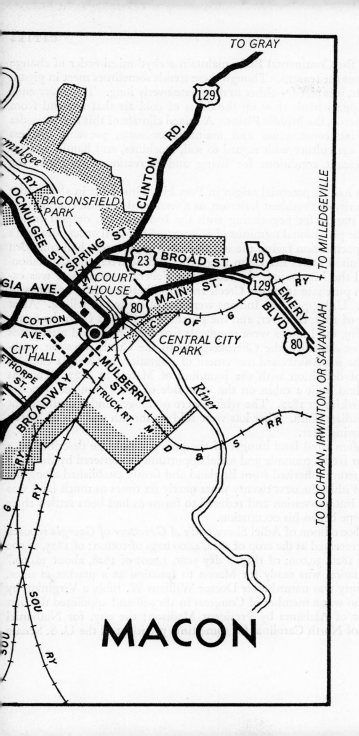

air from the Continental Plain maintain a rhythmical order of change throughout the seasons. Though these trends sometimes meet in gigantic contest, it is rare for either to dominate overly long. The lower ends of the Appalachians slow up the drifts of cold air that descend from Canada across the Middle Plains. A mixed climate of this sort provides conservative construction and maintenance costs, prevents idleness waste in agriculture with regard to soil, machines, and hands, and insures pleasant conditions for living and recreation throughout the seasons.

Macon had its potential origin in Fort Hawkins, built in 1806 under the authority of President Jefferson, as a westward outpost, trading center, and station for negotiating with the Indians. An outpost fort is always the provisional terminus of an encroaching civil order; the ram's head of pacification facing the unruly. By 1802 Georgia had conceded to the United States her claim to all the land between the Chattahoochee and the Mississippi. In return the Federal government was expected to purchase from the Creek and the Cherokee their holdings in Georgia. Unhappily, the Indians were not interested in selling. After the War of 1812, however, and the purchase of Florida from the Spanish in 1819, the Indians were removed; first the Creek, and afterwards with more difficulty, the Cherokee. With the Creek recession established, the southwestward movement of migration in Georgia came to a state of definition with the founding of Macon in 1823. Thomas Tatum had built a cabin on the west side of the Ocmulgee opposite Fort Hawkins in 1822. The whites were no longer under confinement by the Indian claim. First lots were sold on the 6th and 7th of March the following year.

The often cited land hunger of the period should be described as a desire for fresh economic and social opportunity unfettered by the rigid class structure inherited from England and firmly established along the coast. Within the next twenty years nearly six times as much land was brought into possession and reduced to farms as had been settled since Oglethorpe began his occupation.

The 1860 edition of Adiel Sherwood's *A Gazetteer of Georgia* reports, "Macon received as the crop of 1824, 4,000 bags of cotton; of 1825, 17,000 bags; of 1826, 30,000; of 1827, a dry year, 1,700; of 1828, about 39,000." The situation was ready for Macon to function as a market at once. The county was named after Doctor William W. Bibb, a Virginian by birth who was a member of Congress in 1813-16 and appointed the first governor of Alabama by President Madison; the city, for Nathaniel Macon, of North Carolina, for some time president of the U. S. Senate

—doubtless because so many North Carolinians were among its early citizens.

Macon's location in a rich agricultural section advanced it as a cotton market, especially in connection with the ready transportation to the sea along the Ocmulgee. At first the cotton traveled by flat-bottomed boats propelled by oars. These were poled back painfully from Darien, and usually carried bills of processed goods for the farmers. Later raft-like boats or "cotton boxes" were used, and when these reached Darien they were broken up and sold as lumber. The first sizable boat built in Macon, the *Pioneer,* was poled down to Darien, where machinery was installed. On January 30, 1833, the town held a jubilee when the loaded ship came steaming back, bringing its two barges behind it. But technical changes were moving fast, and the new cities were not hampered by an excess of obsolete machinery and stock which they feared to scrap. Instead of remaining an inland river port, Macon was soon to be transformed into an important railroad center.

Prodded by railroad developments that threatened to skim off the rich plantation trade to Charleston, Savannah secured a charter to construct a railroad to Macon in 1833. After a severe bout with the Southern malady, lack-of-funds, the promoters pushed the railroad to Macon in 1843, and were rewarded with the fabulous cotton trade of the area and all that it meant for mercantile interests. Then the route from Macon to Chattanooga was established. Thus access was gained to Nashville, Louisville, and the Middle West. By 1853 the area southwest of Macon was drawn into its transportation area. And by 1855 the East Tennessee and Georgia Railroad, connecting Dalton with Knoxville, drew the traffic of this ample region from as far north as Richmond, Virginia. Thus by the 1860's Macon was prepared to act as a center of shipping and exchange for a remarkably rich and varied section of the then continental area of the nation.

It could not be foreseen of course that General Sherman would discern the significance of this accessibility to the "smoke house" of the Confederacy. For if these railroads multiplied Georgia's communication and wealth, they also supplied in time of war the means of her undoing: an instructive example of how the arts of peace are translatable into the arts of war. It was the recognition of this reversibility that distinguished Sherman's design from that of the old-line military strategist maneuvering in the field with horse, artillery, and masses of men at arms. It also meant that the course of empire was shifting from the coast. But this was as yet obscure.

In 1836 the Georgia Methodist Conference voted to accept the city's offer of a five-acre site and certain sums of money from its citizens for the establishment of the Georgia Female College, later named Wesleyan. It was not until 1871 that Mount de Sales Academy would be established by the Roman Catholics, and Mercer University moved to Macon from Penfield by the Baptists. But the higher learning as a principle of civil order was established hardly more than a decade after the city arose from the wilderness.

Historical portents came and passed. Ex-President Millard Fillmore was given a ball at the Hotel Lanier in 1854, and the following year Alexander H. Stephens and Stephen A. Douglas addressed large crowds from the balcony of the Union Depot. In 1860 the Belgian Fair and Cotton Planters' Exposition drew crowds of visitors and also representatives from Belgium. If the name seems strange, it should be remembered that Belgium was an industrial pioneer of the Continent, having succumbed to the Industrial Revolution on its side of the English Channel early; and that the Exposition was part of a plan to stimulate direct trade with Europe, and thus escape from the northern financial orbit. But it was too late for the South to establish its own center of commercial mobility.

During the War between the States the Confederate Treasury Department established at Macon a depository—evidence of its role in the war—in which $1,500,000 in gold were stored at one time. When the city was made a distribution center for supplies, quartermaster and commissary departments were established, and the Arsenal moved to Macon from Savannah. Saddles, harness, shot, cannon, and small arms were manufactured.

The city became a haven for the dispossessed refugees of north Georgia and for sick and wounded soldiers from the Confederate Army. Never before had the various human and social factors of the South been so brought together. The group sentiment it developed was to lend energy to the political role of the Solid South in later years.

Macon was not threatened with actual attack until July 30, 1864, and this attack was repulsed. On April 20, 1865, however, after the armistice between General Johnston and General Sherman, and presumably because of faulty communications, the city was forced to go through the rite of surrendering to General James H. Wilson, who had advanced from Columbus. After his capture at Irwinville and on May 13, Jefferson Davis was brought to Macon and lodged in a second-floor room of the Lanier Hotel. A rope had been placed in the room and transportation arranged in the alley below. But Davis, no less quixotic than usual, would not agree to continue his escape, and was later removed to imprisonment at Fortress Monroe.

Macon struggled through the days of Reconstruction, rebuilt its railroads, and resumed its industrial and mercantile position. Railroad shops, foundries, brick, and other plants developed. The establishment of the Bibb Manufacturing Company in 1871 may be seen as a symbol of transition and progress.

The new century was marked by the extension of the city limits, by the construction of public buildings, and by relatively large expenditures on business and residential houses. As the school system grew, exceptionally well staffed and equipped vocational schools developed in a supplementary capacity, for specialized training in the industrial arts. The river levee, begun in 1906, protected the lowlands with their remarkably rich and wide alluvial deposits from floods, and rendered them available at suitable places for manufacturing plants. During the same year the Central of Georgia Railway purchased from the city a site on which it later erected shops costing $1,500,000. Like World War I, World War II brought increased industrial employment to the area, reaching a peak in June, 1944, with 30,000 employed, 19,800 of whom were engaged in war production.

Modern Macon is a comfortable and still relatively unhurried city, with an easy, relaxed atmosphere. The repose of surrounding farmlands has blended evenly with the energies of a center of trade, and even in the crowded downtown district the broad parkways planted in roses, crape myrtle, and palmettoes give an appearance of roominess and ample time. Old brick stores and modern shops framed in vitrolite and chromium are overshadowed by dignified buildings with columns and massive porticoes. Though the newer streets loop about in odd patterns, the plan of the original city was well conceived, with wide thoroughfares running northwest and southeast, and cross streets intersecting at exact right angles. Most cities have grown from a crossroads, which pattern remains obscurely present in them. But Macon, like Columbus and Milledgeville, was conceived in the legislative mind and layed out originally by the surveyor.

The business district has spread to the banks of the now clay-laden Ocmulgee River, which separates East Macon from the city proper, and has pushed the residential section to the hills north and east of the town. One of these districts, Vineville, is especially attractive, with its mixture of ante-bellum and modern houses in a dignified setting of tall trees, boxwood hedges, iron fences, and ivy-covered stone walls. The newer houses are in such suburbs as Ingleside and Shirley Hills, where the rolling langscape lends itself conveniently to building sites. Negroes, who constitute 42 per cent of Macon's population, live in settlements scattered throughout the city, the more prosperous living in the subdivisions of Unionville and Pleasant Hill. Federal Housing Projects in late years have served to sharpen community awareness in the South of the housing inequality that exists generally between the white and Negro populations.

Macon has shared well in the migration of the cotton textile industry to the land where it is king—though now a constitutional monarch—and today this is the city's leading industry, with more than 3,000,000 spindles in place and 50,000 looms. The products of these looms feed a large and growing wearing apparel industry as well as processors of other cotton products. Industries of the area are well diversified; in all, 84 commodities are produced and the Bibb County area has 174 industrial plants ranging from fifteen employees to several thousand each.

The marketing of the Georgia Peach Belt centers in Macon, though peaches are but one of the numerous agricultural products contributing to the economy of the area. Fertile farmlands spreading out from the city produce important quantities of peanuts, pecans, watermelons, and truck or vegetables that contribute to the expanding food-processing and freezing business. In keeping with the tendency towards diversification, farmers in the area are raising Hereford, Black Angus and Guernsey cattle in numbers sufficient to rate cattle as one of the primary farm activities. The wealth of pulpwood in the Macon area is feeding over 1,100 cords daily into the manufacture of container board and structural insulation. The sedimentary kaolins of this section supply valuable raw materials, especially for the production of fine china and agents for processing high-lustre paper.

The city is governed by a mayor-council with three councilmen from each of the city's five wards, and Bibb County is governed by five commissioners. Unified direction over sanitation and public health programs is exercised by the Macon-Bibb County Health Department. The Department is staffed by some fifty-eight technicians who conduct clinics, laboratory tests, and examinations and inspections of food production and distribution. In addition the state operates a District Health Office in Macon. One municipal and three private hospitals total 477 beds, with further construction in progress.

The FARMERS' MARKET of the Georgia Farmers' Market System, operated under the supervision of the Georgia Department of Agriculture, is located on US 41 at the intersection of Oglethorpe Avenue and Third Street. This market was constructed in 1936. It is well patronized by merchants and handlers of fruits and vegetables in central Georgia. Like the Atlanta market, it provides valuable terminal and wholesale service. New impetus was given to the Farmers' Market Program in 1941, and the records show that from 1941 through 1951, the total sales on this market have been around 27½ million dollars. At present the annual sales on the market amount to better than $4,000,000 a year.

POINTS OF INTEREST

1. The CITIZENS AND SOUTHERN NATIONAL BANK, NE. corner of Cherry and Third sts., of hand-made red brick trimmed with Georgia marble and terra cotta, was completed in 1933. The Georgian detail shows the influence of Sir Christopher Wren's Hampton Court Palace. On the northern wall of the main banking room five Murals by Athos Menaboni, an Atlanta artist, depict the original Wesleyan building, old Fort Hawkins, the meeting of James Oglethorpe and Tomochichi, the sailing of the steamship *Savannah,* and the original building of Mercer University. Cherry Street is sometimes referred to as Macon's Fifth Avenue. Its floral parkways give it a quality of spaciousness. The business district is in this area.

2. The MUNICIPAL AUDITORIUM, SW. corner of Cherry and First streets, with a seating capacity of 3,300, was completed in 1925. It was designed in the neo-Classic style by Egerton Swartwout, of New York, and constructed of Indiana limestone at a cost of $500,000. Broad terraces lead to the arched doorways of the main floor, and the gallery level is adorned with massive Doric columns. The copper-covered dome is 156 feet, 6 inches in diameter. The murals above the proscenium, showing historical features of the state and of Macon, are the work of Don Carlos du Bois and Wilbur G. Kurtz, of Atlanta. The Chamber of Commerce is on the ground floor.

The ART ROOM (*open 9:30-4 Mon.–Fri.; 8:30-12 Sat.*), in the basement of the auditorium, contains many of the Indian artifacts excavated at the Ocmulgee National Monument (*see* TOUR 9B).

3. WESLEYAN FINE ARTS CONSERVATORY, College St. between Georgia and Washington aves., consisting of the Conservatory of Music, the School of Art, and the School of Speech, is a part of Wesleyan College, the Liberal Arts College of which was removed from this site to suburban Rivoli in 1928 (*see* TOUR 12). The original building in which the college opened on January 7, 1839, was remodeled into the present structure about 1881, when George I. Seney, a New York philanthropist, made a gift of $125,000 to the institution. The building is ornamented with gables, towers, and wide porches in the Victorian manner; in pleasing contrast is the simple Greek Revival chapel built in 1860. The School of Fine Arts on the College Street campus offers to men and women the Bachelor of Music degree and the Bachelor of Fine Arts, in art and in speech. "These programs provide training in piano, violin, organ, voice, composition, and music education, in painting, ceramics

and sculpture, fashion illustration and dress design, and in acting, play production, general speech and speech correction, and radio." This work is supplemented by courses in the liberal arts taught by members of the faculty at Rivoli. Resident men students are housed in Roberts Hall on the campus. Applicants may enroll as special students in studio subjects without specific entrance requirements, provided the prerequisites for courses are satisfied.

4. WASHINGTON MEMORIAL LIBRARY (*open 12-9 weekdays*), SE. corner College Street and Washington Avenue, was endowed and presented to the city in 1919 by Mrs. Ellen Washington Bellamy in honor of her brother, Hugh Vernon Washington. The glazed terra cotta building, designed in simple neo-Classic style, circulates over a quarter of a million books. In the northern wall is a niche containing a white marble bust of Sidney Lanier. The statue and niche were designed by Gutzon Borglum, and the background murals, illustrating Lanier's poems, were painted by Athos Menaboni. On display are a manuscript and first edition of Lanier's poems, a flute of the poet's, and an invitation to the wedding of Lanier and Mary Day. In the Washington home which once stood here, Thackeray was entertained when he came to Macon in 1856.

5. MERCER UNIVERSITY stretches over a beautiful 65-acre campus lying between Tattnall Square Park and Centennial Stadium. Named for Jesse Mercer (1769-1841), a distinguished Baptist clergyman, Mercer Institute opened on January 14, 1833, at Penfield (*see* TOUR *17*) as a manual labor school with 39 students enrolled. In 1837 the Executive Committee of the Georgia Baptist Convention was given power by the State of Georgia to establish Mercer University. One of the founding fathers of Mercer was Josiah Penfield, a jeweler and silversmith of Savannah, who left a legacy of $2,500 in 1828 for the "education of pious young men for the gospel Ministry." With this sum and an equal amount contributed by Jesse Mercer and others, as provided in the Penfield will, the school began with an emphasis on ministerial education in the classical tradition so characteristic of that day. The manual labor department was abolished in 1844, and in time the academy was discontinued. Today Mercer continues to hold to the tradition of liberal education as it trains one thousand students of both sexes in the arts and sciences, and also prepares them for the ministry, law, premedicine, teaching, business administration, and journalism.

The original building on the present compus, now used as the Administration building, was four years in building due to financial and weather difficulties—and to the historic Chicago fire which destroyed the architect's drawings. During the interval, classes were held in the building which stands on what is now the northeast corner of Second and Mulberry Streets. Fifteen of the buildings have followed consistently the red brick theme of the original structure and are of modified Georgian design. The chief exception is the Hardman Library, which follows classical lines. This building which now honors the mother of former Governor L. G. Hardman (1927-1931), was erected in 1907, completely rebuilt inside in 1937, and enlarged so that its stack space was doubled in 1953. The capacity of the enlarged library is 140,000 volumes. Among the prized collections in Baptist history are the Albert H. Newman collection and the file of the *Christian Index,* established in 1821. In the field of English literature, the Shelley and the Burns collections are among the finest in America. The library has the complete 75-volume file of Niles' *Weekly Register* (1811-1849). The collection of Georgiana is steadily growing. In addition to the Hardman Library, the Law School Library contains 25,000 volumes.

The newer buildings, though faithful to the red brick theme, follow more functional lines than the earlier ones. The Willingham Chapel, built in 1890, was refinished in 1940 and a clock tower erected. In 1948 the seating capacity was expanded to 1200 and a three-manual pipe organ was installed. Since 1940, six new buildings have been constructed, the main campus landscaped, and an intricate pattern of concrete walks laid.

The total endowment of the university is $4,000,000; and, in addition, an appropriation equal to five per cent on a principal of one and one-half million dollars is received each year from the Georgia Baptist Convention, which controls Mercer through an elected board of trustees. The growth from such small beginnings as the Penfield legacy of $2,500 and the Mercer bequest of $40,000 has been made possible, in great measure, by the generous response of friends to appeals for help. Such buildings as Penfield Hall, Roberts Hall, Shorter Hall, Mary Erin Porter Hall, Willingham Chapel, and the Hardman Library perpetuate the memory of some of Mercer's benefactors. The memory of Adiel Sherwood, Mercer's first professor of theology, is perpetuated in Sherwood Hall, the oldest dormitory on the campus. The Willet Science Building, which houses the Department of Biology, is named for Professor Joseph E. Willet, who taught natural science, chemistry, and geology at Mercer for 34 years.

The Columbus Roberts School of Christianity, the Walter F. George School of Law, and the Spright Dowell School of Education are already endowed; and plans are being made to endow a school of business administration.

The Law School, established in 1873, has been a member of the Association of American Law Schools since 1923, and has been approved by the American Bar Association since 1925. In 1947, the Law School was named for Senator Walter F. George of Georgia, one of the most distinguished of its alumni. The Law School is housed in the Ryals Law Building, a modern, well-equipped structure that was completed in 1930.

An initial gift of $100,000 by George W. McCommon (1886-1952) gave enough impetus to the endowment drive of 1951 to assure the success of the School of Education. The goal of $600,000 was exceeded; and Mercer retained her place alongside the University of Georgia and Emory University in the work of training teachers on the graduate level.

6. The HOME OF SIDNEY LANIER (*now serving as a tearoom*), 935 High Street, is marked by a marble tablet set in an ivy-covered terrace. Sidney Lanier (1842-81), Georgia's best-known poet, was born at the home of his grandparents in Macon, to which his parents moved later. His musical talent, developed at an early age under his mother's instruction, soon enabled him to play almost every musical instrument. At the head of his class, Lanier was graduated from Oglethorpe College in 1860, and the following year he accepted a position as tutor there. His hopes for further years of study, in Germany, were shattered by the outbreak of the War between the States. Serving with the Macon Volunteers in Virginia, he was captured on a blockade runner and imprisoned at Point Lookout, Maryland, for four months. Ill with consumption and troubled by poverty, he said that between 1865 and 1870 "pretty much the whole of life had been merely not dying." Though practicing law, he decided after the publication of *Tiger-Lilies,* a novel about his war experiences, not to continue as a "third-rate struggling lawyer . . . ," but to become a poet. He published *Poems* in 1877, was accepted as a flutist by the Peabody Orchestra in Baltimore and prepared his two-volume work *Shakespeare and His Forerunners,* published in 1902. Lectures given as incidents of this work resulted in his receiving the position of Lecturer in English Literature at John Hopkins University in 1879. *The Science of English Verse* (1880) and *The English Novel* (1883) were by-products of his academic instruction.

Failing health forced him to retire in 1881 to the North Carolina mountains, and there he completed two of his best-known poems, "The Marshes of Glynn" and "Sunrise." His poems illustrate his thesis that the laws governing music and verse are formally the same, and that time rather than accent determines verse rhythms. The complete *Poems* were published in 1884, reissued with additions in 1891, and also in 1916. The critical edition of his works in ten volumes was issued in 1946.

7. The CITY HALL, Poplar Street at intersection with Cotton Avenue and First Street, built in 1836 as the Monroe Railroad Bank and remodeled in 1933-35, combines the Classical Revival style of the original building with the strict functionalism of modern construction. The severely modern side entrances are in pleasing contrast with the columns of the principal façade. On both sides of the main entrance are black vitrolite panels inscribed with the history of the Macon area. The building was the State Capitol from November 18, 1864, until March 11, 1865, the date of the last session of the General Assembly of Georgia under the Confederacy.

On the third floor is a museum (*open only on special occasions*) containing prehistoric and historic exhibits and an art collection. The room is used for meetings of the Macon Historical Society and the Macon Art Association.

8. The JOHNSTON (Hay) HOUSE (*private*), SW. corner Georgia Avenue and Spring Street, built about 1855, is a 24-room house in a modified Italian Renaissance style. The interior, with its frescoed ceilings and crystal chandeliers, is finished in solid mahogany and rosewood. William B. Johnston was in charge of the Confederate Treasury's Macon Depository, which held at one time the largest monetary reserve south of Richmond. When visiting Macon in 1856, Thackeray mentioned the house in a letter to his daughters, Anne and Harriett.

9. The RALPH SMALL HOUSE, 156 Rogers Avenue, when started in 1822 faced on what is now Vineville Avenue, across from Fort Hawkins more than a mile. It was completed about 1846, and eventually moved around the corner to its present location. Talbot Hamlin has cited this house in his *Greek Revival Architecture in America* as an example of how the genius of the Greek Revival form lends itself to variations in ornament, taste, and construction in terms of local feeling, skill, and materials. This green-shuttered white frame house has a spacious two-story portico across the front, with a small balcony above the entrance door. Six Doric columns are topped with an entablature bearing a frieze of laurel wreaths, the two end columns being enlarged and square—for aesthetic balance, the others round and fluted. The two square fore-columns are also backed by two similar columns at the interior porch corners, thus creating an effect of depth and mass.

10. OVERLOOK (O'Neil), 988 Bond Street, completed in 1840, was designed for Jerry Cowles, railroad-builder and banker, supposedly by Elam Alexander. Temple-like and surrounded by a Doric colonnade

which supports an entablature ornamented by simple triglyphs on the frieze, the house in its setting of lawn and magnolia and other trees, has a commanding presence overlooking downtown Macon from Coleman Hill. A carriage house and servants' quarters remain on the three acres of grounds and garden.

11. BACONSFIELD PARK, across the river by the bridge at Spring Street, lies (L) along the east bank of the Ocmulgee, and is cherished for its floral gardens. Tennis courts and the zoo are located here. Emery Drive (R) passes the site of old Fort Hawkins. One of its block-houses has been reconstructed with studied attention to exactness in presenting a replica of the original.

12. CENTRAL CITY PARK in Macon proper at the lower end of Walnut Street and along the Ocmulgee's west bank, was first developed in the decade following 1870. It is the site of the Georgia State Fair, of Fat Cattle Shows (in the Livestock Arena), and the Luther Williams Base-ball Park, the home of the Macon Peaches.

POINTS OF INTEREST IN THE ENVIRONS

Lamar Mounds and Village Site, 6.8 m. (see TOUR 9A). Ocmulgee National Monu-ment, 1.1 m. (see TOUR 9B). Georgia Academy for the Blind, 2.3 m.; Wesleyan College for Women, 6.9 m. (see TOUR 12). Georgia Baptist College, 5.5 m. (see TOUR 16).

Savannah

Railroad Stations: Central of Georgia Railway, 301 West Broad Street; Union Station, 419 West Broad Street, for Atlantic Coast Line R.R., Seaboard Air Line Ry., and Southern Ry.; Savannah and Atlanta Railway (freight only), Cohen and West Boundary streets.

Steamship Lines: Connections between all parts of the world, principally freight, with occasional accommodations for a few passengers. South Atlantic Steamship Line, Strachan Shipping Company, Stevens Shipping Company, Smith & Kelly Company, Bull-Insular Lines, Inc., and Seatrain Lines, Inc., located at Central of Georgia docks, transport loaded freight rail cars between Savannah and New York on weekly schedule.

Airport Facilities: Travis Field, municipal, 6½ miles W. of city on US 80, for Eastern Airlines, National Air Lines, and Delta C & S Airlines. Limousine fare $1.29, including tax.

Bus Stations: Union Bus Station, 109 West Broad Street, for Greyhound Lines, Southeastern Stages, Inc., Atlantic Trailways, Savannah Beach Bus Line; Trailways Bus Terminal, Montgomery and Oglethorpe, for Service Coach Trailways.

Motor Freight: Principal companies; connections and service, nationwide. Akers Motor Lines, Inc., US 17, North; Benton Brothers Drayage and Storage (Allied Van Lines), Louisville Road; Central Truck Lines, Inc., Telfair Road; Coastal Transport and Trading Company, 1031 West Gwinnett Street; Fedderwitz Trucking Company, 1031 West Gwinnett Street; Youman's Van and Storage Company (Weathers Brothers Transfer Co., Inc.), 414 East Oglethorpe Street; Arco Storage and Moving, Inc. (Suddath), 124 Randolph Street; Arrow Van Lines (Delcher's), East Broughton Street; Security Moving and Storage, East Bay Street (Mayflower Cross Transit).

Taxis: Fare—30¢ and up. Yellow Cab Company.

City Bus Service: Savannah Transit Company, fare 10¢.

Information Service: Chamber of Commerce, 100 East Bay Street; AAA, Hotel DeSoto, Bull and Liberty Streets; Travelers' Aid, Union Station, 419 West Broad Street.

Accommodations: 8 hotels; 25 tourist courts; 7 tourist homes. Rates slightly higher during winter and early spring.

Radio Stations: WSAV (630 kc.); WFRP (1230 kc.); WTOC (1290 kc.); WCCP (1450 kc.); WDAR (1400 kc.); WJIV (900 kc.).

Television: WSAV-TV and WTOC-TV authorized by FCC; scheduled to begin telecasting in early or mid-1954.

Theaters and Motion Picture Houses: Municipal Auditorium, Hull and Barnard streets, for local productions and occasional road shows; 8 motion picture houses; 4 drive-in theaters; 3 motion picture houses for Negroes.

Golf Courses: Municipal Golf Club, Isle of Hope Road, 18-holes, greens fee $1.00; Mary Calder Golf Club, Bay Street Extension, 9-holes, greens fee $1.00. Open to public,

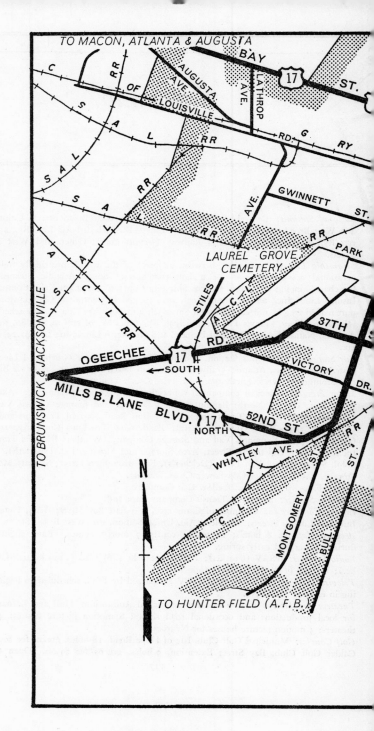

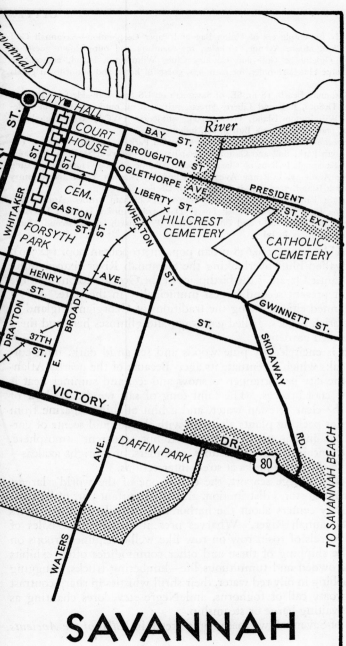

SAVANNAH

though primarily for employees of Union Bag and Paper Corporation—Savannah Golf
and Country Club, Moore Avenue, 18-holes, for members and out-of-town guests of
members only; Oglethorpe Golf and Country Club, Wilmington Island, adjacent to
General Oglethorpe Hotel, 18-holes, for members, guests of hotel, and out-of-town guests
only.

Swimming: Savannah Beach, 18 m. SE. of Savannah on US 80, ocean-side facilities, surf
bathing; Hotel DeSoto, Bull and Liberty Streets, private pool, outdoors; General Oglethorpe Hotel, Wilmington Island, private pool, outdoors; YWCA, West Oglethorpe
Avenue, indoor pool; YMCA, 308 Bull Street, indoor pool.

Additional Recreation: Tennis—Municipal courts, Daffin Park, 1 m. SE. of city on Vic-
tory Drive; Forsyth Park, Bull and Gaston Streets; Baseball—Grayson Stadium, in Daffin
Park, home of Savannah Indians of Class A South Atlantic League; Horseback Riding
—Sa-Hi Riding Academy, DeRenne Avenue; Yachting—Savannah Yacht and Country
Club, Whitemarsh Island, 7 m. SE. of Savannah on US 80.

Annual Events: St. Patrick's Day Celebration, March 17; Chatham Artillery Anniversary,
May 1; Maritime Day, May 22; Armed Forces Day, 3rd Saturday in May; Interstate
Sailboat Regatta, Savannah Yacht and Country Club, Whitemarsh Island, second Thurs-
day, Friday, and Saturday in July.

SAVANNAH (45 alt., 119,638 urban pop., metropolitan pop. 152,900),
built on a walled bluff overlooking the Savannah River sixteen miles
from the Atlantic Ocean, is the birthplace of the Georgia colony and the
oldest and at present second largest municipality in the state. It is a
precisely planned city, showing the traditions of Georgian England in
its compact brick houses, grilled gateways, and glimpses here and there
of half-concealed gardens.

Savannah is encircled by pine woods and set amid dark, moss-cur-
tained live oaks which accentuate its age. Because of the nearby Atlantic Ocean, the city is a stranger to snow and ice, and summer heat is
tempered by cool breezes. The faint tang of salt winds, the hint of
sulphur in the clear artesian water, and a hint of things marine from
fish and oyster packing plants alternate with the languid scents of gardenias and magnolias, to make a varied but recurrent atmosphere.
Luxuriant tropical plants—palmettoes, oleanders, and bright azaleas—
are planted in the broad parks at street intersections.

Traditionally a large seaport, the city is one of the world's largest
markets for naval stores distribution, and an important part of its commercial activity centers about the harbor that extends for some miles
along the Savannah River. Wharves present thousands of bales of
cotton and barrels of rosin row on row like well-disciplined troops on
parade. The shipping of these and other commodities often exhibits
a scene of crowded and tumultuous life—lumbering trucks, chugging
tugboats bobbing in oily red water, their shrill whistles in sharp contrast
with the throaty call of foghorns, and Negro stevedores chanting as
they load a waiting barge or steamship.

The plan of Savannah was based on a sketch in *Villas of the Ancients* by Robert Castell, who died in one of the English debtor prisons that Georgia was founded to relieve. From this sketch James Edward Oglethorpe, founder of the city, and Colonel William Bull, an engineer of South Carolina, designed the Colonial city on a plan which has persisted. For all their contrasting details there is a certain unity in the older Georgian Colonial, Classical Revival, Greek Revival, and Victorian houses, which are built on a level with the sidewalk and often joined in rows. Usually they have three or four stories, including a raised basement, and stairs ascending to a high stoop. Some were constructed of crude brick brought from Europe as ballast in early sailing vessels; others show in their soft colors that they were built of the celebrated Savannah Grey brick from the old kiln of the Hermitage (*see* TOUR *1*).

The most common characteristics are small entrance stoops, recessed fanlighted doorways, delicate iron railings, and tall windows with ornate iron guards covering the lower third of their frames. Frequently an elaborately grilled balcony shows the taste of the French Royalists who fled to Savannah from the Santo Domingo rebellions of the mid-nineteenth century, and in some houses jigsaw woodwork shows the architectural idiom of the latter part of the nineteenth century. High ceilings, intricately carved moldings, handsome mantels of marble, and arched hallways characterize the interiors. In ante-bellum times, offices, dining rooms, and service rooms were in the raised basement, while the second floor was used for drawing rooms and libraries and the upper floor for bedrooms. In the downtown areas these old houses are built close to one another, as in London, England, of the period. To the rear or side of a house there is sometimes a garden enclosed by a wall constructed of brick laid in an openwork pattern, testifying to the traditional English love of privacy. Though often designed in the same architectural tradition, the newer houses of the residential suburbs are distinguished by extensive lawns and masses of shrubbery.

Savannah's social life is as dignified as its buildings, and no other Georgia city has a better established interest in the fine arts. Appreciation of painting is nurtured by the art school and the frequent exhibitions at the Telfair Academy of Arts and Sciences. A winter concert series provides excellent music. The literature, which began with John Wesley's *Collection of Psalms and Hymns* (1737-86), has shifted from romantic looseness in late years to a more analytic realism. The Poetry Society of Georgia was founded in Savannah in 1923.

Education, initiated by Benjamin Ingham's mission school and by George Whitefield's Bethesda Orphanage, has expanded to include a junior college, several private and parochial schools, and an extensive public school sytem. At first the colonists, though welcoming all Protestant groups, excluded Roman Catholics because of the enmity existing between the Georgia colony and Spanish Florida. The city has since become the strongest center of Catholicism in Georgia, much to the enrichment of its cultural pattern, although Protestant church membership is larger.

In Savannah, beneath the hum of the neotechnic age there is always a soft but insistent undertone of the past, of a soil made rich by a lengthy series of human events. The city's early history is identical with that of the colony, for after landing the first settlers on February 12, 1733, Oglethorpe began to lay out the town on a square tract of 15,360 acres to accommodate 240 families. He named the town Savannah, perhaps after the Sawana or Shawnee Indians who once inhabited the river valley, or perhaps—as some think—from the Spanish word *sabana,* meaning flat country, having been applied to the entire coastal plain by Spanish explorers who preceded the English settlers by almost two centuries. Protestant groups from the Continent and also men of affluence who came to the new colony contributed much towards an early cosmopolitanism. East of the town on the river bank the Trustees' Garden of ten acres was established to test plants suitable to the soil and climate of the region and to supply the horticultural needs of the colonists, who were encouraged to establish gardens. Among its specimens were mulberry trees suitable for silk culture, figs, oranges, coffee, tea, camphor, olives, peaches, cotton, medicinal herbs, vegetables, and the vine, especially sorts of grapes productive of wine. Dr. William Houstoun, an eminent botanist of the University of Edinburgh, was chosen by the Trustees to search the South American tropics for adaptable herbs and trees. His collection was shipped to Savannah and introduced into the Garden, but while returning Houstoun died of tropical fever in Jamaica in 1733. Eventually, like a number of Oglethorpe's intentions with regard to slavery and trade, the Garden perished; but recently the Trustees' Garden Club has established another at Trustees' Garden Village on East Broad Street.

After the cultivation of silk, wine, and medicinal herbs had failed, the colonists produced more indigenous commodities and developed a brisk trade with England. In 1744 the first commercial house was established, and soon afterward regular export shipments of rice, hides, and lumber were sent to England. In 1749, the year slavery was introduced, eight small bags—the unit prior to the introduction of the cotton press and bales—of cotton were shipped from this town.

Savannah became the seat of government when Georgia was made a Royal Province in 1754, and two decades of commercial growth and improved trading conditions followed. At the beginning of the Revolution the town had many stubborn Loyalists, but the hot-headed young bloods set up a liberty pole before Tondee's Tavern, shouted approval of the Lexington victory, and organized a battalion headed by Colonel Lachlan McIntosh. When two British war vessels and a transport anchored off Tybee Island in January, 1776, the posture of affairs was such that the Royal Governor, Sir James Wright (1714-86), escaped on one of them to Halifax.

The signing of the Declaration of Independence was celebrated vigorously by the Revolutionists, and in the following year Savannah became the capital of a state so new that it hardly understood its position. On December 27, 1778, however, Colonel Sir Archibald Campbell landed 2,000 British troops a few miles down river to besiege the town. With the help of the surrounding marshes, General Robert Howe and a force of 600 men confidently expected to hold the city. But failing to secure certain passageways through the all but impenetrable marshes—which the British discovered with the help of local intelligence, Howe was taken by surprise on December 29, losing the town and more than half his men. For this negligence, Howe was later court-martialed and, though he was acquitted, his status as a military leader was gone forever. Governor Wright returned, and sought to re-establish British authority. Because Georgia was the infant among the Colonies and thus in many ways more closely related to England as mother than to her twelve older sisters, and because of the terrible nearness of British Florida, and of other regional and integral factors, mixed passions in the colony filled the sails of the Governor's ambition with a favorable wind almost until the final defeat of the British in 1782.

It now became British strategy to attempt to defeat the Colonies by a southern campaign in which one state after another was to be detached from the coastal chain. As a counteraction, in September, 1779, a siege of Savannah was begun by Count d'Estaing's French fleet assisted by American forces under General Benjamin Lincoln. After some weeks, the situation remaining stable, Count d'Estaing, troubled by sickness among his men, the impending autumn hurricanes typical of the area, and the report of approaching British vessels, on October 9 ordered with Gallic impetuosity, a general assault. It was a singular failure in a series of military misadventures suffered by Georgia. More than a thousand casualties resulted among the American and French forces; among these were Count Pulaski and the regional hero, Sergeant Jasper. British losses fell short of two hundred men. Lincoln sought safety in South Carolina with little more than a token of his men left. With the British using Savannah as a center of radial attack, Georgia reverted to a state of nature and became the scene of a bitter struggle to the end between wandering groups of Whigs and Tories. It was a time of spectacular violence in which only men of iron might hope to survive, and of the making of heroes by personal decision and immediate action. Of these were Elijah Clarke, John Twiggs, James Jackson, John Dooly, Patrick Carr, and Nancy Hart. Eventually, Nathanael Greene was made Colonial commander of the southern theater of war, and after his encounter with Cornwallis at Guilford Court House in North Carolina, the tide of British fortune was at the turn. General "Mad Anthony" Wayne was sent to Georgia by General Greene with a Continental force in 1782, and with the help of Colonel James Jackson's Georgia Legion and loyal forces under Colonel Twiggs, he forced the British from Savannah by July. The harm suffered by Savannah and its Colonial area during the Revolution is comparable on the scale of state history to that of Columbus and Atlanta in the War between the States.

But during the the years of conflict Georgia had matured, and a marked period of development followed the Revolution. On October 9, 1783, the first recorded theatrical performance was given as a charity benefit at the Filature (the original silk manufacturing center) by a "Set of Gentlemen" under the direction of Godwin and Kidd, of Charleston, South Carolina. The program consisted of the tragedy *The Fair Penitent,* a play by the English poet laureate Nicholas Rowe (1674-1718) often revived, and the farce *Miss in Her Teens.* The city's first playhouse was built two years later. Savannah was incorporated as a city in 1789, and after Eli Whitney's invention of the cotton gin four years later it sprang into eminence as a cotton center. Tobacco shipped down river from Augusta made Savannah an important tobacco market and outlet. The growth of surrounding plantations and the disposal of Indian lands were other factors in its expansion. In these years came provisions for a water supply and fire protection, the establishment of a cotton exchange, and the incorporation of the Georgia Medical Society.

For defense during the War of 1812, Fort Wayne was strengthened, and Fort Jackson was built down the river; the Chatham Artillery, the Savannah Volunteer Guards, the Republican Blues, and the Georgia Hussars were organized for duty. In May, 1814, the U. S. sloop *Peacock* captured the British warship *Epervier,* brought it into the harbor, and confiscated $10,000 in specie aboard the British ship.

A golden era of prosperity followed the War of 1812. The period from 1817 to 1825, associated with Monroe's eight years as President and often referred to as the "Era of Good Feeling," marked the transition from Jefferson's political views to those of Jackson: from the principle that civil government is best when it governs least to the critical proposition that government must on occasion intervene explicitly on behalf of the unprivileged and exploited. Before the end of the 18th Century a network of roads connected Savannah with Sunbury, Darien, Augusta, Washington, and Louisville. In 1816 the steamboat *Enterprise* carried a Savannah party upstream to Augusta; three years later maritime history was made when on May 22, 1819, the *City of Savannah,* first steamboat to cross the Atlantic, sailed for Liverpool, and visited Copenhagen and St. Petersburg. However, the measure of efficiency in river transportation is shown in the fact that La Fayette, while on his triumphant American tour in 1825, made the journey from Savannah to Augusta by means of a wood-burner, the *Altamaha*—the run lasting forty-four hours, with two hours out for re-fueling en route. The time was then considered record-making.

To lower transportation costs between the Savannah and Ogeechee rivers, the Ogeechee Canal was opened in 1828. In 1833 a charter was secured to run a rail line from Savannah to Macon, and two years later a lateral right to organize banking, by the same company. The lines of the Georgia Railroad and Banking Company reached Macon in 1843, and tapped the rich cotton trade of central Georgia. During this period Savannah, because of its harbor, was the greatest port on the southern seaboard for cotton and naval stores. In 1816 the value of Georgia products shipped through Savannah to other parts of the nation and to foreign countries was ten million dollars and two years later the sum had reached fourteen. The trade which was first well established around 1744 by the commercial house of Harris and Habersham, associated with New York, Boston, and Philadelphia, and by 1749 sending vessels direct to Europe, had grown vigorously as the War between the States approached. The history of Savannah became more and more a function of the port of that name.

During this period Savannah developed a sectionalism that made it respond instantly to the war cry in December, 1860. The schism of Whigs and Tories no longer lacerated the heart of the region. Upon adoption of the Ordinance of Secession, Savannah men seized Fort Jackson, and in March, 1861, the Confederate flag floated over the customhouse. On April 10, 1862, however, Fort Pulaski was taken by Federal forces, and served in connection with the Union navy as a wedge for regional attack and as a painful obstruction to the use of Savannah as a sorely needed artery of Confederate commerce. On December 13, 1864, Sherman took Fort McAllister and on the 17th demanded the surrender of Savannah; but General W. J. Hardee and his 10,000 troops continued to skirmish three days longer before they evacuated the city by means of a new pontoon bridge to Hutchinson Island, leaving in addition to much war matériel 31,000 bales of cotton "for avaricious speculators to fight over." On December 21, Union troops occupied Savannah.

With the abolition of slavery and the collapse of great plantations, the port ceased to function. But despite all the hardships of Reconstruction and an appalling yellow fever epidemic in 1876, the wounds of war were healing—except among those who made a daily ritual of opening them —and affairs began to take a positive turn as was shown by the increased crops, improved bank credits, and greater railroad facilities of 1879. Alien capital sought high rates of profit such as always are present in a region materially resourceful but financially disabled; cotton and tobacco prices climbed again to ante-bellum heights, and the surrounding pine forests created flourishing lumber and naval enterprises. With the establishment of the Naval Stores Exchange in 1882, Savannah became the leading turpentine and rosin port.

Not until the twentieth century had brought a decline in the production of cotton and naval stores did the city turn to manufacturing. During World War I, boom prices caused shipyards to be hastily built along the waterfront, but a cataclysmic fall in business followed the boll weevil's destruction of cotton in 1921. By 1926, however, control of the pest had caused an upsurge of life again in the port. In 1938 exports, including naval stores, cotton, tobacco, corn, sugar, lumber, and other products, were valued at $19,000,000. The chief imports were fertilizer materials and petroleum products.

In World War II Savannah again came fully into its own as a strategic maritime center. The same logic of transportation and distribution that guided Sherman into northwest Georgia and finally to Savannah— now developed complexly in the form of rail- and highways to Chicago —poured a cornucopia of agricultural and industrial products through Savannah as a middle outlet between New Orleans and Baltimore. During the war years, 1941-45, vast stores of munitions and other matériel were channeled through the Port of Savannah to serve both American forces and the allies abroad. Indeed the economic geography of the war could be followed in terms of Lend-Lease supply ships taking the southern circle to England, then of those conveying ammunition, tanks, guns, planes and other sinews of war for the landing on the African coast, and afterwards of cargoes for the prelude to the end, the Normandy Invasion. As it chugged in and about, *Cynthia II,* one of four tugs commonly active in the port, became a sign in miniature of the tireless energy and push of the war years. In 1942 during the apex of the submarine menace a hush fell over the port. But though the

Oglethorpe, the first ship off the ways of the Southeastern Shipbuilding Company, was a submarine casualty, it was merely one of a succession of cargo boats—comprising 88 Liberty ships, 13 AVI's, 25 minesweepers, 4 submarine rescue vessels, and 7 seagoing barges—built at Savannah. A set of stacks belching smoke was progressively becoming a more appropriate symbol of Savannah's economic energy, and of a new culture in keeping with this sort of prosperity, than the white columns sentimentally associated with the past. For the industries that came during World War II, in addition to shipbuilding, had in greater part come to stay.

With approximately ten miles of developed and potential port sites, many large industrial firms have located their plants on the river banks, being served by a deep channel that permits ships of any size to use the land-locked port, some twenty miles up from the Atlantic Ocean. The port is equipped to handle all types of commerce to and from Savannah and points in the South and Southeast as well as in regions more centrally located in the nation. Typical of commodities moving through the port are petroleum and petroleum products, sugar, lumber, cotton and cotton goods, naval stores, chemicals for fertilizers and fertilizers, bagging paper and paper goods, clay and fuller's earth, sodium sulphate, iron and steel parts, scrap iron and steel, tea from India, rosin for South Africa, and pit props for Belgium. And there are many others.

In 1949 Governor Herman Talmadge purchased for the State of Georgia from the Federal government for $808,100 the Quartermaster Depot, the original cost of which was in the vicinity of six millions. The tract included at the time of purchase 407 acres of land with 37 warehouse buildings, and 42 others, all of permanent construction, eight miles of railroad track, and other facilities. In all, what is now the State Port has 4,238 feet of river front. Additional facilities in the form of transit sheds, docks, five ship berths, a cotton compress, a stationary gantry crane of 100-tons lift, a 35-ton locomotive movable crane, a 110-ton diesel locomotive for switching work, and some two hundred thousand dollars worth of fork lifts and conveyors are among additions made by the State Port Authority. Aware of the commercial significance of the new port, *The New York Times,* for Monday, February 4, 1952, carried a news story which observed in part: "The port program is part of a general southern regional move to obtain a larger share of the country's export and import trade as it affects the rapidly growing industrialization and improved farming practices in the South." Among the industries that have made use of the warehouse space at the state docks is the Tetley Tea Company, which has spent three-quarters of a million dollars remodeling for a modern tea-plant. With the state's five berths, the river port in general will have a census of twenty-seven, most of which are equal to any in the country.

The Savannah area is served by twenty-six truck lines, and five major railroads which are: the Atlantic Coast Line Railroad, the Central of Georgia Railway Company, the Seaboard Air Line Railroad Company, the Savannah and Atlanta Railway Company, and the Southern Railway System. The Central of Georgia and the Savannah and Atlanta companies maintain headquarters at Savannah. In 1951 the Seaboard dedicated a new railroad bridge across the Savannah with a 140-foot central lift span which permits the largest ships to sail upriver to the new state docks. On March 5, 1953, Mrs. Eugene Talmadge opened a throttle that began construction work on the Eugene Talmadge Memorial Bridge, designed to remove a lengthy kink in US 17 between Savannah and the South Carolina shore, when completed. An interchange at the Hutchinson Island side will make its 2,018 acres accessible by highway as well as by railroad. The bridge will leave the Savannah side at West Boundary Street. On April 8, 1952, the Hunter Air Force Base was translated from a World War II emergency facility to a Type I or permanent Air Force installation. At that time it was the home of the 38th Air Division made up of the 2nd and 308th Bombardment Wings plus the Second Air Base Group and supporting units.

Chatham County, of which Savannah is the county seat, was named for William Pitt, the Earl of Chatham, defender of the rights of the Colonies during their struggle for liberty. The gently rolling terrain of Chatham County, and of southeast Georgia in general, is favorable for dairying, livestock raising, truck growing, poultry raising, and general farming. The prevailing soil, lying a few feet above sea level, but with natural drainage by creeks and canals, is of the Norfolk series, commonly considered one of the best light truck soil types of the Atlantic Coastal Plain. With an average of nearly fifty inches of rain annually and frequent coastal showers during the heat of summer, the area has an established normal temperature of 49.8° for January and of 80.9° for July. These factors favor year-around farming and industrial efficiency as well as outdoor recreational activities.

In general, it should be observed that with all its commercial and industrial success Savannah is still governed by an air of courtesy and of detachment, sure signs of traditional confidence. A large and leisurely dinner at 2 P.M., sailing parties and turtle egg hunts for visitors, business conferences over iced drinks—such customs give an air of composure and pleasant ease to a city which is still old-fashioned southern in its style of conduct, if no longer in its modes of production and volume of commerce.

POINTS OF INTEREST
(BULL STREET)

Along BULL STREET, which forms the central axis of the city, are five squares that in the original plan were designed as centers of defense against Spanish and Indian invasion. Now two centuries old, these small parks embody Savannah's characteristic, semitropical and hence lush growth, subdued to the precise lines of a formal beauty. Italian cypresses, tall cabbage palmettoes, blossoming bays, and English yews are among the trees that increase the depth of a natural growth of oaks. A geographic picture of the original Savannah, redrawn from Peter Gordon's print by Paul W. Porterfield, exhibits it as a combination of neat squares trimmed from the enclosing fabric of wilderness. Flower beds are bright in season with flame and other azaleas, with glossy green-leaved and white wax-blossomed gardenias, and with both single-colored and variegated camellias. Paths through the grassy plots are lined with benches that offer an invitation to rest and contemplation, and in many of the parks monuments to past heroes create a sense of the continuous ebb and flow of life.

1. CITY HALL, at the head of Bull Street on Bay Street, a massive gray-stone building with a green stained-glass dome, is designed in the neo-Classic style typical of civic architecture since the early part of the twentieth century; it was built in 1905 to replace a building erected in 1799.

Tablets on either side of the entrance commemorate Savannah's role in maritime history, one of the sailing in 1819 of the *City of Savannah,* the other of the *John Randolph.* The successful use of steam in coast-wise vessels prompted William Scarborough and several Savannah merchants to organize the Savannah Steamship Company which was formed on December 19, 1818.

The *Savannah,* equipped with paddle wheels made to fold up fan-wise and be laid away on deck when using sail, was constructed at Corlear's Hook, New York, and reached Savannah on March 28, 1819. Sailing from Savannah on May 22, 1819, the vessel reached Liverpool on June 20, having been fourteen days under steam, the rest under sail lest the fuel supply be exhausted. From Liverpool the Savannah went to Copenhagen, Stockholm, and St. Petersburg, Russia, and then to Cronstadt and Arendal in Norway. The ship returned to Savannah in twenty-five days, nineteen of them by steam. But the expedition was so costly that the merchants lost interest in the vessel's transoceanic use, and it was converted into a sailing packet that plied the coast of the United States until lost off Long Island in 1822. In the National Museum, Washington, D. C., are the log book and a cylinder of this ship, in honor of which President Franklin D. Roosevelt in 1935 proclaimed May 22 as National Maritime Day. A model of the ship may be seen inside the Hall.

The *John Randolph* was the first ironclad ship in American waters. John Laird, of Birkenhead, England, made the plates on order for Gazaway B. Lamar, a Savannah banker and cotton merchant, and it was put together in Savannah and launched in 1834. Its floating seemed to the spectators a contravention of the very roots of common sense.

2. UNITED STATES CUSTOMHOUSE, 3 East Bay Street, a large building of granite blocks, was designed by John S. Norris in the style of the Greek Revival and erected in 1850 on the site of the colony's first public building. The six monolithic granite columns of the stately portico are capped with carved tobacco leaves instead of the usual acanthus. On this site in 1736 John Wesley preached his first sermon in Savannah; the event is commemorated by a tablet on the corner of the Bull Street side. The tablet on the corner of the Bay Street façade marks the site of a small frame house that Oglethorpe used for headquarters.

3. JOHNSON SQUARE, Bull Street between Bryan and Congress streets, was laid out in 1733 and named for Governor Johnson of South Carolina, a friend of Oglethorpe's. One of the original parks, it was a center of early community life, surrounded by the church, the House for Strangers, the Public Mill, the Public Bake Oven, the Public Store, and nearby, the Public Well. The NATHANAEL GREENE MONUMENT, in the center of the park, is erected over the grave of the famous Revolutionary general (*see* TOUR *14*) and his son. The monument, designed by William Strickland, is a tall white marble shaft on a granite base, shaft and base forming a Roman sword. The cornerstone was laid by La Fayette in 1825. A SUNDIAL commemorates the bicentennial of Georgia and honors Colonel William Bull, who assisted Oglethorpe in designing Savannah. Presented to the city by the Sons of Colonial Wars on February 12, 1933, it replaces the first public sundial, from which early settlers read the hours.

4. CHRIST EPISCOPAL CHURCH, Bull Street between E. St. Julian and E. Congress (facing Johnson Square), home of the first congregation organized in the colony (1733), is a Greek Revival building with stucco-covered brick walls half hidden by vines. The present structure, the third on the site, reproduces an earlier church built in 1838 according to a plan furnished by James Hamilton Cooper, and destroyed by fire

in 1897. A double flight of steps leads to a large Ionic portico and above the three classic portals are panels embellished with festoons. Around three sides of the interior is a graceful balcony supported by small columns.

Among the early ministers was John Wesley, who came in 1736 as a Church of England missionary and established what is believed to be the first organized Protestant Sunday School in the world. But his arbitrary attitude made him unpopular with both colonists and Indians, and he was indicted on ten counts for his interference in the secular affairs of the colony. He returned to England in 1737, an embittered man. The minister who followed Wesley was George Whitefield, whose benevolent disposition and numerous charities made him as much beloved as Wesley was not.

BROUGHTON STREET, intersecting Bull Street one block South of Congress Street, is Savannah's principal shopping district.

5. WRIGHT SQUARE, Bull Street between State and York streets, another of the original squares, was laid out in 1733 as Upper Square. Later its name was changed to honor Sir James Wright, last Governor of the Royal Province of Georgia, who fled when the Revolutionary War first stirred Savannah but returned when the British captured the city. In the center of the square is the GORDON MEMORIAL, a large granite and marble monument designed by W. F. Pietch, of New York. Four pink marble columns, rising from a massive granite base, are grouped about a tall bronze urn. About the columns are four cherubs that support a granite globe. The memorial was erected to honor William W. Gordon, an influential citizen who was the first president of the Central Railroad & Banking Company of Georgia. He lost his life while engaged in the construction of the Central of Georgia Railway.

The TOMOCHICHI MARKER, in the southeast corner of the square, honors the venerable, kindly Yamacraw chief who befriended the first settlers. On May 21, 1733, with the half-Indian Mary Musgrove acting as interpreter, Tomochichi signed the formal treaty permitting Oglethorpe to settle his colonists. In April 1734, with his wife, his nephew, and several tribesmen, he accompanied Oglethorpe to England, where he was received by King George II at Kensington and by the Archbishop of Canterbury at Lambeth palace. Excited throngs gathered to see the Indians during their tour, and they enlisted valuable English patronage for the colony. Portraits of Tomochichi show him as a man of grave and commanding appearance.

6. LUTHERAN CHURCH OF THE ASCENSION, Bull Street between E. State and E. President streets, was built in 1843 upon the site of the first wooden church erected in 1756 by a pious group of Salzburgers, refugees who

fled from Salzburg, Bavaria, to Georgia because of the new colony's tolerance for persecuted sects. Most of the Salzburgers soon went to Ebenezer, but some remained in Savannah and formed the Lutheran congregation in 1744.

7. The w. w. GORDON HOUSE (*private*), northeast corner of Bull Street and Oglethorpe Avenue, a stuccoed brick dwelling with a small Ionic portico, is an admirable example of Classical Revival architecture. Although a third story and side porch have been added, they have not marred the fine proportions of the façade and the entrance portico. The interior shows numerous excellent details in the African black-marble mantels, mahogany doors, and handsome cornices. The building, originally owned by Judge J. M. Wayne, was sold before its completion in 1829 to his nephew-in-law, William W. Gordon. The house has opened its doors to such celebrities as Alexander H. Stephens, Admirals Dewey and Schley, and Presidents McKinley and Taft. Juliette Low, *née* Juliette Gordon, founder of the Girl Scouts of America, spent her childhood here.

8. INDEPENDENT PRESBYTERIAN CHURCH, SW. corner Bull Street and W. Oglethorpe Avenue, is a finely proportioned white granite building of late Georgian Colonial design, distinguished by its arched windows, well-designed portico, and a steeple in the Christopher Wren style. The granite Doric columns of the portico support an elaborate wooden entablature and a pediment with a shell-like design reminiscent of the Adam style. Above the portico a graceful clock tower rises from a square base through three classically adorned octagonal tiers to a tall spire. The interior is notable for the classic ornamentation of the segmental, vaulted ceiling and for the unusually high pulpit which stands before a pleasing Georgian window. In the rear the Ralph Adams Cram addition replaces the manse where in 1885 Ellen Axson, granddaughter of the pastor, became the first wife of Woodrow Wilson. The present building, constructed in 1889-90, is a copy of a former one erected 1815-19, and destroyed by fire in 1889.

The congregation was formed in 1755, about two decades after Presbyterianism was introduced into the colony by the Scottish Highlanders who were imported to defend Savannah against Spanish Florida. A branch of the Scottish Presbyterian Church, it has always remained independent of the American organization.

9. CHIPPEWA SQUARE, Bull Street between Hull and Perry streets, was laid out in 1813 and named for the Battle of Chippewa, an American victory over the British in the War of 1812. The OGLETHORPE MONUMENT, in the center of the park, is a massive bronze statue of the man whose philanthropy and shrewdness caused Georgia to be founded.

The monument, designed by Daniel Chester French with a base by Henry Bacon—both men associated with the Lincoln Memorial in Washington, D. C.—was erected in 1910 by the State of Georgia and the City of Savannah.

10. The BARROW HOUSE (*private*), SW. corner Bull and W. McDonough streets, erected between 1835 and 1840, is an excellent example of neo-Classic architecture. Although a third story has been added and the balcony heightened, the building retains its distinctive proportions.

11. MADISON SQUARE, Bull Street between Harris and Charlton streets, was laid out in 1839 and named for President James Madison. The JASPER MONUMENT, in the square's center, honors the Revolutionary hero, Sergeant William Jasper, who won distinction by his gallantry at Fort Moultrie and was mortally wounded in the Siege of Savannah in 1779. Two OLD CANNON, at the south end, mark the junction of two early roads, one from Augusta and the other from Darien (now the Ogeechee Road).

12. The MELDRIM HOUSE (*private*), NW. corner Bull and W. Macon streets, is a massive stuccoed brick dwelling with Gothic Revival oriel windows, intricate ironwork, and crenelated roof. On three sides are piazzas with flagstone floors. The house, which with its garden and servants' quarters occupies an entire block, was built in 1856 by Charles Green, a British subject, grandfather of the novelists Anne and Julian Green. During the Federal occupation of 1864, General Sherman made his headquarters here, and it was from here that he dispatched to President Lincoln the message offering Savannah as a Christmas present. It is now the Parish House of St. John's Episcopal Church.

13. ST. JOHN'S EPISCOPAL CHURCH, SW. corner of Bull and W. Macon streets, a stuccoed brick edifice of Gothic Revival design, was built in 1852. In the tall wooden steeple are chimes which were saved from destruction during Federal occupation of the city by a special plea to President Lincoln. The chimes are generally played at twilight and can be heard throughout most of the city.

14. MONTEREY SQUARE, Bull Street between Taylor and Gordon streets, was laid out in 1848 and named in honor of the American capture of Monterey in 1846 during the Mexican War. The PULASKI MONUMENT, centering the square, was erected in 1855 to honor Count Casimir Pulaski, the Polish nobleman who aided the American cause during the Revolution and met his death during the Siege of Savannah in 1779. The monument was designed by Robert E. Launitz.

Though without historic importance, the houses surrounding the square are interesting for their typical nineteenth century design.

15. The HENRY JACKSON HOUSE (*private*), NE. corner of Bull and

E. Gaston streets, is the home of the Oglethorpe Club. Built about 1840, with massive brownstone steps ascending to the high main floor, the house is an example of Classical Revival architecture. The large dining rooms in the basement were originally kitchens. One of its owners was Confederate General Henry R. Jackson, chargé d'affaires to Austria from 1853 to 1858, minister to Mexico during 1885-86, and author of the locally celebrated poem "The Red Old Hills of Georgia."

16. ARMSTRONG COLLEGE, 447 Bull Street, was organized in 1935 as a city-owned and supported two-year junior college. The faculty of forty-five is made up of both part-time and full-time teaching personnel. The day and adult evening college enrollments average 500 to 600 students a quarter. It is fully accredited by the Southern Association of Colleges and Secondary Schools.

The college and the administration building are named for George F. Armstrong, whose widow gave their former home to the city as the first college building. Herschel V. Jenkins Hall, facing beautiful Forsyth Park, provides space for classrooms and an auditorium. It is named for the President of the *Savannah Morning News* who has served several terms as the chairman of the college's governing board. The Lane Building bears the name of the late Mills B. Lane, founder of the Citizens and Southern National Bank, who donated the building to the college. The science building is named for a former mayor of the city, the late Thomas Gamble, and the Hunt Building, housing the Home Economics program and the Student Center, is a memorial to John W. Hunt. Hodgson Hall, the library of the Georgia Historical Society, also houses the college library. It was originally given to the Georgia Historical Society in 1876 by Margaret Telfair Hodgson in memory of her husband, William B. Hodgson. The Georgia Historical Society, organized in 1839, has a vigorous membership and has published many early letters and records.

Armstrong College offers the usual arts college courses that are pre-requisites to the professions, and in addition offers semi-professional programs in business administration, home economics, nursing, and secretarial work. The college also co-operates with local businesses and industries, such as the Union Bag and Paper Corporation, in offering special courses for their employees.

17. WARREN G. CANDLER MEMORIAL HOSPITAL, W. Gaston Street between Drayton and Abercorn streets and extending to Huntingdon Street, is the outgrowth of a hospital for seamen founded in 1819—a time when, because of growing commerce in the harbor, sailors of many nations were evident on Savannah's streets. In 1835 the institution was incorporated as the Savannah Poor House and Hospital, but is now

owned by the Methodist Church and operated as a general hospital. A tall iron fence surrounds the wooded grounds, through which a center drive leads to the main building, erected in 1877 on the foundation of an earlier building.

18. FORSYTH PARK, Gaston Street between Whitaker and Drayton streets extending to Park Avenue, is a twenty-acre tract named for Governor John Forsyth. The park was laid out in 1851 according to the design of a Bavarian landscape gardener, William Bischoff. French influence is evident in the plan and in the large white center fountain. In spring the park is gay with wistaria, dogwood, and the warmth of azaleas, and the shrubs are astir with the explorations of squirrels and the quick short motions of pigeons. Summers it is identified with the rich scent of the magnolia.

The park extends beyond its original limits through the Savannah Militia parade ground equipped with practice fields, tennis courts, and playground facilities for children. On the central walkway of this section, known as the Park Extension, are two monuments, one honoring the dead of the War between the States, the other the veterans of the Spanish-American War. The CONFEDERATE MONUMENT is a lofty sandstone pyramid surmounted by the bronze figure of a Confederate soldier. The original design for the memorial was the work of Robert Reid, of Montreal, but later much ornamentation was removed and a marble figure representing Judgment was replaced by that of a soldier, designed by David Richardson. Within the iron-railed enclosure are memorial busts of the Confederate General Lafayette McLaws and Brigadier General Francis S. Barton. The SPANISH-AMERICAN MEMORIAL is a large bronze figure of a soldier overlooking the long avenue south of the park.

19. The CHATHAM ARTILLERY BARRACKS, SE. corner Bull Street and E. Park Avenue, houses one of the oldest artillery organizations in continuous service. It is a long, low, cream brick building with double doors through which the parade ground is visible. Old records show that the company was organized May 1, 1786, by veterans of the American Revolution, and that it was engaged actively in the Indian campaign the following October, and also served in the War of 1812. On the paved walk in front of the building are two brass six-pound cannon, presented to the artillery by George Washington soon after his visit to Savannah in 1791.

20. SAVANNAH PUBLIC LIBRARY (*open 9 A.M.-9:30 P.M. weekdays*), 2002 Bull Street, is a massive two-story granite structure with heavy columns flanking the entrance. It contains comfortable reading rooms, a reference room, and a children's room.

The institution is an outgrowth of the Savannah Library Society, organized in 1809 to replace a circulating library eleven years older. After the Georgia Historical Society was founded in 1839, the two associations occupied the same quarters, and in 1847 they were united in organization. In 1902 the joint society offered its facilities to Savannah as a public library if the city would provide for maintenance; consequently, Hodgson Hall served as the Public Library until 1916, when the Savannah Public Library was built with funds from the Carnegie Foundation. This library is one of the few Carnegie-aided institutions that does not bear the donor's name.

(*EAST OF BULL STREET*)

FACTORS ROW, E. Bay Street between Bull and Abercorn streets, was named for the cotton factors who made the nineteenth century a period of flourishing trade for Savannah. To be "on the Bay" was assurance of business prestige. The old red brick buildings, straggling along the bluff, are only two stories high on the Bay Street front but are four stories in the rear where their foundations reach the wharf level. Here iron balconies overhang the river front, and iron bridges cross the cobblestones of the ramps leading to River Street. The retaining walls along the bluff are made from stones brought from England as ballast in early sailing vessels. With its steep heights, its weathered bricks, and broken ironwork dark against the water, this section suggests the atmosphere of Old World seaports.

21. The OLD HARBOR LIGHT, NW. corner E. Bay and E. Broad streets at the foot of Emmett Park, is a small cast-iron beacon erected in 1852 to guide ships into the harbor, now disused for many years.

22. The SITE OF FORT WAYNE, NE. corner E. Bay and E. Broad Streets, is now occupied by the municipal gas plant. Though built in 1762, the fort was not of great military importance until the Revolutionary period, when it was named for "Mad Anthony" Wayne. After the city had fallen into their hands, the British strengthened it in 1799, and the Americans rebuilt it for defense during the War of 1812. Encircling a high bluff and overlooking what was once a marshy plain are the massive buttressed brick walls, built during the second alteration. They still appear redoubtable with their old black cannon, relics of the fort, pointing seaward.

The fort was built on the original site of the Trustees' Garden, which covered ten acres.

23. SITE OF THE FILATURE (headquarters of the silk industry), E. St. Julian Street between Lincoln and Abercorn streets, is now Cassell's Row, a cluster of small brick houses with high stoops and handsome

iron banisters. The barnlike Filature, where apprentices were instructed in silk weaving, was erected in 1751, but two decades later the industry failed and the building was converted into an assembly and dance hall.

24. The PINK HOUSE, 23 Abercorn Street, is so named because of the pinkish stucco covering its old brick walls. Of Georgian Colonial design, with a low-stooped, columned portico and a fine Palladian window over the entrance, it was built in 1771 for James Habersham, Jr. In 1812 additions were made, and the building became the Planters' Bank, the first state bank in Georgia. In 1865 it was used as headquarters by General York, a Federal officer. It is now a tearoom.

25. The RICHARDSON-OWENS HOUSE (*private*), 124 Abercorn Street, was begun by an unknown architect in 1816 and finished three years later by William Jay, the celebrated English architect. A stuccoed brick dwelling with corner quoins, arched second-story windows, and paneled parapet above the main cornice, it is praised by architects as Savannah's finest example of the Regency style. Notable exterior details are a beautiful wrought-iron balcony and a graceful columned entrance portico in the Ionic order reached by a winding double stairway. The yard is enclosed by a balustrade with classic urns on the corner posts. Details of the interior are Grecian.

When the late owner, Miss Margaret Thomas, died in 1951, it was learned that her will assigned the house to the Telfair Academy of Arts and Sciences.

26. The DAVENPORT HOUSE (*private*), 324 E. State Street, one of Savannah's best examples of late Georgian Colonial architecture, was built soon after Isaiah Davenport, son of the noted English potter, acquired the lot in 1812. Its curving, double-entrance stairs with wrought-iron banisters and its dormer windows suggest houses of eighteenth-century London.

27. The McINTOSH HOUSE (*private*), 110 E. Oglethorpe Avenue, built about 1764, is generally conceded to be the oldest brick house in the state. As Eppinger's Inn it was a popular rendezvous for Colonial leaders, but Revolutionary patriots closed it because of the proprietor's Tory sympathies. On August 1, 1782, after the British had evacuated the city, the Georgia legislature held its first meeting in the Long Room on the second floor. This room, the scene of many important public meetings, was divided into a number of small rooms when the interior was remodeled. A third story and some decorative ironwork, added in the nineteenth century, have somewhat altered the Georgian Colonial simplicity of the dwelling, which now stands inconspicuously in a group of modern commercial buildings.

Later the house was occupied by Lachlan McIntosh, who won popularity leading Savannah's forces but passed behind a cloud when he fatally wounded Button Gwinnett, one of Georgia's signers of the Declaration of Independence, in a duel that was bred from political faction. In 1791, during the debt-ridden McIntosh's precarious occupancy, George Washington visited in this house.

28. COLONIAL PARK CEMETERY, between Oglethorpe Avenue and Perry Lane, laid out in 1753, was for many years the colony's only public burying ground, that is, until 1852. The cemetery was defaced when General Sherman's men used it for stabling horses. In 1896 the ground was landscaped as a municipal park. Among the distinguished men buried here are Hugh McCall (1767-1824), Georgia's first historian; Dennis L. Cottineau de Kerloguen, who assisted John Paul Jones, during the epic engagement between the *Serapis* and the *Bon Homme Richard;* and Edward Greene Malbone (1777-1807), who in his short career painted more than three hundred miniatures.

29. The W. W. OWENS HOUSE, NW. corner Abercorn and E. McDonough streets, is one of the older houses showing the French influence brought to Savannah in the mid-nineteenth century by French Royalists fleeing the Santo Domingo massacres. Decorative features of the old brick house are the iron balconies and the ironwork set in the lower portion of the window frames.

30. CATHEDRAL OF ST. JOHN THE BAPTIST, NE. corner Abercorn and E. Harris streets, is one of the largest Roman Catholic cathedrals in the Southeast. The building, which shows Gothic influence, is an imposing white stucco structure, with two tall spires. The present cathedral, completed in 1876, was partly destroyed by fire in 1898 and rebuilt two years later around the original walls.

31. The LOW HOUSE, 329 Abercorn Street facing La Fayette Square, a Classical Revival brownstone structure with an iron grillwork balustrade guarding the lower windows, was built about 1847 for Andrew Low, a cotton factor. It is now state headquarters for the Georgia Society of the Colonial Dames of America. The front garden, retaining its original hour-glass pattern, is enclosed by an iron picket fence. William Makepeace Thackeray visited this home in 1853 and again in 1856, when he came to Savannah to give his readings. A letter that he wrote at the drawing-room desk speaks of the tranquility of the city at that time and of its broad, shady streets. General Robert E. Lee visited here in 1870 while he was touring the South for his health. In the drawing room on March 12, 1912, Mrs. Juliette Gordon Low (1860-1927), daughter-in-law of Andrew Low, organized a small group of Girl Guides, later called Girl Scouts. Other troops were formed, and

Mrs. Low opened National Headquarters in Washington the following year. On her birthday, October 31, she is honored nationwide as the founder of the Girl Scouts of America. The Girl Scout headquarters, directly back of the Low House, is the first established in America.

(WEST OF BULL STREET)

32. SITE OF OGLETHORPE'S FIRST CAMP, on Yamacraw Bluff, in the small park on the north side of W. Bay Street, is marked by a marble bench placed by the Colonial Dames.

33. An OLD COBBLESTONE ROADWAY, W. Bay and Barnard Streets, descends to the level of the broad river where century-old buildings with stone masonry and iron railings stand clear and commanding against the bluff.

34. TELFAIR ACADEMY OF ARTS AND SCIENCES *(open 12-5 Mon.; 10-5 Tues.-Sat.; 3-5 Sun. and Thanksgiving Day)*, 121 Barnard Street, is one of the finest art galleries in the South. The stuccoed brick building, believed to have been designed by William Jay about 1820, suggests an eighteenth-century Italian villa, with its belt cornice, high attic parapet, heavy Corinthian portico, and pedestaled figures. The building, which stands on the site of the Royal Government House, was bequeathed in 1875 by Mary Telfair, sister of the original owner, to the Georgia Historical Society, which opened the academy in 1885. Since 1920 this gallery has been conducted by the Telfair Academy of Arts and Sciences Corporation.

35. The GILES BECU HOUSE *(private)*, 120 W. Oglethorpe Avenue, is an unpretentious two-story frame structure with chamfered porch posts built sometime before 1800 by Giles Becu.

36. The WARING HOUSE *(private)*, 127 W. Oglethorpe Avenue, constructed of brick in 1816, is notable for its Georgian Colonial doorway, iron balcony, and fine Palladian window.

37. The MCALPIN HOUSE *(private)*, 230 Barnard Street, was designed and built by Henry McAlpin about 1835. Of elaborate Greek Revival design, it is impressive because of its massive Corinthian columns and the curved sandstone steps at each end. It was constructed of Savannah Grey brick from the Hermitage kilns, but this virtue has since been obscured in stucco. Its owner at the time of Sherman's occupation of the city, Aaron Champion, a wealthy banker, hid his gold hoard here in a cistern, and none suspecting this clandestine relation between the house and wealth, he afterward recovered it all except a single ten-dollar gold piece, perhaps exacted by the spirit of the well for its rectitude.

38. HERTY FOUNDATION LABORATORY, Southeastern Shipyard, was estab-

lished in 1932 as a pilot plant to demonstrate the feasibility of making paper pulp from Georgia pine. The plant was directed by Charles H. Herty (1867-1938), a native of Milledgeville and a nationally known chemist who, possessing scientific vision and undiscouraged by the prevailing "common sense" of the day, secured the co-operation of the Industrial Commission of Savannah, Inc., the Chemical Foundation of New York, and the State of Georgia, in his experimental work. Since Herty's death, the laboratory has been conducted by the Herty Foundation, the committee members of which are appointed by the governor of the state.

Dr. Herty discovered that second-growth pines, before the development of the heartwood, do not contain more gum than red spruce, the northern wood previously used for high-grade newsprint paper. Since in Georgia there are extensive areas suited for little else than reforestation, and because the sort of pines used for paper reproduce themselves here three times faster than spruce in its northern range—which means that the Southeast has added enormously to its neotechnic productive scope by becoming a major source of pulp—the future economic significance of Herty's discoveries could hardly be measured, in any intelligent sense, by a mere citation of monetary statistics, impressive though they may be. Successful experiments were also conducted in making fine paper from the black and tupelo gums.

If someone were to advance the notion that the future of Savannah is far more likely to evolve from the Herty Laboratory than to revolve around the port of that name, it would perhaps be a step in the right direction, and nearer to truth than likely phrases usually are.

(YAMACRAW)

YAMACRAW, along the west side of W. Broad Street, stands on the site of an Indian village of the same name, where Oglethorpe parleyed with the Indians.

39. WEST BROAD STREET NEGRO SCHOOL, 111 W. Broad Street, the first Negro public school in Savannah, was established in 1878 by the board of education and replaced Beach Institute, founded eleven years earlier· by the American Missionary Association. The building, a three-story stuccoed brick house of Classical Revival style, is another of the buildings attributed to William Jay. Distinctive details are the Doric portico, the ironwork, the rear façade cresting, the graceful hall columns, and a white Adam mantel. The house was built about 1818 for William Scarborough, whose mercantile interest made him one of the owners of the *S. S. Savannah.*

40. The FIRST BRYAN BAPTIST CHURCH (Negro), 565 W. Bryan Street,

dates from 1785, when Andrew Bryan, a slave who had been baptized by the noted Negro pastor George Leile, began preaching to a group of Negroes in the barn of his master's plantation, Brampton (*see* TOUR *1*). He soon had a following in Savannah where Reverend Abraham Marshall, a white missionary, baptized forty-five additional members in 1788. Organizing them into the First African Baptist Church, he ordained Andrew Bryan as their first pastor. Despite many hardships, during which the Negroes resumed worship at Brampton for two years, the congregation was able to purchase the lot on which this church stands, for a permanent house of worship in 1797. Outgrowing this building, the congregation moved to Franklin Square in 1832, but it proved to be a year of dissension. Most of the members returned to the old site under the leadership of their pastor, Andrew Marshall, calling themselves the Third African Baptist Church and later the First Bryan Baptist Church. The original frame building has been replaced by a brick one.

POINTS OF INTEREST IN THE ENVIRONS

TOUR *1*

Savannah—Thunderbolt—Fort Pulaski—Savannah Beach, US 80, 18.5 m.

(This tour begins on VICTORY DRIVE, at Bull Street, which intersection is reached from the downtown area by taking Whitaker Street south to West Victory Drive, then making a left turn and going east two blocks to Victory Drive and Bull.)

In the environs of Savannah attractive residential suburbs are grouped about the curve of a river or on a tree-crowned bluff. The newer suburban houses in the modern American style are trim on their well-kept lawns planted in shrubbery, and many have their own docks and boat houses in the rear. The intricate waterways and salt-water rivers afford good fishing, crabbing, and swimming.

Many Negroes who have found that their daily necessities may be conveniently found along the river have formed permanent, self-sustaining communities near the white settlements.

Victory Drive (US 80), built as a memorial to the Savannah soldiers of World War I, extends east from the city to Thunderbolt. The twin thoroughfare has a central parkway planted in azaleas and lined with tall palmettoes like giant sentinels against the even skyline.

DAFFIN PARK, *1 m.* (R), is an exceptionally large municipal park, with a fresh-water lake for swimming, tennis courts, an emergency landing field, and Grayson Stadium, home of the Savannah Indians, of the South Atlantic Baseball League.

At *1.5 m.* is a junction with Bee Road.

Right on this road to GEORGIA HUSSARS HEADQUARTERS (*private*), *0.1 m.,* a large yellow brick building housing a unit of the 108th Georgia Cavalry. According to claim, this unit is the second oldest military organization in the United States. On February 13, 1936, the Georgia Hussars celebrated their 200th anniversary, claiming that their organization is an outgrowth of the Oglethorpe Rangers, founded by General Oglethorpe on February 13, 1736, to protect Savannah against raids by Spaniards and Indians. Though it is not known when this cavalry troop became the Georgia Hussars, records indicate that the name was used as early as 1796.

At *2 m.* on US 80 is the junction with Skidaway Road (*see* ENVIRONS TOUR 2, below).

THUNDERBOLT, *3.2 m.,* incorporated as Wassaw, was originally a small Indian settlement whose name derived from the tradition that lightning once struck here and started a spring. The quaint harbor with its fishing boats, yachts, and other small craft speaks idiomatically of the sea.

1. Left from Thunderbolt on Bonaventure Road to BONAVENTURE, *1.5 m.* (R) Savannah's beautiful historic cemetery. Cloaked somberly in gray moss, the branches of old oaks meet like Gothic arches above the drives and faint tombstones. Even in spring, when crimson azaleas and white and pink camellias lend the cemetery splashes of color, it is the neutral tone of trailing moss and weathered stone that most truly reflects Bonaventure. Brown fallen leaves and here and there, in season, a purple wistaria blossom or one of the yellow jessamine, float past like hours without an arrow, on the sluggish river.

2. Right from Thunderbolt on a paved road to GEORGIA STATE COLLEGE (Negro), *1.2 m.* (L), a unit of the University System of Georgia. On its campus, shaded by moss-covered oaks and bordered on the south by a tidewater stream, are thirty buildings valued at more than a million dollars. The buildings are of wood, concrete, or red brick, and most of them show either a modified Georgian or Greek Revival influence. A few of the frame buildings were houses of the old Postell Plantation. Adjacent to the campus is a sizable farm where students carry out agricultural routines and problems in connection with college courses in agriculture.

Courses in the following are offered: Arts and Sciences, Agriculture, Business, Home Economics, Industrial Education, and Teacher Training. The college is accredited by the Southern Association of Colleges and Secondary Schools and by the Georgia State Department of Education. It is a member of the Association of Colleges and Secondary

Schools for Negro Youth. Special courses have also been offered under the G. I. Bill of Rights in carpentry, auto-mechanics, masonry, quantity cookery, painting, electricity, steam fitting, radio, and poultry raising. Chartered in 1890 as a land-grant college, the school was opened for a preliminary session at Athens in 1891 and was transferred to this campus the following year.

Between Thunderbolt and Savannah Beach, US 80 is a causeway, lined with palmettoes and oleanders. It crosses wide marshes, wooded islands, and dark tidal rivers.

The Route crosses the Wilmington River, up which small craft move slowly, and passes to Whitemarsh Island, a heavily-wooded island where many struggles occurred during the War between the States. The Federals desired it as an entrance way to the southern plantations and communities, rich with supplies.

At Whitemarsh take the left-hand road to OATLAND ISLAND, about 1.5 m. to a large building which was formerly the National Conductors' Home for retired members, but now this and sixteen other permanent buildings house the Technical Development Division of the Communicable Disease Center of the U. S. Public Health Service.

US 80 crosses Turner's Creek to WILMINGTON ISLAND, which is higher than the other islands and is forested with pine and moss-covered oaks. It is the site of many private estates, two golf courses, and the modern, well-appointed General Oglethorpe Hotel.

At SOUTH-END POINT on Wilmington Island, Confederate breastworks are still visible on the site where General A. R. Lawton massed defenses to cover approaches to Savannah from the Wilmington River. At this time the island was divided into small plantations. From the mouth of the river there is an excellent view overlooking Wassaw Sound and the Atlantic Ocean.

McQueen Island is reached by crossing Bull River, the largest of the tidal streams connecting the Savannah River with Wassaw Sound and the Atlantic Ocean.

Towards the end of McQueen Island the rose-brick walls (L) of Fort Pulaski are visible.

Turn L. at the flagpole and entrance, and continue across the bridge, over the South Channel of the Savannah River, to FORT PULASKI NATIONAL MONUMENT on Cockspur Island (*open to the public daily, 8:30 A.M. to 5:30 P.M., throughout the year except on Christmas Day; attendants; by arrangement in advance organizations and groups are given special service; nominal charge for all persons over 12, but children under 12 admitted free when in charge of an adult; groups of school children between the ages of 12 and 18 charged Federal tax only*).

Fort Pulaski is one of the best preserved fortresses constructed for coast defense during the first half of the nineteenth century. It was established as a national monument on October 13, 1924, by presidential proclamation, after being abandoned since the Spanish-American War. In 1933 it passed from the War Department to the supervision of the National Park Service of the U. S. Department of the Interior. Today the monument area includes 5,427.39 acres on McQueen and Cockspur Island. The fort, facing seaward and guarding the entrance to the Savannah River, is itself encircled by two moats spanned by drawbridges. On the ground between the moats are breastworks, large earthen mounds on which grow cactus, thorn ash, sweet myrtles, and cassena berries. Because of their crescent shape these mounds are called, technically, *demilunes* (Fr., half-moons).

Entrance to the inner fort is through the portcullis, a dark, vaulted brick passage leading from the drawbridge. The massive brick walls of the fortification, from 7 to 11 feet thick and 32 feet high, enclose a green parade ground with officers' quarters, arched casemates, and bombproof chambers, each arranged to mount a cannon which was fired through an embrasure in the outer wall. The floors of these chambers are of Georgia pine, with all nailheads covered by wooden pegs to prevent them from giving off sparks. A four-foot layer of sand and shell covering the lead roof of the fort forms the terreplein, which serves to protect the casemates and to make an upper platform on which other guns can be mounted. In early days rain, filtering through the sand and shell, was stored in large cisterns as a water supply.

Fort Pulaski was the third fortification erected on Cockspur Island, the first being Fort George, a small block structure built in 1761 and dismantled in 1776 by American patriots. On the ruins of this garrison Fort Greene, a second small fort, was erected in 1794 but was swept away by the great hurricane of 1804. The sites of these earlier forts cannot be exactly identified because time and weather have altered the shape of the island. The War of 1812 had published the need of coastal defense, and in 1816 Congress established a Board of Engineers for Seacoast Fortifications. As a part of this development, Cockspur Island was selected as the place for a new fort in the first part of the 1820's. Brigadier General Simon Bernard, Napoleon's chief engineer, was associated with the new fortification movement from 1816 to 1831. Work actually began in 1829 and continued as planned until 1831, when Lieutenant J. F. K. Mansfield, taking command at Cockspur Island, revised Bernard's plan, and completed the fort during the fourteen years of his supervision. Robert E. Lee's first assignment after graduation from West Point was to Cockspur Island, where as an officer of engineers he assisted with the preliminary plan until 1831. In 1833 the new fort was named Pulaski in honor of Count Casimir Pulaski, who served the American cause in the Revolution and died at the siege of Savannah.

The shell-torn masonry at the eastern end of the fortification recalls the dramatic part that Fort Pulaski played not only in the War between the States but in the annals of military defense. Joseph E. Brown, Governor of Georgia, learning that Federal soldiers were being assigned to Fort Sumter, sent A. R. Lawton, then colonel of the 1st Volunteer Regiment, to occupy the ungarrisoned Fort Pulaski on January 3, 1861. (Since Georgia did not formally secede from the Union until January 19, technically the command was an act of treason.) Federal batteries of the new rifled cannon, and other sorts, were set up on Tybee Island early in 1862. On April 11, after thirty hours of sustained bombardment, during which the southeastern angle and wall of Fort Pulaski were effectively breached, Colonel Charles H. Olmstead, the 25-year-old Confederate commander, surrendered sometime after the noon hour. A fortress believed to be a model of its sort and impregnable to cannon fire had been destroyed in a brief interval by the discovery of a new industrial technique, the rifling of cannon barrels. The loss of 385 men with their officers, 48 cannon, and both ammunition and supplies, was incidental in importance.

Without adequate industrial means, and thus crucially dependent on England and the Continent for the matériel of war, the South actually suffered irreparable harm when the mouth of the port at Savannah was sealed against foreign trade. There is no common measure between field strategy and the domain of economic warfare, and yet one may suppose that the freezing of the port to trade was equivalent to the loss of a tidy number of major battles.

When John Wesley came to Georgia as a missionary, he landed on Cockspur Island—then known as Peeper Island—on February 6, 1736. The Georgia Society, Colonial Dames of America, has placed a memorial cross on the site where it is believed Wesley knelt to thank God for a safe voyage. On the detached tip point of Cockspur Island is the abandoned Cockspur Light, which for many years served to mark the river channel.

Where US 80 crosses Lazaretto Creek, on the Tybee Island side is (L) the site of the Federal Battery that briefly reduced Fort Pulaski and thus technically emended the rules of combat.

FORT SCREVEN, *17 m.*, known first as Fort Graham, became an active army post on March 3, 1898, the reservation area having been bought much earlier from John Screven and J. C. Rowland by Congressional acts of 1808 and 1820. A circular drive leads from the fort area to TYBEE LIGHTHOUSE, which marks the mouth of the Savannah River. This point dates from Colonial times, for here in 1753 General Ogle-thorpe built a tower "constructed of the best pine, strongly timbered, raised upon cedar piles, a brickwork around the bottom." Before 1755 a brick tower was erected but not lighted, and it was not until 1791 that adjustments were made and a light installed. Partly destroyed and its light extinguished by Confederate forces in 1862, the lighthouse was rebuilt five years later.

The route continues over Tybee Island to the Atlantic Ocean.

At *18.5 m.* is SAVANNAH BEACH, the popular playground and summer resort where swimming, fishing, boating, and a number of other out-door sports are available. It has adequate hotel and cottage accommo-dations. The beach is at the southern end of Tybee Island, which is a V-shaped sandbar running 3.8 miles along the Atlantic and 2.5 miles up the Savannah River.

During the War between the States, while preparing for the knock-out blow to Fort Pulaski, the Federals landed cannon on the south end of the island, and spent painful days dragging them through the ob-structing marshes to the position opposite Pulaski.

TOUR 2

Savannah—Wormsloe—Fort Wimberley—Bethesda; Skidaway Road, La Roche Avenue, and Ferguson Avenue, 11.2 m.

Two miles E. of Bull Street, Skidaway Road runs S. from Victory Drive *o m.* At *1 m.* is the junction with La Roche Avenue; L. on La Roche Avenue.

ISLE OF HOPE, *6 m.*, an attractive year-round settlement situated on a crescent-shaped bluff above the river, began as the summer colony of Parkerburg in 1840 and was given its present name in 1898. Steam transportation service was made available and amusement concessions were built and operated by the railroad. In the summer months chil-dren play in the shallow waters while their mothers gossip beneath the large oak trees. Motorboats putter about the small wooden docks, where drying bathing suits and crabbing nets blow in the breeze.

At *6.5 m.*, at the narrow neck of Isle of Hope (R), A. M. Barbee began his famous DIAMOND BACK TERRAPIN FARM in 1893. It developed until thousands of terrapins were shipped annually to northern markets. The beautifully marked terrapins are not salable until they are between five and nine years old.

Immediately past this point the road makes a sharp turn (R).

WORMSLOE (*private*), 7.7 *m*. (L), is renowned not only for its gardens but also as one of Georgia's few colonial plantations that has remained in the possession of the same family for centuries. Soon after the founding of the colony in 1733, Noble Jones received from the Georgia trustees a grant of 500 acres, but it was not formally certified by the royal government until 1756. Jones set out mulberry trees for the culture of silkworms—hence the name "Wormsloe." Because the tract was strategically situated on the inland waterway leading south to Spanish territory, General Oglethorpe selected it as the site for a garrison. Noble Jones was placed in command of a small wooden fort built under his direction to guard the narrows of the Skidaway River. In 1763 Jones received a second grant of 500 acres from the crown adjacent to the first, but only 300 acres of this second tract are included in the 800 acres of Wormsloe.

One of the most prominent names in the history of the estate is that of George Wymberly Jones DeRenne, who began a library of Georgia history. DeRenne, born Jones, added to his name a French modification of Van Deren, the name of his maternal grandmother, and became known as G. W. J. DeRenne. The library begun by him was destroyed by the bummers who lagged behind Sherman's army, but the owner immediately began to reconstruct it. This second collection was bequeathed to his son Everard, who willed it to the state, and it now forms the basis of the literature and history collection of the library in the state capitol. Book collecting was on the way to becoming a generic trait when his son, Wymberley Jones DeRenne, in 1891 began to assemble a third library, containing rare volumes, maps, old documents, manuscripts, and engravings. This library was housed in a white stone building at Wormsloe until its sale by Wymberley Wormsloe DeRenne in 1938 to the University of Georgia. It now forms a special collection in the university library at Athens.

WORMSLOE HOUSE, enlarged around the middle of the nineteenth century on earlier tabby foundations, was remodeled some ten years or so ago for Dr. and Mrs. Craig Barrow. Mrs. Barrow is the daughter of Wymberley Jones DeRenne and present owner of the estate. The house, overlooking the Isle of Hope River, contains ante-bellum mantels and many other details of interest. The grounds, carpeted with large-leaf Algerian ivy, are shaded by lofty oaks that form an effective relief for the azaleas and camellias, many of which have grown as large as young trees. Behind the house a series of formal walled gardens introduces an interesting note of definition.

An oak-bordered drive leads more than a mile from the arched entrance gate to FORT WIMBERLEY, a ruined tabby fortification built in 1741 to replace the earlier wooden structure guarding the narrows of the Skidaway River. (It was this later fort, equipped with four brass cannon, that Mary Jones commanded when the Spanish and Indians attacked. In places the ruined walls stand as high as eight feet. It is believed that the bastions, which extended from each corner, and the powder chamber were roofed over but that the main part of the enclosure was open. Although two centuries have weathered the tabby walls, the embrasures through which the colonists fired are still distinct. For many months a Confederate battalion stationed here successfully prevented Federal ships from passing on the inland water route.)

At *8.7 m.* is the intersection with Ferguson Avenue; L. on Ferguson Avenue.

BETHESDA (*open*), *11.2 m.*, the oldest existing orphanage in America, occupies a group of substantial Georgian Colonial buildings set on a bluff overlooking a tidal river. The landscaping follows the scheme initiated by the Trustees' Garden Club when the orphanage was opened in 1740 by George Whitefield and James Habersham, acting colonial governor. A small, well-proportioned GEORGIAN CHAPEL, presented in 1924 by the Georgia Society of Colonial Dames of America, is a reproduction of Whitefield's church in England.

Bethesda, meaning House of Mercy, was established as an asylum for needy boys and girls. Although the land was granted by the Georgia trustees for an orphanage, the institution functioned primarily as a school and was among the most successful enterprises of the colonists. Besides the rudiments: writing, reading, and arithmetic, instruction was given in religion, trades, and especially agriculture, *e.g.* the care and culture of silkworms. This and the Salzburgers' orphanage at Ebenezer might be reasonably referred to as the region's first agricultural schools. Around 1746 historical sources speak of Bethesda as a "Latin school," and because the English clergy were college bred, training on the grammatical level may well have included much Latin. At the death of Whitefield in 1770 the grant was bequeathed to Selina, Countess of Huntingdon, who had helped the school with its monetary problems. Two years later she sent students from her seminary in Wales, supposing that Bethesda might be transformed into a mission school for training evangelists. This plan, however, failed, and when she died in 1791 it came about that the orphanage was discontinued, whereupon it was claimed by the state government, and committed to a board of trustees.

In 1801 the school was reopened by the trustees, who were members of the philanthropic Union Society. This society goes back to 1750 when it was founded in Savannah by three men, each of a different religion—Peter Tondee, a Catholic; Abraham Sheftal, a Jew; and Richard Milledge, a Protestant—for charitable purposes that included the care of orphans. Four years later, however, the building burned and the property was sold, and it was not until 1855 that the Union Society actually bought the property and revived the historic institution. During the War between the States the buildings were used as a military hospital, and at the close of the war were occupied by freed Negro slaves. Since its restoration to the Union Society in 1867, Bethesda has continued its work without interruption.

Jasper Spring, *1.6 m.;* Site of the Hermitage, *1.9 m.;* Union Paper and Bag Co., *2.5 m.;* Irene Mound, *5.7 m.;* Silk Hope Plantation, *5.9 m.;* Savannah Sugar Refinery, *8.3 m.* (*see* STATE TOUR *1*).

*

PART TWO

TOURS

*

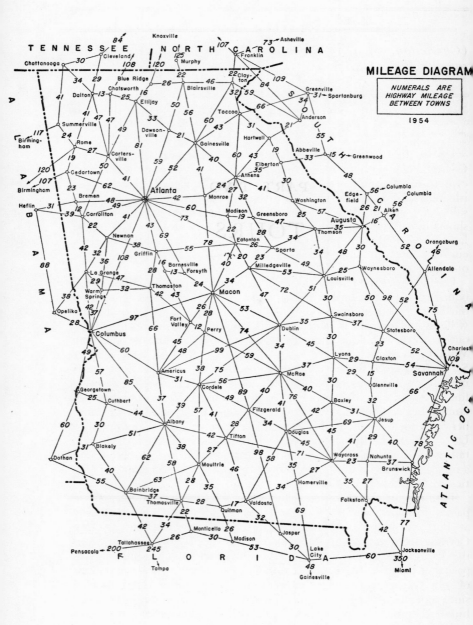

MILEAGE DIAGRAM

NUMERALS ARE
HIGHWAY MILEAGE
BETWEEN TOWNS

1954

TOUR I

(Charleston, S. C.)—Savannah—Darien—Brunswick—(Jacksonville, Fla.); US 17.

South Carolina Line to Florida Line about 134 m.—Roadbed hard-surfaced throughout. Seaboard Air Line Ry. roughly parallels route. All types of accommodations in Savannah and Brunswick; limited elsewhere.

US 17, the Coastal Highway, crosses the lowest part of the Georgia Coastal Plain with its many tidal creeks and its swamps dense with cypress, tupelo, and bay trees. Giant live oaks hung with ghostly Spanish moss add a note of timeless mystery. Along the route are many salt water marshes that vary in color from the light green of tender shoots in early spring to the yellow of dying grass in fall. The higher land is wooded with pine and palmetto whose dark shadows move curiously upon the light sandy soil which seems to flow endlessly without depth.

US 17 crosses the red waters of the SAVANNAH RIVER, *0 m.,* the natural boundary between South Carolina and Georgia, on bridges which link one delta island with another. A high causeway lined with swamp willows and myrtles is built across the islands. These fertile islands, once covered with flourishing rice fields, are now a part of the Savannah Wildlife Refuge established in April 1927 by the Fish and Wildlife Service of the U. S. Department of the Interior. Of the 12,900 acres making up this former rice field area about half fall inside the Georgia line. Savannah Refuge is an especially favorable location on the Atlantic Flyway, and all sorts of waterfowl, but principally ducks, numbering in the forty thousands, concentrate upon it in the winter months. US 17 bisects the Refuge and one often sees mallard, black duck, pintail, wood duck, ruddy duck, and teal in addition to ibis, heron, and a mixture of other wading birds, from the road. No recreational facilities are available in this area.

Through an entrance gate (L), *2 m.,* a half-mile, oak-lined drive passes through a semitropical garden to the SAVANNAH SUGAR REFINERY at Port Wentworth. Manufacturing the widely distributed Dixie Crystals from raw sugar mostly from the tropics but in part from the Everglades at Clewiston, Florida, this factory has a melting capacity of about 3,000,000 and a storage capacity of 120,000,000 pounds of raw sugar daily. The capacity has been more than doubled since operations began in July of 1917, and currently over seven hundred employees are engaged in the daily production of some thirty carloads of refined sugar. Around the plant is a fifteen-acre mill village with a hospital and also a hotel which however is exclusively for the use of employees and guests of the company.

At *4 m.* is the junction with a graded road.

Left on this road to WHITEHALL PLANTATION (*private*), *0.5 m.*, on land granted to Joseph Gibbons in 1759. A green-shuttered, white frame house (L) is set in a beautiful grove of large oaks along the Savannah River.

At *5.3 m.* is the junction with a sandy road.

Left on this road to IRENE MOUND, *0.7 m.*, on the bank of Pipemakers' Creek. Archeological exploration has revealed, six feet below the surface, what is believed to have been the cellar of the schoolhouse of the Indian mission established in 1735 by John Wesley, Benjamin Ingham, and the Moravians. Nearby was the Indian Village of New Yamacraw, founded by Chief Tomochichi after the white man's occupation of Savannah.

At *7.3 m.* is the junction with a paved road.

Left on this road to the largest manufacturing unit of the UNION BAG & PAPER CORPORATION, which extended its operations to the South as a result of Charles Herty's experiments in the production of paper from Georgia slash pine pulp. This plant manufactures a daily output of 1,350 tons of kraft paper and paperboard as well as thirty-five million bags. It currently employs about five thousand people whose total annual wages are in excess of $15,000,000.

At *7.4 m.* is the junction with a sandy road.

Left on this road to the SITE OF THE HERMITAGE (L), *1 m.* In the early Colonial period negotiations between Oglethorpe and Tomochichi reserved this land as the Indians' hunting ground. In 1750, however, a 100-acre tract was granted to Joseph Ottolenghe, who was employed by the trustees of the colony to further the silk industry in Savannah. This plantation, which has changed hands many times, has been used for rice culture, brick burning, lumbering, and as the site for a Colonial tavern.

In the early part of the nineteenth century it was purchased by a Scotsman, Henry McAlpin, who utilized the clay soil to manufacture the famous "Savannah Grey" brick used in many structures of the city. Whenever an old house is torn down these brick are eagerly sought after for new buildings by those who have a sense of age and beauty. In 1820 McAlpin facilitated the shipping of his brick by constructing from the kilns to the river a rough horsecar railroad, one of the earliest in America. For many years his brick manor designed in the Regency style, with its curving, double-entrance stairway, was a standard of perfection for architects. Gradually, however, the place fell to ruin from neglect and vandalism, and in the middle 1930's Henry Ford bought all of the buildings of the plantation. For a while it was rumored that he would restore them and thus enrich the historical imagination of Georgia, but he decided to raze them, and used the brick in building a house on the Ogeechee River near Ways (*see below*). Two of the slave huts were restored and placed on display at the Ford historical center in Dearborn, Michigan. All that remains of the plantation is an impressive avenue of oaks, and a collection of photographs and measured drawings in the Library of Congress.

A small wooden shelter (R) covers JASPER SPRING, *8.7 m.,* where Sergeant William Jasper, aided by Sergeant John Newton, captured ten British soldiers who were taking American prisoners to Savannah to be hanged. Jasper was killed in the Battle of Savannah, and a large monument to him stands in the center of Madison Square in that city.

SAVANNAH, *10.3 m.* (21 alt., 119,638 pop.) (*see* SAVANNAH).

Points of Interest: Telfair Academy of Arts and Sciences, Herty Pulp and Paper Laboratory, Armstrong Junior College, Atlantic Coast Line Docks, Bethesda Orphanage, Wormsloe, and others.

Savannah is at the junction with US 80 (*see* TOUR *9*) and with State 21 (*see* TOUR *14*).

SILK HOPE PLANTATION (R), *16.2 m.,* is part of the 500-acre tract granted in 1756 to James Habersham, who in 1750 had been appointed silk commissioner by the Colonial trustees in London. One of the first industrial enterprises in Georgia was the manufacture of silk thread at the filature in Savannah. So great was the confidence in the suitability of Georgia's coastal climate for silkworm culture that the figure of a silkworm was placed on the great seal of the colony. With its vast fields in white mulberry trees and its gardens designed by an English horticulturist, Silk Hope was a noted silk plantation. Eventually the hope in silk declined, and was replaced by the cultivation of rice and indigo which encouraged the use of slave labor. During the early part of the twentieth century lumber companies cut much of the timber. This is a typical example of decline in this area.

US 17 crosses the LITTLE OGEECHEE RIVER, *17.6 m.,* one of the numerous salt-water estuaries indenting the Georgia coast. Its still, black water reflects the moss-covered branches of the black gum, oak, and tupelo trees that crowd its banks. This small river provides some good fishing.

At *18.5 m.* is the entrance (L) to LEBANON (*private*), originally a part of the Colonial holdings by grants from George II to James Devaux and Philip Delegal in 1756 and 1758 but now owned by Mrs. Mills B. Lane. The plantation house is white clapboard, placed upon a raised basement, and with double mounted galleries extending around the front and sides of its two-story construction. It was built in the early part of the nineteenth century. Mrs. Lane in restoring the original house added a Georgian wing, and has added an extensive garden of broadleaf evergreens and other semitropical shrubs and flowers, which extends to the Little Ogeechee River.

HOPETON (L), *21.2 m.,* is a farm on the site of a Colonial plantation.

Of the original plantation buildings, only the ante-bellum slave cabins remain; Negro laborers live in these small, whitewashed, frame huts with clay chimneys.

At *22.3 m.* is the junction with a private road.

Left on this road to WILD HERN PLANTATION (*private*), *3 m.* (R), a large tract of land which was granted in 1755 by King George II to Francis Harris, a Savannah merchant, and remained in the family until 1935 when it was bought by Mr. and Mrs. Shelby Myrick of Savannah. The original grant hangs in the house, specifying a thousand acres, more or less; and the house itself is in the story-and-a-half Colonial style, built over a brick basement, with sloping roof and dormer windows. It is today basically unchanged. All the old timbers, the English bricks, and some of the flooring and side paneling remain as they were. At the southeast corner of the house is a tall palm tree that was planted by Elizabeth Harris in 1780 when she came to Wild Hern as a bride.

The plantation was named Wild Hern for the Hampshire, England, estate of Mary Goodall, who married Colonel Harris. Hern is the old contraction for heron in England.

The BARBOUR LATHROP PLANT INTRODUCTION GARDEN, *23 m.* (R), is a 53-acre experimental station or garden, devoted to the testing and propagation of new plant introductions of possible value to the horticultural or agricultural welfare of the people of the United States. The garden was established in 1920 by the U. S. Department of Agriculture, the land being donated to the Department by Mr. Barbour Lathrop who was greatly interested in the possibilities of bamboo as a new crop for southern growers. The donation of the land included a well-developed bamboo grove which is visible from the highway. It resembles a low hill completely covered with ferns. This grove is the growth of a single plant of the Timber bamboo, the largest culms of which attain a height of sixty or seventy feet, with basal diameters of five to six inches. It is maintained as a demonstration planting and is one of the best developed of its sort in the Eastern United States. Considerable quantities of material have been made available to those investigating the strength and other properties of the canes.

In addition to the original bamboo planting, about 170 other varieties of bamboo have been established. These vary greatly in size, hardiness, and other features. The smallest varieties are low-growing types suitable for use as ground covers like grass, while the largest are tropical sorts that attain a height of a hundred and twenty feet and are a foot in diameter. Some varieties are peculiarly suited for planting to prevent soil erosion, others may have value for forages, some produce the edible shoots of commerce, others produce canes of value for use as tool or broom handles, staffs, fishing poles and rods, support for radio and TV antennas, flag poles, mast and boom for sail boats, stakes for plants and for making fish nets; and a quantity of bamboo is used in making furniture, porch and window shades, and to panel rooms. The garden has furnished the Herty Foundation Laboratory, in Savannah, with many tons of bamboo material, which has facilitated the work of the laboratory in the development of practical commercial processes for the production of paper and textiles from bamboo pulp.

Many new and little known plants and trees are also growing in the garden, such as Chinese chestnuts, varieties of pears, persimmons, and some fiber plants and plants with medicinal properties. Experiments have been conducted with the Chinese waternut which has long been an important part of many Chinese recipes. The experimental and cultural information formulated by the garden has often resulted in the commercial production of new plants and crops. Notable among these in addition to bamboo are tung oil trees, new lawn grasses for the South, and a blight-resistant pear of superior quality.

A marker (R) at 24.7 m. indicates the SITE OF THE KING'S FERRY REVOLUTIONARY ENGAGEMENT. Colonel John White, with Captain George Melvin and Captain A. G. Elholm and three soldiers, on the night of October 1, 1779, determined to capture the five vessels and 130 men of Captain French, a British commander. French, intending to reinforce General Augustine Prevost and attack Savannah, had landed his forces at this point on the Ogeechee River twenty miles from the city, arranging the ships to protect him against a sea attack.

A short distance away, the six patriots built many watch fires at such intervals as to convince the British that they were surrounded by a large force. Throughout the night the stratagem was furthered by much shifting, marching between fires, and loud calls to imaginary sentinels. White then rode alone to the British camp and told French that the American troops demanded unconditional surrender as the price of his life. The frightened British commander agreed, thanking him for his humanity. The five vessels were burned and the British were conducted to Sunbury under the "protection" of two of the Americans, while White, who was ostensibly in the rear restraining his impatient forces, was collecting the surrounding militia.

US 17 crosses the Kings Ferry Bridge, 24.8 m., over the OGEECHEE RIVER.

At 27.3 m. is the junction with the Ways Station Road.

1. Left on this road is WAYS, 0.5 m., a model community which was developed by the late Henry Ford according to the plan of the one at Dearborn, Michigan. Beginning his operations here in 1925 with the purchase of several old plantations, Ford added to his holdings until he had a total of 70,000 acres in Bryan and Chatham counties.

The Ways Station road continues to what was formerly the HENRY FORD ESTATE, 1.5 m., composed of the old Richmond, Cherry Hill, Whitehall, and Strathy Hall plantations, all on the Ogeechee River in a setting of large, moss-covered oaks. At Richmond, Ford built a house of the "Savannah Grey" bricks he obtained from the Hermitage.

After Mr. Ford's death these properties were assigned to the Ford Foundation, a colossal enterprise which supports worthy causes in the realm of education, and were sold to the International Paper Co. of New York City; specifically to the Southern Kraft Timberland Corporation, in 1951. The entire area has been placed under permanent forest management by that company. There is no information to suggest that Mr. Ford's social program will be continued at any time in the future.

On a bluff overlooking the Ogeechee River is the SITE OF HARDWICK, 7 m. After John Reynolds, first Royal Governor of the colony (1754-57), had selected the site in 1755, he obtained appropriations for public works and the entertainment of Indians and had William DeBrahm, noted French engineer, plan the town. The Governor initiated a movement to change the Colonial seat of government from Savannah to Hardwick, and many lots were granted and sold before the plan was abandoned. The town became a trading village and later the seat of Bryan County. After the county seat was removed in 1814, Hardwick began to decline and, despite an effort at revival in 1866, became one of Georgia's dead towns.

The SITE OF FORT MCALLISTER, *8 m.,* is on the Ogeechee River opposite Genesis Point. This earthwork, erected by the Confederates, was one of the principal defenses of Savannah and withstood attacks during 1862 and 1863. On December 13, 1864, however, the fort was taken by General William B. Hazen after Major George W. Anderson had made a gallant but unsuccessful effort to defend it with 200 men. After this defeat General Hardee withdrew his Confederate forces from Savannah.

2. Right from the junction on a paved road to the RICHMOND HILL FISH HATCHERY, *0.3 m.,* one of the five hatcheries controlled by the State Game and Fish Commission. This location was known earlier as the Henry Ford Fish Hatchery, the 75-acre tract having been donated to the state by Henry Ford. It is currently engaged in hatching bass, bream, and crappie.

FREEDMEN'S GROVE (L), *37.4 m.,* is a Negro settlement on land deeded by the owner to his former slaves immediately after the War between the States. Although this was not a common practice, there are several instances of such gifts in Georgia.

MIDWAY, *40.9 m.* (30 alt., 228 pop.), a small, oak-shaded village, was once the religious center of a large plantation area known as the Midway District. The site is about midway between Savannah and Darien, but the name may have been derived from the English river Medway. In 1695 a group of Puritans from Dorchester, Massachusetts, moved to South Carolina to conduct missionary work among the Indians. There they founded another settlement called Dorchester, but, because of an unhealthful climate, sent scouting parties to look for a site in Georgia. In 1752 two families came to settle in the district, and by 1771 there were thirty-eight families and five single men on grants totaling more than 32,000 acres. These Puritan settlers were among the first in the colony to oppose the British. The first church, a log structure, was established in 1754. Congregational in polity but served by Presbyterian ministers, it was the religious center not only of the Puritans, but of the prosperous rice planters of the district. The roads that led to Midway became thoroughfares of fashion as the landowners drove leisurely in their carriages to the little church.

MIDWAY CHURCH (L), a white clapboarded structure, 40 feet wide and 60 feet long, is surrounded by a grove of moss-covered oaks. The exterior, reminiscent of a Colonial New England meeting house, has a double row of shuttered, small-paned windows. In the pedimented front gable end are two small circular openings. Surmounting the roof is a slender square tower with crowning belfry and octagonal spire. This building, the fourth on the same site, was erected in 1792, and the old slave gallery and high pulpit remain unchanged. For a period of six weeks in 1864 General Judson Kilpatrick's cavalry encamped about the church and made raids over the countryside. Later a part of Sherman's army used the little building as a slaughterhouse. The melodeon, used as a meat block by the soldiers, now serves as a communion table. Regular services are no longer held, but each year on April 26, Confederate Memorial Day, descendants of the early members gather for a meeting. Speeches are made, communion is received from the original service, and flowers are placed upon the graves in the cemetery across the road.

Among the early pastors of the congregation was Abiel Holmes, father of Oliver Wendell Holmes, and Jedidiah Morse, father of S. F. B. Morse. The membership of the church, which never exceeded 150 at any one time, numbered among its communicants Lyman Hall and Button Gwinnett, signers of the Declaration of Independence. With the decline of the plantation system after the War between the States, the importance of Midway ended.

In the section of the village called Black Midway is a Negro church with a wooden hand pointing heavenward from the steeple.

Left from Midway on the Dorchester road is DORCHESTER, 2 m. (30 alt., 220 pop.), settled by a group of the Puritans who came from Dorchester, South Carolina. They were the organizers of Midway Church and worshiped there until they formed their own congregation in 1781.

At 6 m. is a fork.

1. Left from the fork to the SITE OF SUNBURY, 4 m., which was established in 1758 soon after Mark Carr, friend of James Oglethorpe, had conveyed 300 acres of his original 500-acre grant to a group of trustees. They laid out a rectangular town with three public squares and 496 lots, and by 1769 Sunbury was a busy river port rivaling Savannah. Sunbury Academy, established in 1788, became the finest in this part of the state. The town began to decline with the shift of population inland and the growing importance of Savannah. It is believed that one of the earliest Masonic lodge meetings in America was held on this site in 1734 with Oglethorpe as master. Here are the REMAINS OF FORT MORRIS, built for defense in 1776, now overgrown with wild myrtle and cedar trees. The Continental troops who garrisoned the fort offered spirited resistance to British attacks, but Sunbury was virtually destroyed.

2. Right from the fork to COLONEL'S ISLAND, 5 m., between the mainland and St. Catherines Island. In 1773 William Bartram, the botanist, explored Colonel's Island and mentioned its shell mounds in *Travels through North and South Carolina, Georgia, East and West Florida*:

"These sea shells, through length of time, and the subtle penetrating effects of the air, which dissolve them to earth, render these ridges very fertile; and, when clear of their trees, and cultivated, they become profusely productive of almost every kind of vegetable. Here are also large plantations of indigo, corn, and potatoes, with many other sorts of esculent plants. I observed, among the shells of the conical mounds, fragments of earthen vessels, and of other utensils, the manufacture of the ancients; about the center of one of them, the rim of an earthen pot appeared among the shells and earth, which I carefully removed, and drew it out, almost whole; this pot was curiously wrought all over the outside, representing basket work, and was undoubtedly esteemed a very ingenious performance, by the people, at the age of its construction."

Across St. Catherines Sound, OSSABAW and ST. CATHERINES ISLANDS can be seen. These are two of the islands known to the Spanish settlers as the Golden Isles of Guale, which included only six of the coastal chain: Ossabaw, St. Catherines, Sapelo, St. Simons, Jekyll, and Cumberland.

St. Catherines Island was the first of the Golden Isles to be settled by the Spanish. When Menendez de Aviles came to this island he was well received by the Indian chief, Guale. Among the Jesuit missionaries who followed the soldiers was Brother Domingo Augustine, who in 1568 translated the catechism and wrote a grammar in the native Yamassee language. In 1680, however, the Spanish outpost was moved farther south, and pirates and hostile Indians sacked or burned all of the buildings. In 1733 the island became a hunting preserve for the Indians.

In 1749 Thomas Bosomworth, who had come as a clergyman to the colony and who had married Mary Musgrove, Oglethorpe's half-Indian interpreter, met with a council of seventeen *micos* (chiefs) at Frederica (*see* TOUR *1A*) and induced them to acknowledge his wife Empress of the Creek and her kinsman Melatche, Emperor, since both were relatives of their former ruler, Chief Brim. Mary claimed as her right the three hunting islands, because, she declared, the Creek gave them to her and because the Colonial trustees had not paid her in full for her services nor for money which she had advanced. Her claim was at first not recognized by the colony, but after ten years of delay Governor Ellis was directed to pay her more than two thousand pounds and to acknowledge her right to St. Catherines Island, upon which she was living.

The Bosomworths later sold the island to Button Gwinnett, who, it is believed, built the tabby house which has lately been remodeled. The simple lines of the structure have been preserved, and the original mantels, stairways, and other details have been used wherever possible. After Gwinnett's death the island was returned to the Bosomworths, who are buried there.

The SITE OF CEDAR HILL (R), *44.9 m.,* is where the Colonial estate of General Daniel Stewart, Revolutionary patriot existed. General Stewart was the grandfather of Martha Bulloch, who married Theodore Roosevelt, of New York, and so became the mother of President Theodore Roosevelt and the grandmother of Mrs. Franklin D. Roosevelt.

EULONIA, *61.2 m.* (25 alt., 300 pop.), is a center of the naval stores industry. The longleaf and slash pine trees of the surrounding sandy plain are tapped for gum resin, which is distilled into turpentine, leaving a residue of hard rosin (*see* TOUR *4*). Here giant live oaks arch over the highway.

At *62.2 m.* is the junction with State 99, hard-surfaced, the Darien-Crescent Road.

Left on this road to CRESCENT, 4.5 m. From the crescent-shaped bluff is a clear view of CREIGHTON ISLAND and of SAPELO (Sp. *Zapala*) ISLAND, the latter the property of Richard J. Reynolds of Winston-Salem, N. C. During Spanish occupation it was the seat of the San Jose Mission, which became the Spanish frontier after the abandonment of St. Catherines in 1680. From 1733 to 1759 the island was reserved for the Indians. In 1786 it was purchased by five French Royalist refugees, of whom the better known are de Boisfeuillet and Poulain du Bignon, who attempted to establish a communal society. The partnership was dissolved because of dissension in 1802. The northern end of the island was sold to the Marquis de Montelet, a refugee from the slave uprisings of Santo Domingo, who established a new home, Le Châtelet, a name corrupted by the Negroes into Chocolate. Ruins of this so-called "Little Castle" still exist.

Thomas Spalding, the son of James Spalding—originally of County Perth, Scotland, who had settled at Frederica on St. Simons Island, purchased 4,000 acres on the southern end of the island and in 1802 began his house, SOUTH END. Among the first to plant cotton, grow cane, and manufacture sugar, he had by 1843 become very wealthy and owned most of the island. When Spalding died in 1851, South End Plantation was left to his grandson and namesake, Thomas Spalding. During the War between the States the island was abandoned, but afterwards the Spaldings moved back to what was left of the old place after the usual Federal outrages. Eventually it passed out of their hands and in 1914 was carefully rebuilt in its former character by Howard E. Coffin, a former vice-president of the Hudson Motor Co. Mr. Reynolds bought the island in 1934. On Barn Creek are octagonal TABBY RUINS, of which one building has been carefully restored.

Tabby (Sp. *tapia*, mud or cement) is a building material made by grinding burned oyster shells for the necessary supply of lime, and mixing the substance with sand, shells, and water. The tabby formula of Thomas Spalding called for equal parts of ground shells, lime, and sand; whole oyster shells, frequently taken from the numerous Indian mounds, were always added as a binder. Since it is known that this medium was used by both the Spanish and the English, the origin of such ruins has been the subject of much uncertainty.

Across the creek from the northern end of Sapelo Island is the small, heavily wooded BLACKBEARD'S ISLAND, now designated as The Blackbeard Island Wildlife Refuge. The island was named for Blackbeard, an English pirate, who tied his bushy black beard into small tails with ribbon. In order to inspire terror he often looped the beard tails behind his ears or stuck under his hat lighted strands of hemp dipped in a solution of saltpeter and limewater. This smoldering fiber gave the appearance of smoke coming from his ears. He began his career in the West Indies during the War of Spanish Succession and about 1716 is thought to have made his headquarters on this island. He terrorized the coast of Georgia, Carolina, and Virginia until he was killed in a hand-to-hand combat by a British lieutenant in 1718. From 1840 until 1910 the island was used as a Government quarantine station. In 1934 explorers obtained permission to look for the pirate's treasure, of which Blackbeard had said that nobody but himself and the devil knew where it was, and the longest liver should take all.

The route continues through small settlements.

The RIDGE is a residential section where most of the houses face a tidal river.

Left from the Ridge on a shell road to the THICKET, *1.5 m.,* an old plantation on which are the TABBY RUINS of eight buildings. The ruins on this site are believed by many to have been the Tolomato Mission, founded in 1595 by Pedro Ruiz, and one of the largest in Georgia. At Tolomato began the Indian uprising of 1597 which spread through Guale. The mission, however, remained until 1686, when the Spanish retired south of St. Marys River. Though it is known that Tolomato was located in this vicinity, the preponderance of evidence today suggests that the ruins are old sugar mills built about 1816 by William Carnochan of the Savannah firm of Carnochan and Mitchell, possibly with the aid of the wealthy planter Thomas Spalding.

At the Darien golf course, *16.3 m.,* is a junction with a dirt road; L. on this road to the junction with another road, *0.3 m.;* L. on this second road, at Lower Bluff, to the site of FORT KING GEORGE (R), *0.5 m.,* easily identified by the pits and refuse mounds of an old sawmill and by several large live oaks. Nothing remains of the twenty-foot-square, gabled blockhouse, erected in 1721 to protect the colonies from the encroachments of the French and Spanish. Garrisoned by His Majesty's Independent Company, this was the first English settlement on Georgia land. Fire almost destroyed the fort in 1727; although it was rebuilt, the plea of South Carolina caused the removal of the troops to that colony. Upon Lower Bluff the Scottish founders of Darien landed in 1736 and built their first houses and church. In 1938 the legislature purchased the site for a state park, but it has remained undeveloped.

The side route proceeds to Darien, *16.8 m.*

DARIEN, 72.7 *m.* (15 alt., 1,380 pop.), seat of McIntosh County, is a drowsy old town on a bluff high above the northern bank of the Altamaha River. At the foot of the bluff are tabby warehouses, docks, shipyards, and canneries, about which the weather-faded shrimp boats anchor and spread their nets to dry. Old frame houses with fragrant gardens are enclosed by picket fences. Along the streets, shadowed by live oaks, pass Portuguese fishermen, Negro shrimpers who speak an almost unintelligible dialect, and lumbermen from the pine forests.

In 1735 the trustees for the colony procured a parliamentary grant to found a group of military colonies in Georgia for the protection of the southern frontier against the Spanish and their Indian partisans. Oglethorpe's agent recruited between one hundred and two hundred people, a part of whom were women and children, from the Scottish Highlands where much unrest continued as an aftermath of the Jacobite rebellion of 1715. The character and accomplishments of this group were exceptionally high, especially in military leadership. After a stormy voyage on the *Prince of Wales* the settlers landed in Savannah in January, 1736. In April they proceeded down the coast and after preparing temporary huts, began the construction of a fort which mounted four cannon. The names which stand out in this group are those of John Mohr McIntosh, the principal leader; Hugh Mackay; and their religious leader, John McLeod.

Because of the large plantations and the commerce afforded by the harbor as the years passed, Darien became a prosperous community. Its greatest period of development followed the War of 1812, when several large sawmills cut timber from the forest of the Altamaha for the building of navy vessels. Many sailboats from foreign ports took on cargoes of timber. Some of the stone ballast which they unloaded is still visible along the river bank. Although in later times its important trade was taken by other ports with better railroad facilities, the town still depends largely on its waterfront industries. In 1818 the Bank of Darien was chartered and later branches were established in Savannah, Augusta, Milledgeville, Macon, and St. Marys. At one time this institution was one of the largest and most reliable financial agents in the South.

Near the courthouse is OGLETHORPE'S OAK, a tree so immense that its wide symmetry of branches is said to have sheltered an entire company of General Oglethorpe's soldiers who encamped there.

The HIGHLANDER MONUMENT (L), W. of the courthouse, is a pink marble monument designed by R. Tait MacKenzie and erected by the Colonial Dames of the State of Georgia, the St. Andrew's Society of Savannah, and the Society of Colonial Wars. Ornamented with the Scottish thistle and the Georgia cherokee rose, it bears a bronze panel depicting a group of Scottish Highlanders.

The PRESBYTERIAN CHURCH was established in 1736 under the supervision of John McLeod, a minister who came with the colonists from Scotland. Although the present edifice, a brick building with a tall steeple, was not built until 1870, it contains the records of the original congregation.

The name of the wide ALTAMAHA RIVER, 75 *m.,* is an alteration of Altama (Ind., Way to the Tama Country); Tama was a village at a point where the Oconee and Ocmulgee rivers flow together to form the Altamaha. A very interesting and singular evergreen shrub originated in this area, known variously as the Lost Gordonia, or Franklinia. Technically it is GORDONIA (FRANKLINIA) *alatamaha,* a member of the tea family, and hence a cousin of the camellia by its common tie to the *Theaceae.* It was first found along the river by John Bartram of Philadelphia, who assigned it the name *Franklinia alatamaha* in honor of Benjamin Franklin. John's son William Bartram again found it in 1778 while on an expedition in this area, but in spite of constant search the shrub has never been seen again in its native habitat. All the plants now existing are reputed to be from the ones which John Bartram took to his famous Garden in Philadelphia. The long and oval foliage is dark green, and five or more inches in length, turning reddish in autumn, like its other cousin of the tea family, Japanese Cleyera. Its magnolia-like, creamy flowers, accentuated by a dense array of yellow stamens, appear in late summer or early autumn at a time when little else of definite character is in bloom. It may grow to twenty feet as a sub-tree, but more often it develops as a shrub with several trunks. If given protection it is hardy as far north as Boston.

The river channels are divided by delta lowlands, known as Butler, General, and Champney islands. They were owned by Colonel T. L. Huston, part owner of the New York Yankees, until his death in 1938, when his son, A. T. Huston, inherited the property.

On the northern end of Butler Island (R) is the HUSTON HOUSE (*private*), a two-story, white frame dwelling, with dormer windows and a gabled roof designed in the manner of a New England Colonial house. The house is on the old Pierce Butler rice plantation, where the actress Fanny Kemble spent part of her time in Georgia (*see* TOUR *1A*). South of the house is an ivy-covered brick chimney (R), the REMAINS OF AN OLD RICE MILL built by Butler.

The old drainage system of the Pierce Butler plantation was replaced by modern dikes and drainage ditches to regulate the spring and fall freshets of the river and reclaim many acres of fertile land. This property was purchased in 1950 by Richard J. Reynolds of Winston-Salem, N. C., who has continued Huston's agricultural experiments on the island, in part, by devoting extensive acreage to the growing of iceberg lettuce. The property has been further improved by remodeling the house and renovating the drainage system.

The highway, passing through heavily wooded swamp country, was built over the old roadbed of the Georgia Coastal & Piedmont Railway.

At 78 *m.* is the junction with a shell road.

Right on this road through a wood dense with laurel, cedar, and dogwood to BOYS ESTATE, GEORGIA (*0.5 m.*), located on the area of the former Santo Domingo State Park, which was made available by the Georgia legislature for the establishment of the "town." The total area makes up some 363 acres. Boys Estate, Georgia, patterned after the famous Boys Town, Nebraska, and Boys Ranch, Texas, has been started on the wooded elevation of giant live oaks, tall yellow pines, red-berried hollies and cassena bushes, magnolia, and dogwood overlooking the Altamaha River and Delta. In this area there are about 155 acres, while the remainder of the tract is composed of ante-bellum rice fields extending to the banks of the Altamaha. The eastern boundary of the Estate is the slave-built Brunswick-Altamaha Canal that was originally designed for transportation from Brunswick to Darien, though never finished. During Colonial days the land was part of the Elizafield Plantation of Hugh Frazier Grant and for many years was planted to rice or indigo. In 1925 it was bought by Cator Woolford, of Atlanta, who donated the land to the state. The preservation of the tract as a park has resulted in a fine stand of virgin timber. Much of the jungle-like tangle of undergrowth has been cleared and the Estate is a haven for wildlife natural to coastal Georgia. Tabby Ruins believed by some to be the foundations of Santo Domingo de Talaxe, a Spanish mission erected in 1604, but by others to be the remains of sugar houses from plantation days, along with the Grant Family

Cemetery enclosed by a moss-covered tabby wall, are being preserved as a part of the community.

At present there are three cottages, Friendly, Albany, and Macon, a Spanish type building that was on the original park land, the Jesse M. Donaldson P. O. Building, a public works building, and several barns. The long range plan of the town includes a number of cottages, a school, general store, bank, chapel, hospital, recreation building, town hall, and other community developments.

Not on an area-quota basis, the acceptance of boys is on the basis of need and available room. Applications come from various sources, including the Advisory Trustees, court and welfare agencies, clubs, churches, parents, and relatives, and often by request of the boys themselves. After a boy has begun residence at the Estate he is under no compulsion to remain, and is free to go and come, subject to the town's regulations and ordinances. These are made by officials who are elected from among the boys who are the citizens. A guardianship is assumed by the Board of Managing Trustees which supersedes parental or other claims, and a boy will not be accepted as a parolee or probation case from a court, but only on condition that the court relinquish its jurisdiction. When a boy terminates his residence, the guardianship of the Trustees ends.

Upon arrival a new citizen is helped to become adjusted to the town and the other boys as effortlessly as possible. The boys govern themselves. The most important office-holder is the mayor, who officiates at public ceremonies, presides over the city council with its five members, and is vested with executive authority. Meeting twice each month, the council passes laws if needed, and a police chief and his officers enforce the laws while a city judge deals with the citizens violating them. A city treasurer works over the financial problems, and the president of the chamber of commerce plans suitable hospitality for visitors and is busy in many other ways such as planning livestock shows and arranging for the dedication of buildings. Aspirants for office campaign vigorously for weeks prior to the yearly election in September.

A new cottage now under construction will increase the census of the Estate to ninety citizens. Founded in 1945 the Estate has grown, and in 1953 the state-wide campaign for operation funds fixed its aim on $100,000. "This is the only place I know of in the state where a homeless boy has the opportunity to be cared for, educated, and taught to become a real citizen," said Mr. James V. Carmichael, chairman of the board of trustees for Boys Estate.

At *4 m.* on the shell road is the estate of CATOR WOOLFORD (*private*), on the site of Hopeton, the 2,000-acre plantation of John Couper and James Hamilton. The two-story tabby house, ALTAMA, erected in 1857, is of simple design with a low front portico. Restoration, begun by William du Pont and completed by Woolford, has preserved the fine proportions of the building. John Couper's son, James Hamilton Couper, who was made manager of Hopeton in 1816, developed it into one of the most flourishing plantations along the coast. Couper was one of the first southern planters to make use of improved technical methods. He set up a sugar mill with machinery imported from England in 1829. In 1834, establishing a cotton seed oil mill at Mobile, Alabama, and next year one at Natchez, Mississippi, he was, probably, the first to extract oil from cotton seed. This oil venture was not a financial success however, and the mills were discontinued in 1836. Giving his attention to the cultivation of rice after 1838, he introduced a diking and drainage system that was a model for other rice growers. Having inherited his father's plantation at Cannon's Point on St. Simons Island, at one time he had under his management around 1,500 slaves, an exceptional number in anybody's reckoning.

U. S. NAVAL AUXILIARY AIR STATION at GLYNCO, *84 m.,* (R) was constructed to provide the Navy with a base of operation for airships engaged in in-shore patrol and anti-submarine warfare. In the summer of 1942 a site was selected approximately 6 miles north of Brunswick, Georgia, for the proposed Naval Air Station. Construction began in September of that year and the station was commissioned in January, 1943. The following month the first Airship Squadron arrived at Glynco and started its operation. During the war years, Glynco served as an integral part of the anti-submarine network. Squadrons based at Glynco flew countless missions covering convoys and in search for the German menace, the U-Boat. Throughout these thousands of hours of patrol, not a single airship was lost while on convoy duty.

With the conclusion of World War II, Glynco was utilized as an airplane and aeronautical storage point. The two airship hangars, which are the largest wooden structures in the world, were ideal for the storage of hundreds of airplanes and other material. During this period when millions of military personnel were returned to civilian life, activity at Glynco was sharply reduced. In July of 1945 the station was reclassified as a Naval Air Facility and over a period of several years was reduced to a maintenance status. At the outbreak of the police action in Korea the Navy began to swell its ranks and increased emphasis was placed on the airship program. Additional personnel was added to Glynco and in August, 1951, Airship Squadron TWO was transferred from Naval Air Station Lakehurst, N. J., to Glynco. At this time Glynco was placed in a full operating status, and in January, 1952, was reclassified as a Naval Auxiliary Air Station.

The future holds evidence of increased expansion for this station. The Naval Airship Training Unit, which trains all Lighter-than-Air pilots in the Navy, is scheduled to be transferred from Naval Air Station Lakehurst, at Lakehurst, New Jersey, to Glynco early this summer. A Combat Information Center School will be established upon the completion of construction which is already underway. This school will utilize jet aircraft in the training of naval officers to man the Combat Information Centers of naval warships. It is in these centers that information is received and interpreted to determine the movement of friendly and enemy forces.

HERCULES NAVAL STORES PLANT (R). The Hercules Powder Company operates at Brunswick the largest naval stores plant of its sort in the U. S. Started in 1920 on a minor scale, this plant now makes more han two hundred different products from the rosin extracted from pine stumps.

CHAMBER OF COMMERCE BUILDING (R) (formerly the Visitors' Club) occupies a low Spanish-type building with arched porches, red-tiled roof, and high towers. This serves as an information center for tourists.

At this point is the junction (L) with the new BRUNSWICK–ST. SIMONS CAUSEWAY, dedicated June 9, 1950. The Causeway to St. Simons is a toll road: fifty cents for car and passengers, round trip (*see* TOUR *1A*).

Under LANIER'S OAK (L), a gnarled live oak at the edge of the salt-water swamp, Lanier is said to have been moved to conceive his poem "The Marshes of Glynn."

BRUNSWICK

Railroads: Brunswick is the terminus of two trunk-line railroads, The Atlantic Coast Line and the Southern. The Seaboard Airline Railroad has convenient operating arrangements with the Atlantic Coast Line at Thalmann and with the Southern at Everett City.

Bus Lines: The Atlantic Greyhound Lines operate north and south to Richmond and Jacksonville. Service Coach Lines operate west and northwest to Waycross and Baxley. Georgia City Coaches operate a street bus line in Brunswick and to St. Simons and Sea islands.

Air Lines: Delta–C. & S. and Eastern Air Lines have a total of seven arrivals and departures daily.

Hotels: 6 in Brunswick; 5 on St. Simons Island; one on Sea Island.

Amusements: Surf-bathing, water sports, tennis, golf, horseback-riding, fishing, and hunting. The Howard E. Coffin Recreational Park has a swimming pool, tennis courts, and softball courts.

Steamships: The Strachan Shipping Co. operates both coastwise and foreign steamship service from Brunswick.

Inland Waterway: Brunswick is located on the great inland water-way, and many yachts, barges and other craft use this protected route between New York and Florida.

BRUNSWICK, *90.1 m.* (14 alt., 17,954 pop.), seat of Glynn County, is a busy seaport with the gayety of a resort city. The city includes forty-two manufacturing and processing establishments, the principal prod-ucts of which are: naval stores, pulp, shipbuilding, plywood, creosoted timbers, paint and varnish, lumber products; fresh frozen and breaded shrimp, crab, and other seafood; ice, mill and building supplies, ship repairs, and garments. It is Georgia's second seaport in importance, and has a natural landlocked harbor of 31 square miles area. The Brunswick Pulp and Paper Co., jointly owned by the Meade and Scott paper interests, has a large pulp plant at Brunswick, where 140,000 tons of bleached sulphate wood pulp are produced annually. This plant recently made a $5,250,000 expansion. TIME magazine for December 10, 1951, speaks of Brunswick as one of the three important seafood centers in the Southeast. Since seven important local industries are dependent upon pine and other forest products, the citizens of Glynn and adjoining counties have organized an effective association for timber protection, with fire-control aided by radio and telephone. A colorful feature of the seafood industry is the fleet of small boats, decorated by their Portuguese owners with bright pennants and figureheads, that bring shrimp to factories along East River.

A few houses in Brunswick are of Georgian Colonial architecture, but most are either Victorian structures or Spanish-type bungalows. Brunswick has a semitropical climate, with a mean annual temperature of 68.4° and an average rainfall of fifty inches. Its straight, broad streets are shaded by live oaks and divided by parkways planted with palms, dogwood, and native shrubs and evergreens. The parks and squares, part of the original plan, are named for English places and Colonial benefactors. The Howard E. Coffin Recreational Park consists of seven acres of reclaimed land fronting on a tidewater stream in the direction of the Marshes of Glynn. The portion of the park not used for its swimming pool, tennis courts, and other recreational facilities is well landscaped with palms and other semitropical plants.

In 1742, six years after Frederica had been founded on St. Simons Island (*see* TOUR 1A), Mark Carr established a plantation on the present site of the city. It was not until 1771, however, that the council of the Royal Province of Georgia decided to build a town on the mainland. A rectangular tract of 385 acres was set aside, a survey ordered, and the town named for King George III, of the House of Brunswick (Hanover). The first lot was granted in 1772, and Glynn Academy, one of the three oldest public schools in the state, was chartered in 1778. It is still in existence. Brunswick was prosperous in 1862, when the Confederate government ordered its evacuation because of the difficulty of fortifying it. Glynn County, of which Brunswick is the county seat, was named in honor of John Glynn, a member of Parliament, who sympathized with the colonists in their struggle for independence. The city was incorporated February 22, 1856.

The OGLETHORPE HOTEL, N. W. corner Newcastle and F streets, is a brick building with a wide porch and round towers. This building, designed by Stanford White and erected in 1885, has since been remodeled.

In the center of QUEENS SQUARE, intersection of Newcastle and Mans field streets, (one of the well-landscaped parks), is a large Celtic cross, a monument to James Edward Oglethorpe.

The CITY HALL, 1227 Newcastle St., erected in 1889, is built of brick in the German Romanesque style.

The PRESBYTERIAN CHURCH, 603 George St., erected about 1871, is a simple structure of modified Gothic design. It is the city's oldest church built for a white congregation.

WRIGHT SQUARE, intersection of Norwich and George streets, was used as a cemetery until 1850. Among the old graves is that of Benjamin Hart, husband of the Revolutionary patriot Nancy Hart (*see* TOUR *3A*). The Harts moved here after the war and aided in the development of the town.

At Brunswick is the junction with US 341 (*see* TOUR *12*).

From the bridge over TURTLE RIVER, 95.2 *m.*, a tidewater arm of the Atlantic Ocean, is a broad view including the Brunswick water front and in the distance the faint outlines of ST. SIMONS ISLAND (*see* TOUR *1A*) and of JEKYLL ISLAND, the smallest of the Golden Isles.

BLYTHE ISLAND, 95.9 *m.*, has been developed as a residential subdivision of Brunswick. About two-thirds of the island is privately owned. Part of the remaining 1,000 acres, which belongs to the U. S. War Department, is used as a target range by the National Guard.

Turn left on State 50, about *11 m.*, to the bridge connecting the mainland with the JEKYLL ISLAND STATE PARK (*accommodations of all sorts*); it is expected that the bridge now under construction will be completed some time in 1954, at which time the park will formally open. Once the home of the Jekyll Island Club, owned and operated by a group of American multi-millionaires as a scene adapted to their peculiar needs in life which have been described in a recent witty book called *The Last Resorts*, this southern playground fell upon uncertain days and was condemned by the state in 1946. From that time until 1949 the state operated the island as a vacation retreat, but the financial loss involved suggested the need of some other arrangement for its administration.

Early in 1950 the state created the Jekyll Island State Park Authority by an Act of the Legislature which set up a five-man organization with the responsibility of subdividing and subletting to Georgia residents certain sections of the island in order to gain the means with which to develop and to maintain the rest of the island as a seaside park. In 1951 the Authority was able to secure the authorization of a bridge to connect the island to the mainland, but its construction was delayed by the steel shortage. However, now that the bridge is well advanced, though whether it will be one of the newly authorized toll-bridges or not remains undetermined, the first business and residential lots have been plotted and will be offered on long-term leases to state residents. Roads are now being cleared by convict labor that will connect the bridge and beach with the section where the tycoons built their winter homes, commonly called "cottages." According to a recent (1953) article in the *Journal-Constitution,* "The authority plans to rent several of these 'cottages'—like the 22-bedroom Crane house—to Georgia corporations on 10-year leases to use as vacation spots for employees. It is also seeking a lessee for the clubhouse, annex and Sans Souci apartments." The Authority expects to negotiate the lease of the Jekyll Island Club House and Annex together with the Morgan Apartments to hotel interests in time for these accommodations to be available when the bridge is complete.

The Act creating the Authority provides that each of Georgia's 159 counties, subject to certain requirements of the Act, may obtain a rent free lot for charitable purposes. One section of the island will be set apart as a business district, and another for the special use of Negroes. The Authority has used the interim period to renovate the major buildings on the island. With the help of the State Highway Department and the Forestry Department work has progressed measurably on the preparation of roads and the clearing of the parkland. Upon the opening of the park, 9 miles of scenic beach, hundreds of acres of parkland woods, swimming pools, tennis courts, golf courses, and camping sites for youth organizations will be available.

At *100.4 m.* is the junction with US 84 (*see* TOUR 5).

At *117.1 m.* is the junction with a dirt road.

Right on this road to REFUGE PLANTATION (*private*), *2 m.*, a 5,000-acre tract granted by George III to John Houstoun McIntosh, who settled here in 1765. The house, built of hand-hewn timbers in 1798, has a gabled roof with two dormer windows. The chamfered wood columns that support the porch roof rest upon the ground, and behind them is a balcony with wooden balustrades. Double entrance steps lead to the balcony. The old kitchen is connected with the house by a covered passage, and the brick fireplace, with its hanging rod and cooking iron, is still intact. This house now belongs to Mrs. D. J. Hebard of Philadelphia.

WOODBINE, *118.9 m.* (14 alt., 750 pop.), on the banks of the Satilla River, was incorporated in 1893 and became the seat of Camden County in 1923.

KINGSLAND, *130.7 m.* (34 alt., 1,169 pop.), was established as a flag station on the Seaboard Air Line Railway in 1894.

Left on State 40 to Scotchville, about *5 m.* and then left on 40 S. to Crooked River State Park, the only inland park in Georgia where salt water fishing is available. Across the river and opposite the park proper lie several hundred acres of marsh which provide excellent marsh hen hunting. The hunting season opens October 1 and closes November 30. The bag limit is fifteen. There is playground equipment available for children, and for adults supervised boating, fishing, swimming, hiking, and picnicking. For reservations to cabins address the superintendent, Crooked River State Park, Kingsland, Georgia. There are no general admission charges or fishing fees for Georgia State Parks.

Adjacent to Crooked River is Santa Maria Mission State Park Area which contains the most impressive TABBY RUINS on the coast. These ruins, two stories high and 75 feet wide by 150 feet long, stand in a grove of cedar and oak trees entwined by garlands of muscadine vines. They seem to be divided into three large rooms and were evidently of two stories. There are thirty small, vertical windows to light the second floor of the room on the north, and free-standing square columns on each side of the middle room. Some believe them to be remains of Santa Maria Mission, built about 1570 by Menendez de Aviles and his followers; others, that they were sugar houses built about 1825 by John Houstoun

McIntosh, whose plantation New Canaan was established here during the War of 1812.

At *10.7 m.* on State 40 is st. marys (15 alt., 1,348 pop.), an old sea town occupying an eminence on the St. Marys River. A wide street lined with oaks and wind-scarred cedars leads to the docks and the beautiful wide stretch of the river.

After its incorporation in 1802—following several half centuries of Spanish, French, and English occupation and struggle—St. Marys grew rapidly as timber was sent to shipbuilding centers for the construction of U. S. Navy vessels. Its nearness to the Spanish territory of Florida required the presence of customs collectors and other Federal officials, who, with the planters, established a standard of culture unusual in pioneer Georgia. With the advent of steamships and the development of railroads, St. Marys lost its commercial energy and today is occupied with supplying fish and shrimp to sea-food canneries.

The presbyterian church, NW corner Osborne and Congress streets, is a frame structure with a high basement and a square tower. Erected in 1808, it is one of the oldest churches in the state. At first the organization was a community church but was incorporated as a Presbyterian church in 1818. For many years it served also as a school, the Old Academy, and it still houses the library and old church records.

orange hall (*private*), SW. corner Osborne and Congress streets, is a two-story house of Greek Revival design set on well-landscaped grounds enclosed by a picket fence. Its columns are imitated in miniature in the porch balustrade. The immense basement kitchen has the original fireplace fitted with crane and built-in ovens. The three-story house was built between 1832 and 1837 by Horace S. Pratt when he was serving his last term as pastor of the Presbyterian Church.

Visible from the harbor of St. Marys is the southern end of cumberland island (*private*), the largest of the Georgia islands. It is owned largely by members of the Carnegie family, who have done much to preserve and to improve its natural beauty.

US 17 crosses the St. Marys River, *134.7 m.,* under an arch into the State of Florida, 32 miles north of Jacksonville.

TOUR I A

Junction US 17—Bloody Marsh Battlefield—Sea Island—Frederica; 11.5 m., St. Simons Causeway, Sea Island Rd., and Frederica Rd.

Georgia City Coaches Bus Line operates from Brunswick to St. Simons, and Sea Island. Nine trips daily throughout the week. Fare 65¢ round trip, and 45¢ one way—Shell and paved highways—Good hotels, motor and ocean courts, cottages and lunchrooms; recreational facilities of all sorts: fishing, hunting, golf, surf bathing, swimming pools, etc., winter and summer.

St. Simons Island, the small adjacent Sea Island, and more recently Jekyll Island are, with the exception of Tybee, Georgia's only coastal islands open to the public. St. Simons has been a popular summer resort for Georgia people for years; Sea Island, more recently developed, offering a luxurious hotel life, is widely known in the North as a winter retreat. On these beautiful islands wooded stretches of moss-draped live oaks and glossy-leafed cassenas mingle with lively plantings of crape myrtle and pink and white oleanders. Evergreens in a wide assortment and vivid flowers grow the year round in the mild climate.

East from its junction with US 17 (*see* TOUR *1*) at the Brunswick Chamber of Commerce, *o m.,* just north of Brunswick (*inquire for information and local maps*), the route crosses the new Brunswick–St. Simons Causeway (*toll 50¢ round trip for car and passengers*). Bordered with shrubbery, the causeway stretches across land reclaimed from the Marshes of Glynn and tidal rivers.

GASCOIGNE BLUFF is a low, wooded, shell-covered bank overlooking the Frederica River. It is named for Captain James Gascoigne, a commander of the man-of-war *Hawk,* which convoyed the two ships bringing settlers to Georgia in 1736. Known as the Great Embarkation, this company included Oglethorpe, making his second trip to America, John and Charles Wesley, and a tidy group of Moravians and Lutheran Salzburgers. The authors of *Empire Builders of Georgia* have this to say of the texture of Oglethorpe's colonists, "Nationalities represented in the colony included Jews and Gentiles, English, Germans, Scotch, Irish, French, Italians, Swiss, Portuguese, and perhaps others. There were also men and women of varied professions: vinedressers, silk workers, Indian traders, doctors, bakers, ministers, carpenters, bricklayers, shoemakers, shopkeepers, and numerous other occupational groups." The settlers were mostly people suffering from the closed economy of England, or refugees from another sort of poverty, religious intolerance. This goes far toward explaining the heady winds of self-reliance that circulate through the annals of Georgia as well as why the life of the great plantations never thoroughly dominated the social imagination of the people—except in the pages of the romantic historians.

After leading his charges to Savannah, Gascoigne brought his ship to St. Simons. He was placed in charge of the ships that Oglethorpe had stationed in the protected water below the bluff to defend the Georgia coast. This bluff was the scene of numerous bloody struggles between the English colonists and Spanish-Indian forces.

North of the Frederica Bridge on Gascoigne Bluff is the MARINA (*open to the public with boats and bait available*) of the St. Simons Boating and Fishing Club. Further inland in this direction, through an impressive grove of trees is the American Legion Home. Two typical slave cabins nearby are used at present by the Cassina Garden Club.

HAMILTON PLANTATION is a short distance farther. The estate was first established about 1793 by James Hamilton, one of the largest planters associated with the island, on land granted by King George II to Captain Gascoigne. According to Fanny Kemble, the estate became "by far the finest on St. Simons Island." In 1857 it was purchased by James Hamilton Couper who assigned it to the management of his brother, William Couper. During the War between the States the estate suffered from the passions of the day and afterwards from unavoidable neglect until eventually, after passing through the hands of a number of owners, it was acquired by the South Georgia Conference of the Methodist Episcopal Church for use as the South Georgia Conference Grounds. It has in recent years undergone considerable rehabilitation, and is now known as Epworth-by-the-Sea (*rooms, meals, recreational facilities; open to the public*) in honor of Charles and John Wesley, founders of the faith.

In a southerly direction by Kings Way Road is (R) the SEA ISLAND YACHT CLUB (*reservations for meals accepted; open the year round*). The Frederica River, part of the inland water route from Norfolk, Virginia, to Key West, Florida, is about two hundred yards west of the club. On its opposite shore is Olsen's Yacht Yard where yachts from all parts dock while visiting St. Simons and the other Golden Isles. In the quiet waters near the wharf of the Sea Island Yacht Club, the U. S. Coast Guard has established a yacht basin and maintains both motor and manual-power lifeboats.

The SEA ISLAND GOLF CLUB is on Kings Way towards the intersection (R) with Retreat Avenue. This club comprises two nine-hole golf courses: one is a typical inland links, with fairways bordered with somber oaks and open pines; the other, built along the edge of the water, resembles an English seaside course with sand traps and stubborn water hazards. The clubhouse is built around the tabby walls of an old barn which once served Retreat Plantation.

Retreat Plantation, once engrossing the southern part of the island, was the original Colonial grant to James Spalding, a Scot who came to Georgia in 1760. About 1775 the plantation with its Colonial mansion was bought by Major William Page, of South Carolina, who left it to his daughter Anne, wife of Thomas Butler King, planter, Congressman, and one of the promoters of the Southern Pacific Railroad. Under the management of the Kings, Retreat became well-known for the excellence of its sea-island cotton, the first grown in the United States. An olive tree, a few exotic plants, and an avenue of majestic live oaks are reminders of the extensive plantation which John James Audubon admired, when, compelled to land on St. Simons from his schooner *Agnes,* he was met by King on the beach and invited to dinner at Retreat. The old Retreat Slave Cemetery lies near the ninth green of the golf course.

ST. SIMONS VILLAGE is nearby. It is a permanent resort colony with accommodations offered by hotels, tourist courts, cottages, restaurants, etc. The St. Simons Chamber of Commerce, the public library, and the theatre are in the Old Casino building across from the public pier. Nearby is the New Casino where swimming, bowling, shuffleboard, and dancing offer an occasion for pleasant hours.

The pier extends into St. Simons Sound (Brunswick Harbor) from the foot of Mallory Street; Jekyll Island (*see* TOUR *1*) is visible across the sound. The St. Simons Lighthouse, marking the approach to the port at Brunswick, was first established in 1808, but during the War between the States it was destroyed by the Confederates as a defense measure, and not replaced until 1871. Near the lighthouse is the marked site of Fort St. Simons which was a part of Oglethorpe's military defense, being connected with Fort Frederica to the north by a road.

The KING AND PRINCE HOTEL (*open year round*) in the direction of East Beach is directly on the Atlantic Ocean. This is the largest of the hotels on St. Simons Island, and is well-known for the variety of its seashore diversions.

The U. S. COAST GUARD STATION is located on the south end of East Beach, about a mile from the village and beyond the hotel.

BLOODY MARSH BATTLEFIELD is on Demere Road. Here occurred an event which contributed measurably towards breaking the grip of Spain on Georgia territory. On June 28, 1742, a Spanish fleet of fifty-one vessels with three thousand men under the command of Don Manuel de Montiano anchored off St. Simons Bar; after testing the bar thirty-six ships sailed into the harbor on July 5 under a four-hour bombardment from Fort St. Simons. Oglethorpe, however, realizing that his troops needed to be drawn together for strength, spiked the St. Simons guns and retreated towards Frederica, the stronger position. The Spanish landed and possessed the fort at once.

Two days later Montiano sent out a scouting group to investigate the terrain between Fort St. Simons and Fort Frederica where Oglethorpe had some nine hundred men: British Regulars, Marines, Indians, Highlanders, and Rangers. The Spanish came within a short distance of Frederica when they were driven back by Oglethorpe who prepared his men for further attack. The Spanish soon sent three hundred grenadiers to break the resistance. Oglethorpe's men retreated, but left a detachment ambushed in the dense thickets. By one of those strange accidents which figure so crucially in history, the Spanish decided that the English were demoralized, and so detecting nothing in that immense silence where they had stopped, stacked arms and prepared to eat in front of the ambush. At this favorable moment for the British, a Scotch cap was raised on a stick as the sign of assault. The Spanish were so hopelessly at odds that they lost two hundred men; and the lot of Spain began to settle in the balance.

KELVIN GROVE PLANTATION was later established in this area. Originally owned by Thomas Cater, it belonged at one time to James P. Postell, well-known collector of shells. The plantation now belongs to Mrs. Maxfield Parrish, wife of the painter, whose house stands near the battlefield marker. Chants sung as rhythms by Negro crews, in the lively days when plantations used to race by boat against each other on festive occasions, have been collected and published by Mrs. Parrish in her book *Slave Songs of the Georgia Sea Islands*.

The MCKINNON AIR FIELD lies between this area and Retreat Avenue (*Delta and Eastern airlines*), and serves both Brunswick and St. Simons. It was constructed by the U. S. Navy during World War II to be used as a training base.

SEA ISLAND is reached by continuing along Sea Island Road and across the Sea Island Causeway. It is now a well-known resort developed by the late Howard E. Coffin. At the center of a group of stucco buildings on landscaped grounds is the CLOISTER HOTEL, designed by Addison Mizner in a modified Spanish style. The terrace of the Cloister Apartment Annex faces the water, where private boats can be anchored. On the beach side of the hotel is the casino, overlooking the ocean, and adjoining it is an outdoor swimming pool used summer and winter. Left from the Cloister on Sea Island Drive is a residential colony along the beach.

The SEA ISLAND FISHING CAMP is located on the north end of the island.

Return to intersection with the Frederica Road, then turn right. GLYNN HAVEN ESTATES, on Frederica Road (L), is a small colony built around a lake.

The SITE OF OGLETHORPE'S FARM is at the intersection of Frederica Road with Couper Road (L); it is indicated by a stone marker. Orange Hall, the two-story building that Oglethorpe erected on the original 50-acre tract, was the only home that Oglethorpe ever owned in America; for apparently he preferred the military exercises of Frederica to the mercantile and religious interests in Savannah.

At this point turn left.

CHRIST EPISCOPAL CHURCH (L) is a low, gabled, frame structure, surrounded by the graves of early settlers and soldiers, and set in a grove of moss-hung, giant live oaks. This congregation was established as a mission of the Church of England in 1736. Both Charles and John Wesley preached in the first church. While he was fulfilling his office of secretary to Oglethorpe on St. Simons Island, Charles had his historical break with Oglethorpe with the result that Charles left for Savannah and, later, for England. The present church was built in 1884 by Anson Phelps Dodge, Jr., as a memorial to his first wife. WESLEY OAK, a large tree shading the church yard, is commonly accepted as the place where the Wesleys preached to colonists and friendly Indians.

The RUINS OF FORT FREDERICA, now the FORT FREDERICA NATIONAL MONUMENT, are about a mile farther on. It consists at present of two small tabby chambers surmounted by a low parapet, thus reduced by the passage of years and the wash of the nearby river. In 1736, for purposes of expansion and defense, Oglethorpe established here as a military outpost the town and fort named in honor of Frederick, Prince of Wales, and only son of George II. Selecting a site on the southern branch of the Altamaha River (known locally as the Frederica River), he erected a fort on a small bluff ten feet above high water mark, at a strategic point commanding a curve of the river. Shortly the temporary fort was replaced by a four-bastioned fortification with tabby walls. Like Caesar, Oglethorpe described the details of this strategic act, saying that he had enclosed the whole town in which there were some very good houses, that it was half a hexagon with two bastions and two half bastions and towers after Monsieur Vauban's method upon the point of each bastion. He added that the walls were of earth faced with timber, ten feet high in the lowest place and thirteen in the highest and the timbers from eight inches to a foot thick; there was a wet ditch ten feet wide. It was a right little, tight little fort.

After the Peace of Aix-la-Chapelle in 1748 the political situation was so composed that Frederica, dedicated to the arts of war, had no function, and hence fell quickly into disorder. In 1754 Frederica had taken on the stillness of a doomed town: houses without inhabitants, barracks without martial life, guns fallen from their carriages, and streets all but lost again to the laurel and the oak.

The remains of the Citadel were acquired by the Georgia Chapter of the Colonial Dames of America in 1903; later the Fort Frederica Association added a tract of eighty acres. This area with the fort was turned over to the Federal Government on September 10, 1945, and now makes up the Fort Frederica National Monument. This includes the fort site, the walled area of the town, and a burying ground to the east. The moat surrounding the town, the cemetery, portions of the citadel, and part of the barracks have survived. At present public facilities are limited. The monument is now administered by the National Park Service of the U. S. Department of the Interior on behalf of the people of the United States.

Nearby is the Frederica Yacht Club (*reservations accepted for meals*). The Club has achieved a well-deserved fame for its seafood and steak dinners.

Return along the route.

About fifty yards beyond Christ Church is a monument placed by R. S. Abbot, a St. Simons Negro, in honor of his father and aunt. Abbot, seeking opportunity, went to Chicago where he eventually became owner of the newspaper, *Chicago Defender*. Gossip has it that he left with a quarter and came back with a million dollars.

At this point, turn left on a shell road which leads by the DODGE HOME FOR BOYS.

WEST POINT PLANTATION and the PINK CHAPEL (*open to the public*) are only a short distance. West Point Plantation was the home of Colonel William Hazzard, and though the house disappeared long ago, a number of tabby ruins were discovered when Mr. and Mrs. Maxwell Berry cleared the bluff on the Frederica River as a site for a plantation. Historical evidence supports the theory that the largest building with its dependencies, later uncovered, was a Catholic chapel center; and since the inside walls of the principal structure were of a warm hue, it was named suitably enough Pink Chapel.

On the return, at the junction of Frederica Road with Couper Road, turn on Couper Road. About a half mile on Couper Road is (R) the junction with Village Road.

THE SALZBURGER VILLAGE, known locally as the German Village, is about a mile on this road. The Salzburgers who came under Oglethorpe's protection in search of religious freedom were artisans and horticulturalists. Each was given fifty acres and a mulberry tree, and they are justly celebrated for their silk culture, which they continued after others had become discouraged, until just before the War for Independence. They are generally credited with having nurtured the peach in the New World. People in the locality claim that the road which leads on to the Preece Fishing Camp on Village Creek is all that is left of those originally planned by Oglethorpe.

At about 5 m. on Couper Road is a fork.

1. HAMPTON POINT is left from the fork about two miles, at the northern end of the island. Here are the ruins of the house and garden of the old Hampton Plantation, one of the Georgia estates of Major Pierce Butler. The Major was a man of parts, having been a member of the Continental Congress (1787-88), of the Constitutional Convention

(1787), and a United States Senator from South Carolina (1789-96 and 1803-04). Major Butler lived on this plantation during the winters from 1795 to 1815, and in 1804 was visited by Aaron Burr, who was seeking asylum after his duel with Alexander Hamilton. Butler's plantation was almost self-sustaining, for his slaves were skilled in a variety of domestic and agricultural arts. After amassing a fortune, Butler moved to Philadelphia, and "the big house" was almost in ruins by 1838, when Pierce Butler, grandson of the founder, brought Frances Anne (Fanny) Kemble, his English actress wife, to live at Hampton. Mrs. Butler was not sympathetic to the institution of slavery, whether benevolent or not; she expressed her animus in bitter letters to her friends. It was the winter of 1838-39, spent here and on Butler Island (*see* TOUR *1*), which she described in her *Journal of a Residence on a Georgia Plantation*. Following the War between the States, Frances Butler Leigh, Fanny Kemble's daughter, came to live on the Georgia plantation. Her *Ten Years on a Georgian Plantation Since the War* gives a softer picture of plantation life than her mother's book. The house, its orange groves, and gardens have no existence now except in the records of the past.

2. Right from the fork *1.5 m.* is CANNON'S POINT, the site of the plantation which the Scottish John Couper, Georgia statesman, bought in 1793. He developed his plantation into what has been called Georgia's first agricultural experiment station. He planted every tree, flower, and shrub which he believed would grow in this semitropical climate. His two hundred olive trees, though five months in transit from France, did so well that a good grade of oil was pressed from the fruit. Little remains that can be unequivocally established as having belonged to the culture of the estate.

Taylor's Fishing Camp is just to the right of the entrance gate to Cannon's Point.

Little St. Simons Island, across the Hampton River, is visible from this point.

TOUR 2

(Chattanooga, Tenn.) — Dalton — Atlanta — Griffin — Perry — Valdosta — (Lake City, Fla.); US 41.

Tennessee Line to Florida Line, about 385 m. — Roadbed hard-surfaced throughout. This route is undergoing reconstruction as a four-lane highway. From Emerson to Atlanta the four-lane construction is complete. The Nashville, Chattanooga & St. Louis R.R. parallels route between Tennessee Line and Atlanta; the Central of Georgia Ry. between Atlanta and Griffin; and the Southern Ry. between Griffin and Fort Valley, also between Cordele and the Florida Line — All types of accommodations in cities; limited elsewhere, except for motor courts and motels which are increasingly available. Note: Route between Barnesville and Perry carries State 7 and US 341 markers.

Section a. TENNESSEE LINE *to* ATLANTA, *about 112 m.,* US 41.

Between Chattanooga and Atlanta US 41, known as the Dixie Highway, winds through the green Appalachian Valley where the mountains multi-sloped and wooded to the crest, suggest repose and ancient wisdom. This valley was the heart of the Cherokee Nation until 1838, when thousands of these Indians were displaced from their homes as the surge of white population flowed westward. The highway closely follows the route taken in 1864 by General Sherman in his Dalton-to-Atlanta campaign, when Federal forces drove the Confederates to Atlanta and ravaged a strip of land sixty miles wide through the state.

But in the past, at least, the destructiveness of war was relative, and few marks remain. Today northwest Georgia is exceptionally alive with fresh productive energies. The area around Atlanta is of course a story in itself. The northwest corner, with a growing season of 180-210 days of frost-free weather, situated partly in a limestone area, has been traditionally agricultural for two hundred years. An increasing annual income is derived from such farm products as cotton, corn, small grains, and fruit. Stimulated by the U. S. Soil Service and the State Extension agents, extensive pastures of perennial grasses and dairy herds of selectively bred cattle are becoming increasingly evident. When the pasture sequences are properly arranged, grazing throughout the year is now common practice. The area, especially in the mineral belt around Cartersville, is an exceptionally rich and varied mineral community, containing such sorts as limestone, talc, iron, manganese, barite, potash, ochre, shale, bauxite, cement, and slate; and a large number of workers are engaged in mining and processing these materials. Textile mills have grown increasingly and tended increasingly to diversify their products in recent years. The addition of a super-highway and the completion of the Allatoona Dam, which began the production of hydroelectric power in January, 1950, should turn this quiet corner of Georgia into a model center of the industrial arts. So far, the best instances of American neotechnic culture are the result of an expanding industrial program that is surrounded by an area of complementary advance in agricultural resources and skill.

RINGGOLD, about 7 m. (785 alt., 1,192 pop.), seat of Catoosa County, and incorporated in 1847, was almost entirely destroyed in the Chattanooga campaign.

TUNNEL HILL, 15 m. (853 alt., 255 pop.), grew up as a development of the Western & Atlantic Railroad. Here, on November 27, 1863, the last battle of Sherman's Chattanooga campaign was fought.

Right from Tunnel Hill about 0.5 m. to the OLD TUNNEL (reached by walking along the tracks), one of the first tunnels in the South, built as part of the Western & Atlantic Railroad. The old stone structure, no longer used since the construction of a new tunnel nearby, was hewn with pick and axe through the Chattoogata (local pronunciation Chat toóga) Ridge. Work commenced in 1848 and the first train passed through in 1850.

DALTON, about 22 m. (775 alt., 986 pop.), seat of Whitfield County, is second only to Rome as a manufacturing center for northwestern Georgia. This is also becoming a section of pastures and well-bred herds of cattle, and increasingly of poultry and hogs. Strawberries are plentiful in season and make up a considerable item in the local income.

Dalton was incorporated in 1847 and became the county seat when Whitfield County was formed in 1851. In this period the town developed as a shipping point for the copper mined at Ducktown, Tennessee, and during the 1800's the ore was hauled to Dalton in wagon trains.

Encircled by the blue ranges of the Cohutta Mountains, its streets lined with shade-casting trees, Dalton has an air of quiet detachment in spring and summer, when oaks, elms, and weeping willows move crisply in the cool mountain breezes. The factories stand along the railroad track apart from the residential area.

The textile industry has shown in recent years a steady up-trend in Dalton. It now manufactures thread, tire fabrics, yarn, duck, drill, full-fashioned hosiery, and osnaburg. It is the center of the candlewick-bedspread industry, which brings to northwestern Georgia an annual income of several million dollars. The first impetus was given to the tufting industry in 1919 by Mrs. M. G. Cannon, Jr., of Dalton, who persuaded New York department stores to take an interest in its products. A part of this work goes on in country homes, and along the highway tufted spreads, pillow cases, bath mats, and rugs are hung on display from clotheslines and fences. Spreads are also made in the Dalton factories, both by hand and machinery, for sale to outside markets.

CABIN CRAFTS PLANT (*open to visitors on weekdays, 8* A.M.-*5* P.M.), 120 East Morris Street at the railroad tracks, employs over 400 workers in the manufacturing and finishing of tufted products.

The HUFF HOUSE (*private*), 71 Selvidge St., served during the winter of 1864 as headquarters of General Joseph E. Johnston between the Chattanooga and Atlanta campaigns. Johnston's occupancy is commemorated by a small bronze plaque on the front lawn. The white-trimmed cottage, with four gables, has been altered but little since then.

RESACA, about *38 m.* (654 alt., 159 pop.), was first named Dublin by the Irish laborers who constructed the state railroad and built a large camp at the site of the present town. After the Mexican War the town was renamed by returned veterans in memory of their victory at the battle of Resaca de la Palma. In May, 1864, this town was the scene of the first major engagement resulting from Sherman's turning movement through Snake Creek Gap, which forced Johnston to abandon his advanced position along Rocky Face Ridge. The CONFEDERATE CEMETERY here contains the graves of 500 soldiers.

The OOSTANAULA RIVER, about *39 m.* (*excellent fishing for bream, black bass, goggled-eyed perch, and, in smaller quantities, rainbow trout*), is about *1.5 m.* from the MEMORIAL ARCH at the Calhoun city limits.

Facing the arch is a bronze STATUE OF SEQUOYAH (1770-1843), inventor of the Cherokee alphabet. The son of an Indian trader of Dutch ancestry and his Cherokee wife, Sequoyah bore the American name of George Gist, sometimes corrupted to Guess. He spent his boyhood in Tennessee and later moved to this section of Georgia. A skilled silversmith, he had his name written by a friend so that he could fashion a die to stamp his articles. This signature led him to ponder over the white men's "talking leaves," and to work out an alphabet for his people.

It is known that he spent twelve years (1809-21) devising a system of eighty-five characters, each representing a monosyllable of the Cherokee language. The Indians scorned his invention until he proved that he could communicate with his six-year-old daughter by means of the marks. The Council of Chiefs then approved his work, and soon thousands had learned to read and write. The *Book of Genesis* was printed, and a newspaper, the *Cherokee Phoenix,* was published.

Left from the Sequoyah statue on a good road to a massive granite shaft with bronze plaques indicating the SITE OF NEW ECHOTA (L), *1.8 m.,* the capital of the Cherokee Nation. In 1819 the Cherokees selected this place for their assemblies, and on October 20, 1820, they met here and adopted a republican form of government. The national assembly which they formed consisted of a council and a national committee of which John Ross was elected president. On November 12, 1825, the council resolved to build a permanent capital on the assembly site, which was surveyed and marked off in lots. A school and a courthouse were built, as well as other establishments, and in 1828 the citizens established the *Cherokee Phoenix,* their own newspaper printed in Sequoyah's syllabary as well as in English.

Near New Echota in 1821 the Moravian church set up the Oothcaloga Mission, which continued its work among the Indians until 1833, when the missions were closed by order of the state. This was a phase of the state's strategy to acquire the Cherokee lands. On December 28, 1828, the state had passed a law extending its jurisdiction over their territory. Ten years later, despite much intercession for the Cherokee and their recognition as a nation by the Federal government, Georgia succeeded in securing permission to remove the Indians. When this perfidious concession had been made, General Winfield Scott set up his headquarters at New Echota and effected, with the aid of 4,000 Federal and state troops and 4,000 volunteers, a ruthless removal of 13,000 Cherokees to the West.

CALHOUN, about *43 m.* (657 alt., 3,231 pop.), seat of Gordon County, is a trim town. Its original name, Oothcaloga (Ind., at the place of the Beaver dams), was changed in 1850 to honor John Caldwell Calhoun, Secretary of State under President Tyler. The town was incorporated in 1852. In the direct path of Sherman's march, it was almost completely destroyed in 1864, but was rebuilt after the war. This is an excellent dairy and poultry area, which ships large quantities of dairy products and eggs. It manufactures textiles, brick, tile, and lumber, and is a purchasing center for the hardwood that abounds in this section.

ADAIRSVILLE, about *50 m.* (708 alt., 916 pop.), has red brick shops with small wooden arcades that cover the sidewalk around the central square of the town.

Right from the railroad station at Adairsville to the first road across the railroad tracks, *0.1 m.;* R. on this road which roughly parallels the tracks, to the junction with another road at a brick store, *5.3 m.;* right on this road to BARNSLEY GARDENS (originally called Woodlands), *8.3 m.* (L). In the 1850's Godfrey Barnsley, from Derbyshire, England, who became a wealthy cotton exporter in Savannah, bought 10,000 acres here, and began the small frame house which still stands to the right of the main structure. Among the group of plantation buildings, in once formal gardens now fallen into a riot of confusion, are the ruins of the imposing brick house, begun in 1859 but never completed when the War between the States interrupted its construction. It stands roofless as the result of a windstorm, its central tower crumbling, its classic Palladian windows, now with loose hanging shutters, staring without speculation like sightless eyes. Part at least of the gardens was done by P. J. Berckmans, the noted Belgian botanist and landscape gardener who established *Fruitlands* in Augusta. Berckmans introduced English and Japanese yews, Nordmann's fir, and a California redwood among other exotics of the time. Stately hemlocks, Scotch rowans, and giant lindens add depth and character to the setting, and a more delicate feature is introduced by a profusion of shrub roses, including double sorts of the Cherokee. Barnsley's fortune was destroyed by the War, and though he returned to Savannah after the peace to mend his affairs, death intervened. In 1942 what remained of the estate, which had been reduced to less than a fifth of its acres, was sold to Mr. and Mrs. G. C. Phillips, and is now leased to tenants.

It is said that Augusta Evans Wilson was so affected by the image of Barnsley Gardens that it appears as the setting of her novel *St. Elmo* (*see* COLUMBUS).

CARTERSVILLE, about 70 *m.* (787 alt., 7,270 pop.), seat of Bartow County, is the center of the Bartow County mineral belt, and, except for textiles, the industries that center about the town mostly depend upon this rich store of natural wealth. The town was founded in 1832 on the site of the railroad underpass south of this point and was called Birmingham for the English coal and iron city. Later moved to its present center, and incorporated in 1850, it was named Cartersville for Farish Carter, a prominent landowner of the vicinity. Only two houses survived the Federal occupation in 1864.

FRIENDSHIP MONUMENT, in a public square by the railroad tracks, is a small monument on a rock foundation, erected by Mark A. Cooper at old Etowah in 1860 as a tribute to thirty-eight "friends and creditors." In the panic of 1857, when Cooper was forced to buy his partner's interest in the Etowah Manufacturing and Mining Company for $200,000, his friends endorsed his notes. Three years later he returned the paid notes and erected the monument, which was moved to Cartersville in 1927.

1. Left from Cartersville is the gigantic ALLATOONA DAM and RESERVOIR, the first step in a comprehensive plan for the development of the water resources of the Alabama-Coosa river system. Although World War II delayed the start of actual construction until 1946, it was authorized by Congress in the Flood Control Act of 1941. The system was designed by the U. S. Army Corps of Engineers, and constructed by a number of private contractors, among which was the Hardaway Contracting Company of Columbus, Georgia. The drama of construction came to an end in December of 1949 when the reservoir began to fill, and power production began in January, 1950. It was dedicated on October 15, 1952, by Lieutenant General Lewis A. Pick, Chief of Engineers, who said in part, "It is the first large multiple-purpose project to be completed by the Corps of Engineers in the State of Georgia, and we take pride in the construction of this modern structure as we dedicate it to the purposes for which it was constructed. Today's ceremony, however, has a deeper significance. The history of this project is an outstanding example of cooperation by Federal, state, and local interests. It will stand always as an impressive tribute to that cooperation and to all who contributed to it—to the constructive leaders who recognized the need for control and improvement of the rivers of this basin; to the individuals and civic groups who gave their support; and to the other Federal agencies with whom we have worked in closest harmony." Thus the American people have been presented with what is a symbol and at the same time an actual example of their neotechnic culture, the Allatoona Dam.

The cost of the Allatoona Project totaled up to around $32,000,000. The dam is being operated under the supervision of the Mobile District of the South Atlantic Division of the U. S. Army's Corps of Engineers.

Allatoona Dam is a concrete gravity-type structure on a curved axis. The spillway is controlled by eleven tainter gates, and four large sluices and one smaller sluiceway permit the direct release of water through the dam. The powerhouse is situated on the left bank of the stream, and the switchyard and transformer substation are placed between the dam and the powerhouse. The water area of the reservoir is technically divided into three strata: the bottom or "permanent pool" level of the reservoir, which is always kept full to supply the minimum water pressure necessary to operate the power plant; the middle or "power drawdown" level which controls stream flow; and the top level or "flood storage" portion which is empty except when flood waters are under storage. Water passes beyond the dam itself by one of three ways: penstocks or tubes leading to the turbines, spillway gates, and sluices. In the generation of hydro-electric power, the reserved water flows through the gate-controlled intake section of the dam by way of large pipes (or penstocks), then rotates the turbines in the powerhouse, and discharges through the draft tubes to the channel of the river below the dam. The turbines operate directly with generators that produce power, thus converting the flow of the water into electrical current, and the electric power, being stepped up in voltage by transformers, is carried away from the powerhouse by a line leading from the switchyard.

The statistical image of the dam follows. Stream: drainage area, 1,110 square miles; flow (average 1898-1945), 2.210 cubic feet per second. Reservoir: length of shoreline at normal summer level, 180 miles; surface area at normal summer level, 10,550 acres; amount of water at normal summer level, 101,483,000,000 gallons; storage reserved for flood regulation, 116,839,000,000 gallons. Dam: Total length at roadway level, 1,250 feet; elevation, roadway on top of dam 880 feet above sea level; crest of spillway, 835 feet; stilling basin floor, 690 feet. Powerhouse: two main power units, 36,000 KW each; one service power unit, 2,000 KW; additional main power units to be installed, one 36,000 KW unit; average total yearly output, 171,000,000 KWH.

The primary purpose of the dam is to hold back the floodwaters of the upper Etowah River in order to lessen floods in the lower Etowah Valley and in particular to reduce flood levels at Rome, where the Etowah and Oostanaula River join to form the Coosa River. As described above, the secondary purpose is the generation of power, the earnings of which will more than pay for the cost of construction and the interest on the sum within a reasonable interval. Water stored during the periods of greatest rainfall is released at dry times to increase the flow for power production at the site and at the plants of the Alabama Power Company on the Coosa River, and to help navigation on the Alabama River. Thirdly, additional benefits are derived from measures employed for reforestation, soil erosion control, water conservation, preservation of fish and wildlife, and malarial mosquito control. The extensive recreational area and facilities provided, perhaps make the greatest impression on the imagination of the people.

The mild and open climate makes some form of recreation pleasant throughout the year. The state of Georgia has under development two park areas—Redtop Mountain State Park (white) and George Washington Carver State Park (Negro)—containing some 2,000 acres. Bartow, Cherokee, and Cobb counties are each developing areas for public use. At present eight sites have been leased to private concerns to provide additional boating, docking facilities, fishing equipment and supplies, food, and overnight accommodations. Sites have been granted to Boy and Girl Scout troops, the YMCA, and other non-profit organizations to provide outdoor recreation for underprivileged children. A number of sites have been leased to private clubs, of which the Atlanta Yacht Club with clubhouse, docks, swimming beach, and parking area, is a model. So far some two hundred sites have been leased to individuals for cottages, and these increase steadily. The construction of public parks by state, county, and local agencies is encouraged, and these are given every possible help towards making the area available for the use of the American people.

From Cartersville take US 411 (L)—(when the new bypass on US 41 is completed around Cartersville, it will intersect directly with US 411 and State 20 (L) —about 3 m. to junction with paved State 20 (R), then to junction with paved Right Bank Access Road, now designated as State 294 N. Continue on this road to intersection with a paved spur (L) to Bartow County Public Use Area (*swimming beaches, bath houses, drinking water, picnic areas, trails*). Or straight ahead on State 294 N. to Cooper Branch Public Use Area (L) (*drinking water, comfort stations, picnic areas*); and to Bill's Boat House—Cooper Branch Landing (L) (*concessions, drinking water, comfort stations, public boat launching ramps, fishing camps: dock, boats, tackle, bait*). Along a ridge of Pine Mountain on Overlook Area there is a fine open view of the Dam, of a wide sweep of the Reservoir, and of the Etowah River and Valley. This road terminates at the Dam in the Dam Site Area (*concessions, drinking water, comfort stations, picnic area*). In the Exhibit Room of the Administration Building, located near the main parking area just north of the Overlook Area, is an instructive display of engineering features of the project, historical sites, and objects found in the reservoir area, and of prehistoric cultures of the Allatoona Basin.

On State 20, a dirt road leads beyond Rogers Creek to the intersection with a gravel road (R) to The Wilderness Camp (Stamp Creek Landing)—(*concessions, drinking water, comfort station, public boat launching ramps, fishing camps: dock, boats, tackle, bait*); 2.3 m. by water to the Dam Site area.

For roads into the area south of the Dam Site, *see* below.

2. Right from Cartersville on Main St., which follows State 61, to the junction with a dirt road, 0.2 m.; L. 0.9 m. on this road to the junction with another dirt road; L. 1.2 m. on this road to the Tumlin residence (L). From this house a lane leads to the ETOWAH INDIAN MOUNDS, on the property of Mr. Lewis Tumlin.

Grouped about the site of an Indian village are two large ceremonial mounds. Originally there were three large mounds and three burial mounds. These mounds were surrounded by a moat. The mound, on which it is supposed a temple was built, was explored by the Bureau of American Ethnology in 1882 and again in 1925-27 by Warren K. Moorehead, Director of Archeology at Phillips Academy, Andover, Massachusetts. The largest mound, which was evidently built for the public house or chief's dwelling, has not been explored. Sixty-five feet high and covering almost three acres, this is one of the largest aboriginal mounds in the United States.

From the site, principally from the smallest mounds, have been excavated many bones, stone effigies of human beings and eagles, clay idol heads, bone awls, and hundreds of shells, ornaments, and weapons. Since Moorehead unearthed artifacts made of copper from Lake Superior, pottery from Tennessee, and shells from the Gulf Coast, he concluded that these Indians were traders. He judged the mounds were built of soil taken from the great moat.

On State 61 at Pettit's Creek, 2.6 m., is a junction with a road; L. 1 m. on this road to WALNUT GROVE (*private*), built in the 1840's by R. M. Young. The house of slave-made brick, with its square white columns and two-story portico, is distinguished by large boxwoods. The aged woodwork of the interior was made from black walnut trees on the plantation. Walnut Grove was the childhood home of General P. M. B. Young, who was one of the youngest major generals of the Confederacy. General Young afterwards served in the U. S. House of Representatives, and was appointed consul general to Russia in 1885 by President Cleveland. He was minister to Guatemala and Honduras in 1893.

On State 61 at Shaw's Store, a frame structure, is the junction with the Euharlee Rd., *2.7 m.*

Right (*straight ahead*) *5 m.* from Shaw's Store on the Euharlee Rd. is VALLEY VIEW (L) (*private*), its entrance marked by two stone pillars and a gate; now the home of Mrs. Sproull Fouché. A driveway leads from the entrance through dense woods to the house, which looks out into the distance over a wide and deep valley. An iron gate opens to the garden where Carolina cherry laurels and boxwoods grow. Dwarf and tree box, English laurel, spruce and fir trees, crape myrtle, gardenia, and forsythia stand out boldly against the warm red bricks of the house.

The house, built by Colonel J. C. Sproull around 1840, has white, two-story Ionic columns extending across the front of the porch and around it on the two ends of the main house. A one-story hanging balcony also extends around the front and two ends of the house in a similar manner. The iron balustrade has been missing from the balcony since the day Union soldiers removed it to the Cooper Iron Works near Cartersville, to be cast into cannon balls. At the back the house has been extended, at a reduced height, by two opposite and parallel wings, the rooms of which open upon a continuous gallery supported by square columns, the whole elevated above an U-shaped court looking to the vegetable gardens, slave quarters, and a brick water tank, with open fields leveling off into the distance. As one looks out from the focal center on the gallery immediately behind the main house and down the court, the resulting optical impression is so sharply enclosed and detached in content from the present that one expects to hear a bell toll and to see the slaves returning from the fields—even with a tractor insistently at work in the near distance.

There is a Latin aphorism that art softens manners, but the arts of war as exercised by the Union army in this area were a notable exception. General George W. Schofield occupied the second floor for three months and kept his horses in one of the front rooms below, where his soldiers converted the grand piano into a feed trough. Confederate sharpshooters may have contributed to this striking expedient.

3. Left from Cartersville on US 411 to a junction with a road, *14.3 m.,* near the village of Pine Log; L. on this road to the entrance (L) to IN THE VALLEY, *17.1 m.,* once the home of Corra Harris (1869-1935), the Georgia novelist, who is best known for *A Circuit Rider's Wife,* a novel describing her days as the wife of a young minister. Hollywood used the scene at and around In the Valley to film a story made from her life and several of her published works, which was released on the screen in 1951 as *I'd Climb the Highest Mountain.*

From the entrance, the road winds *1 m.* through fields and woods to the rambling log house set on a knoll surrounded by pines. Near the house is the log study where Mrs. Harris wrote, and just across from the house is the CORRA HARRIS MEMORIAL CHAPEL, built of local stone, and designed by Ralph Adams Cram, architect for the Cathedral of St. John the Divine in New York. Her tomb is set into the floor at the foot of the altar. The chapel was erected in 1936 as a memorial by three of her nephews. In the Valley now belongs to Mr. and Mrs. Elbert Smith, Jr.

The ETOWAH RIVER, about *71.3 m.*, receives the regulated overflow from the Allatoona Dam. About two miles beyond the river is (L) an intersection with paved State 294 S., the Powerhouse Road, which leads to the south side of the Dam. On this road about *1 m.* from US 41, (R) an unpaved road leads over Bethany Bridge to RED TOP MOUNTAIN STATE PARK (L), now under development by the state (*swimming beaches, bath houses, tent and trailer camp area, concessions, drinking water, comfort stations, picnic areas, foot trails, public boat launching ramp, boats for rent, boat docks*).

At EMERSON, *4 m.* from Cartersville, begins the new four-lane highway route of US 41. (A new bridge is now under construction, November, 1952, over the Etowah River south of Cartersville. US 41 will be relocated to pass east of Cartersville and return to the old route north of the town.) From Emerson what was formerly US 41 is now State 293 through Acworth. Until the new route is stabilized on the maps it will be necessary to make inquiries along the new highway about villages and towns formerly designated as on US 41.

ALLATOONA has existed as a village since the 1830's when gold was discovered in the vicinity. Allatoona Landing of the Allatoona Reservoir Area is located here (L) (*concessions, drinking water, comfort stations, children's playground, public boat launching ramps, fishing camps: dock, boats, tackle, bait*); distance by water from Allatoona Dam, *4.8 m.*

By State 293, or watch for spur (L) near Bartow County Line from new US 41, State 3, to Block House Area of Allatoona Reservoir (*public boat launching ramps*). Continue to US Highway 41 Area (*public boat launching ramps*), and farther (L) an unpaved road leads to Groover's Marina—Tanyard Creek Landing—(*concessions, drinking water, comfort stations, public boat launching ramps, fishing camps: dock, boats, tackle, bait*); distance by water from Allatoona Dam, *5.7 m.*

ACWORTH, *80.1 m.* on State 293, (915 alt., 1,466 pop.) or L. at the junction of State 92 from new US 41, State 3, is a small town with a line of red brick stores along the highway; incorporated in 1860.

On State 92 between new US 41 and Acworth is the Cobb County Public Use Area at the Acworth Sub-Impounding Dam (R)—pool elevation 848 ft.—(*public boat launching ramps*); distance by water to Allatoona Dam, *10.5 m.*

State 92 from Acworth (L), a gravel road, makes a junction in about *4 m.* (L) with another gravel road which leads to King's Camp—Glade Farm Landing— of the Allatoona Area (*overnight accommodations, concessions, drinking water, comfort stations, public boat launching ramps: docks, boats, tackle, bait*); distance by water from Allatoona Dam, *4.6 m.* A short distance farther there is a junction with a dirt road (L) which leads to the GEORGE WASHINGTON CARVER STATE PARK (Negro) (*swimming beaches, bath houses, drinking water, comfort stations, picnic areas, trails, scenic boat rides, docks, boats, fishing*).

About *1 m.* farther on State 92 is a gravel road (L) which goes to Galt's Ferry Landing of the Allatoona Area (*concessions, drinking water, comfort stations, public boat launching ramps, fishing camps: docks, boats, tackle, bait*); distance by water from Allatoona Dam, *7.1 m.*

State 92 intersects with State 205, turn L. and continue to Victoria. The Lovingood Bridge Landing is a few miles farther (*concessions, drinking water, comfort stations, public boat ramps, fishing camps: docks, boats, tackle, bait*).

Just beyond Little River Bridge on State 205 (L) is Little River Landing of the Allatoona Area (*overnight accommodations, concessions, drinking water, comfort stations, scenic boat rides, public boat launching ramps, fishing camps: dock, boats, tackle, bait*); distance by water to Allatoona Dam, *14.7 m.*

On State 205 near the village of Univeter there is a junction with a road (L) which leads to State 20 (L); continue on State 20 about *2 m.* to the junction with another road (L) to Cherokee County Public Use Area (*swimming beaches, picnic areas, public boat launching ramps*); distance by water from Allatoona Dam, *16.0 m.*

KENNESAW, about *87 m.* (1,093 alt., 564 pop.), was for many years known as Big Shanty because it was the site of the Big Shanty Distillery Company. The village was not incorporated until 1887, when it was given its present name. Close to the railroad tracks (L), marked and enclosed by a fence, is the site where the engine *General* was seized by Andrews' raiders (*see* Atlanta).

Four miles south of Kennesaw (*when travelling on new US 41 watch for a signpost 1 m. south of Kennesaw*) is (R) the KENNESAW NATIONAL MONUMENT BATTLEFIELD PARK. The Park Office and Museum is situated near the point where the highway passes the northern tip of Big Kennesaw Mountain (1,809 alt.). Since 1933 the Park has been administered by the National Park Service of the U. S. Department of the Interior. It has increased from a battlefield site of sixty acres in 1917 to its present area of 3,094.21 acres as a battlefield park, and now covers the scene of the Battle of Kennesaw Mountain—June 19 to July 3, 1864, the first major engagement of the Dalton-Atlanta campaign. Big and Little Kennesaw mountains, the Park Museum and Office, the Kolb Farm and House, and Cheatham Hill are included in this area.

From Park Headquarters a double road of a mile and a half in length has been built to a cleared area just below the summit of Big Kennesaw Mountain. This point of elevation affords a superb sweep of the battle area below, and contributes effectively towards translating the map of the battle into a concrete image made up of actual places. The road was formally opened with the cutting of a ribbon on Easter Sunday, 1952. Trails have been cleared through the park area, some of which afford an excellent picture of the elaborate earthworks which featured the Confederate defense. A number of services are available at the Park Office.

By the summer of 1863, after the capture of Vicksburg by Grant on July 4, Federal forces were in possession of the Mississippi River.

Meanwhile the Union forces centered around Nashville gained control of Tennessee by a decisive action late in November which resulted in the fall of Chattanooga. The Confederate Army had entrenched at Dalton, where General Joseph E. Johnston had taken over the command on December 27, 1863. It was not until May 7, 1864, that Sherman with an army of around 100,000 men took the initiative against Johnston's forces of some 50,000 by an attack at Dalton. Johnston proved himself a subtle and mobile master of the strategy of evasion and delay, the only course left to him, because the larger Federal forces tirelessly outflanked him, thus threatening to cut his line of communication and supplies from Atlanta. Johnston would make a stand, the Federal forces would flow around his left and right; he would retreat and dig in again.

After Johnston evacuated Allatoona, he entrenched his army on Kennesaw, Lost, and Pine mountains, thus forming a triangle for the protection of Marietta and his supply line, the railroad. It was here finally that the first engagement, involving the combined corps of both armies, was to take place. Sherman had decided to give up his flanking movements and make a major threat.

The terrain of Johnston's position was hilly and densely wooded, with tangled vines overrunning the slopes of the mountains. In addition an easterly spring rain of almost three weeks had further increased the burden of movement. Unable to make a concentrated advance, Sherman divided his troops to cover all of the Confederate positions and slogged doggedly towards the entrenched Confederates, attacking the line between Kennesaw and Pine mountains on June 14, 1864. After a day's heavy fighting, the Confederates abandoned the position on Pine Mountain and by the next day were entrenched between Kennesaw and Lost mountains. The Union forces continued to edge forward to such an extent that the Confederates were forced to retreat from Lost Mountain. Johnston then centered his forces on Kennesaw Mountain, with Hood covering the town of Marietta and Hardee protecting the railroad. As Sherman now struck for the Confederate left flank, Hood on June 22 made an attack at Kolb Farm with the intention of diverting the Federal movement, but he was repulsed severely and forced to take up a position at a hill south of the Marietta-Dallas Road.

Sherman decided to split the Confederate center and then deal with the dispersed flanks of Johnston's army piecemeal. The Army of the Cumberland under Thomas was to make an assault on the Confederate center at the hill south of the Marietta-Dallas Road (now called Cheatham Hill), defended by General Cheatham, while James B. McPherson's Army of Tennessee was to engage the Confederate center at the south end of Little Kennesaw Mountain. It was expected that this double wedge-action if undertaken simultaneously would prevent one section of the Confederate Army from supporting the other. The attack came on June 27. It was stubborn and sustained on both sides, but the Federals were driven back with a loss of some 2,500 men, while the Confederate generals, Hardee and Loring, though they bore the brunt of the attack, were so well barricaded that they lost only 808 men.

After the failure of this gambit, Sherman returned to his less brilliant but more effective routine of outflanking Johnston. Johnston, unable to protect his rear because of the excess of Union men, was forced to abandon Kennesaw Mountain on July 2 and to retreat towards Atlanta for its protection. At the time of his retreat, Johnston's left was farther from Atlanta than Sherman's right.

With the scene of action in this unsteady light, Johnston received a telegram from Richmond on July 17 relieving him of his command and appointing General John B. Hood in his place. General Hood was a man of decision if not strategy. Four battles costly for the Confederacy followed one another in an impetuous sequence, and on September 2 the Union Army entered Atlanta. With no effective core of energy left except that of Lee in Virginia whom Grant held minutely engaged, with the army deprived of its richest remaining source of equipment, food, and manpower, the Confederacy sank hopelessly into its final agony. Sherman's March to the Sea was without significant resistance, and in December he presented the city of Savannah to Lincoln as a "Christmas gift."

MARIETTA, about 92 m.—or from Atlanta 20 m.—(1,118 alt., 20,687 pop.), seat of Cobb County, is built about an old-fashioned town square. Marietta came into existence in 1832 when Cobb County was created from Cherokee land, but it was not incorporated until 1834. The town grew rapidly in the 1840's, and in the 1850's hotels were built for summer residents who came from the state's lowlands for the sake of the cooler days and fresh mountain nights. Its second period of pronounced growth began with the construction of Government Aircraft Plant No. 6 (see below) during World War II and later with the reorganization of the plant by the Lockheed Aircraft Corporation after the outbreak of the Korean War.

In addition to the routine bustle of a town situated near a large industrial unit, on Saturdays Marietta's town square is further enlivened by farmers and their families who come in from the surrounding farms to buy and sell. The local farms supply garden truck, dairy products, eggs, and especially poultry; for north Georgia's first magnitude broiler industry extends into this area.

The MARIETTA NATIONAL CEMETERY, Washington St. five blocks left of the public square, is a well-kept plot of twenty-four acres surrounded by a high stone wall. There are 10,158 Union soldiers buried here, the graves row on row, each marked with a headstone; at intervals are memorial monuments erected by home states. Large oaks and dark magnolias, supported by a shrubbery of southern evergreens, relieved in season by roses and other colorful flowers, maintain an elegiac quiet over the Union dead.

The CONFEDERATE CEMETERY, Powder Springs St. one-half mile south of the public square, is a section of the inclusive city cemetery. On the slope of a hill are more than three thousand graves indicated by rows of marble slabs, most of them unmarked. Old cedars and magnolias create an atmosphere of age and of rest from former passion and decision.

The ALICE McLELLAN BIRNEY MEMORIAL stands on the high school grounds on Winn St. Alice Birney, whose girlhood home was in Marietta, was the founder of the National Congress of Parents and Teachers. The Memorial, a sundial on a base of Georgia marble with a stone court, signifies a woman who was wise enough to know that humanity it badly served when the state's educational policy so works as to estrange the child from the family.

The LOCKHEED AIRCRAFT CORPORATION (Georgia Division) and (adjacent) the DOBBINS AIR FORCE BASE are on (R) US Highway 41 E, about 2 m. from its intersection with the Roswell Road.

Government Aircraft Plant No. 6 was built during World War II in a brief thirteen months between March, 1942, and April, 1943, and operated for the duration of the war by the Bell Aircraft Corporation for the purpose of building Boeing-designed B-29's, the famed Superfortresses of World War II. After the war, production ceased at the plant, but it was used to store machine tools belonging to the Army Air Force as a preparedness step in case of future need.

With the outbreak of the Korean War rumors spread in the area that the plant, locally known as the Bell Bomber Plant, would reopen. Eventually rumor became fact and it was announced that the Army Air Force had requested the Lockheed Aircraft Corporation to clear the plant for production. It was to begin operations with the modification and reconditioning of B-29's, but finally to build the new six-engine B-47 Stratojet, with a top speed calculated at 600 m.p.h.

Dobbins Air Force Base, originally begun as a commercial airfield by Cobb County, was named in honor of Captain Charles Dobbins, of Marietta, a pilot who lost his life in World War II. The area now occupied by Lockheed and the Dobbins Air Base was originally a single tract of several thousand acres. But with the reactivation of the plant the area was technically divided into two sections: Dobbins Base, under the Continental Air Command for flight use, and the production area, under Lockheed which operates it for the Air Material Command on a fixed fee basis, i.e., the company builds planes for the estimated cost plus a fixed fee for doing the work; Lockheed gets only the original contract fee whether base costs rise or not. In test flights planes use the runway of the Dobbins Base. Fifty acres are covered by the main buildings alone of the factory, with a second level underground.

With its employees now numbering around 11,000, the renewal of the plant placed a heavy burden on Cobb County utilities, housing, and other civic and area services. The company has taken on a constructive role in meeting these needs in co-operation with local authorities. Cobb County and Southeastern manufacturers and merchants will secure a generous part of the cost of the B-47's since more than fifty per cent of the manufacture of the plane will be regionally subcontracted. But doubtless the most important contribution in a regional sense is not so much the increase in per capita income but rather the expansion of industrial skills among the workers. In addition an actual training program has been formally maintained. For in the making of a complex and exact product many steady and rigorous skills become finally unified in the thing made, and the B-47 Stratojet is not only exact and complex but extremely so. From the focal point of a neotechnic civilization, the plant is one of the more significant "schools" in modern Georgia.

At Marietta is a junction with State 5 (*see* TOUR *13*).

ATLANTA, about *112 m.* (1,050 alt., 331,314 pop.) (*see* ATLANTA).

Atlanta is at the junction with US 78 (*see* TOUR *8*), with US 29 (*see* TOUR *3*), with US 42 (*see* TOUR *12*), with US 23 (*see* TOUR *7*), and with US 19 (*see* TOUR *6*), which unites with US 41 between this point and Griffin.

Section b. ATLANTA *to* FLORIDA LINE, *about 256 m., US 41 to Barnesville, US 341 from Barnesville to Perry, and US 41 from Perry to the Florida Line.*

South of Atlanta, *o m.,* US 41 crosses an agricultural section of the rolling Piedmont region, beautiful in spring with the pink blossoms of peach orchards. Most of the houses between Atlanta and Griffin were destroyed by Sherman's forces before they turned eastward a few miles above Griffin and swept on to Savannah and the sea. South of Griffin the people were more fortunate in saving their homes, though they too saw the wreck of the system that had raised them to power and prosperity. From the Piedmont belt the route crosses the Fall Line and continues over the westerly side of the Coastal Plain. The staple crops are cotton, corn, tobacco, and peanuts. Pecans take a minor position. With the increase in grass and legume pastures beef and dairy cattle have increased. This area has from 210 to 240 days and over of frost-free weather.

The FAIR OF 1850 (*conducted tour: adults $1.00, children 50¢*) is a small but exceptional historical museum owned by Colonel John W. West. The seven buildings housing the museum were brought from various sections of Georgia. Included in the collection are early firearms, vehicles, household effects, clothing, and documents. The bake oven in the side of the chimney, the smoke-jack, the crane, the trivet, and the dutch-oven; a full set of gunsmith's tools, a complete shoe shop, and farm equipment—give a cross section of life in the 1850's from the instrumental point of view.

The museum stands on the SITE OF THE BATTLE OF JONESBORO, a combat lasting two days, August 31 and September 1, 1864, in which resistance by Hardee was broken down by Sherman, and the southern army forced to evacuate the Atlanta area.

JONESBORO, *17.3 m.* (905 alt., 1,741 pop.), seat of Clayton County, is often identified as a source of scenes for Margaret Mitchell's Pulitzer Prize novel, *Gone With the Wind,* but Miss Mitchell always insisted that Tara Plantation was entirely a figure of the imagination.

The KELL HOUSE (*private*), *29 m.,* was the home of Captain John Mc-Intosh Kell, a naval officer under Commodore Perry on his expedition to Japan, later a captain in the Confederate navy, executive officer of the *Alabama,* and an adjutant general of the state. Standing 200 yards (L) from the highway, the simple, white frame house is unusual chiefly for its iron-railed porch, with steps at both ends. It was while visiting in this house that Sidney Lanier (*see* MACON) wrote his lyric "Corn."

The GEORGIA AGRICULTURAL EXPERIMENT STATION, about *37 m.,* began to function at Athens in 1888, a year after an act of Congress appropriated to each state $15,000 annually in connection with agricultural colleges. A year later the Station was moved to Experiment near Griffin, the people of Spalding County having contributed 130 acres of land and $4,000. Since that time, the Station has grown rapidly, until now it owns approximately 1,200 acres and also holds under lease another 16,000 acres. Both buildings and equipment have increased, and the Station now employs a staff of ninety technically trained persons as well as clerks, skilled laborers, and others.

The Georgia Mountain Experiment Station at Blairsville was established as a branch of this Station in 1930, with around 370 acres, for the purpose of research in the agricultural needs of the mountain region. Since late 1938, the Station has operated, under a co-operative and license agreement, a 15,000-acre tract of Federal land in the western corner of Putnam County. This is an area of research work in forestry, beef cattle, and pasture. Parts of this tract are also used by the Agronomy Department to produce and to increase foundation seed stocks for distribution to the farmers of the state.

Station work includes rsearch conducted by eleven departments: Agronomy, Agricultural Economics, Agricultural Engineering, Animal Industry, Botany, Chemistry, Entomology, Food Processing, Home Economics, Horticulture, and the Primary Plant Introduction Station.

Investigations are made with field crops, fruit, vegetables, small grain, pastures, melons, beef cattle, dairy cattle, sheep, and hogs. Studies are made of the processing and use of food. Insect and disease control is investigated. Breeding Programs include the development and testing of new and improved varieties of plants.

Among the crops developed and released are Dixie Crimson Clover, Empire Cotton, Truhart Perfection Pimiento, Chancellor and Sanford wheat, and Georgia 101 and 103 corn. Dixie Crimson Clover and Empire Cotton are worth millions annually to the farmers of the state.

GRIFFIN, about *39 m.* (965 alt., 13,982 pop.), seat of Spalding County, is a center of brisk textile activities. The mills, however, have been built apart from the business and residential sections and do not detract from the clear perspective of the city. Although its age is shown by numerous houses and buildings, Griffin is more suggestive of the new industrial South than it is of ante-bellum days. Along the streets and parkways so many iris bloom in the spring that it is called the Iris City.

The land on which Griffin is built was part of the Creek territory through which the half-Indian chief William McIntosh (*see* TOUR *10*) blazed a trail in 1812, when he led the lower Creek against the British. The town was not laid out until twenty-eight years later, when Colonel Lewis Lawrence Griffin purchased 800 acres and reserved twenty-two of them for churches, parks, and public buildings. The Dundee Mills, Inc., were organized in 1888. From a small beginning, they have become one of the largest producers of towels in the world, along with corduroy, diapers, cotton flannel, and table damask. The company employs around 3,300 persons and uses some 50,000 bales of cotton annually. Griffin has about a dozen other textile mills, large and small, engaged in manufacturing an exceptional range of textile products, mostly cotton. The city has an annual industrial payroll of fourteen million dollars.

Cash crops in the order of importance are peaches, small grain, crimson clover, cotton, and pimientos. The Pomona Products Co. and Community Canning Plants as well as nearness to Atlanta markets have stimulated vegetable production. In addition to the above leading crops, Spalding County has surged forward in the production of small grain and lespedeza seed. In the five years from 1946 to 1950, dairying doubled, beef production tripled, 7,000 acres were seeded in permanent pasture, and 10,000 acres planted for temporary grazing. The growth in sericea lespedeza and kudzu for supplementary grazing has been notable. Poultry for egg production is on the increase because of the steady demand for hatching eggs. The Georgia Experiment Station's work in the production and processing of small fruits and berries has contributed greatly to the success of these fruits in the area. This picture of a diversified and expanding agriculture holds forth great promise for the health and happiness of the people of Georgia.

The POMONA PRODUCTS COMPANY PLANT (*open to visitors*), on Pimiento Avenue, one block off Meriwether Street, is one of the country's major pimiento canneries, producing an average of ten million cans annually. The chances are high that whenever a can of pimientos is opened it is a Pomona product. The pimiento season is from the first part of August to the middle of November, but the plant operates about nine months a year by packing other fruits and vegetables.

The MUNICIPAL PARK (*18-hole golf course, weekdays 50¢, Sundays $1.00; playground; swimming pool, adults 25¢, children 15¢; picnic facilities; bridle paths*), on S. 9th St., contains thousands of iris plants. The two hundred acres that make up Municipal Park include an eighteen-hole golf course with rustic club house, large natural areas and woodland with landscaped and sequestered sections, open lawn and meadow, and a pure fresh-water stream fed by springs. There are easily accessible picnic grounds, parking areas, and comfort stations in addition to tables, benches, outdoor cooking ovens, a wading pool for small children, swings and other play apparatus, a supply of good drinking water, and shelters. Inside the park are also lighted tennis courts, an open-air dance pavilion, and a concrete swimming pool with bathhouse, lockers, and showers.

The Negro park consisting of forty-six acres has an outdoor concrete swimming pool and bathhouse, an open-air dance pavilion, beautiful natural picnic grounds, and play space for children.

HAWKES LIBRARY, 210 S. 6th St., is a two-story red brick building of English design with a well-equipped auditorium on the second floor. Built in 1916 with a $10,000 gift from the late Albert King Hawkes of Atlanta and a $5,000 appropriation from the city, it now has a circulating department of some sixteen thousand books and a reading room with fifty subscriptions to leading magazines and newspapers. The library has a research department and a complete section for children.

At Griffin US 19 (*see* TOUR 6) branches R. from US 41.

BARNESVILLE, about *54 m.* (859 alt., 4,185 pop.), seat of Lamar County, was founded in 1826 by Gideon Barnes, a popular tavern keeper of pioneer days. The tavern stood on the old Alabama Road, originally an Indian trail which, in the early part of the nineteenth century, was widened to form a highway for stagecoaches. Barnesville has cotton mills, facilities for pecan shelling, several planing and lumber mills, and a furniture factory.

GORDON MILITARY COLLEGE, five blocks R. of the city square, is a non-sectarian school offering a six-year course in high school and college work. Its extensive campus and red brick buildings were formerly those of a state agricultural and mechanical school. Established in 1852 as the Barnesville Male and Female High School, this college was renamed later in honor of the Confederate general, John B. Gordon. Military training was introduced in 1880, and training now consists of Basic and Senior ROTC units leading to a reserve commission. Approximately 125 boarding students and 210 day students are enrolled. The school offers the 8th grade, four years of high school and two years of college work.

At Barnesville US 41 turns L. to Forsyth and Macon (*see* TOUR *12*).

TOUR *2 continues from Barnesville to Perry on* US 341.

Right from Barnesville on hard-surfaced State 18 to the GACHET HOME, *3 m.,* where General de La Fayette paused for a night on his tour of the South in 1825. This two-story, rectangular, white house, built in 1823, has hand-hewn shutters, hand-carved banisters, and wooden pegs instead of nails. The interior, with its three rooms opening on each side of a broad central stairhall, is notable for its timber ceilings.

ROBERTA, about *83 m.* (487 alt., 673 pop.), is a trading village for farmers. In the center of Roberta is the BEN HAWKINS MONUMENT, erected in 1930 by the U. S. Government to commemorate the life and services of this Indian agent (*see* HAWKINSVILLE, TOUR *12*).

Roberta is at the junction with US 80 (*see* TOUR *9*).

The FORT VALLEY STATE COLLEGE (Negro), about *99 m.,* has as its antecedents the Fort Valley Normal and Industrial School and the State Teachers and Agricultural College at Forsyth. When the Fort Valley institution began in 1895, it had as its first principal John W. Davidson, a graduate of Atlanta University. A gift of $5,000 from the Anna Jeanes Foundation in 1903 was used for the building of a girls' dormitory, Jeanes Hall; and this sum was matched by an equal amount from the General Education Board. With the election of Henry Alexander Hunt, who was also an Atlanta University graduate, as the second principal, in 1904 the school entered a period of steady growth and expansion. Collis P. Huntington, the railroad financier, contributed $25,-000 for a girls' dormitory in 1908 which was named Huntington Hall in his honor.

In 1919 the institution became affiliated with the American Church Institute, an agency of the Protestant Episcopal Church, and this relationship continued until 1939 when the school passed from church to state supervision. Funds came in from a number of educational foundations during this period and from other contributions in both large and small amounts. Ohio Hall was built in 1930 with funds contributed by Episcopalians resident in Ohio. A number of other important buildings were constructed in this period, and at the time of Principal Hunt's death in 1938, the school was in a well-advanced state of operation.

On July 1, 1939, the Fort Valley Normal and Industrial School and the State Teachers and Agricultural College at Forsyth were merged under state control to form the present Fort Valley State College at Fort Valley. It was officially designated the Land-Grant college for Negroes by the Georgia Legislature in 1949.

The college offers a B.S. in Education and also in other subjects including Agriculture, and a B.A. in English, History, or Sociology. Accredited by the Southern Association of Colleges and Secondary Schools and by the State Department of Education of the State of Georgia, it has a complete four-year curriculum. The enrollment for the summer quarter of 1950 was 1,828 students, and the enrollment of regular students for the academic year 1950-51 was 716.

The grounds of the college make up 500 acres, of which thirty are used for the main campus. The Athletic Field of about six acres in size is equipped for football, basketball, volleyball, track, and other games. A 95-acre farm occupies the south part of the grounds. Together with substantial appropriations from the College budget, a recent grant from the Carnegie Corporation has made it possible to increase the book collection from 5,000 volumes to 16,000 as well as to maintain an excellent subscription list of newspapers and periodicals. The Carnegie Library was built with funds provided by the Carnegie Foundation in 1925. At present the offices of the Registrar, the Dean, the Business Manager, and the President of the College are located on the first floor of the Library.

FORT VALLEY, about *100 m.* (525 alt., 6,820 pop.), the seat of Peach County, developed slowly around an academy and church established about 1836. When a railroad reached the town in 1851, it began to grow more rapidly and was incorporated in 1856.

Peach County is one of the leading peach-growing areas in an extensive section that is famous for its pink blossoms in April. Hal Steed in his book *Georgia: Unfinished State,* in celebrating Fort Valley and its peaches, makes the challenging claim that the peach industry is one of the oldest forms of diversified farming in Georgia. Peach County also has pecans, garden vegetables, and melons as well as cattle, all edging up on corn and cotton.

At Fort Valley is the junction with State 49 (*see* TOUR 2B).

PERRY, about *112 m.* (355 alt., 3,849 pop.), seat of Houston County, was incorporated in 1824. Two well-preserved landmarks are the FIRST

METHODIST CHURCH, a white frame structure erected in 1827, and the PRESBYTERIAN CHURCH, built in 1849.

At Perry TOUR 2 leaves US 341 (*see* TOUR *12*) and returns (R) to US 41 *to* Valdosta and the Florida Line.

VIENNA (pronounced Vy-enna), about *140 m.* (350 alt., 2,202 pop.), seat of Dooly County, was first called Berrien and later Centreville; it was incorporated under its present name in 1841. The county had been created from Creek territory twenty years earlier and named for the Revolutionary soldier Colonel John Dooly, who was killed in 1780 by Tories at his home near Augusta.

Vienna is a center for pecan shelling, vegetable canning, and the shipping of truck produce. Though the town is not in the area usually associated with Georgia peaches, this fruit and also pimientos are an important source of income.

CORDELE, about *150 m.* (336 alt., 9,462 pop.), the seat of Crisp County, was founded in 1888 as a railroad junction and is now served by three large lines—the Georgia Southern and Florida, the Atlantic Coast Line, and the Seaboard Air Line; and the lesser Albany and Northern. As a result of this confluence of railroads, Cordele has developed rapidly in recent years as a center of industry and agricultural production and marketing. Industrial plants include cotton mills, a foundry and steel mill, pecan shellers, peanut processers and shellers, cotton oil presses, lumber mills, and fertilizer factories as well as various implement and machine works. But the agricultural products are even more diversified than the industrial.

The CORDELE STATE FARMERS MARKET, *1 m.* north of Cordele on US 41, is operated under the supervision of Georgia's Department of Agriculture. Farmers and civic leaders in Cordele worked with the State Commissioner of Agriculture, the city, the Crisp County Commissioners, and the county agent to establish a marketing program for the entire Middle Southwest Georgia area. Growers from all sections of the producing area haul their products to the market, but especially watermelons and cantaloupes. More than 1,700 cars of watermelons are shipped during the season from the market. In a recent year watermelons led the sales with $924,000; then sweet potatoes at $125,000; a total of 368,000 pounds of pecans sold at auction for $88,320; and finally cantaloupes, among the major items, at $76,500. In addition cucumbers, onions, squash, beans, field peas, sweet corn, tomatoes, and butter beans made up a considerable volume. The Farm Bureau and the various agricultural agencies have planned a commodity program to make produce available for the greater part of the year.

A new $100,000 grading building has just been completed and loading areas have been paved. The use of graders, as well as sweet potato washing and waxing machines, by a group of farmers, has established a reputation for Cordele Market sweet potatoes. In the first six months of 1952, sales on the market totaled $796,000.

The Watermelon Festival in Cordele comes sometime just after the first week in June and lasts into July. This month-long movable feast is complete with a queen and a gala ball. Cordele deserves to be called the Watermelon Capital of the South.

Right from Cordele on paved US 280 to the Crisp County HYDROELECTRIC POWER DAM AND PLANT, *6 m.*, built, owned, and operated by Crisp County. In 1927 a group of citizens initiated a five-year development program that included a proposed hydroelectric power dam across the Flint River, which drains an area of 3,500 square miles. The plant was chartered in 1925 by an amendment to the state constitution, and was financed by a quarter million dollar county bond issue. The act provided for the creation of a Crisp County Power Commission, composed of seven members: three county commissioners, and the other four elected by the grand jury in alternates of two for two years. Full and final authority is vested in the Commission in all matters pertaining to the construction and operation of the project on behalf of the people of Crisp County.

Construction began in October, 1928; the generation of power August 1, 1930. After twenty years of operation the plant is serving about five thousand consumers, of which more than two thousand are rural, and is producing a gross revenue of one-half million dollars. The plant makes Crisp County stand high in regard to the percentage of farm electrification.

GEORGIA VETERANS MEMORIAL STATE PARK, R. from Cordele *10 m.* on US 280, State 30, and then L., is a 1,000-acre tract of parkland on the shores of Lake Blackshear (*swimming, dock, boating, fishing, water supply system, day use area: picnic grounds and children's playground, two overnight cabins,* and *seven vacation cabins; for reservations, address the superintendent, Georgia Veterans Memorial State Park, Cordele, Georgia*).

In 1946 the Commissioners of Crisp County purchased the 1,000-acre area, deeding the land to the state in honor of Georgia's dead of World Wars I and II. Seventy miles of roads, lined with trees that are curtained with Spanish moss, wind around the 8,000-acre lake that has been created by the dam of the Crisp County Power Plant. Among sportsmen this area has an established reputation for the excellence of its fishing. Outside of the park boundary many privately owned cabins have been built along the lake. A Veterans' Memorial Building, completely equipped with restaurant and fountain facilities, has recently been completed and is now in operation. The building is large enough for meetings and conventions. Winter quarters are provided for race horses in the park, and racing tracks have been built.

The SCHOOL BOY PATROL SAFETY SCHOOL, located in the park on Lake Blackshear, is operated by the Georgia State Patrol for school patrols throughout the state. Patrols are treated to a week of recreation and lessons in safety. Accommodations include a completely modern kitchen, well-equipped clinic, new swimming pool, open recreation hall, and comfortable barracks-type buildings.

Left from Cordele on State 257 (part of the Blackshear Road constructed in 1814 by General Andrew Jackson's orders) *10 m.* to the GEORGE WALTON EXPERIMENTAL FOREST (*open to the public*) of the CORDELE-TIFTON FOREST AND RESEARCH

CENTER. On January 2, 1947, the Southeastern Forest Experiment Station of the U. S. Forest Service, signed a 50-year lease, rent free, on 4,000 acres of timberland in Dooly County, with owner Holt E. Walton, of Cordele. The tract was named in honor of George Walton, one of Georgia's three signers of the Declaration of Independence. The transaction, marking a forward step in southern forest research, has brought the scientist and the timber producer together in order to determine and to demonstrate methods of growing better timber faster on a large scale. Mr. Walton is carrying out the plans developed by the research foresters.

The timber of the George Walton Experimental Forest is representative of the eleven million-acre belt of longleaf slash pine of the Middle Coastal Plain of Georgia. Running in a northeasterly-southwesterly direction from the Florida Line to the Savannah River, it constitutes the highly fertile, gently rolling country that lies between the flatwoods of the south and the Piedmont of the north. In this area potential growth rates for pine rank with the highest in the nation. The experimental forest contains over 500 acres of planted slash pine, from eighteen years downward, and in various spacings from the traditionally wide of the naval stores industry to the narrowest which is suitable for quantity production of small items. It so happened that Mr. Walton made a large planting years ago which fits perfectly into the current research program.

In addition to timber a second basic source of forest income is forage. This research feature is centered at Tifton (see below), with extensive field installations of 2,000 acres near Alapaha, on US 82, some twenty-five miles to the east of Tifton. On this area of state-owned land, the Southeastern Forest Experiment Station, the Bureau of Plant Industry, Soils, and Agricultural Engineering, the Bureau of Animal Industry, and the state of Georgia are co-operating on a variety of range and reseeding projects. Among the projects already in progress some seven years are managing native forest ranges profitably; the introduction of improved forage species for added grazing profits; the integration of timber and stock on a single holding; and the use of reseeded strips as effective fire barriers.

ASHBURN, about *170 m.* (450 alt., 2,918 pop.), seat of Turner County, is typical of the newer southern Georgia towns; its small frame houses are set back from wide streets and shaded by large trees. This town, surrounded by a productive agricultural region, is a poultry and livestock center.

At SYCAMORE, about *172 m.* (415 alt., 634 pop.), is the junction with State 32, L. (*see* TOUR 2C).

The ABRAHAM BALDWIN AGRICULTURAL COLLEGE (R), about *188 m.,* was named in honor of Abraham Baldwin, a Georgia delegate to the constitutional convention in 1787 at Philadelphia, who shared a tradition of civil wisdom with Thomas Jefferson. His interest in education in early Georgia is aptly exhibited in this statement: "As it is the distinguishing happiness of free government that civil order should be the result of choice and not necessity, and the common wishes of the people become the law of the land, their public prosperity and even existence, very much depends upon suitably forming the minds and morals of their citizens."

Administration Building and Museum, Jefferson Davis Memorial Park

Yard Buildings at Liberty Hall, Alexander H. Stephens Memorial State Park

The Chapel on the grounds of the Warm Springs Foundation

The Barbecue and Cafeteria on Overlook Hill, Ida Cason Gardens

The Club House, Ida Cason Gardens

Painting by Athos Menaboni on west wall of the Club House, Ida Cason Gardens

Georgia is one of the world's strategic sources of Naval Stores

Lush Pastures are a common sight in Georgia

Irrigation is becoming an accepted agricultural technique in Georgia

Peach Orchard near Macon

Corn is one of the staple crops in Georgia

Cultivating Cotton: The "Iron Mule" replaces its epic counterpart

In spite of Crop Diversification, Cotton is still King

The Administration Building at Mercer University, built in 1871, Macon

The institution is a coeducational junior college maintained by the University System of Georgia. Originally one of the state's agricultural and mechanical high schools, it became, as technical needs grew more complex, the State College for men in 1924, and the present agricultural college in 1933. Several hundred students are engaged in a two-year course of studies based on scientific farming and home making. Demonstration and experimental work at the Georgia Coastal Plain Experiment Station supplies an important working laboratory for the domestic and agricultural arts.

The GEORGIA COASTAL PLAIN EXPERIMENT STATION, about *189 m.*, is a unit of the College of Agriculture, University System of Georgia. In co-operation with various state and Federal agricultural agencies, the station promotes efficient methods of agriculture and animal husbandry. Primary emphasis has been given to work with beef cattle, hogs, cotton, peanuts, corn, grasses, legumes, a variety of vegetables, sweet potatoes, blueberries, and muscadine grapes.

In addition to providing research results to farm people through the county agricultural agents, the vocational agricultural teachers, and other workers, the station provides much information to farmers directly. Organized groups of farmers visit the station year after year, to make a survey of its procedures and to observe experimental results. Co-operative short courses also bring thousands of other farmers to see the station's exemplary work at first hand. Interviews with staff members about problems as they arise are numberless.

TIFTON, about *190 m.* (370 alt., 6,831 pop.), seat of Tift County, was incorporated in 1891; both town and county were named for Nelson Tift, Georgia member of the U. S. Congress (1868-69).

Tifton stands high among the top seven tobacco markets in Georgia according to the 1951 report of the Georgia Department of Agriculture. Farmers sold 12,410,434 pounds for a total sum of $5,910,399.30, at an average price of 47.62 cents a pound.

Besides being a row crop tobacco is a cash crop. The farmer brings the leaf to the market, and when the auctioneer knocks it down to the highest bidder, an identification tag is attached to the lot, and payment is the next transaction. When the boll weevil forced farmers in 1917 to look to new crops, tobacco made steady gains until today tobacco stands next to cotton as a cash crop. Tobacco raising is a family enterprise. All hands are required in planting the seed bed at the proper time in winter, setting the plants when the weather is in season, cultivating, stripping the leaves, keeping the heat in the curing barn right, and at last hauling the cured leaf to the market.

Although Tifton is primarily known as a tobacco market, it is an important market also for pecans and peanuts, with two large peanut-shelling establishments. Several of the large canning companies, such as Campbell Soup, grow their own tomato plants near Tifton, shipping them out by the millions. Other vegetable plants are brought on in the mild climate and shipped elsewhere for spring and fall planting.

The TIFTON FARMERS MARKET, supervised by the Georgia State Department of Agriculture, serves for the most part as a feeder market where dealers can buy directly from local producers. It began operation in 1942. Sales have increased gradually and now amount to about $800,000 annually.

The PLANT OF THE IMPERIAL TOBACCO COMPANY OF GREAT BRITAIN AND IRELAND, First St. (R) is a processing center for redrying the tobacco purchased in Georgia. Since the duty in England on American-grown tobacco is at present $12.50 a pound when it contains above ten per cent moisture but $25 a pound when the moisture content is less, the plant reduces the natural moisture and introduces a regulated amount artificially, which at the same time makes the tobacco seaworthy. Savannah serves as the shipping point on the seaboard.

Tifton is a honey section along with a number of others in Georgia. Bees are shipped to most of the apple growing sections and even to Canada for the purpose of increasing the yield of fruit.

Left from Tifton on paved State 50 to a branch of the ARMOUR MEAT-PACKING PLANT (*open to visitors*), *1.2 m.* The volume of livestock has increased to such an extent that the plant can operate almost continuously, processing hogs, cattle, and poultry. Products are shipped directly to branch distribution points throughout the southeastern section.

ADEL, about *213 m.* (246 alt., 2,776 pop.), seat of Cook County, was incorporated in 1900. It is a tobacco market and also the headquarters of the Sowega (coined from Southwestern Georgia) Melon Growers Co-operative Association, owned by a group of farmers.

VALDOSTA, *237 m.* (215 alt., 20,046 pop.), is one of the most prosperous small cities of Georgia. A railroad center with seven branch lines of three systems, it has extensive railroad shops. Other industrial establishments include cotton mills, machine shops, feed mills, peanut-shelling plants, fertilizer works, sawmills, planing mills, a barrel factory, and a diversity of other industries, amounting to some sixty-five. Valdosta is the headquarters of the American Turpentine Farmers Association Co-operative, and claims for itself the capital position of the Georgia-Florida flue-cured tobacco belt.

The well-wooded country affords excellent hunting, and eighty-five clear-water lakes within easy motoring distance provide abundant water sports. Though the town is not a winter resort, it is becoming increasingly popular as a stopping place for people on the way to Florida.

Before 1860 the county seat, about four miles west of the present site, was called Troupville in honor of Governor George M. Troup (*see* TOUR 9). In 1859 when the first railroad through the area was laid out, Troupville was by-passed. The citizens lost no time in moving to the railroad and named the new site for the Governor's estate, *Val d'Osta*. In 1860 the town was incorporated under its present name.

VALDOSTA STATE COLLEGE, Patterson St., a coeducational, senior college of the University System of Georgia, has a physical plant of eight white stucco buildings of the Spanish-mission type of architecture, on a sixty-acre campus wooded with pine groves. Opened in 1913 as the South Georgia Normal College, it began granting degrees in 1923 when its name was changed to the Georgia State Womans College. By action of the Board of Regents in January of 1950, the name was changed again, and it was made a coeducational college of arts and sciences conferring both the A.B. and the B.S. degree. The college has an enrollment in excess of four hundred and a faculty of forty-one.

EMORY JUNIOR COLLEGE, Patterson St., housed in seven buildings of modified Georgian design on a 43-acre campus, was formerly a branch of Emory University (*see* ATLANTA). These buildings consist of four dormitories, an administration building, an indoor swimming pool, and a gymnasium. The gymnasium was donated by the Federal government for the use of veterans attending college under the G. I. Bill of Rights.

The first classes were held in 1928, when the college was opened through the co-operation of the people of Valdosta, the South Georgia Conference of the Methodist Episcopal Church, South, and the trustees of Emory University. In 1942 the college closed and remained closed for the duration of the war, but it reopened in the autumn of 1946. It has recently been taken over by the University System of Georgia.

The VALDOSTA FARMERS MARKET, supervised by the Georgia State Department of Agriculture, has operated continuously since 1936 receiving and distributing fruit and vegetables produced in the area. It is rather on the seasonal side, handling more tomatoes and watermelons than any other commodity. Total sales for the period 1941-1951 run around $14,000,000.

At Valdosta is the junction with US 84 (*see* TOUR 5).

At about 245 m. (L) is the entrance to TWIN LAKES (*swimming, fishing, and dancing*), a resort hotel of Spanish design, a casino, and a tourist camp beside two large lakes surrounded by great moss-draped trees.

At about 256 m. US 41 crosses the Florida Line, at a point some 38 miles north of Lake City, Florida.

TOUR 2A

Dalton—Chatsworth—Fort Mountain State Park—Ellijay; 34.2 m., State 52 and US 76, hard surfaced complete.

Between Dalton and Chatsworth this route leads through the broad farmlands and low, timbered hills of the beautiful Appalachian Valley. The vague blue mass of the Cohutta Mountains, visible for miles across the highway ahead, takes definite shape at the entrance to the Chattahoochee National Forest just east of Chatsworth. Here peaks, almost four thousand feet above sea level, are green with a heavy growth of pines and hardwood trees. In the deep, fertile valleys are the homes of a hardy people, descendants of English settlers. Elizabethan terms are still used not only in the ballads, but also in everyday speech.

State 52 (L) from DALTON. US 76 branches east at Dalton from US 41 (*see* TOUR 2), and is then continuous with State 52 to Ellijay. *o m.*

SPRING PLACE, 9.6 *m.* (730 alt., 214 pop.), named for the spring here, was the seat of Murray County until 1913, when the county government was moved to Chatsworth.

THE SITE OF A MORAVIAN MISSION (R), established by the Moravians from Salem, North Carolina, is marked by a small granite slab. In 1799 missionaries were authorized by the Society of United Brethren (Moravians) to spread their doctrines among the Cherokee; permission was granted by the U. S. government in 1800, and the mission at Spring Place was opened March 26, 1802. The land was donated by Joseph Vann, half Scot and half Cherokee Indian, whom the Cherokee had made a tribal chief. The mission school remained open until 1833 when the Cherokee lands were distributed by lottery (*see* TOUR 2). After the government had paid the Moravians $2,878 for the property, the building was converted into a courthouse.

CHIEF VANN HOUSE, across the street from the mission site (L), was built about 1790.

Active throughout his life in furthering Christianity among the Indians, Vann befriended the Moravian missionaries and sent his children to their school. At the time of the Cherokee eviction, Joseph Vann received an eviction notice on February 23, 1835, and on March 2 was forced from the house by Captain W. N. Bishop and a detachment of the Georgia Guard in order that Absalom Bishop, brother of the captain, might have possession. Vann eventually accepted a sum from the Federal government and left for the Indian Territory. At the foot of the driveway is a D. A. R. marker recording the trial and acquittal in this house of John Howard Payne, author of the lyric "Home Sweet Home." After a visit to Chief John Ross, Payne, who was a champion of the Cherokee cause, had begun to study tribal customs and legends to be included in a Cherokee history. He was accused of sedition, seized by the Georgia Guard, and imprisoned for twelve days in a log cabin near the Vann house.

The red brick dwelling, standing on high ground, is dilapidated but shows many details of fine workmanship. From a short distance the house presents a commanding appearance with its end chimneys, its fanlighted doorway, its fine modillioned cornice, and its windows with white stone lintels and sills. The red bricks are softened with age except where they are obscured by the clinging plaster of pilasters removed long ago. Inside neglect has left many marks. The mantels that conform to the modified Georgian style of the house are cracked, and only a few fragments of the old paper cling to the wall. Above the doorways of the lower hall are fanlights of fine workmanship, and the interior paneling is carved by skilled hands. Beneath the recessed windows are removable panels that open upon cubbyholes of considerable size. Most striking of all the interior features is the hanging stairway that ascends upward two stories from the center hall.

The Georgia Historical Commission is now restoring the house.

In CHATSWORTH, *11.8 m.* (approx. 800 alt., 1,214 pop.), a trim and orderly village, the most prominent buildings are the red brick Murray County Courthouse and the jail, which stand on a green lawn (L). The chief industry is talc mining, carried on by three processing plants. Talc layers, ranging from five to fifty feet in thickness can be traced for hundreds of feet along their strike, and are mined by digging a tunnel into the mountain until a vein is struck and then following the vein. The mineral is blasted out and hauled in small tramcars to the grinding mills, where it is reduced to a powder of very fine mesh and bagged for shipping. Georgia talc is used in the manufacture of soapstone pencils for industrial marking, in filler materials, in foundry dusting, and in the preparation of toilet talcum powder.

From Chatsworth the mountains no longer appear a vague blue but are revealed as a solid mass of green. As the road winds up over wooded Fort Mountain, it affords one superb view after another of the valley below. For the fisherman the streams are filled with rainbow, brown, and red-eyed trout, bass, bream, and shell-crackers, and for the huntsman the woods offer deer, fox, rabbit, quail, doves, and ducks in season.

The LAKE CONASAUGA RECREATION AREA, L. from Chatsworth on US 411 to Eton and then R. on a Forest Service Road some *10 m.*, then L. about *3 m.*, and then L. about *4 m.*, is located near the top of Grassy Mountain (alt. 3,200) in Murray County. It is one of the major recreation areas of the Chattahoochee National Forest, maintained by the U. S. Forest Service. Consisting of a 25-acre artificial lake with shore developments for picnicking and camping, it contains numerous picnic units, camping units, three shelters, two parking areas, a bathhouse, toilets, and garbage pits. (It can also be approached by US 76, about *15 m.* east of Chatsworth and before Ellijay, L. on a Forest Service Road.) Inquire for further information from the U. S. Forest Ranger in Blue Ridge. At *19.2 m.* is a junction with a dirt road.

Left on this road *1.8 m.* to FORT MOUNTAIN STATE PARK (*picnic area, with sheltered barbecue pit, furnished cabin except for linens, trading post*). This area of 1,954 acres around a rugged mountain peak is being developed by the Georgia Department of State Parks in co-operation with the U. S. Forest Service. Fort Mountain has an elevation of 2,855 feet, and there is a lake of seventeen acres. A magnificent forest growth of hickory, pine, oak, red maple, persimmon, and sourwood trees covers the mountainsides, and the rhododendron, mountain laurel, dogwood, and wild azalea that bloom along the roadside in spring are followed in fall by goldenrod and purple asters. There are about three and a half miles of highway in the park and numerous mountain trails. The lake which has the exceptional altitude of 2,850 feet offers because of its clear cold water excellent bass and trout fishing. From a high stone tower, built by the U. S. Forest Service to detect forest fires, is a fine panorama of the highland region. Encircling the crest of the mountain is a low stone wall, the ruins presumably of an old fortification from which the mountain takes its name. Very low, never rising above two feet, the wall is fifteen hundred feet long and twelve feet thick at the base. Pits, believed to be part of the defense works, occur at regular intervals, and there are traces of a gateway that may well have opened to a spring thirteen hundred feet away.

Speculation about the people who built the ruin has produced a number of theories. One is that it was built by De Soto's men while on one of their gold-seeking expeditions, or some other Spaniards; another considers it the work of British agents during the Revolution; and still a third, that of Dr. A. J. Waring, of Savannah, a collaborator with the Smithsonian Institution, judges them to be entirely Indian in origin and quite old, as early as the 12th or 13th century. It is suitable that an enigma should reside in the center of so much primitive grandeur.

The park is open throughout the year with a resident superintendent in charge. Children's playground equipment was recently added. Inquiries concerning the facilities of the park should be addressed to the superintendent, Fort Mountain State Park, Chatsworth Georgia. There are no general admission charges or fishing fees to be paid in Georgia's state parks.

ELLIJAY, *34.2 m.* (1,298 alt., 1,527 pop.) (*see* TOUR *13*), is at a junction with State 5.

TOUR 2B

Fort Valley—Montezuma—Andersonville—Americus; 48 m., State 49.

Roadbed hard surfaced throughout—Central of Georgia Ry. parallels route—Limited accommodations.

State 49 connects towns noted for their ante-bellum houses, passes the site of a large Confederate prison camp, and runs through a clay-loam section, bordered for many miles with peach orchards. In spring the countryside is pink with flowering peaches; in harvest season it bustles with activity. Picking begins at an early hour and lasts until dark; for when the peaches begin to ripen there is no pause. At packing sheds along the way large trucks are loaded with fruit, principally for points north.

State 49 branches R. from US 41 in FORT VALLEY (*see* TOUR *2*), *0 m.*

Memorial Highway, a five-mile stretch of State 49 on either side of Marshallville, is bordered by camellia and crape myrtle and dedicated to the early settlers of the community.

MARSHALLVILLE, *8 m.* (500 alt., 1,121 pop.), was settled by the descendants of colonists who came to Orangeburg, South Carolina, in the 1730's. Around 1830 these people decided to move to the new western lands, and part of the group came to this area, where they bought thousands of acres, and set out peach trees, grapevines, and flowering bulbs, especially hyacinths.

The FREDERICK-WADE HOUSE (*private*), Main Street, is a white frame structure (R) with a tall, square-columned portico and a hanging balcony. It was built about 1845 by Daniel Frederick who came here in 1832 as one of the original settlers. A grand-nephew of the builder, John Donald Wade now lives in the Frederick House; a former professor of English at the University of Georgia, he is the author of two biographies, *Augustus Baldwin Longstreet* and *John Wesley.*

The SLAPPEY HOUSE (*private*), Main Street (L), has a Doric portico, a fine Palladian doorway, a second-story porch, and a hipped shingle roof. It was built in the 1860's by George H. Slappey, one of the original settlers.

The MCCASKILL-RUMPH HOUSE (*private*), on McCaskill Street is a red brick structure (R) with Doric columns and a double gallery. Built about 1855, it later came through marriage into the possession of Lewis A. Rumph, who about 1875 developed a delicious white peach with a red suffusion. A variant from a Chinese clingstone seed, this peach, named the Georgia Belle for Mrs. Belle Hall, half sister of Mrs. Rumph, has become a staple crop throughout the southern peach area.

Left from Marshallville on Main St., a hard-surfaced road, to a junction with a dirt road, *1.5 m.;* (L) *2.5 m.* on this second road to WILLOW LAKE FARM, formerly the plantation of Samuel H. Rumph. The spreading, one-story white house, fronted by a beautiful garden with large boxwoods, is reached by a walk lined with dwarf box. Here Samuel Rumph (1851-1922) established the first commercial peach orchard in Georgia. In 1875 he produced the large, copper-colored peach that he named Elberta after his wife. Propagated from a Chinese clingstone pollinated supposedly by an Early Crawford, the Elberta is a yellow freestone peach of exceptional firmness which makes it suitable for shipping.

On the first dirt road, *2.5 m.* from the junction, is the LEWIS RUMPH HOUSE (*private*), erected in the 1830's by Lewis A. Rumph's father, one of the first of the Orangeburg colonists. Immense boxwoods border the front yard of the square, clapboard house, which originally had only two rooms upstairs. But two more were added after Rumph, a widower with five children, married Mrs. Benjamin D. Plant, a widow with three. To separate the boys from the girls, no connection was made between the older and the newer rooms, which were reached by an additional stairway in the rear of the hall. Friends of the family insist, though, that the barrier was no foe to romance, since young Samuel Rumph later married one of the Plant girls.

From Marshallville to Montezuma, State 49 follows a ridge overlooking the beautiful Flint River valley. The unusually good air circulation here tends to prevent damaging frosts and is largely responsible for the vigorous appearance of the orchards.

The narrow, two-story CROCKER HOUSE (*private*), *17.5 m.* (L), was built in the 1830's. Its white boards are set flush around the porch but overlap on the rest of the house, a characteristic of many nineteenth-century houses.

MONTEZUMA, *23.9 m.* (184 alt., 2,921 pop.), is a pleasant town with frame and brick houses set back from the tree-shaded streets. There are several elaborate neo-classic dwellings built during the twentieth century. Montezuma is known for peaches. In 1950 John T. McKenzie built a large community packing shed which is being used by a number of small growers and one or two of the larger. Operations at this packing shed are typical of the enterprise. In 1951 about 700 cars of peaches were shipped from Montezuma and it was considered an average year. Among the industrial establishments are a fertilizer plant; the Montezuma Knitting Mill (locally owned and managed), manufacturing products sold under the trade names of OTIS and E-Z; the Vanta Corporation making baby and children's clothes; a cottonseed-oil mill; and a planing mill. Local capital built Southern Frozen Foods which is the largest quick-freezing plant in this section. Largely things grown locally are frozen by the plant such as turnips, peas, kale, okra, collards, peppers, and others.

Montezuma began to develop in 1851, when the Central of Georgia Railway was built through the region, and was incorporated in 1854. In 1883 when the muddy Flint River was found to be navigable, two steamship companies were established, and the *Montezuma* and the *Ida* began making biweekly trips to the Gulf of Mexico. The sandy, shifting bed of the river, however, made navigation so uncertain that when the two boats sank they were not replaced.

The town site was part of the Indian reserve officially granted to Buckee Barnard by the Treaty of Indian Springs in 1821. Buckee was a son of Timpoochee Barnard, chief of the Uchee and a major in the U. S. Army during the War of 1812; he was a grandson of Timothy Barnard, an English trader who became interpreter to the Creek and deputy Indian agent for Benjamin Hawkins. From 1780 to about 1820 Timothy owned the land of Macon County and helped lay out a stage-coach route from Columbus to St. Marys by way of this point. Because of the prominence of the Barnard family, four of Timpoochee's children were allowed to retain their land, three of the reservations being within Macon County.

Montezuma has a reputation for its artesian water and particularly for its well in the middle of the town.

OGLETHORPE, 25.9 m. (299 alt., 1,204 pop.), seat of Macon County, was incorporated in 1849. When the southwestern division of the Central of Georgia Railway was completed to Oglethorpe in 1851, the town expanded rapidly and was considered the "metropolis" of southwest Georgia. Its period of prosperity, however, was short-lived, the zenith of its progress being reached about 1855, a year after it became the seat of county government. The extension of the railroad to Americus and a severe smallpox epidemic resulted in the town's decline.

There are many artesian wells in this section. Prior to the installation of waterworks in Oglethorpe, one public well supplied water for most of the town's inhabitants, and housewives paid "toting" fees to have the water fetched.

The COLONEL GEORGE FISH HOUSE (*private*), Randolph St., built about 1850, is a one-story structure with a high basement and two pairs of stairs leading to a small, sharply elevated porch. The octagonal stone chimneys are unusual.

The HANSELL-KEEN HOUSE (*private*), Randolph St., is a square two-story house erected in the 1840's, with a simple, pedimented classic portico, and a Palladian doorway opening on the left.

The ANDERSONVILLE NATIONAL CEMETERY (*picnic grounds outside cemetery walls*), *34.9 m.* (L), comprises twenty-eight acres surrounded by an ivy-covered brick wall. Limerock driveways lead through the grounds, beautiful with rolling lawns, magnolias, oaks, and willows. Indicated by small markers are the graves of 13,741 soldiers, many of whom died while imprisoned in the Andersonville Confederate Prison camp. Throughout the cemetery are monuments erected by northern states in memory of their dead.

Right from the cemetery and across the railroad is ANDERSONVILLE, *0.2 m.* (394 alt., 281 pop.). In the center of town is a MONUMENT TO CAPTAIN HENRY WIRZ, the Confederate commandant in charge of the Andersonville Prison. In 1865, soon after the close of the war, Wirz was seized in his Andersonville home and taken to Washington, D. C., where he was tried on thirteen charges by a military commission that sat for three months. In spite of the testimony of witnesses that he was not responsible for the suffering and misery within the camp, he was found guilty of maliciously conspiring to kill and torture the prisoners and was hanged on November 10. Doubtless a heavy thumb was on the scale of justice and the captain made to serve as a scapegoat. Carved on the monument, erected by the United Daughters of the Confederacy as a protest against his execution, is a quotation from a speech made by Jefferson Davis in 1888: "When time shall have softened passion and prejudice, when reason shall have stripped the mask of misrepresentation, then justice holding evenly her scales will require much of past censure and praise to change places." Captain Wirz is buried in Mount Olivet Cemetery, Washington, D. C.

The ANDERSONVILLE PRISON PARK (L) *35.4 m.*, is the site of Camp Sumter, one of the largest Confederate prison camps. From the iron gate limestone driveways, shaded by pines, oaks, willows, and cedars, wind through the eighty-acre park, which is neatly maintained by the Federal government. Throughout the area northern states have erected monuments to honor their soldiers who were imprisoned here. Surrounding the prison site are the breastworks, now overgrown with grass. Stone posts mark the four corners of the prison stockade and white cement posts indicate its outline. In the caretaker's house, a two-story white building overlooking the park, is a drawing by a prisoner named O'Dea depicting the hardships of prison life. The land was presented to the United States in 1910 by the Women's Relief Corps, an auxiliary of the Grand Army of the Republic.

The stockade and hospital of the camp built to accommodate 10,000 men, began to receive prisoners on March 1, 1864, but were crowded beyond their capacity almost at once. In the thirteen months the prison was used 49,485 men were enclosed there, as many as 33,000 at one time. Because of the crowded conditions, shortage of food in the South, and the lack of medicines—which were contraband of war, many prisoners contracted scurvy and gangrene. Others, strangers to the southern diet of cornbread, contracted what is now called pellagra. Steadily increasing day in and day out, the death rate reached its apex on August 23, with ninety-seven for one day. By this time, happily, provision had been made to remove the prisoners to other camps or to return them to the North without the usual exchange for Confederate prisoners. With the coming of October only 4,000 were left. Despite attempts to counteract diseases with the few fresh vegetables obtainable and an acid beer made of molasses and corn meal, 12,462 prisoners died.

In the center of the park is PROVIDENCE SPRING, acclaimed by the Union soldiers as a direct answer to prayer. Tortured by thirst, when in August (1864)—a hot month in a dry year—a drought dried up the source of their water, the prisoners prayed through a night and a day for rain, and on the evening of the second day it fell, a heavy rain continuing all night. A small puddle of water persisted next morning. Instead of seeping into the ground it grew larger. The downpour had opened an old spring that had been clogged for years. A stone pavilion was erected in 1901 to cover the spring which has been made into a fountain.

AMERICUS, 48 m. (360 alt., 11,389 pop.) (see TOUR 6), is at the junction with US 19.

TOUR 2C

Sycamore—Irwinville—Fitzgerald; 26.6 m., State 32 and State 107. Hard surfaced from Sycamore to Fitzgerald.

Traversing the wiregrass region, this route passes through a distinctly rural section where small farms of diversified crops are broken by tracts of longleaf pines. The countryside is flat and somewhat swampy, with scatterings of scrub palmettoes over the land. In spring the roadsides are yellow with tall-necked pitcher plants and fragrant with a trailing pinkish-white honeysuckle. Near Irwinville is the site of Jefferson Davis' capture by Federal troops.

SYCAMORE, 0 m. (415 alt., 624 pop.), is at the junction with US 41 (see TOUR 2).

IRWINVILLE, 17 m. (448 alt., 300 pop.), was made the seat of Irwin

County in 1831 and named for Jared Irwin, the Governor of Georgia (1806-9) who rescinded the Yazoo Act (*see* TOUR *4*). In 1906 the county seat was changed by legislative act to Ocilla.

The town is the center of the IRWINVILLE FARMS, a rehabilitation project of what is now the Farmers Home Administration, of the U. S. Department of Agriculture. The project, on ten thousand acres of the finest South Georgia lands, extends along the highway east and west from Irwinville and for several miles south on the Tifton Road. In 1934, when the project was organized (under what was then the Rural Rehabilitation Corporation), only a small part of the land was under cultivation, the major part being forest, swampland, and outlying tracts that had formerly been cultivated. After the original tenant houses had been repaired and painted, thirty-four rehabilitation families began farming on land which they hoped eventually to own. Fences were built, land cleared, and preparations made to plant the first crops. Many new houses and barns were constructed afterwards. The four- and five-room cottages are of frame construction, painted white with green roofs, and are surrounded by shrubbery and flowers. Diversified farming was stressed, and the tenants were required to plant cotton, corn, tobacco, peanuts, and potatoes. The raising of poultry, cattle, and hogs also was encouraged. Tenants were added as time went on.

According to the plan of operation, every tenant was assigned a tract of 60 to 125 acres that he was required to cultivate; the acreage varied according to the size of the family and the type of land. All supplies, seed, and fertilizer were charged and paid for later from crop proceeds. According to a recent statement from the Farmers Home Administration Office in Atlanta, the Irwinville Farms project is a leader among these establishments; more than fifty per cent of the obligations have been paid off completely, and others are making regular payments. After paying off his debts, the farmer is released from supervision, and the government's function if any, is entirely advisory. The school house that was built by the Rural Rehabilitation Corporation has been deeded to the county for local use.

Left from Irwinville to JEFFERSON DAVIS MEMORIAL STATE PARK, *1 m.*, an area of some twelve acres commemorating the site where the president of the Confederacy was taken prisoner by Federal troops at the close of the war. After seeing Davis arrested, the father of James D. Clements (who was later one of the actual donors of the park site) vowed to commit the land to the people of the South. A stone marker designates the exact spot on which Davis was captured.

The CONFEDERATE MUSEUM, of modified Southern Colonial style, contains a collection of documents relating to the Confederacy and relics of the War between the States. A superintendent is on duty to answer questions. The site of the park is pleasingly located near a trailing brook in a grove of Georgia longleaf pine. Paths interlace the adjoining woodland which is in the center of some of the finest farmlands in Georgia.

The DAVIS MONUMENT, a granite shaft surmounted with a bronze bust of Davis, bears on its side a bas-relief panel depicting his capture. Davis had left Washington, Georgia, where his last cabinet meeting was held, and with his family was on the way to a southern port. Early in the morning of May 10, 1865, he was overtaken by Union soldiers and sent to Fortress Monroe.

To the right of the monument a small stream can be crossed to the skirmish ground, a hillside covered with a growth of wiregrass and tall yellow pines. A brief engagement occurred here in the early morning of May 10 between a detachment of the Michigan cavalry, attempting to cut off the Davis party, and a body of Wisconsin cavalry on the same mission. Each, mistaking the other for Confederate forces, opened fire, and harm was done before daylight permitted identification. A marker indicates this spot.

At Irwinville is the junction with State 107, on which the route turns L.

FITZGERALD, 26.6 m. (275 alt., 8,130 pop.), is in the midst of the wiregrass section; it is the county seat of Ben Hill County, and at the same time the only town and post office in the county. The town has a number of industries: a large cotton mill making auto upholstery, shops of the Atlantic Coast Line Railroad, other cotton mills, two tobacco markets—the Fitzgerald and the Farmers, and warehouses. Agriculture, however, is the chief interest, centering around cotton, peanuts, tobacco, blue lupine, cattle, and naval stores. But the indisputably exceptional thing about Fitzgerald is the manner of its founding.

In 1894, when there was a drought in the middle west, Governor William J. Northen of Georgia organized a relief committee that shipped flour, corn, and meat for free distribution in the suffering states. This friendly gesture, coming from a one-time enemy state, appealed to a group of Union veterans who were eager to settle in the South. In 1895 the veterans formed a stock company, the American Soldiers' Colony Association, which purchased fifty thousand acres of land. It was an area of virgin pine and wiregrass, but it was fertile land that was untouched by the plow and it promised warm winters and no drought. Whole families, bringing their household pets and furnishings, came to Georgia in covered wagons, by boat, on horseback, and in carriages; one family from Nebraska floated a raft down the Mississippi and then pushed across Mississippi, Alabama, and west Georgia to the new Eden. Among the first families was Mrs. E. C. Fox and her daughters. Leaving Nebraska on April 20, 1895, and traveling by means of two wagons and two buggies, they arrived after three months on July 24. The place where the new town was to grow was a tiny lumber camp called Swan with a population of four men and a boy, according to a story one of the Fox daughters wrote for the *Fitzgerald Leader* some years ago. At first the newcomers built rough slab houses in "Shacktown," but when they did begin the building of the town there was nothing hit or miss about it.

The town was laid off precisely in a square with two central bisecting avenues (Main and Central): the streets bounding this square area were named for Federal and Confederate war vessels (Sultana, Roanoke, Merrimac, and Monitor), the streets running north and south for Union and Confederate generals, and those running east and west for southern trees and rivers. This symmetrical plan remains basically the same to-day. The hotel was named the Lee-Grant, and Fitzgerald's recreation area is known as Blue and Gray Park. The town became a trading center and was incorporated in 1896. Eventually Southerners began to move in and the two peoples became assimilated into one.

Left from Fitzgerald on US 129 to the BOWEN MILL HATCHERY and QUAIL FARM, about *8 m.* Supervised by the State Game and Fish Commission, this hatchery provides bream, bass, and crappie. The Quail Farm is in the same location.

TOUR 3

*(Anderson, S. C.)—Hartwell—Athens—Atlanta—LaGrange—
West Point—(Montgomery, Ala.); US 29.*

---

*South Carolina Line to Alabama Line, 204.2 m.—Roadbed hard-surfaced throughout.
Seaboard Air Line Ry. parallels route between Athens and Atlanta; Atlanta & West Point
between Atlanta and West Point. All types of accommodations in Atlanta; limited elsewhere, except for cabins and motor courts.*

Section a. SOUTH CAROLINA LINE *to* ATLANTA, *119.7 m.*

This route crosses the upper Piedmont Plateau, where rolling hills of red clay are often covered with fields of cotton and corn. Forests that once covered the entire region have been largely cleared, and the remaining trees are mostly second-growth pines. As a result of the deforestation and the heavy seasonal rains that make muddy torrents of the creeks and rivers, the area has suffered from serious erosion. Row crops, planted year after year without a program of rotation, have aggravated the situation. But a government project for the conservation of soil, which was centered around Athens, and the work of the state agricultural agencies have begun to show noticeable effects. Here and there fields are green with cover crops, and cattle on clover and fescue have displaced cotton and corn. Most of the farms average about seventy-five acres in size, and the farmhouses are usually small, unpainted frame structures. Skirmishes occurred in this region during both the Revolution and the War between the States, and through it trekked the Indians as refugees from the white man during the Cherokee Removal.

US 29 crosses the SAVANNAH RIVER, *o m.,* about fourteen miles southwest of Anderson, South Carolina. At this point on the river, which was established in the charter of the colony as the boundary line between Georgia and South Carolina, a ferry was operated as early as 1790, when Thomas Shockley bought a quarter acre of land to be used as the landing. A great freshet one year washed up some apples near the ferry landing with the result that next year seedlings appeared, of which one proved to be a distinct apple, yellow, with a bright crimson cheek, firm and sweet. Given the name Shockley, the apple became widely cultivated. Later known as Brown's Ferry, after a family that owned it in the 1820's, the ferry ran until a toll bridge replaced it in 1917. The bridge was purchased by Georgia and South Carolina nine years later and the toll discontinued.

The F. G. STOWERS HOUSE (*private*), *1.5 m.* (L), built about 1840, is one of the oldest residences in this section. On a slight rise that affords a view of the outlying territory, this single-story, white frame structure has a deep veranda adorned with small, square columns extending around three sides. The double front door is set in a Palladian frame ornamented with pilasters. The house is on the site of the old Oak Bower Post Office that was served by the Star Stagecoach between Athens and Anderson, South Carolina.

The NANCY HART MARKER (L), *5.4 m.,* at the intersection with a road, bears a bronze tablet commemorating the bravery of the Georgia Revolutionary heroine (*see* TOUR *3A*). Both the town of Hartwell and Hart County are named for her.

HARTWELL, *6.6 m.* (838 alt., 2,964 pop.), incorporated in 1856, is the seat of Hart County, the only County in the state named for a woman. Hartwell and Hart County industrial plants are engaged in a wide variety of activities, which include a large cotton mill (426 looms), two garment plants, a large rayon weaving plant (600 looms), a mica mining plant, two feed mills, six seed cleaning, treating and storage houses, cotton gins, lumber mills, and hatcheries. Dairying has become one of the leading enterprises of the county. A dairy cattle improvement program has been developed which includes the artificial insemination of dairy cows by the Northeast Georgia Artificial Breeders Association;

herds are being improved by the purchase of purebred heifers. Hart County has a widely diversified agriculture. A wide variety of vegetables and fruits are grown, and community canning plants are set up in most sections. With three-fourths of its farmers taking part, the county stands high in what it has accomplished in soil conservation. Cotton is still an important crop, but farmers are planting more and more small grain—oats, barley, wheat—followed by annual lespedeza which is both an important cash and feed crop. Crimson clover flourishes in Hart County. Since both climate and soil make year-round grazing practicable, Kentucky 31 fescue and ladino clover are becoming increasingly important and popular crops.

The American Legion Recreation Center for Hart County, just out of Hartwell, has a nine-hole golf course with grass greens, tennis courts, a lake for recreation and fishing, a swimming pool, and picnic center.

The marked SITE OF AH-YEH-LI A-LO-HEE (Ind., center of the world) (L) *9.5 m.*, was once a Cherokee assembly ground. Indian trails radiated in many directions from this point, which became an important trading post, with a large traffic in hides, furs, and blankets.

FRANKLIN SPRINGS, *21.8 m.* (approx. 750 alt., 182 pop.), is an incorporated town. The town is named for Franklin County in which it is located and the three springs that are found near its center. Two of the springs are rich in mineral content, iron being strong in one, and sulphur in the other, while the third is mineral-free; the three are within a few hundred yards of each other.

After the War between the States, Franklin Springs was developed as a health resort and two hotels were built to provide room and board for those who wished to enjoy the curative benefits of its waters. Cottages were built, and a skating rink for recreation. In 1918 the Pentecostal Holiness Church acquired this resort property, including the two hotels, the skating rink, and some eighty acres of land, mostly in forest. On January 1, 1919, the Franklin Springs Institute (literary and Bible school of the church) began its first session. It was developed into an accredited junior college, now known as EMMANUEL COLLEGE, of 200 students, with a physical plant consisting of an extensive campus and buildings valued at $500,000. Although it is owned by the Pentecostal Holiness Church, its student body is not restricted to this denomination. It is accredited by the State Department of Education and the University of Georgia, and is a member of The American Association of Junior Colleges, The Southern Association of Junior Colleges, and The Georgia Association of Junior Colleges.

In 1919 the Pentecostal Holiness Church also built and equipped a modern printing plant, where are printed the official organ of the church called the *Pentecostal Holiness Advocate* (a 16-page weekly), a monthly young people's paper, a quarterly preachers' magazine, and the Sunday School literature used by the church.

The springs are open to visitors, though no hotel facilities are at present available for the public.

DANIELSVILLE, *33.3 m.* (760 alt., 296 pop.), seat of Madison County, was incorporated in 1818 and named for Allen Daniel, a captain in the Revolutionary Army and later brigadier general in the state militia. It is an agricultural region where small farms are cultivated by the owners or by white tenants; few Negroes live in this section.

In the public square is the CRAWFORD W. LONG MONUMENT, a white marble effigy of the celebrated doctor who first used ether as an anesthetic during an operation. The statue, erected in 1936, the ninety-fourth anniversary of the event, shows Dr. Long standing before a small cabinet.

At Danielsville is the junction with State 98 (*see* TOUR *3A*).

Right from the Danielsville courthouse on a dirt road to the BIRTHPLACE OF DR. CRAWFORD W. LONG (*private*), *0.2 m.* (L), a small two-story clapboarded house with raised basement, tall brick end chimneys, and a low front porch supported on hand-hewn posts.

Southwest of Danielsville is the site of the old 104,000-acre SANDY CREEK DEMONSTRATION PROJECT which was operated by the Soil Conservation Service, and its predecessor, the Soil Erosion Service, from 1934 to 1938. It is a triangular area, with the towns of Commerce, Comer, and Athens as its vertices, and lies in Madison, Jackson, and Clark counties. It was the first of its kind to be set up in Georgia. Although it was discontinued in 1938, many of the conservation measures which were applied during its operation are still in evidence. Hand-high pine seedlings planted then are now 40 feet or more tall and are six to twelve inches in diameter. Fields of kudzu and sericea lespedeza are still producing hay and grazing while protecting the soil from erosion. Many of the old terraces and water disposal areas are continuing to function efficiently. Gullies that were planted to various kinds of vegetation are now completely stabilized.

The entire project area is now included in the Oconee River and Broad River Soil Conservation Districts. Farmers who co-operated with SCS while the project was in operation are now working whole-heartedly with the districts, and are doing for themselves with technical assistance from the Soil Conservation Service, many of the things the Government did for them during that period of depression. The demonstration project served the important function of creating an erosion consciousness among the farmers. A great majority of them are now following the sound conservation principle of using the land within its capability and treating it in accordance with its needs for protection and improvement. Together with the other soil conservation district co-operators, they are revolutionizing Georgia's agriculture.

ATHENS, 47.7 m. (660 alt., 28,180 pop.), (see ATHENS). Points of Interest: University of Georgia, ante-bellum houses.

Athens is at the junction with US 129 (see TOUR 16) and with US 78 (see TOUR 8), which coincides with US 29 for about ten miles west of Athens.

WINDER, 72 m. (969 alt., 4,604 pop.), is the seat of Barrow County, created in 1914 from parts of Walton, Jackson, and Gwinnett counties. The town developed around a tavern advertised by an enormous liquor jug and was known as Jug Tavern until 1893, when it was incorporated and given its present name. A skirmish occurred here on August 3, 1864, between Confederate cavalry and the 14th Illinois cavalry.

On the fringe of the city limits is FORT YARGO STATE PARK, a 2,000-acre tract of government-owned wooded land. The initial appropriation for the park was made by the General Assembly in 1951. It is at present listed by the Department of State Parks as undeveloped.

Winder's progress in manufacturing is reflected in the annual industrial payroll of $3,880,000. Barrow County has nine clothing manufacturers, six of whom are located in Winder. In addition a waistbands plant, two furniture factories, and a blanket mill add to the industrial income of the town.

Barrow County has 94,009 acres in farm production, of which 43,793 are in crop land, 22,618 in pulpwood, 15,150 in permanent pasture, 2,100 in temporary grazing, 200 in kudzu, 825 miles of terracing, 111 acres in wildlife, and 125 acres in fescue grass. As compared to seven in 1944, there are now fifty-four dairies in operation. Herds of Black Angus, Hereford, and other cattle are on pasture. At Sales Barn auctions livestock producers were paid a total of $432,000, not including the sales by FFA and 4-H Club members to the extent of $35,000. In common with other areas of northeast Georgia, the broiler industry has been making strides in this vicinity, with houses of 10,000 to 16,000 birds dotting the hillsides. The egg-production rate has climbed above fifty thousand, and hogs and turkey are in good supply.

Right from Winder on paved State 11 to JEFFERSON, 13.1 m. (800 alt., 2,040 pop.), the seat of Jackson County; it was created in 1796. Incorporated in 1806, the town had several hundred inhabitants when Dr. Crawford W. Long (1815-78), performed here the first operation in which sulphuric ether was used as an anesthetic, on March 30, 1842. Two markers on the front of a red brick store on the west side of the public square indicate the SITE OF DR. LONG'S OFFICE where the operation was performed; some claim that the operation occurred under a mulberry tree in front of the office.

After receiving his medical education at the University of Pennsylvania and serving his internship in New York, Dr. Long came to practice in Jefferson. According to Dr. Long's account, after James V. Venable had consulted him on several occasions about removing two small tumors from his neck: ". . . I mentioned to him . . . the probability that the operation might be performed without pain, and proposed operating on him while under the influence of ether. He consented. . . . The ether was given to Mr. Venable on a towel, and when fully under its influence, I extirpated the tumor. . . . He gave no evidence of suffering during the operation, and assured me after it was over that he did not experience the slightest degree of pain from its performance."

Long remained in Jefferson eleven years before he moved to Athens, where he lived from 1851 until his death in 1878.

The HARRISON HOTEL, SE. corner of the square, was built about 1835, probably by Joshua A. Randolph. The two-story, gray frame Greek Revival structure has verandas running the full length of the façade on both floors, forming a square-columned portico.

LAWRENCEVILLE, *89.5 m.* (1,082 alt., 2,932 pop.), made the seat of Gwinnett County in 1821, is a rambling town of frame houses. It was named for Captain James Lawrence, remembered for his last words, "Don't give up the ship." These were spoken after he had been mortally wounded in an engagement between the *Chesapeake* under his command and the British *Shannon* in the War of 1812.

On September 15, 1831, Samuel A. Worcester, Elizur Butler, and other New England missionaries to the Cherokee were tried in Lawrenceville for residing in the Cherokee land and for encouraging the Indians to make a stand against the seizure of their land. Found guilty, they were sentenced to the state penitentiary, where they remained until 1833 in spite of a reversal of the verdict in 1832 by the U. S. Supreme Court.

In the corners of the courthouse square are small red brick buildings, and around the square is an iron fence. In 1849 an act of the legislature authorized the justices of the inferior court of the county to deed the four corner lots to responsible citizens, provided they build and maintain a fence around the square. The buildings are used as offices by lawyers.

HIGHTOWER TRAIL MARKER, *102 m.,* on the line between DeKalb and Gwinnett counties, indicates the route of an Indian trail between the sites of the present Athens, Georgia, and Gadsen, Alabama.

DECATUR, *112.9 m.* (1,049 alt., 21,635 pop.), the seat of DeKalb County and a residential suburb of Atlanta, appears unlike other towns of the Old South except for the majestic oaks that shade its streets. Decatur was incorporated on December 10, 1823, and soon became a prosperous town. In 1837 the citizens, disliking the smoke and clatter of trains, refused to allow the Western & Atlantic Railroad to come within the city limits. The tracks were built to a site that became the settlement of Terminus, later incorporated in 1843 as Marthasville, and in 1845 reincorporated and named Atlanta (*see* ATLANTA), which became the railroad center of the Southeast. The land of this section was settled by English, Scottish, and Irish people from Virginia and the Carolinas, industrious farmers who owned few slaves.

On July 21, 1864, the day following the Battle of Peachtree Creek (*see* ATLANTA), General James B. McPherson brought Sherman's rear guard into Decatur and placed his supply wagons in the cemetery, about which he constructed earthworks on three sides. On July 22 General Joseph Wheeler made a fierce assault, drove McPherson through the northern limits of the town, and captured more than two hundred prisoners. Only an urgent call to support General W. J. Hardee farther west prevented the destruction of a large section of the Federal wagon trains.

The gray granite DE KALB COUNTY COURTHOUSE is surrounded by the principal banking and commercial houses, and serves as a seat of activity for local politics and, on Saturday, as a gathering place for farmers who have come to trade. On the northwest corner of the courthouse square is a small granite monument honoring Stephen Decatur, the naval hero for whom the town is named.

AGNES SCOTT COLLEGE, E. College Ave., is a four-year, non-sectarian, liberal arts college for women, awarding the bachelor of arts degree. Facing the street and overlooking an expanse of lawn shaded by oaks and magnolias are the older red brick buildings, some with wide, columned verandas. To the rear of these are the newer red brick and limestone buildings, constructed in the collegiate Gothic style. The campus covers fifty-five acres and includes about forty buildings.

Agnes Scott's CARNEGIE LIBRARY is housed in a red brick building trimmed with Indiana limestone, in the Gothic style. The book stacks have a capacity of 120,000 volumes. Cubicles among the stacks permit space for individual research work, and seminar rooms provide for group study. Other features of the library are an exhibition room for paintings and a projection room for motion pictures. An outdoor reading terrace is reached from the upper reading room by a stone stairway.

While Agnes Scott is a privately controlled liberal arts college, it is also a part of a larger group of institutions which form the University Center in Georgia. In the group are Emory University, Georgia Institute of Technology, the University of Georgia at Athens, Columbia Theological Seminary, the Atlanta Art Association, and Agnes Scott College. Chief features of this co-operative program are reciprocity in library services, exchange of instructors, administration of grants for research, and the reduction of duplication and overlapping in certain bailiwicks of instruction.

The college is an outgrowth of Decatur Female Seminary, organized in 1889 by members of the Decatur Presbyterian Church, under the leadership of the Reverend F. H. Gaines. It was named Agnes Scott for the mother of Colonel George W. Scott, of Decatur, who in 1890 donated $40,000 for a permanent endowment and six years later became its president. In 1906 the school was chartered as a college; in 1907, admitted to the Southern Association of Colleges; and in 1920, recognized by the Association of American Universities.

Agnes Scott has a limited enrollment of five hundred students. To-day the total assets of the college are in the neighborhood of $7,000,000, of which nearly $3,000,000 are in endowment. The remaining sum is represented by the campus and buildings. A large part of the income from endowment is used to provide scholarships for worthy students.

Left from College Ave. in Decatur on Columbia Dr. to COLUMBIA THEOLOGICAL SEMINARY (R), *1 m.* Three theological buildings and nine faculty houses are on a 57-acre campus of rolling woodland. The school buildings are of red brick trimmed with gray limestone. In addition to the bachelor of divinity degree, the seminary offers the degree of master of theology and doctor of theology. With a student body of 220 men, the theological virtues are cultivated in the fields of biblical, historical, systematic, and practical theology.

The school was organized in 1828 at Lexington (*see* TOUR 8) by the Presbyterian Synods of Georgia and South Carolina. In 1850 it was removed to Columbia, South Carolina, and remained there until 1927, when it was removed to Decatur. It is owned by the Presbyterian Synods of Georgia, South Carolina, Alabama, and Mississippi, and is controlled by a board of directors.

At Decatur is a junction with US 78 (*see* TOUR 8).

ATLANTA, *119.7 m.* (1,050 alt., 331,314 pop.) (*see* ATLANTA).

Points of Interest: State Capitol, Georgia School of Technology, Emory University, Atlanta University (Negro), Cyclorama of the Battle of Atlanta, and others.

Atlanta is the junction with US 41 (*see* TOUR 2), with US 19 (*see* TOUR 6), with US 23 (*see* TOUR 7), and with US 78 (*see* TOUR 8).

Section b. ATLANTA *to* ALABAMA LINE, *84.5 m., US 29.*

Southwest of Atlanta, *o m.,* the route passes through a part of the middle Georgia section where cotton plantations formerly flourished. In Newnan and LaGrange are many ante-bellum houses. Since the

War between the States, textile mills have increased in this section, and soil conservation and crop diversification have worked some impressive changes. Cotton is still a basic product; but the red clay hills, formerly eroded and worn out by excessive one-crop planting, are giving way in one and another place to green rotation of legumes and grass, and to permanent pasture.

Headquarters, Third Army is stationed at FORT MCPHERSON (R), *4.2 m.*, a U. S. Army Post, whose red brick barracks and military buildings are visible behind a high fence. After the fall of Atlanta, the post was established by the Federal government on the site of the old muster ground used by the Georgia militia—now the site of Spelman College in Atlanta. The post was named for James Birdseye McPherson, the Union general who was killed during the battle of Atlanta. In 1885 the fort was moved from Atlanta to its present quarters. The 236-acre reservation was occupied during World War I by the 305th Motor Repair Unit, and during World War II by a Reception and Induction Center.

EAST POINT, *6 m.* (1,060 alt., 21,080 pop.), once the eastern terminus of the Atlanta & West Point Railroad, was incorporated in 1887. On this site, one of the key points of the Confederate line of defense, cannon, forts, and a powder magazine were established.

COLLEGE PARK, *7.8 m.* (1,060 alt., 14,435 pop.), was incorporated as Manchester in 1891, but was renamed in 1895 after the opening here of Cox College.

GEORGIA MILITARY ACADEMY (L), N. Main St., visible through the Gothic entrance arch, has a 32-acre campus with well-equipped buildings, a parade ground, and athletic fields. This school was founded in 1900 by Colonel John C. Woodward. The enrollment of about 750, including day students, represents half the states of the Union and a number of foreign countries. Georgia Military Academy has the following divisions: both junior and senior units of ROTC; grammar school; high school; and junior college. The ROTC unit was established in 1916, and the academy has been continuously designated an honor school for more than twenty-five years.

PALMETTO, *23.7 m.* (1,045 alt., 1,257 pop.), incorporated in 1854, was called Palmetto Station when, on September 21, 1864, General John B. Hood brought his 40,000 men here and began preparations for an aggressive campaign to cut the Federal lines of communication. Jefferson Davis, President of the Confederacy, visited him here, promised all possible assistance, and reviewed his troops, assuring them that they would make Sherman's retreat "more disastrous than was that of Napoleon from Moscow." Hood's plan was to march north on the supposition that Sherman would be diverted into following him. But Sherman, with the granary of the Confederacy in front of him, was not troubled by Hood's threat to his supply line. It was not a serious task to reach Savannah and the Federal fleet, living on the country along the way.

At *35.9 m.* is the junction with the paved Roscoe Road.

Right on this road to the HETTIE JANE DUNAWAY GARDENS (*adm. 50¢; blooming season April–June; lunch, tea, or dinner by reservation at Blue Bonnet Lodge*), *7 m.* The garden is reached by a road that winds over the crest of a two-hundred-foot ridge from Windy Hill, the guest house at the main entrance. Numerous varieties of Georgia flowers, trees, plants, and shrubs as well as many from other sections of the world that adapt themselves to the Georgia soil are planted in the 20-acre garden. In season it is brilliant with wild azaleas, thousands of Paul's Scarlet and American Pillar roses, dogwood, honeysuckle, and other blooming plants. Landscaped by Cagle and Monroe, the garden has been planted to take advantage of the rugged outcroppings of rocks and boulders.

BLUE BONNET LODGE is a century-old one-story building with end chimneys and a spacious living room in which are the original fireboard and beamed ceiling. Surrounding the house are sunken gardens with rock-bordered lily pools and a wishing well. Seven springs have been used as a part of the landscaping plan to form a series of reflecting pools. The rock swimming pool, formed by a dip in the hillside slope, is fed by sparkling spring water. Other natural and landscaped features add further interest to the garden.

NEWNAN, *36.3 m.* (957 alt., 8,218 pop.), seat of Coweta County, is a city of handsome ante-bellum and modern houses and well-kept churches. After the formation of the county from Creek lands gained by the Treaty of Indian Springs in 1825, a small settlement named Bullsboro developed in 1827. Though this village was two and one-half miles to the northeast of this site, it was the beginning of the town. In 1828 the Baptists of Bullsboro acquired several acres within what are now the present boundaries of Newnan and built a church. Other sects followed; soon the whole village had moved to the new site, and the settlement was named after General Daniel Newnan, veteran of the War of 1812. Newnan became so prosperous that by the 1850's planters built large white dwellings and set up industrial plants.

Newnan has produced two distinguished governors for the state. Governor William Y. Atkinson (1894-1898) was the promoter of the first state college for women, Georgia Normal and Industrial College (changed in 1890 to Georgia State College for Women), at Milledgeville. Ellis G. Arnall was the liberal governor (1942-1946) during part of the Roosevelt administration and World War II.

One of the richest cities in America on a per capita basis, Newnan is a textile and generally well-developed industrial city, and also a livestock center in a rich agricultural area of diversified farming. At present, over 75,000 acres are under cultivation, 187,974 in timber and woodland, and thousands of acres in peaches and apples, in Coweta County; with the average farm around 127 acres in size. According to a preliminary survey in January, 1952, the income from 4-H projects was $27,584.27; from cotton and cotton seed, $2,200,000; and from livestock, livestock products, and other crops, $1,599,443. The principal raw products of the area are: feed crops, cotton, dairy products, livestock, poultry, small grains, peaches, apples, lumber, pulpwood, hardwood, and a variety of minerals. Newnan is served by the Central of Georgia Railway Co. and the Atlantic & West Point R.R. Co.

Among the public buildings are: the Municipal Auditorium, the Carnegie Library, a city gymnasium, a well-staffed hospital, and a Welfare Building, 22 East Broad Street, devoted exclusively to the use of the county, in which are the offices of the county farm agent, the soil conservation engineer, the Farmers Home administrator, and the Production and Marketing Administration. On the southeast corner of the courthouse square is a marker indicating that the McINTOSH TRAIL passed through Newnan. This Indian trail ran northward from an Indian agency on the Flint River to the McIntosh Reserve in Carroll County (*see* TOUR *10*). There it connected with the other trails, one running eastward by way of Indian Springs to Augusta, the other westward to Talladega, Alabama.

The CALHOUN HOUSE (*private*), 72 Greenville St., built in 1848, is an imposing red brick house with white columns across both the front and back. Originally the home of Dr. Andrew Bonaparte Calhoun, the house has remained in the family to the present.

ROSEMARY (*private*), 9 Jefferson St., has a front garden designed in 1859 by P. J. Berckmans, a Belgian landscape artist who settled in Georgia (and a distinguished breeder of fruits and ornamentals). It is the only original boxwood garden in Newnan today. The garden is dominated by two giant magnolias, one of which is entirely covered with wistaria. The original cottage, built in 1823, was moved in 1914 to another part of the property to make room for a modern house; the garden plan, however, remained intact.

A RED BRICK RESIDENCE (*private*), 73 College St., was once the laboratory building of College Temple, a college for women, chartered in 1854. During 1864 the three buildings were used as a hospital for both Confederate and Union soldiers. The college became defunct in 1888.

At MORELAND, 42.9 *m*. (937 alt., 306 pop.), is the junction with State 41 and US 27 Alt.; turn (L) for short route to WARM SPRINGS, and FRANKLIN D. ROOSEVELT STATE PARK; also IDA CASON GARDENS, 2 *m*. south of Chipley. (*See* TOUR *10*.) Four miles below Greenville keep on

State 41 to Warm Springs; or turn (R) with US 27 Alt. as it leaves
State 41, to Chipley, *4 m.* to Franklin D. Roosevelt State Park.

HOGANSVILLE, *53 m.* (715 alt., 3,769 pop.), on the old McIntosh Trail,
was an industrial town even before its incorporation in 1870. A settlement grew up around the village of the textile mill established here in
1828 by David Norwood. When the Atlanta & West Point Railroad
was completed in 1854 community activities began to center around the
railroad station; new settlers arrived, and soon the town was one of
the best cotton markets in western Georgia. Industrial plants and with
them a number of textile mills were established in the twentieth century.

LAGRANGE, *66.7 m.* (786 alt., 25,025 pop.), seat of Troup County, is
known for both textile manufacturing and the character of its architecture. Here the modern, industrial South has been superimposed
upon the Old South of the plantation era without obscuring the charm
of the classically designed houses, formal gardens, and wealth of magnolias, water oaks, and elms.

In the early nineteenth century LaGrange was a settlement of log
cabins. Gradually larger houses were built until, by the second quarter
of the century, there were many ample houses with broad, columned
porches. On his visit to America in 1825 the Marquis de La Fayette,
spending two weeks in Georgia as the guest of Governor George M.
Troup, was impressed with the similarity of the Creek lands of western
Georgia to his own estate, La Grange, in France. In his honor the
town, incorporated in 1828 as the county seat, was called LaGrange.

Widely known for its many textile products, the city is also becoming
an important retail trade center for western Georgia and eastern Alabama. Among the cotton textile products are: tire cord; belt ducking;
ducks, drills, and twill fabrics; color-fast chenille and tufted rugs; bath
mats, bath sets, towels, industrial wiping cloths; and industrial, mechanical, and commercial yarns. Nylon and rayon fabrics are also
manufactured. LaGrange and Troup County, however, are active agriculturally as well as industrially. With a climate that favors year-round
grazing, livestock production is fast becoming one of the area's leading
agricultural commodities. For the year ending August 31, 1951, cash
sales at the Livestock Market amounted to more than a million and a
half dollars. All of the staple row crops can be raised in the county,
and uncleared lands abound in timber and pulpwood.

The GEORGE HEARD HOUSE (*private*), 206 Broad St., is a two-story, white
frame house of classic simplicity with double porches, tall shuttered
windows, and Doric columns on three sides. It is surrounded by oaks,

elms, and boxwood, and a boxwood-lined walk leads to the porch.

The SEGREST HOUSE (*private*), 311 Vernon St., visible (L) from Broad St. at the end of Trinity Ave., is a house of closely fitted white boards and has heavy Doric columns across its porch, but it departs from tradition in not having a small balcony above the porch. The large bushes of white, pink, and variegated camellias, which bloom soon after Christmas, are typical of the age and character of the house.

THE OAKS (*private*), 1103 Vernon St., built in 1845, is a Greek Revival house with a façade adorned with six massive Doric columns. The house, which has a hanging balcony and a widow's walk, is especially notable for the curving stairway inside and for the mantels of black Italian marble. It now belongs to Mrs. Francis J. Dodd, whose son, Lamar Dodd, the artist, is well known for his paintings.

BELLEVUE (*private*), 204 McLendon Ave., visible (R) from Broad St. at the head of McLendon Ave., was for several years the home of Benjamin H. Hill, who acquired the site in 1853. Here Jefferson Davis was entertained, and here Hill was arrested by Federal soldiers. The white frame house, with tall Ionic columns and massive, carved cornices, stands on land once part of a 12,000-acre plantation. Boxwood hedges outline the gardens on both sides of the white sand walk, which is flanked by superb magnolias. The interior is admired for its spacious rooms, its walnut stairway, its drawing-room mantel of black marble, and its high ceilings decorated with various floral patterns.

Benjamin Harvey Hill (1823-82), though opposed to secession, supported the Confederate cause during the war. Although he strove to protect the interest of Georgia during the Reconstruction, he advised submission to the inevitable and thus became estranged from the embittered people. Nevertheless, in 1875 he was elected to the U. S. House of Representatives. A fearless and eloquent speaker, he was a strong influence in persuading President Hayes to withdraw the Federal military from the South. Elected to the U. S. Senate in 1877, he held office until his death five years later. The house is now restored as a clubhouse for the LaGrange Woman's Club.

LAGRANGE COLLEGE (L), Broad St. extending back to Vernon St., is the third oldest Protestant institution of higher education for women in America, according to the Research Staff of the Library of Congress. It is the oldest in Georgia. Now a fully accredited four-year college, it was established as the LaGrange Female Academy by Thomas Stanley in 1831. It became LaGrange Female Institute in 1847, LaGrange Female College in 1851, and LaGrange College in 1934. It first began conferring degrees in 1843. Oreon Smith Hall has four ivy-covered columns known to the students as Matthew, Mark, Luke, and John.

HILLS AND DALES (*private*), Vernon St. (R), the estate of Mr. and Mrs. Fuller Callaway, Jr. Built in 1916 by the late Fuller E. Callaway, it is an extension of the famed Ferrell Gardens started in 1841 by Sarah Coleman Ferrell.

LaGrange is served by two railroads and one commercial air line. Callaway Airport, owned jointly by the city and the county, is located three miles from the downtown section. Southern Airways provides six flights daily. The airport was built by the government as an emergency landing during World War II. Three runways with taxi strips are paved and measure 150 feet in width and 5,000 feet in length. The Civil Aeronautics Administration in co-operation with the city and county has built and commissioned a communication station, which makes available weather reports and information to aircraft in flight. Automatic lighting is provided for night flights.

Both the American Legion Course and the Highland Country Club have nine-hole golf courses, that of the latter designed by Donald Ross. Favorable climate permits playing almost any day. The city is exceptionally well provided with swimming pools.

The CALLAWAY MILL COMMUNITY, covering several blocks in southwestern LaGrange, includes in its area some of the red brick buildings of the Callaway Mills, white frame cottages for mill employees, a community house, a YMCA and both indoor and outdoor swimming pools. In the center of the community village is an 8-acre park surrounding the 97-foot CALLAWAY MEMORIAL TOWER, a structure of red brick and limestone with a clock on each of its four faces. It was designed in the manner of the Campanile of St. Mark's in Venice, and erected by employees in 1929 as a memorial to Fuller E. Callaway, Sr., founder of the Callaway Mills, who died in 1928.

The Callaway Mills, established in 1900 with the building of the Unity Cotton Mills, comprise eight industrial plants in LaGrange, one in Manchester, and one in Milstead. The company employs between four and five thousand people and manufactures more than a hundred major products, including yarns, fabrics, rugs, and towels.

At LaGrange is a junction with US 27 (*see* TOUR *10*).

Between LaGrange and West Point the land is thickly wooded in pine and oak, and small truck farms take the place of large crop areas. Lettuce, tomatoes, and cabbage have to a great extent replaced cotton.

The CANNONVILLE DEMONSTRATION PROJECT, 70.2 *m.,* is one of five similar projects operated in Georgia by the U. S. Soil Conservation Service from 1934 to 1938. This project included approximately 30,000 acres of privately owned land. The purpose was to demonstrate to the 175 families living within its area, land use practices which would prevent further soil wastage through increasing erosion. Trained technicians made detailed soil surveys and assisted the farmers in planning their farms. Terracing equipment, tractors, seeds, plants, WPA labor, and other services were furnished by the government to speed up the establishment of erosion-control measures.

Many measures applied during the life of the project may still be seen. Chief among these are reforested areas and kudzu fields. Terraces, waterways, sericea lespedeza, pasture improvement, woodland management demonstrations, and others are still in evidence.

Closed in 1938, the project is now included in the Pine Mountain Soil Conservation District. Farmers are benefiting today from the lessons learned while the demonstration was in progress, and are developing improved programs in co-operation with soil conservation districts. Grassland farming, forest fire protection, woodland management, and other modern steps essential to conservation farming are rapidly replacing a system of farming which exhausted the soil and caused soil loss on uncontrolled water sheds.

WEST POINT, *83.9 m.* (576 alt., 4,076 pop.), on the banks of the Chattahoochee River, is an industrial town. When the site of West Point was first acquired by the state in 1825 there was a trading post here known as Franklin, where both Creek and Cherokee exchanged furs for firearms and liquor. After the first store was built in 1829, the post grew into a town that was incorporated as Franklin in 1831; but since it was the westernmost point on the Chattahoochee River in Georgia, its name was changed to West Point the following year. With the completion of the Montgomery & West Point Railroad in 1851 and of the Atlanta & West Point Railroad in 1854, West Point developed as an important cotton market. During the War between the States the town was sacked, and the toll bridge and railroad trestle were destroyed. It was, however, the first Georgia city to be released from military control after the war, and it immediately began a period of industrial activity.

At West Point is the home office of the West Point Manufacturing Company which consists of the Lanett Bleachery & Dye Works, the West Point Utilization Company, the Lanett Mill, the Shawmut Mill, the Langdale Mill, the Fairfax Mill, and the Riverdale Mill, all within a radius of a few miles, some across the state line in Alabama. The business was begun in 1866 by LaFayette Lanier with an estimated 150 employees, 6,000 spindles, and 98 looms; in 1949 it had 8,207 employees, 204,856 spindles, and 5,075 looms. A complex of services, medical and social, are maintained by the company for the benefit of its employees.

For many years West Point experienced heavy damage to property from the high waters of the Chattahoochee River. After the flood of

1919, Smith Lanier employed hydraulic engineers, who made surveys and recommended the construction of a lake and a series of dams to reduce the flood hazard and encourage further industrial development. A flood control project, begun in 1933 by the C. W. A. was continued under the F. E. R. A. and finally taken over by the U. S. War Department, which spent approximately $591,000 from W. P. A. funds on stream clearance, drainage, levee construction, and bridge work. There has not been a serious flood since the project was completed in 1939.

The GRIGGS HOUSE (*private*), W. Tenth St., built about 1857, is a square-pillared, white frame house set in the center of cedars, boxwood, and wistaria. It is on the SITE OF THE BATTLE OF WEST POINT, which lies partly in Georgia and partly in Alabama. On a hill rising behind the house are the REMAINS OF FORT TYLER, breastworks made to protect the city from the fire of Federal guns. General Wilson quotes Colonel La Grange's description of the fort as "a remarkably strong bastioned earthwork 35 yards square, surrounded by a ditch 12 feet wide and 10 feet deep, situated on a commanding eminence protected by an imperfect abatis and mounting two 32-pounders and two field guns." On Easter, April 16, 1865, Confederate forces under General Robert C. Tyler, who was killed, held the fort for several hours against a brigade of Federal soldiers under Colonel O. H. La Grange. This force was a flanking detachment of General James H. Wilson's cavalry corps which had been ordered to raid the Confederate depots and manufactories in Georgia and Alabama.

At *84.5 m.* US 29 crosses the Alabama Line at a point 23 miles east of Opelika, Alabama.

TOUR 3A

Royston—Elberton—(Abbeville, S. C.); State 17 and State 72.

This tour crosses a land of rolling red clay hills devoted principally to agriculture. In Elbert County are several old houses associated with pioneer and Revolutionary days. The vicinity of Elberton is noted for its large deposits of granite, Georgia's second most important mineral resource.

At ROYSTON, *0 m.* (898 alt., 2,039 pop.) 13 miles west of Hartwell, (*see* TOUR 3), US 29 intersects State 17. Left on State 17.

ELBERTON, *20 m.* (706 alt., 6,772 pop.), was settled during the 1780's by pioneers who came from Virginia and the Carolinas with gun and axe to open up the Cherokee lands. The town was named for General Samuel Elbert, the Revolutionary soldier who took Fort Oglethorpe and was governor of the state in 1785. When Elbert County was created in 1790 Elberton became the county seat but did not begin to prosper until a railroad was run through this section after the War between the States. Its most rapid growth began after the first granite quarry was opened in 1882. It is now one of the largest granite finishing and shipping points in the state. More than fifteen hundred workers are employed in the operation of the quarries and finishing sheds in the vicinity, almost all of which are locally owned. Additional stimulus to the industrial life of the town was given by the establishment of a large silk mill in 1926.

The OLIVER HOUSE (*private*), McIntosh St. (L) between Church and Edward sts., was built in 1840. The white frame house, with its two-story gallery porch, three dormer windows, and square columns, is of an architectural type characteristic of the Louisiana low country but rarely found in Georgia. The main veranda, which is on the second floor, is ornamented with banisters and reached by a curving double stairway at one side.

The HEARD HOUSE (*private*), Heard St. (R) between Thomas and Tusten sts., is a white frame house with eight slender square columns and a classic pediment; a small balcony overhangs the main doorway. The house was built between 1820 and 1830.

The JAMES HOUSE (*private*), 340 Heard St., is the oldest of Elberton's ante-bellum houses. Built about 1820, it has a gabled roof and classic portico with pediment and heavy square columns characteristic of the early Republican architecture of this section. Pleasing details are the banisters surrounding the floor of the portico.

From Elberton on State 17 to the junction with an unimproved dirt road, 8.9 m.; (L) on this road to the gateway (R) with two tall stone columns marking the entrance to NANCY HART PARK, a state park listed as undeveloped by the Georgia Department of Parks. Formerly maintained by a local chapter of the D. A. R., it was given to the state several years ago. The park consists of five acres of the original four hundred granted to Benjamin Hart, Nancy's husband, and has been kept in its natural state—a woodland of dark oaks and pines, especially beautiful in spring when the white dogwood blooms.

Continue south of Elberton on State 17 2 m. and then turn left on State 72 (which now becomes the principal route) to MIDDLETON, 5 m., (approx. 600 alt., 144 pop.). R. from Middleton to the junction with a dirt road 2.2 m.; R. on this road to (R) the WILLIAM ALLEN HOUSE (*private*), 5.1 m. The two-story frame Georgian Colonial house, set well back and not visible from the road, has a long veranda with a central porch on the second story surmounted by a gable pediment. Built in 1785, this is conceded to be the oldest house now standing in Elbert County.

Continue on State 72 about 5 m. to the junction with a road (L) to HEARDMONT (600 alt., 350 pop.), about 3 m., named for Stephen Heard from Hanover County, Virginia, president of the Executive Council in 1780. For his services he was awarded 2,343 acres of land in Wilkes County. Heard is buried at Heardmont in the old Heard Cemetery, surrounded by a 10-acre park owned by the local Stephen Heard Chapter of the D. A. R.

An old Cherokee trail once led from here to the Savannah River ford that was crossed by the settlers from Virginia and the Carolinas after the opening of great tracts in this section. A blockhouse was built here that helped the early settlers resist the British.

A road continues from Heardmont to RUCKERSVILLE (approx. 750 alt., 74 pop.), about 10 m., incorporated in 1822 and one of the oldest settlements in Elbert County. Here the Bank of Ruckersville, the first in the state to issue notes that passed at par, was established by Joseph Rucker, who is believed to have been Georgia's first tycoon.

State 72 crosses the Savannah River in about 2 m. beyond the turn to Heardmont and continues to Abbeville, South Carolina, which is about sixteen miles from the Savannah, and to points East.

1. Right from Ruckersville to (R) the old JOSEPH RUCKER HOUSE (*private*), 0.2 m., begun in 1806 on a grant received from the state in 1795. The original house was built of logs with rock and mud chimneys. In 1812 the lean-to room and shed in the rear were added and, in 1820, the right wing and the permanent brick end chimneys. The fine avenue of cedars and Virginia boxwood was set out in 1825. In this house was born Tinsley White Rucker, Jr., a prominent lawyer and member for two months of the U. S. House of Representatives; and Joseph Rucker Lamar, Associate Justice of the U. S. Supreme Court.

2. Left from Ruckersville to VAN'S CREEK CHURCH (L), 0.3 m., organized in 1785, the second oldest Baptist Church in Georgia. Dozier Thornton came into the wilderness here in 1784 to bring the Word to the Indians and a few early settlers. The church was built in 1800. The present building, with clapboard exterior, two entrances, and steep gable roof, is the third on the site. Old records speaks of its being "puritanical in creed and fanatical in government."

TOUR 4

(Columbia, S. C.)—Augusta—Louisville—Baxley—Waycross —Folkston—(Jacksonville, Fla.); US 1.

South Carolina Line to Florida Line, 222.5 m.—Atlantic Coast Line R.R. parallels route from Waycross to the Florida Line—All types of accommodations in Augusta and Way-cross, hotel accommodations in Louisville; limited elsewhere, except for motor courts and motels at Folkston.

US 1 begins in the Fall Line Hills, traverses the Middle Coastal Plain, and finally enters the Flat Wood Region in Appling County and so continues until it ends, in its Georgia range, on the edge of the Okefe-nokee Swamp, a genuine wonderland of primitive nature. Between Augusta and Louisville it follows an Uchee trail that later became a stagecoach route. Before the War between the States, this region was a part of the great plantation belt, where slave labor was abundant. Some of the old houses date back almost to the Revolution, and there is a lingering grace and mellow charm about them. After the war, how-ever, share cropping developed as an economic substitute for the old plantation program, and the insistent planting of row crops has plun-dered the soil, with results which, at their worst, have been described in Erskine Caldwell's *Tobacco Road*. Dire signs of poverty and estab-lished or once-established wealth are sometimes found strangely as-sorted. But new agricultural techniques strengthened by the demands of World War II and the new industrial markets in Georgia are evi-dent, though cotton continues to be the principal field crop. A growing period of from 210 to 240 or more days favors long-season crops. What is most likely to hold the eye of the traveller new to cotton and its culture is the sight of Negroes in late August and early September, with red bandannas or wide straw hats on their heads and long burlap sacks slung from their shoulders, bending low over the stalks to pick the soft white staple from the bolls. Fewer mules are evident than fancy might expect; in their place more and more are tractors, espe-cially the lighter models.

Interwoven with fields of cotton, tobacco, sugar cane, and peanuts are farmhouses, some of them shakily balanced on rock supports; with rusty plantation dinner bells on tall posts, wells with a sweep (or wind-lass) and oaken buckets, and gourds swinging from crosspieces on high poles to provide nesting places for the martins that keep the hawks at a distance from the chickens. Frequently the porches are boarded in to old loose cotton piled there until enough for a bale has been picked. Economic change, however, is shown not only by more and more fresh paint, and that modern symbol of prosperity that has replaced the lightning rod, the television antenna, but also by the increase of modern compact houses, small but suited to the mild climate.

Climatic conditions in this area are such that both labor and machinery can be kept in nearly continuous operation. And this fact joined with increased credit for farming before and during World War II is evident in better fields and more machinery, some of which in its complexity can only bewilder the uninitiated eye. The returning soldiers have brought back new skills, especially in terms of electrical power, mechanics, and also management.

US 1 crosses the Savannah River, *o m.,* the boundary between South Carolina and Georgia, over a free bridge.

AUGUSTA, *0.5 m.* (143 alt., 71,508 pop.) (*see* AUGUSTA).

Points of Interest: The Hill, University of Georgia School of Medicine, Junior College of Augusta, Paine College (Negro), Haines Institute (Negro), Cotton Exchange.

Augusta is at the junction with US 78 (*see* TOUR *8*) and US 25 (*see* TOUR *15*).

At *15 m.* is a junction with the Bath Road.

Right on this road is BATH, *0.5 m.* (410 alt., 30 pop.).
This village, formerly known as Richmond Bath, developed in the early part of the nineteenth century as a summer resort because the cold, clear water of the spring was thought to possess medicinal qualities. In ante-bellum days this retreat of wealthy planters was celebrated for its old mansions and its hospitality. When malaria in low-lying Burke County caused "third day chills and fever," many families retired here.
Most of the old buildings have been destroyed, and only the decaying manse and the well-preserved PRESBYTERIAN CHURCH remain. The church is a square white clapboard structure designed by James Trowbridge, of Boston, and built about 1820. The hand-made pulpit and pews, the slave-gallery at the side, and the bell hanging in the square steeple, all remain unchanged. For eight years, beginning in 1843, the Reverend Francis R. Goulding served as minister of this church. In the manse next door he wrote *Young Marooners* and, before Elias Howe's invention, was working to perfect a sewing machine. He failed, however, because he did not place the eye of the needle near its point.
In the churchyard is the BATH CEMETERY, its oldest stone bearing the date September 20, 1816.

WRENS, *33.3 m.* (423 alt., 1,380 pop.), was established in 1884, when the Augusta Southern Railroad was laid. The founder, W. J. Wren, inherited the land from his grandfather who, according to local tradition, had obtained it in exchange for two blind horses. Though chiefly a trading point for the surrounding agricultural region, the town has several industrial units.

Wrens was the boyhood home of Erskine Caldwell, who is known not only for his novels, including *Tobacco Road* and *God's Little Acre,* but for numerous short stories dealing with the tenant farmer. With his father, a Presbyterian minister and teacher, Caldwell visited over the countryside and observed at first hand the manners and morals of the sharecroppers. When challenged for the social realism of his work, Caldwell replied, "It is no more obscene than life." His works present an effective combination of the old-fashioned Protestant conscience and modern sociological case histories. The author definitely does not belong to the lavender and old lace school of southern fiction.

POPE HILL (*private*), a white clapboard house on the eastern edge of the town, was erected about 1850. Here Jefferson Davis, after his capture by Union forces, was allowed to stop for breakfast. Although the front has been considerably altered by the addition of a porch and portecochere, the outlines of the original small stoop can still be seen in the paneling on both sides of the front door. During the nineteenth century the residence served as an inn and a relay station where stagecoaches changed horses.

The OLIPHANT HOME (*private*), *35.1 m.* (R), is a plantation house built between 1820 and 1830. A story-and-a-half structure of wide clapboards, it has a center hall flanked by two high-ceiled rooms; later rooms have been added on each side of the front porch. The kitchen, originally standing at a distance from the house, has been moved nearer the back porch. From the rear of the "big house" a lane leads between the double row of slave cabins, which are sagging and weather-worn but held up by their massive stone chimneys.

The OLD WHIGHAM PLACE (*private*), *42.4 m.,* (R) is a gaunt, high standing frame structure with a one-story porch advanced from the front and a kitchen ell from the side. Broad end chimneys dwindle to narrow, tall flues above the roof. An original grant in the possession of the Whigham family shows that the land was owned by their family in 1790, and it is believed that the house was built some time near that date. It remained in the possession of the Whigham family until 1910.

The GOBERT HOUSE (*private*), *46.4 m.,* (L) was built between 1796 and 1800 by Benjamin Gobert, a political refugee from France. The one-story frame house has a steep roof and double doors opening on a front porch. The interior has wide board ceilings and chair rails around the wall.

LOUISVILLE, *48.3 m.* (337 alt., 2,231 pop.), seat of Jefferson County, succeeded Savannah and Augusta as Georgia's capital. The Georgia constitution of 1789 provided for a convention five years later, and when it met in 1795 it decided among other things that the capital of the state should be Louisville.

The town was laid out in 1786 on a 1,000-acre tract purchased by the state for the establishment of a capital. The first statehouse was completed in 1796 in time for a session of the legislature, and the last session was held there in 1805 before Milledgeville became the capital. A troop of cavalry was sent from Washington, D. C., to escort the treasury and records of state when they were hauled by wagon in 1807 to Milledgeville.

The streets were numbered and named before Louisville was populated. It was decreed by a legislative enactment that the town should be laid off "after the style of the streets of Philadelphia." The streets today are wide and shady, in an orderly pattern; every approach to it is upgrade, for it was also required that it should be "far above the unhealthy swampy vapors." Louisville was named in honor of Louis XVI of France as a mark of appreciation for France's help in the Revolution.

The JEFFERSON COUNTY COURTHOUSE, E. Broad St., built from materials of the old state capitol, occupies the site of that building. In front of the courthouse is the marked SITE WHERE THE YAZOO PAPERS WERE BURNED on February 15, 1796, after an impressive ceremony in the presence of the Governor and members of both legislative bodies. Speculative land companies had bought from Georgia 35,000,000 acres of land in the present states of Mississippi and Alabama near the Yazoo River for less than one and a half cents an acre. A state-wide wave of indignation caused the passage of a legislative act to rescind the sale and to destroy all records of the transaction. Later the U. S. Supreme Court declared this act of the Georgia Legislature unconstitutional, and in 1814 a settlement was made with the claimants.

In the LOUISVILLE CITY CEMETERY, W. 7th St., is a tall granite monument marking the grave of Herschel V. Johnson, Governor of Georgia (1853-57), judge of the superior court, and a candidate in 1860 for vice president of the United States. Near the cemetery is a small granite marker on the SITE OF THE LOUISVILLE ACADEMY, chartered in 1796. One of the ten original institutions chosen to make up the University System of Georgia, it was built on a land grant of several hundred acres, a part of which is still held by the institution today.

The OLD SLAVE MARKET, Broad St., was probably built around 1800, though tradition claims that it is older than the town and was built in 1758 at the convergence of two Indian trails, one running westerly from the coast, the other inland north and south. Made of heavy timbers, the structure has a roof about twenty feet square supported by square posts. Hanging in the market house is a bell, sent in 1772 by the King of France as a gift to a convent in New Orleans, which was captured by pirates and sold at Savannah, and later was sent to the new capital. Since the market house was the place of public sales, it is a matter of course that slaves were sold there when offered at public auction.

When Sherman was in this part of the state in 1864, General Slocum and his troops made Louisville their headquarters. The business section was burnt and many of the old landmarks and buildings, but not the Old Market and the house used by the general as a residence.

The ROGER LAWSON ESTATE (L), 5th St. R. of State 24, just within the city limits, has a two-story clapboard house standing on a hill at the end of a long avenue of oaks. It has a two-story pedimented portico with upper gallery, and windows flanked by batten shutters. A double row of slave quarters lines the red clay road which leads to the entrance. Roger Lawson, who received this land as a grant and called it Mount Pleasant, built the house—originally a one-story structure—in 1764 and converted it into a fort during the Revolution. In the early nineteenth century, a subsequent owner enlarged the house but retained the simple design of the original structure in its paneling and wood trim. It is now the property of Mrs. E. N. Willie.

Though cotton is the chief preoccupation of the area, Louisville has a fertilizer plant, a freezer locker plant, cottonseed oil mills, cotton gins, a furniture factory, a garment factory, and a creamery. There is a municipally owned golf course and a children's playground. Fishing and hunting in the vicinity are good.

At Louisville is the junction with State 24 (*see* TOUR *14*).

SWAINSBORO, 78.7 *m.* (318 alt., 4,300 pop.), seat of Emanuel County, was incorporated in 1853. Among the industrial plants are saw mills, planing mills, cotton gins, turpentine stills, machine shops, and warehouses. Hogs, turkeys, chickens, and goats are exported in large numbers.

Swainsboro is at the junction with US 80 (*see* TOUR *9*).

Emanuel County, created in 1812 and named for David Emanuel, Revolutionary soldier and President of the Senate in Georgia in 1801, covers 1,000 square miles; because of its size citizens often refer to it as the State of Emanuel. The county produces large quantities of naval stores, sweet potatoes, corn, nuts, sugar cane, hay, and velvet beans. This diversity favors a four-year program of crop rotation, which agricultural agencies have been promoting.

Below Swainsboro the road stretches through the solemn piney woods or wiregrass section, the last part of Georgia to be developed. In the mid-nineteenth century small farmers from the Carolinas were attracted to this region by the lumber of the pine forests. Relatively few Negroes live here, and the land is worked by independent owners, who grow cotton as the principal money crop. Since the price of cotton has frequently failed to meet production costs, the farmers have suffered acutely. Cigarette tobacco, however, has been introduced on a large scale, and has provided a rewarding cash crop in the pine barrens.

LYONS, *107.6 m.* (254 alt., 2,799 pop.), seat of Toombs County, was chartered in 1897. Tobacco, cotton, and corn are raised on the surrounding farms, and there are extensive timberlands in the area as well as several tobacco markets.

Right from Lyons on US 280 is MOUNT VERNON, *17 m.*, where BREWTON-PARKER COLLEGE is located on the dividing line between the towns of Mount Vernon and Ailey. The college was established in 1904 through the efforts of Dr. J. C. Brewton and Mr. C. B. Parker, of McRae. It was first named Union Baptist Institute, then in 1912 it became Brewton-Parker Institute, and finally in 1927 Brewton-Parker Junior College. After the high school was abandoned in 1948, the institution functioned only as a junior college. The school was formerly operated by twenty-one Baptist associations, but in 1949 the Baptist Convention of Georgia assumed control of the college.

Many ministerial students and church workers have received their training at Brewton-Parker. The enrollment in 1951 was 160. The endowment of the school is approximately $140,000, and the faculty has nine members.

Left from Lyons on State 30 is REIDSVILLE, *15 m.* (200 alt., 1,266 pop.), which has been the seat of Tatnall County since 1832, though it was not incorporated until 1838. Tatnall County was named for General Josiah Tatnall, Revolutionary patriot and Governor of Georgia.

Right from Reidsville on State 147 to the new STATE PENITENTIARY, *22.8 m.*, a model prison constructed by P. W. A. funds under the supervision of the Prison Commission of Georgia and completed in 1936. Tucker and Howell of Atlanta were the architects. From the outside this massive and dignified white concrete structure looks like a modern office building. Above the two fluted columns of the entrance is a bas-relief panel by Julian Harris, a Georgia sculptor, depicting various activities of prison life; justice usually represented as a feminine deity with scales and sword has been expressed by the figure of a man with a powerful physique.

With a frontage of 1,020 feet and a depth of 842 feet, the building contains 8 units with accommodations for 2,000 prisoners. The units on the right are for white prisoners, on the left for Negroes. (Young boys are committed to the Boys Industrial Institute at Toccoa, Georgia. Most of the maximum security prisoners are placed in the Rock Quarry Prison Branch at Buford, Georgia.) Two large recreational fields are provided for exercise on the grounds of the prison where games are played by the inmates under close supervision.

Since the prison is almost completely isolated from large industrial cities, the plant was designed to be a self-sufficient unit. Ample storage space is provided for emergency as well as daily needs, and spare parts for all mechanical equipment are kept in stock. Prisoners cultivate the food crops on a 4,800-acre tract of land surrounding the prison and adjoining the old state prison farm. In the machine shops trades are taught to the prisoners as a part of the rehabilitation program. The automobile tag plant was moved here from the old state penitentiary at Milledgeville.

The plans and specifications of the building meet the standards set by the U. S. Bureau of Prisons. When the prison was built it was agreed with the Federal government that the state should pay 70 per cent of the cost, and this payment was completed in 1942. The building cost $1,281,980 and with its equipment the total came to $1,500,000. Since then a housing project for the custodial officers has been built at the prison together with other improvements including a chapel on the grounds, a recreational hall for movies, and sundry other buildings, totaling another $1,250,000. This prison has gone a long way toward answering the criticism leveled at the Georgia convict camps and chaingangs by other parts of the nation.

BAXLEY, *138.4 m.* (206 alt., 3,409 pop.), seat of Appling County, was incorporated in 1875. Increased transportation facilities have made it a marketing and shipping center for the products of the surrounding area—tobacco, naval stores, lumbers, pecans, and syrup. Tobacco warehouses provide ample marketing facilities for the growers of the surrounding district. In 1951 6,056,516 pounds were sold for $2,646,858.02 at an average price of 43.70 cents per pound.

Resin from the slashed pines is brought to the turpentine stills to be converted into hard rosin and crude turpentine. The unpainted frame sheds are crowded with barrels of amber-colored rosin, and the loading platform is gummed with resin drippings. Recently, a widespread co-operative test of surgical tape was begun by Filtered Rosin Products, Inc., of Baxley, together with a major manufacturer of adhesive tape, Appling General Hospital, and other hospitals, for the purpose of discovering skin reaction to the new tape. A special rosin formula has been developed which when combined with rubber has a texture suitable for surgical use, it is believed. The rosin company has also been investigating chewing-gum bases, and resins for grease and alkali-proof tiles for floors.

Caroline Miller was living in Baxley when she wrote *Lamb in His Bosom,* a story of pioneer life in back country Georgia during the Revolution. Published in 1933, it was awarded the Pulitzer Prize in 1934.

At Baxley is the junction with US 341 (*see* TOUR *12*).

At about *142 m.* (or *4 m.* from Baxley) US 1 passes through the BAXLEY STATE FOREST, where the Georgia Forestry Commission is conducting a program of studies on the advantages obtainable from the controlled management of forest lands. The 1,000-acre area was acquired from Nellie, Samuel, and Joseph Neeley by Appling County and turned over to the Commission July 15, 1937.

ALMA, *156.7 m.* (195 alt., 2,586 pop.), incorporated in 1926, is the seat of Bacon County, which was created in 1914.

Right from Alma on State 32 is DOUGLAS, *22 m.*, where SOUTH GEORGIA COLLEGE is located. South Georgia College is a unit of the University System of Georgia. It is a coeducational junior college offering two years of college work as a preparation for most fields of specialization. Terminal courses in secretarial work, home economics, and general education are also offered. The enrollment usually runs around 400 students, and in 1951 the faculty members numbered twenty-two. South Georgia College is the oldest state-supported junior college in Georgia.

Near Waycross the farmhouses appear better kept, electricity is more generally available, and with it modern conveniences. Some 450 new homes have been built in Alma within the last decade.

Throughout the wiregrass section the poorer tenant farmers formerly raised "piney woods" cattle and "razorback" hogs—inferior breeds allowed to roam and graze as they could. But the agricultural agencies step by step, after patient years, have brought about an improvement in breeding, care, and sanitation. The county contains 20,000 acres in pasture, 19,000 cattle—500 registered—and 1,300 tractors in use. In addition there are 9 sawmills, 1 large planing mill, and a million and a half is done annually in turpentine sales. The cash sales in tobacco run around $1,000,000.

WAYCROSS, *183.4 m.* (138 alt., 18,899 pop.), with large oaks shading the streets, is a clean, well-paved, and progressive city that owes its development as well as its name to its being the converging point of several railroads and five highways.

In 1818 settlers began to claim the land near Kettle Creek, now a part of Waycross, and to build blockhouses and fortifications for protection against the Indians. By 1825 the land had been acquired from the Indians and granted to individuals under the lottery system initiated in Georgia in the early part of the nineteenth century after the disposal of the lands lying west of the Chattahoochee River. The officials of the state were determined that land should be parceled out in small tracts free of charge, and Governor Troup expressed their policy when he said, "Men and the soil constitute the strength and wealth of nations, and the faster you plant men, the faster you can draw on both." After the land had been surveyed and charted into parcels, usually of 212.5 acres, it was distributed by lot. Each citizen was given one chance and heads of families had two, but since there were more citizens than parcels of land in every lottery, many people drew blanks. As late as 1870 Waycross was only a railroad junction with fifty inhabitants and a few scattered houses, but within one generation it became an important commercial center of southern Georgia.

Throughout a belt seventy-five miles wide, beginning at Savannah and running through Waycross to Bainbridge, bee culture has become so extensive that Georgia leads the South in the production of honey and packaged bees for establishing new hives. Pollination is of course essential to orchards and field crops for the production of fruit and seeds, and in addition the cash income is considerable. In 1947, which was less than an average year, about 6,000,000 pounds of honey brought a sales total of $2,000,000; 1,600,000 pounds of packaged bees for shipment brought in another half million, and to this should be added $70,000 for queen bees, to be used in re-queening weak colonies. The blossoms of the tupelo tree provide a heavy amber-colored honey, and the small white blossoms of the gallberry bushes give a clear, almost white sort. These local sorts are as distinguished as the better known clover and orange varieties.

Among the industries of Waycross are the production and processing of naval stores, the marketing of furs, the processing of lumber, and pecan shelling, as well as tobacco warehousing. Whereas in 1935-1936, 3,000,000 pounds of tobacco sold in Waycross for $826,000, in 1951, according to the Georgia Department of Agriculture, 5,773,466 pounds brought $2,831,997.74 at an average of 49.05 cents per pound. Of the pelts marketed, raccoon is by far the leader; others are opossum, mink, muskrat, skunk, gray fox, otter, red fox, weasel, wildcat, and deer.

Waycross was the host on July 17, 1952, to the world premiere of *Lure of the Wilderness,* a film made in the Okefenokee Swamp and based on Vereen Bell's novel *Swamp Water.* An earlier film by Hollywood carried the same name as the novel.

The Headquarters Office of the OKEFENOKEE NATIONAL WILDLIFE REFUGE is located in the Federal Building in Waycross, where arrangements can be made to visit the Refuge area. There are three entrances to the Refuge at which recreational facilities are provided (*see* below and TOUR 4A).

ATLANTIC COAST LINE RAILROAD SHOPS, on US 1 at the southern limits of the city, cover many acres of land and represent an investment of several million dollars. Being the line's largest shops, they employ hundreds of skilled mechanics and laborers. Numbers of fruit and vegetable cars are iced and rerouted at the diversion yard.

Right from Waycross on State 50 to WINONA PARK, *3 m.,* a popular recreation center with beautiful winding drives and a large lake surrounded by tall pines.

At Waycross is the junction with US 84 (*see* TOUR 5).

About *8 m.* from Waycross is an area generally indicated on present maps as the COASTAL FLATWOODS UTILIZATION PROJECT. A state forest and a state park are now located in this area. The WAYCROSS STATE FOREST, under the supervision of the Georgia Forestry Commission, consists of 37,731 acres. It was leased from the U. S. Soil Conservation Service for fifty years, October 5, 1938, with the right to three successive fifteen-year renewal terms at the option of the state. This is a demonstration forest for the purpose of conducting controlled investigations in the scientific management of forest land, reforestation, and soil conservation. The forest area of Georgia is greater in extent than that of any other state east of the Mississippi River, and its products make up a major part of the economy of the state.

The LAURA S. WALKER STATE PARK is about ten miles from WAYCROSS (L), then *7 m.*, (*trading post, picnic area, fishing, boating, cabins, mess hall; for reservations write to Superintendent, Laura S. Walker State Park, Waycross, Georgia*). This 160-acre park is noted for its organized group camping arrangements which are located on Lake Walker; it is open during the entire year, and the mild climate favors all sorts of outdoor sports. There are four groups of four cabins each, and each cabin is provided with eight bunks with individual lockers for the occupants. Four bathhouses are equipped with showers, washstands, and toilets. Hot and cold running water and electricity are always available. Two of the cabins are reserved for camp personnel. The mess hall has a completely equipped dining room and kitchen, refrigeration room, storage room, and a small room used as quarters by kitchen help.

Right on State 177, across the tracks of the Atlantic Coast Line, *5 m.* to the northern entrance of the OKEFENOKEE NATIONAL WILDLIFE REFUGE, which was established in March of 1937 by a presidential order; it covers 331,894 acres (*see* TOUR *4A* and TOUR 5, Fargo). The swampland begins to appear along this paved highway, and with it the exotic wildlife, now under the protection of the Fish and Wildlife Service, that is typical of the area.

The OKEFENOKEE SWAMP PARK, a concessionaire of the government, is at the end of this highway (*trading post, guides for regular boat trips, boats, and fishing*). On the edge of the weird and decidedly startling swamp waterways, this park provides a tour at regular intervals during the day by means of power-driven shallow draft boats through water lanes which present a cross-section view of the swamp. A series of wooden walkways are also built over the swampy earth and water for those who wish to examine the life of the swamp at complete leisure. These lead to an eighty foot observation tower below which spreads a unique scene as strange as an image of prehistoric times. Wild animals from the swamp are housed at intervals along the paved walks of the park grounds, and there is a reptile house where one can see at close quarters behind glass the snakes, both deadly and harmless, as well as other reptiles of the area. The management has had the good taste to allow nature to speak for herself here with the greatest simplicity and directness, and the impression is memorable.

FOLKSTON, *218.2 m.* (81 alt., 1,515 pop.), the seat of Charlton County, is the local center for cypress and the new pulp wood industry of the area. The eastern entrance to the Okefenokee Swamp is reached from Folkston by means of State 23 (*see* TOUR *4A*). Motels and tourist courts of exceptional scope and convenience have been built in recent years for the Florida tourist trade. Some have year-round heating and cooling systems, and are furnished with entirely modern equipment.

TOUR 4A

Folkston—Camp Cornelia; 12 m., State 23 and an unnumbered road.

This route leads to CAMP CORNELIA which is the eastern entrance to the OKEFENOKEE NATIONAL WILDLIFE REFUGE, now under the supervision of the Federal Fish and Wildlife Service. At Camp Cornelia the Okefenokee Sportsman's Club, a concessionaire of the government, provides boats and guides for scenic trips and sport fishing. Since the publication of the autobiographical *Travels* of William Bartram in 1791, the Okefenokee has been known as a region of strange jungle-like beauty abounding with plant and animal life, including sorts rarely found elsewhere. Two powers met in Bartram: that of the acute and rigorous observer and that of the perceptive artist. The depth of his vision is shown in this quotation: "Let us rely on Providence, and by studying and contemplating the works and power of the Creator, learn wisdom and understanding in the economy of nature, and be seriously attentive to the divine monitor within." In the scope of his travels he could hardly have found a scene so replete with the signs of the divine art as that reflected for his eyes upon that mirror of nature, the Okefenokee Swamp.

In FOLKSTON, *0 m.* (81 alt., 1,515 pop.), State 23 branches southwest from US 1 (*see* TOUR 4).

At *8 m.* is a junction with a paved road; the route turns R. on this to Camp Cornelia.

Camp Cornelia is on Trail Ridge, which forms the eastern line of the Okefenokee Swamp. From this point the old Canal leads thirteen miles towards the interior of the swamp. Because of the dense growth of cypress, passage is often difficult, though some waterways have been cleared. The western side can be entered from Fargo (*see* TOUR 5). In Georgia the elevation of Trail Ridge above sea level averages around 170 feet; extending from the Satilla River to the headwaters of the Santa Fe River in Florida, it is 130 miles long. Sloping slightly southwest, the swamp in its northeast end is not much more than 120 feet above sea level.

Containing 660 square miles of fresh water, undergrowth, and timber, the swamp extends from a point a few miles south of Waycross into a section several miles south of the Florida Line. Once the hunting ground of the lower Creek and Seminole, its name is a corruption of Owaquaphenoga (Ind., trembling-earth). Geologists believe that the Okefenokee was once a salt-water sound that was eventually shut off from the ocean by the formation of the reef now called Trail Ridge, and that, likely enough, in its earlier stages it resembled the much younger Dismal Swamp in Virginia and North Carolina and also the Florida Everglades.

Despite at least one major effort to domesticate the swamp for man's use it has kept its primitive virtue, though not quite unspoiled. In 1889 the Suwannee Canal Company bought the area from the state for some $62,000, intending to drain it by means of a canal, cut the rich cypress and longleaf pine, and turn the vast "prairies"—submerged and unstable earth covered by a rugged growth of yellow-eyed grass—into farm lands. After spending what is reputed to have been a million dollars digging a canal with steam shovels and dredges, the corporation failed. The next effort was made in 1908 by the Hebard Lumber Company, which forced a railroad built on pilings into the swamp, with branch lines leading to the larger islands and "bays." As areas were cut over, the cost of lumbering even the valuable prime cypress eventually became greater than the profit, and the enterprise came to an end. Mutilated, but still nursing its breath of life, especially in its more remote recesses, the swamp came back into the possession of the state.

In 1937 President Franklin D. Roosevelt issued a presidential order designating the area as a wildlife refuge. A tract of 293,826 acres was acquired by the U. S. Biological Survey from the state at a cost of $400,000, to preserve the primitive beauty of the swamp and to safeguard its wildlife resources. On June 30, 1940, the Bureau of Biological Survey and the Bureau of Fisheries were transferred from the Department of Agriculture to the Department of the Interior and united as the Fish and Wildlife Service. In 1952, according to a statement from the latter authority, the Refuge contained 331,894 acres. The will of the people expressed as lawful authority is able to preserve what severally they are apt to destroy.

The ghostly expanse of the swamp, with cypress, bay, and tupelo gum trees growing from the muck, is broken by several lakes and islands, by acres of "prairies," and by "houses"—clumps of bushes and trees and an impenetrable undergrowth of berries, smilax, and muscadines growing on more solid areas. A network of water runways, leading from cypress bogs to alligator holes, breaks up the sameness of the "prairies." From north to south inside Trail Ridge, some of these have become fixed by names such as Sapling, Carter, Christie, Mizell, and Grand. Perhaps the largest, Grand Prairie covers some fifty square miles and contains Gannett Lake, Buzzards' Roost Lake, Coward Lake, Sego Lake, and many smaller bays and water holes.

Houses are formed and bogs extended by a process of nature known locally as a "blow-up." Gases, formed beneath the water by decaying vegetable matter, force masses of vegetation, some a hundred feet or so square, from the bottom muck. Assisted by the rise and fall of the water level, the surface of the mass, resembling the submerged sediment, rises several inches above the water and acquires a growth of grass, briars, small bushes, and water weeds. With its accumulated plantation, the entire mass floats until snagged by a clump of trees; sometimes it is forced beneath the surface by the pressure of growing cypress roots. In its floating interval this earth-raft collects seeds from cypress and other trees and in time develops into a house. Many never become stable, though, but sway and tremble as if sensitive, at the slightest touch.

The old drainage canal, with its sluggish waters, is bordered by tall tupelo gum, cypress, and dahoon holly trees. Dahoon holly is rich with bright red berries in winter, and its evergreen leaves that are spineless and rounded like the live oak's, produce a feeling of depth against the silver half-light of the Spanish moss. Lucid on its surface but deceptively opaque as to depth, the water is colored dark brown, almost black in the shadows, by the tannic acid of decaying matter. White and golden water lilies, locally called "bonnets," and the flowers of other aquatic plants, cast their bright images on the dark waters.

At the northern end of the canal is Chase Prairie, navigable only by duck punts, light shells poled by men who stand near the stern. The punt must be shallow, drawing only four inches of water, for one grass-shallow after another needs to be skimmed; it must be narrow so that it can be threaded between tupelo roots and cypress knees, knobs built up by the cypress tree around its roots.

Northwest of Chase Prairie is FLOYD'S ISLAND named for General Charles Floyd, who in 1838 was assigned the painfully skittish task of driving the Indians from the larger islands in the swamp. It is one of more than twenty-five flat, white-sand islands, which differ little from the typical mainland. All are overgrown with saw palmetto, huckleberries, gallberries, sedges, and a mixture of herbs, animated in blooming season by the searching toils of the wild honeybee. Longleaf and slash pine command the central parts of the islands, but in the richer soils along the margins thrive magnolia, live oak, bay, and gums. Sometimes the bogs of muck and moss around the islands are so dense that they will bear a man's weight. Here, growing to the unusual height of three feet or more, spotted, greenish pitcher plants ensnare small flies in their tubelike leaves, luring them by means of a sweetish liquor, to imprison them with a protruding lip, and slowly digest them. Blue-flowered pickerelweeds, purple water shields, and dainty white floating hearts add to the variety of the waterways.

On some of these islands the Seminole, driven to this fastness by the relentless pressure of the colonists, have left mounds. A few hardy settlers later ventured here and made a thin living by marketing lumber and pine resin, and raising a few cattle. COWHOUSE ISLAND received its name during the War between the States, when it was used by farmers to hide their cattle from Federal troops foraging on the land. BILLY'S ISLAND, which along with Cowhouse is one of the larger islands, was named for Billy Bowlegs, a Seminole chief.

The Okefenokee is drained by two small rivers. In times of high-water and winds, the St. Marys drains the southeastern end of the swamp; and the Suwannee drifts southwestward to empty into the Gulf of Mexico. As the Suwannee River courses through the swamp, first through high banks and then in open channels, patches of dense shade and brilliant sunshine mottle the dark, cypress-stained waters. Over the whole brooding area the eerie stillness is broken only by the splashing of waterfowl, singing of birds, bellowing of alligators, hooting and screeching of owls, and that faint concerto of mingled sounds known as the "booming of the swamp."

Reports of the Fish and Wildlife Service show that the swamp has become increasingly functional as a winter refuge for migratory water-fowl and birds. The wood (summer) duck, with its brilliant plumage like a pagan wedding garment—though once nearly exterminated by hunters because the flesh is delicious and the feathers prime for tying trout flies—has increased in numbers. More and more of the alert and nervous ring-necked duck, of the slim-necked and long-tailed pintail duck, and of the shy and graceful black duck, come each year for wintering. Though often confused with the black duck and others, the Florida duck does not migrate but having a settled disposition, remains the year-round. Mallards, canvasbacks, buffleheads, hooded mergansers, and green-winged teal, along with others, increase the winter population. Robins, cardinals, woodpeckers, ruby-crowned kinglets, red-winged blackbirds, and brown-headed nut-hatches stir the swamp with their color, flight, and song. Other sorts are the Canada goose, catbird, red-tailed hawk, bald eagle, osprey, Ward's heron, kingfisher, and pied-billed grebe. Fast vanishing species such as the swallow-tailed kite, ivory-billed woodpecker, and the Florida crane are some-times seen.

Alligators, some around ten feet, are found in the canal, the lakes, the river, and in the deeper prairie pools. Their deep-throated bellow-ing is a familiar beat in the rhythm of the swamp. Generally harmless unless needlessly excited, they are a part of the natural economy, useful in keeping mud from accumulating on the lake bottoms and in build-ing wallows that harbor fish.

For years people living near the swamp hunted deer, bears, and wildcats, and trapped otter and raccoons, marketing the pelts in Way-cross which was known for its fur trade. They served as guides for hunters who came seeking Florida bear, the largest mammal of the swamp. Night hunts were often held as a community affair, the men of the surrounding farms bringing their hounds and joining in the pursuit. The government of course had to restrict the exploitation of the swamp's animals in order to restore its natural economy; shorn of his gun, man the hunter is hardly predatory at all. Panthers have been found in the swamp, and there are such oddities as the little Le Conte frog. More than fifty species of fish, including warmouth, pickerel, short-nosed gars, suckers, catfish, jackfish, and large mouth bass, live in its waters. The rare rain-water fish (*Lucania parva*) is one of the many sorts of tiny tropical fish.

As an English Romantic poet might have said—now rests in itself again, all of this vast, troubled soul of nature.

TOUR 5

Junction with US 17—Waycross—Valdosta—Thomasville—Bainbridge—(Dothan, Ala.); US 84.

Junction with US 17 to Alabama Line, 229.6 m.—Atlantic Coast Line R.R. parallels route throughout—Watch for cattle and hogs on the highway—All types of accommodations in cities; limited elsewhere.

US 84 crosses the extreme southern part of Georgia, from the coastal country through the wiregrass section, where pine forests for years have formed the basis of extensive naval-stores operations, to the fertile west-ern farming area, where thrive vegetables, peanuts, and pecans.

In terms of the economic geography of the nation, the Lower Coastal Plain of Georgia has always been one of the most important forest areas, because the American naval-stores industry has centered around the slash and longleaf pines of the southeastern United States. Around seventy per cent of the nation's gum naval-stores come from Georgia, and that is about half of the world's supply. Dr. Charles Herty discovered in his experimental work that second-growth pines contain no more gum before the heartwood has developed than spruce; and hence are as suitable for paper-making as pulp from Canada and Norway. Longleaf pine (*pinus palustris*) is superior to slash (*pinus caribaea*) for lumber, but both produce naval-stores, and slash pine is excellent for pulp. Longleaf pine during its first few years makes only a slight stem growth, but it does elaborate a thick head of needles like a tuft of coarse grass. In this interval the seedling develops an elaborate root system that looks like the relief map of a river and at the same time bores deeply into the hardpan underneath the flat, sandy, and dry soils of the region. Once thoroughly anchored in the earth, it begins the development of its top growth. This tree has an exceptional ability for drawing crude nutriments from far below the surface and for converting them into higher grade products. Thus it is relatively slow in its growth; for generally speaking qualitative change requires a longer time span than any other sort. Select stands of longleaf pine were set aside by the British Crown for the use of the Royal Navy. Reaching sometimes a hundred feet in height and a diameter of two and a half feet, it made excellent masts and spars for sailing vessels, and supplied resinous materials for calking and planking. The raw materials of both longleaf and slash pine can be manufactured into inks, paints, varnishes, pharmaceutical aids, greases, lubricants and emulsions, linoleum, pitch, agencies in paper making besides pulp, and a long list of other technical products.

Georgia pine renews itself about three times faster than its northern equivalents, and slash, which grows best in the low wet margins of the Coastal Plain swamps and rapidly establishes itself on cutover areas, often reaches a diameter of six inches in ten years. Slow to develop heartwood but fast growing and a tough fighter against odds, it is as valuable as longleaf for resin, and in addition makes prime pulp. Since the discovery of the Herty techniques has added pulp to the production of lumber and resin, vast tracts of land formerly considered so hopeless that not even the heart of the land speculator fluttered once at the sight of them, have now become rich technical and economic assets, with both a present and a future.

In the treaty signed with Oglethorpe in 1773, the Indians had agreed to permit white settlements along the coast, but retained their hunting lands in what is now western Georgia. This territory, then covered with virgin forests of hardwood and longleaf pine, was held by the Indians only by waging bitter warfare against the whites. Finally, in 1816, the territory was opened for settlement. The first homesteaders were, for the most part, farmers from Virginia and the Carolinas, probably seeking relief from the rigid caste restrictions in those states. Past Waycross and on the way to Quitman, well-managed farms become more noticeable until finally toward the western end of the tour the preoccupation with naval-stores decreases and rich farms appear that produce cotton, corn, peanuts, sugar cane, and a wide range of vegetables. In the wooded sections small game, including quail, squirrels, raccoons, and wild turkey, is still abundant, and there are a few deer. The Gulf of Mexico and fishing are not far away.

US 84 branches west from its junction with US 17, *0 m.*, at a point 10 miles west of Brunswick (*see* TOUR *1*).

The OLD POST ROAD, *16.1 m.*, designated by a granite marker at the point where it intersects the highway, was originally an Indian trail extending from St. Augustine, Florida, northward through south Georgia into the rolling country known as the Sand Hill section. Mitchell's map of 1756, now in the Library of Congress in Washington, shows this trail. During the Revolution American forces marched along it on their way to attack a British contingent at Fort Tonyn, which was somewhere south of this junction. The road continued to be used as a stagecoach route and post road between Savannah and Florida until the War between the States.

NAHUNTA, *26.1 m.* (66 alt., 739 pop.) was made the seat of Brantley County when it was created in 1920. This area, included in the piney woods or wiregrass section, has a smaller Negro population than any other comparable area in south Georgia. The plantation system was never developed here, and the land is sparsely settled by small independent farmers.

Logs are hauled to the sawmills, which usually are housed in sheds with corrugated iron roofing and brick chimneys. A steam engine with an iron boiler generates power for the circular, coarse-toothed ripsaw, which quickly cuts off the outer part of the log as it is fed onward by a moving carriage. These outer slabs with the dark rough bark are used to fire the boiler, and the inner wood is sawed into planks which are stacked in triangular piles to season. Sawdust is placed in nearby piles where it decays. Many sawmills are temporary structures that can be moved when a section has been cut.

SCHLATTERVILLE (pronounced Slaughterville), *36.8 m.* (133 alt., 25 pop.), is the center of extensive naval-stores operations. From the many swamps in this locality the Hercules Powder Company of Brunswick collects large pine stumps and wreckage called stumpage, from which resin and paper pulp are extracted by a steaming process.

At *41 m.* (L) is the LAURA S. WALKER STATE PARK (*see* TOUR *4*).

WAYCROSS, *49.8 m.* (138 alt., 18,899 pop.), is at the junction with US 1 (*see* TOUR *4*).

RUSKIN, *55.8 m.* (140 alt., 75 pop.), named for John Ruskin, the English opinionist, author, and social reformer, was founded in the 1890's by a Tennessee group who bought 720 acres of land and established a colony here. It was so organized that all property belonged to the society; individuals brought everything they made to a general exchange where they procured all supplies, paying with scrip issued by the colony. Among the enterprises were a community dining room, factories for the production of shoes, brooms, and suspenders, and a newspaper called *The Coming Nation*. A school provided for education up to the twelfth grade, and a light-opera group provided entertainment. As usually happens with communities founded on exceptional ideals and then not rigorously managed, dissension caused the community to break up in 1901, and Ruskin now consists of only a few families that work in Waycross.

HOMERVILLE, *76.5 m.* (176 alt., 1,787 pop.), is the seat of Clinch County; it was incorporated in 1869.

The town is in the heart of the turpentine section. For the conservation of the pines, firebreaks, telephone lines, and watch towers have been established in all parts of the area. This program of fire protection has resulted in a thick regrowth of young slash pines on cutover acres; and hence pulpwood cutting has multiplied greatly, even within the last two years. Capital from outside the state has moved in and made extensive purchases of pulpwood forests.

From spring until early fall the surrounding pine trees are slashed so that the resin will drip into tin cans fastened beneath the cuts, and the air is rich with the pungent smell of the dripping resin. In the stills (*open to visitors*) the resin is distilled into naval-stores—turpentine and hard rosin. Although the production of naval-stores and pulp are the principal industries, cleared areas of land are being prepared for pasture and pure bred cattle. This is a long-time program and requires several years of financial support before the investment returns any profit, but a number of excellent grasses and legumes have been found to do well on the cutover pine lands.

At Homerville is the junction with US 441 and State 89.

Left on US 441 and State 89 is FARGO, *38.4 m.* (116 alt., 275 pop.). On the highway near the Suwannee River is a stone memorial to Stephen Collins Foster (1826-64), composer of "Old Folks at Home," the song celebrating that river.

Although Foster's so-called "Ethiopian songs" caught the quality of Negro melodies so sympathetically that they are generally thought of as folk music, he was a stranger to the South except for a brief journey to New Orleans in 1852. He was raised near Pittsburgh, Pennsylvania.

At *38.9 m.* is a junction with a sandy road.

Left on this road to the western entrance of the OKEFENOKEE NATIONAL WILDLIFE REFUGE, about *15 m.,* which is the headquarters of OKEFENOKEE RECREATIONS, INC. This concessionaire, in addition to providing boats and guides for scenic trips and sport fishing, also rents modern cabins located on the edge of the Swamp for overnight occupancy. The Refuge boundary and headquarters facilities are marked by the characteristic Flying Goose signs of the U. S. Fish and Wildlife Service (*see* TOUR 4 and *4A*).

VALDOSTA, *112.8 m.* (215 alt., 20,046 pop.), is at the junction with US 41 (*see* TOUR 2).

The source of BLUE SPRINGS, *123.9 m.* (R), remains obscure. Picnic pavilions and a concrete swimming pool, filled with the cold, greenish-blue waters of the springs, make this a popular summer recreational ground.

QUITMAN, *131.5 m.* (173 alt., 4,769 pop.), seat of Brooks County, is a pleasant town with shaded streets and well-kept houses. Along the middle of Screven Street, where the business section is centered, is a parkway green with grass and dignified palms and bright with roses the greater part of the year. Many of the principal residential streets are wide and planted with parkways similar to Screven Street. The town makes an immediate impression of order, energy, and progress. Incorporated on December 19, 1859, it was named for General John A. Quitman, who led a troop of Mississippi soldiers to aid Texas in its struggle with Mexico for independence.

For years Quitman has shipped large quantities of hams and sausage and served as a trading center for cotton and corn, but recently it has added peanuts, watermelons, and cantaloupes as well as other vegetables to its trade. It was feelingly celebrated during the War between the States as the smokehouse of the Confederacy. One of the first areas in the state to develop cold storage for the preservation of meat with ice brought in carloads from Savannah, today the town has two large freezer and locker plants and in addition two ice manufacturers. There has been an increase in pasture land and cattle. The *Bankers Farm Bulletin,* of the Sixth Federal Reserve District, in its issue of September, 1952, observes, "Adding livestock to row crop enterprises or shifting to livestock alone requires changing to a farm economy based on pasture, hay, and grains and also requires some long-run planning. A field can be fitted, a cash crop planted and harvested, and the loan paid off in less than a year. Not so with grassland farming. Here two or three years often pass before income is realized from the initial investment in soil-building pastures, fences, and animals. Thus the shift from row crops to animals cannot be made rapidly. It can, however, be made. But a realistic plan for the farm is necessary to insure a successful transition." The Brooks County Agricultural Planning Board has published a booklet listing conservation practices that gives due recognition to the needs of pasture development and livestock improvement as well as to other more inclusive features. On the back it is approved by The Citizens National Bank, of Quitman, which paid for the publication expense. Tobacco has also moved forward as a cash crop, and there are four warehouses operated by one company.

With an average rainfall of some 53 inches, about 254 growing days, and a wide variety of soils, but principally Norfolk and Tifton loams, the county area offers decidedly favorable conditions for farming. Except for wet weather, the mildness of the climate permits an almost continuous use of labor and farm machinery. An Annual County Fair gives an opportunity for competitive displays and serves to present concretely the achievements of the year.

There are some fifteen industries which include a large textile mill and a hosiery mill, a cannery and a well-known meat packing house. The headquarters of a chain of stores operating in south Georgia, Florida, and Alabama is located in Quitman. The town has a new Farmers Produce Market, a Livestock Market, a new Health Center, and a Civic Center that serves as a meeting place for organizations and as a rest center for visitors to the city.

The Quitman Country Club has a nine-hole golf course and a swimming pool, and there is also the West End swimming pool as well as two recreation parks. Fishing is good in the nearby lakes, ponds, and streams, and there is small game—quail, doves, ducks, and squirrels, in season.

The Brooks County Library, with 10,000 volumes, was established in 1880. It now operates a bookmobile to supply books to all sections of the county.

Between Quitman and Thomasville the more prosperous farmers have tobacco barns—narrow, two-story buildings in which the ample leaves are suspended from sticks in tiers reaching to the rafters. In late summer and early fall the air is filled with the aroma of the drying tobacco. After the leaves have dried and turned a golden brown, they are taken to market.

THOMASVILLE, *159.4 m.* (250 alt., 14,424 pop.), is at the junction with US 19 (*see* TOUR 6).

Much of the land in the southwestern part of the state is included in the hunting preserves of several large estates, and it is almost impossible to purchase the land in this section. Some small farms here are cultivated by tenants.

GREENWOOD (open during Rose Show in spring), *170.8 m.*, is the 20,000-acre estate (L) of the Whitneys. It was once the plantation home of Thomas Jones, who acquired the land in 1827 and in 1835 engaged John Wind, an English architect, to build the house. It took nine years to complete the house, which is set in a grove of oaks, palmettoes, and magnolias. It has a finely proportioned pedimented and galleried portico with fluted Ionic columns that are free-standing, a fine metal railing at the second story, and a large magnolia rosette in the pediment. Wind is reputed to have carved much of the interior woodwork himself. Stanford White planned the two wings and the formal Italian garden on the right of the house.

CAIRO (pronounced kay-ro), *173.4 m.* (237 alt., 5,577 pop.), incorporated in 1870, is a progressive town with a modern business section contrasting sharply with the many old-fashioned houses in the residential district. In 1905 the town was made the seat of the newly created Grady County, which was named for Henry W. Grady, the noted Georgia orator and political leader.

Flower gardens here contain prized plants of pink and white camellias, locally known as japonicas, and many of the semitropical flowers of Florida also grow in Cairo, especially poinsettias and fleecy pink coral vines.

For fifty years Cairo has been the largest producing center for pure cane syrup in America. It is said to ship almost all of the world's supply of collard seed. Other industries include pecan shelling, peanut grinding, and cucumber brining and pickling. In recent years okra growing has increased enormously. A large processing plant is operated here by a nationally known soup concern, and fresh okra is supplied to markets throughout the eastern half of the nation. Both cigarette and cigar types of tobacco have shown an annual increase. The county holds a very high position in the production of eggs.

A center of the new tung-oil industry, the town has a mill for extracting oil from tung nuts. The domestic industry centers around the gulf coastal areas, which resemble in soil and climate the section in China that has in the past produced the bulk of the world's supply. Tung trees planted in groves or growing more commonly in hedgerows along the fences are striking in spring with their pearl-white or pinkish-lavender blossoms. Some of the older trees are thirty-five feet high and have a limb spread of forty-five feet, but in the young groves crops grow between the rows. Like peaches the young trees begin to bear when they are three years old, but unlike peaches the poison in the tree, especially concentrated in the nuts, protects it from insect pests. Reduced by the autumn freeze of 1950, the industry is still alive, supplying domestic oil for varnishes, soap, oilcloth, linoleum, brake linings, insulation for cables and dynamos, and a great many other strategic uses. In 1908 the first tung trees were planted here and at the Georgia Experiment Station near Griffin.

BAINBRIDGE, *198.1 m.* (110 alt., 7,562 pop.), seat of Decatur County, is memorable for the large number of giant water and live oaks along its streets and parks. The town is near the site of old Fort Hughes, an earthwork used by General Andrew Jackson's soldiers during the Indian wars (1817-21) in the territory of the Flint and Chattahoochee rivers. It is believed that a white settlement was established in the bend of the Flint River as early as 1810, but the town of Bainbridge was not chartered until December 22, 1829. It was named in honor of William Bainbridge, commander of the frigate *Constitution*.

The principal industries of the city are the manufacturing of bottles, washing machines, clay by-products, and the processing of lumber. Bainbridge is the home of the Georgia Factory for the Blind, Clark Thread Mill, and Ward-Stilson, Inc.

At the time of the lumber boom in the early part of the twentieth century, a thriving lumber industry made Bainbridge one of the wealthiest towns in the state. So many forests in the county were depleted, however, that agriculture superseded lumbering.

Right from Bainbridge on State 97 which parallels the Flint River (R) to the site of the JIM WOODRUFF DAM, now under construction by the U. S. Corps of Engineers, about 23 *m.* The Jim Woodruff Dam is located on the Apalachicola River about a fifth of a mile below the confluence of the Chattahoochee and Flint rivers which together form the Apalachicola River. It is about a half mile upstream from the US 90 bridge over the Apalachicola River and will be visible from the bridge. The actual dam site is accessible from Chattahoochee, Florida, about a mile and a half northwest of the town. The Jim Woodruff Dam is the first part of the authorized plan for improvement of the Apalachicola, Chattahoochee, and Flint rivers in Florida, Georgia, and Alabama. In addition to the Jim Woodruff Dam the plan includes the Upper Columbia Lock and Dam, the Fort Benning Lock and Dam, and also the Buford Dam.

The Jim Woodruff Dam has as its dual purpose the production of hydroelectric power and the provision of a 9-foot by 100-foot navigable channel on the lower Chattahoochee and Flint rivers. When the dam is complete the resulting lake will offer recreational opportunities similar to those developed in connection with the Allatoona project (*see* TOUR 2).

The dam will be about a mile in length with a maximum head of 33 feet and the resulting lake will cover 37,500 acres, with a shore line of around 243 miles in length. According to plans, the basic features of the dam are: 1. a concrete gravity type overflow section 1,634 feet long; 2. a gated spillway section 760 feet in length, containing sixteen 40-foot by 30.5-foot vertical lift gates operated by a gantry crane; 3. a powerhouse 267-feet by 151.5-feet containing three 10,000-kilowatt generating units; 4. a navigation lock 82 feet by 450 feet long with a maximum lift of 33 feet; and 5. an earth fill dike 3,310 feet long on one end where the switchyard will be built.

At Bainbridge is a junction with US 27 (*see* TOUR *10*).

Left from Bainbridge on US 27 to Attapulgus and the PLANT OF THE AT-TAPULGUS CLAY COMPANY (*open to visitors*), *13 m.* This is one of the largest mines for fuller's earth, a medium used in the purification of oils.

On the bridge across the dark waters of the Flint River, *199.1 m.,* is a marker (*R*) designating the place where Andrew Jackson crossed in 1818, when he was concluding his campaign against the Seminole in the South.

The highway crosses the THREE NOTCH ROAD, *215.4 m.,* which was named for the three notches made on trees by advance scouts who blazed the trail as early as 1800. This road led to Fort Scott, built in 1816 on the banks of the Flint River near the Georgia-Florida Line. From this fort in 1818 Jackson launched his unauthorized campaign into Florida against the Seminole. This act, which was tacitly allowed by the government, very nearly involved the United States in a war with Spain and Great Britain because of the claims of these nations to West Florida. No trace of Fort Scott remains.

DONALSONVILLE, *218.5 m.* (139 alt., 2,569 pop.), incorporated in 1897, seat of Seminole County, is the center of an area producing agricultural products, lumber, and naval stores. Large peanut shellers are in opera-tion. A Farmers' Market was established in 1950.

Left from Donalsonville on hard-surfaced State 91 to an old SUSPENSION BRIDGE, *12 m.,* one of the very few remaining in the south.

In Seminole County game is plentiful, especially deer, fox, and quail. The CHATTAHOOCHEE RIVER, *229.6 m.,* the boundary between Georgia and Albama, is spanned by a free bridge about 22 miles east of Dothan, Alabama.

TOUR 6

(Asheville, N. C.)—Blairsville—Dahlonega—Atlanta—Griffin—Albany—Thomasville—(Monticello, Fla.); US 19.

North Carolina Line to Florida Line 363.2 m.—Central of Georgia Ry. parallels route between Atlanta and Thomaston, and between Americus and Albany; the Atlantic Coast Line R.R. between Albany and Thomasville—All types of accommodations in cities; limited elsewhere.

Section a. NORTH CAROLINA LINE *to* ATLANTA; *121.5 m., US 19.*

In the northeastern section of Georgia, US 19, the Appalachian Scenic Highway, crosses a solitary and spectacularly beautiful region encompassed by darkly wooded and majestic mountains. Since no railroad has ever traversed this section, isolation has caused the settlers of the green valleys to be individualistic and boldly independent. Georgia's ubiquitous corn and cotton have always had place in the lower half of this area, but ten years ago there would have been no more to say, commercially, about this region. Since then Georgia's sixty million dollar a year broiler industry, with its economic center about Gainesville in Hall County, has developed in this general vicinity. Not only has the broiler industry become Georgia's number two cash crop, thus standing just below cotton; it has also made its way to first place among broiler regions in the nation, statewise. Cherokee, Forsyth, and Hall counties constitute the areas of greatest concentration, according to current economic maps.

Of course such a large enterprise has a variety of methods, both in production and financing, but one of the ways of arranging for the production of broilers is, doubtless, the key to its exceptionally rapid development. The grower builds at his own expense a relatively narrow but usually long house with a low pitched roof. Generally, he can then make an arrangement with one of the poultry feed dealers to supply him with day-old chicks and feed, and often also to guarantee him a certain fixed profit on the chickens that reach the broiler stage. According to the U. S. Classes for Dressed Chicken, broilers are chickens about eight to twelve weeks old, and in weight not over two and one-half pounds; and hence it is possible to raise four "crops" during a twelvemonth period, though three is the normal tempo. In contrast, the growing of beef cattle is a long term procedure, requiring the building up of pastures and the acquisition of costly stock; thus it pays no returns for a number of years, and requires a considerable capital outlay.

But the broiler industry requires a minimum of capital and of time before the young broilers can be converted into cash.

Marketing is left to the dealer. On this level the capital investment becomes stiffer and more skill in management is required. But dressing and processing plants have grown up in sufficient number, giving a fresh economic energy to the towns.

When the broiler house litter is cleaned out, it can be spread on the land, and if balanced with phosphate, and perhaps some potash, becomes an agent in the organic enrichment of the soil. A further step is for the grower to acquire capital from broilers, meanwhile enriching his land, and then, planting pasture, to shift his productive level to cattle raising.

Outward signs of the new prosperity can be seen on all sides not only in the typical broiler houses, but also in the spruce new houses, reconditioned farms, newly fenced green fields, paved roads, and recently built school houses. The enterprise has a touch of that material magic that has always deeply moved the American imagination. Like a plant from the soil a sound culture can only grow from a potential base. Men boldly independent and individualistic can turn to this enterprise without let or hindrance. The limit of its growth is the saturation of the market. .

Although Georgia as a whole has been Democratic, some of the counties in this section are Republican, and during the War between the States gave many soldiers to the Union ranks. Confederate deserters often found sanctuary here. Union County takes its name from this disposition.

Near the North Carolina Line this route passes through a segment of the Chattahoochee National Forest; in this former Cherokee Indian territory are Vogel State Park and Neels Gap, the best vantage points in the state for views. South of the national forest lie three towns of sharply contrasting history: Dahlonega, the center of the principal gold mining in Georgia; Cumming, the region's most self-sufficient and independent mountain community; and Roswell, whose early houses were built and maintained by once powerful commercial families from the coast.

At *4 m.* the highway actually cuts across a northeast arm of the NOTTELY LAKE AREA, a part of the Tennessee Valley Authority Project. In fact US 19-129 roughly parallels this lake from the North Carolina Line to Blairsville, with the lake on the right. Nottely Dam, completed in 1942, is located in Union County on the Nottely River, a tributary of the Hiwassee, about 21 miles above its confluence with that river. The dam is in a rugged mountain gorge with abutments rising steeply from the narrow flood plain.

Nottely Dam is 184 feet high, 2,300 feet long. The dam is an earth and rock structure with an impervious rolled earth core supported on both sides by rock fill. It contains 1,552,300 cubic yards of earth and rock fill and 17,700 cubic yards of concrete. An overflow, chute type of spillway of reinforced concrete cuts through the low embankment along the ridge that forms the left abutment. A Georgia county road, which leaves US 19 (R) just before reaching Ivylog settlement, crosses the dam and is carried on a bridge across the spillway approach just upstream from the weir crest. A tunnel connecting with an outlet control works extends through the left abutment for the regulation of discharge from the lake. At this point is Nottely Dam Boat Dock (*12 boats, outboard motors, bait, and tackle; address R. L. Head, Box 54, Blairsville*). At maximum operating level the lake has an area of 4,290 acres, and a total storage capacity of 184,400 acre-feet.

When first built, no generating equipment was installed in either Chatuge (*see below*) or Nottely dams. But using the stored water of each through an aggregate of about 1,000 feet of head in nine downstream plants added 60,000 kilowatts of firm power to the TVA system. At the present time generators are being installed in both plants. The one in Nottely will rate 14,000 kilowatts. The deciding factor for including these two dams in the emergency program of World War II was their ability to create substantial additional power in the system without waiting for the manufacture of generating equipment. The dams are well adapted to multipurpose operation and provide holdover storage for dry years and contribute to flood control. Nottely Lake, draining an area of 214 square miles, extends twenty miles and has a shoreline of 106 miles. Among the other recreation centers located on its shoreline are: Young Cane Creek Cabins (*3 boats, bait, cabins; address J. H. MacFee, Blairsville*); *Lake Nottely Cottages* (*5 boats, cabins; address W. T. Stroud, Rt. 3 Blairsville*); Lake Side Springs Cabins (*9 boats, cabins; address R. L. Head, Box 54, Blairsville*); Canal Lake Camp (*tackle, lunches, meals, cabins; address A. M. McAfee, Rt. 3, Blairsville*).

BLAIRSVILLE, *11.1 m.*, (1,892 alt., 430 pop.), is the seat of Union County. It was laid out in 1838 immediately after the Cherokee Removal, and until 1910 was a focal point for gold-mining activities. The southern section of the town, at the foot of Mount Wellborn, is honeycombed with shafts, now unsafe because the shoring timbers have decayed.

The Office of the Forest Ranger of the Brasstown Ranger District of the Chattahoochee National Forest is located in Blairsville. This district comprises 139,277 acres in Union, Towns, and Fannin counties. Inquire here for information about available forest recreation areas, camps, etc.

Left from Blairsville on US 76 to the junction with a narrow country road, *5.8 m.;* R. on this road *2.3 m.* to TRACK ROCK GAP (approx. 2,250 alt.). On the summit of the ridge (R) are several soapstone boulders bearing many carved figures of unknown origin. According to Cherokee legends, these petroglyphs had been placed here by an earlier people before the first Cherokee entered the region.

At *8.1 m.* on US 76 in Towns County is YOUNG HARRIS (1,928 alt., 450 pop.), the site of YOUNG HARRIS COLLEGE AND ACADEMY (from the campus an 8-mile hiking trail leads to the summit of Mount Enotah or Brasstown Bald). This coeducational college, maintained by the Methodist Episcopal Church, has eleven brick buildings set on a wooded, fifteen acre campus. The institution, organized through the philanthropic efforts of Young L. G. Harris, of Athens, was originally opened in 1886 in an old store building. The library building, constructed of bricks molded of native clay by students, contains the library of Sam Jones, the evangelist, and the Merle Mann collection of Indian artifacts collected from all the states in the Union, and from Mexico and Canada. The school owns 1,200 acres of the surrounding hills and valley, of which 200 acres are in cultivation and pastures. A large number of students pay part of their expenses working for the school.

Before reaching Hiawassee the highway cuts across CHATUGE LAKE. The dam is located on the Hiwassee River, in Clay County, North Carolina. It was built in 1942 as a part of the TVA system. The length of Chatuge Lake is 13 miles, a major part of which is in Georgia, and the length of the shore line is 132 miles. The surface area of the lake at maximum operating level is 7,150 acres, and total storage 247,900 acre-feet. The North Carolina–Georgia line cuts through Chatuge Lake, and the two states have a reciprocal agreement by which the fishing license of either is recognized anywhere on the lake. Recreation centers: Hendrix Dock (*12 boats, bait, tackle, lunches, cabins; address D. R. Hendrix, Young Harris*); Thurman & Caldwell Dock (*25 boats, bait, tackle, lunches, meals, cabins; address same, Rt. 1, Young Harris*); Shady Rest Cabins (*5 boats, bait, lunches, cabins; address Al Youngblood, Box 37, Hiawassee*); Teague's Camp (*4 boats, bait, cabins; address J. D. Teague, Rt. 1, Young Harris*); Homefolks Cafe & Cottages (*8 boats, lunches, meals, cabins; address M. A. Burns, Hiawassee*). At present generators are being installed in this system as well as at Nottely (*see above*); the Chatuge Dam will have a rated capacity of 10,000 kilowatts. The Chatuge area is in the Blue Ridge physiographic province of the Appalachian Highlands, a region characterized by ruggedness and sharp topographic relief; rocks of the area are pre-Cambrian.

HIAWASSEE, *16.6 m.* (1,984 alt., 375 pop.), is a small mountain town. The Hiawassee Mountain Fair, open to all northeast Georgia mountain counties, is held here the latter part of August.

At *18.9 m.* is a junction with State 75; R. on State 75 to a junction with a graveled road, State 66, *26 m.;* R. on this road to SUMMIT OF MOUNT ENOTAH, *33 m.* (4,784 alt.), the highest peak in Georgia. This mountain is heavily wooded except for the bare summit, which is surmounted with the U. S. Forest Service's forty-foot lookout tower. The mountain, locally known as Brasstown

Bald, was named for a nearby settlement called Brasstown, a misinterpretation of the Indian name which meant town of the green valley.

The ENOTAH GLADES PICNIC AREA, near Brasstown Bald, contains a small parking area, walled spring, picnic tables, and toilets. Inquire at the office of the District Forest Ranger in Blairsville for further information.

The MOUNTAIN EXPERIMENT STATION, *14.2 m.*, was established as a branch of the Experiment Station at Griffin (*see* TOUR 2) in 1930. On the 370 acres of fertile soil are the mechanics building, office and storage structure, and livestock barns. The needs of the mountain region are studied at this station.

From a point at *17.1 m.* is an excellent view of Mount Enotah, easily identified by the lookout tower on its summit.

VOGEL STATE PARK (*swimming, picnicking, boating, hiking, fishing, horseback riding, children's playground, museum, cabins, restaurant, inn, trading post*), *22.6 m.*, R. on State 180, is a 248-acre recreation area maintained by the Georgia Department of State Parks. It lies in the heart of the 661,910-acre Chattahoochee National Forest, and is one of the more popular Georgia parks because of its lake and heavily wooded forest.

Shortly after the turn of the century Fred and August Vogel bought a 65,000-acre tract of land here as a source of tanbark for a leather factory in Milwaukee. About this time it was discovered that concentrated tannic acid from the quebracho tree of South America was more economical. In 1928 the Vogel brothers donated 248 acres to the state for a park. Horseback riders or hikers can explore the beautiful mountain trails leading to such scenic areas as Neels Gap, Brasstown Bald, the Appalachian Trail, and Lake Winfield Scott.

LAKE TRAHLYTA (*fishing, swimming, boating, bath house, dock, swim float, official diving boards*) covers an area of about 40 acres at the northern entrance to the park. The park has twenty-seven cottages which can each accommodate two to eight persons or more; with modern equipment for housekeeping except linen: electric stove, electric refrigerator, and hot water heaters. (Superintendent in charge begins accepting reservation March 1. Reservations cannot be made for more than two weeks at any time or less than one between June 15 and September 15; address Blairsville.) The park officially opens on April 15 and closes October 15. The Walasiyi Inn is described below.

Right from Vogel State Park on a winding graveled road to 22-acre LAKE WINFIELD SCOTT, *6.7 m.*, in a beautiful setting of hardwood trees that are reflected in its clear green water. The lake named for Winfield Scott, the officer in charge of the Cherokee Removal in 1838 and general of the U. S. armies (1841-61), is the center of one of the Chattahoochee National Forest recreation areas. It provides numerous picnic and camp units, four shelters, a parking area, a bath house, an educational building, a caretaker's cabin, toilets, garbage pits, and water systems.

The WOODY GAP PICNIC AREA is at the point where the Appalachian Trail (*see* TOUR *13A*) crosses State 60. It provides picnic tables, fireplaces, and toilets.

At WOODY GAP (approx. 3,300 alt.), *12.8 m.*, is a junction with the Appalachian Trail (*see* TOUR *13A*).

At *18 m.* the side route rejoins US 19.

NOTTELY FALLS (L), *25.5 m.* is formed by a small creek that descends 105 feet over gray rocks into the dense shadows of the hemlocks that cover the mountain side.

The NOTTELY PICNIC GROUNDS (*comfort station, picnic shelter, outdoor fireplaces*), *25.8 m.*, is a twelve-acre tract within Vogel State Park. From the grounds well-marked trails lead to nearby points of scenic vantage.

US 19 crosses the Blue Ridge at NEELS GAP, the southern entrance to Vogel State Park, *26.1 m.* (3,108 alt.), where the Walasiyi Inn is located. The inn can take care of thirty guests overnight; it serves three meals a day. (Address the manager for reservations at Blairsville.) This gap through the Appalachian Highlands affords broad views of green valleys and mountain ranges extending far into the distance. In spring and early summer the hillsides are splashed with white dogwood, flame azalea, and rhododendron. A park service ranger stationed here gives information on the many points of interest. Until recently the gap was known as Frogtown Gap.

The APPALACHIAN TRAIL (*see* TOUR *13A*), famous hiking route which crosses the highway at this point, leads through the wildest and most remote parts of the mountains from the Tate Mountain Estates near Jasper (*see* TOUR *13*) to the summit of Mount Katahdin in Maine.

At *26.4 m.* is a junction with a graded and well-marked foot trail.

Right on this trail through the Chattahoochee National Forest to the head of DE SOTO FALLS, *3 m.*, which plunge more than 400 feet down the green slope of the mountain side.

CHESTATEE KNOLL CAMP SITE (*open-air fireplaces, shelter huts, pure water*), *30.7 m.*, is maintained by the Forest Service for free use by the public.

At *32.7 m.* is a junction with US 129.

Left on this road at *6.2 m.* is a point affording an excellent view of MOUNT YONAH (3,173 ft. alt.), its towering cliffs crowned with a steel lookout tower for forest rangers. This land was a hunting ground for the Cherokee, who named the mountain Yonah (Ind., bear).

CLEVELAND, *11.2 m.* (1,571 alt., 589 pop.), is the seat of White County, and a gold mine area.

TRUETT-MCCONNELL JUNIOR COLLEGE grants an Associate in Arts diploma representing two years of work toward an A. B. degree in several fields: English, Business Education, Industrial Education, Elementary Education, Science, and History.

With an endowment estimated at $105,238, the college has five buildings, two of which serve for administrative and class-room purposes and three for dormitories. The faculty has eleven members.

George W. Truett and Fred C. McConnell, in whose honor the school is named, were natives of this mountain region whose faith and courage expressed itself concretely in the establishment of a religious school in north Georgia sixty years ago. Changing conditions resulted in the closing of the school. But the death of Dr. Truett in 1944 stimulated Georgia Baptists to revive his vision of Christian education for the young people of the mountains. After careful consideration, the Georgia Baptist Convention authorized the establishment of a Junior College in north Georgia. On July 23, 1946, the school was formally established at Cleveland.

Left from Cleveland on State 75, at *19.2 m.* the road enters the western side of the beautiful NACOOCHEE VALLEY (1,349 alt.), a fertile tract lying along the headwaters of the Chattahoochee and Sautee rivers. Legend claims the valley is named for Nacoochee, an Indian maiden who kept a fatal tryst here with her lover.

At *19.04 m.* beside a bridge over the Chattahoochee River, is the junction with a country road.

Right *0.3 m.* on this road across the bridge to the NACOOCHEE INDIAN MOUND, 100 yards R. of the road, on private property. This mound is 190 feet long, 150 feet wide, and 20 feet high. Exploration by the Heye Foundation in 1915 revealed a dog pot and many pottery vessels that indicate an advanced cultural development of the makers. According to tradition, this mound was the center of the ancient Cherokee town of Guaxule (pronounced Wah-zú-lee), said to have been visited by De Soto in 1540. In 1838 American gold miners uncovered a nearby subterranean village of more than thirty log houses. The logs were well preserved and showed evidence of having been notched by sharp metal tools. The village may have been made by Spanish gold seekers who penetrated this region after De Soto's ill-fated expedition.

The UNICOI GAP PICNIC SPOT, maintained by the U. S. Forest Service, of the Chattahoochee National Forest, about *7 m.* north of Helen where State 75 crosses the Appalachian Trail (*see* TOUR *13A*), consists of a small parking area, spring, two picnic tables with benches, and fireplaces.

At *21.3 m.* on State 75 is HELEN (1,400 alt., 191 pop.), a cool valley town (*two good hotels; golf course, swimming pool*) where pleasant cottages contrast with shabby old frame dwellings. The latter once housed the employees of a large lumber mill. After the mill was removed, Helen became increasingly popular as a summer resort. TRAY MOUNTAIN (4,389 alt.) is accessible by motor, and a Forest Service Road parallels the Chattahoochee River, which abounds with rainbow trout and black bass. Here the headwaters of the Chattahoochee are clear, though farther down the water is red with clay.

DAHLONEGA (pronounced Dah-láhn-e-ga), *46.9 m.* (1,484 alt., 2,152 pop.), seat of Lumpkin County, is a trading center for mountaineers, who come to town on Saturdays to buy their supplies. The name of the town, suggested by the gold deposits of the surrounding area, is derived from Taulonica (Cher. yellow metal). Sometimes, after heavy rains, small particles of gold are found in the streets.

Although legend says that a gold nugget was found in this vicinity about 1818, the gold fields were not discovered until 1828 or 1829. Almost at once this Cherokee territory was cluttered with the shanties of rugged pre-49'ers, who brought in their train the usual gamblers, con men, and other gaudy accessories of an early gold strike.

During these intrusions on Indian land, Georgia sent out the militia to protect the Indians, it is said. But in 1830 the state acquired the Cherokee territory and during 1831-32 divided it into forty-acre "gold lots" which were disposed of by lottery. There was little regard for private property, however, and the miners panned gold where they found it. Lumpkin County was created in 1832 and a year later Dahlonega was settled at a place called Licklog for a hollowed log filled with salt for livestock. New settlers were arriving daily, and soon all roads leading to the town were lined with huts. At one time there were from ten to fifteen thousand miners within a radius of a few miles.

The first important discovery of gold in the United States occurred in the Dahlonega fields. The Federal government established a mint here which operated from 1837 until 1861, when it was closed because of Georgia's break with the Union. During this period 1,378,710 pieces of gold valued at $6,106,569 were struck; every coin was marked with a prominent D on the reverse side just above the date. Recently H. A. Alexander, of Atlanta, gave the state a complete series of these coins: half-eagles ($5) for each year between 1838 and 1861; quarter-eagles ($2.50) for the years between 1839 and 1859, except 1858 when there was none; a three dollar piece for 1854; and a one dollar coin for the years 1849 to 1861. (The coins are now in the keeping of the Secretary of State.) Of the $17,749,937 taken from Georgia dirt in the period 1830-1933, almost $16,000,000 came from the Dahlonega fields. In 1935 a few mines produced gold valued at $34,790, and there have been sporadic efforts since then, but the increase in labor costs and other production factors have advanced the cost of mining beyond the current set value of gold. People still pan out a bit now and then for fun and their own use.

LUMPKIN COUNTY COURTHOUSE, on the town square, is a two-story structure built in 1833-36 with materials hauled by oxcart from Augusta. The red brick of the walls are now painted red. The lower part of the two-story portico with its white columns is enclosed by walls with a doorway in front in addition to the one on the porch level above. The S's on each façade are metal clamps placed at the ends of wrought-iron rods, inserted about fifty years ago to prevent spreading of the walls.

NORTH GEORGIA COLLEGE, located on the site of the Mint, is the state's only senior military college. A unit of the State University System, the institution has an enrollment of some 600 young men and women, with women comprising approximately one-sixth of the student body. The Department of the Army has long classified North Georgia as one of the eight strictly military colleges of the nation, and recently its program was recognized by the Department of Defense in connection with the Universal Military Training and Service Act (1951). This school is unique in that, while being under military organization, it has been coeducational since its founding. A college of arts and sciences at the bachelor's level, North Georgia's program is widely recognized academically and fully meets the requirements of the Southern Association of Colleges.

Price Memorial Hall, erected in 1880, stands on the original foundations of the old government mint. The original building was burned in 1878, but the granite foundation remained intact. After the War between the States, Federal authorities offered the old mint building to the state for educational purposes, in conformity with the Morrill Act of 1862 "donating public lands to the several states and territories which may provide colleges for the benefit of agricultural and mechanical arts." The school was opened on January 6, 1873, as a land grant college and was known as North Georgia Agricultural College until 1930, when it was legally changed to North Georgia College. With the mint as a nucleus, the College embraces at present a modern plant of fifteen buildings and 198 acres of rolling woodland campus. Agricultural courses are no longer offered, but otherwise the school has remained true to the general principles of its founders.

This section has followed Gainesville in the production of commercial broilers. Dahlonega has three completely modern hatcheries. The industry has meant a great deal to the area, and stepped up the living standards of the rural people. Along with the broiler industry, there has been an increase in truck cropping, cattle, and permanent pasture.

Dahlonega has long been celebrated as a place where the hot days of summer in the larger cities can be left behind. There is hardly a night in summer when one does not need a blanket. The Smith House (hotel) is widely known over the state.

The Chestatee Ranger District of the Chattahoochee National Forest has a U. S. Forest Ranger's office in Dahlonega. This district comprises 101,804 acres in Dawson, Fannin, Gilmer, Lumpkin, and White counties. Inquire about recreation facilities in the forest area.

CAMP WAHSEGA, is an organization camp located in Lumpkin County on a Forest Service Road, about ten miles NW. of Dahlonega. It was constructed and for a time operated by the U. S. Forest Service, but at present it is under special use permit to the Georgia Extension Service, and has been used by 4-H Clubs as a summer camp and by the Department of the U. S. Army in connection with their Ranger Training Program. Improvements consist of a swimming pool, dining and recreation hall, dispensary, caretaker's house, administration building, shower and toilet building, sixteen cabins, and a play area. Inquire at the U. S. Forest Ranger's Office in Dahlonega.

DAWSONVILLE, *61.6 m.* (1,425 alt., 318 pop.), the county seat of Dawson County, is a trading center for the farmers of this vicinity. Incorporated in 1859, it was named for William C. Dawson, who served in the U. S. Senate from 1849 to 1855. The chief natural resource of the county is hardwood, and the principal agricultural products are cotton, corn, small grains, apples, peaches, hay, cattle, sorghum cane, and poultry.

Right from Dawsonville on paved State 53 to a junction with paved State 183, *2.9 m.;* R. on this road about *10 m.* to its junction with State 52. Near this point is AMICALOLA FALLS STATE PARK consisting of 239 highly scenic acres. One of Georgia's seven Natural Wonders, these falls are the highest in Georgia, with a total drop of 729 feet. Formed by a sparkling mountain stream plunging down the side of Amicalola ridge, the falls contain seven different cascades, some of which are hidden by the dense growth surrounding the falls. The Indian meaning of the name is tumbling waters. There is a small lake at the top of the falls.
A picnic area, shelters, and grills have been constructed near the foot of the falls, but it is currently a day-use area until further development. A gravel road leads to the top of the falls, which are visible, however, from the highway. The park is located on the Appalachian Trail that extends from Mt. Oglethorpe to Mt. Katahdin in Maine.

CUMMING, *79.1 m.* (approx. 1,225, 1,264 pop.), seat of Forsyth County, was founded in 1832 and named for William Cumming, an officer in the War of 1812. A large poultry processing plant capable of handling twenty thousand head of poultry a day has been established in the town, and this has greatly stimulated the production of broilers and fryers in the area. Cotton and corn are staples of the county. Sometimes at corn planting time one may see the men laying off the fields with mule and plow and the women in poke-bonnets doing the small work with hoes, though modern machinery is increasing. Fields of fescue and clover are evident, sometimes extensively, and herds of cattle and dairy barns increase along the way. As a side product of the broiler industry, along the highway between Cumming and Roswell appear neat fields of boxwood planted in orderly rows. These are to be sold in Atlanta, or bought up by larger nurseries for distribution. Boxwoods are pernickety about their soil, and especially need mulch, but the compost from the broiler houses makes them flourish. Tufts of cotton, blown from trucks on the way to market or the gin, at times spot the edges of the highway with white.

At about *98 m.* (R) is the site of the LEBANON BAPTIST CHURCH, originally built in 1827, the oldest church in the Roswell area.

ROSWELL, *100.7 m.* (1,000 alt., 2,213 pop.), extending for about two miles along the highway, has stood high, serene, and quietly beautiful for more than a century on the bluffs just north of the Chattahoochee River. Here begins the swell of the foothills that climb toward the Great Smokies in North Carolina. Roswell is much like the little adopted girl who referred to herself as a "chosen child," having been deliberately founded by a group of Savannah and Darien people as a place of summer residence to escape from the malarial coast. Roswell King, who was born in Connecticut in 1765 but removed to Darien in 1788, was sent by the influential Bank of Darien, around 1820, to inspect its gold claims near Dahlonega and in North Carolina. Making the trip on horseback, he crossed at the ford on the Chattahoochee River near Vickery Creek (now Big Creek) and noted both the excellent, fresh climate and the available waterpower at the falls in the creek— factors that influenced his decision to establish a factory for cotton thread here, and a residential town.

By 1835 he had acquired sufficient land for his purposes. The cotton factory was in operation around 1837 or 1839. A letter dated April 14, 1847, concerning it, refers to "high prices, but cotton dividends fair." In regard to the residential development, in addition to the workers' homes, he sought to establish others by offering a number of acres to friends from the coast who would come to Roswell for the summer months. Among these were the group generally referred to in historical documents as the "original founders": his son—Barrington King, his widowed daughter—Eliza King Hand, Archibald Smith, John Dunwody, Nathaniel A. Pratt, and James S. Bulloch. An unusual aspect of Roswell is that all six of the houses built by the original founders are intact as well as the Presbyterian Church of the period, although the Old Academy has been replaced by a modern school building (*see* below).

With the arrival of Sherman's occupying forces after the Battle of Kennesaw Mountain, the cotton mills were destroyed, and also the Ivy Mill, established in 1858 for the manufacture of woolen cloth, and known during the war for its "Roswell Gray." According to the Georgia State Marker commemorating the mills, the women operatives were sent North during hostilities to insure that their skills would not be of further aid to the South. The spur railroad from Atlanta that served the old mills was destroyed by Federal forces, and nothing remains but an embankment at the river. Although the mills were rebuilt after the war and have been in continuous operation since, Roswell has never recovered its original industrial vigor, but it does remain an unusually pleasant residential town in what is now the Atlanta metropolitan region. It was incorporated in 1854.

COLONIAL PLACE (*private*), on a knoll at the end of Goulding Street, leading right from North Roswell, was the home of the Reverend Francis R. Goulding, minister at the Presbyterian Church and author of two books beloved by boys, *Young Marooners* (1852) and *Marooners' Island* (1869), also published in England and Scotland. Built by Goulding about 1857, the house is a red painted brick building with a Palladian doorway and white shutters. Roswell citizens maintain stoutly that Goulding also invented the first sewing machine. But if so, he failed to secure a patent or to receive official credit for it.

In North Roswell, just beyond the Chevrolet agency on US 19, is the house built by Archibald Smith (L), one of the original founders, about 1844. Of frame construction, with two-story white columns, the house faces a hardwood park of several acres. An unusual feature of particular interest is its group of small buildings to the side and rear, typical of the economy of the period. In most instances, these small functional buildings have fallen victim to decay, but here they are still standing, thus preserving much of the original scene.

Just before the WORLD WAR II MONUMENT—with flagstaff and circle of boxwoods—to the side of US 19, turn right to Magnolia Street and continue at its end, on Pine Grove Road, to the factory of the ROSWELL SEATING COMPANY (*open to visitors*), probably the only exclusive producer of ecclesiastical furniture in the Southeast. After preparation at Mercer University, the Reverend R. M. Donehoo took a local church, but finding the salary meager, he undertook to supplement it by establishing a building-and-supply trade. When materials grew scarce in World War I, the future became troubled until the Baptist Church in Roswell commissioned him to build new pews for it. The Methodist Church followed next, and since then the business has grown steadily until it now distributes its furniture throughout the southeastern region.

In Old Roswell at the first stoplight on US 19 and at the corner of the new bank is a marker indicating a left turn to the street leading to the OLD CEMETERY, and OLD BRICK APARTMENTS which were built around 1839 for the workers at the Roswell Mills. At the site of the apartments is a Georgia Historical Marker which gives a brief account of Roswell's early industrial history. At this point a street turns right to the new mill, beyond which can be seen the spectral walls of the old mill burnt by Federal orders. The cemetery, now in a state of serious neglect, contains the graves of early Roswell citizens, including that of its founder, Roswell King.

Just beyond the stoplight on US 19 is (R) the town square, land-scaped by the W. P. A. as a memorial to the early founders, which contains at center, the FOUNDERS MONUMENT of laid stone, erected by the Roswell Chapter of the U. D. C., listing the names of the "original founders"; and, at the far end the CENTENNIAL MARKER, giving a short history of the early settlement. Still in operation, the ROSWELL STORE (L) dates from the early mill days.

Right, at the end of the park to BARRINGTON HALL (*open to visitors except Sundays*), located on a commanding elevation that dominates Old Roswell and historical Mimosa Boulevard. A handsome sunburst gate at the top of a flight of steps from the street opens upon a long walkway leading through old oaks and cedars to the house, and thence left to the English gardens, notable for their circular planting of more-than-a-century-old boxwoods in the upper garden. The house, designed by a Connecticut architect, was built about 1842 by Barrington King, son of Roswell King. With its majestic columns surrounding three sides of the house and its "captain's walk" in New England style on the roof, it is the most dramatically placed and the most dignified of Roswell's Greek Revival houses. Wide verandas, Doric columns, and shuttered windows extending from the floor almost to the ceiling, recall the severe good taste and established dignity of the great plantation days. The grounds contain many shrubs and flowers, and there is an original brick smokehouse in the rear. The interior has not suffered at the hand of renovators, and hence retains its original integrity.

Right around the park to Mimosa Boulevard and then left on Bulloch Avenue to MIMOSA HALL (*private*). This is the second house on the site. The original house, almost an exact duplicate of Bulloch Hall and built of timber, was destroyed by fire in the autumn of 1842 on the night of its housewarming, because a careless workman left a beam exposed in one of the chimneys. Rebuilt by its owner, John Dunwody, one of the original founders, the new house was finished in 1847 and named Phoenix Hall; but later Mimosa.

The present building is of homemade brick overlaid with a plaster which the passing years have tempered to a delicate golden tint. Fashioned in the Greek temple style, it has a two-story portico with four monumental Doric columns supporting a high pediment.

It is notable for the front courtyard and the long wide entrance paved with stone, and for its many old trees, including Virginia cedars, magnolias, hollies, and giant oaks, as well as for its boxwoods, flowering shrubs, and varied sorts of broadleaf evergreens. A blight of recent years that has been spreading through the Southeast has destroyed almost all of the mimosas (*Albizzia julibrissin*). But the profusion of old trees and of suitably arranged shrubs preserves the style of its original scene, so that the house, though softened by time, must still appear to-day much as it did when it first quickened in the imagination of its builder.

At the end of Bulloch Avenue on a slight elevation is BULLOCH HALL (*private*), a Greek Revival clapboard house built about 1842 by James Stephen Bulloch, one of the original founders. It has a portico with four tall Doric columns and pilasters. Bulloch's second wife, married in 1832, was Martha Elliott. Martha, their second daughter, married Theodore Roosevelt at Bulloch Hall. Their son Theodore Roosevelt was the twenty-fifth president of the United States. Elliott Roosevelt, another child of Theodore Roosevelt and Martha Bulloch, was the father of Anna Eleanor Roosevelt, who married her fifth cousin, Franklin Delano Roosevelt. Medora Perkerson's *White Columns in Georgia* contains a lively account of the Roosevelt wedding at Bulloch Hall, of President Theodore Roosevelt's visit years later, and of Eleanor Roosevelt's visit a few years ago.

On Mimosa Boulevard across from the northwest corner of the park (L), is HOLLY HILL, an example of the raised-cottage type of architecture (*see* AUGUSTA). Its construction was supervised by Barrington King on behalf of his friend, Robert Adam Lewis, of Savannah. Built between 1842 and 1847, it is generously proportioned, with all of the rooms eighteen feet square and with wide halls extending the lengths of the three floors. The high columned front gallery at the second floor level, except for the flight of wide steps, is exactly duplicated in the rear. Among the fireplaces of the ground floor rooms is the immense one in the rear that originally served as a kitchen in the old order of household arts.

The OLD PRESBYTERIAN CHURCH, about midway along Mimosa Boulevard (R), was built about 1840 under the direction of Nathaniel A. Pratt, its first minister and one of the original founders. It is a small, white frame structure with Doric columns supporting a Greek pediment, above which is a small boxlike bell tower. Religion being so much a familial rite in the Old South, at the rear is a slave gallery where the servants might worship with their masters. At the opposite end is a high pulpit reached by a small double stairway. The simple design and sense of good workmanship strongly suggests a New England hand.

During the War between the States the communion linen, with its lily-of-the-valley pattern, and the silver communion service were secluded from Yankee eyes, and are still in use today. A cabinet door made into a checkerboard is a memorandum of the use of the church as a hospital by Federal soldiers.

GREAT OAKS (*private*), across the street from the church, was built by the Reverend Nathaniel A. Pratt. Timber was cut at the same time and made ready for the original houses, though that allotted for this house was destroyed by fire. But rich warm bricks from native clay were made at Brickyard Hill just southwest of the house site, and so it came about conveniently enough that this house was built of brick. It is a well-proportioned house of modified Georgian colonial design, built around 1840. The school across from Great Oaks stands on the site of the original academy.

ALLENBROOK, on US 19 along the descent to the river (L), is on part of the site of the old Ivy Mill. Constructed of warm red brick, it was located on a commanding height just above Vickery Creek (now Big Creek) near the Chattahoochee. The terrace in the rear leads to precipitous trails bordered by native rhododendrons that reach their blooming crest in May.

The CHATTAHOOCHEE RIVER, *102.7 m.* muddy with red Georgia clay from the eroded croplands, is spanned by the ROSWELL BRIDGE, built in 1924.

Between Roswell and Buckhead US 19 leads through a variously wooded section, which, however, is being steadily assimilated by suburban expansion into the needs of metropolitan Atlanta.

The marked SITE OF THE HIGHTOWER TRAIL (L) *105 m.,* at a road intersection, just by the first store from the bridge, is one of the oldest and most important Indian trails in north Georgia. It was formerly recognized as the boundary between the lands of the Cherokee Nation and the Creek Confederacy.

SANDY SPRINGS, *108.6 m.,* is a small unincorporated community.

ATLANTA, *121.5 m.* (1,050 alt., 331,314 pop.)

Points of Interest: State Capitol, Cyclorama of the Battle of Atlanta, Georgia School of Technology, Emory University, Agnes Scott College (Decatur), Oglethorpe University, Atlanta University (Negro).

Atlanta is the junction with US 78 (*see* TOUR *8*), with US 29 (*see* TOUR *3*), with US 23 (*see* TOUR *7*), and with US 41 (*see* TOUR *2*), with which US 19 unites between Atlanta and Griffin.

Section b. GRIFFIN *to* FLORIDA LINE; *202.4 m., US 19.*

South of GRIFFIN *0 m.* (965 alt., 13,982 pop.), the highway crosses an area where important crops are cotton, peaches, and pecans, with tobacco on the increase. The peach area around Thomaston is beautiful in spring when the blossoming orchards line the highway with delicate pink. In the vicinity of Albany the pecan orchards have large trees set apart at regular intervals with permanent grass underneath, or sometimes with either cotton, corn, hay, or peas between the rows.

Pecans are members of the hickory family, and though their native area is usually pictured on a tree-map as lower Illinois and Indiana; west Kentucky and Tennessee; northwest Alabama; north Mississippi; northeast Texas and Oklahoma; southeast Kansas; and all of Missouri and Arkansas—nevertheless they have become both well established and celebrated in Georgia. Actually, an account of a squirrel-hunting expedition in Georgia before the turn of the century happens incidentally to mention a woods of pecans and magnolia, where on a hot day the hunter made sleepy by the heavy-scented magnolia blossoms fell into a brief but Rip Van Winkle-like sleep. As for orchards, according to information on hand, the first one on record before the twentieth century was that of the Jim Bacon place in De Witt, Mitchell County, just across the Dougherty county line.

Development got under way soon after the opening of the 1900's, with the heaviest plantings made between 1900 and 1915, making the oldest trees in commercial orchards between thirty and forty-five years old. Probably due to improved soil conditions and research by the experiment stations, the annual production of pecans in Georgia has doubled since 1935, though the age of the trees is a contributing factor. Notable among improvements in harvesting is the tree-shaker, which developed during the acute shortage of labor in World War II. The device is an eccentric and piston on a tractor and is attached to the tree by a cable. Set in motion, the device shakes the tree and a shower of nuts follows. Though not as colorful as sending the children into the limbs to shake them, while the parents gather the nuts, this process is many times more efficient than that method, or shaking the limbs by hand and using long bamboo poles. Pecans are not very obliging about dropping, even in a stiff wind.

Principally, there are two classes of pecans: the seedling sorts and the "named" varieties which include, among others, the Schley, Stuart, Moore, Moneymaker, Teche, Brooks, Farler, Frotscher, Success, and Mahan. Around Albany the more popular are Schley, Stuart, Moore, and Moneymaker. Seedlings are small and hard-shelled, being sold mostly for use in the confectionery trade. The named varieties when graded command the highest prices. Since it is difficult to imagine the market for pecans as ever reaching a saturation stage, the future seems limitless.

On the lower part of this route are a popular year-round resort and a winter playground patronized by wealthy visitors. Below Thomasville the Spanish moss, palmettoes, and dark waters of the semitropics begin to appear.

ZEBULON, *11.4 m.* (approx. 900 alt., 539 pop.), was incorporated in 1825 as the seat of Pike County. Both were named for General Zebulon Montgomery Pike, who was distinguished for his discovery of the peak afterwards known as Pikes Peak; he was killed in action in the War of 1812. The principal products of Pike County are: corn, cotton, peppers, and especially peaches.

SILVERTOWN, *20.8 m.* (approx. 900 alt., 3,387 pop.), is the site of Martha Mills (*open to visitors*), a branch of the B. F. Goodrich Company, tire manufacturers. Housed in two red brick and limestone buildings, the mills represent one of the world's largest plants for the exclusive manufacture of tire cord. With 130,000 spindles in operation, 400 bales of cotton are used daily.

Eight hundred families are accommodated in houses that are individual in design and color, each being furnished with modern bathroom and kitchen equipment. The lawns and parks are trimly landscaped in a setting of pine groves. Recreational facilities include tennis and softball courts and a standard baseball field with a steel and concrete grandstand seating 1,500.

The SILVERTOWN SCHOOLS consist of three modern brick buildings accommodating over six hundred pupils and twenty-three teachers.

The COMMUNITY CENTER, a handsome red brick building in the center of the village, houses several business enterprises and a motion picture house that seats 750.

CRYSTAL HILL (*open to public at times during the winter; inquire at Thomaston Chamber of Commerce*), the estate of Mr. and Mrs. Albert T. Matthews, comprises seventy-two acres of native woodland distinguished by the planting of wild flowers and shrubs and by the addition of gardens, lakes, and pools. One section of the five-mile winding drive through the estate is bordered by gardenias; in summer their white blossoms saturate the air with an oily fragrance that mingles with the drier scent of the fluffy pink mimosa blooms. The crystal rock formation found on the property has been used in the construction of rock gardens, pools, and a mill house. The drives in the open are in large part lined with the dark green of the dignified box. Camellias and azaleas are both featured, and among the peahens the peacock treads his vain but stately minuet.

THOMASTON, *26.8 m.* (700 alt., 6,580 pop.), seat of Upson County, is an industrial town in the center of a peach-growing section. The town was founded in 1825 and named for General Jett Thomas (1776-1817) who built the statehouse at Milledgeville (*see* TOUR *14*) and served with distinction in the War of 1812 as the captain of an artillery company under General John Floyd. In recognition of his services he was made a major general in the state militia after the war and the legislature presented him with a jeweled sword.

The Thomaston Mills, founded in 1899, are made up of allied plants, including a bleachery, at East Thomaston. Locally owned, they have been managed by the same family for two generations. The mills produce nationally known sheets and pillowcases, fine combed shirtings, hose and belt ducks, high speed machine bag closing thread, cotton and rayon tire cord, damask, and other products.

Livestock, including both dairy and beef cattle, has taken an important position. Many peach orchards have been converted into improved pasture land. The red clay subsoil is well suited to grass and legumes, and even when wet supports grazing cattle without undue damage to the grass while retaining the roots of the clovers which are often uprooted in more open soils. Because of the mildness of the climate its pastures can be grazed twelve months in the year. A variety of pasture crops thrive, of which the principal ones are: crimson, ladino, white dutch, bur, and hop clovers; sericea, Kobe, and Korean lespedeza; kudzu; dallas, rye, and fescue grasses. Common lespedeza and Bermuda grass are natives. Channing Cope in his book *Front Porch Farmer* has given a lively personal account of how these crops can be managed for year-round grazing. These assets are being developed in Upson County which is noted for its herds of registered and purebred Hereford and Black Angus cattle. The Georgia Farm Products Sales Corporation provides a convenient market for all sorts of livestock through auctions at its sales barns. Pecans, peppers, peaches, and other fruits and vegetables furnish extra income for the farmers.

At the Country Club is a nine-hole golf course, and swimming facilities and picnic grounds are available at nearby Barker's Springs. Fishing and hunting are good in season.

At *41 m.* is the junction with US 80 (*see* TOUR *9*), which coincides with US 19 between this point and *45.5 m.* where US 80 branches R.

BUTLER, *55.5 m.* (650 alt., 1,182 pop.), seat of Taylor County, was incorporated in 1854 and named for General William Orlando Butler (1791-1880), who succeeded Scott as commander of the U. S. Army in Mexico and was nominated for vice president in 1848. The county, created in 1852 and named for Zachary Taylor, twelfth president of the United States, included the land of Fort Laurens, which guarded an old Indian agency. This reservation, five miles square, was established for the Creeks in the latter part of the eighteenth century.

ELLAVILLE, *79.8 m.* (555 alt., 886 pop.), incorporated in 1859, is the seat of Schley County, which yields lumber and a variety of farm products.

Between *89.3 m* and *90.3 m.* is MEMORIAL MILE, dedicated by the Garden Club of Americus to the Sumter County World War veterans. More than two hundred granite slabs have been placed at regular intervals on each side of the highway, and shrubs have been planted between them. At the death of a veteran, a bronze plate bearing his name and rank is added to one of the granite markers.

AMERICUS, *93.3 m.* (360 alt., 11,389 pop.), seat of Sumter County and one of the most prosperous towns in this area, has a neat residential section built on gently sloping wooded hills. The county, named for the Revolutionary general Thomas Sumter, was created in 1831, and Americus was founded the following year on the site of the Creek agency granary.

Sumter County produces small grain, peanuts, cotton, and pecans in quantity. The sale of pigs in its local livestock pens runs into a good round figure. Industrially, the town has furniture manufacturers, basket and hamper works, lumber mills, peanut and cotton seed crushing mills, grain dealers, and a branch of the Manhattan Shirt Co. which employs 540 people.

Americus has a new 110-bed hospital, and a Carnegie Library, while the county has a new 456-acre Experiment Station area purchased by its citizens and donated to the State Board of Regents.

In this vicinity are bauxite and kaolin mines and thousands of acres of young pine trees. Twenty-two distinct types of soil encourage diversification in crops.

GEORGIA SOUTHWESTERN COLLEGE is a coeducational junior college with about 350 students. Opened in 1908, it functioned as an agricultural and mechanical high school until 1924 when normal courses were added. In 1929 all high school work was abandoned and in 1932 the institution became a unit of the University System of Georgia. The eight main buildings on its campus are of brick.

LEESBURG, *119 m.* (282 alt., 659 pop.), in 1872 became the seat of Lee County; both were named for Colonel Henry (Lighthorse Harry) Lee, who captured Augusta from the British in 1781. The surrounding agricultural area ranks high in the production of peanuts and pears.

At *127.7* is a junction with paved State 91.

Left on this road to CHEHAW STATE PARK (*picnic areas, each with shelter, cooking fireplace, and running water; children's playground*), 2 m., a 600-acre tract, it is at present principally a day-use area. It is enclosed on two sides by a large clear-water bayou formed by the confluence of the Kinchefoonee and Cuckalee creeks. The setting appears almost tropical, with moss-festooned trees growing along the banks of the lake. It is open the year-round, with a resident super-intendent in charge.

Given to the state by Dougherty County, the park was named for the Chiha, or Chehaw, a tribe of Creek who lived here. Arrowheads, spearheads, toma-hawks, hoes, drills, scrapers, and clay pipes have been found along the banks of one of the creeks and in the neighboring fields. Because of the variety of work-manship in the artifacts, it is believed that this section was occupied at several distinct periods. The scientist, Dr. John R. Swinton, found their name men-tioned in the *Chronicle of De Soto*.

ALBANY, *130.1 m.* (184 alt., 31,155 pop.), seat of Dougherty County, is a rapidly developing city of wide streets, commanding oaks, and trim modern residences as well as old houses. Despite its languorous semi-tropical setting, accented by profuse plantings of palmettoes and pink-blossoming coral vines, Albany is a brisk town. Though not a per-manent tourist colony, it is a popular stopover point for visitors, who enjoy the golf, swimming, and dancing at nearby Radium Springs.

In the surrounding region are so many acres of paper-shell pecans that a number of packing and shelling plants have been established in Albany for the nuts which ripen in October. Spanish peanuts used in the manufacture of candy and the pest-proof tung nuts (*see* TOUR 5) are also produced in Dougherty County. Albany is the home of the Southern Field Trials, and the site of the spring training camp for the St. Louis Cardinals B, C, and D teams. The town has a modern hos-pital with 154 beds, and there are modern motels and tourists courts in and about its area.

The site for Albany was purchased in 1836 by Alexander Shotwell, a New Jersey Quaker, who commissioned surveyors to lay out a town. In the same year Nelson Tift, accompanied by other men, brought goods from Apalachicola, Florida, up the Flint River, landed at the Albany Site, and began the construction of the first log buildings. The infant city was named for Albany, New York, both being located at the navi-gation head of the rivers on which they stand. Stern wheel steamers came up the Flint and returned to the Gulf with cargoes of cotton; what could not be handled by the small stern-wheelers was floated downstream in long "cotton boxes," built of rough boards and pitched with tar.

The Henry T. McIntosh Collection of Indian artifacts is housed in a wing of the Carnegie Library.

The BRIDGE HOUSE, on Front St., is a two-story brick building erected in 1857 by Tift at the time he built the first bridge over the Flint River. The approach to the bridge was through an archway in the center of this structure, on one side of which was Tift's office and on the other, quarters for the toll taker. Shortly before the War between the States the bridge was burned, and during the war this building was turned into a meat-packing house for Confederate troops. Later it was re-modeled and decorated for Albany's first theatre, where Laura Keene and E. A. Sothern (father of E. H. Sothern) appeared in *She Stoops to Conquer* and *Our American Cousin*. Shakespeare was presented by the Crisp family, including Charles F. Crisp (1845-96), who later served as Speaker of the U. S. House of Representatives during the fifty-second and fifty-third Congress.

With the conclusion of slavery the extensive cotton plantations were broken up into smaller farms; and the boll-weevil infestation of 1915 forced the farmers to take thought, and thus resulted in the introduc-tion of diversified farming. Pecans, cotton, peanuts, watermelons, cantaloupes, peaches, and various other products do well in the local soil. The presence of a meat-packing company has increased the rais-ing of beef cattle. An Annual Fat Cattle Show is sponsored by the Albany Chamber of Commerce. Other major industries include the Clark Thread Company which operates its largest plant in Albany; a farm equipment plant, two hosiery mills; textile mills and railroad re-pair shops.

Four miles southwest of the city is Albany Airport, with three paved runways. Clearly lighted, the field has a weather bureau, administra-tion building, and three hangers. Albany Air Service maintains a shop for complete service on private planes.

Four miles east of Albany is Turner Field, an Air Force Training Base during World War II, which was reactivated in September, 1947. It has a complement of 4,500 officers and men.

Located southeast of Albany on the Mock Road is the Marine Depot, a supply depot for all of the southeastern states; it has an area of ap-proximately 3,677 acres.

ALBANY STATE COLLEGE (Negro) is a four-year coeducational institu-tion approved by the State Department of Education, the Board of Regents, and The Southern Association of Colleges and Secondary Schools. It offers work leading to both the Bachelor of Arts and the Bachelor of Science degrees in the Division of Arts and Sciences; also the degree of Bachelor of Science in Elementary Education. The col-lege has an average of 450 students each quarter, and has sixty-four faculty and staff members. With the newly constructed dormitory for men, McIntosh Hall, there are thirteen buildings.

Left from Albany on paved State 50 to the CUDAHY PACKING PLANT (*open to visitors*), *1 m.*, which opened in September, 1936. The building (L) has two stories of glass masonry set on a high concrete basement. Since the air is con-ditioned and the walls transmit light, no windows are needed. This plant has an annual capacity of 50,000 cattle and 350,000 hogs; it produces meat, lard, hides, and serves as a market for butter, eggs, cheese, and poultry. The animals are slaughtered on the top floor. As the carcasses pass along moving trolleys, they are skinned, split, and prepared for the coolers without a stop. When sufficiently chilled they are passed along to the cutting floor and prepared for shipment. Almost all of the beef is sold fresh, but a large portion of the pork is cured and smoked. Separate buildings are maintained for the power plant, dressing rooms for the four hundred employees, and government inspectors' offices. Livestock raisers are encouraged by the management to use improved methods of animal breeding and feeding.

RADIUM SPRINGS, *134.4 m.*, is a popular Georgia resort. The bowl of clear blue water, once called Skywater by the Creeks, flows from an unknown depth at the rate of 70,000 gallons a minute at a constant temperature of 68°. There is a swimming pool and an 18-hole golf course; fishing in the nearby Flint River and horseback riding along bridle paths.

CAMILLA, *157.3 m.* (167 alt., 3,745 pop.), is the seat of Mitchell County; it was laid out in 1857. The county was named for David B. Mitchell, Governor of Georgia (1809-13 and 1815-17), and the town for his daughter. The marker in the center of the main street designates the SITE OF THE HAWTHORNE TRAIL, blazed in 1818 by William Hawthorne when he was seeking a short route from North Carolina to Florida. Two years later he made a trip over the trail, broadened it, and settled with his family near Cairo.

The Mitchell County Livestock Company has newly completed a sales and auction barn, the first sales of which were held on July 24, 1952. Buyers are able to look over the day's offering by means of a spectator's catwalk over the lines of stock pens, before going to the arena. The auction market has an air-cooled sales arena, with theater-type seats, completely enclosed stock pens, and an ample parking area.

Left from Camilla on paved State 37 to MOULTRIE, *27 m.* (340 alt., 11,639 pop.), seat of Colquitt County. The town was incorporated in 1859, three years after the creation of the county, and was named for General William Moultrie, who successfully defended Sullivan's Island against the British fleet when Sir Peter Parker attacked Charles Town, South Carolina, during the Revolutionary War. The town is located at the head of the Ochlocknee River on slightly rolling, sandy-loam hills; it has an average growing season of 258 days. Moultrie has forty-three industries of different types. Included are cotton and oil mills, the most modern sulphuric plant in the Southeast, fertilizer works, bedding and garment plants, and other factories processing the raw materials used in south Georgia. The Georgia Peanut Company handles one-third of the peanuts used in the national production of edible peanut products, and is now getting ready a new plant for refining peanut oil to be used for cooking and salad dressing. One of the oldest industries is the Riverside Manufacturing Company, locally financed and under the same management as the Moultrie Cotton Mills and the

Riverside Bedding Company. Riverside manufactures industrial uniforms, a term applied to the work shirts, trousers, and coveralls used by workers where standard clothing is required.

Noted for its progress in livestock and pasture development, Moultrie is a hub for livestock auctions and sales. A purebred sale is held monthly and breeders from the Southeast come to buy and sell. The first Annual State Fat Barrow Show was held in 1948. Tobacco is a major crop, and each year a Southeast Tobacco Festival, lasting three days and featuring an all-day series of events each day, is celebrated around the middle of August. A Southeast Tobacco Queen is selected annually from among the youthful beauties of the general area. Forty thousand people attended the fifth festival in 1952. In 1951 farmers sold 11,630,-120 pounds of tobacco for $5,221,725.72 which is an average of 44.90 cents a pound.

The STATE FARMERS MARKET, which operates under the supervision of the Georgia Department of Agriculture, was opened in 1946, and has operated continuously, with current sales amounting to more than a million dollars annually. Though it functions throughout the year, the major items are cabbage, watermelons, cantaloupe, and others of this sort, which are marketed primarily over a brief period in the spring and early summer. During the six years this market has been in operation, the total sales have amounted to about five and one-third million dollars.

Moultrie has a municipal swimming pool, lighted tennis courts, softball fields, playgrounds, and a nine-hole golf course.

SWIFT & COMPANY MEAT-PACKING PLANT (*open to visitors*), *1 m*. N. of the courthouse, is a modern structure of brick and reinforced concrete. Some seven hundred workers are employed in the preparation of meats and meat products.

PELHAM, *166.3 m*. (355 alt., 4,365 pop.), began in 1870 when J. L. Hand established a sawmill and turpentine business here. The settlement that developed on the site was incorporated in 1881 and named for Major John Pelham, who commanded "Jeb" Stuart's Horse Artillery while in his teens, during the War between the States. The town has peanut-shelling plants, an oil mill, a canning plant, a fertilizer plant, lumber mills, and cotton gins. In 1951 farmers sold 6,252,296 pounds of tobacco for $2,753,681.79 at an average of 44.04 cents a pound.

The STATE FARMERS MARKET, operated under the supervision of the Georgia Department of Agriculture, is a seasonal market intended largely to take care of the big tomato crop typical of this area. It began in 1941, and the sales amount to an average of about one-half million dollars annually. A report from the Georgia Department of Commerce NEWSLETTER for August, 1952, states that, with a smaller acreage of tomatoes in 1952 than in 1951, growers sold more than 85,000 bushels for over a half million dollars—$200,000 more than in 1951. Buyers from the North and East were on hand for the market season which lasted a month.

THOMASVILLE, *189.6 m*. (250 alt., 14,424 pop.), seat of Thomas County, was incorporated in 1826, a year after the creation of the county, and, like Thomaston (*see* above), was named for General Jett Thomas. Because of its position at the intersection of a number of principal highways, large companies have made it a distributing center, and its department stores resemble those of a much larger city. There are thirty or more manufacturers, with from twenty-five to six hundred workers each, of such products as textiles, lumber woodworking, castings, iron work, silica, brick, peanut oil and butter, steam boilers, prepared foods, and others. As the South increases the mechanization on its farms, more and more labor from the farm areas will need to find employment in an expanding industrial program.

With only occasional days when the temperature falls to freezing, the winters are short and mild, and breezes from the Gulf of Mexico for the most part modify the summer heat. Flowers are in bloom for most of the year; the telephone poles are covered with climbing Paul's Scarlet roses, and the streets lined with Red Radiance roses.

The Annual Thomasville Rose Show is held on the last Friday in April, each year. Begun in 1922, this festival of "The City of Roses" attracts over thirty thousand visitors annually. Many of the Thomasville gardens, the displays of the nurseries, and the gardens of the winter residents are open to the public by arranged tours. Perhaps no undisputed monarch exists in the realm of flowers, but the rose is most frequently referred to as its queen. The Camellia Show usually takes place after the middle of January. Thomasville has quite a number of nurseries engaged in propagating roses, camellias, azaleas, and other ornamental shrubs.

Outsiders began coming to Thomasville about eighty-five years ago, and from 1875 until the noted Piney Woods Hotel burned in 1900, there were many transient visitors. A number of northern capitalists bought large estates and built impressive winter homes, which are maintained in the style of old southern plantations. They engross some 150,000 acres, of which a part is under cultivation and the rest kept as hunting preserves. Many of the estates have fine stands of unusually tall longleaf pine. Pine Tree Boulevard, completely encircling the city within a radius of two miles, passes several of these estates.

Hunting and fishing are popular sports around Thomasville. The preserves and the surrounding forests abound with quail, wild turkeys, deer, ducks, and doves, and numerous nearby lakes afford excellent fishing. Predatory animals of the section are plentiful. The Georgia-Florida Amateur Field Trials for bird dogs are held in the spring.

The GREAT OAK, corner of East Monroe and North Crawford sts., has a top spread of 170 feet, a height of 55 feet, and a circumference of 22 feet at four feet from the ground; tree surgeons estimate that it is 270 years old. It has been enrolled as the 24th ranking member of the National Live-Oak Association.

Continued growth in agriculture is assured by the fertile fields, experienced farmers, the mild climate with 260 growing days a year, and the variety of staple and truck crops in cultivation. One of the larger meat packing plants of the Southeast, which happens to be independently owned, is located in Thomasville, and along with other livestock markets in the city, it provides a daily cash market for hogs and beef. Hams, bacon, sausage, and other packing plant products are processed locally.

The STATE FARMERS MARKET, on US 84, a part of the state's farm marketing system that is controlled by the State Department of Agriculture, is one of the earlier markets, having been opened for business in 1936, and operated continuously since then. It is perhaps the most progressive market in the entire system, and has contributed measurably towards bringing about crop diversification in its area. Produce dealers and brokers maintain buying facilities and offices on the market grounds throughout the year. For example, the Merchants Building, one of several produce buildings used at the market, provides offices and room for produce buyers and brokers who, buying direct from the farmers, then grade and repack, to ship by rail and truck to customers in various parts of the nation. Hundreds of refrigerated trucks visit this market each year to pick up fresh vegetables for distribution in the North and East.

An examination of the records shows that in 1941 only $413,000 worth of produce was handled on the market, though in 1951 the amount had climbed to $4,329,000, while the total of sales for the ten-year period is about $23,000,000. In the past two or three years the facilities have been much improved, and because of its location and the loyal support of the business interests of the section, the market operates almost continuously at full capacity.

The MARK HANNA HOUSE (*private*), N. Dawson St., is a victorian structure built in 1877 and later enlarged by Hanna. During the winter of 1895-96, Republican leaders came here to confer with the noted statesman and formulated the plan that carried William McKinley to the White House. McKinley was a guest in this house when he was nominated for the presidency.

ARCHBOLD MEMORIAL HOSPITAL, on Gordon St. near the rim of the city, was given to Thomasville by John F. Archbold in memory of his father, John D. Archbold. The three-story stucco building, showing Spanish influence in its architecture, is set back on a lawn above which rise some exceptionally fine pines. Given by Archbold as a memorial to his mother, the nurses' home is connected with the main building. The property represents a total investment of more than a million dollars, and is spoken of proudly as the best hospital south of Johns Hopkins.

At Thomasville is the junction with US 84 (*see* TOUR 5).

1. Left from Thomasville on Clay Street Road to the VASHTI INDUSTRIAL SCHOOL, 2 *m.,* which includes twenty buildings on 97 acres of land, forty of which are under cultivation to provide vegetables, fruit, meat, eggs, and dairy products. A boarding school founded in 1903 for dependent girls of good character, it is named for Mrs. Vashti Blasengame, the mother of the school's first donor. Limited to 120 girls from ten to eighteen years of age, the school has grades running from the fifth through high school, and is accredited by the Georgia State Board of Education. In addition to the usual courses on home economics and in commercial subjects, courses are offered in industrial arts, music, and in the Bible. The Mary Floyd Pavilion provides for skating, folk dancing, parties, picnics, and other activities. Courts exist for tennis, basketball and soft ball, and there is a swimming pool. A full-time director of Christian education teaches Bible classes and directs and correlates the school's religious activities.

The school is under the jurisdiction of the Woman's Division of Christian Services of the Methodist Church.

2. Right from Thomasville on the lower Cairo Road to BOXHALL (*open during Rose Show*), 3.5 *m.,* a 500-acre estate (R). The red brick house, set on a wide expanse of lawn, is the original structure built in 1830 by the McIntyre family.

3. Left from Thomasville on State 35, US 319, to (L) HOLLYWOOD PLANTATION (*open during Rose Show*), 1 *m.,* which is unusually beautiful because of its profuse setting. The design of the house is based upon that of Monticello, Thomas Jefferson's home in Virginia.

At 2 *m.* is a junction (R) with Pine Tree Boulevard, which runs for thirteen miles, completely encircling Thomasville.

BIRDWOOD (*private*), 3 *m.* (R), is the estate of Cameron W. Forbes, a grandson of Ralph Waldo Emerson, and Ambassador to Japan, 1931-32.

MILLPOND PLANTATION (*open during Rose Show*), 4 *m.* (L) was named for Linton's Mill, which was on the land when the 10,000 acres of the estate were bought. The house of Spanish Colonial design has an exceptionally varied number of gardens, one of which has a rose walk, a long avenue bordered by many varieties of roses against a background of climbing roses trained on posts.

4. Right from Thomasville on US 319 to ELSOMA (*open during Rose Show*), 3 *m.,* a winter estate (R) of 4,000 acres. From the entrance gates, marked by a planting of Spanish bayonets, wild azaleas, and wistaria vines, a winding driveway leads through a sweep of pines mixed with magnolias and oaks to the house. Its porch is outlined by a delicate iron railing, and several dormer windows accent the high pitched roof. Beyond the terrace on the south side is an old-fashioned garden with tea olives, camellias, azaleas, and other ornamentals and flowers.

INWOOD PLANTATION (*open during Rose Show*), across the road (L) from Elsoma, is a 1,000-acre estate with entrance gates banked in native shrubs, flowers, and trees. A circular drive, bordered by a clipped hedge and magnolia trees, leads to the low, rambling stucco house and the nearby azalea and rose gardens.

MELROSE (*open during Rose Show*), 4.9 *m.,* is bordered by fences on which

Cherokee roses and yellow jasmine vines are trained. Wide expanses of lawn, spreading from the winding approach to the house, are shaded by large oaks, magnolias, redbuds, crape myrtle, and flowering peach trees. The residence is a rambling, buff-colored frame house trimmed in white and covered with wistaria. The central portion, constructed of logs and covered with clapboards, was on the site when H. M. Hanna, Sr., bought the estate in the 1890's. The Rose Garden is west of the house.

PEBBLE HILL PLANTATION (*open during Rose Show*), *5.4 m.*, is an estate (R) enclosed by fences covered with Cherokee roses. The planting is in agreement with the natural setting of pine forest, on land that was granted to James Johnson in 1810. From the residence, paths lead to the flower gardens. A fine herd of Jersey cattle is housed by the red brick barn. Mrs. Parker Poe, the owner, has made a real contribution to the improvement of cattle breeding in Georgia. The inspection yard of the barn is surrounded by a serpentine wall on which wistaria has been trained.

GREENWOOD is another well-known estate of this locale (*see* TOUR 5).

At *202.4 m.* US 19 crosses the Florida Line at a point 8 miles north of Monticello, Florida.

TOUR 7

(Franklin, N. C.)—Dillard—Clarkesville—Cornelia—Gaines-ville—Atlanta; US 23.

North Carolina Line to Atlanta, 118.4 m.—Tallulah Falls R.R. parallels route between N. C. Line and Cornelia; the Southern Ry. between Cornelia and Atlanta—All types of accommodations—Many summer hotels and boarding houses.

US 23 crosses a corner of the Chattahoochee National Forest in the lower slopes of the Blue Ridge Mountains, which vary in altitude from 800 to almost 5,000 feet. The broad views of wooded valleys, with blue mountain ranges, waterfalls, and clear, calm lakes combine to make this one of the most beautiful regions in the state. At times the road winds along the sides of wooded slopes, brightened in spring by the delicate pink and white blossoms of mountain laurel and rhododendron and in fall by brilliant red and yellow leaves.

This northeastern corner of Georgia is a popular summer resort area, where many private cottages, summer hotels, and fishing camps have been built along the shores of lakes. Rabun County is famous for its Tallulah Falls gorge where a chain of lakes makes up the hydroelectric area of the Georgia Power Company on the Tallulah and Tugalo rivers. In the valleys land has been cleared for pastures, truck gardens, and apple or peach orchards.

Near Gainesville are rolling foothills, where agriculture is extensive and industry well advanced. Gainesville is the economic center of the north Georgia commercial broiler industry which is now the largest in the nation statewise and is Georgia's number two cash crop. There are several small, prosperous factory towns along the southern part of the route.

US 23 crosses the North Carolina Line, *o m.,* at a point in the CHATTAHOOCHEE NATIONAL FOREST more than thirteen miles south of Franklin, North Carolina.

At *0.7 m.* is a junction with paved State 246 which leads to ESTATOAH FALLS (R), about *2.5 m.,* formed by the waters of Middle Creek cascading between the feathery foliage of hemlocks.

Many points along the road afford sweeping views of valleys and surrounding hills. Occasionally sheep and cows are visible grazing in pastures enclosed by split-rail fences. The mountain woodlands are redolent with the clean, sharp scent of pine and the earthy odors of damp mold.

DILLARD, *2 m.* (2,250 alt., 250 pop.), is a mountain trading village. There are three tourist homes, two of which serve meals. The State Farmers Market, operated under the supervision of the Georgia State Department of Agriculture, is located on the highway; it was established in 1951.

RABUN GAP, *3 m.* (approx. 2,100 alt., 264 pop.), a small settlement in a narrow pass through the highland, was formerly known only for its surrounding scenery, but in recent years it has become known by association with the nearby school.

The RABUN GAP-NACOOCHEE SCHOOL (R), *2.3 m.,* is a boarding high school that offers five years of vocational and academic training. The modified Georgian style red brick buildings with their columned porticos are set on a hill with the mountains as a background, and the 1,800-acre school farm for agricultural instruction lies partly on the opposite side of the highway in a circular valley at the head of the Little Tennessee River.

The boarding school and farm of 200 acres where students, both men and women, pay for their education by farm and domestic work is the center of the system. In the outer circle of 1,600 acres is the farm settlement school. Here whole families receive both agricultural instruction and a living in return for their labor. Sixteen families, admitted in rotation for ten-year periods, are each provided with forty acres of land, a modern six-room cottage, a barn, and outhouses. In conformity with approved methods of agriculture the farms are operated on a sharecrop basis and the farmers assisted in marketing their products, purchasing supplies, and keeping accounts. Next to the boarding-school farm is the elementary day school, for children of the surrounding district. The institution is supported by the Synod of Georgia, Presbyterian Church, by private donations, and by an agreement with the Rabun County School System.

MOUNTAIN CITY, 5 m. (2,200 alt., 600 pop.), is at the point of the Blue Ridge Divide. The Mountain City Packing Company is noted for its apples. There are a number of tourist houses serving meals.

On US 23 at about 6 m. is a sign (R) indicating the road to BLACK ROCK MOUNTAIN STATE PARK, about 2 m., road unpaved. The park area consists of 1,100 acres. It goes to the very top of Black Rock Mountain, the bald summit of which rises sharply above the wooded lower slopes, and there is a picnic area here overlooking the surrounding country. The park is now under development.

CLAYTON, 9.3 m. (1,959 alt., 1,302 pop.), is a well-kept town the main street of which is lined with hotels that provide good accommodations for summer visitors. Clayton was incorporated in 1823 as the seat of Rabun County, which had been created in 1819 from Cherokee lands. With relatively little agriculture and few industries, the county has become a typical mountain recreation area. It was settled principally by New Englanders who previously had lived in the mountains of Virginia, and by a few Tories who escaped to the mountains at the time of the Revolution.

In this section July and August, the warmest months, have an average temperature of 73.9°, which means cool days and refreshing nights. Month by month the distribution of rainfall is roughly the same, the average for the year being 70.96 inches, which is in sharp contrast, for example, with Augusta's 43.20, Atlanta's 47.58, or even Valdosta's 49.23. When summer brings parching days to Atlanta, towards late afternoon it is a common experience to see the sky blacken in the north, and if the thunderheads do not reach so far, at least to benefit from the fresh breath of the northerly storm.

Within the radius of a few miles from Clayton as a point there are twelves lakes (*boating, swimming, fishing*), six of them formed in the process of power development by the Georgia Power Company. Camping facilities in the Chattahoochee National Forest are easily accessible, and fish are plentiful in the mountain streams. The state's Lake Burton Hatchery on Moccasin Creek supplies trout, bass, and bream for stocking streams. Trails have been built through the country by the U. S. Forest Service, and there is a wealth of picnic areas, equipped in some instances with tables and outdoor ovens. It is a land of forest-clad mountains, shaded dells, sparkling waterfalls, rippling streams, and serene lakes with a plenitude of cool bays and inlets.

The Weavers of Rabun, a group located in the Betty Creek Section, have established a reputation for unusual designs in fabrics. Their products are sold in New York's Rockefeller Center. Visitors are welcome and it is interesting to watch these skilled workers with their hand-operated looms.

The Tallulah Ranger District of the Chattahoochee National Forest has a District Ranger's office in Clayton. This district is made up of 147,179 acres in Rabun County. Inquire for information about available recreation facilities in the area.

1. Right from Clayton on US 76, about 7 m. is HILLS FISHING CAMP (R) at the thumb tip of Lake Burton's five fingers. The LAKE BURTON PLAYHOUSE is left from the camp, on the north side of the lake. (Left from Hills Fishing Camp is an unpaved road that skirts the east side of Lake Burton until it joins the Tiger Road: L. to Tiger, R. to Nacoochee Lake.) About a half mile farther where the road cuts the index finger of Lake Burton is JONES FISHING CAMP. About two and a half miles farther turn right at a sign to LA PRADE FISHING CAMP, about six miles. This road runs along the west side of Lake Burton.

With a shore line of sixty-five miles, Lake Burton is the largest of the lakes in the Georgia Power Company's chain that ends with the Yonah development. From the head of Lake Burton to Yonah the river distance is thirty-seven and a half miles, with a total fall of 1,198 feet. Lake Burton has by equivalence, a water storage capacity of 97,400,000 kilowatt hours. The waters of the lake cover a 2,700-acre area, and the power plant has a capacity of 6,120 kilowatts. At La Prade Fishing Camp the road continues to an intersection (L) where a road turns in to CAMP CHEROKEE FOR BOYS. After a short distance the road intersects (L) with the Tiger Road and continues to the north side of NACOOCHEE LAKE. With a capacity of 4,800 kilowatts, the dam and powerhouse were the last units built in the power series. Beyond Nacoochee Lake is LAKE RABUN which has become a celebrated week-end and vacation spot. The lake shore is dotted with homes and boat houses. Not far from the upper end of this water area is the RABUN BEACH RECREATION AREA (L), maintained by the U. S. Forest Service as a part of the Chattahoochee National Forest. It provides numerous picnic and trailer camp units, a large parking area, shelters, a bathhouse, water system, garbage pits, and toilets. Both HALLS BOATHOUSE and WALLS BOATHOUSE (R) are about midway, tucked in a land-pocket of the lake. Mathis Dam backs up the waters that form Lake Rabun. The route ends at LAKEMONT (*see* below) after winding through some of the most beautiful forest terrain in the whole of north Georgia.

2. Left from Clayton on War Woman Rd. to SCREAMER MOUNTAIN, 2 m. (2,925 alt.), named for an Indian who broke away from the tribe during the Cherokee Removal march.

At 4 m. is WAR WOMAN DELL PICNIC AREA. The road, the dell, and the creek are named for War Woman, an Indian woman who was friendly to the whites and once saved the early settlers from a raid. It provides a parking area, picnic tables with benches and fireplaces, two shelters with tables and fireplaces, a water system, and toilets; and is a part of the U. S. Forest Service in the Chattahoochee National Forest.

To RABUN BALD (4,717 alt.), turn left at War Woman Dell on a gravel road and continue for about seven miles, take left at marked Hail Ridge Road for about eight miles, take right at sign for about three miles. Rabun Bald, the second highest peak in the state, has a summit from which one can see into North Carolina, South Carolina, and Georgia.

TIGER, *11.9 m.* (approx. 1,800 alt., 269 pop.), is named for a Cherokee chief, Tiger Tail. Take road L. to GLASSY MOUNTAIN (3,821 alt.), the Bridge Creek (Tiger) Road, and follow signs. This road, referred to above under Clayton, leads to Lake Burton and to Nacoochee Lake.

LAKEMONT, *17.3 m.* (approx. 1,700 alt., 75 pop.), a small settlement, serves as the post office for a summer colony on the shores of Lake Rabun. It has three motor courts, a cafe, and two grocery stores.

At *17.6 m.* is a junction with a graveled road.

Right on this road to the LAKEMONT SUMMER COLONY, *1 m.* (*see* lake tour under Clayton above), composed principally of Atlanta people. Houses of wood or local stone, each with its own boathouse and bathing pier, are built along the slopes that encircle Lake Rabun. In summer this otherwise tranquil lake is a busy surface of canoes, motorboats, and aquaplanes.

Winding US 23 crosses the Tallulah River, and runs parallel to it for almost five miles before recrossing it. The bed of the river is rugged and almost dry because the flow from Lake Rabun has been diverted by means of Terrora Tunnel, cut 5,300 feet through a mountain. The TERRORA POWERHOUSE, (R) with a capacity of 16,000 kilowatts, is located at the head of the Tallulah Reservoir and receives its water through the tunnel.

At *22.6 m.* the highway which formerly crossed the Tallulah Falls Dam now crosses on a new cement bridge immediately below the dam that impounds the waters of the Tallulah River. To the left over the sheer rock precipice of 1,000 feet, the river once formed a beautiful falls. Today only a small stream rills its way over the sharp rocks and flows through the deep gorge that was earlier cut by the torrent of impetuous water. Tallulah Tunnel, also cut through the heart of a mountain, diverts the course of the Tallulah River for 6,663 feet and carries the water nearly a mile and a half. At the TALLULAH POWERHOUSE, with a capacity of 72,000 kilowatts, penstocks 1,200 feet long bring the water from the tunnel down the side of the gorge to the powerhouse. An inclined railway of 1,165 feet in length along the 608-foot wall of the canyon affords passengers a magnificent view of the gorge.

TALLULAH FALLS, *22.7 m.* (1,629 alt., 239 pop.), is a small settlement on the Tallulah River near the southern end of the dam.

TALLULAH FALLS SCHOOL, INC. (*open 9-5*), *23 m.,* owned and operated by the Georgia Federation of Women's Clubs, occupies (R) eighteen rock and timber buildings grouped at different levels on the side of Cherokee Mountain. From this point are sweeping views, not only of the nearby Georgia mountains, but of the distant blue ranges of Tennessee, North Carolina, and South Carolina.

The school, which opened in 1909 with twenty-one pupils and one teacher, housed in a small building, now has a student body of about 250, a faculty of 15, and 500 acres of land, with a plant valued at $300,-000. Although the institution is operated under the state school system and receives public funds, it is also aided by private donations and, in crafts and home economics, by the Smith-Hughes Fund.

The curriculum includes courses from the first through the twelfth grade. All the work of the school is done by the students as a part of their training, with assignments regularly changed for diversification of interest and well-rounded development. Since the school is small, personal attention can be given to developing character and civil duty. It operates on the principle that every waking hour of an adolescent's time may be advantageously used by a carefully correlated system of study, work, and play; that patriotism and religion should share in the curriculum with academic attainment, though the school is not denominational.

About one-half of the students come from remote districts and live at the school, while the others are day students.

TALLULAH POINT, *23.1 m.* (2,000 alt.), is a vantage point for the best view of TALLULAH GORGE, which extends in a huge semicircle from Tallulah Dam. The steep, rugged walls of the canyon are covered with a natural growth of trees and shrubs. In the distance (NE) Rabun Bald in Georgia and Round Mountain in South Carolina are visible on clear days.

A granite marker (R) at the entrance to Clarkesville indicates that this is the supposed ROUTE OF DE SOTO when, with 500 Spanish and Portuguese soldiers and 200 Cherokee burden bearers, he passed through this region in 1540. So confusing are the varied accounts of his travels that historians have been unable to establish conclusively the exact places he visited. It is believed that De Soto entered the region now Georgia at its southwest corner, marched in a northeasterly direction in search of gold, and stopped at an Indian village somewhere between the present Augusta and Columbia, South Carolina. "Thence he marched northwestward," writes E. M. Coulter in *Georgia: A Short History,* "and either entered North Carolina before he turned to the southwest, or he took a shorter cut through the Nacoochee Valley of northern Georgia. It seems rather certain that he departed down the Coosa River, passing by the future location of Rome."

At about *25.9 m.* (R) on US 23 is the PANTHER CREEK PICNIC AREA of the Chattahoochee National Forest, maintained by the U. S. Forest Service. This area of about six acres in Habersham County contains a parking area, two shelters with five tables, individual picnic tables with benches and fireplaces, a water system, and toilets. Inquire for further information from District Ranger's office in Clayton or Clarkesville.

CLARKESVILLE *35.9 m.* (1,372 alt., 1,106 pop.), seat of Habersham County, was named for John C. Clarke (1766-1832), a Revolutionary soldier and Governor of Georgia (1819-23). This small town, in an almost level valley among the mountains, was a fashionable summer resort in the nineteenth century. The town is a center for apples and peaches.

At Clarkesville is located the NORTH GEORGIA TRADE SCHOOL in the plant which, though originally that of the state Agricultural and Mechanical College, had later been used by the National Youth Administration. Recognizing that slight means existed for training in the mechanical and service trades, the members of the State Board of Education approved a plan in 1944 for a system of trade schools as a part of the Georgia regional education program. The establishment has a brick administration building, dormitories, a library, and buildings for the use of the farm that contributes to the needs of the institution. Land, buildings, and equipment have a value of some $500,000.

Instructors are chosen on the basis of their acquired technical skill in actual trade routines, and adjust themselves to teaching at the school. Such techniques are offered in the school as: automobile mechanics, automobile painting and body repairing, bricklaying, electrical skills, machine shop practice, photography, radio and television repairing and servicing, refrigeration, shoe repairing, watch and clock repairing, wood working, and secretarial training. Though Georgia residents pay no tuition, there is a monthly fee of around forty dollars for room, board, and other costs. Nonresidents, if admitted, pay an additional fifteen dollars a month tuition.

The Chattooga Ranger District of the U. S. Forest Service of the Chattahoochee National Forest has a District Ranger's office in Clarkesville. It comprises 100,082 acres in Banks, Habersham, Stephens, Towns, Union, and White counties. Inquire about facilities available for recreation in this forest area.

DEMOREST, *41 m.* (1,469 alt., 1,166 pop.), developed about PIEDMONT COLLEGE (L), one of the earliest schools for montain boys and girls. This accredited four-year college confers the bachelor's degree in liberal arts, and science. Founded in 1897 by a Methodist circuit rider, it is now under the auspices of the Congregational church, and has an enrollment of around 300 students. Since the denomination has few adherents in the South, financial support, other than tuition, comes chiefly from New England. Enlarged and reorganized in 1903, the college has buildings and equipment valued at $150,000. On the seal of the college is a radiant cross imposed against a mountain range, with the word LUX on a scroll under the cross.

DEMOREST SPRINGS, in a public park 150 feet L. of the highway, is a group of six mineral springs. Within a few feet of one another, each is marked with a metal plate describing its mineral properties.

CORNELIA, *44.5 m.* (1,537 alt., 2,424 pop.), incorporated in 1887, is in the center of the apple-growing section of northeast Georgia. It is known as the home of the Big Red Apple. The road from Cornelia to Baldwin is lined with apple orchards, and in the summer and autumn, cider is sold at roadside stands.

Left from Cornelia on US 123, about *2 m.,* to (R) the CHENOCETAH PICNIC AREA, maintained by the U. S. Forest Service of the Chattahoochee National Forest. This small picnic area located near Lake Russell contains a parking area, a picnic shelter, picnic tables, fireplaces, a water system, and toilets.

The nearby LAKE RUSSELL RECREATION AREA is built around a 100-acre artificial lake. In the process of development, its facilities now consist of a parking area, bathhouses, a community picnic unit with fireplaces and tables, individual picnic tables with fireplaces, and toilets.

The FERN SPRINGS PICNIC AREA, on US 123 at about *6 m.* (R), is a popular one. Its facilities consist of a parking area, three shelters, a community unit with fireplaces and tables, individual tables with fireplaces, a spring and springhouse, garbage pits, and toilets.

The GEORGE WASHINGTON CARVER PICNIC AREA (for Negroes), on US 123 at about *7 m.,* has a parking area, picnic tables with fireplaces, an excellent spring, a garbage pit, and toilets.

Inquire for further information about the RUSSELL WILDLIFE AREA and about the above places, at the office of the District Ranger in Clarkesville.

At Cornelia is a junction with State 13 (*see* TOUR 7A).

In NEW HOLLAND, *68.9 m.* (approx. 1,200 alt., 1,618 pop.), is the home of one of the Pacolet plants, textile manufacturers. The other unit is in Gainesville. The plant with the accompanying village and lake is a model of functional neatness. Once the site of a well-known summer resort around New Holland Spring, the town is now entirely industrial.

GAINESVILLE, *70.5 m.* (1,254 alt., 11,936 pop.), in the foothills of the Blue Ridge, is the seat of Hall County, created in 1818 and named for Lyman Hall, one of the three Georgia signers of the Declaration of Independence. Incorporated in 1821, the town was named for General

Edmund Pendleton Gaines, who as commandant of Fort Stoddart in Alabama arrested Aaron Burr (when he sought refuge in Georgia after the death of Alexander Hamilton in the famous duel between the two), defended Fort Erie in the War of 1812, and served in the Black Hawk and Seminole wars. General James Longstreet, of Confederate fame, lived his last years in Gainesville and is buried in Altavista Cemetery, on the west side of the town.

At first the town grew slowly, though it did have a colorful but short-lived gold rush in 1829. Moreover two destructive fires swept the town, one in 1873 and the other in 1876. But the great stimulus to development came after the War between the States with the construction of the Charlotte & Atlanta Air Line Railroad, now the Southern Railway. With the installation of a municipal power plant in 1889, Gainesville became the first town south of Baltimore with electrically lighted streets. By the 1890's farm products were brought to market from the mountains in such bulk that the town became an important chicken and egg market.

On April 6, 1936, a terrific tornado struck three miles west, ravaging a path eight miles long and about a mile wide through the heart of the city. Destruction within the defined area could hardly have been more complete had it resulted from one of the instruments of modern aerial war. Nearly a thousand structures were destroyed or damaged, almost as many people injured, more than seven hundred made homeless, and around two hundred killed. This was the second disaster from wind in the town's annals, a tornado in 1903 having resulted in the loss of both property and lives. The work of rehabilitation began at once, however, and this included the landscaping and replanting of the town square and the renovation of the surrounding business section. Despite a property loss amounting to an estimated sixteen million dollars, the town arose again from its ruin with such renewed energy as to vie with Atlanta for the phoenix as a civic emblem.

Among the new buildings in the town's center are two structures of white Georgia marble housing the city and county authorities, each occupying a square block between Bradford Street and S. Green Street. The new Federal Building and post office is located just off the corner of this public area at S. Green and Spring streets. Completed in 1950, the new Civic Building, containing the Youth Center and the headquarters of the local National Guard unit, has a main auditorium seating 1,500 for meetings or 500 for meals, and other smaller meeting rooms. A division office of the Georgia Highway Patrol has a squad of cars operating from the local station at Gainesville.

The Chattahoochee Ridge which makes a rugged backbone through

Hall County is the dividing line between waters moving to the Atlantic Ocean and those flowing to the Gulf of Mexico. It is said that some houses are so situated that water from one side of the roof flows to the Atlantic, that from the other to the Gulf. Being in the Piedmont Plateau, Hall County and Gainesville are contained by a rolling to hilly terrain with numerous ridges and valleys of irregular extent. Winters with average monthly readings of 40° and summers of an average 73° are decidedly temperate; summer nights are nearly always refreshing. Annual rainfall totals around fifty-four inches, and the growing season free of killing frost varies around two hundred days as a norm. With this sort of climate and soil which is productive if properly managed, the economy of the Gainesville area has been traditionally agricultural. Hogs and cattle are on the increase, and dairy products, small grains, apples, vegetables, and corn are produced in commercial quantities. In 1950 there were 2,522 farms, the total acres of which amounted to 187,-712 in an approximate area of 272,640 acres. A shift has been made in the last decade from the preoccupation with cotton and corn to poultry and livestock, with a decided trend towards grass-farming in place of row-crops. This has resulted in fewer small farms and a greater increase of acreage for each farm and in more owner-operated farms, which is a neat reversal of the Roman adage that one should admire a large farm but own a small one. Population-wise, however, this tendency has brought about a relative decline in farming activities, except in Forsyth County.

A major factor in the above equation is the new poultry industry in the area. In the last ten years the production of commercial broilers has grown from a mere infant to an Atlas supporting a new world of prosperity on its shoulders. It is now Georgia's #2 cash-crop, and the largest enterprise of its sort in the nation. Most of the non-white and many of the white farm workers have been absorbed by the new industry, but others displaced by the shifts in farm practice have had to migrate to more densely industrialized areas.

One of the largest commercial broiler enterprises centers around the name of Jewell in Gainesville, the structure of which is actually a relief map of the industry as a whole. It raises its own laying hens, hatches the eggs, farms out the chickens to qualified growers, and collects and freezes the fryers twelve weeks later for packaged sales. In a recent year over 12,000,000 pounds of frozen chickens were distributed all over the nation and to distant markets outside. The image of a chicken stamped on the town's current automobile tags signifies increased retail sales, new homes, better living standards, money in deposit and savings accounts, and an increase in college educations for the young heirs of the industry. Doubtless the title "The World's Broiler Capital" will replace the older "Queen City of the Mountains." The narrow and low-pitched but often extremely long broiler houses extend along the highways that enter and leave Gainesville.

The other principal industries in Gainesville are textiles, leather, manufacture of shoes, of saddles, of apparel, and of livestock and poultry feeds. Both the Pacolet plants, the Gainesville Mill and the one north at New Holland, manufacture an exceptional range of cotton products such as twills for army fatigues and Boy Scout uniforms, drapery fabrics, sheetings, cloth for chenille bedspreads, upholstery, boat sail drill, moleskin, pique, sateen, and window-shade fabric. Owen Osborne produces full-fashioned nylon hosiery, and the Gaybourn Mills, nylon thread.

Developed by the Navy during World War II and the site of a part of the work done in developing the Ground Controlled Approach radar system, the airport is now municipally owned. Two runways, each 4,000 feet in length and 150 feet wide, are equipped with L-6 light systems with beacon and field boundary lights, Bartow high intensity runway lights, and instrument approach lights at the ends of the runways. Complete receiving equipment is included in the control tower facilities.

Recreational facilities include three municipal swimming pools, a nine-hole municipal golf course and clubhouse, fields at all town schools, baseball and softball diamonds, and football fields. In addition the three largest textile plants have gymnasiums and full-time recreational directors for their communities. The Hall County Library includes a motorized branch library, the "Bookmobile," that circulates throughout the county to serve its rural readers.

The Supervisor's Headquarters of the Chattahoochee National Forest Section of the U. S. National Forest Service is located in Gainesville. Address inquiries about the recreation areas of the forest to this office.

BRENAU COLLEGE, E. Washington Street, one block R. of the highway, is now an endowed, completely accredited, non-sectarian college for women offering the A.B. degree. Brenau was chartered in 1878 as the Georgia Baptist Seminary and opened in 1879. Because of financial difficulties it was sold in 1886 to A. W. Van Hoose to be used as a private non-sectarian school. H. J. Pearce bought a half interest in 1893 and acquired sole possession in 1913. In 1917 the school was deeded to a board of trustees which secured an endowment of $700,000 through the contributions of Mrs. Aurora Strong Hunt and others.

Covering an area of about thirty-five acres the campus contains thirty buildings and faculty homes. Able to accommodate four hundred students, it is a well-contained college, the distinctive features of which are "The Brenau College Plan of Education for Women," and the national sororities that occupy college-owned houses. Brenau's student body usually has representatives from most of the states in the Union and a number of foreign countries.

To reach the RIVERSIDE MILITARY ACADEMY, at Brenau College take Pryor St. to the City Park, turn left here to N. Green St., then right on N. Green St. a bit to Morningside Drive which runs into Riverside Drive; continue on Riverside Drive to the Academy. Founded in 1907 as a military school, its twelve buildings, most of them of red brick in the Gothic style, are on a 250-acre campus near a bend of the Chattahoochee River. Students are at Gainesville during the spring and fall, but in the winter months the student body moves to the Florida campus near Miami, thus benefiting from the best seasons of both climates. Academic work meets the requirements of the Southern Association of Colleges and Secondary Schools. With an average enrollment of 500 students, the school is non-sectarian and has a self-perpetuating board of trustees.

The FACTORY OF THE CHICOPEE MANUFACTURING CORPORATION (R), 74 m., established in 1927, is a subsidiary of Johnson and Johnson, manufacturing tobacco cloth and a gauze used in surgical dressings. According to a report from the Gainesville Chamber of Commerce, it employs around 650 persons and is the third large textile plant of the area. The mill village is outstanding among communities of this sort and is widely known as a model of the planned center. Designed by landscape architects and engineers, the physical exhibit of the village is strikingly neat.

FLOWERY BRANCH, 80.5 m. (1,122 alt., 610 pop.), built along the highway, is the site of a furniture manufacturing plant. A green frame building (L) houses the HIGH ACRES MOUNTAIN GUILD (*open to visitors*), weavers of hand-woven rugs, place mats, and bags, from cotton waste products obtained from cotton mills; and of both rayon and nylon place mats and hand bags from the waste products of garment makers. Rugs special in either color or design or size are made to order. The Guild also carries a wide stock of other gift items, not made by its workers. A story is told of a Georgia woman who upon examining a bag sent by a friend from Holland, found tucked inside of it the trade-mark of the Guild. Whether fact or fancy, the story indicates something of the industry's shipping range.

The BUFORD DAM RESERVOIR AREA will when completed be contained by a section between—roughly—Cornelia, Dahlonega, and Buford, with the dam at BUFORD (1,205 alt., 3,812 pop.), in Gwinnett County. A part of the system authorized by the River and Harbor Act of July 24, 1946, the Buford Project is intended principally to serve the following neotechnic ends: to provide flood protection for the valley below it, to increase the flow for navigation in the Apalachicola River in low seasons, to generate hydroelectric power—estimated at 154,800,000 kilowatt hours of energy in a normal year, and to assure an adequate water supply to meet the municipal and industrial needs of metropolitan Atlanta. Ground was broken to start the project in March of 1950, but though the work is considerably advanced, the dam itself has not yet been actually set. With the completion of the dam, the Chattahoochee River may have less of Lanier's headstrong music in it, but it will have as compensation the rhythmical hum of the electric meter as its energy flows into modern industrial enterprises.

According to a folder from the U. S. Army's Corps of Engineers—who are in charge of the technical construction—in addition to its industrial utility the Buford Lake Area will offer a complex of recreational developments for the people. Studies are now under way by the Engineers in co-operation with the National Park Service, the U. S. Fish and Wildlife Service, the U. S. Public Health Service, and the State of Georgia, to determine the best use of the area for overnight camps, picnic grounds, and other recreational facilities. Near Cartersville the Allatoona Dam Reservoir Area (*see* TOUR 2) is already a telling example of what Federal and state agencies can do to enrich the leisure hours of the people. If wisely ordered, the use of nature need not be the mutilation of nature.

ATLANTA, *118.4 m.* (1,050 alt., 331,314 pop.) (*see* ATLANTA).

Points of Interest: State Capitol, Georgia School of Technology, Emory University, Oglethorpe University, Atlanta University (Negro), Cyclorama of the Battle of Atlanta, and others.

Atlanta is at the junction with US 41 (*see* TOUR 2), with US 19 (*see* TOUR 6), with US 29 (*see* TOUR 3), and with US 78 (*see* TOUR 8).

TOUR 7A

Cornelia—Toccoa—(Greenville, S. C.); US 123, State 13

Cornelia to South Carolina Line, 25.9 m.—Southern Ry. parallels route—Limited accommodations.

US 123, State 13, leads through the foothills of the Blue Ridge. Fair timberlands of pine and oak are broken by small farms, with patches of cotton, corn, and vegetables growing on the steep hillsides. In recent years important educational institutions have been established in this neighborhood and tourists have made the section a popular summer resort. The Yonah development of the Georgia Power Company is immediately north of Toccoa.

US 123 branches east from US 23 (*see* TOUR 7) in CORNELIA, *0 m.* (1,537 alt., 2,424 pop.).

From a point at approximately *14.7 m.* CURRAHEE (Ind., standing alone) MOUNTAIN (1,740 alt.), an outlying peak of the Blue Ridge chain, can be seen in the distance (L).

TOCCOA, *17.7* (1,094 alt., 6,781 pop.), seat of Stephens County, is a prosperous mountain town, incorporated in 1875. Toccoa serves as a trading center for the surrounding farm and orchard area. Participating in the programs of the State Extension Service, the county has both farm and home demonstration agents as well as offices in Toccoa of the Farm Security Administration, the Stephens County Conservation Association, and the Soil Conservation Service, which are all signs of an alert agricultural progress. With some twenty-three industrial plants, there is a wide range of manufactured products such as furniture, thread, earth-moving equipment, metal furniture, playground equipment, garments, chenille bedspreads, lumber, and stone.

The town has a large swimming pool and recreational area with all types of outdoor games supervised by the Stephens Youth Service Council. Camp Mikell, a summer camp sponsored by the Episcopal Church, is located about six miles north of Toccoa. The Le Tourneau Airport, one mile east of Toccoa, provides runways and hangar accommodations. With lights for night use, the east-west runway is 3,200 feet and the northeast-southwest runway is 2,700 feet; work is in progress to lengthen the latter to 5,000 feet.

The COOL SPRINGS PICNIC AREA is a small but popular one located on the Forest Development Road to Black Mountain Tower about eight miles north of Toccoa. It has a picnic area, a good spring, two shelters with tables, individual picnic units with tables and fireplaces, toilets, and a garbage pit. It is maintained by the U. S. Forest Service of the Chattahoochee National Forest.

1. Left from Toccoa on State 17 to the junction *1 m.* to a road which winds among low hills; L. on this road to TOCCOA FALLS INSTITUTE, *1.4 m.,* an accredited four-year high school for boys and girls, and four-year Bible College. It was founded in 1911 as a nonsectarian institution by the Reverend R. A. Forrest, a Presbyterian minister, and in 1950 had a student body numbering 400 and a staff of 35. The school has some sixty buildings in all and is surrounded by a 1,100-acre tract of land, part of which serves as a farm and dairy to supply student needs. Vocational courses include training in wood shop, machine shop,

electrical and sheet-metal work practices, and in commercial skills; also home economics, farm and dairy practices. The school is practically a self-sustaining community as it has its own powerhouse, dairy, post office, telephone system, laundry, and infirmary. An exceptional number of mountain plants grow in the area around the school.

Near the Institute is TOCCOA FALLS, on the school property; it cascades in a lace-like veil of mist over a precipice 186 feet high. A path leads to the rock wall behind the falls, and another follows a rustic stairway to the top, which affords a view of Toccoa and the surrounding country. Below the falls the ravine through which the creek flows is banked with masses of fern, brightened in spring by rhododendron and mountain laurel.

2. Left from Toccoa on the unpaved Prather Road to the PRATHER HOUSE (*private*), 6 *m.*, one of the three houses that Devereaux Jarrett, who came to north Georgia from Virginia and accumulated a large amount of property, built about 1850 for his children. The two-story, hip-roofed white clapboard house, crowning a hill that overlooks the Tugalo River, has a wide porch with square white columns on the front and two sides. A small, balustraded balcony overhangs a Palladian doorway. In this house General Robert Toombs (*see* TOUR 8), Secretary of State for the Confederacy, took refuge on his flight from Union soldiers after the downfall of the Confederacy. Hidden by his friend, Major Joseph Prather, he was not discovered, and was able to escape to Europe. He returned and died without having taken the oath of allegiance to the United States.

At *24.1 m.* is the junction with the unpaved River Road.

Left on this road to JARRETT MANOR, a large, two-story frame house (R) built in 1775 by Jesse Walton. Soon afterward the Walton family, with the exception of one member, was massacred by Indians. The house was then bought by James R. Wylie, who sold it to Devereaux Jarrett about 1800; it has since remained in the possession of the Jarrett family. For a number of years before the War between the States, the manor was used as an inn on a stagecoach route and was called Travelers' Rest.

Measuring 100 feet across the front, the house is flanked by massive end chimneys, one of brick and the other of stone, and has twin flights of stone steps leading to the low, columned porch. Despite the fact that its hand-hewn clapboards have never been painted, the house is well preserved.

The interior is so constructed that the rooms open one into another without a central hallway, and each of the three front rooms opens directly on the porch. In the basement the old kitchen has a flagstone floor and a large fireplace, and in the attic there are slits used by early occupants to fire on Indian intruders. Handmade tables, beds, and cupboards show sensitive carving, and English locks bear the royal crown and crest; relics include a powder horn, candle molds, snuffers, and saddlebags that belonged to George Jarrett, and records of the family real estate and business transactions bearing the names of George Walton, Robert Toombs, Alexander Stephens, and Jefferson Davis.

US 123 crosses the Tugalo River, *25.9 m.*, about 61 miles west of Greenville, South Carolina.

TOUR 8

(Aiken, S. C.)—Augusta—Washington—Athens—Monroe—
Atlanta—Villa Rica—Tallapoosa—(Heflin, Ala.); US 78.

South Carolina Line to Alabama Line, 242 m.—Georgia R.R. parallels route between Augusta and Thomson; Seaboard Air Line Ry. between Athens and junction with US 29; Southern Ry. between Atlanta and Alabama Line—All types of accommodations in cities; limited elsewhere.

Section a. SOUTH CAROLINA LINE *to* ATLANTA, *174.7 m., US 78.*

US 78 crosses the low, red-clay hills of the Piedmont Plateau, where fields of corn and cotton are separated by forest tracts. This upper portion of Georgia's broad cotton belt was once divided into large plantations, and in Washington and Athens there are still many ante-bellum houses with typical columns. Even when shabby they have a nostalgic beauty in their settings of magnolia trees, boxwood, and flowers.

Stone Mountain with its colossal but unfinished Confederate Memorial is on this route.

US 78 crosses the SAVANNAH RIVER, *0 m.,* the boundary between South Carolina and Georgia, 17 miles southwest of Aiken, South Carolina.

AUGUSTA, *0.5 m.* (143 alt., 71,508 pop.), *(see* AUGUSTA).

Points of Interest: The Hill, University of Georgia School of Medicine, Junior College of Augusta, Paine College (Negro), Haines Institute (Negro), Cotton Exchange.

Augusta is at the junction with US 25 *(see* TOUR *15)* and with US 1 *(see* TOUR *4).*

HARLEM, *23.1 m.* (542 alt., 1,033 pop.), is the junction with State 47, paved.

Right on State 47 to Appling, *10.2 m.* (263 alt., 300 pop.), the seat of agricultural Columbia County, laid out in 1790. In front of the courthouse is the GRAVE OF DANIEL MARSHALL, an Anabaptist missionary who baptized many converts and established several churches.

Right from Appling on a dirt road *(difficult in bad weather)* to the junction with a country road, *10.9 m.* on this road to another junction, *12.6 m.;* L. on this road to a third junction, *12.8 m.;* R. on this to old KIOKEE CHURCH, *13.3 m.,* a square building of handmade brick with rough stone steps. It was erected in 1772 for the congregation of the Anabaptist Church of the Kiokee, organized that year by Daniel Marshall and incorporated in 1789. The interior, with its hand-hewn pews and gallery, has the austerity of the pioneer house of worship.

The Anabaptists were a religious sect that arose in Zurich around 1521 among the followers of Zwingli. They asserted principally: that infant baptism had no basis in Scripture and was without effect, that the church was composed of only

Library Building, Wesleyan College, Macon

Indian Mound, Ocmulgee National Monument, Macon

The Owen-Thomas House, Savannah

Entrance Gate to historic Wormsloe Plantation near Savannah

Moat surrounding historic Fort Pulaski, Cockspur Island near Savannah

Oaks and Spanish Moss in Bonaventure Cemetery, Savannah

View of Savannah Plant of the Union Bag and Paper Corporation

Savannah State Docks and Warehouses

Tybee Lighthouse at Fort Screven near Savannah

Midway Church, the fourth on the site, built in 1792

Old Rice Mill at Darien

the saints; *i.e.,* of those who were true Christians, having been baptized strictly on confession of faith, and that there should be no union of church and state; and hence, no interference by the state in church affairs. When, in conformity with an act of 1758 establishing the Church of England as official, Marshall was indicted, he defended himself so effectively that he was released, and continued his work unmolested until his death in 1784.

THOMSON, *36.2 m.* (540 alt., 3,489 pop.), seat of McDuffie County since 1879, was incorporated in 1820 and named for J. Edgar Thomson, a Philadelphia engineer who surveyed the route of the Georgia Railroad. The chief products are cotton, corn, crates, barrels, pine timber, and textiles.

HICKORY HILL (*private*), about two blocks L. from the Methodist Church (R), is the former estate of Thomas E. Watson. From the main gateway a walk leads past a circular lily pool to the house, set in a deep grove of trees, many of which Watson selected himself and had planted. Four fluted white columns with Ionic capitals support the roof of the gabled pediment; above the ornate recessed doorway is a small balcony, and an open veranda runs around almost three sides of the house. The house was erected soon after the War between the States and in 1900 was bought by Watson, who added the Greek portico. The house of his grandfather, Thomas Miles Watson, where Watson was born, is some three miles outside the town. "It did not in the least," he said, "resemble a Grecian Temple which had been sent into exile, and which was striving unsuccessfully to look at ease among corn-cribs, cowpens, horse-stables, pig-sties, chicken-houses, Negro cabins, and worm-fenced cotton fields." But when he chose his own house, it was Greek Revival in style, or at least he made it so. Consistency, however, is commonly owned to be the virtue of small minds while paradox is the first principle of genius.

Born in 1856 and living until 1922, Watson was a controlling factor in Georgia politics for a quarter of a century. A man of positive character and entirely articulate, he inspired an intense devotion in his partisans and an equally measured hatred in his opponents. Although the shadow that he cast in Georgia's political forum has recently grown less defined—like an old Brady photograph, still politicians today prefer not to be visited by the ghost of Caesar on the eve of battle.

Embittered by a defeat that he attributed to a false count, Watson withdrew from the Democratic party and became identified with the Agrarian movement, fostering the county unit system of voting in Georgia to assure protection to rural interests. The farmers whose cause he championed were inveterate readers of his *Weekly Jeffersonian,* though in its pages the idiom carried more of the image of

Jackson than it did of Mr. Jefferson. In 1890 he was elected to the
U. S. Congress, where he advocated the use of automatic couplers on
railroad cars; and introduced the first resolution for rural free delivery,
thus bringing Sears, Roebuck to rural areas—an act that had deeper
economic significance than has perhaps been recognized. In 1896 Watson was a candidate for vice president of the United States on the Populist party ticket with William Jennings Bryan; in 1904 he entered the
campaign for president on the same ticket. He died while serving in
the U. S. Senate, to which he had been elected on the Democratic
ticket in 1920.

Perhaps the most judicious and at the same time interesting book
about Watson is C. Vann Woodward's *Tom Watson: Agrarian Rebel,*
published in 1938.

At 58.7 m. is the junction with State 47, hard-surfaced.

Right on this road to SMYRNA CHURCH (Methodist, but originally Presbyterian),
4 m., one of the oldest congregations in the state. In February, 1793, John
Talbot deeded two acres of land to the congregation, and a frame building was
built shortly afterwards, the second of this locale. The present church was built
in 1910.

Right from Smyrna Church on the Old Augusta Road to a point at *1 m.;* R.
from the road about *0.3 m.* in the woods to the GRAVE OF ABRAHAM SIMONS, a
Jewish Revolutionary soldier. In 1827 his widow, Nancy Mills Simons, married
the Reverend Jesse Mercer and used the Simons' fortune to establish Mercer
University, a Baptist institution in Macon.

At *5 m.* on State 47 is MOUNT PLEASANT (*private*), once part of the John Talbot
plantation. The two-story frame house, built about 1790, has its four original end
chimneys. Sold to Thomas P. Burdette in 1857, it is now owned by his son
J. L. Burdette.

Not more than fifty feet left of the house is a two-room, barnlike structure,
ELI WHITNEY'S WORKSHOP, which was moved from the Miller-Whitney plantation.
One way or another John Lyon began to manufacture the cotton gin in Columbia
County, but after lengthy and expensive litigation, Whitney's prior claim was
established.

An old plantation road leads from Mount Pleasant to the adjoining MILLER-
WHITNEY PLANTATION, where the Eli Whitney workshop stood up to 1810 when
it was moved to its present site. After inventing the cotton gin in 1793, Whitney
formed a partnership to manufacture the "cotton engines" with Phineas Miller,
who tutored General Nathanael Greene's children and later married his widow
(*see* TOUR *14*). In 1796 Miller bought 822 acres of land so that Whitney might
perfect his model in seclusion. Here the inventor built his workshop, perfected
his machine, and established the first public gin. He made machines for cotton
growers on a royalty basis, but Georgia planters, angered by the high 33⅓ per
cent toll, preferred to get their gins from those who had appropriated Whitney's
ideas.

In 1811 the Wilkes Manufacturing Company built on this land a two-story
unit for the manufacturing of cotton cloth. Bolton's Factory, as it was then
known, was one of the first textile plants established in the South.

WASHINGTON, 60.7 m. (618 alt., 3,802 pop.), was laid out in 1780. The first town in the nation to be incorporated as Washington, it was for a time the principal town in the upcountry north of Augusta. Many fine old houses and the tree-shaded streets give this town an air of established tradition.

Actually, the history of Wilkes County reaches well back to 1773 when settlers began to arrive from Virginia, North Carolina, and South Carolina. When the British occupied Savannah and Augusta, Stephen Heard, for a time Acting Governor of the state, moved both the state documents and the State Seal to his home, Heard's Fort, for safekeeping, so that for an interval at least, it served in effect as the capital of the state. Among the distinguished names associated with the county are those of Stephen Heard, Elijah Clark, Nancy Hart, Jesse Mercer, Micajah Williamson, Robert Toombs, Alexander Stephens, and John Archibald Campbell, a list extending from the Revolution to the War between the States.

In the last decade the agricultural economy of the area has changed over from cotton and general cropping to grasslands and livestock. At present some 20,000 acres of established pasture contribute to the production of meat, milk, and other livestock products. Begun as recently as 1950, the Wilkes County Stockyard now has an annual sales-average of $1,750,000, representing the returns from around 15,000 head of cattle and about 5,000 head of hogs. As a result of the Norman Plan, introduced by Colonel Earle Norman of Washington-Wilkes, any qualified boy or girl can own purebred stock. Because of the extensive forest and in the interest of improved lumbering, the county has three fire towers and also fire-fighting equipment, with a County Forest Ranger in charge of the conservation program. The area is unusually rich in hardwood: sycamore, gum, yellow poplar, beech, oak, walnut, cherry, cottonwood, and basswood. Indifferently encouraged in the past, industry in late years has begun to grow, and includes, among others, such manufactured products as garments, processed milk and derivatives, plastic raincoats, and a well-known candy. When completed, the Clark Hill Dam power project by increasing the power potential should accelerate this development.

In addition to a nine-hole golf course, the Country Club, located on a 109-acre tract, has a pleasant lake for swimming, boating, and fishing. The surrounding countryside offers a wealth of opportunity for hunting and fishing.

US 78 passes along the main thoroughfare, and even though passing through briefly, one cannot fail to recognize from the character of the old houses along the way how much of Georgia history has a local habitation here. A more leisurely survey is even more rewarding.

US 78 enters E. Robert Toombs Avenue by the Wilkes Motel (L), passes on to Main Street which is continuous with the Avenue, and leaves on the Lexington Road R. of a small triangular park.

The BARNETT-SLATON HOUSE, set well back (L) from the street (just past the Wilkes Motel), in an informal grove, was built in 1820. A two-story frame house with a broad, one-story porch, it was later occupied by Samuel Barnett, who served as railroad commissioner of Georgia in 1879. When Woodrow Wilson's father came to Washington on occasion as visiting pastor to the Presbyterian church, small Woodrow often came with him to stay a few days with the Barnetts.

The ROBERT TOOMBS HOUSE (*private*), Robert Toombs Ave. (L), erected between 1794 and 1801, was bought and remodeled by Robert Toombs in 1837. Two-story Doric columns define the broad front porch, and French windows open into cool, high-ceiled rooms where the appointments remain much as they were in the 1860's.

The house is easily identified by Toombs Oak, a large, gnarled tree around which the paved sidewalk curves in a semicircle. This is the tree from which it is said Union troops vainly hoped to hang the fiery general, who is often called the unreconstructed rebel.

Robert Augustus Toombs (1810-85), statesman, orator, and military officer, was born in Wilkes County and later made his home in Washington. According to Medora Perkerson in *White Columns in Georgia,* "At the University of Georgia he had rebelled against the too-strict discipline of the time and had not been allowed to graduate. There is a legend that he delivered an address under an oak tree outside the chapel, attracting more visitors than the commencement exercise inside. The tree, now dead, was ever afterward called the Toombs Oak. Toombs was later graduated from Union College in New York and studied law at the University of Virginia. Many years later the University of Georgia offered him a degree which it was his pleasure to decline." After a number of terms in the Georgia Legislature, in 1844 he was elected to the U. S. House of Representatives, where he was influential in passing the compromise acts of 1850 that did much to quiet the southern unrest arising from the Wilmot Proviso. In 1853 he became a United States senator. As the War between the States came on, he declared for secession. Appointed Secretary of State of the Confederacy, he resigned in 1861 after a short term of service to become commander of a Georgia brigade in Virginia, and distinguished himself for bravery at Antietam. After the War had ended, General Toombs, refusing to swear allegiance to the Union, escaped to New Orleans, and became a refugee in London. Returning to Washington in 1867, he rebuilt his law practice and fought for the maintenance of popular rights. He dominated the legislative conference of 1877 that repudiated the carpetbag rule and revised the state constitution.

Toombs was a master of spoken words with a sharp gift for making effective phrases. His warm and happy disposition gained many friends over the nation as well as in his home town. His home was seldom without guests. After the War when there was a movement to build a hotel in Washington, he indignantly opposed it, saying, "If a respectable man comes to town, he can stay at my house. If he isn't respectable, we don't want him here."

The MARIA RANDOLPH-COLLEY HOUSE (L) corner of Poplar Drive, has a two-columned Doric porch with a pilastered front door. The duplicate door above opens to an iron-railed balcony. On each side of the entrance hall are two large rooms, and the hall leads to a ballroom extending the entire length of the house.

The PRESBYTERIAN CHURCH (L), 312 Robert Toombs Ave., more New England than southern in appearance, was built in 1825 under the leadership of Alexander Hamilton Webster of Connecticut who had come to Washington to teach in the Academy. Quaint features of the church are the balustrade around the organ in the back of the church and the early pulpit lamp.

The HOME OF MRS. SARAH HILLHOUSE (*private*), opposite the Presbyterian Church, is a white frame house of two stories with a long porch flanked by wings, each containing one room. Set back from the street, the house is almost hidden among large magnolia trees. Following her husband after his death in 1804 as the editor of the *Washington Monitor,* Sarah Hillhouse, who once lived here, was the first woman newspaper editor in the South.

The ALEXANDER HOUSE (*private*)—turn R. on N. Alexander Ave. and continue past the Woman's Club (begun around 1787 by the Revolutionary soldier, Colonel Micajah Williamson) one-half block to a paved lane (R)—is a two-story brick building of common bond with an entrance in the gable end and Palladian window. Built in 1808 by Felix and William Gilbert of Virginia, it is one of the oldest brick houses north of Augusta.

The PRESBYTERIAN POPLAR, on the Alexander estate, is what remains of a once magnificent poplar tree, originally large enough to hide a man on horseback. John Springer, the first Presbyterian minister to be ordained on Georgia soil, was ordained under this tree on July 22, 1790.

The THOMAS WINGFIELD HOUSE (*private*), on State 17, was built in the 1790's by Thomas Wingfield of Virginia. The house (R) set on broad grounds, is an excellent example of Greek Revival architecture, with wide porches and tall Doric columns. Enclosing the front yard is a white picket fence, and in the rear the slave quarters of the early 1800's stand much as they were in that period.

The THOMAS HOLLEY CHIVERS TREE, 200 Chapman St. at the end of S. Alexander Ave., was planted by Chivers, Georgia's neglected poet, who was a friend of Edgar Allan Poe. The Chivers family home was five miles out from town, but a sister of Thomas Chivers lived where the holly, now of unusual size, was planted.

The LINDSEY HOUSE (*private*), 212 Liberty St. and S. Alexander Ave., has a Doric colonnade and a hanging balcony which also extends around the house, which is actually two houses combined into one, with two identical front doors. This was once the home of Duncan G. Campbell who drafted the treaty covering the removal of the Cherokee Indians from Georgia, and who introduced an early bill in the Legislature advocating higher education for women. His son John Archibald Campbell was a Supreme Court Justice from 1853 to 1861.

The MARY WILLIS MEMORIAL LIBRARY (*open 11-1, 3-6 daily*), at the intersection of Liberty and Jefferson, opened in 1889 as the first free public library serving both town and county alike. It was presented to Washington and to Wilkes County by Dr. Frank Willis as a memorial to his only daughter.

The WILKES COUNTY COURTHOUSE, on the N. side of the Public Square, was built in 1904 on the approximate site of the old Heard house, where Jefferson Davis held the last cabinet meeting of the Confederacy on May 5, 1865. On the second floor of the courthouse the local chapter of the United Daughters of the Confederacy maintains a museum of war relics, including the camp chest used by Jefferson Davis and a uniform and trunk that belonged to General Toombs.

On the courthouse grounds is a granite boulder on which the John Nelson land grant is recorded, which is the oldest grant in the county; and also the capstone from Bolton's Factory (*see* above), established in 1811 on Upton's Creek.

The WASHINGTON MARKET, W. Robert Toombs Ave., (L), is on the site of an early inn. Underneath are the hand-hewn timbers, old burnt brick, massive beams of the inn, and the rock vault with a heavy iron door and an outsized lock where the gold and mail pouches were deposited for the stagecoach. Washington still had stagecoach service until 1870, though the railroad arrived in 1850.

The TUPPER-BARNETT HOUSE, W. Robert Toombs Ave. (R), opposite the bus station, has a two-story Doric colonnade around the building—eighteen columns in all—and a graceful, divided stairway to the main entrance. The daylight basement floor served in part as a kitchen and in part as an office for the cotton business, while the second and third floors served as the residence. This was the home of Dr. Henry Allen Tupper, grandfather of the wife of General George Marshall. Dr. Tupper was pastor of the Baptist Church for twenty years and during that time sent his salary to the Baptist Mission Board.

The BARCLAY POPLAR, beyond the Baptist Church (R), is said to be the one on which Polly Barclay, the first woman to be hanged in Georgia, was executed May 30, 1806, for shooting her husband. The local story is that she rode to the scene wearing a silk dress and sitting on her coffin. Such a story deserves a good ballad, in any case.

The PEMBROKE POPE HOUSE (*private*), W. Robert Toombs Ave., is a handsome Greek Revival building (R) with large Doric columns. It is one of the few inland houses to have the "widow's walk" common to the coast. Inside a closet of the older portion of the house is the date 1818. The extensive gardens embrace the SITE OF HAYWOOD (R. of the house), the birthplace of Eliza Frances Andrews (1840-1931), botanist, educator, author—the first woman ever elected to the International Academy of Science. She was the author of the *War Time Diary of a Georgia Girl*.

ST. JOSEPH'S HOME FOR BOYS (L), on an elevated site at the convergence of W. Robert Toombs Ave. and Lexington Ave., is a Roman Catholic orphanage built on the estate of Jesse Mercer, the Baptist Minister who published *The Christian Index* from 1832 to 1840 and after whom Mercer University was named. The frame house facing the highway is the old Mercer home, and next to it is a modern red brick building that serves the orphan boys of the Savannah-Atlanta diocese. At the front is a small triangular plot called Mercer Park.

The IRVIN-ORR HOUSE, on Lexington Road (R), some distance back from the road, its white Corinthian columns partly screened by oak and magnolia, was the home of the Irvin family. Young Lieutenant Irvin was primarily responsible for General Toombs' eventual escape from the Union forces that sought to take him by surprise in his home.

LEXINGTON, 85.2 m. (756 alt., 514 pop.), seat of Oglethorpe County, was incorporated in 1806 and named for the town in Massachusetts. Three governors of Georgia—George Mathews (1793-96), Wilson Lumpkin (1831-35), and George R. Gilmer (1829-31 and 1837-39)—were from this county.

The LUMPKIN HOUSE (*private*), on the eastern edge of the town, is the old home of Joseph Henry and Wilson Lumpkin, brothers who became prominent in state politics during the nineteenth century and were co-founders of the Lumpkin Law School, now a part of the University of Georgia. Atlanta was first named Marthasville in honor of

Governor Lumpkin's daughter Martha. Joseph Lumpkin was first chief justice of the Georgia Supreme Court.

The PRESBYTERIAN CHURCH, one block R. from the highway, serves what is believed to be the oldest Presbyterian congregation in the Synod of Georgia. The original church, known as Bethsalem, was organized in 1785 two miles from town. When the church was moved to Lexington in 1822, the members erected on this site a white frame building that was replaced by the present one in 1896.

Across the street from the church is the old PRESBYTERIAN MANSE where the Reverend Thomas Goulding, the father of Francis Goulding, conducted the first classes of Columbia Theological Seminary during his ministry of the church. Later the school was moved to Columbia, South Carolina, and in 1927 it was established on its present site in Decatur (*see* TOUR *3*).

In the outskirts of Lexington, two blocks L. from the courthouse, is the old GEORGE R. GILMER HOME (*private*). Gilmer was twice governor of Georgia; during his second administration the Cherokee were finally moved to lands west of the Mississippi River. The house, set far back from the road in a grove of cedars, oaks, and cherry laurels, and known as The Cedars, is a two-story white clapboard structure with a Doric-columned portico fronting upon the garden. The main part of the house was built about 1800, and the two-story wing added in 1840 when Gilmer bought the place.

CRAWFORD, *88.2 m.* (approx. 757 alt., 555 pop.), named for the Georgia statesman William H. Crawford, developed around the railroad station intended to serve Lexington, whose citizens had objected to the noise and smoke of the locomotives. The CRAWFORD MEMORIAL (R), next to the railroad station, is a granite shaft presented to the town by Colonel Charles J. Haden, of Athens, and unveiled in 1933.

The SITE OF WOODLAWN (R), *88.8 m.*, was Crawford's old plantation home during the latter half of his life. The house, built by him in 1804, burned down in 1936 at the time the Crawford Memorial Association was planning to make it the center of a memorial park. In a plot at this site, enclosed by a stone wall is the GRAVE OF WILLIAM H. CRAWFORD (1772-1834).

He was a United States Senator, Minister to France, Secretary of War under Madison, Secretary of the Treasury under Monroe, and a leading Democratic-Republican candidate for the presidency in 1824. A kindly but sternly righteous man, he fought two duels in the 1800's in confirmation of his principles. President Monroe visited him at Woodlawn in 1819, when, it is said, they discussed the policies which led to the formulation of the Monroe Doctrine. After a stroke of paralysis, Crawford retired from public life and practiced law in Lexington.

CHEROKEE CORNER (R), 93 m., was so named because here the boundary line between the Cherokee and the Creek lands formed an angle from which distances were reckoned. So the situation stood in the survey of 1773, when much of their land was possessed by the white people. Behind the old Methodist Church is the Cherokee Corner Marker.

ATHENS, 101.8 m. (705 alt., 28,180 pop.), (see ATHENS).

Points of Interest: University of Georgia, ante-bellum homes, and others.

Athens is at the junction with US 129 (see TOUR 16) and with US 29 (see TOUR 3), which unites with US 78 for about ten miles.

MONROE, 129.2 m. (910 alt., 4,542 pop.), seat of Walton County, was incorporated on November 30, 1821. Walton County is primarily agricultural, much of the prosperity of the area being due directly to the well-organized county agricultural program. Annually an agricultural prospectus formulated by farmers, businessmen, and technical experts is promoted by the Walton County Farm Bureau and the Walton County Agricultural Program. In 1952, for example, the program embraced cotton, dairy feed, feed crops and pastures, diversified farming —poultry, hogs, beef cattle, pimiento peppers, sweet potatoes, truck farming, and seed—soil erosion control, the home and health, and recreation. The production of turkeys has grown from a sale of $36,-000 for 6,000 in 1945 to $150,000 for 35,000 in 1951. But cotton remains the basic cash-crop, with a census of some twenty thousand bales in 1951 resulting in a sales-figure of around four and one-half millions.

Monroe itself offers many of the advantages ordinarily found in a town of much larger size; for not only does it serve as a trade center for the agricultural area surrounding it but also includes a sizable list of industries. Ground has recently been broken for an extensive health center, and the city maintains a recreational program, with a full-time director and assistant. Two Federal Housing projects at a cost of $700,-000 have been completed, and all of the town's streets are being resurfaced. Among the larger industries are the Walton Cotton Mill, with around 600 workers, and the Monroe Cotton Mills, with some 400. The Carwood Manufacturing Co., makers of coats, and the Southeastern Garment Co., manufacturers of sportswear, make up another list of 200 employees between them. In addition there are around twenty additional industries of greater and less size.

Monroe and Walton County have long been known for their high rating in the production of cotton. In recognition of this record the National Cotton Council recently chose Walton County to introduce the Cotton Festival. At the local Festival held annually around August 1, a Maid of Cotton is chosen to represent the county in the state competition, and a Junior Maid for home rule. The festivities also include a parade with floats, and a barbecue and dance.

The HOME OF HENRY D. McDANIEL (*private*), McDaniel St., is a large red brick house with classic portico. McDaniel was a captain in the Confederate army and a governor of the state (1883-86).

Adjoining the grounds of the McDaniel house is the SELMAN HOUSE, a notable example of Greek Revival architecture, built in the early 1800's by Walter Briscoe, a pioneer settler. The original front stoop has been replaced by a wide porch extending across the front and along two sides. Above the main entrance is a small balcony, and the doorways on both levels are surmounted by shapely fanlights. Overhanging mimosa and black locust trees border the winding walk leading to the house.

STONE MOUNTAIN (1,686 alt.), *158.4 m.*, is the largest exposed granite dome (L) in North America. Rising 650 feet above the surrounding Piedmont Plateau, the mountain is two miles long, has a circumference of more than seven miles at the base, and is estimated to weigh 1,250,-000,000 tons, although geologists surmise that the visible mass is only a fraction of the whole formation. Its gray, almost bare, elliptical surface is of a greenish hue because of the resident moss and lichen on the surface.

According to the calculations of the geologists, Stone Mountain took form about two hundred million years ago as a subterranean molten mass, and its gradual appearance above the earth's surface has resulted from erosion. Running through the dome in two principal directions and giving the surface a streaked appearance are crevices formed probably by the contraction of the molten mass when it began to cool. The sides have been streaked by iron oxide and organic matter carried down by rain water from the top.

Before Georgia was settled, Stone Mountain had been used as a signal tower by the Indians of the section. In 1790 Alexander McGillivray, a Creek chief of white and Indian parentage, met here the tribesmen who were to go with him to New York to parley with government officials. By 1825, however, white settlers had a stagecoach terminus at the mountain and a hotel at the western base. The locale became a popular resort, and before 1842 Cloud's Tower, 165 feet high, was erected on the summit to afford a broader view of the surrounding country. The mountain was in the possession of first one owner and then another, but in 1887 it was acquired by Samuel Hoyt Venable and other members of Venable Brothers, who quarried the granite for use in the construction of bridges, buildings, and roadways. In the 1920's the Ku Klux Klan held state-wide conclaves on top of the mountain, and there have been sporadic exhibitions since on a lesser scale, when fissures in public morality have allowed this disorder in the body civil to escape from quarantine.

The unfinished figure of Robert E. Lee on his horse Traveller measures 130 feet from the crown of his hat to the horses hoof, approximately the height of a ten-story building. Appearing in rough outline are the head of Jefferson Davis (L) and that of Stonewall Jackson (R). Tons of granite removed during the carving, and serving in some sort as a measure of the immense amount of labor involved, form a ridge at the base of the work.

Across the road from the memorial is a small museum, where information may be had, and souvenirs are sold. The museum contains a model of the project and plaster molds of some of the figures, including those of Lee, Jackson, and Davis. An inspection of these working models reveals some of the knotty technical problems that the sculptors had to unravel. Against a background so vast the figures needed to be of gigantic size and required an appreciable change of scale from head to foot, since the feet are so much nearer the spectator's eye.

In 1915 a movement began to assume definition among the membership of the United Daughters of the Confederacy to invite Gutzon Borglum (1871-1941) to consider the practicability of carving on the mountain a memorial figure of General Robert E. Lee. Gutzon Borglum was trained both at home and in London and Paris where he was much influenced by Rodin. A man with an imagination on the heroic level, his technique of expression tended more towards the pictorial in sculpture than the plastic. Among other notable works, he did the *Sheridan Monument* in Washington, the *Lincoln Monument* in Newark, and the *Apostles* in New York's Cathedral of St. John the Divine, though doubtless he is generally best known for his titanic portraits of Washington, Jefferson, Lincoln, and Theodore Roosevelt carved on Mount Rushmore, South Dakota.

Borglum, challenged by the complex of technical skills needed to cope with such a mass of stone, as well as urged on by his heroic bent, agreed to undertake the project, but suggested something more in proportion with the bulk of the mountain than a single figure of Lee. The temper of his intention can be seen from this part of his report: "It seems to me that the only fitting memorial to the South of 1861-65 by the equally great South of today, is to reconstruct as best we can the great characters of those days, and in colossal proportions, carve them in high and full relief, in action, mounted and on foot, moving across the granite mountain in the arrangement of two wings of an army, following the mountain contour, moving naturally across its face to the East. These figures should be in scale with the mountain; they must be visible and easily read for miles; and their likeness must be recognized and maintained. The groupings represent the official heads of the South—officers, cavalry, artillery, and infantry."

As with Michelangelo, Borglum's artistic courage impelled him to seek for nothing less than the archetypes of eternity in his material, except that where Michelangelo attempted to educe them from the realm of God and the angels and to express them in images from the Scriptures, Borglum undertook to unfold from a mountain a multitude of persons and events like a stream in full flood. Speaking of the scope of the design, his wife Mary Borglum says, "Beginning on the right of the precipice near its top, and sweeping downward and across, were the Confederate armies mobilizing around their leaders. Above were artillery appearing at the summit as if coming from beyond, and dropping down over to the left across the precipice in the lifelike procession of men, guns, and horses. On the left of these were the cavalry in full motion, while in the center, where the cliff bulged outward, was the colossal group, 200 feet in height, representing the principal chieftains of the Confederacy, among them Robert E. Lee, Stonewall Jackson and the President of the Confederacy, Jefferson Davis. Swinging away to the left were the columns of the Confederate infantry." From the beginning this full-crested sea of poetry did not conform evenly with the sort of retrospective piety that is accustomed to presenting the Confederacy to itself in terms of images taken from the subdued light of Tennyson's *Idylls of the King*. But enthusiasm, especially when well-stoked by promotion, always covers its members in a seamless garment —for a time at least.

His plan was accepted and the Stone Mountain Monumental Association organized. Samuel H. Venable, with his sister Mrs. Frank T. Mason, and his nieces Mrs. Priestly Orme and Mrs. Walter G. Roper, donated the northeast side of the mountain, a gift estimated at more than a million dollars. And on May 20, 1916, it was dedicated as a memorial. Meanwhile the dark shadows of World War I gathered over the project and it was postponed.

Finally, on June 3, 1923, Borglum put the first drill into the granite, and the conversion of modern engineering into an instrument of fine art had begun. Before carving began the workmen had traced the outlines of the giant figures from a photograph of the model projected on the mountain side. One-acre in size, this projection was produced from a two-inch stereopticon slide by means of a specially prepared triple-lens projection lamp which, weighing about a ton, had to be made fast to a solid foundation to avoid tremors in the image from vibration. Thereafter day after day, Borglum was suspended by steel cables over the mountain side, where he not only supervised the work of his artists and stonecutters but also did much of the carving himself. Thus a new stint was added to the labors of Hercules.

Partially completed, the head of Lee was dramatically unveiled on his birthday, January 19, 1924. "The ceremony," says keen-witted Hal Steed in *Georgia: Unfinished State,* "was preceded by a lavish Georgia breakfast. Borglum was host. He seated his distinguished guests at tables set on Lee's massive shoulder. This was a publicity gesture—and a knockout. Not every layman could take in the artistic scope of the project. But to the dullest imagination the spectacle of a human figure so huge that a group could dine comfortably on its shoulders was sensational. The sheer audacity of the conception left them breathless."

Like *Gone with the Wind,* the magic of the action began to ferment in the nation's fancy. For reasons that he must have found sufficiently prudent, President Coolidge approved a measure permitting the striking of five million memorial half-dollars, which began to appear in 1925. As Steed remarks, the resolution was introduced by Congressman McFadden of Pennsylvania in the House and by Senator Reed Smoot of Utah in the Senate, both Republicans. Momentarily at least, a common blood seemed to flow through the various regional hearts of the country. Selling for a dollar to help cover the operating costs, the coins bore designs adapted from the project by Borglum.

But eventually the serpent and old Adam appeared in the garden. Soon after the unveiling ceremony a violent discord burst out among the members of the Stone Mountain Monumental Association, apparently not unlike the purely personal pride and regional conflicts that flared up in the Confederacy itself. Somehow Borglum discovered that he was to be made a scapegoat to be driven into the wilderness in order to purge the situation of its corrosive passions, stone cutters being set to complete his models. Nothing could have been more completely designed to outrage the integrity of an artist than an administrative step of this sort. Borglum destroyed all of his working models except a completed figure of Jefferson Davis and, leaving the monument on which he had worked seven years, escaped across the state line, a refugee just ahead of the sheriff. There is a great confusion of causes in all this, no doubt; but in any event the South lost a work of undoubted genius. Mary Borglum's *Give the Man Room: the Story of Gutzon*

Borglum, published in 1952, places Borglum's life on public record. Another sculptor, Augustus Lukeman, was engaged and began work on a reduced group of mounted officers moving in linear order at a quick-step, with General Lee, his head uncovered, at front, as their leader. This was like a sparrow's nest after the eagle's aerie. When another head of Lee had been completed, Borglum's work was blasted away like a worthless fault of stone. By this time the funds were exhausted and public enthusiasm had grown tepid. The work was left in 1928 as it now appears. Lukeman died sometime soon afterward. Since the terms of the gift included a time-clause for completion of the memorial, eventually the deed reverted to the donors.

When Governor Eugene Talmadge was in office he secured a legislative act authorizing the appointment of a State Park Authority, whose duty it was to develop a memorial park at Stone Mountain. The members of the Authority were negotiating a loan with the Reconstruction Finance Corporation when World War II terminated the transaction. In 1949 the Korean outbreak again broke off negotiations with private bankers in New York. A resolution authorizing the Governor to buy the mountain—when in his opinion the surplus in the State Treasury should allow it—and to assign it to the Authority for development, was passed by the General Assembly in January, 1951. At present the future of the park depends on this condition. Meanwhile further efforts are afoot for a loan to complete the carving and other work needed for the intended park.

At *159.4 m.* is a junction with a paved road.

Left on this road at *0.5 m.* to a junction with a footpath; L. on this among granite boulders and scrub pines up the gradually sloping southwestern side of Stone Mountain to the summit *1 m.*

AVONDALE ESTATES, *168 m.* (approx. 1,025 alt., 1,070 pop.) (*see* TOUR *17*).

DECATUR, *168.9 m.* (1,049 alt., 21,635 pop.) (*see* TOUR *3*), is at a junction with US 29.

ATLANTA, *174.7 m.* (1,050 alt., 331,314 pop.) (*see* ATLANTA).

Points of Interest: State Capitol, Cyclorama of the Battle of Atlanta, Georgia School of Technology, Agnes Scott College, Emory University, Oglethorpe University, Atlanta University (Negro).

Atlanta is at the junction with US 41 (*see* TOUR 2), with US 19 (*see* TOUR 6), with US 29 (*see* TOUR *3*), and with US 23 (*see* TOUR 7).

Section b. ATLANTA *to* ALABAMA LINE *67.3 m., US 78.*

West of ATLANTA, *0 m.* the highway winds through sweeping hills and broad, forest-bordered fields. Dark cedars, somber pine groves, dun fields, and unpainted, slate-colored farmhouses are brightened in spring by the pink and white of blossoming fruit trees, in fall by the white of cotton. In some places the yellowish clay banks along the roadside sparkle in the sunlight with mica particles.

In the towns along the route are the gleaming oil tanks and smoking chimneys of new factories. Most of these villages have no central squares, but sprawl along the railroad; their main streets are lined with stores that have tin awnings projecting over the sidewalk and with frame cottages having jigsaw banisters around their porches and composition roofs of gaudy colors.

The highway crosses the sluggish red waters of the CHATTAHOOCHEE RIVER, *10.5 m.*, which inspired Sidney Lanier's poem "The Song of the Chattahoochee."

AUSTELL, *17.9 m.* (927 alt., 1,413 pop.), an industrial town incorporated in 1885, was named for General Alfred Austell, who founded in Atlanta in 1865 the first national bank in the southern states. The principal industries in the town are furniture manufacturing, textiles, paper products, a wood working shop, a grist and feed mill, and a feed bag reprocessing plant. Among the municipal features are the Austell Youth Center, the Sweetwater Valley Public Library, and the Austell Hospital with 30 beds.

1. Right from Austell on paved State 6, in CLARKSDALE, *1.6 m.* (approx. 920 alt., 600 pop.), is THE CLARK (O.N.T.) THREAD COMPANY, INC. In the large red brick mill building (L), about 800 people are employed. To the left of the mill, electrically lighted drives wind through the model village.

2. Left from Austell on a good dirt road to FACTORY SHOALS (*picnicking, swimming, boating, and fishing*), *3.5 m.*, a recreational development named for the Manchester Cotton Mills, destroyed by Federal forces during the War between the States. Tall trees grow within the enclosure formed by the brick walls that are overgrown with flowering vines.

LITHIA SPRINGS (*swimming pool, 9-hole golf course, picnic grounds, club house, steak and chicken dinners by arrangement*), *18.9 m.*, is a recreational resort (L). The water for the swimming pool is supplied from Austell and is recirculated through a purification plant at the rate of 12,000 gallons an hour. The picnic grounds have free grills, and both tables and benches are provided. In the club house, which may be rented for exclusive use, is a dance floor that will accommodate over a hundred couples. During the latter part of the nineteenth century this resort was known as Salt Spring and was popular with southerners in summer and northerners in winter. A short railroad brought visitors from Austell to the Sweetwater Park Hotel here.

LITHIA SPRINGS VILLAGE, *20 m.* (1,054 alt., 222 pop.), developed because of the nearby spring. During the 1880's Henry Grady (1850-89), orator and journalist (*see* ATLANTA), became actively interested in the resort and was instrumental in establishing here the Piedmont Chautauqua and a large auditorium to accommodate the crowds it drew.

DOUGLASVILLE, *26.8 m.* (1,250 alt., 3,400 pop.), seat of Douglas County, was incorporated in 1875 and, like the county, was named for Stephen A. Douglas, Lincoln's opponent.

The NEW HOPE PRIMITIVE BAPTIST CHURCH (R), *37.1 m.,* was organized in 1826, the year the Creek were removed from the region. This plain, white frame building, recently erected, is said to contain the original pulpit and pew. The service has remained virtually unchanged for the last 110 years, and the ceremony of foot washing is still performed upon occasion.

VILLA RICA (Sp. rich town), *38.1 m.* (1,156 alt., 1,703 pop.), is the oldest town in northwest Georgia. Gold discovered here in 1826 attracted settlers.

West of Villa Rica US 78 is divided into State 8 and State 8A; continue on State 8.

BREMEN, *52.9 m.* (1,416 alt., 2,299 pop.), is an industrial town incorporated in 1883 and named for the German city. The town developed at the intersection of the Georgia Pacific Railroad with the Chattanooga, Rome & Columbus Railroad, later bought by the Central of Georgia Railway.

At Bremen is the junction with US 27 (*see* TOUR *10*).

TALLAPOOSA, *61.9 m.* (1,159 alt., 2,826 pop.), was incorporated in 1860 but grew slowly until 1884, when northerners became interested in developing the gold, silver, copper, and other mineral deposits found here, and in building a resort around a spring of lithia water. In 1887 the Tallapoosa Land, Mining & Manufacturing Company was formed; lakes, parks, drives, and 8,000 city lots were laid out; industries were established; and excursions were run from Kansas City, Chicago, New York, and other cities. This boom reached its peak in 1891, when the partial depletion of the mines and the confusion of involved litigation caused a decline.

US 78 crosses the Alabama Line, *67.3 m.,* about 35 miles east of Anniston, Alabama. This line was designated as the western boundary of Georgia in 1802 by a treaty between the state and Federal governments. According to its terms, Georgia ceded all lands west of the line (the present states of Alabama and Mississippi) to the United States. In return, the Federal authorities agreed to extinguish all Indian claims to lands within the state "whenever it could be peaceably done on reasonable terms" and to transport the Indians westward. This provision almost resulted in war between Georgia and the United States. The

Cherokee Removal was not completed until 1838, although the Upper
Creek had been forced out in 1825-26.

TOUR 9

*Savannah — Dublin — Macon — Talbotton — Columbus — (Mont-
gomery, Ala.); US 80.*

*Savannah to Alabama Line, 286.3 m. — Roadbed hard-surfaced throughout — Watch for
cattle on highways in eastern part of route — Dublin, Macon & Savannah R.R. parallels
route between Dublin and Macon; Central of Georgia Ry. between Geneva and Columbus
— All types of accommodations in Savannah, Swainsboro, Macon, and Columbus; limited
elsewhere.*

Section a. SAVANNAH to MACON, 185.3 m., US 80

On the outskirts of Savannah US 80 is lined with burlap and cotton
bag factories, tanneries, fertilizer plants, and paper mills, as well as acres
of marshy land covered by pines, scrub palmettoes, and moss-hung
oaks. The sandy soil is not well adapted to agriculture, and the highway has been constructed over reclaimed land. Large cotton, turpentine, oil, and tobacco trucks, going to and from Savannah, speed past
old mule-drawn wagons that creak along the shoulders of the highway
with only two wheels on the pavement.

Alternating with the grayed dwellings of Negroes and of tenant
farmers are the larger and better constructed houses of landowners. In
the marshes weeping willow trees droop gracefully. Small game is
plentiful in the surrounding fields, and the sluggish Ogeechee River,
spreading through heavily wooded swamps, provides good fishing.

Midway across the state the route runs through almost level country,
dips at times into hollows at creek levels, and moves through a sandy
terrain of scrub oaks and scrawny pines, known as the "pine barrens."
The soil is poor for cultivation, and farmhouses are widely separated.

SAVANNAH, *o m.* (21-65 alt., 119,638 pop.) (*see* SAVANNAH).

Points of Interest: Telfair Academy of Arts and Sciences, Armstrong
Junior College, Atlantic Coast Line Docks, Herty Pulp and Paper
Laboratory, Bethesda Orphanage, Wormsloe, and others.

Savannah is at a junction with US 17 (*see* TOUR *1*) and with State 21
(*see* TOUR *14*).

Jencks' Bridge, *21.4 m.,* spans the dark and sandy-bottomed Ogeechee
River which runs through swampy pine lands. Near the bridge is a

FISHING CAMP (*tourist accommodations; fishing, picnicking*); shad caught here are marketed in Savannah or shipped to the North.

STATESBORO, *52.6 m.* (218-250 alt., 6,097 pop.), was laid out in 1803 as the seat of Bulloch County, but records of the superior court show that its first session was held here in 1797. Statesboro was on the line of General Sherman's march to the sea during the War between the States, and Federal soldiers stopped here briefly.

Agriculturally, the town is in the center of an important tobacco, peanut, and hog area, and timber is generally available. It serves as a trading center for naval stores and farm products, and has gins, lumber mills, cotton warehouses, and other industries.

Left from Statesboro on US 25, State 73, to GEORGIA TEACHERS COLLEGE, *1.5 m.*, a unit of the University System of Georgia. The academic buildings are set on a large campus, planted with trees and shrubbery and containing two lakes and an amphitheater. Formerly operated as one of ten district agricultural and mechanical schools in the state, the institution was converted into the Georgia Normal School in 1924. In 1929 it became South Georgia Teachers College and a four-year institution, and in 1939 it was changed to Georgia Teachers College. The college is in session for four quarters during the year, and offers the B. S. degree in both elementary and secondary education. The enrollment of the winter term runs around 700, and that of the summer quarter around 1,000.

At *59.2 m.* is a junction with US 25 (*see* TOUR *15*).

The CANOOCHEE BAPTIST CHURCH (R), *82.8 m.*, a severe, gabled, white clapboard building erected in 1818, has undergone no alterations. In the cemetery near the church a number of pioneer settlers are buried.

SWAINSBORO, *90.2 m.* (318 alt., 4,300 pop.) (*see* TOUR *4*), is at the junction with US 1.

DUBLIN, *130.3 m.* (106 alt., 10,232 pop.), seat of Laurens County, is a widely spread town with a vigorous, prosperous atmosphere. The town was incorporated in 1812, the year it succeeded Sumterville as the county seat, and was named by an Irishman, Peter (Jonathan) Sawyer, who gave the land for the public buildings. As the distributing point for freight brought up the Oconee River, Dublin was once more important than Macon, but declined when the Central of Georgia Railway was built and denied access to the town by the people of the county.

The town has a golf club, an airport, two private hospitals, and a large Veterans' Hospital. Lumber from the oak, gum, and tupelo trees of the surrounding forests is shipped from Dublin to be used in high-grade cabinet work, including tables, receiving sets, and wall paneling. Besides the plywood plant, there are three fertilizer plants, a cotton oil plant, and a woolen mill as well as other concerns of lesser scale. Laurens County originally grew little besides cotton, but since the advent of the boll weevil in the early 1920's, cotton has been checked and more acres have been planted yearly to corn, peanuts, and sweet potatoes, and with these hogs and cattle have increased.

The town has two hotels and three motor courts. Dublin is separated from East Dublin by the Oconee River.

VALLAMBROSA, *137.3 m.*, was one of the estates of George M. Troup. Only a few crumbling ruins remain of the house, but a spring house built by slaves for Governor Troup's daughter Oralie has been preserved by the D. A. R. Troup, Governor of the state between 1820 and 1826, insistently urged the Federal government to remove the Indians from Georgia. Although by an agreement of 1802 (*see* TOUR *8*) the United States had promised to remove the Indians, when Troup took office in 1823 little or nothing had been done. Protests from the Governor were met by procrastination. Finally, Governor Troup wrote on April 24, 1824: "If nullified by the act of one party, the other party is dissolved—both are free to declare the resumption of his former rights—give us back our lands and we will give you back your money." Again ignored by the government, he issued an ultimatum: "We have exhausted the argument. We will stand by our arms," and ordered the state militia to be in readiness to stop Federal troops at the border. The matter was finally settled without the shedding of patriot blood and in a way satisfactory to the Governor, by the Cherokee Removal of 1838.

JEFFERSONVILLE, *161.3 m.* (526 alt., 787 pop.) seat of Twiggs County, is a marketing center for corn, cotton, livestock, dairy products, and hardwood timber from the surrounding area.

Left from Jeffersonville on an unpaved road to the RICHLAND BAPTIST CHURCH, 5 *m.* The earliest extant minutes of the church cover the period from 1811 to 1821. The large white frame building with square columns was constructed in 1845 when membership numbered only a hundred. Separate doors lead to the slave gallery, which extends around three sides. The most valued possession of the church is the original communion service, more than a hundred years old. There are also a pulpit, a table, and a bench used by the congregation before the present church was built.

DRY BRANCH, *175.3 m.* (approx. 370 alt., 500 pop.), is the center of a kaolin mining district. This clay is used principally in coating enameled paper, and for making chinaware, and automobile tires. The output of kaolin in Georgia annually runs around 284,566 tons, with a value of over a million and a half dollars.

At *181.5* is a junction with State 87 (*see* TOUR *9A*).

At *183.4 m.* is the entrance to the Ocmulgee National Monument (*see* TOUR *9B*).

MACON, *185.3 m.* (334 alt., 70,252 pop.) (*see* MACON).

Points of Interest: Home of Sidney Lanier, Mercer University, Wesleyan Conservatory, and others.

At Macon is a junction with US 41 (*see* TOUR *12*) and with US 129 (*see* TOUR *16*).

Section b. MACON to ALABAMA LINE, 101 m., US 80.

Just west of MACON, *0 m.,* US 80 crosses a prosperous farming section producing cotton, corn, watermelons, and pecans. Midway between Macon and Columbus is a sandy, thinly populated region of unproductive farms and stunted trees; in this area, however, are a number of widely separated old houses that, though unpainted, are well built and quite distinct from the usual tenant house. Near Columbus and the valley of the Chattahoochee River is another region of prosperous farms.

KNOXVILLE, *25.6 m.* (640 alt., 306 pop.), seat of Crawford County, lies to the right of the highway, which passes through the outskirts of the town.

On the courthouse square (L) is the JOANNA TROUTMAN MONUMENT, a granite boulder with a bronze marker, in memory of the Georgia girl who designed the Lone Star Flag of Texas. In 1835 Joanna, then sixteen, learned that a group of Macon men were going to Columbus to join the Georgia battalion, of 120 men, who had volunteered to aid Texas in its fight for independence. She made a white silk flag with one blue star and presented it to them as they passed through Knoxville. On January 8, 1836, the flag was unfurled at Velasco, Texas, and on March 8 was raised over Fort Goliad, when news arrived from Washington that Texas had been recognized as an independent republic. Because the flag figured in the fight for freedom, it was adopted by the first congress of the new Republic of Texas as the official flag.

As the flag was easily soiled, its colors were reversed to a white star on a blue background, which is still the state flag. In 1913 Texas officials removed Joanna Troutman's body from Crawford County to the state cemetery at Austin, Texas, and erected a bronze statue to her memory.

ROBERTA, *26.6 m.* (487 alt., 673 pop.), is a trading village for farmers. In the center of town, one block L. of the highway, is the BEN HAWKINS MONUMENT, placed in 1930 by the U. S. Government to commemorate the life and services of the Indian agent.

Roberta is at the junction with US 341 (*see* TOUR *2*).

At *41 m.* is a junction with US 19 (*see* TOUR 6), which unites with US 80 to a junction at *45.5 m.*

LEONARD HOUSE (*private*), *63.3 m.,* set back from the road (L) and approached by a curved drive, was built about 1845 from lumber that was carefully selected for uniformity of grain. The two-story stucco house, with a hipped roof and a small balcony over the front door, is surrounded by a two-story colonnade.

TALBOTTON, *64.3 m.* (726 alt., 1,175 pop.), seat of Talbot County, was laid out in 1828. During the middle of the nineteenth century the town was an educational center with two schools, LaVert and Collingsworth institutes, that offered advanced courses.

An EPISCOPAL CHURCH, on the highway one block S. of the courthouse square, built in 1848, is considered one of the finest examples of Tudor Gothic architecture in the state. All the nails used were hand-forged and the lumber was hand-hewn. The old-fashioned pipe organ with a hand pump is in perfect condition and is still in use.

About one-half block NW. of the courthouse square is a little frame cabin, the first American HOME OF LAZARUS STRAUS. Driven from Bavaria in the Revolution of 1848, Straus landed in Philadelphia where he bought a small stock of china and then journeyed southward, peddling his wares. When he arrived in Talbotton in 1852, he opened a small store. After the War between the States, Straus and his three sons established a crockery business in New York City and in 1874 took over the crockery department of R. H. Macy & Company, becoming sole owner of the establishment in 1896. One of the sons, Oscar, became Minister to Turkey under President Cleveland and Secretary of Commerce in the Cabinet of President Theodore Roosevelt.

Serving as a community center is STRAUS-LEVERT HALL, College St., one block E. of the highway, a large frame building with tall Doric Columns around three sides. It was formerly LaVert College, established in 1859 and named for Octavia Walton LaVert, granddaughter of George Walton, one of the three Georgia signers of the Declaration of Independence. The building was restored in 1930 by the sons of Isadore Straus.

The PERSONS COTTAGE (*private*), near the southern limits of the town, is an ante-bellum house (R) with a pyramidal roof. Characteristic of this type of house are the wide central hallway, large rooms with high ceilings, and spacious porch. The pyramidal roof appears on several other houses of the town.

Between Talbotton and Geneva, US 80 runs through a sandy country where the vegetation is dwarfed.

GENEVA, *72.4 m.* (581 alt., 209 pop.), was a stagecoach stop during pioneer days.

Left of the railroad is the MORRIS HOUSE, built about 1840 and operated as Kookogy's Tavern for about seventy-five years.

Between Geneva and Columbus, Negroes can often be seen washing clothes near a flowing spring or small creek and beating them with battlin' sticks to loosen the grime. Their equipment consists of a large iron pot for boiling the clothes and a wooden block over which the boiled garments are battered vigorously with wooden paddles. This method of washing clothes is common throughout the more secluded rural sections of the state.

COLUMBUS, *100.5 m.* (250 alt., 79,611 pop.) (*see* COLUMBUS).

Points of Interest: St. Elmo, Wynnton School, Bibb Manufacturing Company Plant, and others.

Columbus is at a junction with US 27 (*see* TOUR *10*).

US 80 crosses the Chattahoochee River, *101 m.*, the Alabama Line, 80 miles east of Montgomery, Alabama.

TOUR 9A

Junction US 80—Cochran—Eastman, 58.4 m.; State 87, US 23 and 129.

Southern Ry. approximately parallels route—limited accommodations.

Between a suburban section of Macon and the town of Eastman, State 87, the Cochran Short Route, crosses a region once thickly populated by pre-Columbian Indians. It leads through a wide expanse of slightly rolling farm land and forests of pine and oak that supply lumber companies with fine timber.

State 87 branches south from its junction with US 80 (*see* TOUR *9*), *0 m.*, at a point about 4 miles east of Macon.

At *0.2 m.* is a junction with the Riggins Mill Road.

Left on this road to a junction with another road, *0.7 m.;* L. on this second road to the TRAINING SCHOOL FOR NEGRO GIRLS (L), *1.2 m.*, a state institution for delinquents under eighteen years. Sponsored by the Georgia Federation of Colored Women's Clubs, the building was erected in 1936 at a cost of $45,000, and later turned over to the state. The institution was not operated for some time, because the General Assembly did not appropriate the required funds. But finally the maintenance funds were forthcoming, and the institution began to operate August 1, 1943, for Negro girls who are committed from the juvenile courts in the state. In 1946 a wing was added to the main building, which increased the capacity to forty or fifty.

At *1.5 m.* on State 87 is the junction with a road.

Right on this road to the LAMAR MOUNDS AND VILLAGE SITE, *1.5 m.*, (*the detached Lamar area is at present closed to the public*) a part of the Ocmulgee National Monument (*see* TOUR 9B). Before the coming of the Creek the Lamar village was probably occupied by the powerful Hitchiti tribes that had lived on the Ocmulgee hundreds of years before De Soto's journey in 1540. Ethnological studies indicate that these people, though they had divergent customs, were of the same linguistic stock as the Creek and were of Muskhogean origin.

A study of their arts, industries, and materials indicates that they attained a high level of cultural development, that their life was well adapted to swamp dwelling, and that they were agriculturists as well as hunters and fishermen. Vast quantities of animal remains and the small stores of maize and beans are evidence that they were primarily hunters. A study of 100,000 potsherds collected from the Lamar village reveals a sharp contrast in design and general features with the pottery from the Macon Plateau (*see* TOUR 9B). The Lamar Indians made large cooking and utility pots decorated with ornate designs by pressing the pots with wooden paddles or stamps before firing them.

The Lamar site, which has two mounds about 20 feet high and 100 feet wide lying 200 yards apart, exactly fits the description of an "ancient Creek village" as sketched by William Bartram in his *Travels* (1793). The conical SPIRAL MOUND (Mound B) is considered unusual because of its truncated top and the spiral path that runs counter-clockwise from the level of the plain to its summit. This mound was perhaps used for ceremonial purposes. Encircling the base is the collar, formed by a slight ridge of earth, and on the summit are surface indications of a building. The pyramidal MOUND A also has a truncated summit, which implies that it, too, was the base of a temple. It has been altered in shape by erosion, modern cultivation, and partial exploration. An earth ramp leads to the summit of the primary structure. Cross-sectional studies of a small part of the mound indicate that it was built in at least two stages.

Small elevations in the surrounding meadows proved to be house sites. One excavated site exhibited many details of structure and revealed much of the daily life of the villagers. The house was built of small sapling timbers inserted upright in puddled blue-clay floors packed hard by the treading of many feet. Material found on the floor indicates that the irregularly spaced wall posts had been thatched with cane and that the thatched roof had been covered by a thin layer of reddish clay loam. Enough data were found to show that these houses, from twenty to twenty-five feet square, were of rather flimsy construction and that they were built on artificial earth mounds with ramped sides. They were of a type not found in the uplands and are believed to have been inhabited at a different time from those of the Macon Plateau. On the floor were found whole pottery vessels, flint implements including highly polished greenstone celts, a pot of charred beans, and several piles of burned corncobs. The evidence suggests that these buildings were hastily abandoned because of fire, which likely enough spread rapidly in the dry thatch.

At *4.8 m.* on State 87 is a junction with a sandy road.

Right on this road to BROWN'S MOUNT, *0.2 m.,* the most striking topographical feature in the sweep of hills overlooking the Ocmulgee River. The high shelf of 1,000 acres rises 180 feet above the plain. In 1870 Charles C. Jones, Jr., historian, described walls and ditches that indicated that an Indian fortification once occupied the summit. Excavations of a red-clay knoll have revealed a round Indian council chamber, thirty feet in diameter and similar to that of the Ocmulgee National Monument. It has the same arrangement of clay seats, only eleven of which remain. No trace of a platform has been found, but the central fire altar is in good condition. Extensive collections of pottery and other artifacts have been taken from around the council chamber. Fossil remains discovered here indicate that this region was at one time a part of the sea bed.

At *5.1 m.* on State 87 is a junction with a dirt road.

Left on this road to a junction with another dirt road at Bond's Store, *0.2 m.;* right on this to a junction, *1.1 m.,* with a country road that runs through the yard of a tenant-house; R. on this road to SHELL ROCK CAVE (R), *1.3 m.,* a large rock shelter with a high shelving roof of limestone. More than twenty varieties of shell-life fossils indicate that it also was once covered by the sea. Several species of extinct starfish have been found, as well as millions of bryozoa, minute stick-like forms found in the composition of limestone. Thick beds of ashes and charcoal under the debris of the floor indicate habitation by Indians at some time. Many shards, artifacts, and charcoal beds excavated at the cave entrance show that the cave dwellers did most of their cooking outdoors. Pottery shows a close relation to that of both the Napier and the Swift Creek villages, and a combination of pottery and flint suggests the Lamar culture mixed with some other. Many implements were made of beautiful red flint or jasper. At a depth of nine or ten feet a thick cluster of rocks weighing three or four tons mark a section of the cave which has collapsed.

J. M. HUBER CORPORATION, *15 m.,* has a modern kaolin clay refining plant (R) in this location. Nearby are the kaolin pits, an extensive open-cut mining operation, which supply the plant. The equipment is capable of moving more than a million cubic yards of over-burden annually from the cut. The Huber Plant was built in the 1930's and has been increased in productive capacity a number of times since then. Huber is now one of the world's largest producers of refined clay, which is used in the paper and rubber industries as well as in insecticides, ceramics, and adhesives. In paper manufacturing, the clays are used to produce the surface on gloss paper and for filling the space between the fibers. The more expensive magazines, known in the trade as "slicks," are usually printed on this sort of paper.

Georgia kaolin is making it unnecessary to import the high grade clays from England formerly used for china and fine papers. Most of the kaolin is shipped out of the state for processing in other centers, but local manufacturing is on the increase.

COCHRAN, *40.2 m.* (342 alt., 3,357 pop.), seat of Bleckley County, was in early days known as Dykesboro, but when incorporated in 1870 it was renamed for Arthur Cochran, who ran the first train through its boundaries. Among the chief industrial units are a textile mill, cotton gins, lumber processing, and a cold storage plant, while corn, cotton, peaches, and lumber are the chief products of the county.

MIDDLE GEORGIA COLLEGE, *41.2 m.*, a coeducational, accredited junior college of Georgia's university system, is on the brow of a hill against a background of tall pines; its red brick, Georgian Colonial buildings are grouped about a court landscaped with shrubs and grass. This site has been occupied by an educational institution since 1885, when New Ebenezer College was opened. In 1917 the state established an agricultural and mechanical school, which burned in 1926. That same year the present buildings were built and the institution was re-opened as Middle Georgia College. It had an enrollment of 373 in 1951.

EASTMAN, *58.4 m.* (357 alt., 3,597 pop.) (*see* TOUR *12*), is at a junction with US 341.

TOUR 9B

Junction with US 80 to Macon Mounds Section of Ocmulgee National Monument; 1.1 m.

The Macon Plateau is part of the OCMULGEE NATIONAL MONUMENT (*open from 8:30 A.M. to 5 P.M. daily; small admission fee except for children and educational groups; guide service; neither picnic nor camping facilities*), a memorial to the Indians of Georgia, supervised by the National Park Service, of the U. S. Department of the Interior. Now owned by the people of the United States, the Monument was established on December 23, 1936. The other part, the Lamar Mounds and Village Site (*not open to the public at present*), was once held by the prehistoric Creeks who were in what is now Georgia at the time of the first Spanish exploration (*see* TOUR *9A*). Analysis of the great mass of material collected in the area indicates six successive occupations extending over a period from probably around 8,000 B.C. until A.D. 1717, thus suggesting the seven buried cities of Troy. These occupational periods have been classified as follows: *Wandering Hunters* (Folsom Period), who supposedly entered America some ten thousand years ago, at the end of the Ice Age; *Shellfish Eaters* (Archaic Period), who, living for the most part on shellfish, were able to stay longer in a given locality, from around 500 B.C. until 100 B.C.; *Early Farmers* (Swift Creek Period), who probably through combining some farming with hunting had time for the arts, 100 B.C. to 900 A.D.; *Master Farmers* (Macon Plateau Period), who were the mound builders, apparently a politic people, 900 A.D.; *Reconquerors* (Lamar Period), who, from among the Early Farmers left in the area, defeated eventually the Master Farmers after some two hundred years; the Indians of the *Spanish, English, and French Influence* (Creek Period), who remained in possession until 1717 A.D., and kept alive a claim to the area until 1821, when it was ceded to the United States.

The monument road branches south from its junction with US 80 and 129, *o m., (see* TOUR 9*)* at a point about 2 miles east of Macon.

At *0.4 m.* are the ADMINISTRATION BUILDING AND MUSEUM (R); compact and functional, they are entirely modern in style. The Museum houses exhibits that have been arranged to explain the features of the Monument area. There is a parking area near these buildings, and behind them are the EARTHLODGE and CORNFIELD MOUND.

The PREHISTORIC CORNFIELD has the appearance of a modern plowed field, due to having hillocks for corn in straight or slightly curving continuous patches with waving troughs and crests. Two small beaten paths, running diagonally through the cultivated plot, indicate a division of the tract into lesser sections. This prehistoric field is significant because it is one of the two examples recorded for North America in archeological literature and is the only one sufficiently well preserved to be of interest to the layman.

The EARTHLODGE, or Council Chamber, is a room forty-two feet in diameter and enclosed within a low, red-clay wall. Against this wall, opposite the entrance, is a large clay platform in the shape of an eagle with folded wings, which has three seats on it, while along the red-clay wall a raised clay bench has forty-seven seats. The arrangement of the seats suggests a ceremonial routine with appropriate precepts. Carved upon the front of each seat is a small dish-shaped receptacle, and in the exact center of the chamber floor is a large claylined firepit. Four huge oak posts support the roof of pine logs, canes, and clay. This Earthlodge has been restored and now appears from both inside and out very much as it must have been a thousand years ago, when religious ceremonies and tribal councils were held there.

There is another parking area near the LESSER TEMPLE MOUND and the GREAT TEMPLE MOUND, which may be reached either by the trail past the Earthlodge or by the road that passes over the Central of Georgia Railroad and near the Southeast Mound. The Great Temple Mound is forty feet above the level of the Macon Plateau and a hundred feet above the level of the river plain. It is estimated that a million basket loads of earth were needed for its building. Evidence indicates that the mound was built in successive stages and that buildings had been constructed on the clay platform of each mound. Exploratory trenches, dug into the side of the mound from the east rim of the plateau, uncovered evidence of a large projecting apron of earth from the plateau level to the top of the mound. The profiled cross-section of the trenches revealed house sites and refuse pits which indicated that the plateau had been occupied before the mound was built.

Beginning at the southeastern toe of the Great Temple Mound and following along the slope to the extreme east of the middle plateau are four terraces forming an extensive amphitheater overlooking the swamps below. The purpose of the terraces is not definitely known, but they may have formed a fortified ramp serving to protect the Macon Plateau. By cutting exploratory trenches through their slopes, archeologists found that these terraces were artificial and that they were built over pits found in a large trench which extended around the Cornfield Mound, starting at one side of the Great Temple Mound and returning to another side of the same mound.

There is another parking area at the FUNERAL MOUND, the first mound to be explored. It has been so excavated as to show in profile its complex structure. Originally 30 feet high and more than 250 feet long, it was partly destroyed in 1841 when the Central of Georgia Railroad was laid and again in 1877 when the cut was widened. Archeological data reveal that it antedates the journey of De Soto in 1540. When exploration was begun, workers first removed the slump dirt from the cut-away portion to enable archeologists to study the structure, which was found to be a composition of five mounds, built one upon another, with a colorful mosaic of clay bands covering the summit and slopes. The colors of the lower bands ranged from yellow to blue and bluish-yellow to slate-gray, but the topmost was a three-foot band of brilliant red clay. The meaning of this use of colored mosaic is not understood. The main portion of each mound was composed of basket-laid sand, and evidences of each basket load were seen in the freshly cut profiles. Post molds and other material found in the top of each mound indicated that some sort of structure had been built on each summit. A CLAY-MOLDED STAIRWAY of fourteen steps leads from the ground level to the summit of the first or core mound. These steps, about six feet wide, show worn surfaces where human feet trod for generations.

From the original red clay soil beneath the first mound six tomb burials were troweled out. In some cases the sides of the tombs were lined with bark or small saplings, and in others, with upright logs which are shown by the dark soil that filled the cavities left by the decaying logs. The bodies in the tombs had been previously exposed until advanced decomposition had set in; then skin and muscles were stripped from the bones, which were wrapped in skin or bark and laid away in the log tombs. The distribution of many shell beads and disc-shaped bone beads over the burials suggested a woven blanket. Little pottery and few flint artifacts were found, but the bone tools included needles, awls, and skewers, and the ornaments, gorgets, pendants, and ear plugs. In the slopes of the successive mounds were found evidences of secondary burial in bark and skin wrappings. Burials that intruded into the slopes of the last mound contained glass beads, knives, and brass trinkets, evidently obtained in trade with early Europeans. There were also many large conch shells and shell cores perforated and strung as necklaces.

There is evidence that the plateau was inhabited in historic times. Excavations on top of the middle section revealed, just below the surface, small trenches two feet deep and one and a half feet wide. When excavated by troweling, this small trench was found to have held posts which formed a regular, five-sided stockade, with logs laid horizontally rather than inserted vertically in the ground, as in the frontier forts built about 1800. Inside was a discolored area with log molds that outlined the storeroom. There was evidence that the posts of the stockade wall had been pulled up and that the cabin had been demolished instead of burned. Both inside and outside the stockade wall were found numerous Indian burials, most of which were primary burials, in which the flexed or extended bodies were interred with many objects.

This section is opposite the parking area of the Great Temple Mound and is known now as the TRADING POST. The presence of rusty parts of flintlocks, bullet molds, iron knives, swords, and axes indicates military occupation; and glass beads, clay pipes, brass and copper ornaments and iridescent pieces of glass must mean trade relationships between the Indians and early European traders. A flattened piece of silver bearing the arms of Phillip IV of Spain was found inside the stockade, and one of the swords from an Indian burial resembled the weapons used by the Spaniards late in the seventeenth century. It is believed that this trading post was built between 1690 and 1715 by English traders.

The pottery of the Macon Plateau is plain and lacks the glossy finish and highly ornate, paddle-marked designs found at the Lamar Village site. Some vessels have impressions of baskets or nets that were used either to mold or mark them before they were baked. They lack the strength of the Lamar pottery, are rough and crudely finished, and are therefore considered as belonging to a less advanced era. Pre-pottery flint implements, excavated from a considerable depth in the plateau soils, are made up of scraping and cutting tools intended for skin dressing. The technique of their handicraft resembles that of the Old Stone Age in Europe and that of the flint tools found in the western plains of the United States in association with Pleistocene mammals.

It is interesting that the clay eagle in the Earthlodge has on its head the cryptic symbolic eye. This cult sign has a wide distribution. Examples have been found from Florida to Oklahoma and Missouri and in Mayan excavations in Mexico and Central America as well as on the copper eagles found in North Georgia. The uncovered details of the Monument area suggest in many ways the characters and scene of Homer's *Iliad,* and so it might have been with these people except that they lacked the written word; for without it the imagination burns with a very low flame, and a culture lacks its apex. It would be fascinating indeed to know what the reflections were in the eagle's eye.

TOUR 10

(Chattanooga, Tenn.) — Rossville — Rome — LaGrange — Columbus — Cuthbert — Bainbridge — (Tallahassee, Fla.); US 27.

Tennessee Line to Florida Line 363.3 m. — Central of Georgia Ry. roughly parallels route between Fort Oglethorpe and Carrollton, and between Chipley and Columbus; Seaboard Air Line Ry. between Columbus and the Florida Line — Limited accommodations except in larger towns.

Section a. TENNESSEE LINE *to* COLUMBUS, 212.2 m., US 27.

Near the Tennessee Line US 27 crosses a region of superb forests and commanding mountains. On the upper part of the route, the sheer sandstone cliffs of the Lookout Range contrast with the dark, wooded ridges of the Appalachian Mountains; in the vicinity of Rome, less rugged mountains rise behind the cornfields and orchards of the Appalachian Valley, with its clay-burdened, meandering rivers. Between this valley and Columbus, Georgia's second largest industrial city, is the rolling red land of the Piedmont Plateau.

Along this route are a soil conservation area, a farm resettlement project, a major state park, an extensive memorial garden in a natural setting, a prosperous textile area, and a well-known mountain school.

There are reminders of both pioneer and wealthy planter; huts almost as crude as those of the early settlers are only a few miles from some of the state's finest Greek Revival mansions.

ROSSVILLE, *0 m.* (approx. 750 alt., 3,892 pop.), an industrial suburb
of Chattanooga, Tennessee, is on the boundary line between Tennessee
and Georgia. The town was named for John Ross, a man of mixed
Scottish and Indian ancestry who for nearly forty years was head of
the Cherokee Nation.

Ross, whose Indian name was Kooweskowe, was only one-eighth
Cherokee. Although he had served under Andrew Jackson and been
identified with the white man's interest, he steadfastly defended the
rights of the Indians to their lands and accompanied them in the removal of 1838. His wife, a full-blooded Cherokee, was among the
many who died on the march. He devoted his life to the education of
the exiled people.

FORT OGLETHORPE, *2.8 m.* (approx. 800 alt.), (L), is an U. S. reserve of
810 acres. Formerly a military training center, it was established in
1903 and named in honor of James E. Oglethorpe, founder of Georgia.
During World War I, it was used as a mobilization and training center,
and many veterans of that War remember it well.

CHICKAMAUGA PARK (*the museum is the focal point for visitors, no
admission fee, free information for self-guided tours, trained historians
on duty at headquarters; no recreation, housing, or restaurant facilities;
open daily, 8 A.M. to 5 P.M.*), *3.6 m.*, established in 1890 by an act of
Congress and administered by the National Park Service, is the Georgia
portion of the greater Chickamauga and Chattanooga National Military
Park of approximately 8,127 acres within the states of Georgia and
Tennessee. For more than three miles US 27 runs through the Chickamauga area planted with trees and flowering shrubs. The Battle of
Chickamauga, fought in September, 1863, has been commemorated by
markers, monuments, tablets, and artillery pieces, to the sum of 1,892.
In fact the battlefield is exceptionally well-marked. The physical features of the park, both open fields and heavily wooded sections, have
been kept in what is practically their wartime condition.

The PARK MUSEUM and headquarters building is situated at the northern entrance to the park. Besides exhibits the Museum contains an
historical library of the War between the States. Some of the chief
points of interest in the area are BLOODY POND, whose waters are said
literally to have flowed with blood; BROTHERTON HOUSE, where a break
occurred in the Union line; KELLY FIELD, scene of heavy fighting during
the battle; state monuments of Alabama, Georgia, Florida, South Carolina, and Kentucky; SNODGRASS HILL, where General George H. Thomas
made his stand; DEFENSE LINE, morning of September 20, scene of fierce
fighting; and WILDER TOWER, Federal Headquarters—now approached
by Glen Kelly Road from the north or Glen Vinard Road near the

lower end of the park (R)—was erected in memory of Wilder's Union brigade; from the top there is a clear view of the park.

The confederate general, Braxton Bragg, evacuated Chattanooga on September 8, 1863. W. S. Rosecrans, the Union general, believing that Bragg was falling back to Rome, divided his own army in an attempt to trap Bragg between two fires. Finding to his surprise that the Confederates had concentrated for an attack on these divided ranks, he quickly reunited his forces before Bragg's subordinates had made the attack, as ordered. The opposing lines were then drawn up facing each other across Chickamauga Creek. General James Longstreet was on his way from Atlanta with reinforcements that would make the Confederate total around 70,000; reinforcements also were being sent by Johnston from Mississippi. Rosecrans had an army estimated at 55,000.

On September 18 skirmishing occurred at Reed's and Alexander's bridges, and during the night almost two-thirds of Bragg's men crossed to the west side of the creek. General Thomas, who held the extreme left of the Union line on the slopes of Missionary Ridge, attempted to capture a Confederate brigade on the morning of the nineteenth and encountered fierce resistance. Sharp artillery fire continued all day along the line.

During the night Longstreet and Hindman arrived with reinforcements. Planned for daybreak of September, the attack was delayed by fog until later in the morning, when General John C. Breckenridge opened an engagement with a charge that was intended to wedge a large force between Rosecrans and Chattanooga. Confederate charges against the log and earthen breastworks of the Union line met with varying degrees of success. Though the Federals were able to repulse the repeated assaults on their left, at the Brotherton house Confederates poured through a breach made by the withdrawal of a division to support Thomas. Rosecrans retreated to Rossville, where he halted the Federal rout, reformed his lines, and drove the Confederates back. Then the Union withdrew in order, to a position near Chattanooga, and Bragg took possession of Lookout Mountain and Missionary Ridge.

Following the Battle of Chickamauga and after the arrival of Grant and Sherman, the battles of Orchard Knob, Lookout Mountain, and Missionary Ridge occurred. All of these are commemorated by reservations within the confines of the greater park, and can be reached from Chattanooga.

The significance of the Battle of Chickamauga does not consist in the tactics of the field, the intensity of the fighting, nor in a relative calculation of the numbers killed, but in its strategic scope. In possession of Chattanooga, the Union army was able effectively to block any attempt against the west on the part of the Confederates, because this opening to Tennessee and Kentucky was essential. On the other hand just the converse was true for the Union. It now held virtually the gate of entry and a supply route to Atlanta, and thus the key to the conquest of the southeastern states, the great under-flank of the Confederacy. With the loss of this section, action around Richmond became like that of men whose arms are short as in a dream.

At *7.1 m.* is the junction with a paved road, at the lower SW end of the park area.

Right on this road to CHICKAMAUGA VILLAGE, 2 *m.* (750 alt., 1,747 pop.), on a site known to the Indians as Crawfish Spring. In 1891, when the town was incorporated it was given its present Indian name, a corruption of Tsikamagi the meaning of which is unknown. Among its industries are a textile mill and a bleachery.

The GORDON LEE HOUSE (*private*), on Cove Rd., is a handsome, twelve-room, grayish-brick house built in the 1850's by James Gordon, grandfather of Gordon Lee, United States Congressman (1905-27). A wide walkway, bordered on each side by two rows of maples planted around 1880, leads to the wide-proportioned Doric-columned Greek portico. Constructed of brick made by slaves, the house has walls eighteen inches thick. The interior has been remodeled and the second-story porch replaced by a balcony. In 1863 General Rosecrans made his headquarters here, and later the house was used as a Union hospital. To the rear (R) is an ivy-covered brick smokehouse and to the side (L) are two of the twelve slave cabins which constituted the quarters.

The GORDON LEE MEMORIAL HIGH SCHOOL, adjoining the Lee House on property donated by Gordon Lee, is a public independent high school for boys and girls. On the twenty-acre campus, sodded in blue grass, is a crescent-shaped drive which leads past the five red brick buildings. Upon his death in 1927 Gordon Lee bequeathed $250,000 to the town for the school. The school is a member of the Southern Association of Colleges and Secondary Schools.

CRAWFISH SPRING, in a ravine across the street from the high school, is a clear spring flowing through natural rock; it was named by the Indians in honor of Chief Crawfish. After the invention of the syllabary by Sequoyah (*see* TOUR 2), the Cherokee nation was divided into districts, each with a council house similar to the white man's courthouse. About 1820 on the bluff above the spring the Indians built a log structure, which was used by the county officials when Walker County was created in 1833. Here Fort Cumming, a blockhouse stockade, was built by the U. S. Government in 1836 to aid in the removal of the Cherokee to the West (*see* TOUR 2). The land surrounding the spring was later bought by James Gordon, who settled here in 1836.

At *20 m.* is a junction with State 143; marker points R. to CLOUD-LAND CANYON STATE PARK (*see* TOUR *11*); at about sixteen miles on this road, there is another marker which indicates the entrance to the park, and about four miles from this marker is a sign pointing right to Sitton's Gulch, a famous lookout point.

LAFAYETTE (pronounced La-Fáy-et), *22 m.* (871 alt., 4,884 pop.), was established as the seat of Walker County in 1835 under the name of Chatooga, later changed to Benton, and then to LaFayette in honor of the French general. Its growth was accelerated when the Chattanooga, Rome & Columbus Railroad was built through the town in 1888. A trading center for farmers, it has among its industries two textile plants and a large hosiery mill operated by local interests. During the War between the States many skirmishes occurred here.

The office of the Forest Ranger of the Armuchee District (52,490 acres in Catoosa, Chattooga, Floyd, Gordon, Walker, and Whitfield counties) of the Chattahoochee National Forest, U. S. Forest Service, is located here. Inquire about recreation facilities available in the area.

TRION, *33.5 m.* (800 alt., 3,028 pop.), was named for a trio of LaFayette businessmen who first settled here in 1847. The town, incorporated in 1863, escaped Federal destruction, but its growth was retarded by the accidental burning of its mills in 1875. It now has a large textile mill and a glove factory.

The NARROWS PICNIC AREA, (L) from Trion by the Narrows Forest Development Road, about *5 m.,* near Narrows Tower, with water and facilities for picnicking. It is maintained by the Armuchee District of the Chattahoochee National Forest, U. S. Forest Service.

In SUMMERVILLE, *39.5 m.* (668 alt., 3,973 pop.), incorporated in 1839 and the seat of Chattooga County, are a large textile mill and a knitting mill that manufactures hosiery. The Chattooga County hospital has thirty-six beds. With grazing ten months in the year, the county has an increasing number of Black Angus and Guernsey blood-lines. It is said to be the home of the Nancy Hanks watermelon; the chief farm crops are corn and cotton.

Right from Summerville on Lyerly St. to State 48; R. on State 48 to the SUMMERVILLE HATCHERY, *4.1 m.,* operated by the State Game and Fish Commission, at the base of Lookout Mountain. Species of fish hatched are rainbow and brown trout, pond fish, bream, and bass. Water is supplied by a single limestone spring with a flow of 1,800 gallons a minute.

The road passes through the village of MENLO, *9 m.* (850 alt., 453 pop.), and continues up the slope of Lookout Mountain to Cloudland where the Cloudland Park Resort Hotel (*swimming, golfing, dancing for guests; open six months for summer interval*), *13.2 m.,* is located on the almost level summit of the mountain (2,000 alt.). From this point is a magnificent view of the rugged countryside; the steep escarpment on the eastern margin of Lookout Plateau descends in sheer cliffs for several hundred feet.

From Cloudland an unpaved road leads to HIGH POINT, *17.2 m.,* a large boulder that overhangs the valley and is an exceptionally fine vantage point for views.

The KARTAH DELL PICNIC AREA, about *3 m.* south of Summerville, on US 27 (R), consists of a two-acre development near Mack White Gap in Chattooga County.

The facilities consist of a parking area, toilets, spring, picnic tables, and fire-places. It is maintained by the Armuchee District of the Chattahoochee National Forest, U. S. Forest Service.

South of Summerville the highway enters a rolling agricultural section. From TAYLOR'S RIDGE, *42.8 m.* (approx. 1,425 alt.), is a view of the Appalachian Valley and Lookout Mountain to the northwest.

The GATE OF OPPORTUNITY (R), *61.5 m.,* is the entrance to the BERRY SCHOOLS (*open 8-6 weekdays; guide service through building and grounds*). The fenced grounds extend for about eight miles along the highway. Replacing the log cabin in which Miss Martha Berry (1866-1942) began her work are sixty impressive buildings housing four distinct units: separate schools for boys and girls, a college, and a project for child and adult education.

From the gate the ROAD OF OPPORTUNITY, a broad avenue of elms planted by Miss Berry and her first pupils, leads to the white Colonial Administration Building which was built by the students, and where President Theodore Roosevelt spoke to them on his visit in 1910. The campus, covering 150 acres of a 30,000-acre tract of forest and farm land, is landscaped with flower gardens and lawns. Shady walks and pleasant drives connect the buildings, some of which are Georgian Colonial in design, some Greek Revival, some Gothic, and others adaptations of the early log cabin. The MOUNT BERRY CHAPEL (non-sectarian) is a brick structure of Georgian Colonial design seating 1,600 persons. Above the entrance is a lofty front tower, topped with a pedimented and arched belfry of three stages, closely modeled after Sir Christopher Wren's Christ Church in Alexandria, Virginia; and there is a fine Palladian window.

From the Administration Building a drive leads right to BERRY COLLEGE, a group of white-columned, red brick buildings built by the school boys from brick they made. This unit was opened in September, 1926, for young men and women from rural districts who were not financially able to attend other colleges. A member of the American Association of Colleges, it provides academic instruction and requires a year of training in agriculture or industry.

The driveway leads from the Berry School Campus to the rustic log cabins of MARTHA BERRY SCHOOL FOR GIRLS, also visible from the highway, and turns right to the Gothic stone buildings donated by Mr. and Mrs. Henry Ford for high school and college girls. Gargoyles ornamenting the towers and cornices reflect the fancy of medieval times. In the library is a stained-glass window depicting scenes from Shakespeare's *Midsummer Night's Dream.* Effective wood carving throughout the buildings enhances the Gothic tone. It is a point of local pride that the stone used in the buildings was quarried near Rome. Among the exhibits of the school are woolen and cotton articles woven by the girls.

From this school the Road to Remembrance leads to a lake fed by mountain springs, to barns where pedigreed cattle are bred, to fields where food crops are cultivated, and through forests to MOUNT BERRY SCHOOL FOR BOYS, where three hundred students, including grown men, receive high school training.

A road leads to the Community House of the POSSUM TROT RURAL COMMUNITY, founded in 1935. In three classroom buildings a model rural graded school, conducted for local children, serves as a practice school for student teachers. The old mountain church, which has passed the century mark, is where Miss Berry started her day school, teaching many adults to read the Bible before she started the Berry Schools. At Possum Trot entire families have a chance for educational improvement as well as instruction in farming, thus developing the liberal and the natural arts in balance. It was here while engaged in her early religious work that Miss Berry became known as the Sunday Lady.

Right from Possum Trot, on the hilltop of Mount Berry (1,800 alt.) within the bounds of the school property, is the HOUSE OF DREAMS, a cottage in which Miss Berry received faculty members, visitors, and students. The associated tower is used as a watchout for fires in the 25,000-acre forest.

These schools for rural people charge an annual fee of $200 for high school work and $250 for college training, but it is possible for many students to work their way. Those paying the cash fee are on a nine-months basis, while the others work out their tuition during the summer. As is well known, tuition never covers more than a fraction of the educational cost; and hence the school must contribute an additional $400 for each student. The annual deficit required for maintenance exceeds $150,000 above income from industries and endowment.

More than 1,100 students from eleven states are matriculated in the four schools, half of them doing college work. In the work period, two eight-hour days a week, these boys and girls care for the grounds, cultivate the farms, or work in the carpentry shops, laundries, dairies, and kitchens. Half of the 140 faculty members are Berry graduates, and all live on the campus where they can give the students careful supervision. Bible study and regular attendance at Sunday school are required of all the students.

Miss Martha Berry began her work by telling Bible stories to the children of her father's tenants. Next she opened a day school, and rode on horseback through the mountain regions to organize sewing classes, Sunday schools, prayer meetings, and other day schools. With the help of Miss Elizabeth Brewster, and her sister Miss Frances Berry, she established a school in a large log cabin on her 300-acre farm. Her first boarding school opened with five boys on January 13, 1902. In turn the boys hewed pine trees, hauled logs, and built a school for girls, which was opened on Thanksgiving Day, 1909. By this time her personal funds were exhausted and she began enlisting her friends, the merchants of Rome, and various philanthropists.

Epidemics, crop failures, and a disastrous fire did not turn Miss Berry from her purpose. She was granted honorary degrees by eight prominent colleges and received many other tributes. In 1925 the President of the United States presented her with the Roosevelt Medal; in 1929 she received the $5,000 *Pictorial Review* award; and in 1931, as the result of a nation-wide poll, she was selected as one of the twelve outstanding women of America. Hers was the happy life that all men seek, and but few achieve: the entire institution signifies this. Since Miss Berry's death in 1942, the Schools have been operated under a Board of Trustees, headed by John A. Sibley, of Atlanta.

Two thousand acres of year-around pasture and a 200-head herd of Angus cattle have been added in recent years to the operating farm land. With 200 purebred Jerseys and 600 Herefords, the addition of the Angus herd makes the number of cattle equal to a thousand. There are also herds of sheep and hogs and flocks of chickens and turkeys.

Berry graduates are now scattered to the four corners of the world and are numbered among those in almost every field. But—and this is critically significant for the good life—the majority have gone back into rural communities.

The BATTEY STATE HOSPITAL, Georgia's $12,000,000 tuberculosis sanitarium, is approximately three miles from the city of Rome, and situated on the northwest corner of the city limits. An agreement with the War Assets Administration transferred Battey General Hospital, after it was closed in December, 1945, and declared surplus, to the State of Georgia to be used for Public Health purposes; *viz.* as a tuberculosis hospital, for the consideration of one dollar. A six-year compliance period between the state and the U. S. Federal Works Agency was satisfactorily concluded January 29, 1953, thereby making the transaction complete. At a meeting of the State Board of Health in April, 1945, Dr. Rufus F. Payne, Superintendent of the State Tuberculosis Sanitarium (1945-1952), was instructed to proceed with necessary changes and to transfer the patients from Alto, the former state sanitarium, as soon as possible. Patients were transferred on June 20, 1946. Battey General Hospital became Battey State Hospital and was officially opened to the public. The 1946 Legislature appropriated $1,000,000 for the first year's operation. For 1953 the amount was $3,062,000.

The institution is comprised of 180 acres and 145 buildings of brick or concrete block construction. Five groups of hospital buildings are interconnected with 17 miles of enclosed passageways. There are five kitchens, six cafeterias (though not all are in use at present), a complete laundry, maintenance and engineering department, and a steam plant with three boilers fired by natural gas, or fuel oil in an emergency.

The hospital facility is completely self-contained, except for water and electricity. Buildings are laid out in a typical army hospital design with approximately 2,500 beds. While more private beds could be used, the hospital is quite suitable for a tuberculosis sanitarium. Each ward has a diet kitchen, two nurses' offices, and a doctor's office. There are administration buildings, personnel quarters, recreation buildings, a guest house, gymnasium, an auditorium with theater facilities, and a pleasant chapel. An athletic field, tennis court, and a swimming pool add to the interest of employment at the hospital.

Complete medical and surgical service, including internal medical service, is provided for the diagnosis and treatment of tuberculosis by the full-time medical and surgical staff. In addition, specialized medical-surgical service is provided by visiting consultants from the Medical College in Augusta and the Emory Medical School. A staff of fifteen trained laboratory technicians do all needed bacteriological tests in the diagnosis and treatment of patients. Dr. Ingrid Stergus, the pathologist, conducts the scientific research and necessary examinations of excised tissues and organs. The dental clinic is made up of two dentists, with the services of a part-time prosthodontist and one hygienist.

The department of nursing care employs 285 graduate and practical nurses and nurse-aides. Each ward operates under a graduate nurse-supervisor, with the necessary staff assigned to her service. A school for aides is conducted at the hospital with daily classroom and actual ward-work. Average classes for Negro and white aides, conducted separately, consist of about 75 students. The culinary department consists of a chief dietitian assisted by four institutional management graduates, and employs 189 persons: chefs, bakers, diet-kitchen supervisors, and serving women.

All patients are served scientifically planned meals in bed, except those few with "exercise privileges" who are served in a cafeteria.

Between-meal refreshments of fruit juice and milk are served in all wards twice a day. A complete laundry service is furnished for patients without charge.

A 1,000-acre farm bought in 1946, and located on US 41, supplies 800 gallons of pasteurized milk daily, and around 800 hogs annually.

Supplied with a teacher from the Floyd County School System, the hospital school provides bedside and classroom instruction for school-age patients on elementary and high school levels, with a diploma issued when schooling is complete. The State Vocational Rehabilitation Service has a branch department in the hospital. Correspondence courses are available for bed patients, while "exercise" patients may attend daily classes in business administration (typing, shorthand, and bookkeeping), homemaking, tailoring, beauty culture, barbering, or watchmaking.

ROME, 63.5 m. (614 alt., 29,615 pop.), seat of Floyd County and the leading industrial city of northwest Georgia, is surrounded by the fertile, rolling plains of Rome Valley. Climate conditions are good, with an average summer temperature of 78° and an average winter temperature of 42.6°. Within its own confines, Rome is a commercial-industrial town, manufacturing bagging, paper boxes, bricks, chenille, cotton textiles, cotton-seed oil, furniture, garments, gloves, hosiery, mattresses, clay pipe, and rayon yarn and a sizable number of other products. There are eight companies to be listed under the heading of machine shops and foundries. Its plants are built away from the principal business section which is on a peninsula where the confluence of the Etowah and Oostanaula rivers forms the Coosa. From this three-river point the residential section spreads in all directions. Built among several rounded hills, the city has wide streets lined with commodious frame houses, old as well as new, and shaded by oak, elm, and other trees.

Because Hernando De Soto, in 1540, is believed to have spent almost a month on the site of Rome, a section of the city was once called De Soto. Coming to north Georgia in the early nineteenth century, the first settlers found here the Indian village of Chiaha, which was a center for negotiations between the Federal government and John Ross, chief of the Cherokee Nation during the period preceding the Cherokee Removal. The Indians were removed in 1838.

The town was founded in 1834 and succeeded Livingston as the county seat in the following year. Its name, drawn by lot, was suggested because like ancient Rome it was built on seven hills. Such business establishments as might be expected in a town so strategically situated sprang up between 1834 and 1861. When Chattanooga, Tennessee, was chosen as the terminus of the Western & Atlantic Railroad, the Rome Railroad (originally the Memphis Branch Railroad and Steamboat Company of Georgia), was built to connect with the Western & Atlantic at Kingston. Stagecoach lines and post roads were established over Indian trails in north Georgia to join other routes at Athens, Milledgeville, Macon, and Augusta.

Between 1845 and 1850, with the development of steamboat and also railroad traffic, Rome became a shipping point as well as a receiving point for cotton, especially later after the establishment of the Howell Cotton Compress about 1870. Around the time of the half-century, James Noble, Sr., a native of Cornwall, England, moved to Rome from Reading, Pennsylvania, with his family, and built a large foundry and machine works. The plant was located between the N. C. & St. L. Railway tracks and the Etowah River, at the end of East 2nd and East 3rd Streets. They manufactured steam engines, nails, and other articles, and later cannon for the Confederacy. The machine lathe that ground these cannon is still in use at the Davis Foundry & Machine Co. Thus this phase of industrial Rome is more than a century old.

Although Floyd had been what is known as a "Union" county, on January 16, 1861, along with the other counties in Georgia, it sent delegates to the secession convention at Milledgeville, and on January 19, 1861, the ordinance of secession was passed by a vote of 208 to 89. The most notable event of the war for Rome took place in May, 1863, when Colonel Abel D. Streight, coming up from northeastern Alabama with 1,466 men, prepared to attack the city. This force was captured by 410 men under General Nathan Bedford Forrest, who by a clever trick convinced Streight that he was outnumbered. A memorial to General Forrest and the event stands at the intersection of Broad Street and Second Avenue. In May of the following year, at the beginning of his Atlanta campaign, General Sherman dispatched cavalrymen under General Kenner Garrard and General Jefferson C. Davis to take Rome. A small Federal force occupied the town during the summer, and in September Sherman sent forces under General John Murray Corse to hold Rome against expected Confederate attacks. On his way to Resaca, Sherman stopped in Rome on October 12; on October 28 he returned to the city and from headquarters here directed his forces until November 2, when he withdrew to Kingston. On November 10 evacuation was begun, and that night all factories that might be useful to the Confederacy, including the Noble Foundry, were destroyed.

Rome has been flooded numbers of times by the high waters of the three rivers. In the spring of 1886, due to heavy winter rains and snows, the city suffered a flood so devastating that events are still reckoned as occurring just before or after it. Steamboats are reported to have made their way from the rivers as far north as Fifth Avenue and Broad Street. The bridge over the Etowah River at Wooley's Station, in Bartow County, broke and swept through Rome, carrying the bridges at Second Avenue and at Broad Street before it. Good Friday of 1886 presented a scene of bleak ruin. One of the functions of the new Allatoona Dam (*see* TOUR 2), near Cartersville, is to reduce to safe levels the flood heights at Rome and along the upper reaches of the Coosa River.

Visible from all parts of the city, the CITY CLOCK TOWER was erected as a pumping station and reservoir in 1871. A year later the clock was added, the bronze bell of which was cast by the Meneely Bell Foundry of West Troy, New York. A new water system, begun in 1892, replaced the old one, but an electric fire system now employs the bell of the clock as an alarm, and antennas for the police radio system have been installed on the tower.

The CAPITOLINE WOLF which was originally placed in front of the Municipal Auditorium, Broad St. at 6th Avenue, was removed to the basement during World War II, but has since been restored. It is a bronze replica of the familiar Roman one showing the mythical founders of ancient Rome, Romulus and Remus, being suckled by a wolf. It was presented by Mussolini when the Georgia city was selected as a site for the Italian Tubize-Chatillon Corporation. The mill and its village, on Chatillon Rd., now belong to the Celanese Corporation of America.

On the lawn of the auditorium is the BATTEY MONUMENT, a memorial to Dr. Robert Battey (1828-95), a surgeon and pioneer in using ovariotomy as a means of correcting a pathological condition. He is famed in medical circles for the operation that has been named in his honor.

ST. MARY'S CATHOLIC CHURCH, N. Broad Street between 9th Ave. and Smith St., suggests a medieval Gothic country chapel. Set back on an elevated lot, the simple granite building is without ornamentation except for a large crucifix and the carved words *Venite Adoremus* above the doorway. Behind the altar is a sixteenth-century oil painting, *Il Giorno,* of the school of Correggio, showing the Madonna and Child, Mary Magdalene, and St. Jerome. The canvas was given to the church by a sister of Miss Martha Berry's who had married Prince Ruspoli, of Rome, Italy.

THE CHIEFTAINS (*private*), 80 Chatillon Rd., is a two-story house of white clapboards laid over the log cabin built in 1794 by Major Ridge, a Cherokee leader whose English name probably was derived from his military rank in the Creek War of 1814. At first a supporter of John Ross against the eviction of the Indians, he later changed sides and on

December 29, 1835, signed a treaty at New Echota by which the Chero-kee ceded all their lands east of the Mississippi. Apparently, the act was in good faith and intended for the good of his people, because when the Indians were moved westward in 1838 he went with them. But the year following he was executed in accordance with a tribal law exacting the death penalty for the sale of lands without the full consent of the tribe.

Major Ridge's trading post and ferry made these grounds a tribal gathering place. Hosts of Cherokees often gathered on the lawn, and negotiations leading to the Treaty of 1835 were made here. A stone marker was erected by the W. P. A. The house is now the residence of the president of the Celanese Corporation and stands on its property.

THORNWOOD (*private*), Alabama Rd., is an ante-bellum house with a Greek portico in front and colonnades at each end, built in 1848 by Colonel Alfred Shorter. The house was bought in 1944 by Mr. and Mrs. W. A. DuPre who added a kitchen wing at the right of the house. The house suffered various occupations during the War between the States, and here and there on white Doric columns and in the attic, there are signs of an idle soldiery.

SHORTER COLLEGE, Shorter Hill off Alabama Road, was founded in 1873 as the Cherokee Baptist Female College, with Alfred Shorter as the president of the Board of Trustees. Because of his sustained in-terest in the college, which included substantial support, the name was changed in 1877 to Shorter College as a memorial to his wife Martha.

The college is a member of the Southern Association of Colleges and Secondary Schools, of the Association of American Colleges, and of the American Council on Education. It has full membership in the Na-tional Association of Schools of Music. Shorter graduates with the B.A. degree are eligible for membership in the American Association of University Women.

In 1911 the college was moved from the buildings now occupied by a high school into the simple red brick buildings on a hill overlooking Rome and the winding rivers. The 150-acre campus provides abun-dantly for sports and recreational activities. Rome Hall contains class-rooms, the general library, laboratories, offices of the faculty, and the administrative personnel. The dormitories, Cooper Hall and Van Hoose Hall, as well as Rome Hall and the Dining Hall, are joined by glass-enclosed corridors so that when the weather is unfavorable stu-dents may go to classes and to meals without discomfort.

Shorter confers the bachelor of arts degree and also a bachelor of music. The catalogue for 1951-52 shows a registration of 290 students, one hundred of whom are special students, mostly from Rome.

MYRTLE HILL CEMETERY, S. Broad St. across the bridge, is on a conical hill rising abruptly from the junction of the rivers. It contains the graves of three founders of the city, and other historical monuments. The grave of the first Mrs. Woodrow Wilson, who was Ellen Axson, the daughter of a Presbyterian minister of Rome, is marked by a simple stone of Carrara marble. Wilson met her while visiting relatives in the city.

Rome has two business colleges, the Carroll Lynn School of Business Administration and the North Georgia Business College. The Rome Off-Campus Center of the University of Georgia takes care of some three hundred or more northwest Georgia students. St. Mary's Parochial School, under the supervision of the Dominican Sisters, has complete courses through the eighth grade for pupils not attending the public schools.

Library facilities include the Carnegie Library with 35,000 volumes, a 5,000-volume library for Negroes, 15,000 volumes in the Maple Street Community Center Library, and the Floyd County Bookmobile service for the rural areas. The city of Rome has a carefully organized and well supervised program of community recreation.

Both the Coosa Country Club and the Callier Springs Club have golf courses that may be used summer or winter, and other recreational facilities. Exceptional opportunities for boating and fishing are available on the three rivers, the Oostanaula and Etowah rivers which join here to form the Coosa. The Allatoona Dam recreation area is only a short distance away at Cartersville (*see* TOUR 2).

Agricultural changes in the last ten years have remade the rural scene in Floyd County and the surrounding Rome trade area. First among these has been the shift from row-crops to hay and pasture. A local seed-processing plant has made both sericea and fescue seed a good cash crop, with 138,000 pounds of fescue seed and probably some 80,000 of sericea in 1952. Along with kudzu, sericea lespedeza has had to play the rôle of red-headed stepchild among the pasture plants in the past, but the drought of 1952 firmly established it as an excellent summer grazing plant.

As with many parts of north Georgia, the county has broiler houses, with a capacity of some 200,000 chicks, but since there is no nearby poultry dressing plant, production does not compare with that in typical broiler sections. Marketing for commercial eggs is better, however, and in 1952 flocks of laying hens totaled 40,000, with an increase to 60,000 indicated for 1953.

Purebred beef-type bulls have increased from six in 1940 to more than 150 today, serving 800 head of purebred beef and 3,000 commercials. Slow to be accepted, artificial insemination has grown in favor. In

1952, 2,000 cows were artificially bred through the Coosa Valley Breeding Association.

The first to be organized, the Coosa River Conservation District embraces eight northwest Georgia counties. Evidence of its success may be
easily inferred from the fact that in 1952 its membership was increased
by 638 farms.

On US 27, 2 *m.* south of Rome, is the FARMERS MARKET, of that city.
Started in 1949, this market serves an extensive section of northwest
Georgia. Though at present the sales are not equal to those of major
markets in the State Department of Agriculture's Farmers Market System, it is growing rapidly.

1. Right from Rome on State 20 to the junction with a wooded road; L. on
this road to RADIO MINERAL SPRINGS, *3 m.,* a small summer resort at the foot of
Mt. Alto. Left from Radio Mineral Springs on a well-marked road to the MOUNT
ALTO SCENIC LOOP, a 25-mile route winding among high, wooded ridges northwest of Rome and reaching the SUMMIT OF MOUNT ALTO (1,529 alt.), which affords an excellent view of the surrounding valleys. The route returns to Rome
on US 411.

2. Right from Rome on US 411 S. to the DARLINGTON SCHOOL, 2.5 *m.,* a boys'
preparatory school, founded in 1905 and named for Joseph P. Darlington, a
teacher in an earlier Rome school. Its red brick buildings with limestone trim
are grouped about a quiet lake on a wooded campus of approximately eighty
acres. The student body numbers around two hundred and fifty.

On WATER CRESS FARM, 7.9 *m.* cress for local use and outside markets has been
raised for more than sixty years.

CAVE SPRING, *13 m.* (662 alt., 959 pop.), on Little Cedar Creek in Vann's
Valley, has broad streets shaded by oaks, bays, and weeping willows. Settlement was begun in 1826 and the town was incorporated in 1852. Two blocks
L. of the main street is the CAVE (*free picnic grounds*), which has always been
a visitor's attraction. The chambers in this series of limestone caves are equipped
with stairs and bridges that lead to a deep pool and various rock formations.
The water from a spring flowing from the cave is piped to the town. A smaller
spring, about fifty yards from the cave, bubbles out of the hillside and forms a
shallow stream that supplies water for a large rock swimming pool.

A short distance from the cave is the GEORGIA SCHOOL FOR THE DEAF, housed in
simple red brick buildings. Established by legislative act in 1847, the school was
opened on July 1, 1848. Georgia began education of the deaf and dumb in 1835,
when several children were sent to the American Asylum at Hartford, Connecticut. In 1846 the principal of Hearn Manual Labor School at Cave Spring
accepted four pupils from the state and this led to the establishment of the state
institution here. A new building program to cost an estimated $1,000,000 is
under way at Cave Spring.

The site of the former AGATE DEMONSTRATION PROJECT is south of Rome
on U. S. Highway 27. It is one of the five projects operated in Georgia
by the Soil Conservation Service during the period of 1934-38. This
project covered an area of about 30,000 acres of privately owned land

and was situated in Floyd and Polk counties. Its purpose was to demonstrate to the 287 farmers living in the project area the most effective methods for controlling erosion through sound land use with adequate supporting practices. Land owners co-operated with the Service by utilizing their land according to plans worked out with trained technicians. Steep and erodible open lands were planted to pine trees, kudzu, sericea lespedeza, and pasture grasses and legumes. Gently sloping and semi-level lands were used for row crops. Terraces and water disposal systems and soil-conserving rotations were established on sloping crop lands. Several hundred acres of crimson clover were planted annually as a winter cover crop.

The project area is now included in the Coosa River Soil Conservation District. Many of the measures applied during the demonstration period are still evident, especially plantings of pine, kudzu, and sericea lespedeza, and established pastures. As a demonstration area, the project afforded the farmers of northwest Georgia an opportunity to see recommended practices in operation under conditions facing them daily on their farms.

LINDALE, 65 m. (652 alt., 3,234 pop.), is an industrial settlement dependent upon the modern well-equipped textile mills of the Pepperell Manufacturing Company, makers of the nationally known Pepperell fabrics. In the village is a large stucco community auditorium, containing game rooms, a motion picture theatre, a tearoom, and a large tiled swimming pool. Also in the village is a modern gymnasium, comparing favorably with any in the South, and on top of one of the highest hills around Lindale is an American Legion Home.

CEDARTOWN, 81.2 m. (809 alt., 9,470 pop.), seat of Polk County, was the site of a Cherokee Indian settlement named for the numerous red cedars growing in the vicinity. When the town was incorporated in 1854, several planters of means had already built homes here. It was not until the 1920's, however, that its chief industrial expansion occurred; in this period its growth began as a textile center, and there are now three major plants employing around 2,000 persons. The products of the seventeen or so industries include iron ore, gray iron castings, woolen and rayon cloth, cotton yarn, zipper fastener tape, upholstered furniture, cotton and rayon tire cord fabric, box board and core paper, vitamins and chemicals, mixed fertilizers, and paper tubes and boxes. Farmers know Cedartown as the home of the Rome Plow Company, makers of steel disc plows and harrows.

A nine-hole golf course adjoins the country club, which is the scene of many adult community activities. The town water works is built over a natural spring at Big Springs Park, and furnishes an estimated

5,000,000 gallons of water daily for town and industrial use. A modern disposal plant takes care of the town's sewage. Peek's Park has a swimming pool, lighted tennis courts, picnic grounds, and a well-equipped playground. Founded in 1923 by Ethel Harpst, the Ethel Harpst Home provides a refuge for needy children. Several spacious buildings of modified Georgian Colonial architecture, the main building with a two-story columned portico, are arranged about a grassed and well-landscaped area. The town has two good hotels, the Wayside Inn with 36 rooms, and the Baldwin with eleven. In addition there are a number of tourist courts.

With a winter mean temperature of 47°, a summer mean temperature of 71°, and an average annual rainfall of 47.5 inches, the area is favorable to year-around grassland farming, and dairying is increasingly replacing row money crops. A new cheese and dairy products plant, started with local capital and now producing 30,000 pounds of cheese a month, has the trade-name, "Pride of Cedartown." The Polk County Egg Co-operative began marketing on July 1, 1952. Farmers bring eggs to the co-op several times a week; candling and grading are done at once, and the eggs are then distributed locally, though a wider market will be developed. Cotton and corn are staples of the area.

Near the city airport are the track and buildings of the fair grounds. The Northwest Georgia Fair is held here annually.

BUCHANAN, 97.9 m. (1,295 alt., 651 pop.), the seat of Haralson County, was chartered in 1857 and named for President James Buchanan. Among the principal products are cotton, corn, peaches, apples, cotton textiles, lumber, garments, and copper products.

BREMEN, 105.4 m. (1,416 alt., 2,299 pop.), is at the junction with US 78 (see TOUR 8).

CARROLLTON, 117.3 m. (1,095 alt., 7,753 pop.), made the seat of Carroll County in 1829, was incorporated in 1856 and became an enterprising commercial center. Busy mills and comfortable homes indicate the town's prosperity. The county lies in a fertile agricultural section, worked by competent farmers, most of whom own their farms and maintain a high record for productivity.

The citizens have developed what may very well be the most interesting example of community organization and planning in the state. The list of its officers, board of directors, permanent staff, and panel or sub-committees numbers over a hundred persons, and represents all of the available sources of leadership and public-spirited organizations in the area. It is known as the Carroll Service Council, and according to its 7th Annual Report in 1950, it is functionally divided into five phases of community action: Social Welfare, Religion, Information, Education and Recreation, and Chamber of Commerce. According to its own definition, "It is the coordinating machinery through which all needs and problems confronting the county are recognized, cleared, and available resources utilized without destroying or impairing the initiative and autonomy of interested groups."

The Social Welfare Panel has as its function the discovery of need and the fixing of attention upon it by the available means of relief. Thus people in the Carroll County area are helped with food, clothing, and medical care. With the help of the Council, advantage has been taken of the Hill Burton Act to construct the half-million dollar Tanner Memorial Hospital, which includes a Negro wing among its thoroughly modern facilities. In 1946 the Federal government passed an act providing aid for the construction of hospitals, by state allotments. The act specified that local groups contribute two-thirds of the needed fund, and the Federal government one-third. The area has an efficient Public Health Service.

Concerned particularly with the rural churches, the Religious Panel encourages more Sunday schools, an increased number of services each month, and the remodeling and beautification of churches. In 1950 a Panel on Information was incorporated in the Council, to tell the Council's story by means of the press, the radio, monthly news bulletins, and other media of communication.

The Education and Recreation Panel might be described as co-functional, and is concerned with the two healths that make for happiness, that of the mind and that of the body. An especially valuable contributon has been made to the community by the organization of non-credit, tuition-free courses offered to adults. Among the agencies co-operating in this have been the Carrollton Merchants' Association, the State Department of Education, West Georgia College, and the public schools, especially the Unity Junior High School. 4-H Club work in Carroll County was initiated by the Council's undertaking to pay the salary of an assistant farm agent for several years. Community workers, students from the college, and members of the Friends' Service Committee, not only encouraged but actually worked together in the construction of the modern and neatly functional Oak Mountain Chapel, which is the first part of the planned community center. The West Georgia Regional Library is an important part of the area's social economy. The Panel on Recreation performs a multiplicity of functions, but specifically it has operated the swimming pool, gymnasium, park, and playgrounds. Besides sponsoring entertainment carnivals, athletic events and contests in the region, the Recreation Panel developed a Water Safety Instructor's course in 1950 in co-operation with the Carroll County Red Cross.

Among the new industries described in the 7th Annual Report are the Stylewise Mill, a textile plant, and Southwire Company, the first plant in Georgia to manufacture copper and aluminum wire and cable for transmission lines. The older Mandeville Mills, Inc. celebrated its fiftieth anniversary in July, 1952, with an open house for the stockholders, employees, and others who have contributed to the success of the mill. Dixie Garment Manufacturing Company, makers of trousers, increased its floor space the same year. Factors contributing to production in the county are the Hills Brothers' pimiento receiving station, which encourages a new cash crop, the modern broiler plant, the canning company, the three lumber mills, and a freezer-locker plant. With REA at the head of the list, co-operatives include the Soil Conservation Association, a Sales Barn, one for livestock, the Fertilizer Plant, the Cotton Producers Association, and the Farmers Mutual Warehouse; and technical services include extension work and county agent, Soil Conservation Service, and a Production & Marketing Administration office.

Right from Carrollton on Maple Street which becomes State 16 to the entrance of WEST GEORGIA JUNIOR COLLEGE, *1.2 m.*, a unit of the University System of Georgia. A co-educational institution organized in 1907 as the fourth Congressional District Agricultural and Mechanical School, it was made a junior college by the Board of Regents in 1933. The enrollment is around four hundred. On the campus are seven red brick buildings with white columns, and ten feet from the entrance is the MCINTOSH MONUMENT (R), erected to General William McIntosh, leader of the Creek Nation. This monument was originally a mounting block at his home (*see* below).

ROOPVILLE, *127.2 m.* (1,253 alt., 202 pop.), is a settlement built around a granite quarry.

1. Right from Roopville on an unpaved road to GOAT ROCK, *1 m.* The deep holes carved in its surface were used as mortars for grinding corn by Creek Indians who inhabited this region until 1825. The vicinity is rich in Indian relics, mostly arrowheads and spearheads, tomahawks, and pottery shards.

2. Left from a tourist camp in Roopville on an unpaved road to the SITE OF THE MCINTOSH RESERVATION, *10 m.*, on which is a monument marking the SITE OF CHIEF WILLIAM MCINTOSH'S HOUSE. This tract of land was given to McIntosh after he had effected cession of Creek lands to the state by the Treaty of Indian Springs, February 12, 1825, in which a faction of the Creeks agreed to part with their lands in Georgia and in return to receive equivalent lands in the West and also $400,000 (*see* TOUR *12*).

McIntosh, a man of Scottish and Indian ancestry, joined the American forces in the War of 1812, served in the Florida campaign, and became a brigadier general. He was a first cousin of Governor George Troup (*see* TOUR 9), whose relentless and violent efforts to evict the Creek caused sharp difficulties for President Monroe and President John Quincy Adams, and something like a state of open hostility between Georgia and the Federal government. The Treaty of Indian Springs enraged the Upper Creeks who had refused to attend the conference. Menawa, a rival leader, was appointed McIntosh's executioner. On April 30, 1825, Menawa with more than a hundred braves arrived at McIntosh's house. All whites were ordered to leave, and Chilly McIntosh, the chief's son escaped with them. When only McIntosh and his second-in-command were left, they were driven out by fire into a fusillade of bullets and were killed instantly.

FRANKLIN, *141.1 m.* (695 alt., 425 pop.), seat of Heard County, on the Chattahoochee River, was a village as early as 1770 but was not incorporated until 1831. The town is dependent on the cotton, corn, granite, and timber of the county. There is no railroad in this area.

At LAGRANGE, *162.5 m.* (729-786 alt., 25,025 pop.), is a junction with US 29 (*see* TOUR *3*).

The IDA CASON GARDENS, *183.6 m.,* or *2 m.* south of Chipley (*admission fee*), on the slopes of Pine Mountain in Harris County, is entered at the Entrance Lodge (and Administration Building) at right. A memorial to Mr. Cason J. Callaway's mother, the gardens have been planned and constructed under the personal care of Mr. and Mrs. Callaway. Cason Callaway is widely known not only in connection with the extensive textile mills centered in LaGrange, but as the sponsor, with a group of associates, of the Callaway Plan whereby small, submarginal farms, distributed over the state, were restored by modern agricultural techniques, to serve as exemplary models of soil conservation and to encourage diversified farming.

At the Gardens, 12,000 acres of variously rugged terrain are being converted by Mrs. Callaway and her landscape architects, Mr. Gilmore Clark and Mr. John Leon Hoffman, into a recreation area where nature is not mutilated but coached towards its native perfection. The transverse axis of the area is established by Mountain Creek Lake which is disposed, roughly, southwest by northeast, and circumscribed by Five Mile Drive.

In the landscaping, thousands of plants and shrubs from the fifteen-year-old nurseries at the Callaway home, Blue Springs, near Hamilton, have been used. Notable among these are Sweet Azalea (*Azalea arborescens*) which, growing to eight feet, has the convenient habit of unfolding sweet, white flowers in midsummer; and also Plumleaf or Summer Scarlet Azalea (*Azalea prunifolia*), native to hilly regions in Georgia on well-drained but moist spots, which has scarlet flowers in July and August. In recognition of his work in propagating the latter, Mr. Callaway received "The Man of the Year in Agriculture" award from the Women's Garden Club of America.

In the area, though especially in more favorable spots, fine gradations and subtle contrasts are being effected by the use of holly, magnolia, rhododendrons, azaleas, ferns, sweet shrub, wild hydrangeas, laurels, wild crabapples, dogwood and plum trees, surges of wild violets, trillium, trout lilies, and the dainty bluet. Many shrubs from sections of China climatically parallel to this area are analogous to native ones, but offer provocative variations in stem, leaf, or fruit, and may be combined with the natives effectively. One of these is Burford holly (*Ilex cornuta Burfordii*), the decidedly dark green lacquer-like leaves of which brilliantly reflect the numerous but large red berries. In all the plantings, existing nature has been so sympathetically observed, and then aided and directed, as to effect a total composition in terms of shape, mass, position, and color.

With over eight miles of shore line in all, the seven lakes cover 250 acres of land. In keeping with the economy of the terrain, the lakes, constructed on various levels, have been connected by spillways and so inter-disposed as to conserve the water available in the area and to keep it fresh and sweet while at the same time providing that note of landscaping interest that only water can effect. The result is suggestive of the aqueduct skills of the Romans, and offers a primary model for the translation of today's instrumental techniques into forms of beauty, with nature as the measure.

At the ENTRANCE LODGE, a road, leading R. past LAKE MOCKINGBIRD (L) and flanked (R) by the 2nd and 1st greens of the nine-hole golf course, arrives after a brief stretch, at the CLUB HOUSE (*golf, fishing, dining [food, in part, from the Garden Farms], etc.; a 124-car parking area; open every day except Mondays*). At the back of the Club House is a full length, two-story porch looking out over Mountain Creek Lake and the golf course. On the upper floor, and occupying most of its length, is the great dining hall, on the west wall of which is a painting by Italian-born but Georgia-adopted Athos Menaboni, of mallards, pintails, and canvas-back ducks flying in high course, south, over Mountain Creek Lake. The Club House has been described architecturally as a late 17th century English provincial inn in style. It is constructed of handmade brick, hand-hewn exposed timbers, and is roofed with rough-cut shakes.

The NINE-HOLE GOLF COURSE, planned by Donald Ross, every fairway of which is either along the lake or recessed in a protected land-niche, offers "fast greens, strategically trapped," and an exciting game.

At the rear of the Club House, "Cleopatra's Barge," a large, flat-bottomed boat able to carry sixty passengers, leaves at stated intervals for a cruise to the far end of Mountain Creek Lake and back. The U-shaped BOATHOUSE, close to the Club House, is in architectural harmony with the other buildings. Its 528-foot length houses over a hundred fishing boats and canoes, and a canal, flowing the entire course of the building, admits boats at one opening and enables them to exit at the other.

From the Club House area, one can turn into Five Mile Drive at a point just below Overlook Hill and Lake Whippoorwill, and, driving along the shore of greater Mountain Creek Lake, past Lake Bobolink and Lake Bluebird, located above the road (L), arrive at MEADOWLARK PICNIC AREA (*wildflower trails, picnic tables, refreshments, rest rooms, and 340-car parking area*), on the side of Mountain Creek Lake opposite the Club House. From this point Five Mile Drive goes past the 8th and 7th greens (R) and by one end of Lake Hummingbird; then it leads in an irregular crook past the 5th, 4th, and 3rd greens (R), to the lower end of Mountain Creek Lake, and around, past the 2nd green, to the Entrance.

At the Entrance, another road (L) leads to the BARBECUE and CAFE-TERIA ON OVERLOOK HILL (*outdoor lunch, refreshments, canoes, rest rooms, and a 140-car parking area*), just above Lake Whippoorwill. A long, open shed (in the style of the other buildings), supported by massive oak posts, provides shelter, and Georgia plantation meats are a star feature of the menu. Lake Whippoorwill, a scene for aquatic sport, is connected to Lake Hummingbird by a waterway navigable by canoes. For those wishing it, a fully-equipped nursery and playhouse, supervised by a practical nurse, is handy, for the very young.

Beyond the Entrance, 2 *m.* south on US 27 at Tip Top (1,037 alt.), is the GARDENS STORE (R), affording a splendid view of the deep and beautiful Pine Mountain Valley, on one side of which is the FRANKLIN D. ROOSEVELT STATE PARK, and where a RURAL COMMUNITY is located. The store sells what is perhaps the choicest list of foods south of the Mason-Dixon Line. Among the items are frozen turkeys, fryers, pheasants, squabs, guinea hens, cornish game hens, and ducks. Baked goods are on display from the store's kitchen. Also there are hams, cheeses from various parts of the world, glassed fruits and pickles, and luxury groceries that are a gourmet's delight. Many items come from the Garden Farms. THE OLD WATER MILL (*visitors welcome*), 7 *m.* south on US 27, supplies whole-grain products that have been water-ground on slow-turning mills. Plants and shrubs, fishing tackle, and books on cooking, fishing, and gardening are on sale. Box lunches are available, and for Saturday night, a special "Take-Home" supper.

Like those from the Gardens generally, profits from the Store are used to maintain and to improve the Ida Cason Gardens.

Left from the Gardens Store is an entrance to the FRANKLIN D. ROOSE-VELT STATE PARK AND CAMP AREA, formerly Pine Mountain State Park (*swimming, picnicking, boating, hiking, fishing, children's play-*

grounds, cabins, restaurant, trading post; open through the year; no general admission charge, or fishing fee). The park is traversed by scenic highway, State 190, which leads to Warm Springs (*12 m.*) and the Little White House (*see* below). Special features are the magnificent vistas overlooking Pine Mountain Valley, the beautiful stone inn, vacation cabins, lake areas, swimming facilities, and mountain trails. In spring the woods are vivid with dogwood, flame azalea, and delicate pink mountain laurel; one section is known for its wild violets.

PINE MOUNTAIN TAVERN, which serves excellent meals at popular prices, is surrounded by stone cottages for the accommodation of overnight guests. As of May 26, 1952, rates at the cottages were $3.00 single and $5.00 double, a night. (*Reservations should be made with the Manager, Franklin D. Roosevelt Tavern, P. O. Chipley, Georgia.*)

Following the suggestion of President Roosevelt, the designer of the swimming pool arranged it in the shape of a Liberty Bell, with the wading pool at the top. It has three official diving boards and water slides; there is a bathhouse of natural stone. Next to the pool is a children's playground, and a free picnic area with shelters and tables.

At Lake Delano, in the "Rural Demonstration Area" of the park, are ten vacation cabins. All are completely furnished for housekeeping and vacationing, except for linens. In 1952 the daily rates were $3.00 per person a day, or weekly rates from $20 to $60, according to the number of guests and the size of the cabin. A deposit is required for a week's reservation of a cabin, and cabins cannot be reserved for more than two weeks or less than one between May 15 and September 15. (*For reservations, housekeeping cabins, and group cabins—see below— address the Superintendent, Franklin D. Roosevelt R. D. A., Chipley, Georgia.*) Near Lake Delano there is another free picnic area with shelters, tables, and a children's playground. The lake was recently stocked with 15,000 bluegilled bream.

Also in the park are two group camping areas with facilities for any organized groups, as church groups, aquatic schools, Boy Scouts, Girl Scouts, Y. M. C. A., fraternities, or clubs. Each camp supplies squad cabins, completely equipped kitchen and dining hall, administration building and infirmary, playgrounds, docks, help quarters, counsellor cabins, and administrative staff quarters. Butane gas heating has been installed and the cabins have heaters, refrigerators, and new furniture. Both areas are located on Lake Franklin.

The entire park area as it is now constituted contains 5,063 acres.

At the northern corner is the site of King's Gap, and near is the SITE OF KING'S GAP VILLAGE, a settlement where a post office was established in 1837 on an old stagecoach route from Columbus to Newnan. Envelopes with the King's Gap cancellation are prized by collectors. The settlement was abandoned when the Central of Georgia Railroad was built around the lower side of Pine Mountain.

The PINE MOUNTAIN RURAL COMMUNITY was also established in the valley area. Its farms and houses are visible from Tip Top. Originally established by the F. E. R. A. as a rehabilitation project for sharecroppers and one-time farmers caught in urban traps by the economic situation, the project included some 13,000 acres of the valley, bounded on the north by Pine Mountain and on the south by Oak Mountain. Some units consisted of sufficient acreage for efficient farming operations and others of smaller acreage for subsistence farming and truck crops for home use. At the time of the settlement, the directors had three objectives for the people of the community: to create opportunities for work, to enable them to produce most of their subsistence, and to provide them with means to supplement their incomes from industrial work through agricultural activities. The guiding idea was that of the self-sustaining, small farm; and hence dairying, cattle, hogs, poultry, fruits, vegetables, and the care and development of woodlands, especially slash and longleaf pine, were encouraged as the elements of a diversified program.

Each unit had a complete dwelling and essential farm buildings to meet the needs of the program. All of these units were sold to individual families on terms of twenty years. The industrial part of the project did not develop well, however, and this has made the small acreage something of a disadvantage, since an adequate farm needs an acreage of a hundred or a hundred and fifty acres. Of the 262 families that purchased these units, 145 have liquidated their indebtedness in full, and only 117 are still financially obligated to the government.

A view from Tip Top of the neat and verdant Pine Mountain Valley suggests that the project taught a useful lesson.

The WARM SPRINGS FOUNDATION AND THE LITTLE WHITE HOUSE, about *11 m.* on State 190. (*For the short route from Atlanta on US 72 Alt., see* TOUR *3.*)

VISITING HOURS AT THE WARM SPRINGS FOUNDATION FOR RELATIVES AND FRIENDS OF PATIENTS: Subject to change, Weekdays, 2 P.M.-5 P.M., and 7:30 P.M.-9:30 P.M.; Sundays and holidays, 10:00 A.M.-12 N., 2:30 P.M.-5 P.M., 7:30 P.M.-9:30 P.M.

ACCOMMODATIONS: One hotel—Warm Springs Hotel, and the Warm Springs Motel, in the village of Warm Springs, about *1 m.* from the Foundation.

TRANSPORTATION: Southern Ry., and the Atlanta, Birmingham & Coast R.R., from Atlanta; Greyhound and Trailway buses, several schedules daily through Warm Springs.

THE LITTLE WHITE HOUSE (*see* below) is open from 9 A.M. to 5 P.M., daily.

The story of Warm Springs goes back to Indian days. According to legend, wounded warriors, seeking its curative effect, were granted a safe-conduct through hostile tribes. Late in the eighteenth century a group of Savannah residents, fleeing a yellow fever epidemic, discovered Warm Springs. By 1832 the place had become one of the South's summer resorts, and a small village had grown up near it. A quick-witted Englishman named Tidmarsh, claiming that he owned the property, saved it from the fire of Sherman's agents. But in 1865 the buildings were reduced to ashes because of a mishap with a bonfire of leaves started by Tidmarsh's wife. The resort was afterwards rebuilt and became a fashionable watering place of the South during the 1880's and 1890's. With the coming of the automobile, however, its fortunes declined, as did that of others like it. In 1924 it was in the possession of Tom Loyless, his niece Georgia Wilkins, and George Foster Peabody, who saw a future for the resort despite its recent decline. Franklin Roosevelt heard about Louis Joseph who, having had infantile paralysis, had apparently benefited greatly from swimming in the warm waters. He decided to make an exploratory trip.

Warm Springs' seed of national prominence began to grow when Roosevelt came down from New York in October, 1924. The story of Roosevelt's early struggle to walk again and to establish the Springs for those having a common need with him, has recently been published as *Roosevelt and the Warm Springs Story,* by Turnley Walker, one of the Springs' "alumni." Walker has described Roosevelt's first time in the pool. "They watched Roosevelt as he pushed away from the far end and then slid slyly behind Louis Joseph, to suddenly catch him by the back of the neck and duck him. Joseph came up sputtering, and his companion's laughter rang out, seeming to fill the little amphitheater of the pool and send an echo up the mountain slope."

Newspaper men came of course and the story became public. Other polios began to arrive—moved by a fresh hope. Roosevelt recognized their need at once, and it is typical of his firm affection for troubled humanity that he unhesitatingly assumed responsibility for their care. Eventually, the most complete hospital in the world for the treatment of post-infectional infantile paralysis would grow from the small pool that Roosevelt had dug for "his gang" because the guests at the old resort objected to them. It is always moral courage, *i.e.,* intelligence directing and love impelling, that makes the world of men move, when it does move.

In 1927, Roosevelt organized the Warm Springs Foundation, a non-profit corporation. Formally, the incorporators were Roosevelt, George Foster Peabody, Basil O'Connor, Herbert N. Straus, and Louis McH. Howe. According to a recent brochure from the Foundation, it was basically defined as having two objectives: (1) to use the natural facilities of Warm Springs and the skill of an able, carefully-selected professional staff for the direct aid of patients; and (2) to pass on to the medical profession and to hospitals throughout the land any useful observations or special methods of proved merit resulting from this specialized work, which might be applied elsewhere. Dr. Leroy Hubbard, of the New York State Board of Health, became the first medical director. He served until December 1, 1931, when Dr. Michael Hoke, Atlanta orthopedist, became surgeon-in-chief, to be followed eventually by Dr. C. E. Irwin, the present chief.

In the first eight months of 1927, friends of the Foundation had donated less than $12,000, and Roosevelt's personal investment was approaching the $200,000-mark. But seventy-one patients were treated that year, and that was the substance to which every other thing was merely a condition. And then the stars began to show more favorable signs. In 1928 kindly Edsel Ford and his wife visited the Springs, and contributed funds for the building of the solarium or glass-enclosed pool. Then in 1930 the Norman Wilson Infirmary was built at a cost of $40,000, raised by patients and their friends and named for a Philadelphia patient who had died.

In 1933, GEORGIA HALL was built at a cost of $125,000, which was donated by the citizens of Georgia. Cason Callaway's work throughout the state on behalf of the fund was an important factor in its success. This long, one-story building of whitewashed brick, with a portico of white Doric columns flanked by two wings, serves as the administration building and contains the executive offices as well as the registration desk. It also contains the dining hall, reception rooms, and recreation rooms. All entrances are level, and doors are wide enough to permit the passage of wheel chairs into the broad corridors. The rear door of the building opens, automatically by means of an electric eye, upon a terrace and broad lawn. This building as well as all the other principal buildings of the Foundation were designed by Henry Toombs of Atlanta, who was Roosevelt's personal choice from its earliest days.

Then construction moved faster. In 1935 two dormitories were built, and the old outdoor dance pavilion was remodeled into a playhouse.

Here movies, provided by Atlanta distributors, are shown on Mondays, Thursdays, and Saturdays. The Chapel was built in 1937 and the Brace Shop in 1938; the School and Occupational Therapy Building the following year. Then came the Medical Building, a big step ahead, which functions as a complete orthopedic hospital; on June 15, 1946, an east wing was added to it, increasing the capacity from fifty-five to 141, which is the greater part of the Foundation's list of 165 at any given time.

There is a Physical Therapy Postgraduate School, to train physical therapists in the specialized care of polio patients. The campus pool, where all hydrotherapy is now given, was erected in 1942. The Foundation has its own heating plant, laundry, commissary, fire department, even its own golf course, and a library.

President Roosevelt took a special delight in visiting his adopted Georgia home. The famous Thanksgiving dinners with patients are a part of the photolore of the nation. On January 30, 1934, the first Birthday Balls in celebration of the President's birthday were organized from coast to coast. More than a million dollars was raised the first year, and they were repeated in 1935, 1936, and 1937. On January 3, 1938, the National Foundation for Infantile Paralysis was formed. With the start of the National Foundation, Georgia Warm Springs became one of its grantees. The bulk of the money raised is left in the hands of local committees for regional use, though a part goes to Warm Springs to aid its specialists in co-operative research and for associated expenses. The March of Dimes—a slogan invented by Eddie Cantor—is now a familiar interval on the January calendar. Basil O'Connor, who stood faithfully by the President's side in the difficult days of the Warm Springs Foundation, became the first president of the National Foundation, a post that he still holds.

President Roosevelt had appointed a research commission in 1937 to determine the need for nationally co-ordinated and financed research. Infantile paralysis had begun to strike hard and frequently, and it struck impartially on all economic levels. Many hospitals throughout the nation have polio wards. But Warm Springs is still the only complete hospital exclusively for infantile paralysis cases. It now has in progress one of the most extensive and well-organized research programs in the history of medicine and surgery.

All patients follow a fixed routine. This usually consists of daily exercises in the pools, swimming, rest periods, massage, and walking. Plaster casts and sometimes surgery are needed for some cases. The Foundation maintains a school for children, and makes every effort to supply any facility that can contribute to normal living. Despite the presence of crutches, wheel chairs, braces, and canes everywhere, the Warm Springs Foundation has the gay atmosphere of a resort and nothing of the austerity of a hospital.

As to the cause of the warmth of the Warm Springs water, which when measured on different occasions by a platinum resistance thermometer, varied at the east source on different days between 87.7° and 88.2° and at the west source between 87.1° and 87.5°, there is a theory. A good theory takes certain known facts and thinks out what else must be true, though not directly known, if they are true. *The Geography of Georgia* supplies a description of this. "Rain gauges were placed on Pine Mountain and other high points in the vicinity. The amount of rainfall was measured and the flow of water from the spring was determined in order to find out the source of the water that formed the springs. It was the opinion of the geologists, that the rain that falls on the higher land penetrates rock strata which carry the water into the earth to a depth of at least 2,800 feet which causes the water to be warmed. The temperature, in this region, increases about one degree for each 90 feet of penetration into the earth. Beneath Warm Springs, where the rock strata carrying the water reach a depth of 2,800 feet, there is a fault or a break in the rock strata lying above it which permits this warm water to reach the surface. Since the water entered the rock strata at an elevation much higher than the springs, the pressure causes the water to flow from a great depth to form Warm Springs."

THE LITTLE WHITE HOUSE (*open from* 9 A.M. *to* 5 P.M., *daily*). President Roosevelt's Georgia home, where he spent some of his happiest days, and where he died on April 12, 1945, has been preserved about as it was on that day. The round-columned white frame cottage of six rooms, planned by the President with the help of Henry Toombs, of Atlanta, was built in 1932. It faces a ravine at the foot of a heavily-wooded mountain. The premises, open to the public since 1948, had been visited in 1952 by travelers from every state and territory and 67 foreign countries. Now owned by the state, the building is carefully maintained in its original simplicity and good taste. The unfinished portrait that Mme. Shoumatoff was working on before President Roosevelt's death has been added, a gift of the artist. In the near-by garage is his Ford, equipped with special hand controls that enabled him to go about the local countryside, in which he had a great interest.

On August 2, 1952, the state, represented by the Franklin D. Roosevelt Warm Springs Memorial Commission, acquired title to the Roosevelt Farm of 573½ acres, which is adjacent to the Little White House. The title was conveyed by deed from the Georgia Warm Springs Foundation, to which the land had been given by President Roosevelt.

On this farm is a demonstration planting of longleaf pine which the owner developed as an example of reforestation, and which has now become a showpiece. At the same time other adjoining parcels of land were acquired by the Commission, bringing the total to some 4,050 acres.

WARM SPRINGS VILLAGE, some *12 m.* on State 190 through the park area and *1 m.* past the Foundation (930 alt., 557 pop.), developed as a railroad junction for the resort of Warm Springs. It was incorporated as Bullochville in 1893 and as Warm Springs in 1924.

Left from Warm Springs on State 41 to COLD SPRINGS, *0.2 m.*, with a flow of almost mineral free water that is well-adapted to fish culture. Here the Federal government maintains a fish hatchery. The station was established in 1903 by the old Bureau of Fisheries, but it is now managed by the Fish and Wildlife Service of the U. S. Department of the Interior, for the propagation of warmwater fishes for stocking farm ponds and other suitable waters.

The station has an area of 35 acres and contains 19 ponds for the production of fish. The source supplying the water is located on the property.

HAMILTON, *188.9 m.* (778 alt., 449 pop.), incorporated as the seat of Harris County in 1828, has several old frame houses built before the War between the States.

Right from Hamilton to BLUE SPRINGS (*private*), *3.5 m.*, the estate of Cason Callaway, industrialist of LaGrange (*see* IDA CASON GARDENS *above*).

LAKE HARDING (*cabins and boats available*), *10.5 m.*, has a 150-mile wooded shore line with many houses. This lake, which covers an area of ten square miles, was created in 1926 by the BARTLETT'S FERRY DAM, owned and operated by the Georgia Power Company.

South of Hamilton US 27 follows an Indian trail through one of the last sections in Georgia taken by the white man.

COLUMBUS, *212.2 m.* (250 alt., 79,661 pop.), (*see* COLUMBUS).

Points of Interest: St. Elmo, Wynnton School, Bibb Manufacturing Company plant, and others.

At Columbus US 27 junctions with US 80 (*see* TOUR 9), and US 27 Alt. US 280 is common with US 27 from Columbus to Cusseta.

Section b. COLUMBUS to FLORIDA LINE, 151.1 m.

South of COLUMBUS, *0 m.*, the land has been seriously eroded, which has had an obstructive effect not only on the farms but upon the towns. In the undamaged areas the land produces an abundance of cotton, pecans, peanuts, and garden truck, and the woods and streams are popular for hunting and fishing. This region, once occupied by the Creek Indians, was settled later than most of Georgia, not by affluent planters, but by farmers, lumberjacks, and trappers.

At *35.5 m.* is a junction with State 85 (*see* TOUR *10A*).

CUSSETA (pronounced Ku-see'ta), *18.7 m.* (540 alt., 571 pop.), was a small village called Sand Town when it was made the seat of the newly created Chattahoochee County in 1854. Incorporated the following year, the town was named for Kasihta, the largest of the Muskhogean Indian trading towns, which had formerly been near by.

LUMPKIN, *39.5 m.* (approx. 500 alt., 1,209 pop.), named for Wilson Lumpkin, Governor of Georgia (1831-35), became the seat of Stewart County in 1828 and was incorporated in 1831.

Thousands of acres of land in Stewart County have been rendered unproductive by erosion. A study of the land revealed that below the topsoil is a 100-foot stratum of very loose clay-sand overlying a layer of blue marl, a harder clay limestone. If the protective covering is worn away, water seeping through the sand to the marl carries the sand with it into the Chattahoochee River and causes a cracking that occurs first about ten feet below the surface. In many places the marl limestone has been worn away almost completely and immense gullies several miles long and several hundred feet deep have been formed. It was estimated in 1939 that almost half of the agricultural land of the county had been so eroded. On certain scientifically farmed tracts the erosion has been checked by terracing and planting kudzu vines in the ditches.

Left from Lumpkin on hard-surfaced State 27 to PROVIDENCE CAVERNS, *7.5 m.*, known as the Grand Canyon of Georgia. The term applies more specifically to the second and largest canyon. The central basin of this octopus-shaped cavern covers more than 3,000 acres, and the chasm is some 300 feet wide and 200 feet deep. Although the gullies are a spectacle of destruction, their magnitude and the delicate color of their vertical walls gives them a curious beauty. Red, yellow, brown, mauve, lavender, jade, ocher, orange, and chalk-white are evident in the different strata of the soil, though white and yellow predominate.

It is believed that the erosion began less than sixty-five years ago, and the gullies have formed with unbelievable rapidity until they have become a serious threat. Red clay, blue marl, shell, and a yellow clay have crumbled away, and the giant of erosion, having eaten into a layer of chalk, seems as insatiable as ever. Trees, leaning outward and awry, cling precariously to the steep walls. Small islands, like bits neglected by the monster, rise upward from the bottom of the vast fissure, and on these a few small pine trees struggle stubbornly to survive.

CUTHBERT, *59.3 m.* (446 alt., 4,025 pop.), seat of Randolph County, is on the fertile plateau between the Flint and Chattahoochee rivers. Soon after the county had been created in 1828, log houses formed a village that was incorporated in 1834.

Cuthbert was one of the earliest settlements in this area after the Lower Creek Indians were expelled. Families moved in from Virginia, the Carolinas, and the older parts of Georgia. The early architectural

style in Cuthbert, as in most of the ante-bellum houses in Georgia, belongs to the classic revival (reflecting a rebirth of interest in historical
Rome and Greece), of the early eighteen hundreds, as distinguished
from the Colonial tradition. Basically, there were two rooms on either
side of a wide hall (the "dog trot" in simple prototypes), and whether
for one or two stories, the plan was the same. The rooms were rather
square and quite high, with no closets. Kitchens were originally in the
back yard, though the twentieth century found many moved up and
attached to the main house. Always on the front and often on three
or more sides, the porches exhibited a decided variety. Roofs were
hipped over the entire house and porches. A noteworthy fact about the
columns is that none in all the many examples was executed in even
approximate accord with their classic models, but their carpenter-builders
did accomplish a simplification of interest and dignity. In the one-story
houses the columns were frequently rectangular, square or octangular:
carpenter variations, which in proportion and spacing are testimony to
the taste and not-so-untutored skill of the owner or the carpenter. In
fact, these houses, almost unvarying in basic plan, have nevertheless considerable variety and accent in their proportion and composition. Their
symmetry and scale constitute a mute declaration of the dignity, or
perhaps the pretension, their owners wished them to express.

To select a few as examples from among many in Cuthbert, the
KEY HOUSE, College Street, is the one-storied type with the colonnade
on the front only. Columns are round and fluted, giving it richness
beyond many similar ones, such as the REYNOLDS HOUSE or BAILEY HOUSE,
on Lumpkin Street. The latter, however, with simpler columns and
detail, have a decided dignity and restraint, and are very appealing
examples of this simple classic mode. None of the houses is open to the
public.

The McWILLIAMS HOUSE, on College Street, is a good example of the
one-story type, with pedimented porch and square columns in center
of front.

ANDREW COLLEGE, on College Street, founded in 1854 and named for
the well-known bishop, was originally Andrew Female College. During the War between the States the college closed its doors to instruction and offered the use of its buildings for a hospital, though some
classes were continued in private homes. The original buildings were
destroyed by a fire in 1892, but within a half-year a new main building
was started; Senior Hall, Cuthbert Hall, and a memorial library were
added later. Its red brick buildings are located, along with the tennis
courts and swimming pool, on a tree-shaded campus of oaks and pecans. Offering courses in literature, piano, organ, voice, dramatics, art,

home economics, and commercial training, it is a member of the Southern Association of Colleges, and of the Methodist University Senate.

The TOOMBS HOUSE (*private*), on Lumpkin St., probably around 1850, and said to be one of the first two frame houses built in the town, has a two-story portico of square plank columns with a hanging balcony. There are rooms on either side of the hall for both floors; the detail is entirely simple.

On the grounds of the McDonald House, on Lumpkin St., is the MCDONALD PECAN, which has been marked by the American Tree Association. The story is that this immense tree was started from a Texas seedling nut planted in 1846. Though more than a century old, it is said to yield from 200 to 1,200 pounds of nuts annually, depending on the year.

Around the City Hall are some interesting period buildings which served as professional offices, usually for law. They are simple little buildings in temple form, with pedimental porches on the entrance end. Good examples of these are Judge Kiddoo's office on College Street and Judge Hood's, on Court Street; both of these men had important rôles during the Confederacy. There are also a number of houses, in various parts of the town, that exhibit interesting patterns of exterior woodwork, apparently in imitation of the ornamental ironwork usually associated with New Orleans.

The Iris Garden, under which, hidden forever, is an old railroad dump-heap, won honorable mention for the Cuthbert Garden Club in a national contest sponsored by *Better Homes and Gardens*. On the south side of College Street, it serves as a children's playground, and also as a scene for the Andrew College Seniors' May Festival. On Easter Sunday mornings, a Community Sunrise Service is held here; spirituals are sung each year by children from the Negro schools on this occasion.

The town has a Carnegie Library, a community hospital, a County Public Health Center, and a modern swimming pool built by the Cuthbert Community Council. The principal industrial establishments are cotton and lumber mills, and the chief county products are corn, cotton, and lumber.

At *72.1 m.* is the junction with State 37.

Right on State 37 is FORT GAINES, *13.2 m.* (166 alt., 1339 pop.), seat of Clay County, established in the early 1800's and named for the stockaded fort here. The quiet little village on a bluff overlooking a bend in the Chattahoochee River suggests a medieval fortress. At the foot of the bluff a graceful cantilever bridge spans the river. Right of the bridge on a large knoll is the SITE OF FORT GAINES, a log fort occupied and successfully defended by General Edmund P. Gaines during the Indian wars.

A short distance after Bluffton on US 27 and before Blakely is the entrance (R) to the KOLOMOKI MOUNDS STATE PARK (*swimming, picnicking, boating, hiking, children's playground, museum of Indian relics, group camp, trading post; open year round*), a 1,283-acre park in Early County. The large mound belongs among the principal ones in the Southeast. Larger than a football field at its base, it rises fifty-seven feet in the form of an elongated rectangular pyramid, so that at its top it is about 156 feet long and sixty-six feet wide.

According to Mr. Jessie D. Jennings, an archaeologist for the National Park Service, the Kolomoki Mounds area is rich in artifacts of the Swift Creek type, an earlier Indian culture of the Southeast. All relics found will be properly cared for, and those of worth will go into a museum, the first unit of which is complete, with exhibits. Archaeological investigations were carried out by qualified persons during the summers of 1948 and 1949, at which time one of the burial mounds was investigated.

The area for the park was deeded to the state by the citizens of Early County. An impounding dam was completed a few years ago, which created the 75-acre lake. A superintendent's residence has been built, and the resident superintendent is in charge at all times. There are no general admission charges or fishing fees in Georgia parks.

BLAKELY, *87.8 m.* (275 alt., 3,234 pop.), seat of Early County, was founded in 1821 and named for Captain Johnston Blakely, a naval officer in the War of 1812. He was commander of the *Wasp* which mysteriously disappeared at sea, but not before it had done more to harass English commerce than any other single ship. Among Blakely's industrial plants are several lumber mills, turpentine stills, and a large peanut-shelling plant. On the courthouse square near the Confederate monument is a CONFEDERATE FLAGPOLE, erected in 1865. It has been broken twice by storms, and is now reinforced by copper wire and set in a concrete base.

From its establishment until around 1900, cotton was the principal and the one cash crop, with 52,569 acres devoted to the crop in 1909. With the invasion of the boll weevil, however, in 1915, the entire cropping system began to change, and cotton has never been the king crop since. Present-day agriculture in Early County is centered around peanuts, though corn, cotton, and livestock play a contributing rôle in making it an important agricultural county. In 1952, some 33,166 acres were in peanuts and around 25 or 30 thousand in cotton.

With the development of new uses and the establishment of steady markets, peanuts have become one of the state's important cash crops. In July small, light-yellow blossoms appear on the English pea-like vines, and nuts begin to form in clusters on the roots. In August the plants are cut and stacked around poles to dry. These haycocks of drying peanuts are visible at frequent intervals along the highways. About four weeks later the nuts are picked, and the vines are compressed into bales of hay. Mechanical planters, pickers, and balers, often owned by a co-operative group, are moved from farm to farm to serve the growers. The nuts are sold either to a mill, where the oil is extracted by a cooking process, or to a peanut-shelling plant. Here, after being separated by a shaker from vine particles and foreign matter, the nuts are taken to shellers, which rapidly separate the kernels from the hulls. The kernels are then carried on conveyors through lines of workers who sit on each side and pick out the imperfect nuts. From the conveyors the nuts fall into chutes that carry them to a lower floor, where they are bagged and weighed, and so made ready for shipment to processing plants and candy factories. In 1947 there were 1,092,000 acres of peanuts harvested in Georgia for the nuts, and an additional 500,000 acres, more or less, were otherwise used, principally for hogging-off. Peanuts make a heavy demand on the soil, but if grown in rotation with other crops properly fertilized, and if cover crops are used in winter, this demand can be met.

Livestock in Early County has made gains during the past twelve years, although work along this line was begun back in the 1920's by some of the more prominent farmers. Today, there are several herds of registered polled and horned Herefords in the county in addition to registered Angus herds and several of Brahman cattle.

Soils and climate of Early County are suitable for almost any type of farming. Approximately 2,000 additional acres were put in pasture during 1952. Livestock men are proud of the fact that they can grow any pasture plant grown in Georgia: fescue, bahia grass, all of the clovers, coastal bermuda, kudzu, and all types of lespedeza in addition to many small grains seeded for winter and spring grazing.

A map published in 1820 shows an old Federal road passing through the county. It is also called the Jackson Trail, because General Jackson's troops in 1818, under the command of Colonel Haynes, crossed the Chattahoochee River from Fort Mitchell in Alabama to Columbus and then followed this road down to Fort Scott.

In COLQUITT, *108.5 m.* (175 alt., 1,664 pop.), created as the seat of Miller County in 1856 and named for Judge Walter T. Colquitt, Georgia statesman and United States Senator, is a trading center for farmers. The chief products are corn and cotton.

BAINBRIDGE, *103.3 m.* (119 alt., 7,562 pop.), is at the junction with US 84 (*see* TOUR 5).

At *151.1 m.* US 27 crosses the Florida Line, 21 miles north of Tallahassee, Florida.

TOUR IOA

Junction with US 27—Fort Benning; Fort Benning Boulevard.

US 27 (US 280) is a Super Highway, four lanes, from Columbus to Cusseta (*see* TOUR *10*), and passes southeast through the Fort Benning Reservation, by the Sand Hill Area (L), and the Harmony Church Area (R). But in order to visit the Main Post Area, one should take Fort Benning Boulevard (R), just after passing beyond the Ft. Benning R.R., and at the highway circle, about three miles from the Columbus Court House. Fort Benning Boulevard leads to OUTPOST #1 (*passes issued here for visitors*).

Now called the Infantry Center, FORT BENNING is America's most complete army post. It is named in honor of a distinguished Confederate army officer, Brigadier General Henry Lewis Benning, jurist and soldier, of Columbus, Georgia. The Infantry School came into being at Fort Benning early in 1918 when the war-time expansion of the U. S. Army indicated a need for a unified center where the existing schools of infantry instruction could be assembled. The Infantry School of Arms was moved from Fort Sill, Oklahoma, to a location on the Macon Road east of Columbus, Georgia, to be joined later by the School of Small Arms from Camp Perry, Ohio. This union formed the nucleus of The Infantry School, with Colonel H. E. Eames as the first Commandant. The School became a permanent establishment in 1922. Since its inception it has grown from an original acreage of 97,000 to some 182,000 acres or about 284 square miles, of which around 12,000 acres are in Alabama. A mean average temperature of 65.2° and an average annual rainfall of 52.12 inches permit year-around training.

Roads, streets, and terrain features are named for units that served in World Wars I and II, for battle areas in France associated with the action of American units, and for individuals killed in action. First used by The Infantry School only as an incident in drawing up terrain exercises, the names are now permanent.

During World War II some 60,000 second lieutenants of infantry were graduated from the Officer Candidate School, and a total of 100,938 officers and enlisted men were graduated from various resident courses, not including 90,237 airborne personnel who completed training under the Airborne Department of The Infantry School.

Following World War II there was a brief leveling-off period, and the Officer Candidate School was moved to Fort Riley, Kansas. With the outbreak of hostilities in Korea, however, The Infantry School was again faced with the needs of a national emergency. Courses were both expanded and accelerated, and the Officer Candidate School was returned to The Infantry School. A Ranger Department has been added.

The following tour touches the major points of interest and is at the same time a register of information. (*Enter Outpost #1, follow Sigerfoos Rd. to Vibbert Ave.*) RUSS POOL (R), the largest swimming pool on the post, is operated for enlisted men, their dependents, and guests, from May through September. It can accommodate 800 persons at one time. Diving boards, spinning tops, and water slides are available for water sports; no admission charge. Named in honor of Colonel Joseph Russ, G-4 supply officer when construction started, it was built in 1922.

(*Turn right on Vibbert Ave. and follow to Anderson St.*) DOUGHBOY STADIUM (L), was built entirely by voluntary soldier labor as a tribute to dead comrades of World War I. Started in 1924, the stadium which seats 10,000, was completed in 1925. GUEST HOUSE (R), World War II type barrack converted to comfortable temporary quarters for visiting relatives of enlisted men, with a house mother to guide and assist visitors during their stay. RED CROSS HEADQUARTERS (R). The POST LOCATOR (L) houses records indicating the unit to which each person at Fort Benning is assigned. POST OFFICE (L). FINANCE OFFICE AND BANK (R), in addition to finance operations, also houses branch offices of the Columbus Bank and Trust, and the First National Bank, of Columbus, Georgia. The GIFT SHOP (R) is operated as a branch of the Post Exchange. The FOOD SERVICE SCHOOL (R), originally called The Cooks and Bakers School, was started in 1921. Here the basic principles of good cooking and also serving are taught. From 1943 to 1948, over 6,000 cooks and bakers graduated. The building is named for Medal-of-Honor winner Private First Class Martin O. May, 77th Infantry Division, who was killed in the Ryukyu Islands. QUARTERMASTER BAKERY (R) was built in the late 1930's, and supplies bread for all troop installations at Fort Benning and Lawson Air Force Base, with a daily average exceeding 8,000 twenty-ounce loaves. CUARTELS (Sp. meaning *barracks for troops*) (L), three, comprising seven separate buildings. With over one-half mile of porch area, the first building, completed in 1929, has the longest known undivided porch in the world. The total troop capacity of the Cuartels is around 6,000 men. In March 1949 the buildings were named for enlisted men awarded the Medal of Honor: Olsen Barracks, for Sergeant Thurman O. Olsen, 3rd Infantry Division, killed in Italy; Wilkins Barracks, for Corporal Edward G. Wilkins, 45th Infantry Division, killed in Germany; McVeigh Barracks, for Sergeant John J. McVeigh, 2nd Infantry Division, killed in France; Towle Barracks, for Private John R. Towle, 82nd Airborne Division, killed in Holland; and Henry Barracks, for Private Robert T. Henry, 1st Infantry Division, killed in Germany.

(*Turn left on Anderson St. and follow to Indianhead Road*) ARMY FIELD FORCES BOARD #3. This board, charged with studying infantry requirements, was originally located at Fort Leavenworth, Kansas. Shortly after World War I the entire board was moved to Fort Benning to continue its work while located close to the home of the Infantry. It is composed of officers especially selected for broad experience and knowledge of infantry matters. A part of the third Cuartel, the building is known as the Shockly Building for Medal-of-Honor winner Private First Class William R. Shockly, 32nd Infantry Division, killed on Luzon in World War II. THEATER #2 (L) is one of the smaller ones scattered about Fort Benning for the convenience of the troops.

(*Turn right on Indianhead Rd. and follow to Bradshaw Rd. in the* LAWSON AFB *area, or turn left on Marchant St. and eliminate both the tour of Lawson and the close-in firing ranges.*) The QUARTERMASTER LAUNDRY (L), built in 1941, is the most completely equipped in the Army, and valued at more than $2,000,000. When operating on three shifts, it can handle laundry for more than 20,000 people a week. The ARMY EDUCATION CENTER (L) offers classes covering the basic elements of education. By means of this center, military personnel who do not have grammar school certificates or high school diplomas, may study for fully accredited ratings from their home schools. Serving as a source of help in the Army's career program, the purpose of the school is to assist commanders of all echelons in raising the educational standards of their organizations. All instruction is given by accredited instructors, and some college-level courses are offered. FAMILY-TYPE HOUSING (R) for enlisted men of the first three grades, sergeant through master-sergeant, of which the greater part are five- and six-room size.

(*Enter* LAWSON AIR FORCE BASE AREA.) Established in 1919 as a lighter-than-air base, it was named in 1931 for Captain William Ross Lawson who was killed at Wright Field in 1923 in an air disaster. A native Georgian, Captain Lawson was an American Ace who distinguished himself with the 41st Escadrille in 1918, in France. Lawson Air Base primarily is concerned with furnishing the necessary air support to The Infantry School's parachute and air-transportability training.

(*Turn right on Bradshaw Road and follow until rejoining Indianhead Road, follow Indianhead Road to Sightseeing Road.*) AIRBORNE

AREA (L). Here are housed all officers and enlisted men attending the airborne courses offered by The Infantry School. All phases of air-borne technique and air-transportability are taught in this general area: parachute jumping, cargo loading and lashing in aircraft, parachute packing, and airborne pathfinder skill. Having begun the first class in 1941, this is the only post in the U. S. training military personnel in the art of parachute jumping; a class of several hundred graduates weekly. On leaving the area, one will note (L) some odd-looking structures, like the fuselage of a plane. Known as "mock-ups," these are duplicates of aircraft used by the Army's airborne elements, and are used to give exact instruction in the proper technique of loading cargo on planes.

(*At Sightseeing Road, turn right to include the close-in firing range area, or continue to Marchant St. and proceed on tour as indicated. To cover close-in range area, turn right on Sightseeing Rd. and follow to Dixie Road, turn left on Dixie Rd. and follow to Edwards St. Ranges in order, are: English, 1000-inch Landscape Range; English, 1000-inch Rifle and Machine Gun Range; Simpson Pistol Range; and Simpson, 1000-inch Landscape Range. Turn left on Edwards St. and follow to vicinity of Marchant and Edwards streets.*)

(*Left from Edwards St., right from Marchant St.*) The JUMP TOWERS have been a Fort Benning landmark since 1942. Student parachutists are lifted to the top of the 250-foot training towers by means of a hoist and then released in a free parachute drop as a training stage prior to making an actual parachute jump.

(*Proceed to Wold Ave. by turning left on Edwards St. from Marchant St. or continue straight ahead on Edwards St. Then turn right on Wold Ave. and follow to 1st Division Road.*) The BUS STATION AND POST EXCHANGE (R) is the hub of Fort Benning's bus transportation, serving as the point of origin for busses to the Harmony Church area, the Sand Hill area, Baker Village, Main Post routes, and Columbus. Behind the Bus Station is the POST EXCHANGE, built in 1939, which operates thirty-five general retail outlets and twenty-two special recreational outlets such as restaurants, bowling alleys, and snack bars. In addition, there are nearly one hundred concessions such as cleaners, watch repair shops, photo studios, and barber shops. Though civilian operated, they are under the supervision of the Post Exchange Officer, who regulates their prices. The POST LIBRARY (R), a T-shaped red brick building, was built in 1944, and now contains over 16,000 books. The average monthly circulation exceeds six thousand, and that of its five branches in other areas of the post, runs over 15,000 monthly. The MAIN THEATER (R), built in 1938, has a seating capacity of 1,500, and is fully air-conditioned. The GAS STATION AND GARAGE (L) is operated as a civilian concession. The INFANTRY SCHOOL BUILDING (R), 400 feet long and more than 100 feet deep, with sound-proofed and air-conditioned classrooms, was built in 1934-35. The Academic Department and school headquarters began to operate here in 1935. It also contains the offices of the Commanding General of The Infantry Center and of some of his principal staff officers. The INFANTRY CENTER CHAPEL (L) was built in 1935 with WPA funds, and dedicated as the Three Faiths Building, for Protestants, Catholics, and Jews. As the Army expanded in World War II, more than one chapel was needed, and the smaller chapel across the street, known as the Catholic Chapel, was built.

(*Turn right on First Division Road to Lumpkin Road, turn right on Lumpkin Rd. to Morrison Rd., turn right on Morrison Rd. to Ingersoll St.*) The OFFICERS MESS (L) was built in 1933 from funds accumulated by previous clubs, individual officer donations, and gifts from outstanding Columbus citizens. The spacious interior contains a ballroom, dining room, cafeteria, and several private dining rooms. In the rear, there is an annex with a barber shop, beauty shop, and the administrative offices; and, also, a dance pavilion, and three swimming pools, a shallow one for children and beginners, a medium-sized one for those past the first, and a deep water pool. The BOOK DEPARTMENT (L), completed in 1938, houses The Infantry School Book Department which handles professional texts.

(*Turn right on Ingersoll St. to Vibbert Ave.*) GOWDY FIELD (R) can accommodate 5,000 baseball spectators. Hank Gowdy, the first major league baseball player voluntarily to enlist in the Army during World War I, returned to Fort Benning during World War II as Special Services Officer, and remained until his retirement in 1944. The MAIN POST EXCHANGE RESTAURANT, SODA, AND SNACK BAR (L), built in 1943, is the largest of the special facilities provided by the Post Exchange. The cafeteria-type restaurant and adjacent soda and snack bar serve nearly 5,000 patrons daily. SERVICE CLUB #1 (R), originally built in 1920 and recently remodeled, is the second-oldest permanent type building on the post. It is the center of enlisted men's activities in after-duty hours, and various types of entertainment are provided. The BRIANT WELLS FIELD HOUSE (L) was built at a cost of $500,000 for the benefit of all military personnel, and measures 204 by 185 feet. Among its facilities are an indoor swimming pool, a handball court, two basketball courts, and a complete gymnasium with adequate spectator seats. It is named in honor of Major General Briant Wells, a former Commandant of The Infantry School and one-time athletic instructor at Fort Benning.

(*Turn right on Vibbert Ave. to the junction Vibbert Ave.—Sigerfoos*

Rd.—1st Division Road. Turn right on 1st Division Rd. to Lumpkin Rd. Turn right on Lumpkin Rd. to Yeager Ave. Turn on Yeager Ave. to Baltzell Ave.) FRENCH POLO FIELD (L) is named for Lieutenant French, crack player, who served with the 29th Infantry Regiment here, and was killed during a game on the field in the early 1920's. The field is used at present primarily for parades and reviews. On the right is another polo field named for Captain Blue, once an instructor in The Infantry School, and also one of the Army's great players.

(Turn left on Baltzell Ave. to Lumpkin Rd.)

The GOLF COURSE (R), constructed and maintained by funds from the Officers Mess, was the scene of the first All-Army Golf Tournament in 1947. At present it is an 18-hole course, but nine more holes are under construction, and plans call for making it a 36-hole course in the future. The new club house was built in 1948. Another golf course is maintained in the Sand Hill area, primarily for the use of enlisted personnel. The ARMY HOSPITAL (R) was completed in 1935. Since then almost twice the original expenditure has been made for improvements and expansion. This hospital, serving military personnel and their dependents, has a 1,500-bed capacity. The wooden frame wards on the left were built during World War II to accommodate the vast number of personnel being trained. At present they house the out-patient clinic, the eye, ear, nose and throat clinic and other allied medical functions.

(Turn right on Lumpkin Road.) The POST SCHOOL, built in 1921, started with three teachers and sixty pupils. Today there are more than sixty teachers and over 1,000 pupils. The school covers all grades from kindergarten through the seventh grade. The COMMANDING GENERAL'S QUARTERS (L) was once the Colonial home of Arthur Bussy, upon whose former plantation the greater part of Fort Benning is located. The architecture of the house is the same today as when it was originally built. The northeast corner of the building is said to cover the grave of Colonel John Tate, who died in 1780 while preparing to lead 400 Creeks to the British Colonials at Augusta, Georgia.

TOUR 11

(Chattanooga, Tenn.) — Trenton — Rising Fawn — (Fort Payne, Ala.); US 11.

Tennessee Line to Alabama Line, 23.6 m. — Road bed hard surfaced — Southern Ry. parallels route throughout — Limited accommodations.

Crossing the extreme northwestern corner of the state, US 11 passes through the narrow limestone valley that lies between Lookout and Sand mountains, the southern end of the great Appalachian Plateau. This rugged region is separated from the rest of Georgia by mountain barriers and at one time, not so long ago, could be reached only from Tennessee or Alabama.

The inhabitants, almost all of whom are native white, are dependent largely on the fruit and vegetables they raise on their 100- or 150-acre farms; they were never part of the slaveholding plantation life, even romantically.

From about 1860 until 1908 coal was mined in this section, and after 1874 the smelting of iron ore was an important industry. After mining slacked off in the 1900's, the principal industrial units left were lumber mills. The towns are little more than hamlets of small frame houses and garden patches, with corn and fruit trees growing along the main streets. There is some dairying, since blue grass and clover, for example, do well on limestone soils, and sheep graze in hilly pastures separated by old stone fences.

US 11 crosses the Tennessee Line, *o m.,* at a point 6 miles southwest of Chattanooga, Tennessee.

LOOKOUT MOUNTAIN (L), ranging in height from 1,750 to 2,392 feet, probably received its name from the high cliffs that afforded a vantage point for observing approaching Indians. Its steep slopes are capped with almost vertical sandstone cliffs, rising from two hundred to three hundred feet and presenting unscalable walls cut into deep gullies by streams flowing from the top of the mountain into the valley. Although the broad plateau at the summit of the ridge is, for the most part, sparsely settled, there is a residential colony at the northern end.

SAND MOUNTAIN (1,630 alt.), is (R) much more extensive than Lookout Mountain and reaches far to the southwest. The mountain plateau is more thickly populated than the other because it has productive soil and farms.

TRENTON, *10.8 m.* (735 alt., 755 pop.), was made the seat of Dade

County in 1840. At that time is was called Salem, but the following year its name was changed to Trenton. The county was created in 1837 and named for Major Francis Langhorne Dade, who, with his entire force, was killed in the Seminole War in Florida.

Right from Trenton on a country road are several old COAL MINES, about 5 m. In general, the coal of this area is of the "steam type," *i.e.* it is a low volatile, high carbon sort. Some mining is still done in the general area, mostly by a family-contract arrangement. The coal tends to occur in thin seams and in irregular deposits, which makes the cost of extraction high. But with the new technique for the production of coal gas, by burning the coal in the mine, there is promise of a future use for the coal deposits. In addition to coal, vast quantities of limestone are available, slate, sandstone of varied hues, commercial clays, and expandable aggregates usable in cement construction work.

Left from Trenton on State 143 which passes down the west side of CLOUDLAND CANYON STATE PARK and under its southern base, where it makes a junction with State 157 (L), which roughly parallels US 11 and ends at Lookout Mountain, Tennessee, on the state line. The park (*picnicking and hiking, open year-around*), Georgia's "Little Grand Canyon," has an area of 2,370 acres, and contains some of the most majestic scenery in the state, though at present it is largely undeveloped. First steps were taken recently, however, towards its development by the construction of a picnic area, including shelter and grills, and by clearing trails for access to the beauties of the area. Cloudland Canyon contains SITTON'S GULCH, which can be reached by State 157. The Gulch, unfortunately not well known even in Georgia, is a spectacular sight because of its imposing bulk and its gray sandstone walls that have been worn perpendicular by Bear Creek. In June these walls are crowned by pink-blossomed rhododendron. Deep within the gorge a magnificent waterfall plunges with a muffled roar in one desperate descent, to the bottom of the gorge. Against the massive, lowering gray cliffs, this cataract, with its veil of shimmering spray, has a delicate and strange beauty.

State 143 continues in an easterly direction and makes a junction (L) with State 193. Just as State 157 roughly parallels US 11, so State 193 parallels State 157, and joins it just short of the town of Lookout Mountain. State 143 continues to Linwood on US 27 (*see* TOUR *10*), about 2 miles above LaFayette.

A short distance beyond the junction of State 143 with State 157 (L), there is another junction of State 143 with State 157 (R). This route continues southwesterly until it makes a junction with State 239 (L) which goes to Cloudland, through an area of great natural beauty, and there joins State 48 to Menlo and Summerville on US 27 (*see* TOUR *10*).

Southwest of Trenton the dark cedars and bare gray cliffs are a somber scene in winter, but in spring the roadsides are resplendent with white dogwood blossoms, golden-anthered white Cherokee roses, and pale pink laurel and rhododendron. The fragrant white and yellow flowers of the honeysuckle vine cover the banks; ferns, anemones, trilliums, and wild violets grow in the deeper woods. In autumn the forest is aglow with the warm, rich colors of hickory, beech, sweet gum, oak, and chinquapin contrasting with the darker pine foliage. The chestnut trees that once added a distinct grandeur to the forest have been destroyed by blight, and nothing is left of them now except, here and there, spectral skeletons.

RISING FAWN, 20 *m.* (793 alt., 246 pop.), was known as Hanna in 1870 when the Wills Valley Railroad, now the Alabama Great Southern, was run through the village. Its name was then changed to Staunton and later to Rising Fawn.

Left from Rising Fawn on the Newsom Highway, a narrow, graveled road, to the RUINS OF THE RISING FAWN FURNACE (L), *1 m.*, erected in 1874. It had a daily capacity of fifty tons and was operated until 1910. At this point the Newsom Highway turns left and, ascending Lookout Mountain, partly encircles JOHNSON'S CROOK, *5 m.*, a great wooded amphitheater formed by a horseshoe bend of the mountain and bounded on all sides except the south by rugged cliffs. This road connects with State 143 just southwest of Cloudland Canyon State Park.

US 11 crosses the Alabama Line, *23.6 m.,* at a point 23 miles northeast of Fort Payne, Alabama.

TOUR 12

Atlanta — McDonough — Forsyth — Macon — Perry — Hawkins-ville — Brunswick; 293.4 m. US 23 from Atlanta to Forsyth. US 23 and US 41 from Forsyth to Macon. US 41 from Macon to Perry. US 341 from Perry to Brunswick.

Southern Ry. parallels route between Atlanta and Jackson, and between Eastman and Brunswick; Central of Georgia Ry. between Forsyth and Macon — All types of accommodations in Atlanta, Macon, and Brunswick; limited elsewhere.

Section a. ATLANTA *to* MACON, 92.9 *m., US 23 from Atlanta to Forsyth; US 23-41 from Forsyth to Macon.*

Through a section that is typical of the Piedmont Plateau of middle Georgia, this route passes red-clay hills, pine woods, pecan groves, and fields of corn and cotton. The few ante-bellum houses remaining are stoutly built and spacious but not elegant.

The land was a stronghold of the Creek before they were evicted by a series of treaties. After they had been removed in 1821, the section became a thriving cotton-plantation area. General Sherman covered part of this route in his march to the sea after the burning of Atlanta. After the war the plantations were divided into small farms, but the section remained agricultural. Industrial development for the most part plays the lesser rôle.

ATLANTA, *0 m.* (1,050 alt., 331,314 pop.) (*See* ATLANTA.)

Points of Interest: State Capitol, Cyclorama of the Battle of Atlanta, Georgia School of Technology, Emory University, Oglethorpe University, Agnes Scott College, Atlanta University (Negro), and others.

Atlanta is at the junction with US 78 (*see* TOUR 8), with US 29 (*see* TOUR 3), with US 41 (*see* TOUR 2), with US 23 (*see* TOUR 7), and with US 19 (*see* TOUR 6).

MCDONOUGH, *28.1 m.* (861 alt., 1,635 pop.), was incorporated in 1833 as the seat of Henry County and was named for Thomas McDonough, the naval officer who had defeated the British on Lake Champlain, September 11, 1814. Early settlers came from the Carolinas by way of Madison over a stagecoach route that followed an Indian trail, now Key's Ferry Road. After the Battle of Atlanta, July 22, 1864, General Sherman divided his army for his march to the sea. One division came through McDonough, destroyed property, and burned the court records.

Although the commerce of McDonough is based primarily on cotton, corn, granite, and cattle, among the chief manufacturing establishments are textile mills. Several of the houses built soon after the incorporation of the town are still standing.

A CORK TREE in the front yard of Judge T. J. Brown's house, Jonesboro St., is about a century old. During the Administration of President James K. Polk the U. S. Department of Agriculture attempted to introduce cork trees for their commercial value. Acorns were imported from Spain and distributed throughout the southern states.

JACKSON, *45.7 m.* (697 alt., 2,053 pop.), seat of Butts County, was incorporated in 1826 and named in honor of James Jackson, Governor of Georgia from 1798 to 1801. Jackson has a new health center sufficiently enlarged to serve the entire county, and a livestock auction barn able to serve several counties in the area. Agriculturally, row-crop farming has been giving way to livestock, dairying, poultry, pasture improvement, and small grains. But the chief products are still cotton, corn, pimiento peppers, and cotton textiles.

The Jackson National Bank, facing the square, stands on the SITE OF THE ROBERT GRIER HOME. Though it is not known exactly when Grier's *Almanac* was begun, residents of Butts County have copies published as early as 1810. Grier died in 1848 and is buried in the family burial ground at his old home near Stark, about five miles northeast of Jackson.

Left from Jackson on State 16 to the junction with a country road, *8 m.;* L. on this road to a fork, *8.3 m.;* R. from the fork to the junction with another

country road, *9 m.;* R. on this to LLOYD SHOAL DAM, *9.2 m.,* erected on the Ocmulgee River in 1910 by the Central of Georgia Power Company (merged with
the Georgia Power Company in 1928). This dam, 100 feet high and more than
500 feet long, develops 22,000 horsepower.

The river is curbed for some fifteen miles, and the backwater covers more
than 3,000 acres of land, leaving small islands in the large reservoir. The lake
has been stocked with fish.

HOLINESS CAMPGROUND (R), *50.3 m.,* has been in use since 1890. A
hotel, a tabernacle, and around 300 cottages are provided for the thousands of people who gather here in summer for revivals of "the old time
religion."

The entrance (R), to INDIAN SPRINGS STATE PARK (*picnicking, hiking,
horseback riding, children's playground, museum of relics, mineral
baths, trading post; officially open from March 1 to December 1*) is at
51.5 m. When Douglas Watson, a government scout, paused here in
1792 to investigate an odor which he thought to be burnt gunpowder,
he found a sulphur spring fed by a small but steady flow from the walls
of a rock. It had long been known to the Indians who gathered here
to drink the water for its curative properties. In 1800 Creek under
General William McIntosh, who was of mixed Scotch and Indian
origin, encamped here.

On January 8, 1821, the Creek signed a treaty here ceding to the
U. S. Government most of their land between the Flint and Ocmulgee
rivers as far north as the Chattahoochee. They reserved only a few
tracts, including 1,000 acres surrounding this spring. In another treaty
signed here by McIntosh on February 12, 1825, the Creek relinquished
all their remaining holdings within the boundaries of Georgia in exchange for $400,000 and acre for acre west of the Mississippi. Although
McIntosh negotiated this treaty as leader of the Creek Confederation,
the Upper Creek repudiated his action and later executed him (*see*
TOUR *10*).

The state disposed of all the Indian lands except ten acres called the
Indian Springs Reserve, which was leased to individuals for development as a summer resort. After the Wigwam Hotel burned in 1921,
the popularity of the resort waned. In 1933 the citizens of Butts County
purchased 122 acres adjoining the reserve and gave it to the state for a
park. The 152 acres now constituting Indian Springs State Park has
been extensively improved with rock buildings and walks, and thousands of native trees and shrubs have been planted under the supervision of the State Forest Service.

Also in the park area is the Butts County 4-H Club Camp, which can
accommodate 100 boys and girls a week, from different sections and

organizations. The bottom floor of the Museum is used as a health bathhouse where heated spring water baths are given.

Near the park are a swimming pool, bowling alley, ferris wheel, and a number of resort hotels.

An old WATER-POWER GRISTMILL, on the highway (R) near the spring, was built in 1873 and called the Alberta Mill. It still has its original grinding rocks and large water wheel. ROCK CASTLE, the old Collier house near by, was built in 1853. Though rock was plentiful in Georgia, comparatively few homes were built of it because skilled stone masons were rare.

The VARNER HOUSE (*private*), a large frame building (L) with a long one-story porch, was erected as a hotel in 1821 under the supervision of McIntosh and Joe Bailey. It has been changed little and still contains some of the original furnishings and the register desk on which the treaty was signed. Beside the porch is McIntosh Rock, the large boulder upon which O-potto-le-yo-holo stood while making a speech of protest against the treaty.

FORSYTH, 67.5 m. (704 alt., 3,125 pop.), seat of Monroe County, is built about a large open courthouse square bordered by red brick buildings with second-story roofs jutting over the sidewalks. It was incorporated in 1822 and named for John Forsyth, Secretary of State under President Jackson and President Van Buren. Its growth was accelerated when the Monroe Railroad was built from Forsyth to Macon in 1834, since products of the vicinity were shipped to Macon for redistribution to other points by means of the Ocmulgee River. Forsyth raised half the capital stock of $200,000 for this venture, now merged with the Central of Georgia, and became the first inland town of the state to be made accessible by a navigable waterway.

There are four textile mills, one garment manufacturing plant, and a creamery. Monroe County is a milk producing and livestock area as well as a center for corn, lumber, and cotton.

HILL ARDEN (*private*), two blocks R. of the highway on S. Lee St., built in 1822, is a Greek Revival house with fluted door facings and elaborate cornices. The interior is notable for a spiral stairway built of mahogany brought from South America. In the garden is a 100-year old cork tree.

BESSIE TIFT COLLEGE, on a sixty-five-acre campus two blocks left of the public square, is a women's college controlled by the Georgia Baptist Convention. Founded in 1847, it was chartered December 21, 1849, as the Forsyth Female Collegiate Institute. The institution was used as an army hospital in 1864-65, and in 1879 it suffered the loss through fire of its principal building, which originally had been that of the Southern

Botanico-Medical College, chartered in 1839. In 1898 the college became the property of the Georgia Baptist Convention, and in 1907 its name was changed to honor its benefactress, Mrs. Bessie Willingham Tift. On March 28, 1946, the college became a member of the Southern Association of Colleges. The State Department of Education has approved the work in teacher training in the granting of certificates. The college confers the B.A., the B.S. in Elementary Education, the B.S. in Home Economics, and there is also an A.B. with a major in music.

The rambling red brick buildings, with wide porches ornamented with white columns, are set on a broad expanse of lawn. With a farm of 173 acres adjoining the campus on the east, the college operates its own dairy and has fresh farm products for its modern and well-equipped kitchens. According to the *Register* for 1950-51, the college had an enrollment of around 234 regular students and 17 special students, the majority of whom were from Georgia.

US 23-41 to Macon, from Forsyth.

At *84.7 m.,* begins a mile stretch, known as the MEMORIAL MILE, which is part of the Dixie Highway Road of Remembrance extending from Sault Sainte Marie, Michigan, to Miami, Florida. At regular intervals along both sides of the memorial mile are cement posts about two feet high, each with a bronze marker bearing the name and record of one of Bibb County's World War soldiers. Pecan trees, crape myrtle, and spirea bushes beautify the spaces between the markers. When the 5,000-mile Dixie Highway was completed, both southern and northern women had become interested in beautifying it as a World War memorial. In February, 1922, the Dixie Highway Road of Remembrance Association planted the first trees here.

WESLEYAN COLLEGE (R), *86 m.,* at Rivoli, was the first college in the world chartered to grant degrees to women. Incorporated December 23, 1836, as The Georgia Female College, the school was opened in Macon on January 7, 1839. In July of 1840, degrees were conferred upon eleven students, among whom was Catherine E. Brewer, later Mrs. C. E. Benson, mother of the late Admiral William S. Benson, U. S. N. On December 19, 1843, the Georgia Conference of the Methodist Church assumed the supervision of the college, and its name was changed by a legislative act to Wesleyan Female College. In 1878 the college was related to the North Georgia, South Georgia, and Florida conferences of the Methodist Episcopal Church, South, and this relationship has continued. In 1919 the word *Female* was struck from the corporate name by a further amendment, and the name became simply Wesleyan College. In September 1928, the Liberal Arts College was removed from its first site on College Street in Macon, to the new

campus in Rivoli, a suburb on the western side of Macon. The buildings on College Street now house the School of Fine Arts, including the
Conservatory of Music, the School of Art, and the School of Speech
(*see* MACON).

The college at Rivoli offers courses leading to the B.A. degree in
thirteen fields and eight interdepartmental majors, and the B.S. in four
professional fields. It is on the approval list of colleges of the Association of American Universities and is an accredited member of the
Southern Association of Colleges and Secondary Schools. The 170-
acre campus of rolling woodland provides a pleasant setting for the
twelve buildings of Georgian Colonial architecture, constructed of red
brick and trimmed in white wood or marble. According to the *Bulletin* for 1951, there were some 338 students in the Liberal Arts College.
Twenty-one states and several foreign countries were represented
among the degree students for 1950-1951. The Wesleyan Tea Room at
the entrance to the campus serves the college family and guests.

Right of the entrance is the CANDLER MEMORIAL LIBRARY, similar in
architectural style to the Hermitage in Savannah. This library, a gift of
Judge John Slaughter Candler, of Atlanta, in memory of his father
and mother, contains 38,500 volumes, subscribes to 220 periodicals, and
has a seating capacity of 250. On the ground floor is the Georgia Room,
which holds a 1,200-volume collection of Georgiana presented in 1930
by the late Honorable Orville A. Park, of Macon, and a collection of
rare Americana made possible through the generosity of the late
Tracy W. McGregor, of Washington, D. C.

GEORGIA ACADEMY FOR THE BLIND (L), *90.6 m.,* is housed in a red brick
building with a modified Greek portico. In addition to the twenty
acres of land at this location, there is a four-acre area at 151 Madison St.,
Macon, on which is located the unit for Negro children, made up of a
large building for the school and a number of shops. White and Negro
children from six to eighteen who are citizens of Georgia, physically
and mentally fit, but with vision defective to such an extent that they
cannot be educated in regular schools, are admitted by application when
approved.

The white division offers the usual academic subjects found in the
public schools and the school is fully accredited by the state accrediting
commission. The school for Negroes, referred to above, is in a three-
story brick building erected in 1882. Since the building is old and not
entirely adequate, plans are under way to build a completely new plant
at a new location, with some 30 acres of land.

In 1851 a movement for the establishment of an institution for the
blind of the state was brought before the public by the Macon press. A

beginning was made possible by private donations, and a small school with four pupils was set up the same year. In 1852 the school was accepted by the state and received legislative appropriations. During the War between the States it was moved to Fort Valley while the school building, then in downtown Macon, was being used as a hospital. The present building, modeled after that of the Philadelphia Institution for the Blind, was built in 1906 at a cost of $100,000. In 1940 it was renovated and additions made at a cost of approximately $50,000.

MACON, 92.9 m. (334 alt., 70,252 pop.) (See MACON.)

Points of Interest: Mercer University, Wesleyan School of Fine Arts, nearby Ocmulgee National Monument, and others.

At Macon is a junction with US 80 (*see* TOUR 9) and with US 129 (*see* TOUR 16).

Section b. MACON *to* BRUNSWICK, *200.5 m., US 41 to Perry,*
then US 341 to Brunswick.

South of MACON, 0 m., the route descends from the Piedmont Plateau into the Coastal Plain, where the trees gradually begin to show gray hanging moss, the streams become dark and sluggish, and the hills recede into level ground. The sandy loam of this section responds readily to fertilizer, and the mild climate makes it possible to produce the year-around, if cover crops are included. Diversified farming has increased, but though vegetables, fruits, and nuts are grown in abundance, cotton still holds the position of #1 cash crop. This route also crosses the wiregrass or piney woods section, where sawmills and turpentine stills are seen at intervals along the highway and in the small towns.

About 2 m. below Macon take State 247 (L) to ROBINS AIR FORCE BASE, *18 m.*, at Warner Robins. Carved from an area that was once farm land and swamp, and now covering a land mass of 6,400 acres, the Robins Air Force Base is the hub of the vast Warner Robins Air Matériel Area, concerned with the maintenance and supply requirements of Air Force installations in Virginia, the Carolinas, Georgia, and Florida. The Georgia installation, activated in 1941, is named for General Augustine Warner Robins, a pioneer officer of the U. S. Air Arm. His system of cataloguing items, formulated in the 1920's, has stood the test of the complex supply lines of World War II, and is still in use.

Under the command of Major General K. E. Tibbetts, also commander of the Warner Robins Air Matériel Area, the base is landlord to several tenant organizations, the largest of which is the 14th Air Force Headquarters. Since 1941 when the base was established close by, the small village of Wellston has grown into the town of Warner Robins with a population of more than 15,000. Both the base and the town are still growing despite the destruction resulting from a recent tornado, in the summer of 1953.

Another Memorial Mile of the Road of Remembrance (*see* above) begins at *8.1 m.*

Between ECHECONNEE, *11.2 m.* (approx. 340 alt., 60 pop.) and Cordele (*see* TOUR 2), the road runs through part of Georgia's peach section, and in late March and early April pink blossoms border the highway. During the harvesting season, May to July, peaches are sorted, packed, and shipped in thousands of crates to many parts of the country. Packing houses (*usually open to visitors*), sometimes little more than loosely constructed sheds, appear frequently.

PERRY, *27.9 m.* (365 alt., 3,849 pop.) (*see* TOUR 2) is at a junction with US 341. Follow US 341 the rest of the way to Brunswick.

CLINCHFIELD, *34.9 m.* (approx. 350 alt., 300 pop.), is an industrial community developed about a CEMENT-MANUFACTURING PLANT. The settlement, formerly called Coreen, was the site of a small limestone plant. In 1924 a Portland cement corporation, finding the material mined here suitable for their needs, bought the land, renamed the settlement, and built a plant along the Southern Railway. It is the largest cement plant in Georgia. The raw materials are soft white limestone, fuller's earth, and clay.

From *35.4 m.* is a view of the QUARRY FACE (L). Here the raw products are loaded into cars by steam shovels and conveyed to the plant over an industrial railroad.

HAWKINSVILLE, *47.8 m.* (235 alt., 3,342 pop.), on the bank of the Ocmulgee River, is the seat of Pulaski County and was named for Benjamin Hawkins. Hawkins was a member of the Continental Congress and was appointed (1796) by Washington as superintendent of all the Indians south of the Ohio. His headquarters were in Georgia, first at Fort Hawkins near Macon, then at Old Agency on the Flint River in Crawford County, where he is buried. He was so eager to teach the Indians improved methods of agriculture that he brought his slaves to Georgia and operated a model farm as a demonstration project, quite like those now maintained by the Department of Agriculture's extension service.

Hawkinsville is a trading center. Its chief products are cotton, corn, fruit, cotton towels, and yarn.

One block R. of the highway on State 11 is the marked SITE OF THE JACKSON TRAIL (R), which Andrew Jackson followed in 1818 when he invaded Florida to suppress the Seminole. One block farther south is the marked SITE OF THE BLACKSHEAR TRAIL (L), laid out in 1814 by General David Blackshear (*see* TOUR 9). This was the first road in Pulaski

County, and documentary evidence indicates that Jackson followed the same course.

About one block from the highway on State 26 is an S-shaped MEMORIAL BRIDGE (L) spanning the Ocmulgee River and dedicated to the World War veterans of the county. Here General Oglethorpe crossed in 1739 on his way to confer with the Indians at Coweta Town near Columbus.

EASTMAN, *66.8 m.* (357 alt., 3,597 pop.), seat of Dodge County, was named for William Pitt Eastman, who gave the land on which the town is built. The first store was operated at the old depôt of the Macon & Brunswick Railroad in 1871, two years before the town was incorporated. The chief products are cotton, hay, turpentine, and pecans.

Eastman is at the junction with State 87, US 23-129 (*see* TOUR 9A).

HELENA, *85.4* (247 alt., 1,027 pop.), was created when the Scottish citizens of McRae refused a right of way to the Southern and Seaboard railways. Helena became the junction for the two railroads, but they are now known as the twin cities of McRae-Helena, because a stranger never knows when he has left one and entered the other.

Left on State 30 *1 m.* and then left on State 31 (US 441-319) briefly, to LITTLE OCMULGEE STATE PARK (*swimming, picnicking, boating, fishing, hiking, horseback riding, cabins, trading post; open year-around*), 1,397 acres. With its rolling sand hills dotted with Georgia pines and small oaks, the park provides a healthy outdoor atmosphere for hiking and picnic parties. The 300-acre lake has been repaired and is open for boating and fishing; it provides excellent fishing, having been stocked with bream, bass, and perch. The club house provides refreshments and a good place for dancing.

McRAE, *86.3 m.* (230 alt., 1,904 pop.), seat of Telfair County, was settled in the mid 1800's by a group of Scottish Presbyterians who came from the Carolinas where they had settled on arriving from the old country. The town is the focus of farm operations in the vicinity. Because the county is a fertile area, agricultural products are diversified, and truck farming, dairying, and poultry raising bring considerable profits. Its chief products are corn, cotton, creamery products, pine, hardwood, honey, lumber, naval stores, and dewberries.

McRae was the home of Eugene Talmadge, Governor of Georgia (1933-1937; 1941-1943). While state commissioner of agriculture he built up a strong following among the farmers and met all opposition with a bluntness and vigor that endeared him to some and made bitter enemies of others.

LUMBER CITY, *104.1 m.* (146 alt., 1,232 pop.), on the Ocmulgee River (*fishing and swimming*), was incorporated in 1889. A number of saw-mills make this town one of the very large shipping points for pine and hardwood lumber in this section of the state.

HAZLEHURST, *111.3 m.* (256 alt., 2,687 pop.), seat of Jeff Davis County, was incorporated in 1891. The STATE FARMERS MARKET, operated under the supervision of the Georgia Department of Agriculture, is one of the smaller markets of the state. It operates seasonally, but serves the use-ful purpose of affording the local grower a market place for dealing directly with the produce dealer. Hazlehurst is a tobacco market for the eastern part of the tobacco belt. According to the Georgia Depart-ment of Agriculture, sales of tobacco at Hazlehurst in 1951 reached 5,363,072 pounds and brought some $2,600,792.23, or an average of 48.49 cents a pound.

BAXLEY, *128.7 m.* (206 alt., 3,409 pop.), is at the junction with US 1 (*see* TOUR *4*).

Southeast of Baxley is the wiregrass section, which slopes gently to-ward the Atlantic Coast. In this part of the state there are no fence laws, and many hogs are branded and put out to graze until hog killing time in winter.

In JESUP, *160.2 m.* (100 alt., 4,605 pop.), incorporated in 1878 and the seat of Wayne County, the sandy streets are shaded by giant oak trees. The chief products are livestock, corn, cotton, timber, naval stores, and milled lumber.

LOVER'S OAK, with a spread of 150 feet, is one of the oldest trees in the state.

The trend in agriculture is toward permanent pasture and livestock. Perhaps attributable to pulp-mill expansion, with famous old Doctor-town in Wayne County now a site, the planting and management of pine trees has increased decidedly. The expansion of the shirt factory, and the acquisition of a furniture factory, a wood-preserving plant, a naval stores plant, and of a pulp mill have advanced the industrial ac-tivity of Jesup. A Farmers Market has recently been built, and its business is heaviest during the green corn season.

BRUNSWICK, *200.5 m.* (11 alt., 17,954 pop.), is the junction with US 17 (*see* TOUR *1*).

TOUR 13

(Knoxville, Tenn.) — Blue Ridge — Ellijay — Canton — Marietta; State 5.

Tennessee Line to Marietta, 95.9 m. — Murphy Branch of the Louisville & Nashville R.R. roughly parallels the route — Limited accommodations.

Between the Tennessee Line and the mining and textile areas around Marietta, this route crosses ridges of the Copperhill basin and the wooded mountains of the Chattahoochee National Forest area and of the Tate region. In spring the mountains are pink with the delicate shades of rhododendron, laurel, and blossoming fruit trees. In autumn the oak leaves, turning a russet color, contrast with the gold of hickory and the dark green of pines and hemlocks, and the meadows are accented with goldenrod, daisies and wild asters. The Tate region is noted for its valuable marble deposits and its summer resorts.

In the mountainous northern sections, the early settlers patiently cultivated their stony acres, owned few slaves, and remained politically and socially apart from the slave-holding cotton planters. Some of the northern counties traditionally poll a strong Republican vote in this otherwise faithfully Democratic state.

State 5 crosses the clear TOCCOA RIVER, *o m.*, the boundary between Georgia and Tennessee, at a point about a hundred miles south of Knoxville, Tennessee.

Between the Tennessee Line and Ellijay State 5 runs through the purchase area of the Chattahoochee National Forest (*see* TOURS 6 and *13A*). The first land was acquired in 1911, immediately after the passage of the Act of March 1, 1911, which provided for the purchase by the United States Government of Lands needed to protect the headwaters of navigable streams. Acquisition of land continued and the area was managed as portions of the Cherokee and Nantahala National Forests until 1936.

The Chattahoochee National Forest was established by President Roosevelt by a Proclamation on July 9, 1936. That portion of the Nantahala National Forest lying in Georgia became the Tallulah Ranger District and the Georgia area of the Cherokee became the Blue Ridge and Toccoa Ranger Districts of the Chattahoochee. In 1937, a fourth Ranger District, the Armuchee was established as a result of additional acquisition in the northwest part of the State. Next came the Toccoa Division of the Tallulah Ranger District which became a part of the

377

Forest, through transfer of lands from the Resettlement Administration in 1938. Two additional ranger districts have been added: one, the Chestatee created in 1950 by dividing the Blue Ridge District to form the Brasstown and Chestatee; and the other, the Chattooga, created in 1952 by removal of the Toccoa Division from the Tallulah. The Chattahoochee now has six ranger districts, with approximately 660,000 acres of land located in twenty counties, and Ranger District Headquarters at Clarkesville, Clayton, Blairsville, Dahlonega, Blue Ridge, and LaFayette. The supervisor's headquarters is in Gainesville.

The Forest was created primarily for the purpose of watershed protection. It has proved its value in that function, as well as other uses which have developed through the years. Timber, recreation, and wildlife use have increased markedly in the past ten years, so that the Forest now is one truly requiring multiple use management.

McCAYSVILLE, *0.1 m.* (1,500 alt., 2,067 pop.), is inhabited principally by the employees of the mines and smelters of a copper company across the river in Copperhill, Tennessee. For some miles southeast of the town, escaping sulphuric fumes from the smelters have destroyed plant life and heavy rains have eroded the earth's surface as deep as the basic mineral formations and igneous rock. Despite the desolation, the scene has a certain stark interest when sunsets wash the ridges with bold colors.

BLUE RIDGE, *11.6 m.* (1,751 alt., 1,718 pop.), seat of Fannin County, was incorporated in 1887 but remained unimportant until 1895, when the Louisville & Nashville Railroad was brought here. It is a trim town, a center for farming, timbering, and mining operations. The serenity of the surrounding mountains has made it popular as a summer resort. This vicinity was a stronghold of the Cherokee, whose occupancy is evident in the arrowheads, spear points, and pottery found here.

The Toccoa U. S. Forest Ranger District of the Chattahoochee National Forest has a District Ranger's office in Blue Ridge. This district comprises 116,486 acres in Fannin, Gilmer, and Murray counties. Inquire for further information about recreation facilities in this forest area.

Left from Blue Ridge on US 76 to BLUE RIDGE LAKE, formed by a power development that has impounded the Toccoa River. Along with Lake Nottely and Lake Chatuge (*see* TOUR 6), Lake Blue Ridge is a part of the Tennessee Valley Authority. Among the public recreation points are: Blue Ridge Dock, at the dam (*12 boats, outboard motors, tackle, lunches; address Hugh Gibby and O. H. Wilson, Rt. 2 Blue Ridge*), and Morganton Point at the intersection of State 60 with US 76 (*20 boats, outboard motors, bait, tackle; address Leslie Collins and Robert Howard, Morganton*). The narrow lake, twelve miles long, has a brilliant blue color, unusual in Georgia; its shore line is populated with private cottages. Rainbow-trout, bream, and smallmouthed black-bass are plentiful; the muskellunge, locally know as jackfish, is caught, some specimens having weighed as much as eighteen pounds. During the winter months wild ducks and geese are hunted at the lake and wild turkeys in the nearby mountains. White-tailed deer are frequently seen.

The PIGEON CREEK PICNIC AREA, east from Blue Ridge to Morganton on US 76, then L. on State 60, is located on State 86 near Wilscot Gap in Fannin County, east of Blue Ridge Lake. Maintained by the Blue Ridge District of the Chattahoochee National Forest, U. S. Forest Service, this area consists of a small glade which has been developed with an excellent spring, picnic tables, fireplaces, a toilet, and garbage pit. It is a favorite stopping place for tourists, truckers, and local residents.

US 76 is joint with State 5 from Blue Ridge to Ellijay.

ELLIJAY, 27 m. (1,298 alt., 1,527 pop.), seat of Gilmer County, is a pleasing, well-kept village built around a grassed square with a rock fountain. It is named for a Cherokee village on this site that was called Elatseyi (Ind., the place of green things), perhaps suggested by the valleys of the Ellijay and Cartecay rivers. Rainbow-trout and black-bass fishing is good along these rivers, which converge near Ellijay to form the Coosawattee River. The town was incorporated in 1834, two years after the creation of the county. In addition to apples and peaches, the area produces corn as well as pine and oak timber.

Ellijay is on the southern boundary of the Chattahoochee National Forest. Here US 76 turns west to Dalton (see TOUR 2), by way of Fort Mountain State Park and Chatsworth (see TOUR 2A). Continue on State 5.

Beneath JASPER, 47.5 m. (1,500 alt., 1,380 pop.), the seat of Pickens County, are the Georgia marble beds. This trading center for farmers was incorporated in 1857 and named for Sergeant William Jasper, a revolutionary hero (see TOUR 1).

Left from Jasper on State 108 which winds through a mountainous region of dense forest and deep ravines to TATE MOUNTAIN ESTATES, 10.4 m., a private resort development. A small summer colony, with homes owned principally by Atlanta people, has been developed on the shores of LAKE SEQUOYAH, which is well stocked with fish.

From MOUNT BURRELL (3,300 alt.), the surrounding area is visible for many miles on all sides. To the north are the towering peaks of Tickanetly Range; to the northeast, the distant ranges of the Great Smoky Mountains of Tennessee and North Carolina; and to the northwest, rising above the lowlands of the Appalachian Valley, is the distant plateau of Lookout Mountain. To the south, past the foothills of the Piedmont region, Kennesaw and Stone mountains, fifty and eighty miles away respectively, are visible on a clear day.

Throughout the woods of the slopes and valleys are azalea, the deep cardinal Indian-pink, rhododendron, laurel, and trailing arbutus. Holly, dogwood, and galax, many sorts of oaks, and hickory, beech, birch, and pine trees flourish.

At 8.7 m. on the graveled road that completely encircles Mount Burrell, from

State 108, is the summit of MOUNT OGLETHORPE (3,290 alt.), a bald mountain crowned by a white marble shaft erected as a memorial to General James E. Oglethorpe, founder of Georgia. The peak affords a spectacular view.

Mount Oglethorpe is the terminus of the 2,050-mile Appalachian Trail (*see* TOUR *13A*).

South of Jasper even the smaller houses are frequently conspicuous because of their white marble chimneys as well as steps and walks, which are striking in contrast with the informal frame buildings.

Near TATE, 52.5 *m.* (approx. 1,300 alt., 2,000 pop.), the home of the Georgia Marble Company (*visitors welcome*), the vast marble quarries are visible from the road. The town was established about 1818 as a tavern site on the old Federal Road and was named Harnageville after the builder and operator of the first tavern which was located on the site of the present Tate family home.

The discovery of marble, of the highest quality and virtually unlimited in quantity and of a wide variety of color, transformed the quiet Long Swamp Valley farming section into an industrial community almost over night. The quarrying and cutting of marble requires men of exceptional skill. In 1884 the Georgia Marble Company was organized for the purpose of quarrying marble, and several manufacturing plants were required to saw, cut, and finish the marble from the various quarries. These companies were: The Southern Marble Company and the Piedmont Marble Company, of Marble Hill; The George B. Sickles Company, of Tate; The Blue Ridge Marble Company, of Nelson; and The Kennesaw Marble Company, of Marietta. In 1905 all of these companies were consolidated into The Georgia Marble Company.

From the first, the transportation of a product, of exceptional weight and bulk as well as value, was a problem. Some of the first blocks quarried were sent to Philadelphia by oxen. As a solution of the transportation problem, the company assisted in organizing the Marietta & North Georgia Railroad, later bought by the Louisville and Nashville; and when the station was built near the quarries it was named Tate, after the Tate family, associated with the quarry.

Although the building committee for the Georgia state capitol did not choose to use the state's native product, within a few years of its decision the states of Minnesota and Rhode Island had constructed their capitols with it, and some years later Utah used the same material, as did Puerto Rico in the 1920's. Aside from its use in hundreds of private memorials such as those for Ringling, DuPont, Pasteur, and Walter Camp, Georgia marble has been widely used in churches, courthouses, post offices, schools, and in fact, in buildings of many sorts over the nation. Among the public buildings are the Chicago Museum of Natural

History (formerly the Field Museum); St. Patrick's Cathedral and the Stock Exchange Building addition in New York; the Corcoran Art Gallery, the Lincoln Memorial, units of the Department of Agriculture, the Pan-American Building, and the Folger Shakespeare Memorial Library, in Washington; and the Federal Reserve banks of Cleveland, Detroit, and Atlanta.

The community of Tate is unincorporated and most of its residents are employees of the Georgia Marble Company, living in company-owned houses. Tate has a fine marble high school building, churches, and a shopping center, and modern conveniences for the residents of the community.

BALL GROUND, 59.5 m. (approx. 1,200 alt., 700 pop.), incorporated in 1883, developed about a small settlement where the Marietta & North Georgia Railroad established a station. At Ball Ground are a marble-finishing plant, a monument works, and several sawmills and cotton gins. The village was named for a large field where the Cherokee played a native game not unlike modern lacrosse. The ball used by the Indians was made of scraped deerskin, moistened and stuffed with deer hair, and sewed tightly with deer's sinews. The rackets were approximately two feet long, the flattened lower end resembling the palm of the hand.

CANTON, 71.1 m. (894 alt., 2,716 pop.), seat of Cherokee County, was incorporated in 1833 as Etowah, but named next year for the Chinese city because two prominent settlers of 1831 tried silk culture, an industry that flourished for a brief period. Although a public school known as Etowah Academy began in 1833, Canton remained small until the Marietta & North Georgia Railroad was run through it in 1879. The staple products are cotton, cotton textiles, corn, talc, timber, and cattle; and in late years it has become a sub-center for Georgia's new broiler industry (see TOUR 7, GAINESVILLE), which reaches into both Pickens and Cherokee counties.

Just below Canton, graveled State 205 (R) leads to the GEORGE WASHINGTON CARVER STATE PARK (Negro), (see TOUR 2).

MARIETTA, 95.9 m. (1,118 alt., 20,867 pop.), is at the junction with US 41 (see TOUR 2).

TOUR 13 A

North Carolina Line—Unicoi Gap—Neels Gap—Amicalola Falls—Mount Oglethorpe; 96.5 m., Appalachian Trail.

Accommodations: There are seven open shelters located at intervals along the trail, and one seasonal hotel. The shelters afford protection from the rain and will take care of from 4 to 8 people; no bunks or other facilities. Camp sites, springs of drinking water (widely separated), and points of interest are marked. The nearest settlements are mostly to the north and west of the trail. A few stores for food supplies—Watch for rattle-snakes and highland moccasins. A guide book for making the entire trip, or in 1-day portions, is obtainable from the Georgia Appalachian Trail Club, P. O. Box 654, Atlanta, Georgia.

The Appalachian Trail is a 2,050-mile hiking route running along the crest of the Appalachian Highland between Mount Katahdin in Maine and the summit of Mount Oglethorpe in north Georgia. It is well blazed and identified by metal markers bearing the symbol of the affiliated Appalachian Trail clubs. On the hundred-mile Georgia section of the route, maintained by the U. S. Forest Service and the Georgia Appalachian Trail Club, are a site of an Indian battle, a national game refuge, and a spectacular waterfall.

The trail passes through a region beautiful for its dense woodlands, its cascades, and for the deep blue color of the Appalachian Highland when seen from the eastern plateau. It is because of this hazy, almost violet hue that the range is called the Blue Ridge. The crests are not level like those in Virginia, but are frequently broken by rounded peaks with the well-worn, gentle slopes characteristic of all old mountains. Although the peaks rise gradually, some are 2,500 feet above the surrounding 2,000-foot elevation. Except for an occasional bald summit or an exposed rock cliff, the entire region is covered densely with hard woods and conifers including pine, spruce, and hemlock.

Many small, rapid streams cross the forests that are lively in spring with the pale pink of rhododendron, the white of dogwood, and the vivid hues of the wild azalea. In autumn the gold and rufous colors of oak and maple, gum and hickory offer glorious vistas of light enclosed within a somber scene.

This part of Georgia was occupied by the Cherokee Nation until 1838, when the Indians were forced to refugee (*see* TOUR 2). In intelligence and culture the Cherokee were one of the most highly developed tribes within the continental United States. Several mounds, a few scattered pictographs, and such musical place names as Enotah, Hiawassee, Toccoa, Unicoi, and Chestatee are among the reminders of their former regional existence.

The Appalachian Trail crosses the North Carolina Line, *o m.,* in BLY GAP (3,840 alt.), just north of RICH KNOB MOUNTAIN, and immediately enters the CHATTAHOOCHEE NATIONAL FOREST (*see* TOURS 6 *and* 13).

At DICK'S CREEK GAP, *8.7 m.* (2,675 alt.), is a junction with US 76 (*see* TOUR 7), the Henry Grady Scenic Highway. This gap can be reached from Clayton (*see* TOUR 7) or Blairsville (*see* TOUR 6).

SNAKE MOUNTAIN, *9.7 m.* (3,365 alt.), has a log hut shelter in fair condition which will accommodate 4 to 6 people.

Cross in ADDIS GAP, *14.1 m.* (3,304 alt.), an old mountain road which leads L. past the abandoned homestead of the Addis family, a primitive Georgia mountain home now in ruins.

South of Addis Gap the crest of the Blue Ridge falls to a relatively low "sag," or as the mountaineers say, "The Swag of the Blue Ridge." In one of the most isolated highland sections, the "swag" is a vantage point for broad, spectacular views. On the east is the placid expanse of Lake Burton (*see* TOUR 7), and on the west, ridge upon ridge marches toward the Great Smoky Mountains.

The Montray Shelter, *19.6 m.,* a log hut in fair condition, similar to the one on Snake Mountain, is on the northern side of TRAY MOUNTAIN. The summit (4,430 alt.) *19.9 m.,* is a scenic vantage point popular with hikers.

INDIAN GRAVE GAP, *22.3 m.* (3,113 alt.), was named for the isolated stone cairn in the level portion of the gap at the junction of the trail with a forest service road. This rounded mound, about two feet high and eight feet in circumference, supposedly marks the grave of an Indian.

UNICOI GAP, *25.1 m.* (2,929 alt.), at the junction of the trail with State 75, can be reached from Cleveland on the south and Young Harris and Hiawassee on the north (*see* TOUR 6). State 75 follows the route of a Colonial trail, which British soldiers from Charleston, South Carolina, and Augusta followed to Fort Loudon on the Tennessee River near the present site of Knoxville. In 1812 a company, formed by coastal traders interested in commerce with the Cherokee Nation, graded the trail and made a toll road called the Unicoi Turnpike. After this a trading post was established in almost every village throughout the Cherokee land.

Just south of Unicoi Gap is the residence of a State of Georgia Wildlife Ranger. Arrangements may be made in advance to have supplies and mail delivered here. (Address: % Wildlife Ranger, Unicoi Gap Ranger Station, Star Route, Robertstown, Georgia.)

ROCKY KNOB, 27.9 m. (about 3,400 alt.), has another log hut, similar to the one on Snake Mountain; in poor condition, though.

CHATTAHOOCHEE GAP, 29.6 m. (3,500 alt.), is within a hundred yards of the spring (L) that is the reputed source of the Chattahoochee River. In its course through the forest the water of the river is clear, not becoming turbid until it reaches the eroded farm areas rather far above Atlanta.

Right from Chattahoochee Gap on the Enotah Trail to the junction with an unblazed path, 0.3 m.; L. on this path about thirty yards to an old CAVE HOUSE, entered by an opening in the face of a steep cliff. The entrance is protected by an artificial stone wall of dry masonry covered with dense, slow-growing lichens. Within the cave, which is large enough for several men to stand erect, are the ashes of long-dead fires. The presence of lichens indicates that many years have passed, and there are a number of theories about the cave. Some believe it was a refuge for Indians during the Cherokee Removal; others, that it served fugitives from military service during the War between the States; still others, that it was a hideaway for desperadoes who raided this region in the 1830's during Dahlonega gold rush days.

On the Enotah Trail at 5.5 m. is the bald summit of MOUNT ENOTAH (4,784 alt.), known locally as Brasstown Bald (see TOUR 6), the highest peak in Georgia.

TESNATEE (Ind., wild turkey) GAP, 39 m. (3,138 alt.), in an isolated and rugged region, was until 1923 the only entrance to the Nottely River valley from the south. In the gap is a U. S. Forest Service open-type log shelter lean-to, in good condition, with wood floor and fireplace, capable of accommodating six people.

NEELS (FROGTOWN) GAP, 44.7 m. (3,125 alt.), is at the junction with US 19 (see TOUR 6) and the southern entrance of VOGEL STATE PARK. Meals and lodging are available from June to October at Walasiyi Inn in Neels Gap. There is a supply concession at Lake Trahlyta in Vogel State Park, approximately 3 m. down mountain to the north, where groceries may be bought.

BLOOD MOUNTAIN, 46.8 m. (4,461 alt.), is a scenic vantage point of popular interest because of its easy accessibility from Neels Gap. On its summit, the highest point of the Appalachian Trail in Georgia, is a stone shelter for hikers; but no water supply.

The name of the mountain commemorates a legendary Indian battle fought on its slopes. Near the summit is the ROCK HOUSE, a cave extending back some fifty feet into the native stone. According to Cherokee legends, the cave gave access to the subterranean dwellings of the Yunwee Chuns Dee (Ind., little folk), an aerial-like people whose magic music was heard on the mountain slopes. Other fabulous people of the region were the Nunne-hee, an invincible race of normal size who always aided those lost or injured on the mountains. The kindly Nunne-hee regarded Cherokee children as their special wards. A treasure is said to be hidden somehow in the House, and Indians in recent years have been known to return to find it.

SLAUGHTER GAP, 47.5 m. (3,800 alt.), the pass between Blood and Slaughter mountains, is the site of the traditional battle for which the mountains were named. During a fierce engagement here the Cherokee are said to have defeated the Creek who were encroaching upon their territory. Quantities of arrowheads and spear points have been found in the gap.

The Appalachian Trail turns left at Slaughter Gap. Straight ahead a trail leads 2.2 m. to Lake Winfield Scott (see TOUR 6), a U. S. Forest Service Recreation Area, which is recommended as a rest stop for through travelers. The lake affords both swimming and fishing, with bathhouse and a small concession open during the summer season; tables and fireplaces, but no sleeping accommodations.

WOODY GAP, 54.7 m. (3,150 alt.), is at the junction with State 60. Water piped from a spring and picnic tables are available. A bronze memorial plaque has been erected in memory of Arthur Woody, who was the first U. S. Forest Ranger in this area and for whose family the gap was named. A side trail leads 0.5 m. to the summit of BLACK MOUNTAIN (3,742 alt.), where there is a Forest Service lookout tower.

From Woody Gap, it is 1.6 m. northwest on State 60 to Suches (pronounced like "such as"), Georgia, location of the U. S. Forest Service Headquarters. Mail and supplies may be received in care of Ranger Headquarters; supplies are obtainable at several general stores; also accommodations may usually be found in private homes in Suches. The main trail follows the south side of Black Mountain.

GOOCH GAP, 58.2 m. (2,784 alt.), is at a junction with the Forest Service Fire Road, which is used as a public highway. It is 2.7 m. (R) on this road to Suches, on State 60.

COOPER GAP, 63 m. (2,828 alt.); here the Trail comes back to and follows the Forest Service Fire Road. Just beyond Cooper Gap, the road enters a 20,000-acre state and Federal wild-life preserve, NOONTOOTLY GAME REFUGE, through a locked gate which is closed to vehicular travel except during fishing and hunting seasons. During the November-December deer hunting season one should beware when in this area and also take the precaution of dressing conspicuously in red cap and shirt. Whether justly or not, deer hunters at least in part, have acquired a reputation for being trigger-happy. Black bears, though introduced some years ago into this region, are rare, but one often encounters white-tailed deer, wild turkeys or ruffed grouse. Although the streams through this area are filled with rainbow and brook trout, the management permits fishing only at stated intervals.

HIGHTOWER GAP (2,800 alt.) is at *66.8 m.* About 200 yards L. of the gap is the source of the Etowah River, which in its upper course is locally called the Hightower River. Both names as well as that of the gap, are corruptions of Itawa, a Cherokee word believed derived from Italwa (Creek, the town where).

HAWK MOUNTAIN, *67.6 m.* (3,619 alt.), lies within the game refuge. On its bald summit is located a Forest Service lookout tower and the forest ranger's house.

SPRINGER MOUNTAIN, *73.4 m.* (3,820 alt.), is on the edge of the game refuge. It is the southernmost peak of the Blue Ridge which comes together at this point after having been split into two ranges below Roanoke, Virginia.

Until the second decade of the twentieth century, when rural churches became more widely distributed, people from several counties gathered on this mountain once each year for religious services that lasted a week or so. The mountaineers toiled daily over the rough roads of this rugged country. Natives still point out PULPIT ROCK, which was used by the preacher.

South of Springer Mountain the trail follows the crest of Amicalola (Ind., tumbling water) Ridge.

NIMBLEWELL GAP, *75.7 m.* (3,100 alt.), is at a junction with the U. S. Forest Service Fire Road that leads L. *10 m.* to State 52.

FROSTY (BUCKTOWN) MOUNTAIN, *77.1 m.* (3,400 alt.), is the location of a U. S. Forest Service lookout tower. An open-type frame shelter constructed by the Georgia Appalachian Trail Club in 1952 is located *.2 m.* beyond the top of the mountain at a spring. It accommodates 4 to 8 people.

AMICALOLA FALLS AND LAKE, *80.2 m.,* are the principal features of Amicalola State Park (*see* TOUR 6).

STATE HIGHWAY 52, *84.7 m.* (approx. 2,000 alt.), is crossed at the Dawson-Gilmer County Line. This locality is known as Southern's Store because a country store long since abandoned once operated here. At this point the Trail leaves the Chattahoochee National Forest. State 52 affords access to the trail from Ellijay (*see* TOUR *13*) on the west, and from US 19 (*see* TOUR 6) on the east.

STATE HIGHWAY 136, *91.4 m.* (2,800 alt.), is crossed at a point near the old Tate Mountain Estates. Jasper is *11.5 m.* to the right. State 136 becomes State 108 at a junction *1.7 m.* in the direction of Jasper.

At a point .4 m. beyond State 136, the Trail turns left along an old dirt road.

MOUNT OGLETHORPE, 96.5 m. (3,290 alt.) (see TOUR 13), is the southern terminus of the Appalachian Trail and the last peak of the main mass of the Appalachian Highland. A marble shaft is located here commemorating the founder of Georgia. Each hiker should register at the registration cylinder, giving name, date, address, hiking club affiliation (if any), and starting point of trip.

TOUR 14

Eatonton—Milledgeville—Louisville—Sylvania—Savannah; 199.3 m., State 24 and State 21.

Savannah & Atlanta R.R. parallels route between Waynesboro and Savannah—All types of accommodations in Savannah; limited elsewhere.

This route reveals the sharp contrast between the typical old southern towns in the western part of the route and the newer sawmill villages near the South Carolina Line. As capitals of the state, both Milledgeville and Louisville were centers of wealth and social life in ante-bellum days. Stately old houses of the plantation era are seen only in the towns, as the route does not follow the early roads.

Near Sandersville are kaolin deposits. Much of this gently rolling sandy land is forested, and in the lowlands trees are covered with hanging moss. Although there are some pecan orchards, the chief crops are cotton, corn, and hay.

In the area south of Sylvania, lumber and turpentine are the principal industrial products, and the small towns with their frame houses sprawled along the railroad tracks look almost like frontier settlements. At intervals the road passes through pine forests where the local scene is so monotonous that it appears to be moving on a revolving belt. Where the land in the low country is swampy, the oak trees are draped in moss.

Near Savannah the road approaches some abandoned settlements of the Salzburgers, Bavarian settlers who played an important part in the early history of the state.

South of EATONTON, o m. (approx. 575 alt., 2,749 pop.) (see TOUR 16), State 24 (US 441) and US 129 are united. At 2 m. US 129 branches R., but State 24 and US 441 continue to Milledgeville.

MILLEDGEVILLE, *21 m.* (326 alt., 8,835 pop.), laid out in 1803 as the site of the state capital, retains the symmetry of its original plan, which was that of a right-angled parallelogram, with eleven parallel streets in one axis and eight in the other. With the exception of Columbia and Liberty streets, portentous words in 1803, the remaining seventeen were named after men prominent in public affairs. All of the streets were a spacious one hundred feet in width, except Washington and Jefferson, each of which had the dignity of an extra twenty feet. Some years ago the names of ten streets established later, were changed, and now are: Thomas, Charlton, Hall, Mitchell, Irwin, Gwinnett, Cobb, Habersham, Walton, and Pickens, with the result that the names of all the streets are also names of counties in Georgia, including Columbia and Liberty. Three twenty-acre plots were called Capitol, Government, and Penitentiary squares, and another plot "reserved for public uses" was later made into Cemetery Square. These squares enclose an area of sixteen city blocks in which are most of the old houses. Capitol Square and Cemetery Square are little changed, but the early penitentiary has been removed and its site is now occupied by the Georgia State College for Women, and Government Square has become a recreation ground for the college.

The houses of Milledgeville typify the development of early nineteenth-century deep-south architecture. The earliest had small single-story stoops; the next had two porches, one above the other, with superimposed columns. When the Greek portico with full two-story columns was introduced, the second-story porch became a balcony. Later mansions were built with broad, many-columned verandas that sometimes extended around three sides of the house. The proportioned classic portico with an elaborate doorway is more characteristic of Milledgeville homes, however, than are the spacious porches seen frequently in Athens and Washington. Although most of these houses are set too near the street, they still give an impression of serenity and traditional assurance.

It is believed that this section was settled by the Hitchiti Indians before the coming of the Creek, and some historians maintain that a point on the eastern bank of the Oconee River, about six miles from present Milledgeville, known as Oconee Town in records dealing with Indian affairs, was the place where De Soto and his men were entertained in the year 1539-40. A nearby Indian council place called Rock Landing was later the unloading point for all goods brought up the river.

Near the landing is the SITE OF FORT FIDIUS, the largest garrison of Federal troops south of the Ohio, which was established here in 1793. Other forts built within the next few years included Fort Wilkinson, a few miles north, where representatives from thirty-two Creek towns signed the Indian treaty of 1802 and thereby ceded the lands of this section to the state.

When the newly acquired Indian territory was being developed under the land-lottery system, Louisville seemed too far east to remain the capital; accordingly, in 1803 the legislature created this town near the center of the state and named it for John Milledge, Revolutionary soldier, who was then Governor. According to an entry in the *Louisville Gazette,* October 9, 1807, the transfer of the treasury and the state records from Louisville to Milledgeville was made by fifteen wagons, escorted by a troop of cavalry sent from the national capital, and Milledgeville became the second Georgia town to be laid out as a state capital.

Except for burning the state penitentiary, General Sherman, in his 1864-march to the sea, spared the city the thorough treatment by fire given to others. In 1868 Atlanta became the capital. From 1871 to 1879 the old capitol building served as the Baldwin County courthouse, but since then it has been used for educational purposes.

The HARRIS HOME (*private*) on West Montgomery St., between Clarke and Columbia streets, was built by Judge Iverson Louis Harris, whose parents came from Virginia. The two-story clapboard dwelling, with heavy chimneys, and a front porch of later Victorian banisters, pendants, and brackets, stands close to the oak-shaded street. Judge Harris planted the double row of oaks on Clark and Hancock streets so that he might walk to his office down a shaded avenue.

The GEORGIA STATE COLLEGE FOR WOMEN, bounded by Clarke, Montgomery, Hancock, and Wilkinson streets, was created by legislative act in 1889 as the Georgia Normal and Industrial College and was opened in 1891. Many private schools had failed to open after the War between the States and there was need of a college with low tuition fees; and hence, the institution grew rapidly. In 1917 the legislature changed the charter to permit the granting of degrees and in 1922 the school was given its present name and became the primary women's college of the state system.

On a generous campus shaded by old oaks are the twenty buildings of the college. Most of them are of red brick trimmed with limestone and adorned with white Corinthian columns. Ten dormitories accommodate some 1,500 students.

The INA DILLARD RUSSELL LIBRARY, on the campus at Clarke and Montgomery streets, has Corinthian columns supporting a Greek pediment. With a capacity of 100,000 volumes, the library includes a collection of source books on Georgia history and a valuable file of old newspapers. On the top floor is the GEORGIA HISTORY MUSEUM (*open*), begun by Amanda Johnson, former head of the history department.

The OLD EXECUTIVE MANSION, center of the block between Hancock and Greene streets, is one of Georgia's more distinguished and better preserved Greek Revival houses. The imposing Ionic portico topped by a classic pediment is balanced by substantial pilasters at the corners of the house; the present cupola with Corinthian corners was not part of the original design. The great door under the portico opens into a square entrance hall. The door on the right of the hall opens into the parlor, the one on the left, into the library. When the governors occupied the mansion, a sixty-foot salon was on the left, with eight large windows, two mantels of black Italian marble, and two mirrors with gilded frames ten feet tall and six feet wide, one hanging on the east end of the salon, the other on the west. The salon is now divided by a hall into two rooms; and though the mantels are intact, the mirrors have disappeared. At the back of the entrance hall is a door opening into the rotunda which is fifty feet high, with a mezzanine floor defined by an outer railing of mahogany; the gilding of the dome reflects light into the interior, thus enhancing the depth. Behind the rotunda is the octagon room.

The house, designed after Palladio, was built in 1838 at a cost of $50,000. An entry in the state treasurer's report, dated March 20, 1837, reads: "John Pell, $100 for the best plan for a house for the residence of the governor, as approved by the committee"; but a similar check made to C. B. McCluskey on April 19, 1837, creates an ambiguity, though it may be that the two men collaborated. Up to 1879 it served as the home of the following governors: George R. Gilmer (1837-39), Charles J. McDonald (1839-43), George W. Crawford (1843-47), George W. Towns (1847-51), Howell Cobb (1851-53), Herschel V. Johnson (1853-57), Joseph E. Brown (1857-63), and Charles J. Jenkins (1865-68). Since 1890 it has been the home of the presidents of the Georgia State College for Women.

The SANFORD-POWELL-BINION HOME (*private*), W. Greene and Clarke sts., is a stately clapboarded Greek Revival house with fourteen Doric columns around the front and sides. Well kept, it is set on a small lawn planted with suitable shrubbery and shade trees. The house was built around 1825 by General John Sanford, who, born in 1798 on land which later became a part of Baldwin County, died at his home in Milledgeville in 1870. In 1831 he was appointed by Governor Gilmer to command the guards who were needed in north Georgia at that time to protect the state gold mines. General Sanford had a special interest in flowers and shrubs. The house was surrounded by boxwood gardens and the general's floral interest resulted in an unusual number of green-houses.

The original design of the house specified four columns, but his wife, who was Maryanne Ridley Blount, of Virginia, matched the general's passion for greenhouses with one for columns so that the number of Doric columns grew from a modest four to an imposing fourteen. Acquiescing with tolerant good humor, the general merely commented, "Got to sell another slave; my wife wants four more columns."

The WILLIAMS-ORME-CRAWFORD HOUSE (*private*), S. Liberty and Washington sts., built in 1820, is distinctive for its pair of two-story Doric columns supporting the pediment of the high portico, its delicate fan-lighted doorways of which the second opens on a simple, railed balcony, and its massive end chimneys. The house is well preserved and its dignified simplicity has not been marred by tasteless additions.

Richard McAllister Orme, from Maryland, moved to Georgia in 1813, and came to Milledgeville in 1815, where five years later he and Seaton Grantland started the *Southern Recorder*. Richard Orme bought the house from John Williams, its builder, in 1836. The present owner of the house is a descendent of Richard Orme's.

The WILLIAMS-JONES-FERGUSON HOUSE (*private*), S. Liberty and Washington sts., a white frame post-Colonial house with excellently pro-portioned front doors opening upon a central portico and with a hang-ing second-story balcony, was built in 1817 by Peter J. Williams. The boxwood hedges and the wistaria vines clinging to the old cedar trees were planted soon after the house was built. Among the rare orna-mentals are two spikenard trees, said to be the same as the spikenard mentioned in the Bible as a source of incense and precious ointment, the one blue, the other pink, and quite rare.

Wales has always been known as a land exceptionally well supplied with ghosts. One is said to have followed the Williams family from Wales to Virginia in 1715, where though ghosts are also plentiful, there is always room for another; and then the ghost migrated to Georgia with the family, where it became a regular house ghost with a fixed location, apparently, for it is said to be there still.

MILLEDGEVILLE CEMETERY, at the end of Liberty Street, is a peaceful and secluded spot made beautiful by shrubs, flowers, and trees, includ-ing eastern yews and Italian cypress. The GRAVE OF GENERAL JETT THOMAS, an officer of the War of 1812, is marked by a monument. An old-fashioned slab built two and a half feet above ground marks the GRAVE OF DAVID BRYDIE MITCHELL, Governor of Georgia (1809-13; 1815-17). In the Lamar lot, identified by a tall monument, are the GRAVE OF ZACHARIAH LAMAR, a wealthy and influential farmer and merchant of ante-bellum Georgia, and the GRAVE OF L. Q. C. LAMAR, SR. (1797-1834), a prominent lawyer and brother of Zachariah Lamar. The oldest date recorded on a tombstone is 1804. The site of the first church (Methodist) erected in Milledgeville is indicated by a marker in the cemetery. There are some interesting examples of wrought iron fencing, one of which has balusters in the shape of oak branches, with terminals in oak leaf and acorn design.

By an act of the Legislature ten commemorative tablets were erected, one of which, in memory of Jonathan Lewis who died in 1831, reads:

> "A wit's a feather and a chief's a rod
> An honest man is the noblest work of God."

Modern legislators might go about noting intently.

The OLD DARIEN BANK, Wilkinson and Greene Streets, is a severe two-story, red brick building with a gable roof and walls two and a half feet thick. The building, erected around 1818 by its owner Griffin Parke as a branch of the Bank of Darien (*see* TOUR *1*), has served many purposes. In 1825 it was the Masonic lodge hall in which La Fayette was entertained. After 1834, when the present Masonic Lodge was built, it was used as the printing office of *The Federal Union,* a newspaper established in 1825 and combined with *The Southern Recorder*—established in 1820—to form *The Union Recorder,* Georgia's oldest weekly newspaper. Since the War between the States it has served as an apartment house, the barracks for the Middle Georgia and Agriculture College, which later became The Georgia Military College, as a tearoom after once again serving as an apartment house, and after that as the Darien Hotel. According to an unsubstantiated story, the committee headed by Eugenius Nesbit that formulated the ordinance of secession met here.

OLD STATE CAPITOL (now Georgia Military College), (*open*), bounded by Wayne, Elberton, Franklin, and Greene Streets, near the business section, is a building of Gothic Revival design with battlemented crestings. The building burned in 1941, but was restored in 1943, and the exterior duplicates the original building, which was constructed by Jett Thomas and John Scott at a cost of $60,000 and completed in 1807 in time for the legislative session. There is a description of the old state Capitol in an 1829 copy of Adiel Sherwood's *Gazetteer,* thus: "The State House stands on an eminence, three-fourths of a mile from the river, exhibiting a tasteful appearance of Gothic architecture. In this are rooms for the Legislature during its sessions, the offices of the Governor, Secretary of State, Treasurer, Comptroller and Surveyor General, besides apartments for Clerks and Committees, and several fireproof rooms for public records. The Representative Hall is 60 by 54 feet, ornamented with full length portraits of General Oglethorpe and La Fayette, and in the Senate Chamber with those of Washington and Jefferson." Smart and Lane were the architects. Of the two later wings, one was added in 1828, the other in 1837.

The secession convention met in the building on January 16, 1861. South Carolina, followed by several other states, had already passed its ordinance of secession in December. Commissioners were present on January 17 from both South Carolina and Alabama to promote secession. The excitement released by the secession of South Carolina had already been celebrated some time before in Atlanta by an all-day firing of cannon, by the ascension of a hot-air balloon (an almost too literal symbol of the common mood), and at night by a torchlight procession. Ex-Governor George W. Crawford, United States Senator Robert Toombs, and T. R. R. Cobb, younger brother of Howell Cobb, upheld the keynote of the convention: "We can make better terms out of the Union than in it." Alexander Stephens (*see* TOUR *17*), later Vice-President of the Confederacy, Ex-Governor Herschel V. Johnson, and Ben Hill, later United States Senator, opposed secession. After several days of debate, the secession ordinance was presented by Eugenius Nesbit, and was carried by 208 to 89, January 19, 1861.

Some weary years afterward and by the time Sherman reached Milledgeville, the State House was quiet, and most of the state documents had been removed to safety. The remaining books and papers were scattered, though many of the more important records were later recovered. During their occupation of Milledgeville, the Union troops held a mock session of the legislature in which they "repealed" the secession ordinance. The story is that Sherman thought this a pleasant bit of fancy when he heard about it later.

The entrance gates on the north and south are built in the same architectural style as the Old Capitol, and their three-pointed arches and battlemented tops serve as a suitable architectural preface to the building as seen from the streets.

To the right of the main driveway is the LA FAYETTE BOULDER, marking the spot where General La Fayette was entertained at a Georgia barbecue on his visit to the capital in March, 1825.

In 1879 the old statehouse was given to the newly-created Middle Georgia Military and Agricultural College, set up as a unit of the state university system. The school, renamed in 1900 the Georgia Military College, is now a junior college with a good military rating as well as membership in the Southern Association of Colleges and Secondary Schools. At present it is not a part of the University System of Georgia, but is controlled by its own board of trustees which is elected by the people of Milledgeville. The old statehouse contains the administrative offices.

ST. STEPHENS EPISCOPAL CHURCH, S. Wayne St., also on the campus, is a small, frame Gothic Revival building built in 1843 after the Parish was organized in 1841. In 1864 the building was partly destroyed by Northern soldiery who used it for stabling horses, poured syrup down the organ, burned some of the pews, and violated the altar. The roof which was destroyed when the old Penitentiary, which had been used as an arsenal and powder magazine, was demolished, has been replaced, and the church renovated. The interior woodwork was done by Captain John Wilcox.

The Chamber of Commerce lists sixty-four buildings and homes in Milledgeville that are of architectural and historic interest. Those familiar with the city will agree that the list is modest.

1. Right from Milledgeville on State 22 to the GEORGIA TRAINING SCHOOL FOR BOYS (*open*), *1.2 m.*, a reform school (L) for delinquents. On a tract of some 600 acres the state has erected a complete physical plant of about two dozen buildings. It was created by an act of the Legislature in 1905 when it was known as the Georgia State Reformatory and was under the supervision of the State Prison Commission. After two other legislative changes, the school was placed under the supervision of the State Department of Welfare. Regular common-school training is provided through the seventh grade and in some instances through the ninth as well, with agricultural and vocational training also.

Separate dormitories and facilities are maintained for white boys and Negro boys. At present the school has 249 white boys, and 144 Negroes out of 296, the remainder of which are at the institution in Augusta where later all Negro boys will be located. Commitments are variable, but none extends beyond the age of twenty-one since those convicted of a crime punishable by death or imprisonment for life are not admitted here.

THE STATE ARMORY, formerly the Georgia State Prison, (R) *2.8 m.* occupies what was the main building of the old prison. The new prison is at Reidsville (*see* TOUR *4*), and the former farm acreage is now used by the Milledgeville State Hospital.

2. Right from Milledgeville on State 29 (US 441) to a junction with a paved private road *1 m.;* left *0.6 m.* on this road to the MILLEDGEVILLE STATE HOSPITAL; its buildings numerous enough to constitute a township, accommodate some 10,-000 patients, not to enumerate the hundreds of employees and trainees necessary to staff the institution. On the institution's several thousand acres of land are numbers of flower gardens and groves of oak and pine trees. The main building, set on a wide expanse of rolling lawn, has a large circular dome of the sort usually associated with capitols and a two-storied Ionic portico. The act establishing the institution was passed by the legislature in December, 1837. At first known as the Lunatic Asylum of the State of Georgia, the hospital was opened in November, 1842, after spending some $45,000. In contrast, the cost of maintenance operations for the fiscal year ending June 30, 1946, was $2,509,377.17,

and additional sums spent for permanent improvements brought the total net cost to $4,829,870.48. Part of this ratio of increase corresponds to that of population, obviously; probably the other part to the modern temper.

On State 29 is LOCKERLY (*private*) at *1.3 m.*, a Greek Revival House (L) built by Judge Daniel R. Tucker about 1839. The house has two stories and a basement, with six Doric columns across the front, and a small upper balcony. The commodious house with its massive columns stands on an eminence and is surrounded by long-established boxwoods and magnolias as well as other trees and shrubs. Extending across the front of the lawn is a wrought-iron fence made in England.

At *1.8 m.* is a junction with the Henry Dawson Allen Memorial Drive. Right on this to (R) ROCKWELL MANSION (*private*), *1.9 m.*, built about 1830 by Colonel W. S. Rockwell, who came from Portland, Maine, and brought with him Joseph Lane, Sr., who was under contract to build a house. The wide expanse of lawn, surrounded by a wrought-iron fence with handsome gateways, is shaded by beautiful oak and magnolia trees. A long flight of steps leads to the central portico, which has four Ionic columns and a delicate grillwork balcony flanked by two Doric pilasters. The elliptical arch fanlight above the door is especially worthy of note. One of the owners of the house was Herschel V. Johnson, Governor of Georgia in 1853 and candidate for Vice-President of the United States in 1860. Mr. Lane, referred to above, was the actual builder of the original Oglethorpe University, completed in 1838.

The SITE OF OGLETHORPE UNIVERSITY, *2.5 m.*, is now occupied by the Allen Invalid Home, a private sanitarium for mental cases. A manual training school was opened here in 1835 and a year later was taken over by the trustees of the newly chartered Oglethorpe University, organized by the Presbyterian Church. Forced to close in 1862 when the students were drained away for the Confederate Army, Oglethorpe never reopened here, but was refounded in Atlanta in 1916 (*see* ATLANTA).

THALIAN HALL (*open*), erected (R) by the Thalian Literary Society, is the only school building which remains, and is now used as one of the hospital buildings. It was used as a hospital during the War between the States. On the second floor is the SIDNEY LANIER ROOM, which the poet occupied as a student. The Memorial Marker stands near Thalian Hall, and has incorporated in it the corner stone of Oglethorpe University which was unearthed by workmen digging a foundation in 1921. Sometime after the War between the States all of the buildings but the one were torn down and the material sold to the state to be used in The Asylum for the Insane (*see above,* MILLEDGEVILLE STATE HOSPITAL), and the stone steps of the Powell Building came from Oglethorpe.

In the Scottsboro community, *5 m.*, is the SCOTT-CARTER-FURMAN-SMITH HOUSE (*private*), a white clapboarded building built by General John Scott in 1806. The general, who came from Virginia to Milledgeville soon after it was established in 1803, first built a house in Milledgeville about 1804, but decided that he preferred the country. Extending around two sides of the long house, the porch is covered with wistaria, and the house itself is almost hidden from view by large trees. A hedge of flowering quince, vivid in early spring, stands where the flower gardens were once located. In 1813 Colonel Farish Carter bought the house and made additions and improvements, among which was the double "breezeway" which forms a cross passage through the center of the house. Carter made presents of building lots from his plantation to friends; thus Scottsboro was formed.

State 24 and State 22 unite for *4.2 m.* east of Milledgeville, and at *25.2 m.* is the eastern junction with State 22 (*see* TOUR *14A*).

BOYKIN HALL (*open*), *31 m.*, a two-story white frame house (L) set well back from the road, was built by Samuel Boykin in 1830. It has a large Palladian doorway with a fanlight above and a double portico, the pediment of which is supported by two Doric columns. Major Francis Boykin, from North Carolina, after serving with Nathanael Greene during the Revolutionary War, acquired in 1785 a tract of land east of the Oconee River. After his death in 1821, one of his sons, Dr Samuel Boykin, practicing medicine in Milledgeville, decided to give up the medical arts in order to manage the plantation. He was the first to discover that sugar could be made from cane grown in the section, which is recorded in Adiel Sherwood's *Gazetteer* for 1829. It was the doctor who built Boykin Hall.

SANDERSVILLE, *50.6 m.* (445 alt., 4,480 pop.), seat of Washington County, was established in 1796 and incorporated in 1812. Like its neighboring towns, Sandersville is pleasantly old-fashioned in its architecture and restful shady streets.

LOUISVILLE, *76.6 m.* (337 alt., 2,231 pop.) (*see* TOUR *4*), is at the junction with US 1.

WAYNESBORO, *102.3 m.* (261 alt., 4,461 pop.), is at the junction with US 25 (*see* TOUR *15*).

SYLVANIA, *139.2 m.* (238 alt., 2,939 pop.), was established in 1847 as the seat of Screven County. Its chief industries are lumbering and the cultivation of cotton, in which the county stands high. It has some twenty gins and around a dozen warehouses.

At Sylvania is the junction with State 21, now the route. South of Sylvania State 21 passes through a level, pine-wooded country, where only an occasional farm or lumbering settlement breaks the ennui of the terrain.

SPRINGFIELD, *171.9 m.* (80 alt., 627 pop.), seat of Effingham County, was founded in 1799. The primary products of the area are corn, cotton, potatoes, and pine.

RINCON (pronounced Rink'-on), *179 m.* (75 alt., 424 pop.), is a small town in a turpentining section.

Left from Rincon on the Ebenezer (Jerusalem Church) Road (*rough but passable*) to a fork, *1.3 m.*; L. from the fork to the junction with another road, *5 m.* R. on this road to JERUSALEM CHURCH, *8 m.* The red brick edifice completed in 1769 has a white boxlike steeple above the front of a high-pitched roof. The old church, in its setting of moss-covered trees, is the only building remaining of the once thriving Lutheran settlement of New Ebenezer.

The trustees of the colony invited the persecuted Salzburgers of Bavaria to come to Georgia, promising to pay their expenses, to allot each family fifty acres of land, and to provide for them until crops could be produced. So pleased were the seventy-eight who came in 1734 to have a refuge that they named their town Ebenezer (Heb., stone of help). But though their number was soon increased by 150 more from the old country, the soil was too infertile for the town to prosper, and in 1736 the colonists began to migrate to a higher ridge near the Savannah River, which they settled as New Ebenezer. More colonists came, the silk culture in which they were especially skilled prospered, and the new town became well established. But the Revolution brought an unfavorable turn of fortune's wheel. New Ebenezer fell into the possession of the British who burnt the houses, destroyed the gardens, and used the church variously, first as a hospital and then to stable horses. An effort to resume life at the town, after the war, failed because the silk industry no longer proved profitable and because of the rising importance of Savannah. It should be remembered, in connection with the above statement, that at one time the number of settlers in Georgia of German origin exceeded those of British extraction, and that the Salzburgers were masters of productive arts useful in a new country, such as the preparation of lumber, the construction of houses, blacksmithing, and skills of the garden and field, including horticulture. Moreover, their religious seriousness, intensified by earlier persecution, caused them to set up group settlements apart from other colonists. It might have been better for the state if these skilful and just people had dominated its cultural pattern completely. Greed seems to have had no part in them; their attitude can be brought to a focus by saying that they turned their hands to work and their minds to God. It is generally admitted that New Ebenezer had the first orphanage and the first organized Sunday School in the colony.

The GOSHEN METHODIST CHURCH, *182 m.*, organized in 1822, is still active. Its building is the only remnant of the old settlement of Goshen which also declined with the rise of Savannah.

At *183.5 m.* is the junction with the Rice Hope Plantation Road.

Left on this road to the SITE OF MULBERRY GROVE, *3 m.*, the former estate of General Nathanael Greene (1742-86), who succeeded Gates as Washington's lieutenant in the South. The land, originally the estate of the loyalist lieutenant-governor, John Graham, was confiscated after the Revolution by the new state of Georgia and presented to Greene who had suffered financially because he endorsed notes to secure supplies for the army when he was quartermaster general. On June 19, 1786, the general died on the estate, but a tradition of hospitality in the high style continued at the house until 1864 when the plantation was virtually destroyed by Sherman's army which apparently was devoid of historical piety except in the instance of a few of its officers, mostly from New England. In 1791 George Washington was a guest at the plantation, and it was here that Eli Whitney invented the cotton gin.

On leaving Yale in 1792, Whitney (1765-1825) came to Georgia to serve as a tutor in a Savannah family, but on his arrival found the position filled. Having made the acquaintance of Mrs. Nathanael Greene on board the ship coming South, he was invited to Mulberry Grove. As it happened, he overheard someone say, "There is a fortune in store for the man who invents a machine for separating the lint of cotton from the seed." Mrs. Greene, noticing his looking interested, pointed to him and said, "You are that man, Mr. Whitney. Anybody able to fix a watch as well as you did mine, has the ingenuity to make any sort of machine." The young man fashioned his own tools, shut himself off in an improvised workshop (*see* TOUR *8*), and spent a winter on the problem. The first machine he showed Mrs. Greene had a revolving cylinder with hooks that caught the cotton and pulled it through a slit in a metal plate, leaving the seed behind; but there was no contrivance for throwing off the separated lint which wrapped around the cylinder. Mrs. Green intuitively picked up a brush and, applying it to the teeth of the machine, caught the lint upon it. So delicately balanced are the destinies of men that there are times when an event of a feather's weight can definitely change the course of human existence.

SAVANNAH, *199.3 m.* (21-65 alt., 119,638 pop.) (*see* SAVANNAH).

Points of Interest: Telfair Academy of Arts and Sciences, Armstrong Junior College, Atlantic Coast Line Docks, Herty Pulp and Paper Laboratory, Bethesda Orphanage, Wormsloe, and others.

Savannah is at the junction with US 80 (*see* TOUR *9*) and with US 17 (*see* TOUR *1*).

TOUR 14A

Junction with State 24—Sparta—Crawfordville; 44.9 m., State 22.

Roadbed hard-surfaced between State 24 and Sparta; road not hard-surfaced between Sparta and Crawfordville—Georgia R.R. parallels route—Limited accommodations.

This route runs through a section that was developed in the latter part of the eighteenth century under the cotton plantation system. It is so remote from the main thoroughfares and railroad centers that it has retained much of its old-fashioned atmosphere, relatively unblemished by the garish signs of modernity. The area is primarily agricultural and produces cotton, corn, livestock, feed crops, pecans, and pine and hardwood timber. Most of the farms are large and are worked by sharecroppers among whom Negroes predominate.

State 22 branches north from its junction with State 24 (*see* TOUR *14*), *0 m.,* at a point about 4 miles east of Milledgeville.

SPARTA, *20.8 m.* (557 alt., 1,954 pop.), was incorporated in 1805 as the seat of Hancock County. The red brick courthouse of late Victorian design overlooks the tree-shaded square of the business section. The narrow streets of the residential section are bordered with elms and lined with clapboard houses built during the early decades of the nineteenth century. Though not carefully maintained, many of the old houses suggest still the pleasant manner of living and the prosperity of the planters who built them.

Dairy products and quantities of lumber are shipped from the surrounding country, while sawmills and planing mills operate in the town. Although cotton is not neglected around Sparta, diversified farming according to advanced agricultural methods has been developed through the local soil conservation and improvement association.

The MIDDLEBROOKS HOUSE (*private*), 510 Rabun Street, has an elliptical front walk bordered with flowers and shaded by dark cedars. A large Greek Revival house with a slender Doric colonnade supporting a pedimented portico, it was built as a dormitory for the Sparta Female Academy, founded in 1832. By 1837 the academy, which was one of the first schools for girls in the South, had 121 pupils and 5 teachers.

The TERRELL HOUSE (*private*), 839 Jones Street, is a two-story, clapboarded building with a beautiful elliptical fanlight over the front door. The irregularities of the fluted Ionic columns, carved from heart pine, indicate the manual art employed in making them. It was built by William Terrell, an early settler from Virginia, while he was a United States Congressman (1817-21). The original small entrance stoop was later extended, resulting in a porch across the front. In the rear is an old smokehouse of field stones.

The HAROLD ROUNTREE HOUSE (*private*), 22.8 m., is a story-and-a-half Georgian Colonial farmhouse (L) with louvered shutters at the windows. Both the interior and exterior walls are of wide boards. Its date is unknown, but it has been established that Aaron Burr stayed overnight in 1807, probably after his arrest in Mississippi, when Federal agents were taking him to Richmond, Virginia, for trial.

At this point is a junction with State 15.

Left on State 15 to a marked INDIAN TRAIL, *4.8 m.*, the route followed by the Creek and other tribes in traveling from Columbus to Augusta.

The MOUNT ZION METHODIST CHURCH (L), *6.3 m.*, is a white frame structure with four square columns, wide floor boards, and covered keyholes. In 1812 Joseph Bryan, an early settler from Connecticut, influenced Nathan S. S. Beman to come to Mount Zion, then a prosperous community, to organize a Presbyterian church. The present building, erected about 1850, became the property of the Methodists in 1903, when the Presbyterian congregation combined with that of Sparta.

Near the church was the noted Mount Zion Academy, a coeducational preparatory school organized about 1813, with "Classical, English and Female departments," an interesting example of mixed classification. Nathan S. S. Beman, the Presbyterian founder, maintained severe discipline by means of the rod. In 1855 the institution became the Mount Zion High School under the leadership of the Reverend C. P. Beman, who had been the first principal of Midway Seminary, which later became Oglethorpe University.

In POWELTON, *35.8 m.* (approx. 500 alt., 150 pop.), an old village, the houses are not Greek Revival, but simple farmhouse types of one or two stories.

The BAPTIST CHURCH (R), at the turn of the road, serves a congregation organized on July 1, 1786, with Silas Mercer as pastor. The white frame auditorium with two towers is the original church edifice. Except for nine months of 1852, the church minutes, carefully inscribed in great ledgers, are complete. Among the many important church conferences held here was the one that organized the Georgia Baptist Convention on June 27, 1822. Nearby is a slave cemetery, with graves marked by rough slabs of field stone. The Negroes buried here were members of the church and once occupied the rear pews.

CRAWFORDVILLE, 44.9 m. (616 alt., 966 pop.) (see TOUR 17), is at the junction with State 12.

TOUR 15

(Saluda,   S.   C.) — Augusta — Waynesboro — Millen — Junction with US 80; US 25.

South Carolina Line to junction with US 80, 75.2 m. — Central of Georgia Ry. parallels route — Limited accommodations.

This route runs through one of the more fertile cotton sections of the state. Long green watermelons and fragrant yellow cantaloupes are grown in abundance, and garden truck of all sorts is produced. Many acres of pecans are planted near Waynesboro. In this level sandy country US 25 occasionally crosses a long red hill, from the crest of which there is a wide view of farm lands and distant hillsides wooded in pine and scrub oak. In the cool, swampy hollows, the dark but clear creeks are bordered with dense thickets of bay, cypress, various sorts of holly, magnolia, and water oak hung with gray moss.

Some of the tenant farmhouses, built on the sites of once commanding plantation houses, are surrounded by trees and shrubbery long established which lend an air of significance to the present very modest buildings. In the vicinity of Waynesboro and Millen are many prosperous-looking farmhouses. The houses in the towns are attractive with neatly trimmed lawns and hedges.

US 25 crosses the Savannah River, *o m.,* the boundary line between South Carolina and Georgia.

AUGUSTA, 0.5 m. (143 alt., 71,508 pop.) (see AUGUSTA).

Points of Interest: The Hill, University of Georgia School of Medicine, Junior College of Augusta, Paine College (Negro), Haines Institute (Negro), Cotton Exchange, and others.

Augusta is at a junction with US 78 (*see* TOUR 8) and with US 1 (*see* TOUR 4).

At *3.6 m.* is a junction with the old Savannah Road.

Left on this road to the COTTAGE CEMETERY (L), *3 m.,* about a fifth of a mile from the highway; here is the GRAVE OF JOSEPH EVE (1760-1835), inventor of a roller cotton gin which was used in the Bahama Islands as early as 1787 to gin long-fibered cotton. Eve moved to Richmond County in 1810 and built his home, The Cottage. Here he manufactured gunpowder, some of which is said to have been used by American forces in the War of 1812; experimented with steam and was granted patents on two steam engines, one in 1818 and the other in 1826; and in 1823, showing himself the complete man, he published a book of poetry.

At *5.2 m.* is a junction with Tobacco Road.

Left *1.9 m.* on this road to the SITE OF NEW SAVANNAH, on a bluff of the Savannah River. Towards the latter part of the eighteenth century, this was an important point for the shipment of tobacco, and scores of boats were loaded from warehouses near by. With the decline of river traffic, however, the settlement's activity vanished. In 1935 the section sprang into new growth when the Federal government began deepening the Savannah River between Augusta and New Savannah. A lock and dam were completed at this point in 1937 at a cost of about two million dollars.

At *9 m.* is a junction of US 25 with the unmarked, red clay TOBACCO ROAD, the supposed locale of Erskine Caldwell's story (*see* TOUR 4). This road once followed a ridge from north Georgia to New Savannah. In the second half of the eighteenth century, tobacco was a major factor in the development of the Southeast, and pioneers from Georgia and the colonies to the north trundled tobacco over this road in mule-drawn hogsheads to the port; here it was loaded on boats for shipment down river to Savannah. Fur and grain were also traded for necessities. Lusty fellows, traveling in caravans and cracking rawhide whips, the traders gained the name of "Georgia crackers," or at least this is one version, and a likely story. Tobacco Road runs through a thinly populated region between indifferently cultivated fields and occasional lopsided shacks. The boll weevil has encouraged the planting of tobacco again.

Left on Tobacco Road to Gracewood Road, *0.2 m.;* R. on this road *0.1 m.* to the GEORGIA TRAINING SCHOOL FOR MENTAL DEFECTIVES (R), housed in some eight cream-colored concrete buildings and several adjunct structures of frame construction. It was established by an act of the Legislature in 1919, with an appropriation of $100,000 for land and buildings. The Tuttle-Newton Orphanage was bought and after needed renovations, the institution opened in July of 1921. In addition to its 325-acre tract, it acquired a 450-acre farm about four miles away on the Old Savannah Road, in 1929.

The school which is ungraded because of the specific situation, is conducted throughout the year. Boys are taught dairying and farming and associated skills; girls are taught housekeeping, meal planning, cooking, telephone exchange operating, sewing, and laundry work.

WAYNESBORO, *31.5 m.* (261 alt., 4,461 pop.), seat of Burke County, laid out as a town in 1783 and incorporated in 1812, was named for General Wayne, known as "Mad Anthony" because of his daring exploits. He served in Georgia during the Revolution and later moved to the state, where he was elected to the U. S. Congress in 1791. After serving less than one term, he was unseated because of a charge of fraudulence in the election, and he did not enter the campaign in the new election. Waynesboro's houses vary in architecture from the dignified Greek Revival type to the modern box-cottage. Once part of the old plantation belt, where landowners kept many slaves as field-hands, the town still has a large Negro population.

At Waynesboro is a junction with State 24 (*see* TOUR *14*).

The town has a STATE FARMERS MARKET which is supervised by the Georgia Department of Agriculture. As yet one of the smaller markets of the state system, it is expected to grow.

Left from Waynesboro on the McBean Road, paved for five miles, to SHELL BLUFF (*inquire way to the actual area*), near which is an unusual geological formation. High above the Savannah are many giant oyster fossils (*Ostrea georgiana*) from 12 to 15 inches long. Authorities claim that the bed, stretching a thousand feet along the river, is of the Eocene age and that it was formed when the Coastal Plain of Georgia was submerged beneath the sea. The landing at Shell Bluff was important when steamboats plied the river between Augusta and Savannah. Now little used, the road was then the main artery of trade for tobacco and other commodities to and from the landing. A section of Confederate breastworks, now covered with trees and vines, is still discernible.

At *43 m.* is the junction with a dirt road.

Right on this road to the junction with another road, *3.1 m.;* L. *0.1 m.* on this road to (R) BELLEVUE PLANTATION (*private*). Set among fine old oaks and a profusion of flowers, the two-story clapboarded house with its flanking wings is one of the more notable Colonial houses in this section. Porter Carswell, who owns the place, has in his possession a warrant for the survey of the land dated 1766, and a grant dated July 7, 1767 to Samuel Eastlake, signed by James Wright, George III's governor for the royal province of Georgia. Since Eastlake was the surveyor, chances are that the land was granted in payment for his services. The house was probably built soon afterward and has remained in the same family.

Built of heart pine and cypress, the house is in a state of excellent preservation. Though altered from time to time, it still has the authentic lines of the original part, with sloping roof supported by square columns, front porch, and extensive wings at both sides. The southern wing, a late addition, is in keeping with the rest of the house, even to the wide floor and ceiling boards. The brick in the massive chimneys is hand-made, and every piece of timber is hand-hewn; the frame is joined with wooden pegs.

The house is pock-marked in several places by bullet holes made during the skirmish at Buckhead Creek in the War between the States. All of the outbuildings and many of the neighboring houses were burned then, but Bellevue was spared, perhaps because women and children from Waynesboro had taken refuge there.

On the first dirt road is BUCKHEAD BAPTIST CHURCH (R), *6.5 m.,* a white frame edifice built about 1800. Four simple, square columns rise from the ground to the roof, and steps extend across the entire front. The church was organized in 1778. It was here in 1831 that the Georgia Baptist Convention passed a resolution to organize the school that became Mercer University (*see* TOUR *17*).

MAGNOLIA SPRINGS STATE PARK (L), *46.5 m.* (*fishing, swimming, bathhouse, casino, beach, and concession stands; picnic shelters, roads, and trails*), has long been known because of the crystal clear water that flows from the spring at an estimated rate of nine million gallons of water a day. Because of the great depth of its origin the water is exceptionally cold. It forms a pool around a dozen feet or more in depth and so clear that fish and marine plants are clearly visible on its bottom. There are two fine lakes for fishing, one of forty acres, the other of fifty.

This is the SITE OF CAMP LAWTON, a Confederate prison established during the autumn of 1864 to relieve the congestion at Andersonville Prison (*see* TOUR *2B*). Across the stream are the breastworks built for the protection of the prison area.

Adjacent is the FISH CULTURAL STATION. It was established in 1950 by the Fish and Wildlife Service of the U. S. Department of the Interior for the propagation of warm-water species, to be used to stock farm ponds and other suitable public and private waters. The station has an area of 107 acres and contains 12 ponds used for the propagation of fish. Water for the ponds is furnished by Magnolia Spring.

MILLEN, *52.4 m.* (160 alt., 3,449 pop.), seat of Jenkins County, was first called Seventy-Nine because of its mileage from Savannah. In 1836 the town was given its present name for Captain John Millen, a civil engineer of the Central of Georgia Railway, which passed here on its route from Savannah to Atlanta and formed a junction with the branch to Augusta, and the town has grown around this center.

Right from Millen on State 17 to the junction with a dirt road, *10.4 m.;* R., *14.4 m.* is BIRDSVILLE, a small village that grew around the ancestral estate of the Francis Jones family, the land of which was a royal grant from George III of England. Avenues around Birdsville are lined with centuries-old oaks, stately with time. Pre-Revolutionary houses standing at the crossroads served the community around the Jones house. The small, gabled frame building served as an inn, stage stop, and post office.

The JONES HOUSE (*private*), of hand-hewn pine timbers with mortised joints held by wooden pegs, was built (R) in 1762; additions in the Greek Revival style were completed in 1847. Recessed between two flanking rooms, the pedimented porch has two interior Corinthian columns and a pair of outside pilasters of the same order. The balcony under the recessed pediment repeats the front iron-grille balustrade of the somewhat elevated first porch, the whole creating an absorbing pattern of symmetry in minor and major repetition.

General Sherman's men overran the place, stripped it as far as possible, and started to burn the house. The mistress of the house who was ill in a room on the second level, not wishing to outlive her house, refused to move. Because of her firmness the soldiers extinguished the fire which was already mounting from a room in the lower story.

At 75.2 *m.* is the junction with US 80 (*see* TOUR 9), at a point 6.6 *m.* west of Statesboro.

TOUR 16

Athens—Watkinsville—Madison—Eatonton—Macon; 91.3 m., US 129; joint with US 441 to Eatonton.

Central of Georgia Railway parallels route—All types of accommodations in Athens and Macon; limited elsewhere.

US 129 is a speedway through an agricultural land where fields of cotton, corn, and sorghum are interspersed with peach orchards and groves of oak and pine. Once a part of the plantation belt, this section has many old houses which, even when shabby, have a persuasive charm. Few remain along the country roadside, but the towns are particularly notable for their examples of ante-bellum architecture.

ATHENS, *o m.* (662 alt., 28,180 pop.) (*see* ATHENS).

Points of Interest: University of Georgia, antebellum homes, and others.

Athens is at the junction with US 78 (*see* TOUR 8) and US 29 (*see* TOUR 3).

At Watkinsville turn R. on State 53 and continue *0.8 m.* to the SOUTH-ERN PIEDMONT CONSERVATION EXPERIMENT STATION (*visitors welcome*). The station was established by the Soil Conservation Service, U. S. D. A., January 1, 1937, as a centrally located, regional cooperative research center for the study of soil and water conservation with regard to the Southern Piedmont area in Alabama, Georgia, and South Carolina. It contains 981 acres of typical Southern Piedmont land. In November, 1952, the station was transferred to the Bureau of Plant Industry, Soils and Agricultural Engineering, U. S. D. A., and in continued cooperation with the Georgia Agricultural Experiment Station. The station's experimental program includes the measurement of rainfall, runoff, and erosion on varied sites with different degrees of past erosion and with varying crops and covers. Actual soil and water losses occurring under average farm conditions are observed and formulated. Such data serve as an index for formulating practical crop and soil management methods, and are widely used throughout the Southeast for that purpose.

Developing and testing a comprehensive series of conservation-type crop rotations is a major project. Data have been formulated thus far for a ten-year period. A number of new grass-legume based rotations have been added in recent years to the series, to test their adaptability for grassland farming in the Southern Piedmont. A considerable portion of the experimental land is devoted to large scale field tests, mechanization studies, pasture development trials, irrigation projects, and farm woodland studies. As a whole, the station functions as an experimental index for progressive land uses.

A 100-acre tract is in use as a tenant-operated conservation farm. The station supplies technical advice and the tenant carries out the program. The tenant's net income increased from $971.00 the first year to $2,058.00 the eighth. Returns to the landlord, *i.e.,* in this case the Federal government, during the eighth year was 16.6 per cent on the investment in land, livestock, and equipment, for the 100-acre tract. Conservation farming techniques are practical and also profitable for both tenant and landlord.

The station is used as a research, demonstration, and educational center by members of the agricultural agencies and colleges, vocational agriculture units and veterans' farm training classes, and also by land conservation students from abroad. Several thousand farmers visit the station annually, usually in organized groups and on Tuesdays and Thursdays, though guided tours can be arranged by appointment on other days.

WATKINSVILLE, 5.4 *m.* (approx. 750 alt., 662 pop.), seat of Oconee County, is a quiet community. The town was founded as the seat of Clarke County in 1802 and became the seat of Oconee County when it was formed from Clarke in 1875.

Opposite the courthouse is the EAGLE HOTEL, a rectangular building with a two-story loggia. In 1789 the building was used as a blockhouse against the Cherokee and called Fort Edwards. Later it was covered inside and out with wide boards and greatly enlarged. It became a tavern in 1801.

MADISON, 28 *m.* (667 alt., 2,489 pop.), seat of Morgan County, was incorporated in 1809 and named for President James Madison. Beneath the arching branches of aged oak trees, the streets have a quiet, shaded repose. Tall white columns and broad, graceful doorways of old houses recall ante-bellum days. Morgan County has always been an agricultural area, the chief products of which are cotton, corn, and cottonseed oil, and there are few industrial interests.

The BURNEY HOME (*private*), 399 N. Main St., is a two-story, white Greek Revival house set among cedars and magnolias. The portico has six fluted Doric columns and a delicately designed balcony that overhangs the entrance; the doorways on both floors are decorated with fanlights and heavy lintels. The house was built about 1845, but additions have been made to the left and to the rear.

SNOWHILL (*private*), on the old Agricultural College Rd., was the home of Lancelot Johnson, inventor of one of the first machines for crushing cottonseed. This device, patented before 1832, contributed to the rapid development of the cottonseed-oil industry. Snowhill is a two-story, white frame house with a deep, columned portico. The fine hedges of boxwood are especially noteworthy.

On the public square is the BRASWELL MONUMENT honoring Benjamin Braswell, who in 1817 provided in his will that thirteen of his slaves be sold to provide "for education of indigent white children" of the town.

Madison is at the junction with State 12 (*see* TOUR *17*).

At *43.7 m.* is a junction with a road.

Right on this road at signs to Indian EAGLE MOUND and to ROCK EAGLE 4-H CAMP. It is one mile to the Indian mound, a mass of loosely piled stones in the shape of an eagle with outspread wings. It measures 102 feet from head to tail and 120 feet across the wings. The body 10 or 12 feet above the surface of the ground, is 60 feet long and 35 feet wide. The proportions of the mound, distinguishable from the high tower built in recent years for the purpose, correspond amazingly well to those of an eagle. The stones of the body are larger than those of the head, and those of the wings are graduated in size; thus proportion and mass are properly balanced and the likeness of an eagle well done. Matthew W. Sterling of the Bureau of American Ethnology has described the mound as the "most perfect effigy mound in North America."

The EAGLE MOUND 4-H CAMP (*follow signs*) SITE is part of the vast 69,000-acre Piedmont Plantation Land Utilization Project. Much of it tax delinquent, the land was severely eroded when bought by the Federal government in 1935 and turned over to the Soil Conservation Service for development. Today the land abounds with wildlife and trees, making it a spacious outdoor classroom for 4-H Camps in forestry, wildlife, and nature study.

According to the prospectus for the center, 72 cottages lining the banks of a 110-acre lake, dining and recreation halls for 1,200, demonstration buildings and workshops, green pastures for the camp's supply of beef, and other facilities, are part of the construction program. The center is being built in units, making it possible for several meetings to be held at once; six cottages make a 100-capacity unit. Other buildings in the plan are an administrative building; camp store and post office; five recreation buildings; two dining halls—one with a 900-capacity and another with 300; three educational, demonstration and exhibit buildings;

one auditorium of 1,200-capacity; an infirmary; a chapel; and other associated buildings. A cottage, it should be noted, is a dormitory unit capable of housing sixteen boys or girls and two counsellors: two bedrooms, eight bunks to the room, counsellors' room, living room, and showers.

All buildings are being constructed for year-around use, and if the camp is used to capacity, it will accommodate 62,400 people annually. This exceeds the present need of the 4-H clubs, but when not in use by 4-H members, Home Demonstration Clubs, Farm Bureau, University of Georgia groups, commodity groups, and others will have access to the facilities. Thus it will serve as an agricultural center for the state.

The construction of the camp has been hastened by Governor Herman Talmadge's transfer of a skilled-prisoners labor camp to Rock Eagle as a work unit and the promise that the state will match all funds raised by 4-H members and their friends. One of these friends was *The Atlanta Journal-Constitution*, with a check for $10,000 which covered the cost of a cottage. Work began June 1, 1952. By August 19, the administration building and guest house were completed, two cottages were dedicated, and work was under way on twelve others. There are some 126,000 boys and girls in the Georgia 4-H membership.

EATONTON, *49.7 m.* (approx. 575 alt., 2,749 pop.), seat of Putnam County, was incorporated in 1809 and named for William Eaton, Revolutionary officer and naval agent to the Barbary States. The town was settled by owners of large plantations and became a seat of ante-bellum culture. A number of old houses remain. Some of the older Negroes who gather around the town square on Saturdays are not unlike Uncle Remus, the popular character created by Joel Chandler Harris (*see* ATLANTA), who was born in Eatonton on December 9, 1848, and lived in the county until a young man. Before the War between the States the region around Eatonton was devoted chiefly to the cultivation of cotton, but now the farmers take an active interest in dairying and in the improvement of livestock and cropland as pasture.

The JOEL CHANDLER HARRIS MONUMENT, on Jefferson St., is near the eastern entrance to the courthouse. Although Harris' character Uncle Remus is fictional, many of his traits were those of Uncle George Terrell, an old slave who baked ginger cookies in his Dutch oven to sell in Eatonton on Saturdays. While the air was filled with the spicy smell of ginger, children used to collect in his cabin and, sitting before a snapping fire, listen to his stories.

The T. G. GREEN HOUSE (*private*), La Fayette St., built about 1845, is the best-preserved old house in town. It has Corinthian columns, a Palladian doorway, and a hipped roof. The garden is bordered with a beautiful boxwood hedge.

PANOLA HALL (*private*), across from the public library on N. Madison St., is a two-story, white-columned Greek Revival house built before 1850. It was the home of Benjamin W. Hunt, scientist and horticulturalist, who came to Georgia from New York in 1876.. The gardens are planted in palms and other tropical flora, and, though the place has fallen on neglect, it still has an air of distinction. Hunt developed a variety of fig and one of muscadine grape, a favorite, that bears his name.

Left from Eatonton on State 16 to the junction with a road, *1.3 m.;* left on this road to BRIAR PATCH FARMS, *5 m.,* a small project started by the F.E.R.A., and then transferred first to the Resettlement and then to the Farm Security Administration. This project was begun in 1934 as a community-type program to reforest badly eroded and submarginal lands, and to provide tenant farmers with a chance to become owners by developing economical units and putting the land to profitable use through the introduction of diversified farming and efficient farm management.
Though a modest project of 7,400 acres, approximately 3,500 acres proved unsuitable for cultivation and were sold as surplus land. The remainder was divided into 22 farm units. Each farmstead was provided with a dwelling and other buildings needed. In addition, five of the units were developed for dairying operations and equipped with dairy barns and milk houses. Poultry raising was a special activity on about half of the farms. Of the 22 units originally developed in this program, 21 have liquidated their indebtedness, and the one remaining is now under the supervision of the Farmers Home Administration. Aside from the direct benefits for the farm owners, the program has established helpful models for flexible agricultural practices generally, and served to indicate how farm financing might be more realistically redefined.

At *51.7 m.* is a junction where US 129 turns right to Gray and US 441 turns left to Milledgeville (*see* TOUR *14*).

GRAY, *75.6 m.* (553 alt., 866 pop.), was made the seat of Jones County in 1905. Its primary products are cotton, corn, peaches, and pimientos. Canneries in season employ several hundred operators.

Right from Gray *6 m.* on State 11 to Wayside, and then west—on an all-weather road marked by signs—*8 m.* to the HITCHITI EXPERIMENTAL FOREST (*visitors welcome*) and its forest station. Established in 1946 by the Forest Service, of the U. S. D. A., the experimental forest has as its purpose the study of how to produce more wood in the depleted forests of the lower Piedmont areas of Georgia, Alabama, and South Carolina. The field laboratory research center is in the 4,735-acre Hitchiti Forest, situated along the east bank of the Ocmulgee River, and named for an Indian tribe of the region.
About 1773 one surge after another of settlers flowed into this region from the coast. Within a half century, the Piedmont was changed from a land of fine oak and hickory forest with an intermixture of beech, maple, chestnut, and shortleaf pine, of clear and cool streams, and an undergrowth of dogwood, azalea, huckleberry, and chinquapin, to a farming country. The rich topsoil with a depth of seven to fifteen inches was washed away, especially as a result of cotton culture and other such row crops. As a result of what man made of nature, the misuse of the land gave rise to an agricultural crisis in the 1880's. But it was the arrival of the boll weevil in 1920 with the consequent flight of farmers from the land that finally resulted in the pines seeding themselves in again upon the tortured

soil. According to a *Guide to the Hitchiti Forest Research Center* (Southeastern Forest Experiment Station, Forest Service, U. S. D. A., 1952), "Mile after mile of former farmland, in unbroken 10-, 20-, and 30-mile stretches has gone back to woods. It is because of this forest that the future of the area is so closely tied to forest production and forest management."

The Research Program has five principal divisions. The Management of Loblolly Pine includes the comparison of management systems on 40-acre compartments, a survey study of reproduction (growth, damage, mortality) in shelterwood stands, and the survival, growth, and development of residual saplings on areas clear cut and planted. The Stand Improvement in Loblolly Pine is concerned with the relationship of growth to stand density, site, and age in thinned and unthinned stands, and with bud and branch pruning. Regeneration is the study of site preparation for hardwood control before planting clear cut areas, field tests of hybrid pines, seed production by stand characteristics, and the behavior and control of honeysuckle. Silvics is the formulation of controlled burning as a silvicultural tool and its effect upon soil. Financial Aspects is a division that has to do with farm woodlot management, relation of harvesting costs to tree size, volume cut per acre, topography, etc., determining conversion values of trees for alternate uses, development of log and tree grades, and a proposed forest valuation, growth studies, land uses, etc.

At Hamilton, the station and the Ida Cason Callaway Foundation (*see* Ida Cason Callaway Gardens, TOUR 2) are conducting jointly a program of tree study based principally on longleaf, slash, loblolly, and shortleaf pines. This project requires a full-time graduate forester.

Left from Gray on State 22 is the village of HADDOCK, *6 m.* (approx. 500 alt., 336 pop.); R. from Haddock on a dirt road to the BLOUNT HOUSE (*private*), *7 m.,* one of the best examples of ante-bellum architecture in the state. This fine old house is of white clapboards with unusual corner pilasters of the Doric order and a pair of two-story columns extending from the corners of the small portico to the overhanging cornice of the pediment. The fluted columns are complete in detail from the plinth and tarus to the astragal and abacus. These columns are backed by pilasters in the same mode. The cornice and pediment are modest. Opening on the porch, and also on the balcony which is railed and balustraded, are wide paneled doors with unusually generous and fine fanlights. The slender and evenly placed windows have louvered blinds. An "eyebrow" window is placed at the south end of the attic. The ceiling and interior walls are ornamented with plaster medallions and cornices of acanthus leaves, and a spiral staircase with mahogany handrail winds from basement to attic. On each side of the fireplace in the living room are semicircular alcoves outlined with gilded acanthus leaves. A picture of the house is to be seen on page 316 of Medora Perkerson's *White Columns in Georgia,* 1952. At the time the above book was published the house belonged to Dr. L. C. Lindsey.

Available sources agree that the house was built by John W. Gordon, a brigadier general in the militia (1835-39), and was designed by Daniel Pratt, a New England architect who became the first great industrialist of Alabama. Construction began in 1828 and lasted five years, not an unusual interval for that period.

CLINTON, 77.6 *m.* (approx. 650 alt., approx. 200 pop.), was the seat of Jones County from 1807, when the county was created, until 1905, when the county offices were removed to Gray because Clinton has no railroad facilities. Before the War between the States the town was surrounded by large plantations and was a center of wealth and culture. The first iron foundry in the state was established here and manufactured 900 cotton gins a year. It was destroyed by General Sherman's forces on their march to the sea. The Clinton Female Seminary, founded in Clinton in 1828 by Thomas B. Slade, lost prestige and declined when Wesleyan College was opened in Macon several years later.

The CLINTON METHODIST CHURCH is one of the oldest churches in middle Georgia, and Macon people attended services here before there was a church in that town. The land on which the church and cemetery stand was deeded to the congregation in 1821. About 1882 the church was remodeled and the slave gallery removed.

GEORGIA BAPTIST COLLEGE (L), 85.8 m., provides junior college courses for Negro boys and girls, and in addition has a department for theological training. It was founded in 1889 through the efforts of the Reverend E. K. Love, pastor of the Savannah Baptist Church, and placed under the Missionary Baptist Convention in 1915. At the Baptist Convention in Athens in 1935, the school was placed under the supervision of a chartered board of white trustees responsible for administrative procedures. This college is maintained by donations from the Central Missionary Board and the Georgia Baptist Missionary and Education Convention, the Georgia Baptist College Foundation, and private contributions.

The campus contained 235 acres until some years ago, when 30 acres were deeded to the City of Macon for development as a recreational park. On the southwestern side of the school grounds, which were a part of the great plantation called Wilburn Hill, are breastworks set up to check the advance of Sherman's forces. The original main building, once the plantation house, was totally destroyed by fire in 1921. The present two-story building was built the next year.

Georgia Baptist College consists of seven buildings, with an eighth under construction in 1952. After the high school department of the college was discontinued in 1949, the college began to devote full time to the Junior College Department, and the Theological Department.

Right from Clinton on State 18, a sand-clay road, which cuts across the PIEDMONT NATIONAL WILDLIFE REFUGE. At 15 m., the western edge of the refuge on State 18, is Dames Ferry (*free*) across the Ocmulgee River. On the western side of the river, State 18 is hard-surfaced to the point where it joins US 41, about a mile south of Forsyth (*see* TOUR 12). The refuge also has an entry road at Round Oak, some six miles north of Gray on State 11, or about fourteen miles south of Monticello. The address of the Refuge Manager is Round Oak, 'phone Gray 2706.

The refuge is located in Jones and Jasper counties which are included in the lower Piedmont Belt, a section that is split by numerous valleys with steep slopes. The greater part of the area is characterized by red clay loam soils weathered in place from crystalline rocks that underlie the midland of Georgia. In general the refuge lies between the Ocmulgee River on the west and State 11 on the east.

The refuge contains 31,192 acres, titles to which have been vested in the United States. Acquisition of the land now included in the refuge was begun in 1934 by the Resettlement Administration and continued by the Farm Security Administration when the former agency was abolished. Acquisition was continued by the latter agency until 1939 and was then transferred to the Fish and Wildlife Service (formerly the Bureau of Biological Survey) by Executive Order No. 8037, dated January 18, 1939.

Such wildlife as deer, raccoon, opossum, rabbit, squirrel, turkey, quail, and mourning dove flourishes in the area, and it was established primarily for these species. Over 140 species of birds have been recorded on the refuge, and among the rarer song birds that occur in numbers are the nuthatch, red-cockaded woodpecker, pileated woodpecker, Bachman's sparrow, yellow-throated warbler, and blue grosbeak. A major portion of the acreage is heavily wooded; however, sufficient areas are kept opened and planted to wildlife foods to assure food and cover for the bobwhite quail and wild turkey, as well as other wildlife in the refuge.

Accommodations are not available on the refuge for the general public. Though the Piedmont Refuge has been established as an inviolate National Wildlife Refuge, during times of surplus wildlife populations certain areas of the refuge may be opened to hunting by the public. Information may be obtained from the Refuge Manager, Round Oak, Georgia.

MACON, *91.3 m.* (334 alt., 70,252 pop.) (*see* MACON).

Points of Interest: Home of Sidney Lanier, Mercer University, Wesleyan Conservatory, Ocmulgee National Monument, and others.

At Macon is a junction with US 80 (*see* TOUR *9*) and with US 23-41 (*see* TOUR *12*); at Macon US 41 goes to Perry, and US 23-129 to Cochran.

TOUR 17

Thomson—Crawfordville—Madison—Covington—Avondale Estates; 128 m., State 12.

Georgia R.R. roughly parallels route—Limited accommodations.

State 12 traverses a section developed late in the eighteenth century with the growth of the middle Georgia cotton plantations. Although, for the most part, these plantations have long since been broken up into small farms cultivated by owner or tenant, signs of the past are evident along the route in a memorial park honoring a forensic hero of the Confederacy, in the site of an educational institution more than a century old, and in the classic ante-bellum houses of Warrenton and Covington. The region between Covington and Avondale Estates has vast stores of granite, and the quarrying of this stone is a thriving industry.

THOMSON, *o m.* (540 alt., 3,489 pop.) (*see* TOUR *8*), is at the junction with US 78.

The streets of WARRENTON, *12.1 m.* (500 alt., 1,442 pop.), are bordered with aged oaks and its lawns and gardens are neat. The seat of Warren County since 1797, it was named for General Joseph Warren, Revolutionary patriot of Massachusetts and author of the *Suffolk Resolves,* who was killed at the Battle of Bunker Hill. Developed around a seven-acre plot of land given to the county for a permanent courthouse and jail, Warrenton was incorporated as a town in 1810 and as a city in 1908. Early in the nineteenth century, it was on the stagecoach route between Augusta and Milledgeville. The principal products of the region are cotton, corn, peaches, pecans, and timber.

An extract from Adiel Sherwood's *Gazetteer* of 1837 reads: "In this town [Warrenton] lived for a number of years, Dr. Bushnell, formerly of Saybrook, Connecticut, inventor of a submarine vessel called the 'Turtle.' By this instrument great damage was done to British ships during the Revolutionary War."

The WALKER HOUSE (*private*), Main Street, built in 1820, is a white clapboard house (L) with green blinds and an intricate balustrade. It is admired by architects for its fine proportions.

The MCGREGOR HOUSE (*private*), one block R. from the public square, is a two-story, gray stuccoed brick building, originally of Georgian Colonial design. The early nineteenth century stoop has been replaced by a Greek portico with four Doric columns. A cement and stone wall, with iron gateway, surrounds the wide gardens, which contain some fine boxwood and cherry laurels trimmed into symmetrical shapes.

The W. W. PILCHER HOUSE (*private*), 209 Main Street, is a two-story, white frame building with Corinthian portico. Though the house has been remodeled since it was built in the early 1800's, the original framework is intact. When General La Fayette stopped in Warrenton in 1825 a masked ball in the house initiated the program of entertainments.

CRAWFORDVILLE, *32.7 m.* (616 alt., 966 pop.), seat of Taliaferro County, was incorporated in 1826. One block from the courthouse is the ALEXANDER H. STEPHENS MEMORIAL STATE PARK (*swimming, picnicking, hiking, children's playground, museum, and trading post*). On a slight knoll just north of the entrance to the park stands LIBERTY HALL (*hostess in charge*), a two-story white frame house with a wide porch across the front and an ell of two rooms at the rear. The grounds surrounding the house are planted with shrubs and flowers to resemble the original gardens. Directly in front of the house is the ALEXANDER STEPHENS MONUMENT, an Italian marble figure on a granite base, and to the left is ALEXANDER STEPHENS' GRAVE enclosed by a wall. A prisoner in 1865, Stephens entered in his diary: "No mortal ever had stronger attachments for his home than I for mine. That old homestead and that quiet lot, Liberty Hall, in Crawfordville, sterile and desolate as they may seem to others, are bound to me by associations tender as heart strings and strong as hooks of steel. There I wish to live and die. Let my last breath be my native air. My native land, my country, the only one that is country to me, is Georgia." Stephens had been elected to the governorship during a famous political struggle, but his strength at that date was at such a low ebb that a trip to Savannah to celebrate the 150th anniversary of the state's founding, resulted in his death on March 4, 1883. After lying in state at the Capitol in Atlanta, he was buried in Oakland Cemetery, but the casket was removed to Liberty Hall in 1885.

Stephens bought Liberty Hall in 1845 from the estate of Williamson Byrd, a relative of his stepmother. In 1872 the old house was torn down, except the two rear rooms, to allow space for the present house. Restoration has been made as faithfully as possible. Stephens' bedroom on the first floor contains his walnut furniture, the round table where he worked, and his wheel chair. Books of his are on the table. The flowered ingrain carpet has been repaired, and the blue-and-gold striped wallpaper has been reproduced. The massive chairs of the dining room have been duplicated from a single remaining chair of the original set. In the library at the rear, Stephens wrote *A Constitutional View of the Late War between the States* (1868-70). At the head of the steps leading from the dining room to the second floor is a chamber known as the Tramps' Room, with beds for wayfarers who were without means, as many were in the days after the war.

To the rear of Liberty Hall are the slave quarters, wine cellar, smokehouse, woodhouse, wash house, and chicken house, all restored. It is the loss of these dependencies that makes many ante-bellum houses look unrooted today, especially the unpretentious ones.

Alexander Hamilton Stephens (1812-83) was born in Taliaferro County. After graduation from the University of Georgia (known as Franklin College in ante-bellum days) in 1832, he studied law, entered state politics, and was elected to Congress in 1843. Abraham Lincoln, a fellow Congressman, wrote on February 2, 1848, "I take up my pen to tell you that Mr. Stephens of Georgia, a little, slim, palefaced con-

sumptive man, with a voice like Logan's, has just completed the best
speech of an hour's length I ever heard. My old, withered eyes are full
of tears yet." One often wonders how men attain greatness of soul,
and there is no final answer, but some of the factors are discernible now
and then. In a recent article in the Magazine of *The Atlanta Journal
and The Atlanta Constitution,* Ralph McGill has undoubtedly captured one of the complex of causes. "Friends helped him attend Franklin College. . . . He led his classes. Greek was a passion with him,
and he took the beauty and the precision of that language and its
discipline into law, to the legislature, to the Federal Congress, and into
the Confederacy. . . ."

Stephens was Vice-President of the Confederacy during the War between the States, after which he retired to Liberty Hall. Here he was
arrested by Union soldiers and taken to Fort Wayne in Boston Harbor,
where he was detained for several months. Elected to the U. S. Senate
in 1866, he was disqualified because of his affiliation with the Confederacy, and he remained out of active politics until 1882, when he became Governor of Georgia.

A small, frail man with a shrill voice and indomitable courage, he
never weighed more than a hundred pounds and spent the last years
of his life in a wheel chair. Although faithful to the Confederacy after
the secession ordinance at Milledgeville on January 19, 1861, Stephens
was against the move. Affectionately called Little Aleck, he was
widely known for his kindness and generosity, and especially for his
faith in youth as is shown by the sums he spent to educate promising
but poor young men and women.

Alexander Stephens Park properly should be divided into three units.
Besides Liberty Hall and the demonstration area referred to below,
there is a third unit which is the original state park, given in part by
the town of Crawfordville as a recreational section.

Memorial Drive overlooks a picnic area containing a circular wading
pool fed by two cold, clear springs. Mercer Drive leads to LAKE LIBERTY.
A bathhouse, built in the same style as Liberty Hall, is equipped with
showers, lockers, and rest rooms. Along Sunset Drive there are other
picnic areas where shelters and barbecue pits are provided.

The ALEXANDER H. STEPHENS RECREATIONAL DEMONSTRATION AREA, adjoining the park, was originally under the jurisdiction of the National
Park Service, but has been turned over to the state. This 937-acre tract
contains facilities for organized group camping sufficient to care for 96
campers plus counselors and other camping staff. The cost per day is
quite modest. Address the Superintendent, Alexander H. Stephens

R. D. A., Crawfordville, Georgia, for reservations or additional information.

At Crawfordville is a junction with State 22 (*see* TOUR *14A*).

Beside a railroad crossing is JEFFERSON HALL (*private*), *43.3 m.*, a well-proportioned two-story Greek Revival house (L) with Ionic columns. The doorway is decorated with ornamental woodwork and surmounted by a wide fanlight. Built by Lemuel Greene around 1830, the house became the center of a thriving village of the same name when the Georgia Railroad made its terminus here about 1838. After the railroad was extended to Augusta, the village began to decline, and Jefferson Hall is now the only remaining house.

BUFFALO LICK, *44.1 m.*, is named for a rock with a salty taste that attracted buffaloes in the early days of the colony. William Bartram (1739-1823) described this place in his *Travels*, published in 1791. Here is the marked CREEK AND CHEROKEE COUNCIL SITE, where meetings were held culminating in the Treaty of Augusta in 1773. The survey of the lands ceded by the Indians to the state began at this place.

UNION POINT, *44.6 m.* (644 alt., 1,724 pop.), is the central point of the Georgia Railroad between Augusta and Atlanta and the junction with a branch line to Athens.

Left of the highway at a railroad crossing is a HOSIERY MILL that has been in operation for nearly fifty years and is owned largely by local capital.

On Carlton Ave. is (R) HAWTHORN HEIGHTS (*private*), named for the hawthorn hedge which surrounds the eight-acre lot. Built 1867-69, the house has a Greek portico in front and a tiled terrace on one side. A tea bush on the front lawn is one of those sent to Washington, D. C., from Japan by Commodore Perry when he opened the ports of that nation in 1854.

Right from Union Point on the Washington Road to the REDMAN THORNTON HOUSE (*private*), *2.6 m.*, on the crest of a hill (L). The story-and-a-half hip-roof building has a pedimented portico supported by square rough stone columns. Although the studdings are filled between with brick, the exterior is finished with weatherboards. This was the first house not a log cabin to be built in Greene County. There is a built-in niche in the wide outside chimney on the north side of the house. Its style is quite reminiscent of earlier buildings in North Carolina and parts of Virginia. Redman Thornton was a great grandson of Matthew Thornton, Virginia signer of The Declaration of Independence.

At *2.8 m.* is the junction with another dirt road; L. on this to the junction with another dirt road, *4.6 m.;* L. on this road to the BETHESDA BAPTIST CHURCH, *5.1 m.*, a two-story brick building, with two corner entrances, built in 1817. At one end of the interior is the old slave gallery. Many Negroes, upon the consent of their masters, became members.

The church was organized in 1775 and until 1817 was known as Whatley's Mill Church. In early days the minister, who was responsible for law and order in the community, required the members of the congregation to come bearing fire arms to service, as a protection against Indian attacks. The minutes show that four militiamen stood guard at each service. The nearby graveyard has been in use since the founding of the church.

Right on State 77 from Union Point about *4 m.* to Woodville, then left about *5 m.* to PENFIELD (approx. 650 alt., 74 pop.), where Mercer Institute, a Baptist school offering classical and theological training, was opened on January 14, 1833. The institution served as a manual labor school in which students earned part of their expenses by doing farm work on the 450-acre tract of land. The promotion of the school began in 1828 when Josiah Penfield, of Savannah, left the Georgia Baptist Convention $2,500 for the education of young ministers, provided that a like amount be raised. Its actual establishment was largely due to the efforts of the Reverend Adiel Sherwood, Baptist minister and author of the *Georgia Gazetteer,* and to the interest of Jesse Mercer, a prominent Baptist clergyman who aided the school with money his wife had inherited from her first husband, Captain Abraham Simons, a Revolutionary soldier (*see* TOUR 8). In 1837 the institution was chartered as a university, and included an academy, a college, and a theological seminary. In 1871 it was moved to Macon.

Three of the original buildings made of hand-made brick are still on the campus. Mercer Chapel, now used as the Penfield Baptist Church, is a Doric-columned building with a Greek pediment. Within are the original pews and a gallery that extends around three sides and divides in half the tall windows. It was restored in 1949. Much like the chapel, Science Hall is used as a public school building, and the old literary society building, Ciceronian Hall, serves as a school auditorium and community house.

The graves of Jesse Mercer, Billington M. Sanders (Mercer's first president), Mrs. Sanders (affectionately known as "Ole Miss"), and others are enclosed by a stone wall with iron gates in a well-kept cemetery, one-fourth of a mile from the village. The cemetery was endowed by the late Colonel James G. Boswell, of California, whose parents are buried here.

An annual pilgrimage to Penfield has become a tradition of the senior class at Mercer since 1949 when the restored chapel was dedicated. William Cary Richards, a young English-born Methodist minister, who established the *Orion* in 1842, also lived in Penfield. This short-lived publication was one of the exceptional literary publications of its day.

In GREENSBORO, *51.9 m.* (598 alt., 2,688 pop.), seat of Greene County, are large cotton mills owned by local capital. The town was laid out for the site of the University of Georgia soon after the creation of the county in 1786. One hundred acres was reserved for the school, and lots were sold for business houses and residences. But before construction began Athens was chosen as the site of Franklin College, later the University of Georgia.

Greensboro is on the site of one of a series of forts built in Greene County to protect the state from the Creek whose reservation was west of the Oconee River. From 1786 until 1802 the county was a buffer between the civilized east and the frontier west where land speculation was rife. From 1789 to 1796 more than three times as much land as the state had acquired from the Indians was granted to speculators. Elijah Clarke, Revolutionary general and Indian fighter, who already owned many acres, saw in the unsettled conditions an opportunity to seize more land for himself and to set up another government. Through the influence of Citizen Genêt, representative of the French Republic, he assembled a group of adventurers to help the French take Florida from the Spanish. When the bubble burst, he marched his hungry vagrants to the Indian land, built forts, laid out a town, and made plans to set up an independent government called the Trans-Oconee Republic. Since Greene County lay beside the land of the new republic, its citizens were in a constant state of anxiety about the new order of civil virtue bordering on the county. Despite stern words from the Federal and state governments, Clarke remained preoccupied with his new state. Eventually President Washington ordered the tolerant Georgia government to use force. Deprived of food by a blockade, the Trans-Oconee Republic concluded its history almost as suddenly as it had begun.

Greensboro, an early cultural center, has a number of noted citizens in its annals. From a plantation near the town, the Reverend Adiel Sherwood (1791-1879) wrote the first of his four editions of *A Gazetteer of the State of Georgia,* now a source book in Georgia history. Augustus B. Longstreet (1790-1870), politician, writer, preacher, and college president, first tried his skill in law here as a young man.

Greene County's prosperity belonged to the years just before the War between the States, the heyday of the plantations. After the war the plantations were worked by share croppers for the most part, and gradually broken into smaller units. The steady drain of cotton on the soil continued for relentless decade after decade, for even the precious guano from Chile, usually applied at the rate of fifty to one hundred pounds to the acre, did nothing for the soil, if it did increase the yield. Erosion ate away the once profitable acres. Then came the mercy of the boll weevil to check man's unreason, as if long-suffering nature, at last tried to the limit, had taken to itself the scales of retribution. By 1938 the situation had become desperate in the county; its population was seeping away like a stream in a parched land.

About that time the U. S. Department of Agriculture began to talk about Greene County as a demonstration area in which county, state, and Federal agencies might work together to restore the land and its people. Eventually, the Unified Farm Program was established. The story of this reconstruction has been told by Arthur Raper in his *Tenants of the Almighty.* "Under the Unified County Program there was an increase of soil-building crops, terraced fields, strip farming. Kudzu and sericea were planted in waterways and on spent hillsides, and eroded lands were retired to forests. New farm dwellings were built, old ones repaired, sanitary privies installed. Screens were put at windows and doors, pumps in wells. There were new barns, too, and permanent fences, pastures cleared and fertilized for additional cows and calves. More brood sows and fattening hogs, brooders for baby chicks, and crates full of eggs for market. Bigger sweet potato hills, larger gardens, pressure cookers by the hundreds and glass jars by the thousands. New schoolhouses and vocational buildings, better-trained teachers, hot lunch programs, a county library and a bookmobile." The restoration of the land carried with it the restoration of the people. As trade mounted in the stores, the merchants knew the cause of the new economic life. A nostalgic yearning for plantation days seems absurd in the face of this very real achievement. Originally the fields had borne from the bounty of nature; this time from the uses of intelligence in co-operation with nature. The re-birth of Greene County was not unique; it was fortunate in having a competent writer on the spot.

The COBB-DAWSON HOUSE (*private*), East and South streets, is a square two-story frame building with a hipped roof. At the entrances, one on each street, is a small porch with Ionic columns. Ornamented with both side- and fanlights, the doorways open into wide hallways that cross in the center of the house. The garden at the rear is luxuriant with shrubbery and old trees covered with wistaria. Thomas W. Cobb built the house in 1810 and in 1829 it was sold to William C. Dawson, who succeeded him as United States Senator.

Diagonally across from the Cobb-Dawson House is the HOME OF THOMAS J. BOWEN (*private*), who charted the Yoruba country in Africa for the British, put the Yoruba language in writing, served as minister in Brazil, and fought in the Indian wars of 1836.

The GREENE COUNTY COURTHOUSE, Main Street (R), a large three-story brick structure with Greek Doric columns, was built in 1848 on a lot acquired from the trustees of the University of Georgia. To the rear of the courthouse is the OLD GREENE COUNTY JAIL, built about 1807 and used until 1895. The walls of the two-story granite building are a precautionary two feet thick, and the cells, dimly lit from small grated windows, are bleakly forbidding. On the upper floor is a trap door used in the hanging of prisoners condemned to death.

Left from Greensboro on State 15 is SILOAM, 6 m. (approx. 600 alt., 324 pop.); L. at the brick stores for one block to a dirt road; right on this road to the junction with another road, 10.5.; L. on this road to BETHANY PRESBYTERIAN CHURCH, 12 m.; the congregation was organized about the time of the formation of Greene

County in 1786. In the little cemetery adjoining the church are the graves of soldiers who took part in the Revolution. Here in 1886 James Woodrow, Presbyterian clergyman and uncle of Woodrow Wilson, was accused of heresy following the publication of his address "Evolution," in which he denied any essential conflict between science and the Bible. Courageously defending his views, Woodrow was exonerated by the Augusta Presbytery, but later the decision was reversed by the state synod, and he was finally forced to resign his position.

At MADISON, 74.3 m. (667 alt., 2,489 pop.), is a junction with US 129-141 (see TOUR 16); and (TOUR 14).

Right from RUTLEDGE, about 83.3 m. (710 alt., 482 pop.), is HARD LABOR CREEK STATE PARK (swimming, picnicking, boating, hiking, fishing, children's playground, group camp, trading post), 2 m. Hard Labor Creek Recreational Demonstration Area, with its 5,816 acres of woodlands and lakes, was laid out by the National Park Service to demonstrate the significance of group camping by means of an established working model. The entire area was deeded by the Federal government to the state in February, 1946.

Fishing and boating are provided by LAKE RUTLEDGE, which has an area of 275 acres and is the larger of the two lakes in the park. Located in this area are the two group camps, CAMP RUTLEDGE and CAMP DANIEL MORGAN. Both are similar to army camps, with central dining hall, infirmary, staff quarters, and other needed facilities. The camps are available to responsible organized groups such as Boy Scouts, Girl Scouts, schools, 4-H Clubs, civic clubs, and churches. Reservations are made through the Superintendent, Hard Labor Creek State Park, Rutledge, Georgia, who will furnish a schedule of rates which are nominal.

Located on 45-acre LAKE BRANTLEY, which has splendid fishing, is the day-use area. This area has picnic and barbecue shelters, and a bathhouse and swimming section. Except for a slight charge for boating and the use of lockers while swimming, equipment, which includes archery, volley ball, horseshoes, and children's playground and toys, is free. Supervised recreation includes swimming, diving, boating, fishing, hiking, picnicking, and community singing and group recreation. The park is listed as open throughout the year. There are no general admission charges or fishing fees in Georgia's state parks.

At about 87.9 m. is the WALTON COUNTY FISH HATCHERY (R) which is operated under the supervision of the State Game and Fish Commission. The species of fish hatched are bream, bass, and crappie.

COVINGTON, 98.9 m. (763 alt., 5,192 pop.), seat of Newton County, was incorporated in 1822 and named for Leonard Covington, a general of the Revolution. Originally it served as a trading center for large-scale planters, but with the development of the cotton mills it has become a prosperous and growing industrial center and a cotton market for the farmers of the section.

The founding of two schools arose from an early interest in education. In March 1835, the Georgia Conference Manual Labor School was opened in Covington with thirty students. Stephen Olin was the president. The school resulted from a suggestion made by "Uncle Allen" Turner at the annual Methodist Conference held in Washington, Georgia, in 1834, that an industrial institution was needed in the state. When Emory College was opened in 1836 at nearby Oxford, the school was relocated there. In 1851 the Southern Masonic Female College was established as a finishing school. The old building served as a hospital during the War between the States and in 1887 was taken over by the city school system which it served until replaced.

On State 12, here known as Floyd Street, are several well-preserved ante-bellum houses.

The McCORMICK NEAL HOME (*private*), 501 Floyd Street, is a pleasing white frame house of Mississippi planter design. It stands on a high basement of brick; a long flight of steps leads to a portico with small fluted Doric columns. The decorative doorway and long windows emphasized by green blinds are distinctive features.

The USHER HOME (*private*) 300 block Floyd Street, a white frame building with six Doric columns across the front, is a fine example of the Greek Revival style. The entrance ornamented with Doric pilasters, the small hanging balcony, and the long windows flanked by green blinds are characteristic details. Built about 1840, the house was occupied for many years by Jack Henderson, son of the Confederate general.

The HOUSE OF GENERAL ROBERT J. HENDERSON (*private*), L. of Floyd Street two blocks E. of the square, is a large, frame, Greek Revival house with fluted Doric columns. The house was built by Carey Wood, an early settler and father-in-law of Henderson (1822-94), who was made a brigadier general for bravery under Joseph E. Johnston in North Carolina.

DIXIE MANOR (*private*), 3 blocks from State 12 at the intersection of Monticello and Church streets, is a red brick house built in 1859 by Colonel Thomas Jones. The small recessed portico has four Ionic columns and a small balcony.

1. Left from Covington, about *12 m.,* on State 36 to the entrance (L) of the 350-acre FUTURE FARMERS OF AMERICA CAMP, on Lake Jackson in Newton County. By 1953 membership, made up from "in-school" students taking vocational agriculture in Georgia high schools, had reached 16,447. At their state conference in

the summer of 1936, the teachers of vocational agriculture voted to establish a recreation and resident project camp. Each FFA chapter in the state made a pledge of $3.00 per member, to be paid within a three to five year period. The site was selected in the spring of 1937, and actual construction began at once. The National Youth Administration was just getting under way, and Dr. M. D. Mobley, then director of vocational education in Georgia, persuaded the NYA to help set up the resident project with a view to acquiring experience from work projects to be set up at the camp. At present the camp has a total of twenty-one buildings, each with electricity and running water. Three are built entirely of granite, and all the granite used for the project was quarried on the camp property. In addition to the cottages which can house up to four hundred campers, there is a supervisor's cottage, three staff cottages, a dining hall, an assembly hall, an infirmary, and a memorial amphitheater. Facilities for recreation include a 3-acre lake for swimming, softball—the camp has two diamonds and a grandstand, table tennis, volleyball, and horseshoe pitching. In season the weekly average is about 350 campers.

According to a statement by the State Department of Education, whose Mr. T. D. Brown is the executive secretary of the Georgia Association of FFA, the purpose of the organization is to develop in rural boys competent leadership in public affairs, to encourage them in the planning and successful completion of exemplary farming projects as parts of a unified program, to stimulate more interest in the intelligent choice of farming as an occupation, to create a love of country life, to develop character traits, to train for useful citizenship, to encourage farm boys to improve the farm home and its surroundings, and to direct significant programs directed to the progressive improvement of agriculture as a body of knowledge and applied skill. It is a special feature of FFA to provide for organized rural recreation programs.

The movement that became FFA began as the Future Farmers of Virginia in 1926, to provide country boys with the confidence and social skill that city boys commonly acquire by means of the numerous social organizations in urban centers. Officially the organization got started at a meeting in Kansas City in the autumn of 1928, and was incorporated under the laws of Virginia that same year, with its present name. In 1953, the Silver Anniversary of the FFA, the organization had associations in all 48 states as well as Puerto Rico and Hawaii, its membership having grown from 1929's 30,000 to 350,000.

Students of vocational agriculture played an important part in the shift from one-crop farming in Georgia to a system of diversified agriculture and a well-established program of soil conservation. Stress has been placed on good pasture management, feed crops, and the improvement of bloodlines in livestock. Also, with increasing mechanization on the farm, a grasp of shop work became essential; for without shop skills readily available the modern farmer pays a high penalty in work stoppage and delay, especially at crucial seasons. In fact, the modern farmer must increasingly co-ordinate in himself something like the knowledge and skills of the physician or surgeon, if he is to survive as an independent agent at a time when collective modes of production, such as those characteristic of industry, threaten to assimilate every phase of action. The leaders of FFA evidently understand the need of technical competence and they also understand apparently the personal and social dignity that accrues to a man from the possession and exercise of knowledge and applied skill. If freedom consists in the steady habit of choosing one's ends, and within the range of one's own diversified but associated skills, of selecting the means apt to accomplish the ends chosen, then the modern farmer has more freedom than his brother, the industrial worker. Farming is more than an occupation; it is a way of life, for the farmer has not only profit from his work but pleasure in it and satisfaction from it.

The New Farmers of America, or NFA is an organization for Negro boys and young men studying agriculture in the sixteen states where separate schools are maintained for Negroes. The NFA site is at Camp John Hope, near Fort Valley (*see* TOUR 2).

2. West of Covington is the Yellow River which because of Channing Cope's Yellow River Farm radio program has become a symbol of rural interest all over Georgia. His book *Front Porch Farmer,* with an introduction by Louis Bromfield, published in 1949, presents a lively and imaginative account of how one man made eroded gullies and starved land live again. It describes a year-round grazing program of perennial legumes and grasses—kudzu, fescue, Bermuda grass, ladino, crimson, and manganese clovers—which can be so managed as to "be operated while the owner sits in an easy chair on his front porch."

Left from Covington on State 81 is PORTERDALE, *3.2 m.* (600 alt., 3,207 pop.), a prosperous textile town on the Yellow River. The frame houses of its several thousand employees line both sides of the highway. These mills go back to 1868.

3. Right from Covington on State 81 is OXFORD, *1.1 m.* (801 alt., 817 pop.), a college town of sandy, oak-shaded streets lined with houses, several of which are more than a hundred years old. The town developed with Emory College, which was the focal point for all activities. During the War between the States, Confederate officers occupied the town, and school buildings were used as a hospital.

EMORY JUNIOR COLLEGE (L) is on the old campus of Emory College. Through the efforts of Ignatius A. Few, the Georgia Methodist Conference was induced to broaden the field of the old Manual Labor School at Covington. As a result, a charter was obtained on January 25, 1836, for an institution to be named Emory College in honor of Bishop John Emory of the Methodist Church. The following year the cornerstone for the first college building was laid on the 1,400-acre campus in Oxford. In 1914 Emory College became the College of Arts and Sciences of Emory University (*see* ATLANTA) and in 1919 was moved to the new campus. The old buildings at Oxford were used as Emory Academy until 1928, when the junior college was established here as a unit of the Emory University system.

From the stone entrance posts a road leads around the quadrangle, surrounded by some ten buildings and shaded by trees planted by graduating classes.

SENEY HALL (L) is a three-story Victorian building of red brick, built in 1881 through contributions from George I. Seney, New York Philanthropist. In the tower is a bell bearing an old Spanish and Latin inscription and engravings of a crucifix and the Virgin Mary. It is said that the bell, originally taken from one of the ships of the Spanish Armada, was presented to Alexander Means in 1841 by Queen Victoria as a token of her interest in the advancement of learning.

EMORY CHAPEL (*open*) has been in use since its construction in 1873. The entrance portico of the small, brown cement building (L) is framed with Doric pilasters and sheltered by a small gabled roof.

PHI GAMMA HALL (*open*) is a cream-colored stucco building (L) with a high basement, its simplified Greek Revival façade having two fluted Ionic and two square Doric columns. It was built about 1851 for the Phi Gamma Literary Society, one of the two societies organized in 1837 by Few. These societies belonged to the great oratorical and forensic tradition of the day which, for the most part based on Greek political wisdom and Roman civil virtue, did so much towards supplying the South with some articulate and resourceful statesmen as distinguished from mere politicians.

FEW HALL (*open*), with four square Doric columns, a pilastered doorway, and a double row of windows on the sides, was erected (R) soon after Phi Gamma Hall for the Few Society.

Left from Emory College entrance on State 81 (R) is the HOME OF ALEXANDER MEANS (*private*), a two-story frame structure set well back in an oak grove and surrounded by an iron fence. The first four rooms were built of hand-hewn logs before Oxford was a town, but the house was later weatherboarded, and additions were made off and on without regard for symmetry. There is some evidence of the Greek Revival idiom in the square-columned portico and the pilastered doorway. Means (1801-85) served as superintendent of the Manual Labor School in Covington, became the fourth president of Emory, and later taught chemistry at Emory and the Atlanta Medical School. Far in advance of the times in regard to electricity, he made what may have been the first electric light bulb in America.

OLD EMORY CHURCH (*private*), on Wesley Street, is a white frame building (L) with two projecting wings forming a cross. It was dedicated by Bishop William Capers in 1841, used as a Confederate hospital from 1862-64, completed in 1876 and restored by Bishop Candler in 1932. For years this was the only church in town, and was used by both students and townspeople.

BRANHAM HEIGHTS (*private*), on Wesley Street, is a two-story frame structure (L) with a Greek portico and two Doric columns. Built in 1840, it came into the possession of the Branham family in 1855. In this house Lucius Q. C. Lamar (1825-93) left his wife and children while he was seeking aid for the Confederacy in England and Russia. Lamar had lived in Oxford with his mother when he attended Emory College and had married Virginia, the daughter of Augustus Longstreet. He practiced law in Covington and other Georgia towns before he moved to Mississippi and became a United States Senator. He was one among a few who had the political wisdom to advocate a closer union between the North and South after the War between the States. Appointed Secretary of the Interior in 1885, he resigned three years later to become an Associate Justice of the U. S. Supreme Court.

CONYERS, *110.3 m.* (909 alt., 2,003 pop.), seat of Rockdale County, was incorporated in 1854. It was the first town in the state to test and win a case for prohibition; the first to have a law requiring people to keep their livestock confined; and the first to have a Presbyterian campground.

Rockdale County was named for an immense vein of granite or granite-gneiss underlying the soil for some 450 square miles and shouldering its way above the surface in various places.

At Conyers is a TRAPPIST MONASTERY (Roman Catholic), consisting of ninety monks. The Trappists are a branch of the Cistercian Order established by Armand de Rancé in 1660, at the Monastery of La Trappe, in Normandy. The discipline includes frequent religious exercises—the first each day at 2 A.M., study and meditation, a simple meatless diet [except in a particular case when for reasons of health the abbot may allow some meat and perhaps eggs], manual labor, prolonged fasts at intervals, and perpetual silence among themselves. Though not numerous, the Trappists have monasteries in a number of countries, and were permanently established in the United States in 1848.

The monastery has a large library which, however, contains only religious books. Bread is baked, a thrifty and productive farm cultivated, houses, walls, and gardens built; in short, a neat economy practiced by the monks, between the orderly and frequent hours of prayer, worship, and meditation on God. There are no radios, newspapers, television, or magazines. That God *is* primarily, and the existence of all other things contingent upon Him, is attested by a sign over a door of the main building that says, "God Above All."

At *116.4* is a junction with a side road.

R. on this road to LITHONIA, *0.1 m.* (954 alt., 1,538 pop.), known for its granite quarrying industries. Many of the local buildings are made of gray stone from these quarries. Believed by some to be older than the Stone Mountain (*see* TOUR *8*) type, Lithonia granite is a highly metamorphic form of gneiss. Quantities of granite in the form of crushed stone or aggregate is used in Georgia for roadwork and in the construction trades generally. Granite dust and grit go into a wide variety of products, though especially brick and cement or building block.

1. Right from Lithonia on a road to PINE MOUNTAIN, *1 m.,* where quarries (*open to visitors*) have been in operation since 1883 and are among the largest and best equipped in the state. The elevation is sometimes called Little Stone Mountain because one side has been blasted away to such an extent as to leave a sheer wall resembling Stone Mountain itself.

2. Right from Lithonia on a paved road to the QUARRY (*open to visitors*) of the Consolidated Quarries Corporation, *3 m.* The solid granite face of this quarry, some 1,000 feet long and around a 100 feet high, is periodically blasted. For this purpose, holes 6 inches in diameter are drilled 100 feet and filled with 16,000 pound charges of dynamite, which loosens about 75,000 tons of stone. By means of electric shovels the rock is loaded on trucks and hauled to the crusher, from which a belt conducts it through revolving and vibrating screens that separate it into sizes ranging from two inches down. The oversized stones are crushed again by a cone crusher. From the stockpiles, underground conveyors carry the stone to the loading bin where it is given a final washing and screening and dumped by means of an automatic hopper into freight cars.

Between Lithonia and Avondale Estates granite outcroppings break the soil at intervals. Along the Georgia Railroad, which parallels this route (R), gondola cars stand weighted with crushed stone, or sturdy cranes swing heavy granite blocks onto flatcars. Houses along the route are often made of native stone.

AVONDALE ESTATES, *128 m.* (approx. 1,025 alt., 1,070 pop.), a residential suburb of Atlanta, was incorporated in 1927.

At Avondale Estates is a junction with US 78 (*see* TOUR *8*).

★

PART THREE

APPENDICES

★

Chronology

1540 Hernando de Soto marched from Florida through part of Georgia and crossed the Savannah River at Silver Bluff, near Augusta.

1560 Tristan de Luna and 300 Spanish soldiers crossed Coosa River and searched for gold in north Georgia.

1562 Jean Ribault of France explored Georgia coast.

1566 Pedro Menendez de Aviles built fort on Santa Catalina (St. Catherines) Island.

1573 Franciscan friars built mission on Cumberland Island.

1595 Franciscans built missions on St. Simons and Jekyll islands and mainland.

1663 Charles II granted to lords proprietors of Carolina land between 31° and 36° N. lat., including present territory of Georgia.

1689 All missions abandoned, forces being withdrawn to strengthen garrison at St. Augustine, Fla.

1717 "Margravate of Azilia" granted to Sir Robert Montgomery; failed through lack of settlers.

1721 Fort King George, first English settlement in territory, built at mouth of Altamaha River.

1732 George II granted charter authorizing settlement of Georgia by imprisoned debtors; first Great Seal made.

1733 February 12, James Edward Oglethorpe and his colonists settled at Yamacraw Bluff; greeted by Tomochichi, Indian chief. May 14, Italian Piedmontese arrived to teach silk culture to colonists. May 21, chiefs of Creek Nation signed treaty ceding to Oglethorpe and colonists all land between the Savannah and Altamaha rivers. July 7, Savannah town court organized; first jury empanelled.

1734 March 17, Salzburgers from Bavaria settled at Ebenezer. April 7, Oglethorpe sailed for England with Tomochichi and several Indian chiefs.

1735 January 9, Trustees established ban on rum and slaves in Georgia. May, Moravian immigrants settled on Savannah River. Augusta founded.

1736 January, Scottish Highlanders settled Darien. February 5, John and Charles Wesley arrived at Savannah with Oglethorpe. February 18, Fort established at Frederica. August 11, Charles Wesley returned to England.

1737 Oglethorpe appointed commander in chief of His Majesty's forces in Georgia and South Carolina. December, John Wesley returned to England.

1738   George Whitefield and James Habersham arrived at Savannah.

1740   March 25, George Whitefield placed first brick on Bethesda Orphan House.
       May 10, Oglethorpe captured Fort San Diego, near St. Augustine, Fla.

1741   Georgia divided into two counties: Savannah County, north; Frederica
       County, south.

1742   July 7, Oglethorpe, with small band of colonists, defeated large Spanish
       force at Battle of Bloody Marsh, St. Simons Island.

1743   Oglethorpe left Georgia permanently. Government of Georgia changed
       from military to civil status, directed by a president and five councillors;
       Frederica County abolished; William Stephens became first president of
       Colony.

1744   First commercial house in Georgia established by James Habersham and
       Francis Harris.

1749   Trustees allowed introduction of slaves into colony.

1751   First Colonial Assembly met at Savannah.

1752   June 23, trustees surrendered charter. Midway settled by Puritans from
       Dorchester, S. C. Estimated Colonial population 4,000 to 5,000, including
       1,500 Negroes.

1754   Georgia became a royal province; Capt John Reynolds, British Navy, ap-
       pointed first royal governor. October 29, Reynolds arrived at Savannah.

1755   First house of commons, elected by Georgians, convened at Savannah.
       Four hundred Acadians banished from Nova Scotia arrive; sent to South
       Carolina the following spring.

1758   Assembly declared official adherence to Church of England. Georgia is
       divided into eight parishes.

1761   George III proclaimed King with great ceremony in Savannah.

1763   April 7, the *Georgia Gazette,* Georgia's first newspaper, issued at Savannah.
       October 7, boundaries of Georgia extended to St. Marys River on south and
       Mississippi River on west. November 10, peace treaty signed at Augusta
       with all Indians in Georgia.

1766   February, Stamp Act riot in Savannah. Estimated population 10,000
       whites and 7,800 Negroes.

1768   Benjamin Franklin appointed Georgia's agent in England.

1772   First Baptist church in Georgia founded at Kiokee Creek.

1773   Creek and Cherokee Indians signed treaty at Augusta ceding to Britain
       2,100,000 acres in Georgia.

1775   January, first Provincial Congress met at Savannah; Archibald Bulloch
       elected president. May 11, patriots seized store of powder at Savannah.
       May 13, Lyman Hall presented credentials as delegate from Georgia, and
       was seated by Continental Congress as representing only his own parish,
       St. Johns. May 17, Continental Congress placed all Georgia except St.
       Johns Parish under ban of colonial nonintercourse. June 22, Council of
       Safety elected by Savannah citizens. July 4, second Provincial Congress
       met at Savannah; Archibald Bulloch re-elected president; official Council of
       Safety appointed. July 20, Continental Congress rescinded ban of Colonial
       nonintercourse. July, Georgia schooner took 9,000 pounds of powder from

British vessel. September 13, Continental Congress seated three Georgia delegates: Houstoun, Bulloch, and Zubly.

1776 February 11, James Wright, Royal Governor, escaped arrest and boarded British ship. April 15, third Provincial Congress adopted temporary constitution. Lyman Hall, George Walton, and Button Gwinnett signed Declaration of Independence.

1777 February 5, first state constitution ratified by Constitutional Convention in Savannah; parishes replaced by counties; president replaced by governor; new seal adopted. May 8, John Adams Treutlen elected first state governor. May 16, Button Gwinnett mortally wounded in duel with Gen. Lachlan McIntosh.

1778 July 24, Edward Telfair and Edward Langworthy signed Articles of Confederation. November, British troops invaded Georgia. December 29, Savannah captured by British.

1779 January, Whig government moved to Augusta. British captured Augusta. February 14, British defeated at Battle of Kettle Creek. February 28, British evacuated Augusta. July 13, Governor Wright returned to Georgia and re-established royal rule. July 24, Supreme Executive Council elected by Whig assembly to exercise executive power instead of governor; John Wereat elected president. September, Colonial troops aided by French fleet besieged Savannah. October 9, Savannah defenders repulsed attack; Count Pulaski and Sgt. William Jasper mortally wounded.

1780 January 4, Richard Howley appointed governor by Whig assembly in opposition to Supreme Executive Council. February 3, Heard's Fort declared temporary capital by Governor Howley. June, Augusta retaken by British.

1781 British forces expelled from Augusta by Col. Henry (Lighthorse Harry) Lee, Gen. Andrew Pickens, and Col. Elijah Clarke.

1782 British withdrew from Savannah; seat of government re-established in Savannah.

1783 February 15, Edward Telfair, John Houstoun, and Gen. Lachlan McIntosh authorized to adjust northern boundary of Georgia. May 31, Creek and Cherokee ceded lands west of the Tugalo River. July 31, legislature established Richmond Academy at Augusta, oldest existing chartered school in Georgia. Georgia extended jurisdiction to Natchez district along Mississippi River.

1784 February 25, University of Georgia endowed, granted 40,000 acres of land.

1785 January 27, University of Georgia chartered. *Augusta Chronicle* founded. Georgia organized Bourbon County along Mississippi River.

1786 Augusta became temporary seat of government. Sea Island cotton introduced on Georgia coast.

1787 Boundary line established between Georgia and South Carolina. Four of Georgia's six elected delegates attended Constitutional Convention at Philadelphia: William Few, Abraham Baldwin, William Pierce, and William Houstoun; Few and Baldwin signed Constitution.

1788 January 2, Georgia ratified Federal Constitution, the fourth state to do so. February 1, Chatham Academy at Savannah chartered.

1789 May, new state constitution adopted.

1790 Population of Georgia 82,548 (U. S. Census).

1791 President Washington visited Augusta and Savannah.

1793 Eli Whitney invented cotton gin at the home of General Nathanael Greene's widow, near Savannah.

1795 January, Georgia legislature passed Yazoo Act, whereby state relinquished claim to 35,000,000 acres of land in present states of Alabama and Mississippi at price of less than 1½¢ an acre. February 25, Joseph Habersham became Postmaster General of U. S. (1795-1801). May, Seat of government moved to Louisville.

1796 Yazoo Act rescinded and all documents pertaining to it were burnt before state capitol at Louisville.

1798 Georgia abolished African slave trade and interstate slave trade, in new state constitution. Act of Congress separated Mississippi territory from Georgia.

1799 Present seal of Georgia adopted.

1800 Population 162,686 (U. S. Census).

1801 First building of University of Georgia erected.

1802 All Georgia lands west of Chattahoochee and of a line running north from the mouth of Uchee Creek to Nickajack Creek ceded to the United States. Creek Indians by Treaty of Fort Wilkinson, ceded tracts south of Altamaha and west of Oconee rivers.

1803 Land lottery system inaugurated by act of legislature.

1804 Milledgeville declared new seat of government. Georgia Medical Society incorporated.

1805 Creek by treaty ceded their remaining lands east of Ocmulgee River except a strip in Old Ocmulgee Fields.

1806 Fort Hawkins, site of Macon, built.

1808 Site for penitentiary selected at Milledgeville.

1810 Population 252,433 (U. S. Census).

1812 Georgia coast towns fortified after U. S. declared war on England.

1814 General Andrew Jackson forced Creek to sign treaty ceding land in southern Georgia.

1815 August 1, William H. Crawford appointed U. S. Secretary of War. Bank of the State of Georgia in Savannah chartered.

1816 April, regular steamboat transportation began on Savannah River. October 22, Crawford appointed U. S. Secretary of the Treasury (1816-25).

1818 Creek ceded 1,500,000 acres south of Altamaha and about headwaters of the Ocmulgee. Tennessee-Georgia boundary line established.

1819 May 22, the *Savannah,* first steamship to cross Atlantic, left Savannah for Liverpool. Senator John Forsyth became U. S. Minister to Spain (1819-23).

1820 Population 340,989 (U. S. Census).

1821 Creek ceded all of their lands east of Flint River.

1824 Charter obtained for Savannah and Ogeechee Canal.

1825 February, by treaty of Indian Springs, Creek ceded all of their lands in

Georgia to U. S. April 30, William McIntosh, Creek chief, slain by Indians for promoting cession of Creek lands. Sequoyah, Cherokee Indian, invented syllabary. La Fayette visited Georgia.

1826   January, Creek chiefs signed new treaty at Washington, ceding to the state of Georgia all lands but 300,000 acres of land east of the Chattahoochee River.

1827   November 15, all remaining Creek lands ceded to U. S. for $28,000. Cherokee adopted a constitution at their capital, New Echota.

1828   December 20, Georgia legislature extended state jurisdiction over Cherokee country.

1828-29   Gold discovered in north Georgia.

1829   Senator John M. Berrien became Attorney General of U. S. (1829-31).

1830   Population 516,823 (U. S. Census). Legislature decreed no white person might live in Cherokee country without license. First medical college in state organized in Augusta.

1831   Missionaries to Cherokee imprisoned after refusing to obtain license; case brought before U. S. Supreme Court. Cherokee lands surveyed by Georgia for distribution by lottery.

1832   Georgia ignored U. S. Supreme Court decision. Cherokee country divided into ten counties.

1833   January, missionaries released by Governor Lumpkin after swearing allegiance to Georgia. Georgia R.R., first to be built in state, chartered. Central of Georgia Railway chartered. Alabama-Georgia boundary line agreed upon.

1834   Senator John Forsyth became U. S. Secretary of State (1834-41).

1835   Oglethorpe College at Milledgeville chartered. Congressman James M. Wayne became Associate Justice of U. S. Supreme Court (1835-1867). December, by New Echota Treaty, Cherokee ceded to state all their lands in Georgia.

1836   Emory College chartered. Wesleyan College chartered as Georgia Female College. Western & Atlantic R.R. chartered, to be built at state expense.

1837   Mercer College chartered. Terminus of Western & Atlantic R.R. located at present site of Atlanta. Branch mint built by U. S. at Dahlonega.

1838   Last of the Cherokee removed from Georgia.

1840   Population 691,392 (U. S. Census).

1842   First operation using ether as anesthetic performed by Dr. Crawford W. Long at Jefferson. State Sanitarium for the insane created at Milledgeville.

1843   Settlement at terminus of Western & Atlantic R.R. chartered as Marthasville. First train ran from Savannah to Macon over Central of Georgia Ry.

1844   Methodist church divided into northern and southern conference over slavery question.

1845   Georgia organized its first supreme court; Joseph Henry Lumpkin, first chief justice. Marthasville incorporated as town of Atlanta.

1846   Georgia sent 898 men to the Mexican War.

1849   Governor George W. Crawford became U. S. Secretary of War (1849-50).

1850   Population 906,185 (U. S. Census).

1857   Former Governor Howell Cobb became U. S. Secretary of the Treasury (1857-60).

1858   Legislature appropriated $100,000 annual income from Western & Atlantic R.R. to maintain free elementary schools.

1860   Population 1,057,286 (U. S. Census). Secession meetings in Georgia.

1861   January 3, Fort Pulaski seized by order of Governor Brown. January 19, Georgia seceded from the Union. January 23, Georgia Congressmen resigned seats. January 24, Federal arsenal at Augusta surrendered to Governor Brown. February 9, Alexander H. Stephens elected Vice President of the Confederacy. March 16, Georgia adopted Confederate constitution. March 23, Georgia adopted new state constitution. November 24, Admiral Dupont, U. S. N., took Tybee Island.

1862   April 10, Fort Pulaski taken by Federal forces.

1863   September 20, Federal forces defeated at battle of Chickamauga.

1864   May 4, General W. T. Sherman opened campaign in Georgia; May 15, Battle of Resaca; June 14, Lieutenant General Leonidas Polk, the "fighting bishop," killed at Pine Mountain; June 27, Battle of Kennesaw Mountain; July 18, General John B. Hood succeeded General Joseph E. Johnston; July 20, Battle of Peachtree Creek; July 22, Battle of Atlanta; General J. B. McPherson and Major General W. H. T. Walker killed; July 28, Battle of Ezra Church; August 31, Battle of Jonesboro; September 2, Sherman occupied Atlanta; November 14, Sherman burned Atlanta and started on march to the sea; December 22, Sherman occupied Savannah.

1865   May 10, Jefferson Davis, President of the Confederate States, captured near Irwinville. October 26, Secession Ordinance repealed by convention at Milledgeville. December 9, Thirteenth Amendment, abolishing slavery, ratified by legislature.

1866   Georgia accepted Whitner-Orr line as Georgia-Florida boundary. State superintendent of education appointed.

1867   April 1, Federal troops under Major General John Pope occupied Third Military District, including Georgia. December 9, Constitutional Convention met at Atlanta. Ku Klux Klan appeared in Georgia. Atlanta University, first of Georgia's Negro colleges, granted charter.

1868   March 11, Convention adopted new state constitution; declared Atlanta state capital. April 20, people ratified new state constitution; Rufus Bullock elected governor. July 21, legislature ratified Fourteenth Amendment; civil government restored. July, six Georgia Congressmen took seats in national House of Representatives; Senators not seated before Congress adjourns. September, Negro members expelled from legislature.

1869   March, Georgia rejected Fifteenth Amendment. March 5, Georgia Congressmen excluded from National House of Representatives. December 22, Georgia again suffered the military yoke.

1870   Population 1,184,109 (U. S. Census). February 2, Fifteenth Amendment ratified by legislature with Negro members again in attendance; Four-

teenth Amendment reratified. July 15, Georgia admitted to the Union.
October 13, legislature established state department of education. December, Congressmen reseated in national House.

1875   State board of health organized.

1877   New state constitution adopted; Atlanta established as permanent capital by referendum.

1879   Flag of state of Georgia adopted by legislature.

1880   Population 1,542,180 (U. S. Census). William Burnham Woods became Associate Justice of U. S. Supreme Court (1880-87).

1881   International Cotton Exposition held in Atlanta.

1885   Georgia School of Technology chartered.

1888   L. Q. C. Lamar became Associate Justice of the U. S. Supreme Court (1888-93).

1889   Present state capitol at Atlanta opened. Agnes Scott College established as Decatur Female Seminary.

1890   Population 1,837,353 (U. S. Census). Chickamauga and Chattanooga Military Park established by Congress.

1893   Hoke Smith appointed Secretary of the Interior by President Cleveland (1893-96). Congressman Thomas E. Watson secured first appropriation for rural free delivery.

1895   International and Cotton States Exposition held in Atlanta.

1897   State library commission established by legislature.

1898   Georgia contributed three regiments to Spanish-American War.

1900   Population 2,216,331 (U. S. Census).

1901   Federal penitentiary established in Atlanta.

1902   Martha Berry Schools for mountain children founded.

1904   Thomas E. Watson nominated for President of U. S. on Populist Ticket. Nominated again in 1908.

1906   Georgia State College of Agriculture established at Athens.

1907   Statewide prohibition adopted.

1908   Convict leasing system abolished. Georgia Agricultural Extension Service began in January.

1910   Population 2,609,121 (U. S. Census).

1911   Joseph R. Lamar became Associate Justice of U. S. Supreme Court (1911-16).

1912   Girl Scouts of America founded at Savannah by Juliette Low. High schools made part of state school system.

1914   Sixth District Federal Reserve Bank established in Atlanta.

1915   Juvenile courts established in counties with population of 60,000 or more.

1916   State highway commission created. Gutzon Borglum engaged to carve Stone Mountain Memorial.

1917-18   Two Army and two National Guard training camps established; 93,321 men and 238 army nurses from Georgia enter War.

1918   Georgia ratified Eighteenth Amendment (Prohibition). Department of Archives and History set up by legislature.

1919   State board of public welfare created.

1920   Population 2,895,832 (U. S. Census). Georgia ratified Nineteenth Amendment (Woman Suffrage).

1921   Boll weevil first seriously damaged cotton crop.

1922   Fort Benning, largest infantry training school in the world, established near Columbus by Federal government.

1925   Candler Field, first airport in state, established at Atlanta.

1926   High Museum of Art established in Atlanta.

1927   Franklin D. Roosevelt organized Warm Springs Foundation.

1928   First commercial airways system in Georgia completed. First concrete-paved state-line-to-state-line highway in Georgia completed.

1930   Population 2,908,506 (U. S. Census).

1931   Reorganization bill passed, consolidating state departments and establishing university system.

1932   Dr. Charles H. Herty's pilot plant established at Savannah for experimental work with Georgia pines.

1933   Georgia celebrated the bicentennial of Oglethorpe's founding of the colony; historical pageant in Savannah.

1934   Caroline Miller won Pulitzer Prize for her book *Lamb in His Bosom*, a novel of local color.

1936   Tornado struck Gainesville, killing about 200 people and destroying an estimated $5,000,000 in property; the New Deal came to the rescue.

1937   March, State department of natural resources created. Legislature established minimum seven-months' term for public schools, with free textbooks. State planning board organized. Social Security Act adopted by Georgia. Margaret Mitchell won Pulitzer Prize for *Gone With the Wind*, a romantic novel of Georgia during the War between the States and Reconstruction. Georgia Soil Conservation Law passed by the legislature. The live oak adopted as the official state tree of Georgia. Okefenokee Swamp Refuge purchased by the Federal government.

1938   State prohibition law repealed.

1939   State board of penal corrections created.

1940   Population 3,123,723 (U. S. Census).

1941   December 8, United States entered World War II. The state became a center for military camps and air centers.

1943   Georgia took first place in the production of velvet beans, peanuts, pimientos, sweet potatoes, watermelons, and pecans.

1945   President Franklin D. Roosevelt died at Warm Springs. Legislature appropriated $1,000,000 to put Teacher Retirement Law, passed in 1943, into effect. New State Constitution adopted.

1946   Child Labor Law passed by legislature.

1947   Little White House at Warm Springs dedicated as a national shrine and deeded to Georgia.

1949   Minimum Foundation Program for the development of educational facilities passed by legislature, also a law providing for secret balloting in all state elections. Pre-marital health examination law provided. $500,000 appropriated by legislature for the expansion and development of the Farmers Market System.

1950 Bill passed to provide statewide juvenile courts. First electric power generated at the Allatoona Dam, constructed by the U. S. Corps of Engineers. Jekyll Island Authority created. Population 3,444,578 (U. S. Census).

1951 State Building Authority created.

INFORMATION ON THE COUNTIES OF GEORGIA

NAME	NAMED FOR	COUNTY SEAT	DATE FORMED	POPU-LATION
Appling	Col. Daniel Appling	Baxley	1818	14,003
Atkinson	Gov. William Y. Atkinson	Pearson	1917	7,362
Bacon	Augustus O. Bacon	Alma	1914	8,940
Baker	Col. John Baker	Newton	1825	5,952
Baldwin	Abraham Baldwin	Milledgeville	1803	29,706
Banks	Dr. Richard E. Banks	Homer	1858	6,935
Barrow	Chanc. David C. Barrow	Winder	1914	13,115
Bartow	Gen. Francis S. Bartow	Cartersville	1832	27,370
Ben Hill	Benjamin H. Hill	Fitzgerald	1906	14,879
Berrien	John M. Berrien	Nashville	1856	13,966
Bibb	Dr. W. W. Bibb	Macon	1822	114,079
Bleckley	Logan E. Bleckley	Cochran	1912	9,218
Brantley	Benjamin D. Brantley	Nahunta	1920	6,387
Brooks	Preston L. Brooks	Quitman	1858	18,169
Bryan	Jonathan Bryan	Pembroke	1793	5,965
Bulloch	Archibald Bulloch	Statesboro	1796	24,862
Burke	Edmund Burke	Waynesboro	1777	23,458
Butts	Capt. Sam Butts	Jackson	1825	9,079
Calhoun	John C. Calhoun	Morgan	1854	8,578
Camden	Earl of Camden	Woodbine	1777	7,339
Candler	Gov. Allen D. Candler	Metter	1914	8,063
Carroll	Charles Carroll	Carrollton	1826	34,112
Catoosa	Catoosa (Ind. name)	Ringgold	1853	15,146
Charlton	Robert M. Charlton	Folkston	1854	4,821
Chatham	Earl of Chatham	Savannah	1777	151,481
Chattahoochee	Chattahoochee River	Cusseta	1854	12,149
Chattooga	Chattooga River	Summerville	1838	21,197
Cherokee	Cherokee Indians	Canton	1831	20,750
Clarke	Gen. Elijah Clarke	Athens	1801	36,550
Clay	Henry Clay	Fort Gaines	1854	5,844
Clayton	Augustine S. Clayton	Jonesboro	1858	22,872

Population figures are from the U. S. 1950 Census of Population, as released September 27, 1951, by the Bureau of the Census, U. S. Department of Commerce.

NAME	NAMED FOR	COUNTY SEAT	DATE FORMED	POPU-LATION
Clinch	Gen. Duncan L. Clinch	Homerville	1850	6,007
Cobb	Thomas W. Cobb	Marietta	1832	61,830
Coffee	Gen. John E. Coffee	Douglas	1854	23,961
Colquitt	Walter T. Colquitt	Moultrie	1856	33,999
Columbia	Christopher Columbus	Appling	1790	9,525
Cook	Gen. Philip Cook	Adel	1918	12,201
Coweta	Chief Coweta	Newnan	1826	27,786
Crawford	William H. Crawford	Knoxville	1822	6,080
Crisp	Charles F. Crisp	Cordele	1905	17,663
Dade	Maj. Francis L. Dade	Trenton	1837	7,364
Dawson	William C. Dawson	Dawsonville	1857	3,712
Decatur	Commander Stephen Decatur	Bainbridge	1823	23,620
DeKalb	Baron De Kalb	Decatur	1822	136,395
Dodge	William E. Dodge	Eastman	1870	17,865
Dooly	Col. John Dooly	Vienna	1821	14,159
Dougherty	Charles Dougherty	Albany	1853	43,617
Douglas	Stephen A. Douglas	Douglasville	1870	12,173
Early	Gov. Peter Early	Blakely	1818	17,413
Echols	Col. Robert M. Echols	Statenville	1858	2,494
Effingham	Lord Effingham	Springfield	1777	9,133
Elbert	Gen. Sam Elbert	Elberton	1790	18,585
Emanuel	Gov. David Emanuel	Swainsboro	1812	19,789
Evans	Gen. Clement A. Evans	Claxton	1914	6,653
Fannin	Col. James W. Fannin	Blue Ridge	1854	15,192
Fayette	Marquis de La Fayette	Fayetteville	1821	7,978
Floyd	Gen. John Floyd	Rome	1832	62,899
Forsyth	Gen. John Forsyth	Cumming	1832	11,005
Franklin	Benjamin Franklin	Carnesville	1784	14,446
Fulton	Hamilton Fulton	Atlanta	1853	473,572
Gilmer	Gov. George R. Gilmer	Ellijay	1832	9,963
Glascock	Gen. Thomas Glascock	Gibson	1857	3,579
Glynn	John Glynn	Brunswick	1777	29,046
Gordon	William W. Gordon	Calhoun	1850	18,922
Grady	Henry W. Grady	Cairo	1905	18,928
Greene	Gen. Nathanael Greene	Greensboro	1786	12,843
Gwinnett	Gov. Button Gwinnett	Lawrenceville	1818	32,320
Habersham	Maj. Joseph Habersham	Clarkesville	1818	16,553
Hall	Gov. Lyman Hall	Gainesville	1818	40,113
Hancock	John Hancock	Sparta	1793	11,052
Haralson	Hugh. A. Haralson	Buchanan	1856	14,680
Harris	Charles Harris	Hamilton	1827	11,265
Hart	Nancy Hart	Hartwell	1853	14,495
Heard	Gov. Stephen Heard	Franklin	1830	6,975

NAME	NAMED FOR	COUNTY SEAT	DATE FORMED	POPU- LATION
Henry	Patrick Henry	McDonough	1821	15,857
Houston	Gov. John Houston	Perry	1821	20,964
Irwin	Gov. Jared Irwin	Ocilla	1818	11,973
Jackson	Gov. James Jackson	Jefferson	1796	18,997
Jasper	Sgt. William Jasper	Monticello	1807	7,473
Jeff Davis	Jefferson Davis	Hazlehurst	1905	9,299
Jefferson	Thomas Jefferson	Louisville	1796	18,855
Jenkins	Gov. Charles J. Jenkins	Millen	1905	10,264
Johnson	Gov. Herschel V. Johnson	Wrightsville	1858	9,893
Jones	James Jones	Gray	1807	7,538
Lamar	L. Q. C. Lamar	Barnesville	1920	10,242
Lanier	Sidney Lanier	Lakeland	1919	5,151
Laurens	Col. John Laurens	Dublin	1807	33,123
Lee	Gen. Richard Henry Lee	Leesburg	1826	6,674
Liberty	American Independence	Hinesville	1777	8,444
Lincoln	Gen. Benjamin Lincoln	Lincolnton	1796	6,462
Long	Dr. Crawford W. Long	Ludowici	1920	3,598
Lowndes	William J. Lowndes	Valdosta	1825	35,211
Lumpkin	Gov. Wilson Lumpkin	Dahlonega	1832	6,574
McDuffie	George McDuffie	Thomson	1870	11,443
McIntosh	McIntosh family	Darien	1793	6,008
Macon	Nathaniel Macon	Oglethorpe	1837	14,213
Madison	Pres. James Madison	Danielsville	1811	12,238
Marion	Gen. Francis Marion	Buena Vista	1827	6,521
Meriwether	Gen. David Meriwether	Greenville	1827	21,055
Miller	Andrew J. Miller	Colquitt	1856	9,023
Mitchell	Gen. Henry Mitchell	Camilla	1857	22,528
Monroe	Pres. James Monroe	Forsyth	1821	10,523
Montgomery	Gen. Richard Montgomery	Mt. Vernon	1793	7,901
Morgan	Gen. Daniel Morgan	Madison	1807	11,899
Murray	Thomas W. Murray	Chatsworth	1832	10,676
Muscogee	Muscogee Indians	Columbus	1826	118,028
Newton	Sgt. John Newton	Covington	1821	20,185
Oconee	Oconee River	Watkinsville	1875	7,009
Oglethorpe	Gen. Oglethorpe	Lexington	1793	9,958
Paulding	John Paulding	Dallas	1832	11,752
Peach	Georgia peach	Fort Valley	1924	11,705
Pickens	Gen. Andrew Pickens	Jasper	1853	8,855
Pierce	Pres. Franklin Pierce	Blackshear	1857	11,112
Pike	Gen. Zebulon M. Pike	Zebulon	1822	8,459
Polk	Pres. James K. Polk	Cedartown	1851	30,976
Pulaski	Count Casimir Pulaski	Hawkinsville	1808	8,808
Putnam	Gen. Israel Putnam	Eatonton	1807	7,731

NAME	NAMED FOR	COUNTY SEAT	DATE FORMED	POPU-LATION
Quitman	Gen. John A. Quitman	Georgetown	1858	3,015
Rabun	Gov. William Rabun	Clayton	1819	7,424
Randolph	John Randolph	Cuthbert	1828	13,804
Richmond	Duke of Richmond	Augusta	1777	108,876
Rockdale	Rockdale Church	Conyers	1870	8,464
Schley	Gov. William Schley	Ellaville	1857	4,036
Screven	Gen. James Screven	Sylvania	1793	18,000
Seminole	Indians	Donalsonville	1920	7,904
Spalding	Hon. Thomas Spalding	Griffin	1851	31,045
Stephens	Gov. Alexander H. Stephens	Toccoa	1905	16,647
Stewart	Gen. Daniel Stewart	Lumpkin	1830	9,194
Sumter	Gen. Thomas Sumter	Americus	1831	24,208
Talbot	Gov. Matthew Talbot	Talbotton	1827	7,687
Taliaferro	Gov. Benjamin Taliaferro	Crawfordville	1825	4,515
Tattnall	Gov. Josiah Tattnall	Reidsville	1801	15,939
Taylor	Pres. Zachary Taylor	Butler	1852	9,113
Telfair	Gov. Edward Telfair	McRae	1807	13,221
Terrell	Dr. William Terrell	Dawson	1856	14,314
Thomas	Gen. Jett Thomas	Thomasville	1825	33,932
Tift	Nelson Tift	Tifton	1905	22,645
Toombs	Gen. Robert Toombs	Lyons	1905	17,382
Towns	Gov. George W. Towns	Hiawassee	1856	4,803
Treutlen	Gov. John A. Treutlen	Soperton	1917	6,522
Troup	Gov. George M. Troup	LaGrange	1826	49,841
Turner	Henry G. Turner	Ashburn	1905	10,479
Twiggs	Gen. John Twiggs	Jeffersonville	1809	8,308
Union	the Union	Blairsville	1832	7,318
Upson	Stephen Upson	Thomaston	1824	25,078
Walker	Maj. Freeman Walker	LaFayette	1833	38,198
Walton	Gov. George Walton	Monroe	1818	20,230
Ware	Nicholas Ware	Waycross	1824	30,289
Warren	Gen. Joseph Warren	Warrenton	1793	8,779
Washington	George Washington	Sandersville	1784	21,012
Wayne	Gen. Anthony Wayne	Jesup	1803	14,248
Webster	Daniel Webster	Preston	1853	4,081
Wheeler	Gen. Joseph Wheeler	Alamo	1912	6,712
White	David T. White	Cleveland	1857	5,951
Whitfield	Rev. George Whitefield	Dalton	1851	34,432
Wilcox	Capt. John Wilcox	Abbeville	1857	10,167
Wilkes	John Wilkes	Washington	1777	12,388
Wilkinson	Gen. James Wilkinson	Irwinton	1803	9,781
Worth	Gen. William J. Worth	Sylvester	1853	19,357

Bibliography

(*The 1940 edition of* Georgia: A Guide to Its Towns and Countryside, *the University of Georgia Press, contains an extensive bibliography which is classified thus: General Information, Description and Travel, Natural Setting, Archeology and Indians, History and Government, Transportation, Agriculture, Social and Economic Conditions, Education, Religion, Folklore, Literature and Journalism, Architecture; Counties, Cities, and Towns.*)

BOOKS OF INTEREST PUBLISHED SINCE 1937

Southern Politics, V. O. Key, Jr., 1949, Alfred A. Knopf, New York; Chapter Six, pp. 106-129 (Georgia: Rule of the Rustics).

The Mind of the South, W. J. Cash, fourth printing, May 1950, Alfred A. Knopf, New York; paperbound edition, Anchor Press.

Georgia: A Short History, E. Merton Coulter, 1947, University of North Carolina Press, Chapel Hill, N. C.

Geography of Georgia, Edward S. Sell, 1950, Harlow Publishing Corp., Oklahoma City and Chattanooga.

Empire Builders of Georgia (Elementary textbook), Suddeth, Osterhout, and Hutcheson, 1951, The Steck Co., Austin, Texas.

Georgia: Unfinished State, Hal Steed, 1942, Alfred A. Knopf, New York.

Sea Islands of Georgia, Count D. Gibson, 1948, University of Georgia Press, Athens, Georgia.

A History of Education in Georgia, Dorothy Orr, 1950, University of North Carolina Press, Chapel Hill, N. C.

The General Who Marched to Hell (Sherman), Earl Miers, 1951, Alfred A. Knopf, New York.

The Savannah, Thomas L. Stokes, 1951, Rinehart & Co., New York.

Building Atlanta's Future (a text), Ivey, Demerath, and Breland, 1948, University of North Carolina Press, Chapel Hill, N. C.

College Life at Old Oglethorpe, Allen P. Tankersley, 1951, University of Georgia Press, Athens, Georgia.

Henry W. Grady: Spokesman of the New South, Raymond B. Nixon, 1943, Alfred A. Knopf, New York.

Tom Watson: Agrarian Rebel, C. Vann Woodward, 1938, The Macmillan Company, New York.

Tenants of the Almighty, Arthur Raper, 1943, The Macmillan Company, New York.

Modern Georgia (A Sociological Study), John C. Meadows, 1946, University of Georgia Press, Athens, Georgia.

White Columns in Georgia, Medora Field Perkerson, 1952, Rinehart & Co., New York.

Give the Man Room: The Story of Gutzon Borglum, R. J. Casey and M. M. Borglum, 1952, Bobbs-Merrill Co., New York.

Roosevelt and the Warm Springs Story, Turnley Walker, 1953, A. A. Wyn, New York.

Columbus on the Chattahoochee, Etta Blanchard Worsley, 1951, Columbus Office Supply Co., Columbus, Georgia.

Up Ahead: A Regional Land Use Plan for Metropolitan Atlanta, Metropolitan Planning Commission, Atlanta, Georgia, February, 1952.

Index

Abraham Baldwin Agricultural College, 200-01
Academy of Richmond County, 68; and Junior College of Augusta, 82
Acworth, 187
Acworth Sub-Impounding Dam—Cobb County Public Use Area, 187
Adairsville, 182
Addis Gap, 383
Adel, 202
Agate Demonstration Area, 339-40
Agnes Scott College, 220
Ah-Yeh-Li A-Loo-Hee, marked site of Indian Assembly Ground, 216
Albany, 274
Albany State College, 275
Alexander H. Stephens Recreational Demonstration Area, 414
Alexander H. Stephens Memorial State Park, 412-14
Alexander House (Washington), 301
Allatoona, 187
Allatoona Dam and Reservoir, 183-85, 187-88
Allatoona Landing (Allatoona Reservoir Area), 187
Allen House (Augusta), 77
Allen, William, House (near Middleton), 230
Allenbrook (Roswell), 269
Alma, 239
Altama, 165
American Turpentine Farmers Association Cooperative, 202
Americus, 273
Amicalola Falls and Lake, 386
Amicalola Falls State Park, 264
Anabaptists, 296
Anderson, Maj. Geo. W., 158
Andersonville, 210
Andersonville National Cemetery, 210
Andersonville Prison Park, 210-11
Andrew College, 355

Andrews, Eliza Frances, *War Time Diary of A Georgia Girl*, 303
Andrews, James J., 48
Antony, Dr. Milton, 76
Appalachian Trail, 260, 382-87
Appling, 296
Archbold Memorial Hospital, 279
Armour Meat Packing Plant (Tifton), 202
Armstrong College (Savannah), 134
Armuchee Nat. Forest Ranger District Office, 378
Ashburn, 200
ATHENS, 1-17
ATLANTA, 19; Battle of, 25; becomes capital, 27; Points of Interest, 32
Atlanta and West Point Railroad, gives access to N.E. Alabama, 24
Atlanta Art Association, 41
Atlanta Constitution, The, established, 27
Atlanta Daily World Bldg., 38
Atlanta Division, Univ. of Ga., 32-33
Atlanta Medical College, 37
Atlanta Municipal Auditorium, 36
Atlanta Public Library, 34
Atlantic Coast Line Railroad Shop (Waycross), 240
Atlanta University, 28, 51-55
Atlanta University System, 51-55
Attapulgus Clay Co., fuller's earth, 254
Audubon, John James, 173-74
AUGUSTA, 63; Points of Interest, 73
Augusta Canal, 80
Augusta Chronicle and Gazette, 68
Augusta Garden Center, 76
Augusta Museum, 75
Augusta National Golf Course, 85
Augusta Public Library, 75
Austell, 311
Aviles, Menendez de, 160, 170
Avondale Estates, 424
Axson, Ellen, grave of, Rome, 338
Azalea Cottage, 84